Contemporary Challenges and Solutions for Mobile and Multimedia Technologies

Ismail Khalil
Johannes Kepler University Linz, Austria

Edgar Weippl
Secure Business Austria – Security Research, Austria

Managing Director:	Lindsay Johnston
Editorial Director:	Joel Gamon
Book Production Manager:	Jennifer Romanchak
Publishing Systems Analyst:	Adrienne Freeland
Assistant Acquisitions Editor:	Kayla Wolfe
Typesetter:	Alyson Zerbe
Cover Design:	Nick Newcomer

Published in the United States of America by
Information Science Reference (an imprint of IGI Global)
701 E. Chocolate Avenue
Hershey PA 17033
Tel: 717-533-8845
Fax: 717-533-8661
E-mail: cust@igi-global.com
Web site: http://www.igi-global.com

Library of Congress Cataloging-in-Publication Data

Contemporary challenges and solutions for mobile and multimedia technologies /
Ismail Khalil and Edgar Weippl, editors.
    p. cm.
 Includes bibliographical references and index.
 Summary: "This book provides comprehensive knowledge on the growth and changes in the field of multimedia and mobile technologies"--Provided by publisher.
 ISBN 978-1-4666-2163-3 (hardcover) -- ISBN 978-1-4666-2164-0 (ebook) -- ISBN 978-1-4666-2165-7 (print & perpetual access) 1. Multimedia communications. 2. Mobile computing. I. Khalil, Ismail, 1960- II. Weippl, Edgar R. TK5105.15.
C656 2012
 621.39'81--dc23
                                2012019422

British Cataloguing in Publication Data
A Cataloguing in Publication record for this book is available from the British Library.

The views expressed in this book are those of the authors, but not necessarily of the publisher.

Table of Contents

Section 2
Commerce

Section 3
Networks

Section 4
Audiovisual Recognition

Detailed Table of Contents

Section 1
Security

Chapter 1

Anjali Sardana, Indian Institute of Technology Roorkee, India
Ramesh C. Joshi, Indian Institute of Technology Roorkee, India

DDoS attacks aim to deny legitimate users of the services. In this paper, the authors introduce dual - level attack detection (D-LAD) scheme for defending against the DDoS attacks. At higher and coarse level, the macroscopic level detectors (MaLAD) attempt to detect congestion inducing attacks which cause apparent slowdown in network functionality. At lower and fine level, the microscopic level detectors (MiLAD) detect sophisticated attacks that cause network performance to degrade gracefully and stealth attacks that remain undetected in transit domain and do not impact the victim. The response mechanism then redirects the suspicious traffic of anomalous flows to honeypot trap for further evaluation. It selectively drops the attack packets and minimizes collateral damage in addressing the DDoS problem. Results demonstrate that this scheme is very effective and provides the quite demanded solution to the DDoS problem.

Chapter 2

Hai Thanh Nguyen, Gjøvik University College, Norway
Katrin Franke, Gjøvik University College, Norway
Slobodan Petrović, Gjøvik University College, Norway

In this paper, the authors propose a new feature selection procedure for intrusion detection, which is based on filter method used in machine learning. They focus on Correlation Feature Selection (CFS) and transform the problem of feature selection by means of CFS measure into a mixed 0-1 linear programming problem with a number of constraints and variables that is linear in the number of full set features. The mixed 0-1 linear programming problem can then be solved by using branch-and-bound algorithm. This feature selection algorithm was compared experimentally with the best-first-CFS and the genetic-algorithm-CFS methods regarding the feature selection capabilities. Classification accuracies obtained after the feature selection by means of the C4.5 and the BayesNet over the KDD CUP'99 dataset were also tested. Experiments show that the authors' method outperforms the best-first-CFS and the genetic-algorithm-CFS methods by removing much more redundant features while keeping the classification accuracies or getting better performances.

In this paper, the author aim to present a threat and risk-driven methodology to security requirements engineering. The chosen approach has a strong focus on gathering, modeling, and analyzing the environment in which a secure ICT-system to be built is located. The knowledge about the environment comprises threat and risk models. As presented in the paper, this security-relevant knowledge is used to assess the adequacy of security mechanisms, which are then selected to establish security requirements.

Good security cannot be achieved through technical means alone and a solid understanding of the issues and how to protect one's self is required from users. Whilst many initiatives, programs and strategies have been proposed to improve the level of information security awareness, most have been directed at organizations. Given people's use of technology is primarily focused between the workplace and home; this paper seeks to understand the knowledge and practice relationship between these environments. Through a developed survey, it was identified that the majority of the learning about information security occurred in the workplace, where clear motivations, such as legislation and regulation, existed. Results found that users were more than willing to engage with such awareness raising initiatives. From a comparison of practice between work and home environments, it was found that this knowledge and practice obtained at the workplace was transferred to the home environment. Given this positive transferability of knowledge and the willingness to learn about how to remain secure, an opportunity exists to move away from specific organizational awareness programs and to move towards awareness raising strategies that will develop an all-round individual security culture for users independent of the environment they are operating in.

Internet users often have usernames and passwords at multiple web sites. To simplify things, many sites support federated identity management, which enables users to have a single account allowing them to log on to different sites by authenticating to a single identity provider. Most identity providers perform authentication using a username and password. Should these credentials be compromised, all of the user's accounts become compromised. Therefore a more secure authentication method is desirable. This paper implements 2-clickAuth, a multimedia-based challenge-response solution which uses a web camera and a camera phone for authentication. Two-dimensional barcodes are used for the communication between phone and computer, which allows 2-clickAuth to transfer relatively large amounts of data in a short period of time. 2-clickAuth is more secure than passwords while easy to use and distribute. 2-clickAuth is a viable alternative to passwords in systems where enhanced security is desired, but availability, ease-of-use, and cost cannot be compromised. This paper implements an identity provider in the OpenID federated identity management system that uses 2-clickAuth for authentication, making 2-clickAuth available to all users of sites that support OpenID, including Facebook, Sourceforge, and MySpace.

Chapter 6

Florian Kohlar, Ruhr University Bochum, Germany

Jörg Schwenk, Ruhr University Bochum, Germany

Meiko Jensen, Ruhr University Bochum, Germany

Sebastian Gajek, Tel Aviv University, Israel

In recent research, two approaches to protect SAML based Federated Identity Management (FIM) against man-in-the-middle attacks have been proposed. One approach is to bind the SAML assertion and the SAML artifact to the public key contained in a TLS client certificate. Another approach is to strengthen the Same Origin Policy of the browser by taking into account the security guarantees TLS gives. This work presents a third approach which is of further interest beyond IDM protocols, especially for mobile devices relying heavily on the security offered by web technologies. By binding the SAML assertion to cryptographically derived values of the TLS session that has been agreed upon between client and the service provider, this approach provides anonymity of the (mobile) browser while allowing Relying Party and Identity Provider to detect the presence of a man-in-the-middle attack.

Chapter 7

Yehia Elrakaiby, TELECOM Bretagne, France

Frédéric Cuppens, TELECOM Bretagne, France

Nora Cuppens-Boulahia, TELECOM Bretagne, France

Pre-obligations denote actions that may be required before access is granted. The successful fulfillment of pre-obligations leads to the authorization of the requested access. Pre-obligations enable a more flexible enforcement of authorization policies. This paper formalizes interactions between the obligation and authorization policy states when pre-obligations are supported and investigates their use in a practical scenario. The main advantage of the presented approach is that it gives pre-obligations both declarative semantics using predicate logic and operational semantics using Event-Condition-Action (ECA) rules. Furthermore, the presented framework enables policy designers to easily choose to evaluate any pre-obligation either (1) statically (an access request is denied if the pre-obligation has not been fulfilled); or (2) dynamically (users are given the possibility to fulfill the pre-obligation after the access request and before access is authorized).

Chapter 8

Teddy Mantoro, International Islamic University Malaysia, Malaysia

Admir Milišić, International Islamic University Malaysia, Malaysia

Media A. Ayu, International Islamic University Malaysia, Malaysia

The widespread of Internet usage has resulted in a greater number and variety of applications involving different types of private information. In order to diminish privacy concerns and strengthen user trust, security improvements in terms of authentication are necessary. The solutions need to be convenient, entailing ease of use and higher mobility. The suggested approach is to make use of the already popular mobile phone and to involve the mobile network, benefiting from Subscriber Identity Module (SIM) card's tamper resistance to become trusted entities guarding personal information and identifying users. Mobile phone's SIM card is convenient for safely storing security parameters essential for secured communication. It becomes secure entity compulsory for getting access to privacy sensitive Internet applications, like those involving money transfers. Utilizing the NFC interface passes the personal user keys only when needed, giving additional strength to the traditional public key cryptography approach in terms of security and portability.

Section 2
Commerce

There are several methodologies, including traditional and agile methodologies, being utilized in current systems development. However, it could be argued that existing development methodologies may not be suitable for mobile commerce applications, as these applications are utilized in different contexts from fixed e-commerce applications. This study proposes a system development methodology for mobile commerce applications. In order to achieve this aim, four objectives are proposed: investigating existing systems development methodologies used to develop mobile commence applications, identifying strengths and weaknesses of existing development methodologies, construction of a suitable methodology for mobile commerce applications, and testing for its applicability and practicality. The research methodology used in the study is the design research, which includes the steps of awareness of problems, suggestion, development, evaluation and conclusion. However, this paper only focuses on the first two phases of the whole study, which are awareness of the problem and making suggestions, while the evaluation and conclusion will be conducted as future works.

Radio Frequency Identification (RFID) has been used since the Second World War to identify "friend or foe" aircrafts. It has become an enabling wireless technology that is widely used in a number of application areas, such as product tracking through manufacturing and assembly, inventory control, and supply chain management (SCM). By 2006, Wal-Mart used RFID for all of its suppliers. The use of RFID in supply chain networks has allowed Wal-Mart to create value through greater visibility in its networks, higher product velocity, reduce human error and labor cost, and more efficient inventory management, which led to the achievement of Quick Response (QR) and improved Customer Relationship Management (CRM) in the supply chain. However, RFID system challenges and uncertain Return-On-Investment (ROI) must be overcome to fully achieve these objectives. This paper introduces RFID technology and its key components and concepts, and presents an RFID middleware solution called FlexRFID that achieves the maximum benefits of RFID technology independently of the interested backend applications. This paper illustrates how RFID technology is used to solve the main problems in SCM, the advantages and key issues when implementing RFID in SCM networks, and the relationship between RFID and the main SCM processes.

Section 3
Networks

Chapter 11

Allam Mousa, An-Najah National University, Palestine

This paper proposes different queuing scenarios to avoid dropping of handoff and new calls in a cellular phone network, which is essential when the network has certain restrictions on the available frequencies. This limitation degrades the performance of the system and more sites are required to achieve the desired capacity and coverage. However, this leads to a higher percentage of call drops during handoff. This paper presents a queuing technique for both new and handoff calls to reduce the probability of call drop in such a system, leading to improvement in QoS. The proposed scenarios show better system performance. The blocking probability is reduced from 2% down to 0.04% for queuing handoff calls and from 2% to 1.14% when queuing new calls using the same technique. The four different presented approaches are: 1) only new calls are queued; 2) only handoff calls are queued; 3) by using all available channels; 4) by using only half. The queuing size also plays an important role for both new and handoff calls.

Chapter 12

Joel Penhoat, Orange Labs, France

Karine Guillouard, Orange Labs, France

Servane Bonjour, Orange Labs, France

Pierrick Seïté, Orange Labs, France

The management of the mobility between radio networks composed of heterogeneous radio technologies, called inter-access mobility management, provides the capability to tie together heterogeneous radio networks into an integrated network. The 3GPP architectures with well-designed inter-access mobility management capabilities are a part of the solution to cope with the growth of the mobile data traffic. This paper reviews the 3GPP architectures to highlight those with these capabilities. In order to evaluate if the mobility management is well-designed into these architectures, the authors describe the phases making up the management of the mobility and design an evaluation grid to assess the integration of these phases into the highlighted architectures. Since the assessment shows the existence of loopholes in the design of the inter-access mobility management, this paper proposes to enhance the 3GPP architectures by implementing a method called Hierarchical and Distributed Handover.

In structured and unstructured Peer-to-Peer (P2P) systems, frequent joining and leaving of peer nodes causes topology mismatch between the P2P logical overlay network and the physical underlay network. This topology mismatch problem generates high volumes of redundant traffic in the network. This paper presents Common Junction Methodology (CJM) to reduce network overhead by optimize the overlay traffic at underlay level. CJM finds common junction between available paths, and traffic is only routed through the common junction and not through the conventional identified paths. CJM does not alter overlay topology and performs without affecting the search scope of the network. Simulation results show that CJM resolves the mismatch problem and significantly reduces redundant P2P traffic up to 87% in the best case for the simulated network. CJM can be implemented over structured or unstructured P2P networks, and also reduces the response time by 53% approximately for the network.

In this paper, the authors discuss the emergence of new technologies related to the topic of the high-speed packet data access in wireless networks. The authors propose an algorithm for MIMO systems that optimizes the number of the transmit antennas according to the user's QoS. Scheduling performance under two types of traffic modes is also discussed: one is voice or web-browsing and the other is for data transfer and streaming data.

Collision is a common problem in Mobile Ad Hoc Networks (MANETs). There are several backoff algorithms that have been proposed to avoid this problem. This paper proposes a new backoff algorithm called the Square Root Backoff (SRB). Moreover, it identifies that no algorithm can perform the best in all cases. Therefore, an adaptive strategy is proposed to choose the best backoff mechanism from a set of mechanisms based on network density and mobility parameters. The proposed adaptive algorithm is implemented in two phases: the offline phase and the online phase. Such design aims at reducing the time complexity of the algorithm by performing some of the computations prior to the actual deploy-ment and of the network. Results from simulations demonstrate that the SRB algorithm achieved better performance than BEB and LB. Moreover, the adaptive backoff algorithm obtains the best throughput and end-to-end delay performance over the other backoff algorithms.

Chapter 16

Naveen Chauhan, National Institute of Technology Hamirpur, India

Lalit K. Awasthi, National Institute of Technology Hamirpur, India

Narottam Chand, National Institute of Technology Hamirpur, India

Ramesh C. Joshi, Indian Institute of Technology Roorkee, India

Manoj Misra, Indian Institute of Technology Roorkee, India

Mobile ad hoc network (MANET) presents a constrained communication environment due to fundamental limitations of client's resources, insufficient wireless bandwidth and users' frequent mobility. MANETs have many distinct characteristics which distinguish them from other wireless networks. Due to frequent network disconnection, data availability is lower than traditional wired networks. Cooperative caching helps MANETs in alleviating the situation of non availability of data. In this paper, the authors present a scheme called global cluster cooperation (GCC) for caching in mobile ad hoc networks. In this scheme, network topology is partitioned into non-overlapping clusters based on the physical network proximity. This approach fully exploits the pull mechanism to facilitate cache sharing in a MANET. Simulation experiments show that GCC mechanism achieves significant improvements in cache hit ratio and average query latency in comparison with other caching strategies.

Chapter 17

Prashant Kumar, National Institute of Technology Hamirpur, India

Naveen Chauhan, National Institute of Technology Hamirpur, India

Lalit K. Awasthi, National Institute of Technology Hamirpur, India

Narottam Chand, National Institute of Technology Hamirpur, India

Mobile Adhoc Networks (MANETs) are very popular solutions where network infrastructure installation is not possible. In MANETs, nodes are mobile, and due to this mobility, topology of the network changes rapidly. This dynamic topology reduces the data availability in MANETs. Cooperative caching provides an attractive solution for this problem. In this paper, a new cooperative caching algorithm, ProCoCa, is proposed. This algorithm is based on a proactive approach. Each node will be associated with a zone and the data of leaving node will be cached. The authors simulate the algorithm on OMNET++ simulator, and simulation results show that ProCoCa improves the data availability as well as overall performance of the network.

Chapter 18

Surender Soni, National Institute of Technology Hamirpur, India

Vivek Katiyar, National Institute of Technology Hamirpur, India

Narottam Chand, National Institute of Technology Hamirpur, India

Wireless Sensor Networks (WSNs) are generally believed to be homogeneous, but some sensor nodes of higher energy can be used to prolong the lifetime and reliability of WSNs. This gives birth to the concept of Heterogeneous Wireless Sensor Networks (HWSNs). Clustering is an important technique to prolong the lifetime of WSNs and to reduce energy consumption as well, by topology management and routing. HWSNs are popular in real deployments (Corchado et al., 2010), and have a large area of coverage. In such scenarios, for better connectivity, the need for multilevel clustering protocols arises.

In this paper, the authors propose an energy-efficient protocol called heterogeneous multilevel clustering and aggregation (HMCA) for HWSNs. HMCA is simulated and compared with existing multilevel clustering protocol EEMC (Jin et al., 2008) for homogeneous WSN. Simulation results demonstrate that the proposed protocol performs better.

Chapter 19

This paper presents an automated provisioning tool for the deployment of sensors within wireless sensor networks (WSN) where we have employed evolutionary approach as a search technique to find the maximal coverage under minimal deployment cost. The coverage area is partitioned into M by N cells to reduce the search space from continuous to discrete by considering the placement of sensors at the centroid of each cell. The author has explored the relationship between various cell's sizes versus the total number of deployed sensors. The experimental results show that when the number of cells to cover the service area from X by X cells to 2X by 2X cells is increased, on average this increases the cost by 3 folds. In this regard, it is due to the increase of the number of required sensors by an average of six folds, while improving the coverage ratio by only 9%. A custom-made graphical user interface (GUI) has been developed and embedded within the proposed automated provisioning tool to illustrate the deployment area with the placed sensors at step of the deployment process.

Section 4
Audiovisual Recognition

Chapter 20

Visemes are the unique facial positions required to produce phonemes, which are the smallest phonetic unit distinguished by the speakers of a particular language. Each language has multiple phonemes and visemes, and each viseme can have multiple phonemes. However, current literature on viseme research indicates that the mapping between phonemes and visemes is many-to-one: there are many phonemes which look alike visually, and hence they fall into the same visemic category. To evaluate the performance of the proposed method, the authors collected a large number of speech visual signal of five Algerian speakers male and female at different moments pronouncing 28 Arabic phonemes. For each frame the lip area is manually located with a rectangle of size proportional to 120*160 and centred on the mouth, and converted to gray scale. Finally, the mean and the standard deviation of the values of the pixels of the lip area are computed by using 20 images for each phoneme sequence to classify the visemes. The pitch analysis is investigated to show its variation for each viseme.

Preface

In this publication, we have assembled an entire year of contributions to the *International Journal of Mobile Computing and Multimedia Communications*. The papers published in the four issues of Vol. 3 of *IJMCMC* span a wide range of subjects, from authentication and intrusion detection to RFID middleware, visual speech recognition, and topology mismatch problems.

The papers in this volume can be divided into several broad categories: 1) security, with the subcategories of authentication, intrusion detection, and security policies; 2) commerce and logistics; 3) network performance in both fixed and ad hoc wireless networks; and 4) audiovisual recognition.

The topic of **security** is addressed from various perspectives:

Dual-Level Attack Detection, Characterization and Response for Networks under DDoS Attacks by Anjali Sardana and Ramesh C. Joshi and *Improving Effectiveness of Intrusion Detection by Correlation Feature Selection* by Hai Than Nguyen, Katrin Franke, and Slobodan Petrović introduce new intrusion detection methods.

Holger Schmidt discusses *Threat and Risk-Driven Security Requirements Engineering*, an approach that places great emphasis on gathering information, analyzing and modeling the environment in which a system is to be built.

Individual user security is the topic of *Establishing a Personalized Information Security Culture*, in which Shuhaili Talib, Nathan L. Clarke, and Steven M. Furnell examine the transfer of security knowledge from workplace to home and propose a new approach to raising awareness about IT security issues.

Another security aspect is authentication and data security. Anna Vapen and Nahid Shahmehri present *2-ClickAuth: Optical Challenge-Response Authentication Using Mobile Handsets*, an interesting approach that uses two-dimensional barcodes in combination with cell phones in federated identity management system, thus reducing the risk of an attacker gaining access to all accounts of one user through one password. Another approach to protecting federated identity management against attacks is presented by Florian Kohlar, Jörg Schwenk, Meiko Jensen, and Sebastian Gajek in *On Cryptographically Strong Bindings of SAML Assertions to Transport Layer Security*. Yehia Elrakaiby, Frédéric Cuppens, and Nora Cuppens-Boulahia present *An Integrated Approach for the Enforcement of Contextual Permissions and Pre-Obligations*. Finally, Teddy Mantoro, Admir Milišić, and Media A. Ayu suggest a novel method for *Online Authentication Using Smart Card Technology in Mobile Phone Infrastructure*.

In their paper, Anjali Sardana and Ramesh C. Joshi introduce a defense against DDoS attacks that operates on two levels: At the higher level, they use macroscopic level detectors to detect congestion-inducing attacks that cause an obvious reduction in network functionality, while at the lower, finer level, microscopic level detectors identify more sophisticated and stealthy attacks that reduce the performance in a less detectable way. The suspicious traffic flows are then rerouted to a honeypot for analysis, which also helps reduce collateral damage in that misclassified legitimate flows can be detected and redirected to the actual server. This is a promising approach for dealing with the common problem of DDoS.

Hai Than Nguyen, Katrin Franke, and Slobodan Petrović present a method for improving the effectiveness of intrusion detection. Their automatic feature selection procedure is based on Correlation Feature Selection (CFS) - a filter method used in machine learning, which can consider correlations between different features and between features and classes. By looking at the CFS measure as an optimization problem that they transformed into a mixed 0-1 linear programming problem with constraints and variables and then solved with the branch-and-bound algorithm, they were able to find the globally optimal subset of relevant features. They evaluated their results by comparing them to two other feature selection methods. The authors were able to show that their method was equally or even more accurate than best-first-CFS and genetic algorithm CFS methods, while also removing considerably more redundant features than the others.

Holger Schmidt deals with the topic of security requirements engineering. His approach is a threat and risk-driven methodology with a heavy focus on gathering, modeling and analyzing the environment of the planned system. The environmental information is used to create threat and risk models, which are then used to select adequate security mechanisms and establish security requirements. The method is embedded into SEPP, a security engineering process based on patterns, and is illustrated with a case study. The author also relates the terminologies of security requirements engineering and of threat and risk analysis to each other to define security-relevant domain knowledge.

In their paper, Shuhaili Talib, Nathan L. Clarke, and Steven M. Furnell describe their work on information security at the individual level. The paper examines the relationship between information security practices at the workplace and at home. A survey showed that as most awareness-raising measures in this domain target organizations, the workplace with its clear regulations and security policies was where people learned most about the topic. However, they also frequently implemented this knowledge in their homes. The authors propose a new approach to security awareness with a user focus that helps individuals develop a comprehensive security culture that they will then employ in all environments in which they operate.

Anna Vapen and Nahid Shahmehri address user security from the perspective of password security. Many Internet users use the same password on many different Web sites, which can give an attacker who captures the password for one site access to all their accounts. The problem is similar with federated identity management systems, where authentication with only a single identity provider using a username and password gives users access to their accounts on various sites. To address this issue, the authors introduce 2-clickAuth, an optical challenge-response authentication solution that uses a Web camera or camera phone and two-dimensional barcodes. They also implement an identity provider that allows users to use 2-clickAuth on all sites that support the OpenID federated identity management system, such as Facebook, MySpace, and Sourceforge.

Florian Kohlar, Jörg Schwenk, Meiko Jensen, and Sebastian Gajek present an approach to protect SAML-based federated identity management against man-in-the-middle attacks, especially for mobile devices that rely heavily on online security measures. Their novel approach allows the mobile browser to remain anonymous while still enabling the identity provider and the relying party, or service provider, to detect man-in-the-middle attacks. They achieve this by binding the SAML assertion to the transport layer security, creating a cryptographically strong dependency.

Contextual permissions and pre-obligations are at the center of the paper by Yehia Elrakaiby, Frédéric Cuppens, and Nora Cuppens-Boulahia. Pre-obligations, i.e., actions that are required before access is granted to a user – such as the payment for a song before access to the download – allow a more flexible enforcement of authorization policies. Therefore, neither traditional access control models nor newer contextual security models, which require a condition to be true at the moment of the access request, support pre-obligations. The authors present a formalized view of the interactions between the obligations and authorization policy sates, providing declarative and operational semantics for pre-obligations. They present a framework that allows policy designers to easily evaluate pre-obligations both statically and dynamically, and demonstrate their approach on a practical example.

E-commerce also needs strong security and privacy protection. Teddy Mantoro, Admir Milišić, and Media A. Ayu present an innovative approach to secure online authentication. Their method uses the infrastructure of the mobile phone network and converts the phone's SIM card into a tamper-resistant storage for security parameters, personal information and user credentials, similar to a smart card. This is combined with public key cryptography. The SIM card can then become a trusted entity that could be used for accessing sensitive applications, such as payments or online banking. The researchers developed two prototypes to demonstrate their approach, which has the added benefit of using a device users are familiar with, which could increase its acceptance.

Two papers exemplify how diverse the application of computing in **commerce** can be. While Muazzan Binsaleh and Shahizan Hassan propose a *Systems Development Methodology for Mobile Commerce Applications*, M. E. Ajana, H. Harroud, M. Boulmalf, and M. Elkoutbi look at the logistical side in *FlexRFID Middleware in the Supply Chain: Strategic Values and Challenges*.

Muazzan Binsaleh and Shahizan Hassan discuss system development methodologies and their suitability for the development of mobile commerce applications, which are used differently from regular e-commerce applications. In their paper, the authors present the first two phases of a study with the objective of proposing a system development methodology for mobile commerce applications. They investigate the currently used development methodologies and analyze their strengths and weaknesses. The paper provides a detailed overview of the methods and aims of the study and analyzes the special requirements arising from developing for mobile devices with small screens and other constraints.

M. E. Ajana, H. Harroud, M. Boulmalf, and M. Elkoutbi discuss the strategic values and challenges of RFID middleware in the supply chain. The paper provides an interesting overview of RFID technology, its components and its key concepts. It discusses how RFID technology can be used in the supply chain management to address typical problems, looking at both the benefits and the key issues. The authors also present FlexRFID, an RFID middleware solution that achieves the maximum benefits of RFID independently of the backend applications.

A very diverse array of **networks** is another big topic in this volume. Several contributions deal with improving performance of phone or data networks: Allam Mousa proposes and compares several *Prioritization Schemes in Queuing Handoff and New Calls to Reducing Call Drops in Cellular Systems*, while J. Penhoat, K. Guillouard, S. Bonjour, and P. Seïté present *A Proposal for Enhancing the Mobility Management in the Future 3GPP Architectures*. Shashi Bhushan, M. Dave, and R. B. Patel present a solution for the topology mismatch problem in P2P networks in *Reducing Network Overhead with Common Junction Methodology*, and Shailendra Mishra and D. S. Chauha propose an algorithm that optimizes the number of transmit antennas used in *Resource Allocation for Multi Access MIMO Systems*.

Two papers in this section address the optimization of wireless sensor networks: Surender Soni, Vivek Katiyar, and Narottam Chand improve energy efficiency and network lifetime in *An Energy-Efficient Multilevel Clustering Algorithm for Heterogeneous Wireless Sensor* Networks, while Sami J. Habib approaches the optimization problem of achieving maximum coverage at minimum cost in the deployment of the sensors in *Analysis of Sensors' Coverage through Application-Specific WSN Provisioning Tool.*

Allam Mousa presents four queuing scenarios designed to improve system performance and quality of service by reducing the probability of call drop for both handoff and new calls in cellular phone networks. By simulating the different scenarios, where either new calls or handoff calls are queued, and either all or half of the available frequencies are used, the author was able to show that the proposed queuing technique reduced blocking probability for both handoff and new calls.

In their paper, J. Penhoat, K. Guillouard, S. Bonjour, and P. Seïté analyze 3GPP architectures and propose a method for improving their mobility management. They reviewed 3GPP architectures and identified five architectures that had well-designed inter-access mobility management capabilities, which they consider part of the solution for coping with the growing mobile data traffic. Their approach involves splitting mobility management into three phases and assessing their integration into the architectures in question using an evaluation grid designed for the purpose. They propose a method called "hierarchical and distributed handover" to address loopholes found in the design of inter-access mobility management.

Shashi Bhushan, M. Dave, and R. B. Patel present a method to reduce network overhead in peer-to-peer (P2P) systems, which is mainly due to a topology mismatch problem between the logical overlay network and the physical underlay that form a P2P system that generates large volumes of redundant traffic. Their Common Junction Methodology (CJM) identifies optimal physical links and routes traffic through these points instead of the previously identified paths between nodes, which become suboptimal due to the frequent connections and disconnections. Their method works for both structured and unstructured P2P networks without modifying the overlay topology and or reducing the search scope of the network. The paper also includes simulation results that show that CJM resolves the mismatch problem and reduces redundant traffic significantly, as well as the response time of the network.

Shailendra Mishra and D. S. Chauha discuss technologies for enabling high-speed packet data access, specifically MIMO. They developed a new scheduling and selection algorithm for MIMO systems to calculate the optimum number of transmit antennas needed to satisfy a user's demands at a given moment. The authors present the results of a simulation carried out to examine the performance of this resource allocation and scheduling method is investigated for two types of traffic nodes: voice or Web browsing on the one hand and data transfer and streaming on the other, modeled as Pareto and Weibull distributions, respectively.

Yaser Khamayseh, Muneer Bani Yassein, Iman I. Badran, and Wail Mardini address the common problem of collision in MANETs. While a number of backoff algorithms have been proposed in the past to avoid the issue, the paper shows that no algorithm is superior in all cases. The authors therefore propose an adaptive algorithm, which chooses the best backoff mechanism for each situation from a set of mechanisms based on network density and mobility parameters. They address the time issue by implementing their algorithm in two phases, an offline phase where the algorithm can perform some computations before being deployed, and the online phase. Several simulations were carried out that showed that the proposed Square Root Backoff (SRB) was superior to the Binary Exponential Backoff (BEB) and the Linear Backoff (LB) in terms of throughput and end-to-end delay performance as well as in overall performance.

The paper by Naveen Chauhan, Lalit K. Awasthi, Narottam Chand, R. C. Joshi, and Manoj Misra deals with another issue of MANETs, frequent disconnections and, as a result, lower data availability than in traditional networks. The authors discuss the special characteristics of mobile ad hoc networks that result from limited resources, insufficient bandwidth and high user mobility, where caching is often the decisive factor for allowing rescue, military or other highly mobile operations to use MANETs successfully. They present their own caching method, where the network topology is partitioned into clusters based on physical proximity in the network. This global cluster cooperation (GCC) method allows them to utilize the pull mechanism fully for cache sharing. Their paper also presents the results of simulations that showed that the GCC mechanism performed better than other caching strategies in terms of message overheads and data accessibility.

Prashant Kumar, Naveen Chauhan, Lalit K. Awasthi, and Narottam Chand present another cooperative caching algorithm that also improves the availability of data and the overall performance of the network. This algorithm, ProCoCa, has a proactive approach. Each node is associated with a zone, and the data of nodes that are leaving a zone is cached by neighboring nodes to ensure that the data is available in the zone even after the node leaves. The results of a simulation showed that ProCoCa outperformed previously used algorithms.

Surender Soni, Vivek Katiyar, and Narottam Chand use multilevel clustering to improve not only the connectivity but also the energy efficiency and lifetime of wireless sensor networks. While there are numerous approaches to multilevel clustering, most only consider homogeneous wireless sensor networks. The authors discuss the strengths of heterogeneous networks and propose HMCA, an energy-efficient multilevel clustering scheme for heterogeneous wireless sensor networks. It is based on an existing multilevel clustering protocol EEMC for homogeneous networks, but outperforms it in a simulation in a number of categories, including energy efficiency, lifetime and data delivery ratio.

Wireless sensor networks are also the topic of Sami J. Habib's contribution, which presents an automated, application-specific provisioning tool for the deployment of sensors in wireless sensor networks that aims to achieve maximum coverage at minimum deployment cost. The coverage problem was modeled as two separate sub-problems, floor plan and placement, which were then combined into one optimization problem. By partitioning the area into M by N cells and assigning sensors into the cells, the author reduced the continuous design space into a discrete one. He then examined the relationship between varying numbers of cells with correspondingly varying sizes used to cover the area and the total number of sensors. He describes the coverage problem and solution process and provides first experimental results.

The final category is dedicated to a fundamental part of **audiovisual recognition**, with the chapter *Primary Research on Arabic Visemes, Analysis in Space, and Frequency Domain*.

The paper by Fatma Zohra Chelali, and Amar Djeradi focuses on the analysis of visemes in Arabic. Visemes are the visible mouth shapes needed to produce phonemes, the smallest phonetic units of any given language. Mapping visemes to phonemes – for linguistic research but also for applications such as lip reading or audiovisual recognition – is not simple, since not only do many phonemes look alike visually, i.e., are in the same visemic category, but also, one phoneme may have different visual forms depending on the neighboring phonemes, which can also influence lip shape. As each language has a different set of phonemes, viseme systems must be defined separately for each. The authors recorded a corpus of Arabic phonemes spoken by male and female Algerian test subjects as the basis for an Arabic viseme system. Using statistical analysis and geometrical parameters such as the height and weight of the lips, and mapping the visemes to the corresponding phonemes, the authors were able to create an Arabic viseme system that allows the recognition of the phonemes included in the corpus.

With the papers in this volume, we have sought to provide insights into the wide range of topics in this field. We hope the research, ideas, findings, and methodologies presented in the contributions are a useful source for students, developers, engineers, researchers, and managers to read about new developments and the state of the art in various application domains, to gain deeper knowledge, and to see the possibilities this field provides.

Ismail Khalil
Johanes Kepler University Linz, Austria

Edgar Weippl
Secure Business Austria - Security Research, Austria

Section 1
Security

Chapter 1
Dual–Level Attack Detection, Characterization, and Response for Networks under DDoS Attacks

Anjali Sardana
Indian Institute of Technology Roorkee, India

Ramesh C. Joshi
Indian Institute of Technology Roorkee, India

ABSTRACT

DDoS attacks aim to deny legitimate users of the services. In this paper, the authors introduce dual - level attack detection (D-LAD) scheme for defending against the DDoS attacks. At higher and coarse level, the macroscopic level detectors (MaLAD) attempt to detect congestion inducing attacks which cause apparent slowdown in network functionality. At lower and fine level, the microscopic level detectors (MiLAD) detect sophisticated attacks that cause network performance to degrade gracefully and stealth attacks that remain undetected in transit domain and do not impact the victim. The response mechanism then redirects the suspicious traffic of anomalous flows to honeypot trap for further evaluation. It selectively drops the attack packets and minimizes collateral damage in addressing the DDoS problem. Results demonstrate that this scheme is very effective and provides the quite demanded solution to the DDoS problem.

INTRODUCTION

Attack detection is the first necessary element of a complete DDoS defense system. The DDoS attack detection problem consists of designating those points in time at which network is expe-riencing an attack. Only by timely detection of DDoS attacks, system can make proper response to escape big loss.

Many techniques have been suggested so far for DDoS attack detection (Bencsath & Vajda, 2004; Blazek, Kim, Rozovskii, & Tartakovsky,

DOI: 10.4018/978-1-4666-2163-3.ch001

2001; Carl, Kesidis, Brooks, & Rai, 2005; Gil & Poletto, 2001; Ioannidis & Bellovin, 2002; Lakhina, Crovella, & Diot, 2005; Mahajan, Floyd, & Wetherall, 2001). Detecting a DDoS attack is relatively easy at the victim network (Bencsath & Vajda, 2004; Blazek et al., 2001; Gil & Poletto, 2001) because it can observe all the attack packets. However, attack packets clog a large part of the network before they are detected at the victim. Early attack detection schemes (Carl et al., 2005; Ioannidis & Bellovin, 2002; Mahajan et al., 2001) unfortunately, have to wait for the flooding to become widespread. Consequently, they are ineffective to fence off the DDoS timely. Moreover, early packet drops can cause collateral damage, as legitimate packets are also dropped with aggregate of attack flows. Many of the present DDoS attack detection techniques are complex, difficult to deploy or lead to computational and memory overheads (Bencsath & Vajda, 2004; Blazek et al., 2001; Carl et al., 2005; Gil & Poletto, 2001; Ioannidis & Bellovin, 2002; Lakhina et al., 2005; Mahajan et al., 2001).

Unlike earlier proposals for attack detection (Bencsath & Vajda, 2004; Blazek et al., 2001; Carl et al., 2005; Gil & Poletto, 2001; Ioannidis & Bellovin, 2002; Lakhina et al., 2005; Mahajan et al., 2001) that are either based on unreliable assumptions or too complicated to implement, our dual-level based scheme is simple to understand and implement. It is capable of handling infiltrating, sophisticated as well as highly distributed attacks and provides a basis for characterization. It adapts to varying network conditions with minimum false alarms.

The rest of the paper is organized as follows. The traffic feature selection is described, followed by an overview of dual-level attack detection (D-LAD) scheme. Design of macroscopic level attack detector is explained next whereas design of microscopic level attack detector is given after that. Then, the overall response technique is discussed and the performance of our proposed scheme is evaluated. Finally, the paper is concluded.

TRAFFIC FEATURE SELECTION

DDoS attacks are launched from distributed sources. Hence the attack traffic is spread across multiple links. As the distance from the victim increases, attack traffic is more diffused and harder to detect because the volume of attack flows are indistinguishable from legitimate flows. Current schemes for early attack detection are based on detecting aggregates causing sustained congestion on communication links (Ioannidis & Bellovin, 2002; Mahajan et al., 2001), imbalance between incoming or outgoing traffic volume on routers (Carl et al., 2005) and probabilistic packet marking techniques. These early detection methods, unfortunately, have to wait for the flooding to become widespread, consequently, they are ineffective to fence off the DDoS timely.

Lakhina et al. (2005) observed that most of traffic anomalies despite their diversity share a common characteristic: they induce a change in distributional aspects of packet header fields (i.e., source address, source port, destination address, and destination port etc called traffic features).

Let an information source have n independent symbols each with probability of choice p_i. Then the entropy H is defined as:

$$H = -\sum_{i=1}^{n} p_i \log_2 p_i \qquad (1)$$

Entropy can be computed on a sample of consecutive packets. The entropy detection method is used to calculate the distribution of randomness of some attributes which are fields in the network packets' headers. These attributes can be values like source IP address, TTL etc. that indicate the packet's properties. Entropy captures in a single value the distributional changes in traffic features, and observing the time series of entropy on the features exposes unusual traffic behavior.

Source IP based entropy algorithms are efficient in case of highly distributed DDoS attacks or highly concentrated high bandwidth attacks. A proficient and sophisticated attacker usually tries to defeat the detection algorithm based on source IP based entropy (Feinstein, Schnackenberg, Balupari, & Kindred, 2003) by secretly producing flooding attack and simulating the monitor's expected normal data flow. After knowing some packet attributes' entropy values, these attackers could use the attack tools to produce some flooding with adjustable entropy values. By guess, test or summary these attackers could probably know the normal entropy range in the monitors and adjust their own flooding to match it, although such stealthy attacks are not easy to realize.

We improve the previous entropy detection algorithms and propose enhanced algorithms for dual level detection: macroscopic detectors are based on entropy calculated over source IP and microscopic detectors are based on entropy calculated over destination IP.

DUAL-LEVEL ATTACK DETECTION SCHEME

System Model

We use transit stub network model (Zegura, Calvert, & Bhattacharjee, 1996; Zegura, Calvert, & Donahoo, 1997) for the Internet as shown in Figure 1.

Transit stub model is based on the hierarchical approach of the Internet (Zegura et al., 1996; Zegura et al., 1997). In such a model, every domain can be classified as either a stub network or a transit network. Backbone ISPs and regional ISPs are examples of transit networks. The traffic generating nodes (end hosts) are only connected to Stub networks. We model the Internet to measure the entropy in transit – stub network. During an attack, the Internet or IP domain is divided into the two networks; one for inside to be protected

Figure 1. Dual-level attack detection, characterization and response

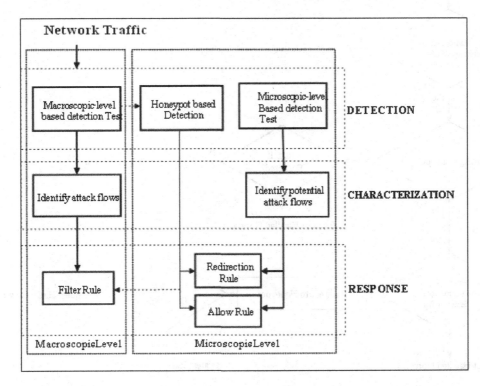

and the other is for outside where attackers may reside. The entropy is measured by recording the dynamics of packets on the border of the two networks. Packets flowing between these two networks may incur to sustain the current value of the entropy if those packets are in harmony with the system or change abruptly if those agitate the system. In the proposed system we keep track of the value of entropy in time to pinpoint the sudden changes in the value. Those changes are regarded as the installation of attacks in the network. Figure 1 shows the modeled dual-level attack detection, characterization and response framework.

Detection Workflow

Figure 2 shows the detection flowchart. Detection algorithms are running on the edge routers of transit and stub network. Macroscopic or largest volume of attacks should be detected early and dropped before they enter the victim network. These attack flows that can create congestion in the network and stress resource utilization in a router and network, which make them crucial to be dropped before they enter the network from an operational standpoint. Macroscopic detectors on edge routers of transit network consistently detect these attacks and do so with a very low false alarm rate. The edge routers of transit network monitor the network traffic by calculating system entropy over source IP aggregates. In the non-attack case, system entropy stays within a stable range. When

Figure 2. Detection flowchart

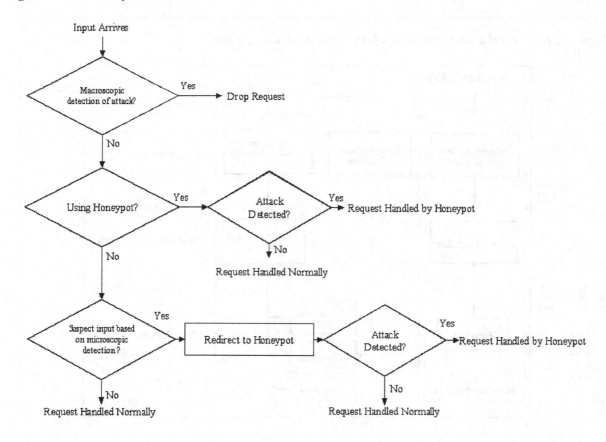

there is an attack, flows are destined on honeypot and entropy based on source IP aggregates (flows) changes dramatically at router, because there is either one flow dominating the router (this indicates concentrated attack and entropy decreases) or multiple flows with a very few packet arrivals in each flow (this indicates distributed attacks and entropy increases).

Microscopic attacks may not necessarily impact the network, but they can have dramatic impact on the victim or server. Microscopic detectors located on edge routers of stub domain are used for such attacks. They enable highly sensitive detection. System entropy based on destination IP based aggregates (flows) is calculated on edge routers of stub domain for servers to be protected. When there is an attack, the system entropy decreases dramatically, because there is one flow dominating the router of the stub domain. In this case, the edge router treats the dominant flow as victim of DDoS attack. Once the victim of DDoS attack is identified, characterization process is triggered and starts to calculate the entropy rate of source IP aggregates on the victim to identify attack flows.

MACROSCOPIC LEVEL ATTACK DETECTOR (MA-LAD)

Macroscopic detectors detect macroscopic attacks which are highly distributed DDoS flooding attacks (e.g., Distributed reflector denial of service attacks) or highly concentrated high bandwidth attacks which induce immediate congestion in the network.

They are located on the edge routers of the transit domains and hence enable early DDoS detection without any traffic observation in the victim network. They make use of computing entropies based on source IP addresses and detect an attack if system entropy crosses threshold limits. If the flows are destined to honeypots, attack is confirmed and corresponding attack flows are

dropped. Thresholds are optimized according to client requirements and network conditions.

Sampling and Detection

Entropy $H(X)$ is used as a parameter to measure traffic feature distributions. Consider a random process $\{X(t), t = j\Delta, j \in N\}$ where Δ, a constant time interval is called time window, N is the set of positive integers, and for each $t, X(t)$ is a random variable. Here $X(t)$ represents the number of packet arrivals for a flow in $\{t - \Delta, t\}$. $X(t)$ As a whole represent our empirical histogram for computing entropy. It is found in our simulation without attack that Entropy $H(X)$ value varies within very narrow limits after slow start phase is over. This variation becomes narrower if we increase Δ i.e., monitoring period. We take average of $H(X)$ and designate that as normal Entropy $H_n(X)$. To detect the attack, the entropy $H_c(X)$ is calculated in shorter time window Δ continuously, whenever there is appreciable deviation from $H_n(X)$ attack is said to be detected (Sardana, Kumar, & Joshi, 2007).

We assume that the system is under attack at time t_a, which means that all attacking sources start emitting packets from this time: the network is in normal state for time $t < t_a$ and turns into attacked state in time t_a. Let t_d denote our estimate on t_a. At time t_d following event triggers

$$(H_c(X) > (H_n(X) + a \times d)) \cup$$
$$(H_c(X) < (H_n(X) - a \times d)) \qquad (2)$$
$$attack = true;$$

Here $a \in I$ where I is set of integers and d is deviation threshold. Tolerance factor or threshold a is a design parameter and d is absolute maximum deviation in Entropy $H(X)$ from average value $H_n(X)$ while profiling for network without attack.

Decision of Optimum Threshold and System Calibration

Many detection tools use a fixed threshold to alarm on anomalous traffic. This method makes sense for some applications. For example, in control systems, there may be a certain tolerance level for products to be considered "acceptable." If this tolerance level is exceeded, then the product is considered "bad." But for network traffic monitoring, the background is continually changing. If the background traffic changes, these thresholds may become meaningless and need to be changed. If the threshold is set too high, entropic range that classifies traffic as legitimate would be broad, then the false alarm rate will be low, but detection rate will be low, too. Similarly, if the threshold set too low may end up detecting most intrusions, but suffer from a high false alarm rate. Therefore, it is critical to update these estimates adaptively. By adaptive threshold we mean that the threshold is updated regularly. Since this adaptive approach continually updates the tolerance factor, the model adjusts to reflect changes in background traffic. By adjusting a baseline, estimates can adjust more or less quickly to changes in the background. Threshold is decided depending on the network conditions. False positives (FP) give the effectiveness of the system whereas false negatives (FN) give a measure of the system reliability. Variation in tolerance factor 'a' has been used to quantify false positives and false negatives which assist in making decisions on optimal value of entropic thresholds (Sardana, Joshi, & Kim, 2008).

Defense Modes

Depending on the threshold or tolerance factor 'a' (refer to Equation 2), the mode of operation is chosen so as to minimize false positives and false negatives. In case of best defense, the value of 'a' and hence the normal entropy bandwidth during attack detection is chosen to be very small. The choice is made to reduce the false negatives to minimum, and is zero in ideal case. Normal and naïve defense have higher values of 'a'; lower detection sensitivity levels and hence lower false positive rate.

System calibration is performed under variable network load by determining optimal entropic thresholds and cut-offs to give minimum false alarms.

Honeypot-Based False Positive and Negative Suppression

We propose the deployment of honeypot along with the server to detect and isolate the attacks that have been crafted to match the statistics of the legitimate traffic. This also reduces false negatives under naïve defense mode of operation and false alarms under best defense mode as follows: If the client load is high, to avoid adverse effects to legitimate traffic (keep FP low); detectors are often tuned in naïve defense mode. Due to the presence of honeypots, attack traffic that lie in permissible entropy range but attempt to exploit the vulnerabilities are directed to honeypots, thus reducing the false negatives. On the other hand, if attack load is also high, detectors are tuned towards best defense mode (reduces false negatives and keeps attack load off the server). Again, due to the presence of honeypot, legitimate traffic that was misclassified by entropic detector will be validated by the honeypot and will be handled correctly by the active server (i.e., a flow that was mistakenly tagged as attack will be served correctly), reducing the false positive. Once value of 'a' is decided, depending upon attacker's aims and defender's needs, optimum entropic thresholds are automatically updated (according to Equation 2) to calibrate the system. Depending on the client load (CL) and attack load (AL) observed during detection, the system can operate in one of the three modes of operation, naive, normal and best.

MICROSCOPIC LEVEL ATTACK DETECTOR (MI-LAD)

Macroscopic level attack detectors are successful in isolating voluminous congestion inducing attack traffic. However, some attacks may not abruptly stress the resources. Slow rate, isotropic attacks that do not cause immediate congestion may go undetected. Moreover, distributional changes captured by entropy observed on source IP alone cannot detect stealthy and sophisticated attacks that are crafted to match statistics of normal traffic. For example, the attackers may simulate the normal network behaviors, e.g. pumping the attack packages as Poisson distribution, to disable macroscopic detectors. Also, how to discriminate DDoS attacks from surge legitimate accessing is a major challenge.

Current volume based detection schemes (Bencsath & Vajda, 2004; Blazek et al., 2001; Gil & Poletto, 2001) for attack detection at the victim cannot detect slow rate, isotropic attacks because these attacks do not cause detectable disruptions in traffic volume. Moreover, solutions (Bencsath & Vajda, 2004; Blazek et al., 2001; Gil & Poletto, 2001) suffer from collateral damage when attack is carried at slow rate or when volume per attack flow is not so high as compared to legitimate flows.

A DDoS attack, regardless of its volume and source, will cause the distribution of destination address to be concentrated on the victim address. In DDoS attack scenario, a single destination IP address (or alternatively, a very, very few number of unique destination IP addresses) receives much more traffic than other normal conditions. Hence, observing the time series of entropy on destination IP exposes unusual traffic behavior which source IP alone could not detect. A decline in entropy of the system in the destination IP address based entropy time series indicates Denial of Service attack.

However, this happens as well when there is a flash crowd or surge of legitimate accessing to one server. Based on router entropy calculation alone, we cannot identify the surge of legitimate accessing from DDoS attacks. In order to detect a DDoS attack, we need to test for changes in our detection feature over time. However, our detection feature is a random variable due to the stochastic nature of Internet traffic. Consequently, we require a mechanism that can accurately discriminate between the onset of a DDoS attack and a temporary random fluctuation in traffic.

We therefore apply cumulative sum (CUSUM) (Basseville & Nikiforov, 1993) to solve this problem. CUSUM is calculated over destination IP address based entropy to detect the attacks. It makes use of the concept of time along with threshold to judge the network condition. If the abnormal condition persists for a certain period or crosses threshold, attack is detected. Destination under attack is identified in case attack is present.

Sampling and Detection

Microscopic attack detectors designate different flow IDs to each unique DestinationIP, DestinationPort encountered in incoming packet. In other words, we define flow as the packets that share same destination address at the edge router of stub network.

Our attack detection algorithm is based on the Sequential Change Point Detection (Basseville & Nikiforov, 1993).

Change Point Detection: CUSUM

In the non parameter CUSUM algorithm, the idea of sequential variation is proposed (Peng, Leckie, & Ramamohanarao, 2003, 2004). To implement that algorithm, one needs to create database containing large amount of legal IP address. The calculation is complicated and has low efficiency. In our improvement, we use the destination IP address based entropy statistics. Because of the nature of entropy, it clearly shows the distribution of destination IP's randomness to entropy calculated on the basis destination IP addresses.

We try to cumulate the entropy according to some rules, thus it will have more accurate DDoS attack detection rate.

In our destination IP address entropy based DDoS attack detection method, suppose Y_n is the destination IP address based system entropy value calculated on edge router or stub at each sampling interval of Δ_n, and the random sequence is extracted as network service random model. In the normal occasion this sequence is independent and distributed. Assume the variation parameter is the average value of the sequence. Before change, this value $E(Y_n) = \alpha$. Before attack, when the network is normal, the distribution of destination IP addresses is stable, and has certain randomness. But when DDoS attack happens on one of the destinations, this average value will decrease suddenly. $E(Y_n)$ will become far smaller than α. Without losing any statistics properties, we transfer the sequence to another random sequence $\{Z_n\}$ with negative average value:

$$\text{Let } Z_n = -(Y_n - \beta) \tag{3}$$

where $\alpha = \beta$. In a given network environment, parameter β is a constant used for producing a negative random sequence $\{Z_n\}$, and thus the entire value of Z_n will not be cumulated along the time. In our detection algorithm, we define that $\beta = \alpha$. When the attack happens, Z_n will suddenly become very large and positive. The detection threshold is the limit for the positive, which is the cumulative value of Z_n.

We use this recursive formula for cumulative sum:

$$S_0 = 0$$

$$S_n = \max(S_{n-1} + Z_n, 0) \tag{4}$$

where S_n represents the cumulative positive value of Z_n. The bigger the S_n, the stronger the attack is.

We calculate the rate of increase of CUSUM as:

$$C_0 = 0$$

$$C_n = (C_{n-1} + 1), (S_n > S_{n-1}) = 0, \text{ otherwise} \tag{5}$$

where C_n represents a counter and signifies the duration of increase in S_n. It uses the concept of time to judge the network condition. The bigger the C_n, higher the probability that there is an attack. The judgment function is:

$$d_n(S_n, C_n) = 1, S_n > T \text{ OR } C_n > T' = 0, \text{ otherwise} \tag{6}$$

where $d_n(S_n, C_n)$ is the judgment function at time n, the value 1 shows that attack happens, while 0 shows the normal case. T and T' are the detection thresholds. We can control the total attack detection time by setting the value of parameter T'. For example, if time window Δ_n is .2s and T'=8, an alarm is generated only when destination IP address based entropy increases for more than 1.6s or destination IP address based entropy increases beyond T, whichever earlier. A sudden traffic increase in short time might still be a normal traffic and should be allowed. But if the networks anomaly lasts for more than 1.6s or longer, the system might be abnormal, and some attacks might happen.

The advantage of this improved algorithm is that it comprises implicitly a concept of process cumulating. The function of cumulating process is to avoid false alarm when the network has something abnormal just at a time point like a surge of legitimate access. Thus the threshold based approach leads to a more real time attack detection. Time based approach emphasizes on time tolerance and ignores network anomalies in some allowable range. Network is regarded abnormal if threshold is reached or tolerable limit defined by time period increases.

OVERALL RESPONSE MECHANISM

The proposed response mechanism works by implementing three rules, namely allow rule, redirect rule and drop rule to advocate the above functionality. Hence, our response mechanism selectively drops the attack packets and minimizes collateral damage in addressing the DDoS problem. It redirects the suspicious traffic of anomalous flows to honeypot trap for further evaluation. Legitimate traffic is directed to servers.

Our approach to DDoS defense involves response methods which are based on results obtained from characterization. The packets belonging to characterized flows as subjected to one of the three packet filter rules. As a first step to response at microscopic-level, the packets belonging to flows identified as attack are subjected to packet filtering depending upon the intensity of attack and user requirements. At microscopic-level, the response module allows the packets to enter the server or redirects them to honeypots depending on the corresponding flow being classified as normal or suspicious attack based on the results of microscopic-level characterization. Honeypots isolate those stealthy and sophisticated attacks that exploit the vulnerabilities and statistical anomaly detector fails to identify. Thus the overall goal of response module is to allow as much traffic into the network as it can tolerate without compromising with the services to the legitimate requests, and block the congestion inducing traffic early in the network.

Filter Rule

A filter rule is used to drop the packets belonging to source IP based flow aggregates that have been characterized as attacks during macroscopic-level characterization. Because the thresholds and baseline estimates established at macroscopic-level are adaptive and minimize false positives, filtering is performed with minimum collateral damage. Because the mechanism generates filtering rules immediately based on the traffic characteristics it gathers from detection and characterization at macroscopic-level, the response is immediate. Filtering reduces the impact of congestion inducing attack traffic almost instantaneously.

Redirect Rule

This rule redirects the packets to honeypots and is applied to flows that have been identified as suspicious attacks as a result of characterization at microscopic-level. Such packets belong to flows that are either destined to honeypots or the source IP address based flow that have same or similar entropy value and their entropy rate is zero or less than threshold and are destined to victim.

If the flow is found to be anomalous at microscopic-level, it is tagged as suspicious attack otherwise it is tagged as normal during characterization. Instead of just dropping the packets corresponding to suspicious attack flows enroute or resetting sessions, they are actively redirected from hostile sources to honeypot. Honeypot server responds to suspicious attack flows in exactly same manner as would the actual server to legitimate clients. Active server and honeypot both are with the same IP. Since the connection with suspicious attack flows is retained, the flows can be treated as legitimate flows and directed to active server if the corresponding flows are found to be belonging to a set of legitimate normal flows in subsequent time windows, but were momentarily misclassified as suspects. Since the packets corresponding to such flows can be transferred back to actual server in subsequent time window, FN are reduced. However if persistently, in many time windows, the flow remains tagged suspicious attack, connection remains directed at honeypot server. Also one can potentially gain more information about the attacker. Since, instead of dropping such flows, they are redirected to honeypots, they can be analyzed before a final response decision is taken. This reduces collateral damage.

A set of flows $F_n - F_n^* + F_s^*$ are subjected to redirection.

Allow Rule

During DDoS attack, there is a need to allow a particular kind of traffic that belongs to legitimate clients to pass through the network and reach the server or destination. The allow rule is used to allow the packets belonging to flows identified as legitimate during the characterization step.

A set of flows $F_n^* + F_S - F_S^*$ are permitted access to the server. The production rules for response are presented in Box 1.

Overall Detection, Characterization and Response Algorithms

The overall algorithm for macroscopic-level detection, characterization and response at the edge router of transit network is presented in Algorithm 1. The overall algorithm for microscopic-level detection, characterization and response at the edge router of stub network is shown in Algorithm 2. The overall scheme is shown in the following sections.

Raising DDoS Attack Alarm at Edge Routers in Transit Stub Network

This corresponds to macroscopic-level detection. We collect source IP based flow samples on the edge router of the transit network for a time window. If the entropy of system changes dramatically or flows are destined to honeypots or both, a DDoS attack is confirmed and alarm is raised at the router.

Handling the DDoS Suspects at Microscopic-Level

We collect destination IP based flow samples on edge router of stub network for a time window. We monitor system entropy as well as contribution of entropy of each destination towards the total system entropy. If the entropy of system decreases dramatically, the victim is identified and alarm is generated.

Discriminating DDoS Attacks from Legitimate Traffic

In case of macroscopic-level characterization, packet arrivals and entropy rate for each source IP based flows are calculated. Set of flows having least or highest measured packet arrivals which share same or very similar entropy and minimal variations in their entropy are attack flows. In case of microscopic-level detection, source IP based flows destined to victim that share same or very similar entropy and minimal variations in their source entropy are suspects and tagged as suspicious attacks. Flows destined to honeypots are also tagged as suspicious attacks.

Box 1.

Production Rules for Response

If
 {Flow identified as attack at macroscopic-level}
   FILTER
 else if
 {Flow destined to honeypot OR identified suspicious attack at microscopic-level}
   REDIRECT
 else ALLOW

Algorithm 1.

---

i. For a time window, initialize the parameters and size of time window.

ii. Count the number of packets from different sources in a time window.

iii. Calculate the system entropy $H(X)$ based on source IP aggregates. Determine the optimum threshold; calibrate the system; detect the attack.

iv. If Attack = true, trigger characterization and start monitoring the individual contribution of entropy of each source IP based flows towards total system entropy.

v. Determine m flows that have highest or least packet arrival rates and contribute least to source IP aggregate based system entropy.

vi. Drop the identified attack flows.

Algorithm 2.

---

i. For a time window, initialize the parameters and size of time window.

ii. Count the number of packets to different destinations.

iii. Calculate the system entropy $H(X)$ based on destination IP aggregates. Apply CUSUM and judgment function.

iv. If Attack = true, identify the victim and start monitoring the source IP flow based entropy for flows destined to victim.

v. Set of source IP based flows that share same or very similar entropy and minimal variations in their entropy such that their entropy rate is zero or less than threshold value are suspects and tagged as suspicious attacks. Moreover flows destined to honeypots are also tagged as suspicious attacks.

vi. The flows tagged as suspicious attacks are directed to honeypots whereas the flows tagged as normal or legitimate are allowed access to servers.

Eliminating DDoS Attack Packets Before They Reach the Target

Packets corresponding to the attack flows identified at macroscopic-level on the edge router of transit network are discarded. In case of microscopic-level, the packets corresponding to flows either tagged as attacks or destined to honeypots are isolated from legitimate traffic and redirected to honeypots. Hence the detection, identification, elimination and isolation of attacks are done before the attack packets reach the target.

PERFORMANCE EVALUATION

Detector Evaluation

In order to evaluate the effectiveness of the DDoS detection mechanism, one must address the following issues. Firstly, it must determine what kind of DDoS attacks can be detected and what fraction of monitored traffic the attacks must be

compromised in order to be detected. Secondly, it should be applicable to wide environments with minor changes in threshold settings. If the method is to be applied in core routers, its per packet computational requirements and memory usage must be modest. The basic parameters for simulation are shown in Table 1.

Experiment Design and Procedure

For the study in this paper, we model the Internet as transit stub network. We choose AT&T networking environment and generate its transit-stub model (Heckmann, Piringer, Schmitt, & Steinmetz, 2003). Our specific model has 3 core routers, 4 transit nodes with 3 stubs per transit and 4 stub nodes, 5 servers and 137 clients (legitimate clients and attackers). The topology considered is similar to the one used traditionally to depict a typical client-server scenario in the Internet. Transit domain edge routers are point of presence (POP) of the ISP and stub domains are customer domains attached to POPs.

Table 1. Basic parameters of simulation

	Parameter	Value
1	Number of legal sources	15-48
2	Number of attackers	1-89
3	Backbone link bandwidth	100 Mbps
5	Bottleneck link bandwidth	10 Mbps
6	Bottleneck link delay	1 msec
7	Access link bw for legitimate clients	1 Mbps
8	Access link delay for legitimate clients	10 msec
9	Server link bandwidth	3 Mbps
10	Server link delay	1 ms
11	Mean attacker rate	0.1-3.0 Mbps (low rate) 3.0 – 6.5 Mbps (moderate rate) > 6.5 Mbps (high rate)
12	Mean client load	0.1-7.0 Mbps (low rate) 7.0-9.0 Mbps (moderate rate) >9.0 Mbps (high rate)

NS2 (Simulator, 2005) topology for AT&T transit stub model has been generated using GT-ITM (Calvert & Zegura, 1997) and extended nam (Figure 3).

Detection of Attack by Ma-LAD

As soon as any event in Equation 2 triggers, attack is said to have occurred. Figure 4 shows entropy profile when network is put under such attack.

The attack is launched with 80 attackers with mean rate varying from.05 to 4 Mbps per attacker. Clearly in first time window after attack is launched at 8 seconds, there is jump in entropy value. The positive jump and persistent high value of entropy as compared to no attack case reflects a distributed attack. Also note that mean attacker rate is low and the flows causing this anomaly are highly distributed and have comparatively lesser frequency than already existing ones.

Threshold Optimization in Ma-LAD

Figure 5 shows the entropy profiles of attacks simulated by 5 attackers generating traffic at the rate of 10 Mbps. Client load varies depending on the number of clients and traffic rate. We model two different workloads, low client load and high client load. In case of low client load, a low value of tolerance factor 'a' easily detects all the attacks and have low false alarms. Higher value of 'a' reduces the false alarms to zero but lower the detection rate as well. However, at high client load, the parameters like detection and false alarm rate become sensitive to tolerance factor 'a'. In case of high client load, at low value of 'a' to maximize detection rate, a large number of false alarms are generated. A very large value of 'a' to minimize false alarms reduces the detection rate to nearly 50%.

Hence, there is a trade-off between detection rate and false alarm rate. These parameters become more sensitive at high client loads. Static or fixed value of tolerance factor 'a' does not work in dynamic network environment. We therefore need to quantify and optimize the value of 'a' (so as to maximize detection rate keeping false alarms low) according to the network environment and subsequently calibrate the detection mechanism.

ROC Analysis

We quantify the tolerance factor 'a' to vary between 2 – 9 for different network scenarios. We generate ROC (receiver operating characteristic) curves to compare the detection performance by varying tolerance factor 'a' in different network environments. We plot ROC curve where each point represents a sensitivity/(100-specificity) (or detection rate/false alarm rate) pair corresponding to a particular value of tolerance factor 'a'.

To plot the ROC curves, we vary attack load in two ways, first, by varying the mean attack rate keeping the number of attackers constant (Figure 6 (a), (b) and (c)) and second, by varying

Figure 3. Simulation topology of AT&T transit stub network used in our experiments

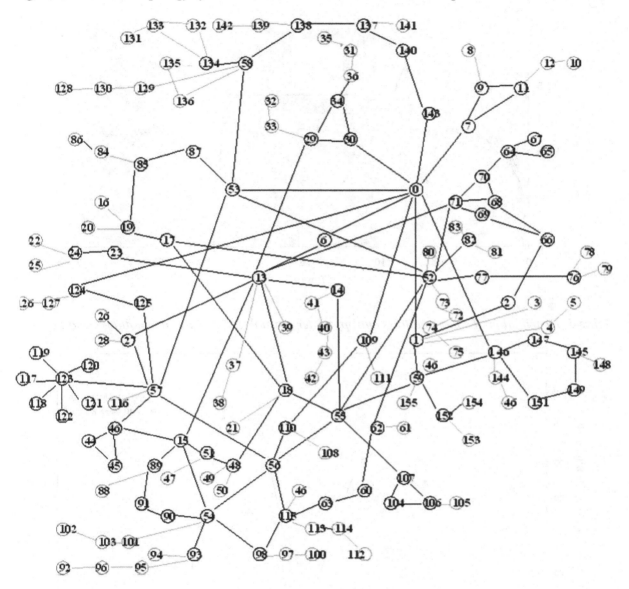

the number of attackers keeping the mean attack rate constant (Figure 6(d), (e) and (f)). In the first case, with 60 attackers and .5 Mbps attack rate, values of a equal to 8 and 9 give largest areas under curve (Figure 6(a)), as the attack rate increases to 2 Mbps, maximum area under curve is obtained by a equal to 7 (Figure 6(b)) and with a further increase in attack load to 5 Mbps, maximum area under curve is obtained at a still lower value of a,

i.e., a = 3 (Figure 6(c)). Hence optimum value of 'a' decreases as the attack load increases. A similar trend is seen in Figure 6(d), (e) and (f) where the attack load increases by increasing the number of attackers, keeping the mean attack rate constant.

On the basis of the above observation, we calibrate our macroscopic level detector to work in one of the three modes of defense, as shown in Table 2.

Figure 4. Entropy distribution for DDoS

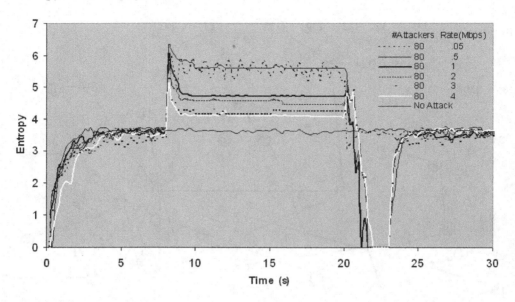

Figure 5. Distribution of source address entropy under normal and typical-DDoS attack conditions

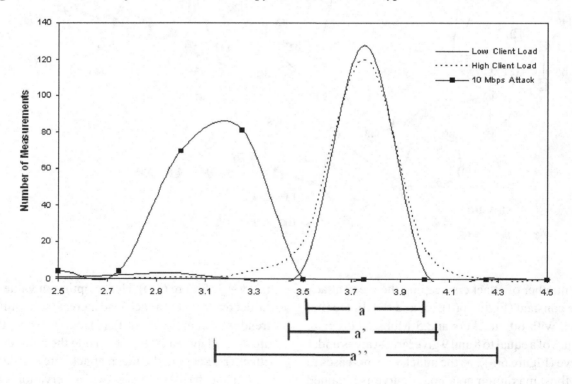

Figure 6. RoC curves

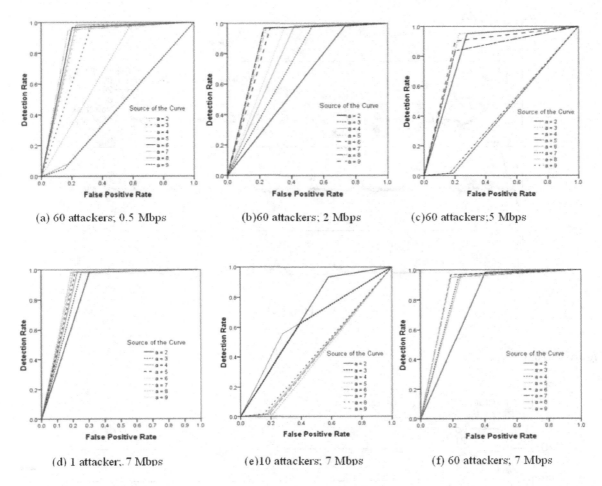

(a) 60 attackers; 0.5 Mbps   (b)60 attackers; 2 Mbps   (c)60 attackers;5 Mbps

(d) 1 attacker;. 7 Mbps   (e)10 attackers; 7 Mbps   (f) 60 attackers; 7 Mbps

Detection of Attack by Mi-LAD

Figure 7 shows the time series of source IP address based system entropy under normal conditions in the absence of attack as well as in the presence of sophisticated DDoS attacks like 20 attackers with attack rate 2 Mbps and 3 Mbps and 80 attackers with 5 Mbps. There is a significant overlap between the time series of source IP address based system entropy for normal and attack conditions which shows that detection of such attacks is not possible based on source IP address based entropy alone. In such cases where source domain entropy does not show remarkable distinction, a significant drop in destination domain entropy clearly detects the presence of the attacks as shown in the figure.

Figure 8 shows the time series value of counter C_n (refer Equation 5) which judges the persistence of abnormal condition in the network over a time period. By setting the threshold T' = 5 for our network environment, when C_n >T', we believe

Table 2. Mapping parameter to mode of operation

Mode of Operation	Tolerance Factor 'a'
Naïve Defense	6 - 9
Normal Defense	4 - 6
Best Defense	2 - 4

Figure 7. Time series entropy

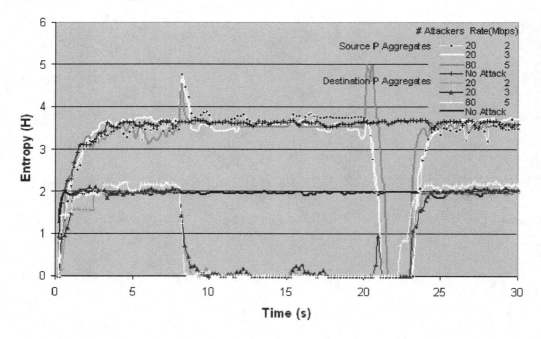

Figure 8. Time series C_n

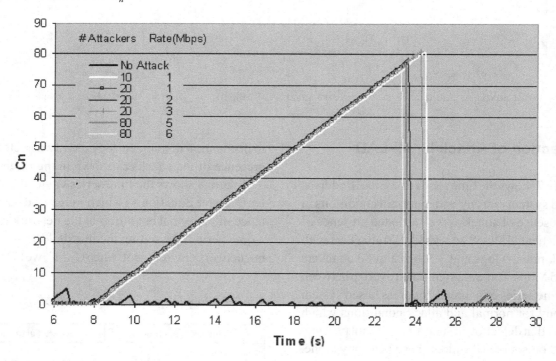

that something abnormal persisted over network tolerance limit and network is attacked. The flash crowds persist for a very small duration and are represented by small positive fluctuations that lie below threshold T' as shown in the figure. Hence, results in the figure justify our claim that the approach is able to differentiate between DDoS attacks and flash crowds.

The judgment function is given in Equation 6. The judgment function is based on two events. As soon as any one of the two events becomes true, the value of judgment function is triggered to 1 and attack is said to have occurred.

Identification of the Victim

We monitor the contribution of each destination IP based flow's entropy towards total system entropy at edge router of stub network where each distinct destination IP corresponds to a server to be protected. Since, the overall decrease in the destination IP based total system entropy triggers the microscopic-level characterization, there is one destination IP based flow that dominates rest of flows, and therefore flow with highest frequency of packet arrivals is victim.

Figure 9 shows time series entropy variation of each destination IP based flow which corresponds to each server in the server pool of five servers to be protected. The attack is simulated with 20 attackers at the rate of 2 Mbps, and starts at 8 seconds. Figure 9 clearly shows that server 118 has the least measured entropy value during the attack period and contributes least to the total system entropy; and hence is the cause of decrease in total system entropy. This implies that server 118 has highest measured frequency of packet arrivals identifying it has victim of the attack.

Figure 10 shows the relationship between different attack strengths and decrease in entropy of the flow identified as victim. The entropy of server 118 decreases in presence of different attack strengths. The higher the strength of attack more is the decrease in the entropy of the victim. It is so because higher the strength of attack more is the frequency of packet arrivals, and lesser the contribution of the flow's entropy in total system entropy.

We simulated the attack with 10 attackers at rate of 1 Mbps and monitored time series entropy of each distinct Source IP based flow destined to server 118. Figure 11 shows that set of source IP

Figure 9. Time series entropy variations of distinct destination IP based flow corresponding to each server

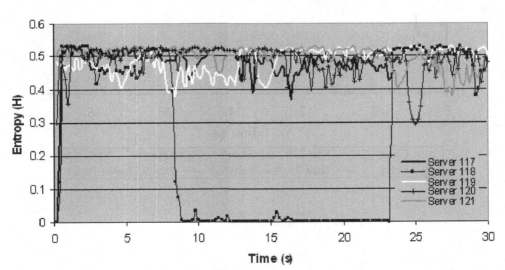

Figure 10. Time series entropy variations showing contribution of victim flow towards total destination IP based system entropy under different attack strengths

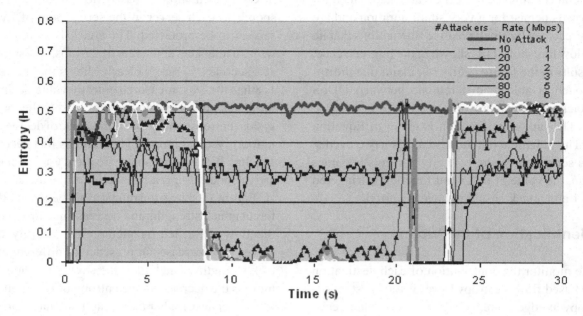

Figure 11. Time series entropy variations of each distinct source IP based flow destined to the victim (server 118) monitored on edge router of stub network ; 10 attackers ;1 Mbps

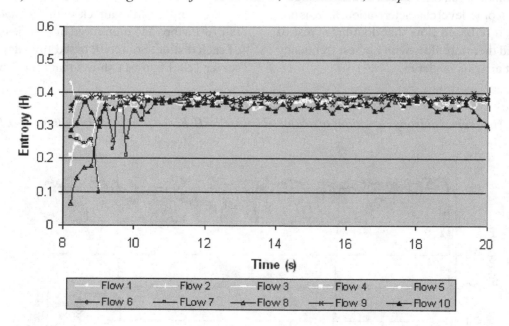

Table 3. Intensity of DoS and DDoS attacks

Thinning Factor	Attack Rate (Mbps)
0	100
10	10
100	1
1000	.1
10000	.01
100000	.001
1000000	.0001

based flows from 1 to 10 share same entropy space and there are minimal variations in their entropy rate. These dominant signals are effortlessly identified tagged as suspicious attacks.

Sensitivity of Detector to Attack Detection

We document the sensitivity of entropy based approach of our detector to DoS and DDoS event detection. We simulate 10 Mbps legitimate traffic originating from 15 clients picked randomly with inter-arrival time of .1 seconds. Attack load is varied from 100 to .0001 Mbps representing thinning factor from 0 to 1000000 respectively. DoS attack is launched with single attacker whereas DDoS attack is launched with 80 attackers sending attack traffic towards victim. Table 3 shows the attack rate corresponding to various thinning factors.

Figure 12 shows that high detection rates are possible for much lower intensities of attack. For example, a detection rate of nearly 98% is possible for DoS and DDoS events comprising only 0.90% of the total traffic. When attack traffic

Figure 12. Sensitivity of detector to attack detection

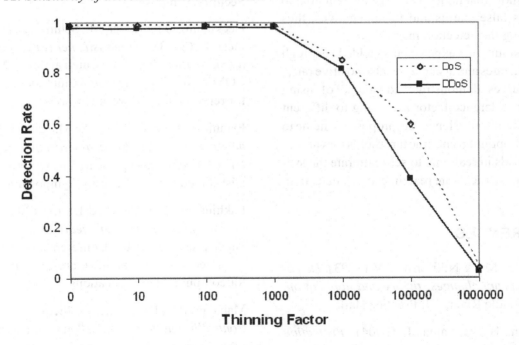

comprises .09% of total traffic on average, the detection is still effective but to a lesser degree.

In summary, the results in this section are encouraging for the use of dual level detection scheme. We find that dual level scheme exposes a lot of anomalies, generates relatively few false alarms, can be tuned to different network environments by optimizing the threshold, and has a high detection rate even when it comprises a small fraction of total traffic.

CONCLUSION

The two step approach is appropriate for detecting a large variety of DDoS attacks. It detects congestion inducing attacks at the early stage, without any collateral damage. Stealthy and sophisticated attacks that remain undetected are detected near the victim. Even very meek rate DDoS attacks are detected reliably early in the network. The results show that honeypots have the potential to suppress false alarms and false negatives, thus improving the detection rate.

The simulation experiments yielded very high detection rates and acceptable false positive rates. ROC curves demonstrate advantage of using optimum tolerance factor according to different attack conditions. Hence, the proposed scheme to calculate optimum entropic thresholds for varying attack loads in real time to self-calibrate the system promises accurate real time attack detection.

REFERENCES

Basseville, M., & Nikiforov, I. V. (1993). *Detection of abrupt changes: theory and application.* Upper Saddle River, NJ: Prentice Hall.

Bencsath, B., & Vajda, I. (2004). *Protection against DDoS attacks based on traffic level measurements.* Paper presented at the International Symposium on Collaborative Technologies.

Blazek, R. B., Kim, H., Rozovskii, B., & Tartakovsky, A. (2001). *A novel approach to detection of denial-of-service attacks via adaptive sequential and batch-sequential change-point detection methods.* Paper presented at the IEEE Workshop Information Assurance and Security.

Calvert, K., & Zegura, E. (1997). *GT internetwork topology models.* GT-ITM.

Carl, G., Kesidis, G., Brooks, R. R., & Rai, S. (2005). *Denial-of-service attack-detection techniques.* Distributed Systems Online.

Feinstein, L., Schnackenberg, D., Balupari, R., & Kindred, D. (2003). *Statistical approaches to DDoS attack detection and response.* Paper presented at the DARPA Information Survivability Conference and Exposition.

Gil, T. M., & Poletto, M. (2001). *MULTOPS: a data-structure for bandwidth attack detection.* Paper presented at the 10th conference on USENIX Security Symposium.

Heckmann, O., Piringer, M., Schmitt, J., & Steinmetz, R. (2003). *On realistic network topologies for simulation.* Paper presented at the ACM SIGCOMM workshop on Models, methods and tools for reproducible network research.

Ioannidis, J., & Bellovin, S. M. (2002). *Implementing pushback: Router-based defense against DDoS attacks.* Paper presented at the Network and Distributed System Security Symposium.

Lakhina, A., Crovella, M., & Diot, C. (2005). *Mining anomalies using traffic feature distributions.* Paper presented at the Conference on Applications, technologies, architectures, and protocols for computer communications.

Mahajan, R., Floyd, S., & Wetherall, D. (2001). *Controlling high-bandwidth flows at the congested router.* Paper presented at the Proc. 9th International Conference on Network Protocols.

Peng, T., Leckie, C., & Ramamohanarao, K. (2003). Detecting distributed denial of service attacks by sharing distributed beliefs. In Safavi-Naini, R., & Seberry, J. (Eds.), *Lecture Notes in Computer Science* (*Vol. 2727*, pp. 214–225). New York: Springer.

Peng, T., Leckie, C., & Ramamohanarao, K. (2004). Proactively detecting distributed denial of service attacks using source IP address monitoring. In Mitrou, N. (Ed.), *Lecture Notes in Computer Science* (pp. 771–782). New York: Springer.

Sardana, A., Joshi, R., & Kim, T. (2008). *Deciding Optimal Entropic Thresholds to Calibrate the Detection Mechanism for Variable Rate DDoS Attacks in ISP Domain.* Paper presented at the International Conference on Information Security and Assurance.

Sardana, A., Kumar, K., & Joshi, R. C. (2007). *Detection and Honeypot Based Redirection to Counter DDoS Attacks in ISP Domain.* Paper presented at the 3rd International Symposium on Information Assurance and Security.

Simulator, N. (2005). *2 (NS2).* Retrieved from http://www.isi.edu/nsnam

Zegura, E. W., Calvert, K. L., & Bhattacharjee, S. (1996). *How to model an internetwork.* Paper presented at the IEEE INFOCOM.

Zegura, E. W., Calvert, K. L., & Donahoo, M. J. (1997). A quantitative comparison of graph-based models for Internet topology. *IEEE/ACM Transactions on Networking (TON), 5*(6), 770–783. doi:10.1109/90.650138

This work was previously published in the International Journal of Mobile Computing and Multimedia Communications, Volume 3, Issue 1, edited by Ismail Khalil and Edgar Weippl, pp. 1-20, copyright 2011 by IGI Publishing (an imprint of IGI Global).

Chapter 2
Improving Effectiveness of Intrusion Detection by Correlation Feature Selection

Hai Thanh Nguyen
Gjøvik University College, Norway

Katrin Franke
Gjøvik University College, Norway

Slobodan Petrović
Gjøvik University College, Norway

ABSTRACT

In this paper, the authors propose a new feature selection procedure for intrusion detection, which is based on filter method used in machine learning. They focus on Correlation Feature Selection (CFS) and transform the problem of feature selection by means of CFS measure into a mixed 0−1 linear programming problem with a number of constraints and variables that is linear in the number of full set features. The mixed 0−1 linear programming problem can then be solved by using branch-and-bound algorithm. This feature selection algorithm was compared experimentally with the best-first-CFS and the genetic-algorithm-CFS methods regarding the feature selection capabilities. Classification accuracies obtained after the feature selection by means of the C4.5 and the BayesNet over the KDD CUP '99 dataset were also tested. Experiments show that the authors' method outperforms the best-first-CFS and the genetic-algorithm-CFS methods by removing much more redundant features while keeping the classification accuracies or getting better performances.

DOI: 10.4018/978-1-4666-2163-3.ch002

INTRODUCTION

Intrusion detection systems (IDS) have become important security tools applied in many contemporary network environments. They gather and analyze information from various sources on hosts and networks in order to identify suspicious activities and generate alerts for an operator. The task of intrusion detection is often analyzed as a pattern recognition problem - an IDS has to tell normal from abnormal behaviour. It is also of interest to further classify abnormal behaviour in order to undertake adequate counter-measures. An IDS can be modeled in various ways (Crescenzo et al., 2005; Gu et al., 2006). A model of this kind usually includes the representation algorithm (for representing incoming data in the space of selected features) and the classification algorithm (for mapping the feature vector representation of the incoming data to elements of a certain set of values, e.g., normal or abnormal etc.). Some IDS, like the models presented in (Gu et al., 2006), also include the feature selection algorithm, which determines the features to be used by the representation algorithm. Even if the feature selection algorithm is not included in the model directly, it is always assumed that such an algorithm is run before the very intrusion detection process.

The quality of the feature selection algorithm is one of the most important factors that affect the effectiveness of an IDS. The goal of the algorithm is to determine the most relevant features of the incoming traffic, whose monitoring would ensure reliable detection of abnormal behaviour. Since the effectiveness of the classification algorithm heavily depends on the number of features, it is of interest to minimize the cardinality of the set of selected features, without dropping potential indicators of abnormal behaviour. Obviously, determining a good set of features is not an easy task. The most of the work in practice is still done manually and the feature selection algorithm depends too much on expert knowledge. Automatic feature selection for intrusion detection remains therefore a great research challenge.

In this paper, we propose an automatic feature selection procedure for intrusion detection purposes based on so-called filter method (Guyon et al., 2006; Liu & Motoda, 2008) used in machine learning. The filter method directly considers statistical characteristics of the data set, such as correlation between a feature and a class or inter-correlation between features, without involving any learning algorithm. We focus on one of the most important filter methods, the Correlation Feature Selection (CFS) measure proposed by Hall (1999).

The CFS measure considers correlation between a feature and a class and inter-correlation between features at the same time. This measure is used successfully in test theory (Ghiselli, 1964) for predicting an external variable of interest. In feature selection, the CFS measure is combined with some search strategies, such as brute force, best first search or genetic algorithm, in order to find the most relevant subset of features. However, the brute force method can only be applied when the number of features is small. When the number of features is large, this method requires huge computational resources. For example, with 50 features the brute force method needs to scan all 2^{50} possible subsets of features. That is impractical in general. With best first search or genetic algorithm, we can deal with high dimensional data sets, but these methods usually give us locally optimal solutions. It is desirable to get globally optimal subset of relevant features by means of the CFS measure with the hope of removing more redundant features and still keeping classification accuracies or even getting better performances.

The feature selection method that we propose in this paper finds the globally optimal subset of relevant features by means of the CFS measure. Firstly, we formulate the problem of feature selection by representing the CFS measure as an optimization problem. We then transform this optimization problem into a polynomial-mixed 0−1 fractional programming (P01FP) problem. We improve the Chang's method (Chang, 2000; Chang, 2001) in order to equivalently reduce this P01FP to a mixed 0−1 linear programming (M01LP) problem (Chang, 2000). Finally, we propose to use the branch-and-bound algorithm to solve this M01LP, whose optimal solution is also the globally optimal subset of relevant features by means of CFS measure.

Any feature selection algorithm selects relevant traffic features based on labeled data. In this research we used the KDD CUP'99 (KDD CUP 1999) data set for this purpose. The full feature set assigned to this data set consists of 41 features. For evaluating the performance of our feature selection approach, two available feature selection methods based on the CFS measure (Chen et al., 2006) were implemented. One was the best-first-CFS method using the best first search strategy to find the locally optimal subset of features by means of the CFS measure. The other one used the genetic algorithm. We called this feature selection approach as a genetic-algorithm-CFS method. To test the overall effectiveness of an IDS employing our feature selection algorithm, 10% of the overall (5 millions) KDD CUP'99 IDS benchmarking labeled data was also used to train and to test C4.5 (Quinlan, 1993) and BayesNet (Duda et al., 2001) machine learning algorithms with 5-folds cross-validation evaluation. Experiments show that an IDS applying our feature selection algorithm outperforms the IDSs implementing the best first and genetic algorithm search strategies in the feature selection process. Our method removes much more redundant features and the classification accuracies with the reduced feature set are kept at the same level or they become even better.

The paper is organized as follows. The next section describes the CFS measure in more detail. We show how to represent the problem of feature

selection by means of the CFS measure as an optimization problem and then as a polynomial mixed 0−1 fractional programming (P01FP) problem. The background regarding P01FP, M01LP problems and Chang's method are also introduced in this section. The new approach is then presented, followed by some experimental results. Finally, the last section summarizes our findings.

BACKGROUND

Correlation Feature Selection Measure

The Correlation Feature Selection (CFS) measure evaluates subsets of features on the basis of the following hypothesis: *"Good feature subsets contain features highly correlated with the classification, yet uncorrelated to each other"* (Hall, 1999). This hypothesis gives rise to two concepts. One is the feature-classification $\left(r_{cf_i}\right)$ correlation and another is the feature-feature $\left(r_{f_i f_j}\right)$ correlation. There exist broadly two measures of the correlation between two random variables: the classical linear correlation and the correlation which is based on information theory (see Appendix A for correlation computation). The feature-classification correlation r_{cf_i} indicates how much a feature f_i is correlated to a target variable C, while the feature-feature correlation $r_{f_i f_j}$ is, as the very name says, the correlation between two features f_i, f_j. The following equation from Ghiselli (1964) used in Hall (1999) gives the merit of a feature subset S consisting of k features:

$$Merit_S(k) = \frac{k\overline{r_{cf}}}{\sqrt{k + k(k-1)\overline{r_{ff}}}} \qquad (1)$$

Here, $\overline{r_{cf}}$ is the average feature-classification correlation, and $\overline{r_{ff}}$ is the average feature-feature correlation, as given below:

$$\overline{r_{cf}} = \frac{r_{cf_1} + r_{cf_2} + \dots + r_{cf_k}}{k}$$

$$\overline{r_{ff}} = \frac{r_{f_1 f_2} + r_{f_1 f_3} + \dots + r_{f_k f_1}}{\dfrac{k(k-1)}{2}}$$

Therefore, we can rewrite (1) as follows:

$$Merit_S(k) = \frac{r_{cf_1} + r_{cf_2} + \dots + r_{cf_k}}{\sqrt{k + 2(r_{f_1 f_2} + r_{f_1 f_3} + \dots + r_{f_k f_1})}} \tag{2}$$

In fact, Equation 1 is Pearson's correlation coefficient, where all variables have been standardized. It shows that the correlation between the feature subset S and the target variable C is a function of the number k of features in the subset S and the magnitude of the inter-correlations among them, together with the magnitude of the correlations between the features and the target variable C. From Equation 1, the following conclusions can be drawn: The higher the correlations between the features and the target variable C, the higher the correlation between the feature subset S and the target variable C; The lower the correlations between the features of the subset S, the higher the correlation between the feature subset S and the target variable C.

Task of Feature Subset Selection by CFS Measure

Suppose that there are n full set features. We need to find the subset S of k features, which has the maximum value of $Merit_S(k)$ over all 2^n possible feature subsets:

$$\max_S \{Merit_S(k), 1 \le k \le n\} \tag{3}$$

When the number of features n is small, we apply the brute force method to scan all these subsets. But when this number becomes large, the heuristic and random search strategies, such as the best first search or genetic algorithm, are usually chosen due to their computational efficiency. Consequently, the given results will always be approximate. It is desirable to get optimal subsets of features. In the sequel, we propose a new method to find these optimal subsets.

Firstly, we formulate the above mentioned task as an optimization problem. We use binary values of the variable x_i in order to indicate the appearance $(x_i = 1)$ or the absence $(x_i = 0)$ of the feature f_i in the optimal subset of features. Therefore, the problem of selecting features by means of the CFS measure can be described as an optimization problem as follows:

$$\max_{x=(x_1, x_2, \dots, x_n)} F(x) = \frac{\displaystyle\sum_{i=1}^{n} r_{cf_i} x_i}{\sqrt{\displaystyle\sum_{i=1}^{n} x_i + \displaystyle\sum_{i \ne j} 2r_{f_i f_j} x_i x_j}} \tag{4}$$

or in parameter form:

$$\max_{x=(x_1,x_2,\dots,x_n)} F(x) = \frac{(\sum_{i=1}^{n} a_i x_i)^2}{\sum_{i=1}^{n} x_i + \sum_{i \neq j} 2b_{ij} x_i x_j} \qquad (5)$$

In the next subsection, we consider the optimization problem stated above as a polynomial mixed 0−1 fractional programming (P01FP) problem and show how to solve it.

Polynomial Mixed 0 − 1 Fractional Programming

A general polynomial mixed *0−1* fractional programming (P01FP) problem (Chang, 2001) is represented as follows:

$$\min \sum_{i=1}^{m} \left(\frac{a_i + \sum_{j=1}^{n} a_{ij} \prod_{k \in J} x_k}{b_i + \sum_{j=1}^{n} b_{ij} \prod_{k \in J} x_k} \right) \qquad (6)$$

subject to the following constraints:

$$\begin{cases} b_i + \sum_{j=1}^{n} b_{ij} \prod_{k \in J} x_k > 0, i = 1,\dots,m, \\ c_p + \sum_{j=1}^{n} c_{pj} \prod_{k \in J} x_k \leq 0, p = 1,\dots,m, \\ x_k \in \{0,1\}, k \in J, \\ a_i, b_i, c_p, a_{ij}, b_{ij}, c_{pj} \in \mathbb{R}. \end{cases}$$

By replacing the denominators in (6) by positive variables $y_i (i = 1\dots m)$, the P01FP then leads to the following equivalent polynomial mixed *0−1* programming problem:

$$\min \sum_{i=1}^{m} \left(a_i y_i + \sum_{j=1}^{n} a_{ij} \prod_{k \in J} x_k y_i \right) \qquad (7)$$

subject to the following constraints:

$$\begin{cases} b_i y_i + \sum_{j=1}^{n} b_{ij} \prod_{k \in J} x_k y_i = 1, i = 1,\dots,m, \\ c_p + \sum_{j=1}^{n} c_{pj} \prod_{k \in J} x_k \leq 0, p = 1,\dots,m, \\ x_k \in \{0,1\}, k \in J, y_i > 0, \\ a_i, b_i, c_p, a_{ij}, b_{ij}, c_{pj} \in \mathbb{R}. \end{cases} \qquad (8)$$

In order to solve this problem, Chang (2001) proposed a linearization technique to transfer the terms

$$\prod_{k \in J} x_k y_i$$

into a set of mixed *0−1* linear inequalities. Based on this technique, the P01FP becomes then a mixed *0−1* linear programming (M01LP) which can be solved by means of the branch-and-bound method to obtain the global solution.

Proposition 1: A polynomial mixed *0−1* term

$$\prod_{k \in J} x_k y_i$$

from (7) can be represented by the following program (Chang, 2000):

$$\min z_i$$

subject to the following constraints:

$$\begin{cases} z_i \geq M(\sum_{k \in J} x_k - |J|) + y_i, \\ z_i \geq 0, \end{cases} \qquad (9)$$

where *M* is a large positive value.

Proposition 2: A polynomial mixed $0-1$ term

$$\prod_{k \in J} x_k y_i$$

from (8) can be represented by a continuous variable v_i, subject to the following linear inequalities (Chang, 2000):

$$\begin{cases} v_i \geq M(\sum_{k \in J} x_k - |J|) + y_i, \\ v_i \leq M(|J| - \sum_{k \in J} x_k) + y_i, \\ 0 \leq v_i \leq M x_i, \end{cases} \quad (10)$$

where M is a large positive value.

In the following, we formulate the optimization problem of the CFS measure (5) as a polynomial mixed $0-1$ fractional programming (P01FP) problem.

Proposition 3: The optimization problem of the CFS measure (5) can be considered as a polynomial mixed $0-1$ fractional programming (P01FP) problem.

Proof. We change the sign of $F(x)$ in (5) to make a minimum problem and decompose the numerator of (5) as follows:

$$(\sum_{i=1}^{n} a_i x_i)^2 = \sum_{i=1}^{n} a_i^2 x_i^2 + \sum_{i \neq j} 2 a_i a_j x_i x_j \quad (11)$$

Therefore, (5) can be written as (6). By applying the Chang's method, we can transform this P01FP problem to the M01LP problem. The number of variables and constraints will depend on the square of n, where n is the number of features. The reason is the number of terms

$$\prod_{k \in J} x_k y$$

which are replaced by the new variables in forms

$$(\sum_{i \neq j} 2 a_i a_j x_i x_j y)$$

or

$$(\sum_{i \neq j} 2 b_{ij} x_i x_j y)$$

is $n(n-1)/2$. The branch-and-bound algorithm can then be used in order to solve this M01LP problem. But the efficiency of the method depends strongly on the number of variables and constraints. The larger the number of variables and constraints an M01LP has, the more complicated the branch-and-bound algorithm is.

In the next section, we present an improvement of the Chang's method to get an M01LP with a linear number of variables and constraints in the number of full set variables. We also give a new search strategy to obtain the relevant subsets of features by means the CFS measure.

OPTIMIZATION OF THE CFS MEASURE

By introducing an additional positive variable, denoted by y, we now consider the following problem equivalent to (5):

$$\min\{-F(x)\} = -\sum_{j=1}^{n} (\sum_{i=1}^{n} a_i a_j x_i) x_j y \quad (12)$$

subject to the following constraints:

$$\begin{cases} y > 0, \\ x = (x_1, x_2, ..., x_n) \in \{0,1\}^n, \\ \sum_{i=1}^{n} x_i y + \sum_{j=1}^{n} (\sum_{i=1, i \neq j}^{n} b_{ji} x_i) x_j y = 1 \end{cases} \quad (13)$$

Here, all the terms $a_i a_j x_i x_j$ in the numerator and the terms $b_{ij} x_i x_j$ in the denominator of (5) have been grouped into the sum

$$(\sum_{j=1}^{n} (\sum_{i=1}^{n} a_i a_j x_i) x_j y)$$

and the sum

$$(\sum_{j=1}^{n} (\sum_{i=1, i \neq j}^{n} b_{ji} x_i) x_j y)$$

respectively. Each sum contains n terms, which will be equivalently replaced by new variables with constraints following the two propositions given below:

Proposition 4: A polynomial mixed *0−1* term

$$(\sum_{i=1}^{n} a_i a_j x_i) x_j y$$

from (12) can be represented by the following program:

$$\min z_i$$

subject to the following constraints:

$$\begin{cases} z_j \geq M(x_j - 1) + (\sum_{i=1}^{n} a_i a_j x_i) y, \\ z_j \geq 0, \end{cases} \quad (14)$$

where M is a large positive value.

Proof.

1. If $x_j = 0$, then

$$z_j \geq M(0 - 1) + (\sum_{i=1}^{n} a_i a_j x_i) y \leq 0$$

will force $\min z_j$ to be zero, because $z_j \geq 0$ and M is a large positive value.

2. If $x_j = 1$, then

$$z_j \geq M(1 - 1) + (\sum_{i=1}^{n} a_i a_j x_i) y \geq 0$$

will force $\min z_j$ to be $(\sum_{i=1}^{n} a_i a_j x_i) y$, because $z_j \geq 0$.

Therefore, the above program on z_j reduces to:

$$\min z_j = \begin{cases} 0, & \text{if } x_j = 0 \\ (\sum_{i=1}^{n} a_i a_j x_i) y, & \text{if } x_j = 1 \end{cases}$$

which is the same as

$$(\sum_{i=1}^{n} a_i a_j x_i) x_j y = \min z_j$$

Proposition 5: A polynomial mixed *0−1* term

$$(\sum_{i=1, i \neq j}^{n} b_{ji} x_i) x_j y$$

from (13) can be represented by a continuous variable v_j, subject to the following linear inequality constraints:

$$\begin{cases} v_j \geq M(x_j - 1) + (\sum_{i=1,i\neq j}^{n} b_{ji}x_i)y, \\ v_j \leq M(1 - x_j) + (\sum_{i=1,i\neq j}^{n} b_{ji}x_i)y \quad (15) \\ 0 \leq v_i \leq Mx_j, \end{cases}$$

where M is a large positive value.

Proof.

1. If $x_j = 0$, then (15) becomes

$$\begin{cases} v_j \geq M(0 - 1) + (\sum_{i=1,i\neq j}^{n} b_{ji}x_i)y, \\ v_j \leq M(1 - 0) + (\sum_{i=1,i\neq j}^{n} b_{ji}x_i)y, \\ 0 \leq v_j \leq 0, \end{cases}$$

v_j is forced to be zero, as M is a large positive value.

2. If $x_j = 1$, then (15) becomes

$$\begin{cases} v_j \geq M(1 - 1) + (\sum_{i=1,i\neq j}^{n} b_{ji}x_i)y, \\ v_j \leq M(1 - 1) + (\sum_{i=1,i\neq j}^{n} b_{ji}x_i)y, \\ 0 \leq v_j \leq M, \end{cases}$$

v_j is forced to be

$$(\sum_{i=1,i\neq j}^{n} b_{ji}x_i)y$$

as M is a large positive value.

Therefore, the constraints on v_j reduce to:

$$v_j = \begin{cases} 0, \quad if \ x_j = 0 \\ (\sum_{i=1,i\neq j}^{n} b_{ji}x_i)y, \ if \ x_j = 1 \end{cases}$$

which is the same as

$$(\sum_{i=1,i\neq j}^{n} b_{ji}x_i)x_jy = v_j$$

We substitute each term x_iy in (13) by new variables t_i satisfying constraints from Proposition 2. Then the total number of variables for the M01LP problem will be $4n+1$, as they are $x_i, y,$ t_i, z_j and $v_j(i, j = 1...n)$. Therefore, the number of constraints on these variables will also be a linear function of n. As we mentioned above, with Chang's method (Chang, 2001) the number of variables and constraints depends on the square of n, thus our new method actually improves his method by reducing the complexity of branch and bound algorithm.

We now present a new search strategy for obtaining subsets of relevant features by means of the CFS measure.

The new search method for subsets of relevant features by means of the CFS measure:

Step 1: Calculate all feature-feature $\left(r_{f_if_j}\right)$ and feature classification $\left(r_{cf_j}\right)$ correlations from the training data set.

Step 2: Construct the optimization problem (4) from the correlations calculated above. In this step, we can use expert knowledge by assigning the value *1* to the variable x_i if the feature f_i is relevant and the value *0* otherwise.

Step 3: Transform the optimization problem of CFS to a mixed *0−1* linear programming (M01LP) problem, which is to be solved by the branch-and-bound algorithm. A non-zero integer value of x_i from the optimal solution indicates the relevance of the feature f_i regarding the CFS measure.

EXPERIMENT

Experimental Setting

For evaluating the performance of our new CFS-based approach, two available feature selection methods based on the CFS measure (Chen, 2006) are implemented. One is the best-first-CFS method, which uses the best-first search strategy to find the locally optimal subset. The other one uses the genetic algorithm for search. Note that the best first search and genetic algorithm may not guarantee to find the globally optimal solution. However, we can overcome this issue with our new method. We did not choose the exhaustive search method since it is not feasible for feature selection from data sets with a large number of features. Even for this experiment we have no access to required computing resource. We applied machine learning algorithms for evaluating the classification accuracy on selected features, since there is no standard IDS.

We performed our experiment using 10% of the overall (5 millions) KDD CUP'99 IDS benchmarking labeled data. This data set contains normal traffic and four main attack classes: (i) Denial of Service (DoS) attacks, (ii) Probe attacks, (iii) User to Root (U2R) attacks and (iv) Remote to Local (R2L) attacks. The number of instances for the four attack classes and normal class is quite different, e.g. the relation of the number of U2R to the number of DoS is $1.3 * 10^{-4}$. Details of the number of class instances are given in Table 1.

Table 1. The partition of KDD CUP'99 dataset used in experiment

Classes	Number of Instances	Percentage
KDD99-normal	97.278	18.30%
KDD99-DoS	391.458	73.74%
KDD99-Probe	41.113	7.74%
KDD99-U2R	52	0.01%
KDD99-R2L	1.126	0.21%
Total	**531.027**	**100%**

In more detail we testified the performance of our newly proposed CFS-based feature selection method as follows:

1. Feature selection is performed on the basis of the whole data set:
    a. Each attack class and the normal class are processed individually, so that a five-class problem can be formulated for feature extraction and classification with one single classifier.
    b. All attack classes are fused so that a two-class problem can be formulated, meaning the feature selection and classification for normal and abnormal traffic is performed. It might be well possible that the attack-recognition results are not satisfactory for all of the classes, since the number of class instances are unevenly distributed, in particular classes U2R and R2L are under-represented. The feature selection algorithm and the classifier, which is used for evaluation of the detection accuracy on selected features, might concentrate only on the most frequent class data and neglect the others. As consequence, we might miss relevant characteristics of the less represented classes.

2. As the attack classes distribute so differently, we preferred to process these attack classes separately. With the specific application of IDS we can also formulate four different two-class problems. Four classifiers shall be derived using specific features for each classifier in order to detect (identify) a particular attack. The rationale for this approach is that we predict the most accurate classification if each of the four intrusion detectors (classifiers) is fine-tuned according to significant features. This approach might also be very effective, since the four light-weight classifiers can be operated in parallel.

For understanding the effect, as mentioned in 1), we conducted a small experiment. The aim was to show that the classifier highly neglected U2R attack instances. In order to do that, we mixed all attack classes to get only one data set and considered five-class (normal, DoS, Probe, U2R and R2L) problem. The C4.5 machine learning algorithm was used as a classifier. We applied 5-folds cross-validation for evaluating the detection accuracy of the C4.5. The result of the experiment is given in Table 2. It can be seen from Table 2 that the C4.5 highly misclassified U2R attack instances with 34.6% error.

In order to perform the experiment 2), we added normal traffic into each attack class to get four data sets: KDD99-normal&DoS, KDD99-normal&Probe, KDD99-normal&U2R and KDD99-normal&R2L. With each data set, we ran

three feature-selection algorithms: our new CFS-based method, the best-first CFS-based and the genetic algorithm CFS-based methods. The numbers of selected features and their identifications are given in Table 3 and Table 4, respectively. We then applied the C4.5 and the BayesNet machine learning algorithm on each original full set as well as each newly obtained data set that includes only those selected features from feature selection algorithms. By applying 5-folds cross-validation evaluation on each data set, the classification accuracies are reported in Table 5 and Table 6.

Our new CFS-based method was compared with the best first-CFS and genetic-algorithm-CFS methods regarding the number of selected features and regarding the classification accuracies of 5-folds cross-validation of BayesNet and C4.5 learning algorithms. Weka tool was used for obtaining the results. In order to solve the M01LP problem, we used TOMLAB tool. All the obtained results are listed in Tables 3, 5 and 6.

Table 3. Number of selected features

Data Set	Full-Set	Our Method	Best-First	GA
KDD99-normal&Dos	41	3	6	11
KDD99-normal&Probe	41	6	7	17
KDD99-normal&U2R	41	1	4	8
KDD99-normal&R2L	41	2	5	8

Table 2. Unclassified instances (UI) by the C4.5 classifier

Classes	Number of UI	Percentage
Normal	65	0.07%
DoS	21	0.01%
Probe	39	0.10%
U2R	18	34.6%
R2L	39	3.46%

Table 4. Identification of selected features (for feature names, see Appendix B)

Data Set	Identifications
KDD99-normal&Dos	5, 6, 12
KDD99-normal&Probe	5, 6, 12, 29, 37, 41
KDD99-normal&U2R	14
KDD99-normal&R2L	10, 22

Table 5. Classification accuracies of C4.5 performed on KDD CUP'99 dataset

Data Set	Full-Set	Our Method	Best-First	GA
KDD99-normal&Dos	97.80	98.89	96.65	96.09
KDD99-normal&Probe	99.98	99.70	99.71	99.89
KDD99-normal&U2R	99.97	99.96	99.97	99.95
KDD99-normal&R2L	98.70	99.11	99.01	98.86
Average	**99.11**	**99.41**	**98.84**	**98.69**

Table 6. Classification accuracies of BayesNet performed on KDD CUP'99 dataset

Data Set	Full-Set	Our Method	Best-First	GA
KDD99-normal&Dos	99.99	98.87	99.09	99.72
KDD99-normal&Probe	98.96	97.63	97.65	99.19
KDD99-normal&U2R	99.85	99.95	99.97	99.93
KDD99-normal&R2L	99.33	98.81	98.95	99.28
Average	**99.53**	**98.82**	**98.91**	**99.52**

Experimental Results

Table 3 shows the number of features selected by our approach and those selected by using the best-first and GA search strategies. The identification of selected features is given in Table 4 (for feature names, see Appendix B). Table 5 and Table 6 summarize the classification accuracies of the BayesNet and the C4.5, respectively, performed on four data sets (see above).

It can be observed from Table 3 that our CFS-based approach selects the smallest number of relevant features in comparison with the full and the feature sets selected by the best-first and GA search strategies. Especially in some cases, our new method compresses the full set of features extremely. For example, only one feature was selected out of 41 features of the KDD99-normal&U2R data set.

In Table 5 and Table 6 it can be observed that with our approach the average classification accuracies are slightly different from the ones obtained by using the best-first search or the genetic algorithm. The absolute difference between them does not overcome 0.69%. In the case of the C4.5 classifier, we got better performance. Even though the gain of classification accuracy is not very high compared to other methods, the overall gain of the feature selection classification procedure lies in significantly improved efficiency and in obtaining the classification results due to reduced number of relevant features.

Therefore, based on all these experiments we can say that in general our new method outperforms the best-first-CFS and genetic-algorithm-CFS methods by removing much more redundant features and still keeping the classification accuracies or even getting better performances. Thus it can be used to find optimal subsets of relevant features by means of the CFS measure for intrusion detection systems.

CONCLUSION

We have proposed a new search method to get the globally optimal subset of relevant features by means of the correlation feature selection

(CFS) measure. Actually we transformed the CFS optimization problem into polynomial mixed $0-1$ fractional programming (P01FP) problem. From this P01FP problem, we then applied our improved Chang's method to get mixed $0-1$ linear programming (M01LP) problem with linear dependence of the number of constraints and variables on the number of features in the full set. We used branch-and-bound algorithm in order to solve that M01LP. Experimental results showed that our approach outperforms the best-first-CFS and genetic-algorithm-CFS methods by removing much more redundant features and still keeping the classification accuracies or even getting better performances.

REFERENCES

Chang, C.-T. (2000). An efficient linearization approach for mixed integer problems. *European Journal of Operational Research, 123,* 652–659. doi:10.1016/S0377-2217(99)00106-X

Chang, C.-T. (2001). On the polynomial mixed 0-1 fractional programming problems. *European Journal of Operational Research, 131*(1), 224–227. doi:10.1016/S0377-2217(00)00097-7

Chen, Y., Li, Y., Cheng, X.-Q., & Guo, L. (2006). Survey and Taxonomy of Feature Selection Algorithms in Intrusion Detection System. In *Proceedings of Inscrypt 2006* (LNCS 4318, pp. 153-167).

Cormen, T. H., Leiserson, C. E., Rivest, R. L., & Stein, C. (2001). *Introduction to Algorithms* (2nd ed.). Cambridge, MA: MIT Press.

Crescenzo, G. D., Ghosh, A., & Talpade, R. (2005). Towards a theory of intrusion detection. In *Proceedings of the 10th European Symposium on Research in Computer Security (ESORICS'05)* (pp. 267-286). New York: Springer.

Duda, R. O., Hart, P. E., & Stork, D. G. (2001). *Pattern Classification.* New York: Wiley-Interscience.

Ghiselli, E. E. (1964). *Theory of Psychological Measurement.* New York: Mc GrawHill.

Gu, G., Fogla, P., Dagon, D., Lee, W., & Skoric, B. (2006). Towards an information-theoretic framework for analyzing intrusion detection systems. In *Proceedings of the 11th European Symposium on Research in Computer Security (ESORICS'06)* (pp. 527-546). New York: Springer.

Guyon, I., Gunn, S., Nikravesh, M., & Zadeh, L. A. (2006). *Feature Extraction: Foundations and Applications.* New York: Springer. doi:10.1007/978-3-540-35488-8

Hall, M. (1999). *Correlation Based Feature Selection for Machine Learning.* Unpublished doctoral dissertation, University of Waikato, Department of Computer Science, Hamilton, New Zealand.

Liu, H., & Motoda, H. (2008). *Computational Methods of Feature Selection.* Boca Raton, FL: CRC.

Quinlan, J. R. (1993). *C4.5: Programs for Machine Learning.* San Francisco: Morgan Kaufmann.

APPENDIX A

Correlation Computation

For continuous class problem: For a pair of random variables (X, Y), the linear correlation coefficient $\rho(X, Y)$ is given by the formula:

$$\rho(X, Y) = \frac{E((X - \mu_X)(Y - \mu_Y))}{\sigma_X \sigma_Y}$$

where μ_X, μ_Y are expected values of variables X and Y, respectively; σ_X, σ_Y are standard deviations; E is the expected value operator.

For discrete class problem: For a pair of random variables (X, Y), the correlation is defined as symmetrical uncertainty $SU(X, Y)$ coefficient by the formula:

$$SU(X, Y) = 2[\frac{H(X) - H(X \mid Y)}{H(X) + H(Y)}]$$

where $H(X)$, $H(Y)$ are the entropy of variables; X and Y, respectively; $H(X|Y)$ is the conditional entropy.

APPENDIX B

Table 7. Names and identifications (ID) of selected features

ID	Names
1	Duration
3	Service
5	src_bytes
6	dst_byte
9	Urgent
10	Hot
11	num_ failed_logins
12	logged_ in
14	root_shell
16	num _root
17	num _file_ creations
22	is _guest _login
26	srv _serror _rate
27	rerror _rate
29	same _srv _rate
31	srv _diff_ host _rate
32	dst_ host _count
33	dst _host_ srv _count
37	dst _host _srv _diff _host _rate
39	dst _host_ srv _serror _rate
41	dst _host_ srv _rerror _rate

Chapter 3
Threat and Risk–Driven Security Requirements Engineering

Holger Schmidt
Technical University of Dortmund, Germany

ABSTRACT

In this paper, the author aim to present a threat and risk-driven methodology to security requirements engineering. The chosen approach has a strong focus on gathering, modeling, and analyzing the environment in which a secure ICT-system to be built is located. The knowledge about the environment comprises threat and risk models. As presented in the paper, this security-relevant knowledge is used to assess the adequacy of security mechanisms, which are then selected to establish security requirements.

INTRODUCTION

Security describes the inability of the environment to have an undesirable effect on an ICT-system (Røstad, Tøndel, Line, & Nordland, 2006). Expressed from the software development point of view, the software of an ICT-system must be constructed in a way such that the ICT-system is protected from the environment.

From the definition of the term security alone the importance of the environment in which an ICT-system is integrated when we deal with security becomes clear. The adequacy of an ICT-system's security mechanisms is strongly influenced by its intended operational environment. Thus, knowledge about the environment must be collected to

support or even allow the decision for particular security mechanisms. Especially knowledge about the malicious part of the environment, i.e., the part that can attack an ICT-system in order to nullify or bypass its security mechanisms, must be gathered, modeled, and assessed.

The gathering and modeling parts involve threat analysis techniques such as Microsoft's STRIDE (Hernan, Lambert, Ostwald, & Shostack, 2006), attack trees by Schneier (1999), and the approach by Fernandez, Red M., Forneron, Uribe, and Rodriguez G. (2007). Threat analysis is applied to identify threats that exploit vulnerabilities of security mechanisms. The assessment part is related to risk analysis techniques such as CORAS by Braber, Hogganvik, Lund, Stølen, and Vraalsen

DOI: 10.4018/978-1-4666-2163-3.ch003

(2007). Risk analysis is used to determine the probability that security mechanisms will work correctly in the intended (malicious) environment.

When constructing secure ICT-systems, it is instrumental to take the environment into account right from the beginning of the software development. Consequently, we focus in this paper on early security requirements engineering. We consider our security engineering process using patterns (SEPP) (Hatebur, Heisel, & Schmidt, 2007; Schmidt, 2010). There, security requirements are elicited, analyzed, and documented so that security mechanisms adequate to establish the security requirements can be selected. SEPP makes use of special patterns called security problem frames for security requirements and concretized security problem frames for security mechanisms. Thus, security requirements are strictly separated from solutions, i.e., security mechanisms.

Results from applying threat and risk analysis techniques heavily influence the process of selecting security mechanisms to establish security requirements. In this paper, we analyze the impact of threat and risk analysis on security requirement engineering. We extend SEPP by a threat and risk-driven procedure to select adequate security mechanisms. We illustrate the procedure using an example software development.

The rest of the paper is organized as follows: In the next section, we introduce a concrete security-critical software development problem. We use this example then to demonstrate security problem frames and concretized security problem frames. Following this, we present the threat and risk analysis extensions to SEPP's requirements analysis phase. Afterwards, we validate this threat and risk-driven approach. Finally, we consider related work followed by a summary and directions for future research.

CASE STUDY

We use the following software development problem as a case study to demonstrate the techniques presented in this paper.

A secure text editor should be developed. The text editor should enable an author to create, edit, open, and save text files. The text files should be stored confidentially. The informal security requirement (SR1) can be described as follows:

Preserve confidentiality of text file except for its file length for honest environment and prevent disclosure to malicious environment.

Note that we decided to focus on storing text files confidentially. The given software development problem can also be interpreted such that the security requirement also covers confidential editing operations, e.g., confidential clipboard copies. To simplify matters, this is not covered in the security requirements analysis presented in this paper. For the same reason, the create and edit functionality of the secure text editor is not covered in our case study. Practically, it is very difficult to develop 100% confidential systems. Hence, as an example, we discuss an SR that allows the secure text editor to leak the text file length.

Problem Frames for Security Requirements Engineering

In earlier publications (cf., Hatebur, Heisel, & Schmidt, 2008; Schmidt, 2010), we presented special patterns defined for structuring, characterizing, and analyzing problems that occur frequently in security engineering. Similar patterns for functional requirements have been proposed by Jackson (2001). They are called problem frames. Accordingly, our patterns are named security problem frames (SPF). SPFs consider security requirements. Furthermore, for each SPF, we defined a set of concretized security problem frames (CSPF) that take generic security mechanisms[1] (e.g., encryption to keep data confidential) into account to prepare the ground for solving a given security problem. Since CSPFs involve first solution approaches, they consider concretized security requirements.

Problem frames, SPFs and CSPFs are graphically depicted by frame diagrams. Figure 1 shows an instance of the frame diagram of the CSPF confidential data storage using password-based symmetric encryption. Instances of frame diagrams are called problem diagrams.

SPFs and CSPFs as well as instances of these frames make use of the same syntactic elements. They consist of a machine domain denoted by a rectangle with two vertical stripes, which represents the software that should be developed in order to fulfill the (concretized) security requirement textually denoted in a dashed oval. According to our case study, the software to be developed is represented by the machine domain *Secure text editor*. The concretized security requirement CSR1 derived from SR1 is stated as follows.

If password is unknown to malicious environment, then confidentiality of text file except for its file length is preserved for honest environment and disclosure to malicious environment is prevented.

The environment in which the software development problem is located is structured by domains, which are graphically denoted by plain rectangles. According to Jackson (2001), we distinguish causal domains that comply with some physical laws, lexical domains that are data representations, and biddable domains that are usually people. In the instantiated frame diagram depicted in Figure 1, a marker "X" indicates that the corresponding domain is a lexical domain, "B" indicates a biddable domain, and "C" indicates a causal domain[2].

The connecting lines between domains represent interfaces that consist of shared phenomena. According to Jackson, we distinguish symbolic phenomena, e.g., data items, causal phenomena,

Figure 1. Instantiated CSPF confidential data storage using password-based symmetric encryption "secure text editor"

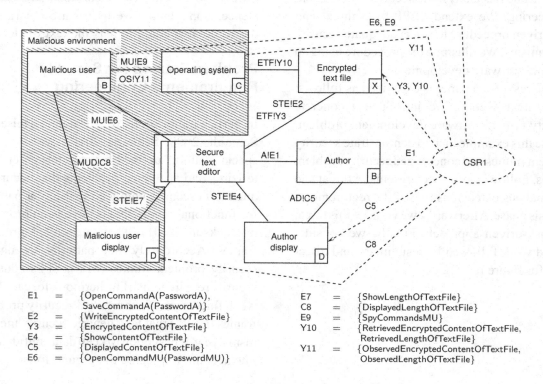

E1	=	{OpenCommandA(PasswordA), SaveCommandA(PasswordA)}
E2	=	{WriteEncryptedContentOfTextFile}
Y3	=	{EncryptedContentOfTextFile}
E4	=	{ShowContentOfTextFile}
C5	=	{DisplayedContentOfTextFile}
E6	=	{OpenCommandMU(PasswordMU)}

E7	=	{ShowLengthOfTextFile}
C8	=	{DisplayedLengthOfTextFile}
E9	=	{SpyCommandsMU}
Y10	=	{RetrievedEncryptedContentOfTextFile, RetrievedLengthOfTextFile}
Y11	=	{ObservedEncryptedContentOfTextFile, ObservedLengthOfTextFile}

e.g., operations, and event phenomena, e.g., events and messages. The sets that contain phenomena are named according to their type: sets with symbolic phenomena begin with the letter "Y", those with causal phenomena with the letter "C", and for event phenomena the letter "E" is used. Additionally, the sets have a consecutive number as suffix. Shared phenomena are observable by at least two domains, but controlled by only one domain. The notation "*STE!E7*" means that the event phenomena of interface *E7* between the domains *Secure text editor* (abbreviated *STE*) and *Encrypted text file* are controlled by the Secure text editor domain.

The environment contained in SPFs and CSPFs as well as instances of them is divided into an honest and a malicious part. The malicious environment of a CSPF is equally modeled to that of the corresponding SPF. Those CSPFs that deal with confidentiality requirements basically consider passive malicious environments to observe the protected assets the confidentiality requirements refer to. In contrast, the CSPFs that treat integrity requirements are equipped with active malicious environments to modify the protected assets the integrity requirements refer to. According to our case study, the domains *Author* and *Author display* and the interfaces *A!E1*, *STE!E4*, and *AD!C5* between these domains and the machine domain represent the honest environment. The domains *Malicious user, Malicious user display,* and *Operating system* together with the interfaces, *STE!E7, MUD!C8, MU!E9, OS!Y11* between them, the interface *MU!E6* between the *Malicious user* domain and the machine domain, and the interface ETF!Y10 between the domains *Operating system* and *Encrypted text file* represent the malicious environment. It is emphasized in Figure 1 as a hashed area.

Because of the encryption mechanism used by the machine domain, the interface *ETF!Y3* between *Secure text editor* and *Encrypted text file* contains the phenomenon *EncryptedContentOfTextFile*. Authors can enter passwords for encrypting and decrypting text files. Therefore, the interface *A!E1* between *Author* and *Secure text editor* contains the phenomena *OpenCommandA(PasswordA)* and *SaveCommandA(PasswordA)*. Malicious users can also enter passwords under the assumption that they cannot guess passwords of honest users. Therefore, the interface *MU!E6* between *Malicious user* and *Secure text editor* contains the phenomenon *OpenCommandMU(PasswordMU)*.

A dashed line represents a requirements reference, and the arrow shows that it is a constraining reference. In the instantiated frame diagram depicted in Figure 1, the CSR refers to all domains except for the machine domain. It constrains the *Encrypted text file* domain and the display domains, because the text files are encrypted by the machine and not shown to the environment.

The environment, i.e., the domains (except for the machine domain) and the interfaces with the phenomena they contain, is described by domain knowledge. We distinguish two kinds of domain knowledge:

- **Facts:** Fixed properties of the environment irrespective of how the machine is built. For example, it is a fact that the secure text editor is running on a public computer.
- **Assumptions:** Conditions that are needed, so that the requirements are accomplishable. For example, one must assume that the authors do not reveal their passwords.

In contrast to domain knowledge, that describes the environment independently of the machine, requirements are expressed by describing the environment after the machine is integrated into it.

SPFs and CSPFs are organized in pattern catalogs, which form a pattern system (Hatebur et al., 2008; Schmidt, 2010). After an SPF is instantiated, the pattern system is used to identify a set of possible CSPFs that can be used to solve the problem characterized by the SPF instance. Moreover, dependencies between security mechanisms (represented by CSPF instances) and security requirements (represented by SPF instances) can be determined.

SPFs are equipped with a formal description of the security requirement, which we call effect. Furthermore, CSPFs are equipped with formally expressed necessary conditions, which must be met by the environment for the security mechanism that the CSPF represents to be applicable. If a necessary condition does not hold, the effect described in the according SPF cannot be established. Necessary conditions can be covered by assumptions.

For reasons of simplicity, we describe the necessary conditions of the CSPF instance in Figure 1 only informally:

- Passwords used by the honest environment must be different from the ones used by the malicious environment. Otherwise, a password-based encryption mechanism is not secure.
- Passwords transmitted by the honest environment to the machine must not be eavesdropped by the malicious environment.
- Passwords used by the honest environment must be transmitted to the machine domain in an integrity-preserving way.
- The text file's content must be transmitted between the machine domain and honest environment confidentially.

The concepts presented in this section, i.e., SPFs, CSPFs, the pattern system, and the effects as well as the necessary conditions, are the basis of our secure software engineering method SEPP (Hatebur et al., 2007; Schmidt, 2010). Additional material such as SPF and CSPF catalogs are available online at http://ls14-www.cs.tu-dortmund. de/schmidt/sepp.html. We describe SEPP's first phase, i.e., security requirements analysis, in more detail.

Security-Relevant Domain Knowledge

In this section, we relate terminology from security requirements engineering and the (C)SPF approach with terminology from threat and risk analysis. The goal is to provide an understanding and a definition of security-relevant domain knowledge. Figure 2 and Figure 3 summarize the terminology and interrelationships using a UML class diagram (UML Revision Task Force, 2009). They are complemented by Table 1 that serves to map a part of the notions contained in the class diagrams to the elements of CSPFs.

Using Zave's and Jackson's terminology (Zave & Jackson, 1997), a system consists of a machine in its environment (see Figure 2). Adopting a holistic view, we consider security to be a system property. Security can only be regarded as a char-

Figure 2. System and countermeasures

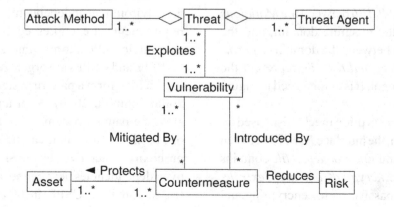

Figure 3. Countermeasures, assets, and threat and risk analysis terminology

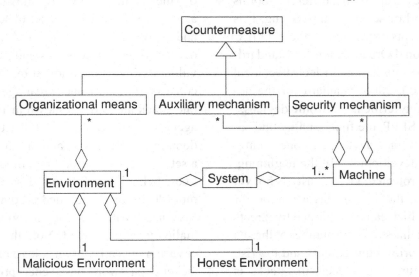

Table 1. Relation between risk/threat notions and CSPF notions

Risk/Threat Notions	CSPF Notions
threat	potential attack to nullify or bypass necessary condition
threat agent	part of malicious environment, i.e., at least one biddable domain and interface
attack method	set of phenomena that are part of the malicious environment
vulnerability	described by necessary condition
security mechanism	described by CSPF
asset	set of lexical domains and/or symbolic phenomena

acteristic of a system. It is not a characteristic of the machine alone.

As depicted in Figure 2 and Figure 3, a countermeasure protects at least one asset, and each countermeasure is a part of the system. Security mechanisms (e.g., encryption and access control mechanisms), auxiliary mechanisms (e.g., mechanisms that obfuscate password fields), and organizational means (e.g., user policies) are countermeasures. The latter are countermeasures that are realized by the biddable part of the environment since this part cannot be influenced by the machine. In contrast, the former two types of countermeasures are realized by the machine. As shown in Table 1, a CSPF describes a security mechanism.

In his PhD thesis, Mayer (2009) gives an overview of the different definitions of threat and risk terminology, and he comes up with consolidated notions in this field. The terminology related to threats and risk presented in this section is based on these notions. Note that risk is commonly defined as

risk = probability of a successful attack
  * loss per successful attack

Since the only variable on the right hand side of this equation is the probability of a successful attack, we focus on this variable when analyzing risk and we omit the constant loss per successful attack. That is, if we refer to risk analysis in connection to the approach presented in this paper, we actually refer to the probability of a successful attack.

Figure 4 serves to clarify the different notions of risk in the field of security engineering. It is inspired by concepts explained in the ISO/IEC 61508 (International Organization for Standardization (ISO) and International Electrotechnical Commission (IEC), 2000) standard for the development of safety-critical electronic devices.

According to SEPP, the functionality and security mechanisms are developed concurrently during software development. In the beginning, the system is unprotected, i.e., security is not yet considered. Thus, the system has a number of vulnerabilities, which can be exploited by threats (see Figure 2). At this stage, the number of threats to nullify the security requirements and the risk that the threats turn into successful attacks is maximal. As shown in Figure 4, we refer to this risk as the unprotected system risk. The goal of security engineering is to reduce this risk by applying countermeasures until a level of tolerable risk is reached. Since it is practically very difficult (if not impossible) to develop completely secure systems, there remains a residual risk. We consider a system secure in a given environment, if the residual risk is lower than the tolerable risk.

Against this background, we now describe Figure 2 in detail. We consider an asset some piece of information to be protected by countermeasures, which mitigates vulnerabilities. Furthermore, a countermeasure possibly introduces a number of other vulnerabilities. As shown in Table 1, an asset is represented by a set of lexical domains and/or symbolic phenomena. A vulnerability is described by a necessary condition. In general, vulnerabilities are exploited by threats. A threat consists of at least one threat agent, and at least one attack method. As shown in Table 1, a threat agent is represented by at least one biddable domain and interface, and an attack method by a set of phenomena. A threat model (e.g., attack trees, Schneier, 1999) that describes a threat in more detail can be regarded as domain knowledge associated with the corresponding part of the malicious environment. Note that the malicious environment can contain at least one potential attacker. A password-based encryption mechanism has several vulnerabilities, e.g., the passwords could be determined using brute force. So, a threat to the mechanism is the possible exploitation of this vulnerability by the attack method brute force.

Since CSPFs introduce security mechanisms, threats to the machine that implements these mechanisms can be considered when a CSPF is instantiated. When instantiating a CSPF, it is possible to model a sophisticated malicious environment, i.e., one that can make use of certain knowledge, e.g., passwords, cryptographic keys, and ciphertexts.

When a security requirements engineering method such as SEPP is applied, which strictly

Figure 4. Risk and risk reduction

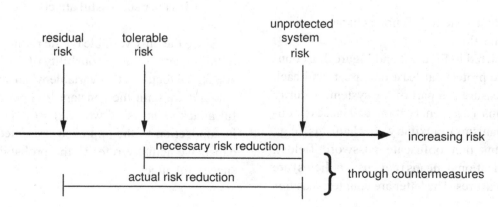

separates security requirements from solutions to these requirements, then risk can be initially considered after first solution approaches are determined. To ensure that a security mechanism works properly, i.e., that it meets the security requirements it is intended to fulfill, necessary conditions must be satisfied. A risk analysis method (e.g., CORAS, Braber et al., 2007) can be used to determine the probability that a selected security mechanism will work properly in the intended (malicious) environment. More precisely, such a method helps to decide if necessary conditions can be assumed to be fulfilled or if they constitute new security requirements, which must be treated by further countermeasures. If the risk that a condition does not hold is not tolerable, then it should be considered as a new security requirement. Otherwise, the necessary condition can be considered as an assumption, and hence becomes part of the security-relevant domain knowledge.

Threat and Risk-Driven Security Requirements Analysis

SEPP constitutes an iterative and incremental pattern-and component-based process to develop secure software. It consists of three phases following a top-down approach until a global platform-independent security architecture is developed in phase three. Then, it takes a bottom-up approach to search for given security components for constructing a global platform-specific security architecture.

SEPP was published first in (Hatebur et al., 2007). A revised version of SEPP that complies with the one presented in this paper is published in (Schmidt, 2010).

We focus in this section on SEPP's first phase, i.e., security requirements analysis. Figure 5 shows an overview of SEPP's security requirements analysis lifecycle. The arrows are annotated with inputs or with conditions (in square brackets). The latter must be true to proceed with the step

the arrow under consideration is pointing at. The arrow pointing at the "End" state is annotated with SEPP's overall output of the first phase.

SEPP starts given a textually described software development problem. SEPP's security requirements analysis phase can be executed in parallel to "normal" requirements engineering (e.g., based on problem frames). Moreover, a set of initial security requirements SR must be determined. For example, the initial security requirements can be obtained using the methods proposed by Gürses et al. (2005) and by Fernandez et al. (2007).

Step 1: Describe Environment

All security-relevant entities contained in the environment and relations between them are modeled using a context diagram (Jackson, 2001). Given a context diagram that emerged from functional requirements analysis, this diagram is extended by security-relevant entities and relations. The result is a context diagram CD_{sec}.

Domain knowledge, i.e., facts and assumptions, about the environment in which the software development problem is located is collected and documented. According to the description given in Section 4, we consider an unprotected system with maximal risk of threats turning into successful attacks. The security-relevant domain knowledge D_{sec} collected in this step comprises basic knowledge about the malicious environment, e.g., about the equipment used by a potential attacker. The result is security-relevant domain knowledge D_{sec} that consists of a set of security-relevant facts F_{sec} and a set of security-relevant assumptions A_{sec}.

Depending on how the set of initial security requirements SR is obtained, the security-relevant domain knowledge is complemented by an attacker model, a threat model, and results from risk analysis. For example, the approach by Fernandez et al. (2007) identifies security requirements by analyzing the threats to the unprotected system.

Figure 5. SEPP's security requirements analysis lifecycle

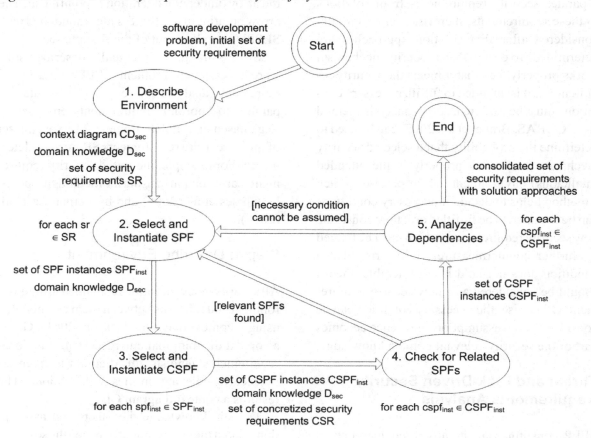

Hence, the result is a set of security requirements and an attacker model as well as a threat model.

Step 2: Select and Instantiate SPF

This step must be executed for each security requirement sr ∈ SR. To determine an SPF that is appropriate for the given environment and the security requirement sr ∈ SR, the latter is compared with the informal descriptions of the security requirement templates of the SPFs contained in our pattern system. The result is a set of SPFs candidates from which the SPF to be instantiated is selected by considering the security-relevant environment represented by CD_{sec} and the security-relevant domain knowledge D_{sec}. More precisely, the context diagram CD_{sec} represents

the environment of a complex problem, which is decomposed into subproblems that fit to SPFs using decomposition operators such as "leave out domain" or "combine several domains into one domain." Thus, an SPF candidate that fits to the decomposed environment of the corresponding subproblem is selected. Afterwards, the SPF is instantiated by assigning concrete values to the domains, phenomena, interfaces, effect, and the security requirement template. The instantiation of an SPF may result in additional security-relevant domain knowledge, which is added to the security-relevant domain knowledge D_{sec}. For example, if in the course of the problem decomposition a domain is split into several domains, domain knowledge about these new domains is collected and documented.

After this step is executed for each security requirement sr $\in$ SR, the result of this step is a set of security problems SPF$_{inst}$ represented as instantiated SPFs. Furthermore, the security-relevant domain knowledge D$_{sec}$ may be updated.

Step 3: Select and Instantiate CSPF

This step must be executed for each SPF instance spf$_{inst}$ $\in$ SPF$_{inst}$. Each SPF instance must be analyzed: one might find out that a security problem is already solved by the environment, e.g., by using a secure network or data storage. Then, a justification and corresponding security-relevant domain knowledge D$_{sec}$ is noted. Otherwise, a generic security mechanism based on the CSPFs that corresponds to the applied SPF is chosen. The pattern system indicates the CSPFs that correspond to an SPF by positions marked with "C" in the SPF's column. From the different generic security mechanisms that are represented by CSPFs, an appropriate CSPF is selected. To decide if a CSPF is appropriate, the security-relevant environment represented by CD$_{sec}$ and the security-relevant domain knowledge D$_{sec}$ is considered. For example, if users should select secrets for an encryption mechanism, a password-based encryption mechanism should take precedence over an encryption-key based mechanism. Furthermore, the selection can be accomplished according to other quality requirements such as usability or performance requirements or according to the presumed development costs of the realizations of the generic security mechanisms represented by the different CSPFs. After a CSPF is selected, it is instantiated by assigning concrete values to the domains, phenomena, interfaces, necessary conditions, and the concretized security requirement template. Domains and phenomena contained in the SPF instance are re-used for the instantiation of the corresponding CSPF. The instantiation of a CSPF may result in additional security-relevant domain knowledge, which must be added to the security-relevant domain knowledge D$_{sec}$, e.g.,

domain knowledge about passwords or cryptographic keys.

After this step is executed for each SPF instance spf$_{inst}$ $\in$ SPF$_{inst}$, the result is a set of CSPF instances CSPF$_{inst}$ and a corresponding set of concretized security requirements CSR. Furthermore, the security-relevant domain knowledge D$_{sec}$ may be updated.

Step 4: Check for Related SPFs

This step must be executed for each CSPF instance cspf$_{inst}$ $\in$ CSPF$_{inst}$. SPFs that are commonly used in combination with the described CSPF are indicated in the pattern system by positions marked with "R" in the CSPF's row. This information helps to find missing security requirements right at the beginning of the security requirements engineering process. After this step is executed for each CSPF instance cspf$_{inst}$ $\in$ CSPF$_{inst}$, the result of this step is a set of related security requirements and a corresponding set of SPFs. The related security requirements are added to the set of security requirements SR and the SPFs are instantiated by returning to the second step.

Step 5: Analyze Dependencies

This step must be executed for each CSPF instance cspf$_{inst}$ $\in$ CSPF$_{inst}$. For each instantiated necessary condition of the CSPF instance, it must be determined if the necessary condition can be assumed, or if it has to be treated using additional countermeasures:

1. The instantiated necessary condition constitutes a vulnerability of the security mechanism represented by the CSPF instance. Threats to the security mechanism must be identified based on the instantiated necessary condition. The result of this substep is a set of threats that exploit the vulnerability described by the necessary condition.

2. For each threat related to the necessary condition under consideration, the risk that the threat turns into a successful attack must be determined. Then, consider the following cases:

   a. **>tolerable risk:** If the risk is higher than the tolerable risk, then the threat should be mitigated by countermeasures.

   b. **≤tolerable risk:** If the risk is not higher than the tolerable risk, then one can assume that the threat does not turn into a successful attack. This means that it is not treated by the system at all.

   c. The result of this substep is a set of threats with associated risk values.

3. For each threat with an associated risk higher than the tolerable risk, find countermeasures to reduce the risk until it becomes tolerable. We must deal with the following three cases:

   a. Introduce an auxiliary mechanism to reduce the risk of the threat resulting in a successful attack. If there remain threats not yet considered by step 3, one executes this step again. Otherwise, the procedure terminates.

   b. Select and instantiate an SPF according to the second step. An SPF can easily be determined using the pattern system: the corresponding positions in the row of the instantiated CSPF are marked with "D". Then, one proceeds with the third step. The CSPF that is then instantiated represents a countermeasure to the threat.

   c. Some threats cannot be treated by the machine, because they are threats executed by the malicious environment on the honest environment. Thus, the application of technical countermeasures, i.e., security mechanisms and auxiliary mechanisms, is impossible. One must either deal with the threat by organizational means, or assume that the threats will not turn into successful

attacks, or the initially chosen security mechanism is not adequate. In the latter case, one must go back to step 1 and select a different CSPF. Otherwise, one must check if there remain threats not yet considered by step 3. If there are remaining threats, one executes this step again. Otherwise, the procedure terminates.

If one cannot find countermeasures sufficient to reduce the risk to a value lower than the tolerable risk, one must go back to the third step and select a different CSPF.

This step is executed for each CSPF instance cspfinst ∈ CSPFinst until all necessary conditions of all CSPF instances can be proved or assumed to hold. The results of this step are consolidated sets SPF and CSPF instances, additional auxiliary mechanisms and organizational means, and security-relevant domain knowledge (i.e., results from threat and risk analysis). Note that the result of the procedure possibly leads to the conclusion that the system cannot be realized because the risk cannot be sufficiently reduced.

All in all, the security requirements analysis method results in a consolidated set of security problems and solution approaches (i.e., generic security mechanisms represented by CSPF instances, auxiliary mechanisms, and organizational means) that additionally cover all dependent and related security problems and corresponding solution approaches, some of which may not have been known initially.

Validation

In the following, we first summarize the results generated by applying the first four steps of SEPP's security requirements analysis phase to the case study according to Section 5.

The security requirement SR1 captured by the CSPF instance shown in Figure 1 will be established by a password-based encryption mechanism applied to the text files. Furthermore, the related security problem of storing text files in an integrity-preserving way is detected. It is analyzed and documented using the SPF integrity-preserving data storage (Schmidt, 2010), and it will be established using a checksum mechanism represented by an instance of the CSPF integrity-preserving data storage using non-keyed hash functions (Schmidt, 2010). Note that the SPF integrity-preserving data storage, the CSPF integrity-preserving data storage using non-keyed hash functions, and their instances are not presented in this paper.

In the fifth step, the instantiated necessary conditions of the instantiated CSPFs are inspected. We begin with the conditions of the instantiated CSPF confidential data storage using password-based symmetric encryption. The first one expresses that passwords used by the honest environment must be different from the ones used by the malicious environment. To bypass this necessary condition, the following threats are found:

- **SR1-NC1-T1:** Malicious environment determines the right passwords (brute force).
- **SR1-NC1-T2:** Malicious environment applies social engineering means to reveal the right passwords.
- **SR1-NC1-T3:** Malicious environment guesses the right passwords.

Note that the security-relevant domain knowledge D_{sec} collected in this step is summarized Table 2 Security-Relevant Domain Knowledge "Secure Text Editor" Table 2. For each threat, the risk that it turns out to become a successful attack is determined. In our case study, the brute force threat SR1-NC1-T1 is assessed to have a risk higher than the tolerable risk, since the encrypted text files are stored on some public storage device. Note, that the statement that public access to the storage device is available is an assumption. Hence, it is added to the security-relevant domain knowledge D_{sec} (see Table 2). Moreover, the risk of the social engineering threat SR1-NC1-T2 is considered higher than the tolerable risk because the authors of the text files are not aware of social engineering attacks (which are an assumption too). In contrast, it is unlikely that the threat SR1-NC1-T3 turns into a successful attack, since the authors select non-trivial passwords. Moreover, passwords are strings and thus, the space of possible passwords is sufficiently large. Therefore, the risk of this threat is lower than the tolerable risk.

For each threat with intolerable risk, countermeasures have to be determined. SR1-NC1-T1 can be prevented by introducing a (functional) auxiliary mechanism that blocks the password dialog after a wrong password has been entered a limited number of times.

Table 2. Security-relevant domain knowledge "secure text editor"

Domain or Phenomenon	Security-Relevant Domain Knowledge D_{sec}	Type
Author	Author selects a non-trivial PasswordA	Assumption
Author	Author does not reveal PasswordA	Assumption
Author	Author stores Encrypted text file on public memory devices	Assumption
Author	Author is not aware of social engineering attacks	Assumption
Malicious user	Malicious user has only very basic technical abilities	Assumption
Malicious user	Malicious user's primary goal is to reveal text files, not to make them unavailable	Assumption
Malicious user	Malicious user does not have the access rights to install programs	Fact
Operating system	Operating system provides tools to reveal length and contents of files	Fact
PasswordA	Space of possible PasswordA is sufficiently large	Assumption

SR1-NC1-T2 threatens none of the machine's interfaces directly. Instead, it is located purely in the biddable environment. Since the biddable part of the environment (in contrast to the lexical and causal parts) cannot be influenced by the machine, countermeasures enforced by the machine are not available. The only available choices to deal with this threat are assuming that the biddable environment is immune against social engineering, installing an organizational policy that instructs authors not to reveal their passwords, or we have to choose a different security mechanism. In our case study, we rely on the mentioned assumption, which becomes a part of the security-relevant domain knowledge D_{sec}.

Since the countermeasure for SR1-NC1-T1 prevents brute force attacks and SR1-NC1-T2 is assumed to never turn into an successful attack, the overall risk for the non-fulfillment of the necessary condition is lower than the tolerable risk, i.e., the residual risk is lower than the tolerable risk. For that reason, the first necessary condition holds.

The second necessary condition expresses that the passwords are transmitted from the honest environment to the machine in a confidentiality-preserving way. To bypass this necessary condition, the following threat is found:

- **SR1-NC2-T1:** Malicious environment eavesdrops on transmission of password.
  The risk for this threat to turn into a successful attack is lower than the tolerable risk, because we expect that the malicious environment has only very basic technical abilities. For that reason, we can assume that the corresponding necessary condition holds. The assumptions on the technical abilities are a part of the security-relevant domain knowledge D_{sec}.
  The third necessary condition expresses that the passwords are transmitted from the honest environment to the machine in an integrity-preserving way. To bypass this

necessary condition, the following threat is found:

- **SR1-NC3-T1:** Malicious environment modifies password during transmission.
  The risk for this threat to turn into a successful attack is lower than the tolerable risk, because the primary goal of the malicious environment is to reveal the encrypted text files, and not to make them unavailable for the honest environment. For that reason, we can assume that the corresponding necessary condition holds.
  The fourth necessary condition expresses that the text file's content must be transmitted between the machine domain and the Author display domain and between the latter and the Author domain confidentially. To bypass this necessary condition, the following threat is found:

- **SR1-NC4-T1:** Malicious environment installs a program (e.g., a computer virus) to eavesdrop on the transmission of text file's content.
  The risk for this threat to turn into a successful attack is lower than the tolerable risk, because the malicious environment does not have the access rights to install a program. For that reason, we can assume that the corresponding necessary condition holds.

In summary, all four necessary conditions hold; either because it is assumed to be unlikely that the threats to these necessary conditions turn into successful attacks or auxiliary mechanisms is introduced to deal with the threats. One can be sufficiently confident that password-based symmetric encryption works properly in the operational environment, except for some residual (but tolerable) risk that the considered threats turn into successful attacks.

Following a similar procedure, additional security-relevant domain knowledge is found to cover the necessary conditions of the second CSPF instance that deals with the problem of storing text files in an integrity-preserving way. We do not present this part of the case study in detail.

As a result of applying SEPP's security requirements analysis phase to the secure text editor example, we have identified and analyzed in detail two security problems. Furthermore, we selected generic solution approaches to solve the security problems based on security-relevant domain knowledge.

RELATED WORK

While Mayer (2009) relates the threat and risk terminology to the security requirements engineering terminology, his approach is not environment-centric and it does not consider the transition from security requirements to security mechanisms. The environment is not explicitly covered because Mayer mainly refers to security requirements engineering methods such as the goal-based Secure Tropos (Giorgini & Mouratidis, 2006, 2007) and KAOS (van Lamsweerde, 2004, 2007) approaches, and SQUARE (Mead, Hough, & Stehney II, 2005) that are rather machine-centric. Consequently, Mayer does not explicitly consider security-relevant domain knowledge.

Asnar, Giorgini, Massacci, and Zannone (2007) propose the Tropos Goal-Risk Framework, an extension of earlier work (Asnar, Giorgini, & Mylopoulos, 2006), to assess risk based on trust relations among actors. Trust, combined with the concept of delegation of the fulfilment of a goal, enables the modeling of responsibility transfer from one actor to another. The authors propose qualitative risk reasoning techniques to support the analyst in evaluating and choosing among different possible sub-goal-trees. Compared to our approach, Asnar et al. do not model threats explicitly. Moreover, the notion of trust is comparable to the assumptions on biddable parts of the environment that we summarize together with

facts under the term security-relevant domain knowledge.

Lin, Nuseibeh, Ince, and Jackson (2004) define so-called anti-requirements and the corresponding abuse frames. An anti-requirement expresses the intentions of a malicious user, and an abuse frame represents a security threat. The authors state that the purpose of anti-requirements and abuse frames is to analyze security threats and derive security requirements. Based on a set of functional requirements and security objectives, the authors propose an iterative threat analysis method which is comparable to our approach to the extent that they identify and tackle vulnerabilities iteratively based on their abuse frames. It is our impression that abuse frames rather compare to problem diagrams than to problem frames. Problem diagrams are problem models that do not constitute patterns. Moreover, risk is not covered by the abuse frames approach, and threat analysis results are not explicitly considered as security-relevant domain knowledge.

Houmb, Georg, France, Bieman, and Jürjens (2005) present a cost-benefit trade-off analysis supported using Bayesian Belief Networks (BBN). According to the authors the "framework separates security concerns from core functionality using aspects. Each treatment strategy is modeled as an aspect model, and then composed with the primary model." The treatment strategies are comparable to the countermeasures in our approach. The properties of the treatment strategies are estimated by variables, which are the input for the BBN. The security level of a system is compared to an acceptance level comprised of the budget, security acceptance criteria, law and regulations, business goals, and policies. This security level is similar to the level of tolerable risk of our approach. In summary, the approach by Houmb et al. supports to justify design decisions based on risk analysis and system threats derived from successfully exploited vulnerabilities.

Sindre and Opdahl (2001) extend the traditional use case approach to also consider misuse cases, which represent behavior not wanted in the system to be developed. Misuse cases are initiated by misusers. A use case diagram contains both, use cases and actors (notated as named ellipses and named stick figures, respectively), as well as misuse cases and misusers (notated as graphically inverted use cases and actors). The definition of mal-activity diagrams (Sindre, 2007) is based on a similar idea. In this work, malicious activities and actors are added to UML activity diagrams in order to model potential attacks. Risk is not covered by the misuse case approach, and threat analysis results are not explicitly considered as security-relevant domain knowledge.

A comprehensive comparison of security requirements engineering approaches with respect to threat, risk, and further issues can be found in (Fabian, Gürses, Heisel, Santen, & Schmidt, 2010).

Note that we are aware of other approaches to threat and risk analysis (e.g., Microsoft STRIDE (Hernan et al., 2006) and SDL (Howard & Lipner, 2006)). However, we do not consider them in detail here.

CONCLUSION AND FUTURE WORK

The paper at hand relates security requirements engineering to threat and risk analysis terminology to elaborate an understanding of security-relevant domain knowledge.

The presented approach is embedded into SEPP, which is extended by a method driven by security-relevant domain knowledge to select adequate security mechanisms. The security-relevant domain knowledge comprises facts and assumptions on the operational environment, especially threat and risk models.

In the future, we would like to extend our SEPP's later phases, i.e., architectural design phases, by an approach similar to the one presented in this paper. We believe that threat and risk analysis must be repeatedly applied throughout the complete software development lifecycle. Moreover, we consider an analysis of the interactions between security requirements and different other kinds of quality requirements such as safety, usability, and performance requirements as a key feature of a software engineering approach to develop highly secure software.

REFERENCES

Asnar, Y., Giorgini, P., Massacci, F., & Zannone, N. (2007). From trust to dependability through risk analysis. In *Proceedings of the international conference on availability, reliability and security (AReS)* (pp. 19-26). Washington, DC: IEEE Computer Society.

Asnar, Y., Giorgini, P., & Mylopoulos, J. (2006). *Risk modelling and reasoning in goal models* (Tech. Rep. No. DIT-06-008). University of Trento, Trento, Italy.

Braber, F., Hogganvik, I., Lund, M. S., Stølen, K., & Vraalsen, F. (2007). Modelbased security analysis in seven steps – a guided tour to the CORAS method. *BT Technology Journal*, *25*(1), 101–117. doi:10.1007/s10550-007-0013-9doi:10.1007/s10550-007-0013-9

Fabian, B., Gürses, S., Heisel, M., Santen, T., & Schmidt, H. (2010). A comparison of security requirements engineering methods. *Requirements Engineering*, *15*(1), 7–40. doi:10.1007/s00766-009-0092-xdoi:10.1007/s00766-009-0092-x

Fernandez, E. B., la Red, M. D. L., Forneron, J., Uribe, V. E., & Rodriguez, G. G. (2007). A secure analysis pattern for handling legal cases. In *Proceedings of the Latin America conference on pattern languages of programming (SugarLoaf-PLoP)*. Retrieved August 9, 2009, from http://sugarloafplop.dsc.upe.br/wwD.zip

Giorgini, P., & Mouratidis, H. (2006). Secure Tropos: dealing effectively with security requirements in the development of multiagent systems. In M. Barley, F. Masacci, H. Mouratidis, & P. Scerri (Eds.), *Safety and security in multi-agent systems – selected papers*. New York: Springer.

Giorgini, P., & Mouratidis, H. (2007). Secure tropos: A security-oriented extension of the tropos methodology. *International Journal of Software Engineering and Knowledge Engineering, 17*(2), 285–309. doi:10.1142/S0218194007003240doi:10.1142/S0218194007003240

Gürses, S., Jahnke, J. H., Obry, C., Onabajo, A., Santen, T., & Price, M. (2005). Eliciting confidentiality requirements in practice. In *Proceedings of the conference of the centre for advanced studies on collaborative research (CASCON)* (pp. 101-116). IBM Press.

Hatebur, D., Heisel, M., & Schmidt, H. (2007). A security engineering process based on patterns. In *Proceedings of the international workshop on secure systems methodologies using patterns (spatterns)* (pp. 734-738). Washington, DC: IEEE Computer Society.

Hatebur, D., Heisel, M., & Schmidt, H. (2008). Analysis and component-based realization of security requirements. In *Proceedings of the international conference on availability, reliability and security (AReS)* (pp. 195-203). Washington, DC: IEEE Computer Society.

Hernan, S., Lambert, S., Ostwald, T., & Shostack, A. (2006, November). *Uncover security design flaws using the STRIDE approach*. Retrieved from http://msdn.microsoft.com/de-de/magazine/cc163519.aspx

Houmb, S. H., Georg, G., France, R., Bieman, J., & Jürjens, J. (2005). Cost-benefit trade-off analysis using BBN for aspect-oriented risk-driven development. In *Proceedings of the IEEE international conference on engineering of complex computer systems (iceccs)*. Washington, DC: IEEE Computer Society.

Howard, M., & Lipner, S. (2006). *The security development lifecycle*. Redmond, WA: Microsoft Press.

International Organization for Standardization (ISO) and International Electrotechnical Commission. (IEC). (2000). *Functional safety of electrical/electronic/programmable electronic safty-relevant systems* (ISO/IEC 61508). Retrieved August 9, 2009, from http://www.iec.ch/61508/

Jackson, M. (2001). *Problem frames. Analyzing and structuring software development problems*. Reading, MA: Addison-Wesley.

Lin, L., Nuseibeh, B., Ince, D., & Jackson, M. (2004). Using abuse frames to bound the scope of security problems. In *Proceedings of the IEEE international requirements engineering conference (RE)* (pp. 354-355). Washington, DC: IEEE Computer Society.

Mayer, N. (2009). *Model-based management of information system security risk*. Unpublished doctoral dissertation, University of Namur. Retrieved August 9, 2009, from http://nmayer.eu/publis/Thesis Mayer 2.0.pdf

Mead, N. R., Hough, E. D., & Stehney, T. R., II. (2005). *Security quality requirements engineering (SQUARE) methodology* (Tech. Rep. No. CMU/SEI-2005-TR-009). Pittsburgh, PA: Carnegie Mellon Software Engineering Institute.

Threat and Risk-Driven Security Requirements Engineering

Røstad, L., Tøndel, I. A., Line, M. B., & Nordland, O. (2006). Safety vs. security. In M. G. Stamatelatos & H. S. Blackman (Eds.), *Proceedings of the international conference on probabilistic safety assessment and management (PSAM)*. New York: ASME Press.

Schmidt, H. (2010). *A pattern-and component-based method to develop secure software*. Berlin: Deutscher Wissenschafts-Verlag (DWV).

Schneier, B. (1999). Attack trees. *Dr. Dobb's Journal*. Retrieved August 9, 2009, from http://www.schneier.com/paper-attacktrees-ddj-ft

Sindre, G. (2007). Mal-activity diagrams for capturing attacks on business processes. In P. Sawyer, B. Paech, & P. Heymans (Eds.), *Proceedings of the international working conference on requirements engineering: Foundation for software quality (REFSQ)* (LNCS 4542, pp. 355-366). New York: Springer.

Sindre, G., & Opdahl, A. L. (2001). Capturing security requirements through misuse cases. In *Proceedings of the Norwegian informatics conference (NIK)*.

UML Revision Task Force. (2009, February). *OMG unified modeling language: Superstructure*. Retrieved August 9, 2009, from http://www.omg.org/spec/UML/2.2/

van Lamsweerde, A. (2004). *Elaborating security requirements by construction of intentional anti-models* (pp. 148–157).

van Lamsweerde, A. (2007). Engineering requirements for system reliability and security. In J. G. M. Broy & C. Hoare (Eds.), *Software system reliability and security* (*Vol. 9*, pp. 196–238). Geneva, Switzerland: IOS Press.

Zave, P., & Jackson, M. (1997). Four dark corners of requirements engineering. *ACM Transactions on Software Engineering and Methodology*, *6*(1), 1–30. doi:10.1145/237432.237434doi:10.1145/237432.237434

ENDNOTES

[1] For reasons of simplicity, we write security mechanism, even if we refer to a generic security mechanism.

[2] Showing domain types in frame instances differs from the original notation by Jackson (2001), which does not indicate the domain types.

This work was previously published in the International Journal of Mobile Computing and Multimedia Communications, Volume 3, Issue 1, edited by Ismail Khalil and Edgar Weippl, pp. 34-49, copyright 2011 by IGI Publishing (an imprint of IGI Global).

Chapter 4
Establishing a Personalized Information Security Culture

Shuhaili Talib
University of Plymouth, UK & International Islamic University, Malaysia

Nathan L. Clarke
University of Plymouth, UK & Edith Cowan University, Australia

Steven M. Furnell
University of Plymouth, UK & Edith Cowan University, Australia

ABSTRACT

Good security cannot be achieved through technical means alone and a solid understanding of the issues and how to protect one's self is required from users. Whilst many initiatives, programs and strategies have been proposed to improve the level of information security awareness, most have been directed at organizations. Given people's use of technology is primarily focused between the workplace and home; this paper seeks to understand the knowledge and practice relationship between these environments. Through a developed survey, it was identified that the majority of the learning about information security occurred in the workplace, where clear motivations, such as legislation and regulation, existed. Results found that users were more than willing to engage with such awareness raising initiatives. From a comparison of practice between work and home environments, it was found that this knowledge and practice obtained at the workplace was transferred to the home environment. Given this positive transferability of knowledge and the willingness to learn about how to remain secure, an opportunity exists to move away from specific organizational awareness programs and to move towards awareness raising strategies that will develop an all-round individual security culture for users independent of the environment they are operating in.

DOI: 10.4018/978-1-4666-2163-3.ch004

INTRODUCTION

The volume and nature of information security threats has evolved, moving away from technical savvy hackers demonstrating their skill, to organized and well established crackers that aim to receive substantial financial rewards for their efforts (Hinde, 2004). This has resulted in an increase in cybercrime activities and subsequent threats end-users find themselves the target of. For example, in the Computer Security Institute (CSI) survey report stated that 52% of organizations had encountered threats in 2007 (Richardson, 2007). Another survey conducted by Harris on behalf of Microsoft and the National Cyber Security Alliance (NCSA) found that 64% of respondents had encountered a Phishing email – a threat rarely encountered 5 years ago (Harris Interactive, 2009). To safeguard users a range of security counter-measures exist. These tools continually evolve in sophistication and increase in number to counter the changing nature of the threats. However, in order for these to operate successfully they inherently rely upon the end-user to be able to deploy, configure and operate them. Unfortunately, it is also a well recognized fact that security is only as strong as the weakest link; and the weakest link is frequently the end-user (Schneier, 2000).

To counter the threat caused by end-users an increased focus has been given towards information security awareness and the need to educate and inform end-users. Within an organizational context, efforts towards improving awareness amongst employees have increased with CSI survey indicating 82% of Enterprise organizations having training programs (Richardson, 2008). Unfortunately, however, this is not necessarily the case for all, with Business Enterprise Regulatory Reform (BERR) Information Security Breach Survey, which largely comprises of small-to-medium sized companies (SMEs), indicating only 40% of their respondents conduct training (Business Enterprise Regulatory Reform, 2008). Whilst many organizations arguably have the resources

to provide such training, should they deem it important to do so, they only represent a (95%) proportion of people who use the Internet. The remaining users are typically home-users or the general public. Worryingly, evidence demonstrate that it is this group of users that are most at risk, with 95% of all attacks being focused upon them (Symantec, 2007). Home users have a variety of resources at their disposal in order to improve their awareness of online threats. All the major Anti-Virus providers, Operating System vendors and government initiatives provide supporting information to the home user (GetSafeOnline, 2009; StaySafeOnline, 2009; WebWise, 2009).

Whilst training programs and initiatives exist within both the workplace and home, little research has been conducted to understand what is being taught and where, the effectiveness of such strategies and to what degree learning styles play a role in achieving good information security practice. Information security awareness can be tackled from a variety of different directions, such as within school, government-sponsored initiatives and security providers; however, this paper will specifically focus upon and investigate behavior, practices and interactions within and between organizations and home environments. The paper is organized as follows: the next section discusses the current state-of-the-art information security awareness and the development of security culture. Next, the methodology of the study is described followed by the presentation of results. Then, main findings of the study are presented along with the conclusion and possible future areas of exploration.

PRIOR WORK IN INFORMATION SECURITY AWARENESS TRAINING

Information security awareness has been given an increasingly important focus within both academic and commercial communities. Organizations are gradually understanding the importance of their information assets and developing strategies to improve awareness throughout the company. Good corporate governance, regulation and legislation have also helped in raising the importance and relevance of good information security policies and practices (R. von Solms & von Solms, 2006). Within academia, focus by researchers has partially moved away from the technical issues towards understanding the end user and developing models and programs that organizations can utilize in developing better awareness (Dlamini, Eloff, & Eloff, 2009).

Interestingly, within academia, current research is suggesting that simple awareness strategies that educate employees about particular security topics through traditional mechanisms such as class-room based teaching, online education and poster/email campaigns are not sufficient in maintaining long-term information security practice (Furnell & Thomson, 2009; Rotvold, 2008). Rather an increasing volume of research is proposing the need to develop an information security culture within the organization – moving away from surface learning and embedding or indoctrinating good practice within employees (Chia, Maynard, & Ruighaver, 2002; Furnell & Thomson, 2009; Schlienger & Teufel, 2003; B. von Solms, 2000). The authors of these studies believe through establishing an information security culture in the organization, long-term security practice can be maintained and moreover, the drive towards awareness and education of security issues becomes self-fulfilling, as employees are engaged and proactive about their practice.

Within the context of home users, awareness raising initiatives have been created. GetSafeOnline is a UK Government-sponsored initiative that provides a blanket-based approach; providing general information about the risks and how to get protected (GetSafeOnline, 2009). The site provides a variety of information from beginnings guides to specific information about relevant threats in a timely fashion. The site is predominately text based information with the addition of occasional

video files. Other countries such as the USA have similar national based websites (StaySafeOnline, 2009). A number of companies that provide security software and operating systems also provide web-based access to resources – largely reading based – to assist in educating and informing home users (McAfee, 2009; Microsoft, 2009).

Arguably, motivating home users into undertaking security training is challenging as security is always a requirement but never actually the primary task the user is trying to achieve. People often do not have the understanding they need to do it and moreover for those that do, they frequently do not have the time or inclination in any case. Worryingly, evidence demonstrates even when users do think they know about security and how to protect themselves, this is often found not to be the case. A joint study by NCSA and Symantec found that while 75% of home users thought they had spam protection, in fact only 42% actually did (National Cyber Security Alliance & Symantec, 2008). This disparity between what they think they have and actually do have illustrates a significant gap in their understanding.

In order to achieve good security awareness considerable research has been undertaken into developing various learning mechanisms, such as: face-to-face training sessions, email messages, online training, video game, intranet-based access and poster campaigns (Cone, Irvine, Thompson, & Nguyen, 2007; European Network and Information Security Agency, 2008; Hawkins, Yen, & Chou, 2000; Spurling, 1995; Wood, 1995). Whilst focus has been given to what and how to educate within organizations, research has identified the importance of measuring the effectiveness of such programs in order to ensure education leads to practice (Chen, Medlin, & Shaw, 2008; Thompson & Von Solms, 1998). The CSI survey reported that 68% of the organizations measure the effectiveness of their awareness training (Richardson, 2008). Unfortunately, no figures were given as to the actual levels of effectiveness of the training. Various approaches have been identified to assist in creating an effective security program, such as, having more user engagement in the process through workshops and providing the training on a continuous basis (Albrechtsen, 2007; Cooper, 2008; Dlamini et al., 2009).

However, whilst such strategies might be possible for organizations to utilize, home users would find it arguably difficult to engage for a multitude of reasons: desire, time, resources and the knowledge they need to, to name but a few. Unfortunately, there is little evidence demonstrating whether home users are in fact knowledgeable about information security and indeed practicing it.

A SURVEY OF END-USER AWARENESS AND PRACTICES

Given the prior literature in the area, it was concluded that it was difficult to determine the effectiveness of training and moreover where and how they received that training. In addition, whilst it could be hypothesized that the majority of training came from organizations, it is not clear exactly to what extent learning from work and home played a role in information security practice in general. A survey was therefore created to assess these factors. A quantitative method of collecting data was chosen for the study in order to maximize the number of respondents across a broad spectrum of industries and roles. The aims of the survey are:

- To understand respondents general levels of security awareness and practice.
- To understand whether they received training from work and if so, what type and how effective it was.
- To understand the relationship between knowledge gained and practice between work and home
- To understand how people learn and what preferences they have towards various learning styles.

The survey consists of four sections: Demographics; Information Security Awareness; Practice at Workplace and Practices at Home. The Practices at Workplace, sought to investigate the current practice of respondents at their workplace. The section also enquired about the type of training that they have attended and what the learning methods that they have experienced had been and what they preferred. Respondents were also asked about the sources of information security knowledge in the workplace. This section provided information about the degree of transferability of information security knowledge between home and the workplace. At the end of the section is a list of common security practices that have been created to understand what their practices at their workplace actually are. The final section on Practices at Home sought to mirror much of the composition of the previous section but with a view to practices and education at home.

The survey was distributed to a wide range of people regardless of location but with the condition that they were in employment and regularly use a computer at home and their workplace. The study was undertaken from 20th August – 7th October 2008 (49 days). The survey collection has been stopped when it reached more than the survey target (300) respondents. The survey was promoted via email, based on the authors' academic contacts, personal contacts, from the word-of-mouth and two mailing lists such as Google and Yahoo groups. A total of 333 responses were obtained and the results are analyzed in the sections that follow.

RESULTS

An analysis of the demographics identified that a fairly even split in responses were received from both genders (55% male; 45% female). It was found that the majority of the respondents (55%) were from the age group 25 to 34 and 81% had at least an undergraduate level of education. This could be due to the personal contacts of the author and those who are in the age group are more likely to be IT literate and have at least an email account. Whilst this proportion of users are clearly not representative of the general population, it is not felt this would bias the results of the survey except to provide perhaps a more informed and educated response to the questions. The results therefore probably indicate a more positive perspective on the use and knowledge of information security than what exists within the general population.

Information Security Awareness

In order to assess the level of security awareness, respondents were asked to rate their perceived level against a five point scale. Almost half of them (49%) rated themselves at high or very high (as illustrated in Figure 1). When tied to the question asking respondents what their level of competency is with Information Technology (IT), where 64% stated that they had at least and advanced level of knowledge, it can be surmised that this group of respondents are well educate and informed about IT and Information Security in general.

In order to better understand what aspects of information security respondents understood, they were asked a couple of questions surrounding their knowledge of security threats and their use of social networking sites. Table 1 presents the results of respondent's awareness of a variety of security threats. Un-surprisingly, the long-standing threats such as Virus and Spam were amongst

the highest selected as being understood and newer threats such as zero-day attacks, Botnets ad Zombies less understood. Interestingly, whilst 70% understood Phishing, a relatively smaller 44% understood Social Engineering of which Phishing is an example of. The list of terms also included a couple of fake terms – Phlopping and Whooping – so that it was possible to identify respondents who might be exaggerating their knowledge or providing arbitrary responses. On the whole, relatively small numbers (7-10%) of respondents thought they had heard and understood the terms. That said it is a little concerning that these terms received any acknowledgement at all.

Social networking is a popular Internet activity, which literature has suggested is a common threat vector when looking to obtain information about people for subsequent use in identity fraud (Adlam, 2009; British Broadcasting Corporation, 2007; Wallop, 2007). Amongst the respondents, 63% indicated they belong to one or more sites. When asked what information they release onto the social network, the respondent group overall appear to be informed and careful about releasing too much information. Table 2 illustrates that whilst 59% and 62% are releasing information regarding their real name and email address; only 7% reveal their full postal address. The most worrying statistic is the 45% releasing their date of birth but along with their name this amount of information is unlikely to result in identity theft.

Figure 1. Perceived level of information security awareness

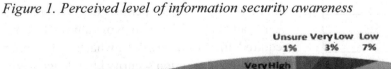
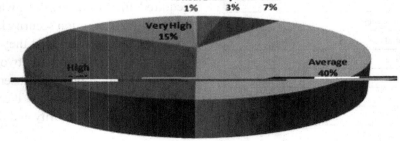

Table 1. Perceived understanding of security threats

Information Security Terms	You Understand It (%)	You Never Heard of It (%)
Virus/Worm	92	0
Trojan horse	80	3
Spam	90	0
Social engineering	44	24
Phishing	70	10
Pharming	24	42
Identity theft	81	8
Key loggers	57	22
Phlopping[a]	7	68
Botnets	33	43
Zombies	33	38
Denial of service	56	24
Packet sniffer	47	37
Whooping[a]	10	59
Hacker	95	1
Zero day attacks	29	44
Cracker	56	24
a. Fake security term		

Table 2. Personal information revealed by social networking

Personal Information	Respondents (%)
Real name	59
Email	62
Real date of birth	45
Full address	8
Phone number	14
Personal blog	22
Special occasions	22
Photographs of yourself	67
Photographs of your family members	37
Photographs of your friends	42
Photographs of your office	7
Photographs of your house	8
None of the above	5
Other	1

Information Security Practices at Workplace

Analysing the participant's responses with reference to their practices within work, 36% stated their organization provided some sort of training with regards to information security. When comparing this to the size of the organization the respondent works for, it was found that 36% came from SMEs and coincidently 36% also came from Enterprise (an Enterprise being defined as those organizations with 250 or greater employees). Whilst this figure is in line with the 40% stated by BERR survey, which largely canvases SMEs, it falls somewhat short of CSI Computer Crime and Security Survey's 80% (whose respondents are largely but not exclusively Enterprises) (Business Enterprise Regulatory Reform, 2008; Richardson, 2008). A further analysis of those responding on behalf of Enterprises shows that relatively few (3%) come from US-based companies – where regulation and legislation have arguably been prime motivators in ensuring staff are appropriately trained. Of the 36% of respondents who stated their organization provided training, 95% also stated they attended the training sessions.

In order to understand more about security practices in the workplace, respondents were asked about the sources of their information security knowledge. The top three information security sources at work are presented in Table 3; with websites and search engines the most popular. Arguably this could be due to many organizations now providing open access to the Internet. This freedom permits the employee to search and locate information of value at the time required. In addition to asking what their top three sources of information security knowledge were, they were also asked what they prefer. Interestingly, the results from these two questions came out identically, illustrating user's already have the freedom of choice when it comes to learning about information security and organizations are

Table 3. Top three sources of information security and learning at work

	Top Three for Information Security in the Workplace		Top Three Most Preferred for Information Security in the Workplace
1	Websites and search engines	1	Websites and search engines
2	Informal discussions with colleagues and professional contacts	2	Information discussions with colleagues and professional contacts
3	Organization's policy	3	Organization's policy

not burdening them with approaches they would not prefer.

From Table 3, it is evident that much of the knowledge for Information Security within a workplace comes from fairly informal means – web searches and informal discussions with colleagues. Interestingly, these results do illustrate the importance and relevant of the organizational policy in informing employees and moreover practice.

This freedom of choice of how to learn comes through again when the respondents were asked about where or how they received their training. 28% of respondents responded that it was through self-study. As illustrated in Figure 2, the remaining options received a fairly even split, indicating that if organizations are willing to invest in training their staff, the methods utilized will vary with no single option being a considered standard. Interestingly, further analysis of these responds when taking into account the size of the organization found that the preferred training type was independent of the organizational size, with SMEs willing to

invest in outside experts as much as Enterprises – countering the standard assumption that SMEs do not have the resources to pay for training and would rely upon less expensive options such as self-study or online training.

Respondents were also asked how frequent they would like to have security training. As Figure 3 illustrates, the largest proportion of users preferred to have an on-demand service, with the majority of the remaining respondents split between monthly, quarterly, half-yearly and yearly. Overall 95% of respondents felt they needed some level of training.

Information Security Practices at Home

In order to compare practice from the workplace and home, respondents were asked a series of questions with respect to their practice at home. When analysing the top three sources of acquiring information security knowledge and what sources they preferred to learn from, it can be seen that

Figure 2. Preferred training type

Figure 3. Respondent preference to having information security training

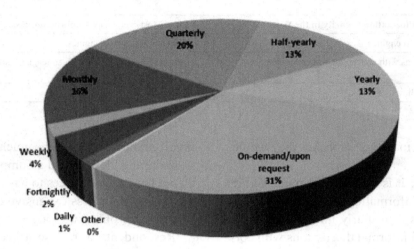

the lists were identical, with web searches coming out first, what they had learnt from the workplace second, and reading newspapers and magazines third (as illustrated in Table 4). Upon reflection, this correlation should be expected as within the home environment you have complete freedom over what and how you learn. The user is not forced through employment to attend training courses or learn in a specific manner depending upon how the organization has decided to implement training. This freedom provides the user with the opportunity of using learning approaches that are preferred and most convenient to the individual. Arguably, without the formal training approaches that organizations utilize it is difficult to understand the depth of learning that goes on at home – with much of the learning likely being a result of news articles and press coverage of a particular event. A further research that focused on the level of understanding of information security knowledge

acquired at home would be required to further explore on this aspect.

That said, the results from Table 4 do illustrate the users are willing and do learn at home. Interestingly, the second most preferred source of information is what they learn from the workplace. Acquiring knowledge about information security within the workplace has an impact upon the level of awareness and learning at home.

In addition to understanding how they learn, respondents were also asked how frequent that learning takes place. Figure 4 presents the breakdown of responses. 71% of respondents undertake some level of training at home with 39% performing this on average on a monthly basis and 25% weekly. Whilst the regularity of the training is somewhat infrequent, given the lack of motivation within the home environment to undertake training, it is encouraging to note

Table 4. Top three sources of information security & learning at home

	Top Three for Information Security at Home			Top Three Most Preferred Sources for Information Security at Home	
1	Websites and search engines		1	Websites and search engines	
2	From what I learnt at my workplace		2	From what I learnt at my workplace	
3	Daily newspaper and Magazines		3	Daily newspaper	

Figure 4. How frequently learning takes place at home

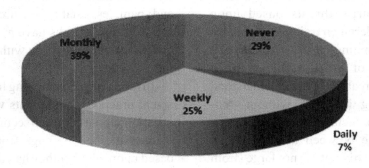

that over two thirds are willing to undertake some level of training at home.

Given that the proportion of users not willing to learn at home and the proportion that learn on a monthly basis make up 68% of the respondents, the need to acquire the knowledge necessary to ensure they remain secure at home is imperative. Arguably therefore, the knowledge users obtain within the workplace and subsequently transfer into the home environment is key to establishing a level of information security awareness for many respondents. Without such transference, a good proportion of home users will have little or no security awareness.

Effectiveness of Information Security Training

Having established training practices at home and the workplace, the survey proceeded to understand the extent to which this training and practice was effective. A total of 115 of the total respondents received training, 115 did not and the remaining claimed that they are not sure they have attended the training. Whilst training, awareness and practice are arguably associated with each other, simply undertaking training or having an awareness of an issue does not necessarily imply practice.

To this end, Figure 5 provides a comparison between those respondents who undertook training and what they considered their level of security awareness is. A total of 67% of respondents who undertook training felt they had a high or very high level of awareness. This compares to just 43% who had not received training. This demonstrates respondents at least perceive they have a better understanding of the information security threats and countermeasures over those that have not received training.

Figure 5. Respondents who attended training and their awareness level

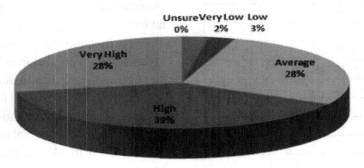

A further analysis of respondents' understanding of various security threats based upon whether they had undertaken training or not also reveals those with training on the whole have a better understanding of terms. As illustrated in Table 5, all security threats were better understood by those with training than those without – unfortunately, this also included the fake terms. Whilst the difference between those that had training and those that did not are not large (from 3%) for many of the terms, it is worth noting the large proportion of respondents in this survey who regard themselves as advanced users. It is therefore anticipated that this difference would be larger under normal circumstances. It is also noticeable that while the difference is small on

well established threats such as viruses, worms and spam; less established threats such as Botnets and Zero-day attacks have a significantly larger difference between those with and without training.

In terms of understanding how training effects actual practice, respondents were asked several questions about common security practices. Table 6 illustrates the findings from these questions based upon whether they had undertaken training or not. More significantly from these results it is identifiable that a bigger difference exists in practice between those that had training and than those that did not. A good example here is the use of strong passwords for user authentication, with 72% of those trained using them but only 45% of those un-trained doing so. Training therefore is arguably having a positive effect not only upon awareness but also on actual practice. Unfortunately however, it is also evident that the level of practice amongst the trained respondents is not necessarily as high as would be liked with certain practices such as changing passwords and reporting incidents as low as 23 and 33% respectively.

In order to understand the effectiveness of users practice at home based upon whether they had received training, participants were asked a series of questions. Table 7 illustrates that practice at home for those respondents with training is significantly better than those without – with practice differing from 7 to 17%. Similarly with the previous question, the level to which trained users are actually following good practice is worryingly low, highlighting some potential concerns over the nature and type of training been undertaken.

Security controls are one of the first defense layers that protect users from security threats. The survey finally tried to understand what kind of security controls were used by respondents while at home. The results are shown in Table 8. Even though respondents do not receive training, 97% of them are using Antivirus at home. This could be related with the results discussed in the previ-

Table 5. Perceived understanding of security threats based upon whether training had been provided

Information Security Terms	Respondents Who Received Training (%)	Respondents Who Did Not Receive Training (%)
Virus/Worm	97	93
Trojan horse	94	77
Spam	94	88
Social engineering	58	40
Phishing	81	67
Pharming	34	20
Identity theft	85	81
Key loggers	72	55
Phlopping[a]	10	5
Botnets	50	28
Zombies	50	30
Denial of service	75	56
Packet sniffer	65	48
Whooping[a]	17	8
Hacker	97	95
Zero day attacks	45	23
Cracker	73	55
a. Fake security term		

Table 6. Information security practice of respondents

Good Security Practices	Respondents Who Received Training (%)	Respondents Who Did Not Receive Training (%)
I log off my computer whenever I leave a computer system	50	37
I backup my data on disks or CDs regularly	35	22
I check that antivirus software is enabled and updated	69	60
I use the organization's firewall protection	72	56
My passwords consists of at least 8 characters and uses the combination of letters (a-z), symbols (!@#$%) and numbers (0-9)	72	45
I keep my password a secret and only I know it	84	61
I change my password regularly	23	9
I scan with antivirus any external disk/thumb drive/USB drive when first plugging it into the computer system	43	27
I report to security incidents to the appropriate parties	33	14
I look for "https://" or the "little gold padlock" before I make financial transaction online	60	54
I protect confidential files with passwords	36	23
I read the privacy statement before I proceed with an action (such as registering with a website, installing an application or financial/online banking transaction)	34	17
I ensure nobody is looking at my keyboard each time I key in my password	57	37

ous section where 92% of them are aware of the virus/worm threats and take necessary action such as installing Antivirus. Overall, there is no significant difference between those who received training and those who did not. However, the results do demonstrate that those trained respondents are still marginally ahead of those who are not in using security controls at home.

DISCUSSION

On the whole, the participants represented a well-informed group of individuals on the topic of Information Security, with respondents generally having a good level of awareness and practice. Care should therefore be given in generalizing these results to a wider population as it is anticipated that the levels of IT and security awareness would be generally lower. Whilst this does not affect the key results of the survey, it is important to realize that the problem of achieving information security

Table 7. Information security practice at home

Good Security Practices	Respondents Who Received Training (%)	Respondents Who Did Not Receive Training (%)
I shred confidential documents before throwing them into the bin	50	38
I change the default password for my router	53	36
I use encryption key to protect my wireless connection	58	51

Table 8. Respondents' use of security controls

Security Controls	Respondents Who Received Training (%)	Respondents Who Did Not Receive Training (%)
Antivirus	98	97
Firewall	78	72
Anti-phishing	45	38
Anti-spyware	75	75
Intrusion Detection Systems (IDS)	20	18
Spam filter	67	66

awareness and practice still remains. Indeed, even within this well educated demographic, 50% of them felt they had an average or lower level of awareness.

Whilst establishing the effectiveness of awareness training is not a simple task, the results have demonstrated that respondents whom have undertaken training are more aware of a greater variety of security issues – particularly threats. With the ever-changing security landscape and people's increasing adoption of technology, the need to maintain up-to-date levels of awareness is imperative if users are to remain secure. Indeed, the last few years alone has seen a significant increase in security threats that focus upon the human-factor, such as Phishing, that countermeasures were unable to protect against. Only through relevant and timely training can security be maintained.

Encouragingly, when looking at the motivations of participants in undertaking some form of education on information security, respondents appear very willing to engage to some degree both in home and workplace environments. Unfortunately, however, the volume and depth of such education is lacking in places – with only 36% of organizations willing to invest in security education and home users arguably lacking in credible, structured learning, given their focus upon web searches and news reports. What is evident from the findings is the participant's freedom of choice when looking to learn about security – both in terms of what they learn and how. Flexibility therefore appears to be an important consideration, so that users are able to learn what topics they want, in a manner or learning style they prefer, at a time and location they feel most comfortable in.

As motivation of home users will inevitable be problematic due to the various constraints of everyday life, focus therefore arguably has to be placed upon what can be achieved in the workplace. With 95% of participants who have training provided; attending, and home users stating that what they learn in the workplace is key to what they practice at home, leveraging workplace learning could potentially be very useful in establishing good security practice independent of the environment. The workplace environment is also better placed to ensure a credible and structured security awareness program is in place to ensure important aspects of knowledge are not missed. Industry therefore has an important role to play in educating employees on the subject of information security awareness; however, it is important to ensure such training is not too specifically focused upon any particular company's processes and is easily generalizable so that employees are able to apply such knowledge within the home environment.

A Personalized Security Awareness Framework

Current approaches to information security awareness are obviously not fit for purpose. Whilst they are certainly better than nothing, they fail in providing the necessary learning for users to become and remain competent. The approach taken thus far by industry and research has focused on what to teach rather than how to, with the effect of awareness strategies that are "one size fits all". This approach left users disappointed as they acquired little new knowledge (Okenyi & Owens, 2007). Studies have also commented on how security awareness training is analogous to fitting a square peg in a round hole (Schultz, 2004).

Within school education it has been long understood that putting the learner at the centre of the learning experience is imperative for effective education. One core concept coming out from this approach is the idea of an individualized or personalized learning plan (Burton, 2007; Dainton, 2004; Department for Children School and Families, 2010; The National Strategies, 2007; Underwood & Banyard, 2008). Personalized learning has been defined as teaching based upon students' need or in other words it is tailor-made into the individuals interests and preferences (Dainton, 2004; Maguire, 2008). Personalized learning also provides the opportunity of understanding how an individual learns, adopting different learning strategies to maximize the effectiveness of education (Sternberg, Grigorenko, & Zhang, 2008). Personalization of learning also enables learners to set their own learning objectives which provide flexibility in the learning process itself (Campbell, Robinson, Neelands, Hewston, & Mazzoli, 2007). Whilst prior literatures suggesting individualized learning can improve learning outcomes; little research has been undertaken in the field of information security education (Brocke & Buddendick, 2005; May, 2008).

When considering the factors or attributes that affect learning, a myriad of internal, external, direct and indirect aspects arise. Figure 6 below illustrates a mind-map of factors that need to be considered if a flexible, individual and robust framework for information security awareness education is to be developed.

CONCLUSION

Achieving good information security awareness in the general population of Internet users is imperative if they are to remain secure and electronic business is to thrive. Unfortunately, educating users about the threats and countermeasures in a dynamic environment like security requires time, resources and motivation. Comparing the home and work environments, it is clear the latter provides more opportunity for such education to take place – with companies motivated to provide training due to changes in legislation, regulation and governance. The survey findings have already demonstrated that leveraging this transference of knowledge from the workplace to home is already underway.

Whilst the workplace provides a good opportunity to educate users about information security, it has also become apparent that care needs to be taken when looking into what they are taught, when they are taught it and how they like to learn. Given the mixture of: differing priorities of business; cost; the varying degrees of prior knowledge of security from employees; and the differing pedagogies required, it follows that a highly flexible framework is required that is capable of tailoring information security awareness training to the individual across all environments: work and home. Future research will focus upon the developing such a framework and in particular look to incorporate other factors such as psychological profiling in order to maximize the learning experience but importantly also ensure that learning follows through to practice.

Figure 6. Factors affecting information security awareness

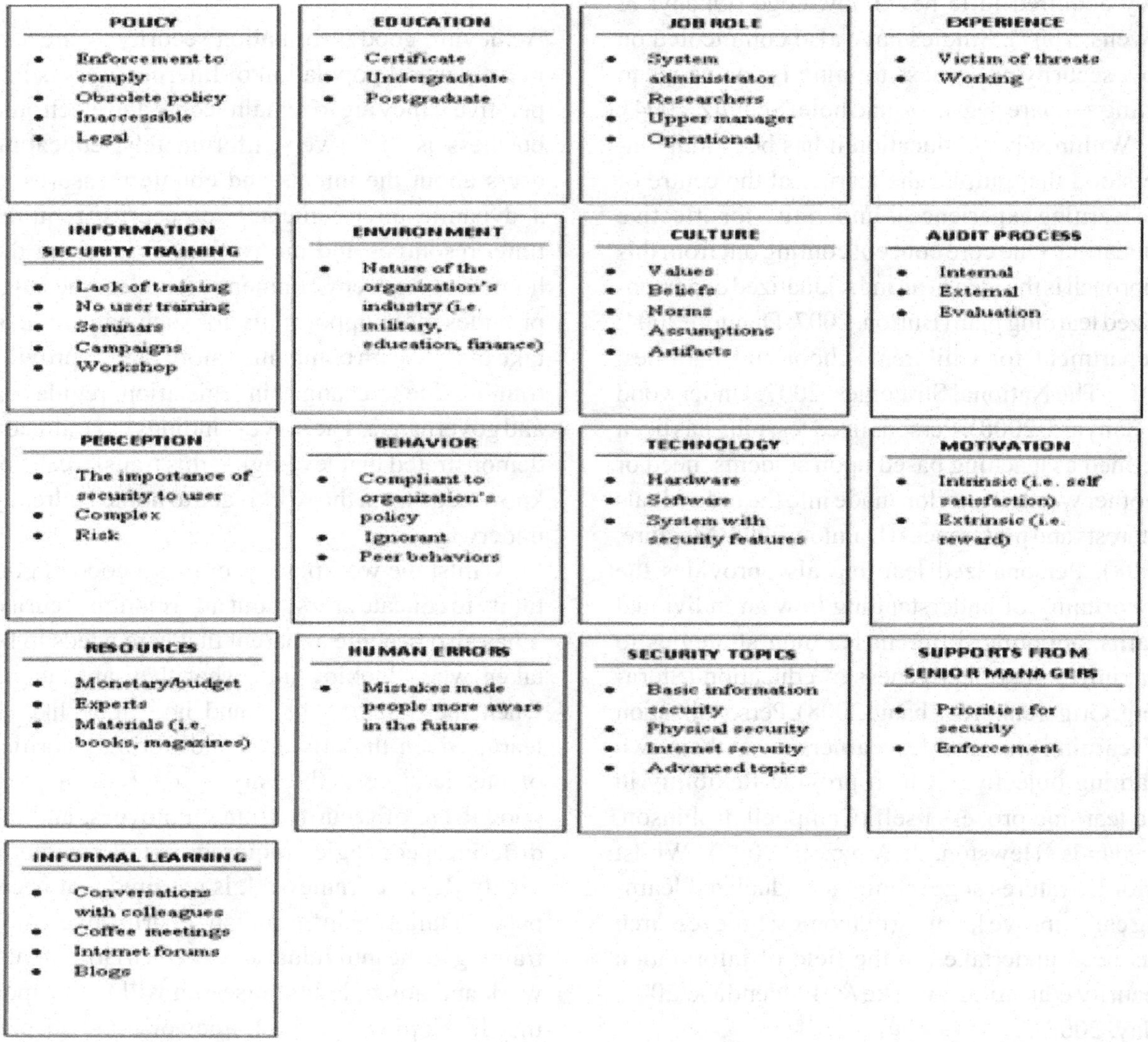

POLICY	EDUCATION	JOB ROLE	EXPERIENCE
• Enforcement to comply • Obsolete policy • Inaccessible • Legal	• Certificate • Undergraduate • Postgraduate	• System administrator • Researchers • Upper manager • Operational	• Victim of threats • Working

INFORMATION SECURITY TRAINING	ENVIRONMENT	CULTURE	AUDIT PROCESS
• Lack of training • No user training • Seminars • Campaigns • Workshop	• Nature of the organization's industry (i.e. military, education, finance)	• Values • Beliefs • Norms • Assumptions • Artifacts	• Internal • External • Evaluation

PERCEPTION	BEHAVIOR	TECHNOLOGY	MOTIVATION
• The importance of security to user • Complex • Risk	• Compliant to organization's policy • Ignorant • Peer behaviors	• Hardware • Software • System with security features	• Intrinsic (i.e. self satisfaction) • Extrinsic (i.e. reward)

RESOURCES	HUMAN ERRORS	SECURITY TOPICS	SUPPORTS FROM SENIOR MANAGERS
• Monetary/budget • Experts • Materials (i.e. books, magazines)	• Mistakes made people more aware in the future	• Basic information security • Physical security • Internet security • Advanced topics	• Priorities for security • Enforcement

INFORMAL LEARNING
• Conversations with colleagues • Coffee meetings • Internet forums • Blogs

REFERENCES

Adlam, D. (2009). *Social networking identity fraud*. Retrieved September 2, 2009, from http://ezinearticles.com/?Social-Networking-Identity-Fraud&id=2730177

Albrechtsen, E. (2007). A qualitative study of users' view on information security. *Computers & Security, 26*(4), 276–289. doi:10.1016/j.cose.2006.11.004

British Broadcasting Corporation. (2007). *Web networkers 'at risk of fraud'*. Retrieved September 2, 2009, from http://news.bbc.co.uk/1/hi/uk/6910826.stm

Brocke, J. v., & Buddendick, C. (2005). *Security awareness management - Foundations and Implementation of security awareness*. Paper presented at the 2005 International Conference on Security and Management (SAM'05), Las Vegas.

Burton, D. (2007). Psycho-pedagogy and personalised learning. *Journal of Education for Teaching: International research and pedagogy, 33*(1), 5-17.

Business Enterprise Regulatory Reform. (2008). *The 9th information security breaches survey*. London: Department for Business Enterprise and Regulatory Reform & Pricewaterhouse Coopers.

Campbell, R. J., Robinson, W., Neelands, J., Hewston, R., & Mazzoli, L. (2007). Personalised learning: Ambiguities in theory and practice. *British Journal of Educational Studies, 55*(2), 135–154. doi:10.1111/j.1467-8527.2007.00370.x

Chen, C. C., Medlin, B. D., & Shaw, R. S. (2008). A cross-cultural investigation of situational information security awareness programs. *Information Management & Computer Security, 16*(4), 360–376. doi:10.1108/09685220810908787

Chia, P. A., Maynard, S. B., & Ruighaver, A. B. (2002). *Understanding organizational security culture*. Paper presented at the Sixth Pacific Asia Conference on Information Systems, Tokyo, Japan.

Cone, B. D., Irvine, C. E., Thompson, M. F., & Nguyen, T. D. (2007). A video game for cyber security training and awareness. *Computers & Security, 26*(1), 63–72. doi:10.1016/j.cose.2006.10.005

Cooper, M. H. (2008). *Information security training: lessons learned along the trail*. Paper presented at the 36th annual ACM SIGUCCS conference on User services conference.

Dainton, S. (2004). Personalised learning. *Symposium Journals, 46*(2), 56-58.

Department for Children School and Families. (2010). *Personalised learning approaches used by schools*. Retrieved May 6, 2010, from http://www.dcsf.gov.uk/research/programmeofresearch/projectinformation.cfm?projectId=14664&type=5&resultspage

Dlamini, M. T., Eloff, J. H. P., & Eloff, M. M. (2009). Information security: The moving target. *Computers & Security, 28*(3/4), 189–198. doi:10.1016/j.cose.2008.11.007

European Network and Information Security Agency. (2008). *The new users' guide: How to raise information security awareness*. European Network and Information Security Agency.

Furnell, S., & Thomson, K.-L. (2009). From culture to disobedience: Recognising the varying user acceptance of IT security. *Computer Fraud & Security, (2)*: 5–10. doi:10.1016/S1361-3723(09)70019-3

GetSafeOnline. (2009). *Get safe online with free, expert advice*. Retrieved July 23, 2009, from http://www.getsafeonline.org/

Harris Interactive. (2009). *Online security and privacy study*. Retrieved July 23, 2009, from http://staysafeonline.mediaroom.com/index.php?s=67

Hawkins, S., Yen, D. C., & Chou, D. C. (2000). Awareness and challenges of Internet security. *Information Management & Computer Security, 8*(3), 131–143. doi:10.1108/09685220010372564

Hinde, S. (2004). Hacking gains momentum. *Computer Fraud & Security,* (11): 13–15. doi:10.1016/S1361-3723(04)00136-8

Maguire, A. (2008). *Achieving real personalised learning: Considerations on blended learning*. Retrieved March 30, 2010, from http://www.thirdforce.com/resources/whitepaper/WP_AMaguire01.pdf

May, C. (2008). Approaches to user education. *Network Security,* (9): 15–17. doi:10.1016/S1353-4858(08)70109-0

McAfee. (2009). *McAfee security tips - 13 ways to protect your system*. Retrieved September 2, 2009, from http://www.mcafee.com/us/threat_center/tips.html

Microsoft. (2009). *Consumer online safety education*. Retrieved September 2, 2009, from http://www.microsoft.com/protect/default.aspx

National Cyber Security Alliance & Symantec. (2008). *NCSA-Symantec national cyber security awareness study newsworthy analysis*.

Okenyi, P. O., & Owens, T. J. (2007). On the Anatomy of Human Hacking. *Information Systems Security, 16*, 302–314. doi:10.1080/10658980701747237

Richardson, R. (2007). 2007 CSI computer crime and security survey. In *Proceedings of the 12th annual computer crime and security survey*. Retrieved August 22, 2008, from http://i.cmpnet.com/v2.gocsi.com/pdf/CSISurvey2007.pdf

Richardson, R. (2008). *2008 CSI computer crime & security survey*. Computer Security Institute.

Rotvold, G. (2008). How to create a security culture in your organization. *Information Management Journal, 42*(6), 32–38.

Schlienger, T., & Teufel, S. (2003). *Analyzing information security culture: Increased trust and appropriate information security culture*. Paper presented at the 14th International Workshop on Database and Expert Systems Applications (DEXA'03), Prague, Czech Republic.

Schneier, B. (2000). *Secrets and lies*. New York: Wiley Publishing, Inc.

Schultz, E. (2004). Security training and awareness--fitting a square peg in a round hole. *Computers & Security, 23*(1), 1–2. doi:10.1016/j.cose.2004.01.002

Spurling, P. (1995). Promoting security awareness and commitment. *Information Management & Computer Security, 3*(2), 20–26. doi:10.1108/09685229510792988

StaySafeOnline. (2009). *Are your defenses up and your instincts honed?* Retrieved July 23, 2009, from http://www.staysafeonline.org/

Sternberg, R. J., Grigorenko, E. L., & Zhang, L.-f. (2008). Styles of learning and thinking matter in instruction and assessment. *Perspectives on Psychological Science, 3*(6), 486–506. doi:10.1111/j.1745-6924.2008.00095.x

Symantec. (2007). *Symantec Internet security threat report - Trends for January - June 2007*. Symantec Corporation.

The National Strategies. (2007). *Leading on intervention: Personalisation questions and answers*. Retrieved March 30, 2010, from http://nationalstrategies.standards.dcsf.gov.uk/downloader/9e2a483e7a1c-9191f017c6ddfe2dfc30.pdf

Thompson, M. E., & Von Solms, R. (1998). Information security awareness: Educating your users effectively. *Information Management & Computer Security, 6*(4), 167–173. doi:10.1108/09685229810227649

Underwood, J., & Banyard, P. (2008). Managers', teachers' and learners' perceptions of personalised learning: evidence from Impact 2007. *Technology, Pedagogy and Education, 17*(3), 233–246. doi:10.1080/14759390802383850

von Solms, B. (2000). Information Security -- The Third Wave? *Computers & Security, 19*(7), 615–620. doi:10.1016/S0167-4048(00)07021-8

von Solms, R., & von Solms, S. H. (2006). Information security governance: Due care. *Computers & Security, 25*(7), 494–497. doi:10.1016/j.cose.2006.08.013

Wallop, H. (2007). *Fears over Facebook identity fraud*. Retrieved September 2, 2009, from http://www.telegraph.co.uk/news/uknews/1556322/Fears-over-Facebook-identity-fraud.html

WebWise. (2009). *The BBC guide to using the Internet*. Retrieved July 23, 2009, from http://www.webwise.com/

Wood, C. C. (1995). Information security awareness raising methods. *Computer Fraud & Security Bulletin*, (6): 13–15. doi:10.1016/0142-0496(95)80197-9

This work was previously published in the International Journal of Mobile Computing and Multimedia Communications, Volume 3, Issue 1, edited by Ismail Khalil and Edgar Weippl, pp. 62-78, copyright 2011 by IGI Publishing (an imprint of IGI Global).

Chapter 5
2-ClickAuth:
Optical Challenge-Response Authentication Using Mobile Handsets

Anna Vapen
Linköping University, Sweden

Nahid Shahmehri
Linköping University, Sweden

ABSTRACT

Internet users often have usernames and passwords at multiple web sites. To simplify things, many sites support federated identity management, which enables users to have a single account allowing them to log on to different sites by authenticating to a single identity provider. Most identity providers perform authentication using a username and password. Should these credentials be compromised, all of the user's accounts become compromised. Therefore a more secure authentication method is desirable. This paper implements 2-clickAuth, a multimedia-based challenge-response solution which uses a web camera and a camera phone for authentication. Two-dimensional barcodes are used for the communication between phone and computer, which allows 2-clickAuth to transfer relatively large amounts of data in a short period of time. 2-clickAuth is more secure than passwords while easy to use and distribute. 2-clickAuth is a viable alternative to passwords in systems where enhanced security is desired, but availability, ease-of-use, and cost cannot be compromised. This paper implements an identity provider in the OpenID federated identity management system that uses 2-clickAuth for authentication, making 2-clickAuth available to all users of sites that support OpenID, including Facebook, Sourceforge, and MySpace.

INTRODUCTION

Today, Internet users have accounts on a wide variety of web sites such as social networks, blog sites, forums and multimedia sites, e.g. YouTube. Usually users log in to these sites using a user-name and a password (Mannan & van Oorschot, 2007). When a user chooses a strong password, which is difficult for an attacker to guess, they often write down the password and/or reuse the same password for every site (Yan, Blackwell, Anderson, & Grant, 2004). This creates a risk

DOI: 10.4018/978-1-4666-2163-3.ch005

since an attacker that captures a password for one site is likely to try the same password on other accounts belonging to the user.

For sites with higher security requirements, we have designed and implemented the authentication solution 2-clickAuth (Vapen, Byers, & Shahmehri, 2010) as an alternative to the standard password-based solution. It offers a higher level of security while retaining the simplicity of passwords.

2-clickAuth is an optical challenge-response solution that uses a camera-equipped mobile phone as a secure hardware token together with a web camera to provide fast, simple, highly available and secure authentication. 2-clickAuth combines text-based and imaged-based data representations with real time video capture of data, in order to provide fast, multimedia-based authentication. Data is transferred both to and from the phone using Quick Response (QR) codes, a two-dimensional barcode type invented by Denso Wave Inc. It has been proven that QR codes can be reliably captured using mobile phone cameras.

To demonstrate and evaluate 2-clickAuth, we have implemented an identity provider for the federated identity management system OpenID, which uses 2-clickAuth for authentication.

The purpose of identity management is to solve the problem of users having many passwords and usernames to remember. One approach to identity management is federated identity management, in which participating sites form a circle of trust, so that if the user is authenticated to one site the other sites will automatically log the user in if the user visits them. A variation on this method uses a third party, often known as an identity provider, which holds information for the user and is responsible for authentication. Such systems are secure if the third party can be trusted (Shim, Bhalla, & Pendyala, 2005).

OpenID is a federated identity management system that uses trusted third parties called OpenID providers. Anyone can start an OpenID provider and the provider decides which login method to use. Some well-known OpenID providers are Google, Microsoft Live and Yahoo (OpenID Foundation, 2010). Web sites that allow users to log in using OpenID are called relying parties. Some well-known relying parties are Facebook, Sourceforge and MySpace (OpenID Foundation, 2010). The number of relying parties in OpenID is constantly increasing (JanRain, 2009).

A related problem is that of untrusted computers. All computers are potentially untrusted since they can contain malware such as key loggers that are capable of capturing user input, including passwords. Even a laptop that is owned and trusted by the user may be attacked if used in an untrusted environment, e.g. an unsafe network. Since computers and the environment may not always be trusted, mobility can create security problems.

When accessing web sites from untrusted computers or in untrusted environments, there is a need for more secure authentication than passwords can provide. This is especially true in federated solutions where the user's password at the identity provider is a valuable asset that can give an attacker access to all web sites where the user has an account. An alternative to passwords should be as easy to use as passwords and should require no special software on the computer, so that it can be used anywhere, including places where the user cannot install software, such as at Internet kiosks or cafés.

2-clickAuth is designed to meet the above requirements concerning security, availability and ease of use.

The remainder of this paper describes the 2-clickAuth solution and its implementation in OpenID. Firstly, we discuss the current state-of-the-art and the design choices made for 2-click-Auth. After that we describe the 2-clickAuth system in detail and the performance of 2-clickAuth. Then we present an evaluation method based on the Electronic Authentication Guideline from NIST (Burr, Dodson, & Polk, 2008) that can be used to evaluate and compare authentication solutions for mobile phones. To conclude this paper we discuss related work, particularly in the area of mobile and optical authentication systems, describe ideas for future work, and present our conclusions.

CURRENT AUTHENTICATION METHODS

Table 1 lists the properties of currently used authentication methods both on and off the web.

For 2-clickAuth, we have chosen to use a challenge-response protocol since it provides higher security than passwords, prevents replay attacks (a risk with passwords and biometrics), is location-independent, and does not allow an attacker to capture and use authentication data while the user is awaiting authentication, which is a possibility with one-time passwords and biometrics.

Challenge-response-based systems often use a hardware security token on which keys can be stored and the response-generating algorithm can run in a tamper-proof environment. Table 2 lists the properties of different hardware tokens.

We have elected to use a mobile phone for 2-clickAuth in order to support the goal of high availability. Because of their prevalence, mobile phones are an excellent platform for something that should be available to users at all times (Aloul, Zahidi, & El-Hajj, 2009). Furthermore, mobile phones have several channels for input and communication (both with the nearby devices through e.g. Bluetooth (Bluetooth SIG Inc, 2010) and directly with remote servers through e.g. a phone

Table 1. Current authentication methods

Methods and Definitions	
Passwords	Secret combination of characters that can be used several times for login.
One-time passwords	Passwords to be used only once that are stored in a list on paper, in an application or generated by a hardware device.
Challenge-response	A challenge generated by a server is sent to the user's device, which calculates a response and sends it back.
Biometrics	Proves a user's identity by physical features of the user, for example a fingerprint (Jain & Ross, 2008). Requires special hardware.
Location based	A user located in a specific area is authorized based on for example mobile phone triangulation, GPS or a connection to a nearby access point (Hazas, Scott, & Krumm, 2004).
Two-factor authentication	A combination of two types of authentication methods.

Table 2. Hardware tokens

Tokens and Definitions	
Smartcard	Tamper resistant hardware, requires a smartcard reader and communicates automatically with the computer.
USB stick	Does not require a specific reader, only a USB port. The USB stick either contains a smartcard chip or runs software used for authentication.
Special-purpose device	Often implemented as a small device with a display and, if allowing user input, a keypad.
Mobile phone	Available to a large number of users, equipped with several channels for input and communication. Can communicate directly with a remote server.
PDA	Similar to a phone, but often with a smaller number of channels available and not as commonly used as phones.

network) that can be used in an authentication solution.

Special-purpose devices could provide higher security and high usability, but such devices would need to be distributed to all users by some means. The practical difficulties and costs associated with distribution of a physical device make special-purpose devices an unattractive choice for the types of applications we want 2-clickAuth to support.

2-CLICKAUTH: OPTICAL CHALLENGE-RESPONSE

2-clickAuth is an optical challenge-response solution where a camera phone is used as a secure hardware token together with a web camera to provide fast, simple, highly available and secure authentication. We have designed 2-clickAuth to be suitable for authentication in federated identity management systems, such as OpenID, but it can be used in any situation where authentication is required.

Authentication

The 2-clickAuth system we have built consists of an OpenID provider, a MIDlet running in the user's phone and a Java Applet that communicates with the computer's web camera. Figure 1 shows how 2-clickAuth is used to log in to an OpenID relying party. To use 2-clickAuth a user must register at the 2-clickAuth OpenID provider.

Every user of 2-clickAuth shares a 128 bit secret key with the 2-clickAuth OpenID provider. This key is generated by the 2-clickAuth MIDlet in the phone and sent to the 2-clickAuth OpenID provider using 2-clickAuth key exchange when the user first registers at the 2-clickAuth OpenID provider. The secret key is part of the HMAC-SHA1 protocol (HMAC is a keyed hash function and SHA1 a cryptographic hash function) (Krawczyk, Bellare, & Canetti, 1997).

When the user wants to log in to an OpenID relying party using 2-clickAuth, authentication proceeds as in Figure 1.

First, the OpenID protocol arranges for the user to be authenticated at the correct OpenID provider:

1. The user types their OpenID (a URL to a personal page at the OpenID provider), as

Figure 1. A user interacting with the 2-clickAuth OpenID provider

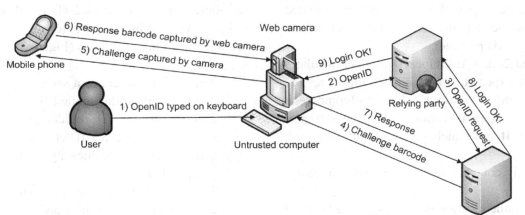

text, into the login form on the relying party's web site in the computer's web browser.

2. The OpenID is sent to the relying party.
3. The relying party sends an OpenID request to the 2-clickAuth OpenID provider and notifies the relying party to redirect the user's browser to the 2-clickAuth OpenID provider login page.

Next, the 2-clickAuth authentication process is executed:

4. The 2-clickAuth OpenID provider calculates a challenge, a 128 bit secure random number. The challenge is presented to the user as a QR code image in the browser.
5. The user opens the 2-clickAuth MIDlet on their phone and captures the QR code using their phone camera. The 2-clickAuth MIDlet interprets the QR code and calculates a response by creating a HMAC-SHA1 keyed hash from the challenge and truncating it to 128 bits. The response is displayed on the phone as a QR code.
6. The user holds the phone display in front of a web camera connected to the computer so that the response can be captured as real-time video frames, by the web camera.
7. The 2-clickAuth Applet in the web browser interprets the QR code image from the video frames captured by the web camera to text and the response is sent to the 2-clickAuth OpenID provider.
8. The 2-clickAuth OpenID provider calculates the expected response using the secret key shared with the user's phone, and compares it to the response captured using the web camera. If they match, the user is authenticated.

Finally, control is returned to the relying party:

9. If authentication is successful, the OpenID provider redirects the user browser back to the relying party.

The reason for truncating the hash used as response is that a smaller amount of data makes the barcode smaller and less dense, and therefore easier to capture and interpret, which makes the login process faster and more reliable. To prevent prediction by an attacker and to resist birthday attacks, the truncated hash should not be smaller than 80 bits or half the hash output length. The HMAC-SHA1 length is normally 160 bits, which gives a recommended smallest truncated length of 80 bits (Krawczyk, Bellare, & Canetti, 1997).

HMAC-SHA1 is designed for message integrity, but is also used in authentication solutions such as the one-time password algorithm HOTP (M'Raihi, Bellare, Hoornaert, Naccache, & Ranen, 2005), in IPsec (Glenn & Madson, 1998) and in TSIG (transaction signatures, mainly for domain name servers) (Eastlake, 2006).

Figure 2 shows the communication between the user's phone, the untrusted computer and a server (which in our implementation is a combination of the OpenID provider and a relying party).

Initialization and Key Exchange

2-clickAuth requires the user and OpenID provider to share a secret key. The key is established by an initial key exchange when the user registers with the OpenID provider. Like authentication, key exchange is done optically using QR codes. A first-time user downloads the 2-clickAuth MIDlet to her phone and initiates it before first using it for authentication, as follows (Figure 3):

1. The MIDlet generates a secret key that is encrypted using the public RSA key of the 2-clickAuth OpenID provider. The RSA key is embedded in the MIDlet (which can be signed to ensure the integrity of the MIDlet and public key).
2. The encrypted key is then shown as a QR code on the phone display and captured by the computer's web camera.

Figure 2. 2-clickAuth authentication

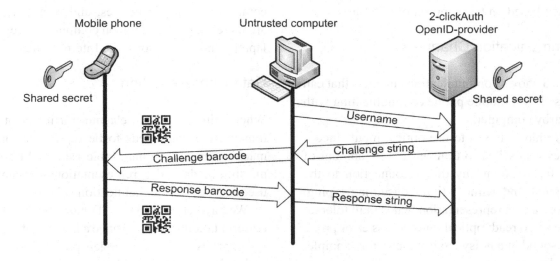

Figure 3. 2-clickAuth key exchange

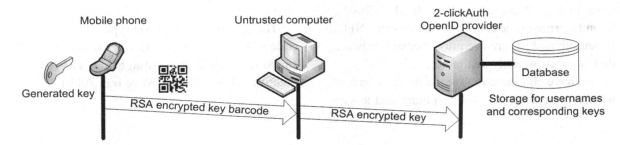

3. The key is transferred to the 2-clickAuth OpenID provider, which decrypts the key and stores it in a database. The user and the OpenID provider now have a shared secret used for 2-clickAuth.

Design Choices for 2-clickAuth

When designing 2-clickAuth the following criteria were considered:

- **Security:** 2-clickAuth shall be resistant to replay attacks and it shall not be possible for malware to fetch arbitrary information from the security token.

- **Availability:** 2-clickAuth shall use a hardware token that the user probably already has. Registration and initialization of the token shall be done online. It shall be possible to use the solution without side channels (such as the token connecting directly to a remote server over the phone network).

- **Usability:** 2-clickAuth should provide a login process so simple and fast that it can compete with passwords.

The security and availability criteria first led to the choice of a challenge-response protocol using a mobile phone as a hardware token. The communication channels, specific algorithms and data representation for 2-clickAuth were then chosen based on the same set of criteria.

Communication Channels

Table 3 shows communication channels that can be used by a mobile phone communicating with a nearby computer.

We have chosen to use optical input since it makes it possible to transfer a large amount of data fast without any direct connection to the computer and without time-consuming typing. Choose a data representation that is fault tolerant and easy to read; optical input is less error prone than sound in a noisy environment, for example, at an Internet café.

Bluetooth can be read from a distance. It can also be used by malware on the untrusted computer to exploit the token (Bose & Shin, 2006). Sound is error-prone in noisy environments. NFC, Bluetooth and infrared require special hardware that is not commonly available.

We have chosen to realize the optical channel with a camera on the mobile phone and a web camera on the computer. Today, cameras are common on mobile phones, and web cameras are increasingly common on computers, even on laptops and in locations like Internet cafés.

Data Representation

When using an optical channel for information transfer, the data needs to be represented in a machine readable format. Table 4 shows different machine readable data representations that can be used in an optical authentication solution.

We have chosen to use 2D barcodes for data representation since they have a higher data storage capacity than 1D barcodes, provide fast and fault tolerant reading without special hardware, are more environment independent than light signals and require less processing than optical character recognition.

The specific 2D barcode type chosen is QR-code (Quick Response Code), which is well suited for mobile phone usage and is already in widespread use (Denso Wave Inc, 2009).

Table 3. Communication channels

Channels and Descriptions	
Bluetooth	Requires a Bluetooth adapter connected to the computer and must be paired with the computer. Can be read from 100 meters and more (Bluetooth SIG Inc, 2010).
Infrared	Short range channel (less than 2 meters) that requires an IR adapter connected to the computer. Not commonly used in modern mobile phones (Infrared Data Association, 2009).
NFC	Near Field Communication. Short range channel (10 cm) built on wireless smartcard technology. New, and not yet common in phones. Has small data capacity and therefore mainly used together with Bluetooth so that pairing is not needed (NFC Forum, 2010).
Cable	Direct data transfer from the mobile phone to the local computer.
Optical	Can be used either with a phone camera (sending data to the phone) or a web camera (sending data to the computer). If in machine readable format, a large amount of data can be captured by the camera.
Manual input	Manual input is when data is transferred between the computer and the token by the user typing on the keyboard/keypad.
Audio	Can be used either with computer speakers and a phone microphone (sending data to the phone) or a phone speaker and a computer microphone (sending data to the computer). Data can be encoded as high frequency "modem sound"

Table 4. Machine readable data representation

Representations and Descriptions	
1D barcode (GS1, 2010)	Data is represented as black and white bars. The code stores 13-20 digits, usually an identification number that is read by a dedicated reader or a phone camera and mapped to a database.
2D barcode	Data is represented as a two-dimensional bit pattern. There are several types of 2D barcodes that are adapted to mobile phones.
Character string	Data is represented as human readable characters and processed using optical character recognition.
Light signals	Blinking lights on the phone display and computer monitor, similar to Morse code.

Security Considerations

There are security risks related to authentication that must be considered. For 2-clickAuth, we consider the following risks: replay attacks, stolen phone, and man-in-the-middle attacks.

Replay Attacks

Barcodes can be captured from a distance if the attacker can see the display and has a camera with which to capture the barcode. The challenge and the response can also be captured by malware on the computer running the 2-clickAuth applet. This risk is mitigated by using random secure numbers for the challenge; they are unpredictable, and the probability of repetition is extremely small.

Stolen Phone

If an attacker steals a phone used for 2-clickAuth, the attacker can either use the application directly or extract the secret key. To mitigate this risk, the phone or the application should be PIN protected. Improved protection of the secret key is part of our future work.

Man-in-the-Middle-Attacks

Man-in-the-middle (MitM) means that an attacker intercepts communication from the client and sends it on to the server (possibly after modifying it). The result is that when the server authenticates the client, the attacker gets authenticated instead.

2-clickAuth currently does not mitigate MitM attacks since mitigation requires either a secure side channel, for example the response being sent via SMS, or more messages to be exchanged between the phone and the computer. Avoiding side channels and limiting the exchange of messages to one in each direction are availability and usability considerations, respectively.

Implementation and Choice of Software

In our implementation (Vapen & Shahmehri, 2009) of the 2-clickAuth OpenID provider and client software, the application on the phone is built as a Java ME MIDlet, which makes it platform independent. The image capturing mechanism is built on the Zxing (Google, 2010) library from Google.

On the server side, the OpenID provider implementation is built on Joid (Google, 2009), an OpenID library from Google, running on a Tomcat web server. All user data (pairs of usernames and keys) are stored in a relational database.

A Java Applet runs in the user's web browser, showing the challenge barcode and a video window in which the user can see the response while showing it to the web camera. The applet does not have access to any secret information such as keys; it only serves as a GUI. Figure 4 shows a screenshot of the 2-clickAuth applet and MIDlet during the authentication process.

Figure 4 shows a user logging in on the 2-clickAuth OpenID provider using a mobile phone. In

Figure 4. Screenshot of a user logging in to the 2-clickAuth OpenID provider using a mobile phone

the upper part of the screen shot the QR code containing the challenge is displayed. Below the challenge is a video window, in which the user can see the same image as the web camera currently is capturing. The video window makes it easy for the user to adjust the phone's position in relation to the web camera, thus speeding up the capturing process.

2-CLICKAUTH PERFORMANCE

One of the criteria for 2-clickAuth was that it should be fast. In order to evaluate the speed of the login method we had a user perform 200 trials of the 2-clickAuth authentication process, and we measured the time elapsed between the application being loaded and a correct response being recorded. Results above 8000 milliseconds were filtered out. The histogram in Figure 5 shows the distribution of the times.

The test shows an average of 6.25 seconds to use 2-clickAuth when logging in to a website. Of this time, approximately 2 seconds are a delay in the image capturing software in the phone when loading the captured image into the MIDlet. The

Figure 5. Authentication speed (milliseconds) when using 2-clickAuth

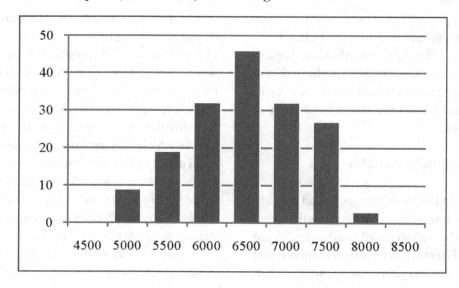

authentication time is also influenced by light conditions. The web camera used here either gives a low resolution image or uses automatic light settings to sharpen the image. As a result, the black parts of a QR code can melt into the white parts, making it impossible to interpret. To solve the problem of automatic light settings and poor image quality, the MIDlet animates the QR code, displaying the white parts in different shades of gray, ranging from pure white to dark gray. This makes the capture process less sensitive to lighting conditions. However, if the optimal shade in a particular light is the last one shown by the MIDlet, authentication may take a few extra seconds.

SECURITY EVALUATION

The Electronic Authentication Guideline from NIST (Burr, Dodson, & Polk, 2008) defines security levels that can be used for evaluating the security of an authentication solution. The NIST levels are general and do not focus specifically on phones. Since there are specific concerns related to phones, we have extended the guidelines to handle phone-specific problems, such as eavesdropping on the short range communication channels. There are also other important factors such as usability and availability, which are not discussed in the guidelines.

Work on evaluating authentication solutions in the area of IMS (IP Multimedia Subsystem) is in progress (Eliasson, Fiedler, & Jorstad, 2009). The IMS evaluation method considers several different factors such as security, simplicity and user friendliness.

We propose an evaluation method based on the NIST guidelines that also take usability and availability into account and that focuses on mobile phone authentication in general, not specifically in the area of IMS. The evaluation method is part of a larger, as-yet-unpublished work on security levels.

Evaluation Method for Mobile Phone Authentication

In our proposed evaluation method, Table 5 is used in conjunction with the list described in the section entitled "Our Evaluation Method" to calculate the security level of a solution. The table and the list can help developers of authentication solutions for mobile phones to evaluate their design choices. The evaluation process determines the level of security of the evaluated solution and provides advice on how to reach a higher level. The process also provides a list of alternative methods and communication channels that could be used to address specific requirements when designing new authentication solutions.

Security Levels

NIST defines four security levels for authentication (1 - 4 where 4 is the highest), which we have summarized here:

Level 1: No identity proof, i.e. authentication as in level 2, but vulnerable to one or several attacks.

Level 2: Single factor authentication. Protection against eavesdropping, replay attacks, and online guessing. For authentication data that is to be reused, e.g. passwords, the data must be tunneled, for example by using SSL, when sending data via the untrusted computer to the remote server. Other methods that do not require tunneling are one-time passwords and challenge-response.

Level 3: Multi-factor authentication with protection against verifier impersonation, MiTM attacks and the attacks from level 2. One-time passwords and challenge-response can be used. Requires the authentication device to be unlocked by the user using a password or biometrics.

Level 4: Possession of a key is proved through a cryptographic protocol. The same rules as for level 3 apply. Tamper-resistant hardware, according to the FIPS-140-2 standard (NIST, 2001), is used.

Our Evaluation Method

Table 5 can be used when evaluating the design of a phone authentication solution. The following list can be used in conjunction with Table 5 to determine the highest security level that a solution can achieve:

- **Channels:** Choose the channels that are used in the solution or known to be available, given the target user group and place. Table 3 lists the equipment needed to establish the optical and audio channels. Note that two channels are needed for challenge-response, since data will be transferred in both directions between the computer and the phone.
- **Unlocking Methods:** Choose a method for locking the phone to protect it when it is not in use (required for level 3 and higher). The phone could be locked with a manual method such as a password or PIN-code or

Table 5. Features of mobile phone communication channels

Features	Factor	Bluetooth	IR	NFC	Cable	Audio	Optical	Manual	Comments
Keylogger resistant	S	•	•	•	•	•	•	(•)	Manual input may be vulnerable to keyloggers when using passwords. Non-HID Bluetooth devices are not vulnerable to keyloggers.
Cannot spread malware	S					•	•	•	
For closed environments	S	(•)	•	•	•	•	•	•	Bluetooth can be eavesdropped from outside a building.
For open environments	S	(•)	(•)	•	•	(•)	(•)	•	Channels in parenthesis can be eavesdropped and replayed by a nearby attacker, if the data is used several times.
For phone unlocking	S					•	•	•	In specific cases a touch screen or fingerprint reader could be used for biometric unlocking.
For noisy environments	U	•	•	•	•		•	•	
For users with poor eyes	U	•	•	•	•	•		•	
For users with shaky hands	U	•	•	•	•	•		•	
Used without extra equipment	A					(•)	(•)	•	An optical channel from the phone to the computer requires a web camera. Audio channels require speakers and a microphone. See Table 3.

The factors S, U and A denotes if the feature is a factor related to security, usability or availability. • denotes that a specific channel has the specific feature. (•) denotes that the channel usually has the feature, but that there are exceptions that are noted in the "Comments" column.

with a biometric method if the phone has a microphone, a camera or other biometric input method.

- **Eavesdropping:** Choose channels that are not vulnerable to replay attacks. Authentication data that is used more than once can be eavesdropped and replayed by an attacker. Table 5 shows which channels can be used in a closed environment, e.g. a room without untrusted people present, and which channels can be used in an open area with untrusted people present. If the data is not reused, any channel can be used.
- **Other Factors:** Choose channels considering facts that are known about the specific system being evaluated. If there is a risk of malware, users with poor eyes etc, check Table 5 for solutions that may be used in the specific cases.
- **Authentication Methods:** In an existing system that is being evaluated it is clear which authentication method or methods are being used. If the system is not yet implemented, there may be different choices of possible methods. Choose all that apply of: passwords (stored on the phone), one-time passwords, and challenge-response. According to NIST, different authentication methods can be used for different security levels. Biometrics may only be used for device unlocking, not as an authentication method for remote authentication. Passwords can reach, at most, level 2. If the phone cannot be locked, all methods can reach level 2 at most. If passwords are used, the information sent via the computer must be tunneled so that it cannot be captured while being transferred over the network. Without tunneling, level 1 is the highest level for passwords.

If the phone does not contain secure hardware certified by the FIPS-140-2 standard (NIST, 2001), level 3 is the highest level. If there are long range

channels available, such as a phone network or Wi-Fi, they can be used as a secure side channel to protect against MiTM attacks. Such protection is needed for level 3 and higher. If there are no available long range channels, mutual authentication or similar methods must be used to prevent MiTM attacks.

Consider the channels chosen in step 1-4, the guidelines regarding authentication methods (step 5), and additional guidelines on MiTM protection and secure hardware as described above. The result will be the security level applicable for the system being tested, together with other channels and techniques that may be used in addition.

Evaluation of 2-clickAuth

Here we use our evaluation method to evaluate 2-clickAuth. We make similar evaluations of the related solutions in the "Related Work" section. Since we do not know all the background details of these systems, the evaluations will be based on what is published. The evaluation of 2-clickAuth has been made using the same level of detail as the other evaluations, in order to make the evaluations comparable and fair.

- **Channels:** For 2-clickAuth, optical channels are used in both directions. Manual input channels are also available, but not used because of the large amount of data being transferred. Side channels are not used.
- **Unlocking Methods:** 2-clickAuth may be used with a PIN-code to lock the phone. Since there is a phone camera available, optical biometrics could also be implemented.
- **Eavesdropping:** Since 2-clickAuth is intended for use by mobile users at different places there is a risk of eavesdropping, but since the data is only used once there is no risk of replay attacks.
- **Other Factors:** 2-clickAuth should be possible to use in noisy environments such as in public places, which is possible when using

image based data transfer. It should also be malware resistant, since data can only be sent as a direct result of user action.

- **Authentication Methods:** 2-clickAuth is designed to use a challenge-response protocol.

By summarizing the choices of channels according to steps 1-4, the decisions in step 5 and additional guidelines in the previous section and in Table 5, it can be stated that 2-clickAuth could reach level 2. To reach level 3, MiTM mitigation such as a side channel must be used.

RELATED WORK

A number of other approaches to strong authentication on the web using mobile phones have been presented over the years. There have also been attempts at optical systems that bear some similarities to 2-clickAuth.

Secure Web Authentication

Secure Web Authentication (SWA) proves that a user owns a specific mobile phone and if the user does, access to a web site is allowed. When a user is going to log in to a web application they are redirected to a trusted third party where they enter a username. A session name, a short string of characters, is then sent to the user's phone via SMS and is simultaneously shown in the web browser. If an attacker manipulates the session name shown in the browser it will not match the session name sent to the phone. After displaying the session name, the WAP browser of the phone is directed to a site where the user can deny or allow the current session, thus using a direct channel from the phone to the trusted third party instead of via the untrusted computer. If the user allows the current session, the user is logged in on the computer (Wu, Garfinkel, & Miller, 2004).

Unlike 2-clickAuth, SWA depends on a side channel. Use of a side channel can increase security, but decreases availability since the user may not have access to (or may not want to access) the mobile phone network. For example, when abroad, the fees for using the phone network can be high, and in such a situation a solution that can be used without connecting to the phone network is less costly for the user. There are also situations when there is no phone network available, for example a CDMA phone will not work on a GSM network.

In SWA, no sensitive information is typed on the computer keyboard. Therefore, there is no keylogger risk. A side channel is used, which require the phone to have WAP support and use the phone network to access the Internet. SWA is intended for use with untrusted computers in public places. Therefore, malware, keyloggers and eavesdropping are potential risks. Using public computers also limits the equipment at hand. Only a keyboard can be expected at the computer side. The environment may be noisy since it is a public place. According to Table 5, manual or optical methods can be used. Manual typing on the computer keyboard of information that is meant to be used more than once should be avoided. Optical or manual unlocking can be used. If used, the solution reaches level 3 because of the side channel. The side channel places SWA on a higher security level than 2-clickAuth. However, WAP access is not always available.

Strong Authentication with Mobile Phone

The Strong Authentication with Mobile Phone (SA) method consists of a several different methods where the user's phone operator is used as a trusted third party. A secret identifier stored on the user's SIM card (Subscriber Identity Module) and listed in the phone operator's user database is used to prove the identity of the user. This secret information is used to calculate session IDs and challenges as described below. When attempting to log in to a web site supporting SA, the user is redirected to the SA server, which acts as a trusted third party. The user then logs in by 1) sending an SMS to the SA server acknowledging that a session ID shown in the computer's browser and one sent to the user's phone is the same, or 2) sending an SMS to the SA server, containing a response calculated by the phone to a challenge shown in the computer's browser and typed into the phone by the user (or sent via Bluetooth), or 3) receiving the challenge from the SA server via SMS, calculating the response with the phone and sending the response to the computer via manual typing or Bluetooth, or 4) using the EAP-SIM protocol for strong authentication via Bluetooth, or 5) using EAP-SIM via SMS. When sending information to the computer a SIM card embedded in a SIM dongle that is connected to the computer can be used instead of a phone, in order to avoid the need for Bluetooth pairing (van Thanh, Jorstad, Jonvik, & van Thuan, 2009).

When using SA with a phone, a side channel (and, in some variants, Bluetooth) is required. Furthermore, SA requires the participation of a mobile phone operator. In contrast, 2-clickAuth requires no side channel and can be implemented by anyone on any website, without involving phone operators.

It is stated that SA needs to be usable. Since the SIM card is used, a PIN code can be assumed for phone unlocking. In earlier versions of SA, the identifier on the SIM card was used as a static password, which was vulnerable to replay attacks. In the new versions, however, replay attacks and eavesdropping are not problems, whether or not Bluetooth is used. However, Bluetooth can spread malware between the phone and the computer. SA can reach level 3 for the EAP-SIM solutions that protect against MiTM attacks. The session ID solution is a simple solution that reaches level 1. The other solutions reach level 2 even if SMS

is used. This is because the SMS channel is not used as a side channel, but as an alternative to short range channels.

Camera-Based Authentication

Camera-Based Authentication is an early image based authentication method that uses dedicated hardware with camera functionality to capture an image with a nonce, a one-time password and a message authentication code added to the image as a bit pattern similar to a 2D barcode (Burnside et al., 2002).

Camera based authentication requires high camera resolution, an initial calibration process, and also requires that the camera is kept completely still during the authenticated session, since pixel mapping is done to be able to capture a very detailed image (Burnside et al., 2002).

2-clickAuth differs from camera based authentication in that it uses a much simpler code and that the camera is only used to capture a single image, once. Because of this, 2-clickAuth can use a much simpler camera that does not need to be kept still at all times.

This solution should not be evaluated using the security levels for phones, since it is used with a dedicated hardware token and not with a phone. However, dedicated hardware may reach level 4 if certified. On the other hand it may be less available and usable than a phone based solution.

QR-TAN

QR-TAN is a variant of TANs (Transaction Authentication Numbers), which are one-time passwords used instead of static passwords in online banking. A drawback with regular TANs is that they do not guarantee that the transaction data is unmodified. QR-TAN is a method using QR codes to assure that the transaction data is unmodified.

When the user has entered transaction data into the bank website, the user is shown a QR code containing the transaction data combined with a nonce from the server and encrypted with a public key of the user's phone. The user captures the QR code using a password protected program in their phone. The phone uses HMAC and a counter value to generate a response as a string of six characters that the user manually enters on the website. The manually-entered string is sent to the server together with the transaction data, proving that it is unmodified (Starnberger, Froihofer, & Goeschka, 2009).

2-clickAuth does not use manual input which makes it possible to transfer more data. On the other hand, QR-TAN does not require a web camera.

QR-TAN is not an authentication method; rather it is a method for transaction signing. Therefore, it cannot be completely evaluated using our method. If adapted to authentication, QR-TAN could achieve similar results to 2-clickAuth, since they both use an optical channel. QR-TAN also uses a manual channel. As seen in Table 5, manual keyboard input on the computer can be used for data that is only used once, as it is in QR-TAN.

Confident

Confident consists of two authentication solutions where the first is a one-time password solution in which the user is presented with ImageShield, a collection of pictures in different categories (for example boats, dogs, people etc). Each picture has an alphabetic character associated with it. The user has chosen three categories beforehand, and when logging in, the user types the characters from the pictures related to the user's pre-chosen categories. The characters and the position of the images on the screen change between each login. When using this method for the first time on a new computer the user must use a one-time password sent by SMS to the user's phone and typed into

the computer's web browser. This proves that the user has access to the phone, and is therefore considered trustworthy.

The second Confident solution is used without ImageShield and lets the user log in with a static password combined with a one-time password sent to the user's mobile phone and typed into the computer's web browser (Confident Technologies Inc, 2010).

One of the Confident variants uses a side channel, combined with a static password. The ImageShield variant of Confident also uses a side channel the first time a user uses a new computer (for users of Internet cafés and kiosks, this could be a frequent occurrence). 2-clickAuth does not use a side channel, nor does it require the user to remember a static password.

Usability is important in the Confident solutions, since they are intended as a more usable alternative to passwords. The one-time password solution may be rated as level 3, because of the side channel. The other variant of Confident, however, relies partly on a static password which can be replayed. Static information typed on the keyboard should be avoided as seen in Table 5. Therefore the solution with the static password ends up at level 2, at most.

Comparison of Current Solutions

While Image Based Authentication and QR-TAN cannot be compared with other solutions depending on the choice of hardware and the area of use, the other solutions described in this section can be compared with each other and with 2-clickAuth. The side channels used in SWA, Confident and two of the SA variants could increase the security levels of these solutions from level 2 to level 3. Reaching level 3 also requires the phone to be locked when not used. This requirement is not discussed in the solutions, but a PIN-code or similar can be assumed. 2-clickAuth reaches level

2, because side channels are not used. For federated identity management, any choice that is more secure than passwords might be a better choice. For more security critical applications, however, a side channel may be needed. Not using a side channel increases the availability of the solution.

Where malware and eavesdropping are potential concerns, manual data transfer is a better choice than for example Bluetooth. Optical channels may be eavesdropped, but cannot spread malware.

FUTURE WORK

Using a smartphone – an enhanced mobile phone similar to a PDA – gives us access to a rich set of input channels and communication channels together with higher processor capacity than with a normal phone. Smartphones usually have high camera resolution, which is also prevalent among modern phones that are not smartphones. The higher camera resolution and the computational capacity would make it possible to improve image processing so that barcodes could be captured and interpreted faster and more efficiently. Smartphones also have large displays that can show large barcodes, which are easy to capture with a web camera.

As mobile phones become more complex there is an increasing risk that phone malware will steal or corrupt sensitive information stored on the phone (Bose & Shin, 2006). As part of future work, investigations will be conducted in order to see if it is possible to protect the 2-clickAuth MIDlet and the shared secret it stores, by using the SIM card of the phone for secure storage of the secret, or if there are other possibilities to protect 2-clickAuth from phone malware.

2-clickAuth is focused primarily on providing a more secure, yet simple, alternative to passwords on untrusted computers, not on creating an authentication method as secure as challenge-response with a dedicated hardware token. However, it is

part of future work to analyze and mitigate the risks associated with running authentication software on a mobile phone.

Another area for future investigation is how to increase the maximum transferrable amount of data by choosing a different barcode type or image interpretation algorithm. A larger amount of data would make it possible to increase security by having longer hashes and keys. It could also allow a higher level of error correction for the barcodes, thus making them easier and faster to interpret.

The speed of the authentication process could be increased by improving the reading algorithm, changing barcode type and experimenting even further with the animation of response barcodes to adjust them to the light settings of different web cameras.

To mitigate man-in-the-middle-attacks, so that 2-clickAuth could be used for applications with high security requirements, such as online banking, 2-clickAuth could use a secure side channel to increase security. Since use of a side channel would reduce availability, 2-clickAuth should be flexible enough to operate both with and without the side channel, depending on the level of security required. Security could also be improved by using trusted hardware on the mobile phone, such as the user's SIM card, to provide secure storage for the secret key, or even for running parts of the application.

In the future we will also explore the usability aspects of 2-clickAuth and conduct usability studies in order to evaluate and ultimately improve the usability of the system.

CONCLUSION

In this paper we have presented 2-clickAuth, a fast and simple authentication solution for the web that is designed to be as easy to use as normal passwords, while also being more secure, particularly in situations where authentication is done using an untrusted computer. 2-clickAuth uses a camera-equipped mobile phone to implement a challenge-response authentication protocol. Data is transferred to and from the mobile phone using two-dimensional barcodes. 2-clickAuth is designed for applications that require better security than plain passwords can provide, but where usability, simplicity and availability cannot be sacrificed.

We have also implemented an OpenID identity provider that uses 2-clickAuth for authentication. This allows 2-clickAuth to be used with any OpenID relying party. In federated identity management systems, such as OpenID, a user needs only to authenticate to the identity provider in order to access any site that participates in the system. Therefore, higher security than normal passwords can provide is desirable. 2-clickAuth is resistant to key loggers and password-capturing malware, but does not sacrifice usability, requires only hardware that most users carry anyway, and requires no special software on the computer that is used for authentication.

Unlike other authentication solutions that use mobile phones, 2-clickAuth does not rely on a side channel. Although use of a side channel would increase security, it would also decrease the availability of the solution, since the user might be unable or unwilling to use the side channel. However, we are investigating the possibility of adding side channels to 2-clickAuth for those situations where sacrificing availability in favor of security is warranted.

2-clickAuth is as yet the only system that uses a web camera in a challenge-response solution. With video chats and similar applications in use today, web cameras are becoming very common. It is also a part of the user experience to be able to login by simply holding up a phone, taking a picture and turning the phone around.

REFERENCES

Aloul, F., Zahidi, S., & El-Hajj, W. (2009). Two factor authentication using mobile phones. In *Proceedings of the IEEE/ACS International Conference on Computer Systems and Applications*, Rabat, Morocco (pp. 641-644).

Bluetooth, S. I. G. Inc. (2010). *Welcome to Bluetooth.org*. Retrieved from https://www.bluetooth.org/apps/content/

Bose, A., & Shin, K. G. (2006). On mobile viruses exploiting messaging and bluetooth services. In *Proceedings of the Securecomm and Workshops*, Baltimore, MD (pp. 1-10).

Burnside, M., Clarke, D., Gassend, B., Kotwal, T., van Dijk, M., Devadas, S., et al. (2002). The untrusted computer problem and camera-based authentication. In *Proceedings of the First International Conference on Pervasive Computing* (pp. 114-124).

Burr, W. E., Dodson, D. F., & Polk, W. T. (2008). *Electronic authentication guideline, recommendations of the National Institute of Standards and Technology*. Retrieved from http://csrc.nist.gov/publications/nistpubs/800-63/SP800-63V1_0_2.pdf

Confident Technologies Inc. (2010). *Intuitive and secure image-based authentication solutions*. Retrieved from http://www.confidenttechnologies.com/

Denso Wave Inc. (2009). *QRCode.com*. Retrieved from http://www.denso-wave.com/qrcode/index-e.html

Eastlake, D. (2006). *HMAC SHA TSIG algorithm identifiers*. Retrieved from http://www.ietf.org/rfc/rfc4635.txt

Eliasson, C., Fiedler, M., & Jorstad, I. (2009). A criteria-based evaluation framework for authentication schemes in IMS. In *Proceedings of the 4th International Conference on Availability, Reliability and Security*, Fukuoka, Japan (pp. 865-869).

Forum, N. F. C. (2010). *NFC forum homepage.* Retrieved from http://www.nfc-forum.org

GS1. (2010). *GS1 barcodes.* Retrieved from http://www.gs1.org/barcodes

Glenn, C., & Madson, R. (1998). *The use of HMAC-SHA-1-96 within ESP and AH.* Retrieved from http://www.ietf.org/rfc/rfc2404.txt

Google. (2009). *Joid.* Retrieved from http://code.google.com/p/joid/

Google. (2010). *ZXing.* Retrieved from http://code.google.com/p/zxing/

Hazas, M., Scott, J., & Krumm, J. (2004). Location-aware computing comes of age. *Computer*, *37*(2), 95–97. doi:10.1109/MC.2004.1266301

Infrared Data Association. (2009). *IRDA: The secure wireless link.* Retrieved from http://www.irda.org/

Jain, A., & Ross, A. (2008). Introduction to biometrics. In Jain, A., Flynn, P., & Ross, A. (Eds.), *Handbook of biometrics* (pp. 1–22). New York, NY: Springer. doi:10.1007/978-0-387-71041-9_1

JanRain. (2009). *Relying party stats as of Jan 1st, 2009.* Retrieved from http://blog.janrain.com/2009/01/relying-party-stats-as-of-jan-1st-2008.html

Krawczyk, H., Bellare, M., & Canetti, R. (1997). *HMAC: Keyed-hashing for message authentication.* Retrieved from http://www.ietf.org/rfc/rfc2104.txt

M'Raihi, D., Bellare, M., Hoornaert, F., Naccache, D., & Ranen, O. (2005). *HOTP: An HMAC-based one-time password algorithm.* Retrieved from http://www.ietf.org/rfc/rfc4226.txt

Mannan, M., & van Oorschot, P. C. (2007). Using a personal device to strengthen password authentication from an untrusted computer. In S. Dietrich & R. Dhamija (Eds.), *Proceedings of the 11th International Conference on Financial Cryptography and the 1st International Workshop on Usable Security* (LNCS 4886, pp. 88-103).

NIST. (2001). *Federal information processing standards publication: Security requirements for cryptographic modules.* Retrieved from http://csrc.nist.gov/publications/fips/fips140-2/fips1402.pdf

Open, I. D. Foundation. (2010). *Get an OpenID.* Retrieved from http://openid.net/get-an-openid

Shim, S. S., Bhalla, G., & Pendyala, V. (2005). Federated identity management. *Computer*, *38*(12), 120–122. doi:10.1109/MC.2005.408

Starnberger, G., Froihofer, L., & Goeschka, K. M. (2009). QR-TAN: Secure mobile transaction authentication. In *Proceedings of the 4th International Workshop on Frontiers in Availability, Reliability and Security*, Fukuoka, Japan (pp. 578-583).

van Thanh, D., Jorstad, I., Jonvik, T., & van Thuan, D. (2009). Strong authentication with mobile phone as security token. In *Proceedings of the 6th IEEE International Conference on Mobile Adhoc and Sensor Systems*, Macau, China (pp. 777-782).

Vapen, A., Byers, D., & Shahmehri, N. (2010). 2-clickAuth - optical challenge-response authentication. In *Proceedings of the 5th International Conference on Availability, Reliability, and Security*, Krakwo, Poland (pp. 79-86).

Vapen, A., & Shahmehri, N. (2009). *Optical challenge-response authentication*. Retrieved from http://www.ida.liu.se/divisions/adit/authentication/

Wu, M., Garfinkel, S., & Miller, R. (2004, July). *Secure web authentication with mobile phones.* Paper presented at DIMACS Workshop on Usable Privacy and Security Software, Piscataway, NJ.

Yan, J., Blackwell, A., Anderson, R., & Grant, A. (2004). Password memorability and security: Empirical results. *IEEE Security & Privacy, 2*(5), 25–31. doi:10.1109/MSP.2004.81

This work was previously published in the International Journal of Mobile Computing and Multimedia Communications, Volume 3, Issue 2, edited by Ismail Khalil and Edgar Weippl, pp. 1-18, copyright 2011 by IGI Publishing (an imprint of IGI Global).

Chapter 6
On Cryptographically Strong Bindings of SAML Assertions to Transport Layer Security

Florian Kohlar
Ruhr University Bochum, Germany

Jörg Schwenk
Ruhr University Bochum, Germany

Meiko Jensen
Ruhr University Bochum, Germany

Sebastian Gajek
Tel Aviv University, Israel

ABSTRACT

In recent research, two approaches to protect SAML based Federated Identity Management (FIM) against man-in-the-middle attacks have been proposed. One approach is to bind the SAML assertion and the SAML artifact to the public key contained in a TLS client certificate. Another approach is to strengthen the Same Origin Policy of the browser by taking into account the security guarantees TLS gives. This work presents a third approach which is of further interest beyond IDM protocols, especially for mobile devices relying heavily on the security offered by web technologies. By binding the SAML assertion to cryptographically derived values of the TLS session that has been agreed upon between client and the service provider, this approach provides anonymity of the (mobile) browser while allowing Relying Party and Identity Provider to detect the presence of a man-in-the-middle attack.

DOI: 10.4018/978-1-4666-2163-3.ch006

INTRODUCTION

In browser-based Federated Identity Management (FIM) protocols, data has to be transported from a trusted third party to the service provider with an intermediate step at the browser. The trusted third party—called Identity Provider (IP)—is asked to issue a security token that is valid for a fixed time period and permits access to some service (hosted by a service provider, in this context called Relying Party (RP). This token is first transmitted to the browser and in a following step transfered to the RP. Data stored in the browser is susceptible to attacks on the Same Origin Policy (SOP) of the browser, like Cross Site Scripting (XSS) or dynamic pharming. Mobile devices are especially vulnerable, since all data sent or received by the device is transmitted "over the Air" and can therefore be easily sniffed. Since the SOP relies on the Domain Name System (DNS), the data can also be accessed by a variety of spoofing attacks, from ARP and IP spoofing to DNS spoofing (Pharming). This even applies if sophisticated security measures are in place (e.g., see the latest attack on Microsoft's, Cardspace, Gajek, Schwenk, & Chen, 2008). Mobile Browsers (Figure 1) in general often lack the latest patches/updates and still contain known and easily exploitable security holes. To protect these devices special security measurements are needed.

Two approaches have been proposed for SAML based Federated Identity Management to counter these attack threats. The first approach is to bind the SAML assertion and the SAML artifact to the TLS client's certificate public key. It was proposed in Gajek (2008) and Gajek, Jager, Manulis, and Schwenk (2008) and has already been adapted for standardization (Klingenstein, 2009). The other approach is to combine the security of TLS with the browser's Same Origin Policy (Gajek, Liao, & Schwenk, 2008). In this paper, we present a third approach which further enhances IDM protocols: We bind the SAML assertion to the

Figure 1. Scheme of a common browser-based

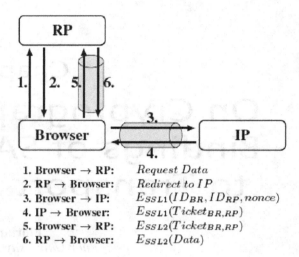

1. Browser → RP:	*Request Data*
2. RP → Browser:	*Redirect to IP*
3. Browser → IP:	$E_{SSL1}(ID_{BR}, ID_{RP}, nonce)$
4. IP → Browser:	$E_{SSL1}(Ticket_{BR,RP})$
5. Browser → RP:	$E_{SSL2}(Ticket_{BR,RP})$
6. RP → Browser:	$E_{SSL2}(Data)$

TLS session that has been agreed upon between client and Relying Party (RP) and as a result rely on the user authentication. Furthermore do we achieve security even in the case, when an adversary is able to impersonate the RP by presenting a valid (e.g., self signed), but different, certificate for the requested RP to the browser. We do so by including the public key as part of the SAML assertion.

(MOBILE) BROWSER-BASED FEDERATED IDENTITY MANAGEMENT PROTOCOLS

The (mobile) browser plays an important role in Federated Identity Management (FIM) standards/ frameworks like Liberty Alliance (Pfitzmann & Waidner, 2003), SAML (OASIS Security Services (SAML) TC) or Microsoft Cardspace (Gajek, Schwenk, & Chen, 2008). This is due to the fact that he can be used as a platform-independent client application with a (commonly) rich set of features, and a provably secure cryptographic functionality: SSL/TLS (Dierks & Allen, 1999, Dierks & Rescorla, 2006). Protocols realizable within the constraints of standard web browsers are called browser-based protocols, and if we speak of browser in the following pages, we refer to both common pc web browsers and web browsers on mobile devices, as they are comparable in functionality. Firefox for example is also available for mobile devices under the name "Firefox mobile". A common security approach in browsers was (and still is) to let the user decide, if he wishes to access untrusted or unsecured data through the browser. But recent studies point out that average-skilled Internet users understand neither server certificates nor browsers' security indicators at all (Dhamija, Tygar, & Hearst, 2006; Schechter, Dhamija, Ozment, & Fischer, 2007; Herzberg, 2009). An adversary may fake the site and disclose the user's password (phishing attacks).

Apart from that problem, another shortcoming is that the user either has to memorize a plethora of passwords (and frequently forgets about them; otherwise; it would be unnecessary to include a "Forgot your password" link in a web application), or use the same low-entropy password in most cases, thus making offline dictionary attacks feasible. In order to alleviate such man-in-the-middle attacks, browser-based FIM protocols have been introduced, basically extending the widely adapted Kerberos protocol (MIT, 2011) for the use in open networks. First migrations are peppered with severe problems (cf. Kormann & Rubin, 2000; Groß, 2003; Soghoian & Jakobsson, 2007; Gajek, Schwenk, & Chen, 2008) and a first attempt to disburden from a client application and make use of browser based capabilities alone are found in Microsoft's Passport protocol (Microsoft, n. d.). Unfortunately, it turned out that the protocol had some deficiencies (Kormann & Rubin, 2000; Slemko, 2001). When the (secure) Kerberos protocol was adapted to the World Wide Web, crucial changes had to be made to transform it into a browser-based protocol:

- User authentication and key agreement have been separated. Thus http cookies, hidden form fields, or URL based mechanisms that contain security tokens are independant from TLS.

- There is no cryptographic trust relationship between the browser and token issuing servers. As any browser (even in Internet kiosks) is sufficient to execute the protocol, cryptographic identifiers (e.g., client certificates) or additional addons could not be used. The http cookie carries the authentication token and any party in possession of the cookie can impersonate the real owner of the token.

In addition, some (unfounded) assumptions have been made, namely that users could somehow determine the authenticity of a web server on the basis of server certificate, and that the Domain Name System (DNS) is an authentic host name resolution protocol. In fact, various Certification Authorities (CAs) have stored their root certificates in browsers and are thus trusted per se. Weak issuing policies can be exploited by adversaries, as a single CA that is careless or corrupted could issue certificates for rogue servers. Moreover, the browser enforces only a weak security policy.

A crucial component in browsers is the Same Origin Policy (SOP). This policy states that web objects, in particular cookies, stored in a browser are accessible by other (active) web objects only under the condition that they are from the same domain. Thus, security policies of browsers heavily rely on DNS.However, many attacks on domain name resolution protocols are present in the wild, ranging from Javascript code that alters a router's configuration (Stamm, Ramzan, & Jakobsson, 2006) to large scale DNS Cache Poisoning attacks (Kaminski, 2008).

Another problem is cross site scripting (XSS) attacks. Due to shortcomings in the application, the adversary injects some malicious code into the response of the application server. Since the code is in the same security context, the SOP does not apply, and the malicious code can break free and access protected objects within the browser's DOM.

ATTACKS AGAINST FIM PROTOCOLS

The original Kerberos protocol and related three party schemes have been intensely studied without finding severe security deficiencies (Boldyreva & Kumar, 2007; Backes, Cervesato, Jaggard, Scedrov, & Tsay, 2006). However, their browser-based offspring—federated identity management protocols—turned out to have some vulner-abilities: In addition to the mentioned Microsoft Passport analyses of Kormann and Rubin (2000), Slemko (2001), and Grob (2003) analyzes SAML, an alternative single sign on protocol, and shows that the protocol is vulnerable to adaptive attacks where the adversary intercepts the authentication token contained in the URL. Groß makes use of the fact that browsers add the URL in a referrer tag into an HTTP response when they are redirected (Note that this is a feature which depends on the security policy of the browser. The default value in today's browsers is set to be turned off, i.e., no referrer tag is sent).

Hence, a man-in-the-middle adversary signal-ing the browser to redirect the request to a rogue server retrieves the authentication token from the referrer tag. The previously described flaw in the SAML protocol has led to a revised version of SAML. Grob and Pfitzmann (2006) analyzed this version, again finding the need for improvements. Similar flaws have been found in the analysis of the Liberty single sign on protocol (Pfitzmann & Waidner, 2003). The authors point out some weak-nesses in presence of man-in-the-middle attacks.

OUR CONTRIBUTION

We solve the above problems by presenting a stron-ger binding of SAML assertions to a specific TLS session. Thus we make use of the strong security guarantees TLS gives. Browser based protocols which employ these bindings are much closer to the original Kerberos protocol.

The main idea is to perform a TLS handshake even when contacting the RP for the first time (this makes sense since the requested data has restricted access). This session is characterized by a TLS master secret, which is only known to the browser and the RP. If the RP issues a redirect to the IP, the browser actively derives a value from this master secret, and sends it together with its authentication to the IP (this value must not threaten the confidentiality of the master secret; this can be achieved e.g., by using a hash value of the master secret). The IP now includes the derived value into the SAML assertion, and signs the assertion.

When the browser sends the SAML assertion to the RP, he must make sure to use the same TLS session as before (this can be achieved by not releasing the TCP connection, or by re-using an old TLS session id and a fast TLS handshake). The RP can now verify that the SAML assertion contains a derived value from the current TLS master secret. From this he can conclude that no man-in-the-middle attack occured in between client and RP.

To prevent man-in-the-middle attacks between client and IP, other means must be used e.g. a special browser plugin, which automatically distinguishes between valid IP certificates and invalid ones, is sufficient (this approach will not work for the link between client and RP, because there will be far too many RPs to give any strict rules on the validity of server certificates).

RELATED WORK

Grob and Pfitzmann propose the Janus profile for SAML artifacts (Grob & Pfitzmann, 2006). Their idea is to employ two artifacts in a consistent way. In that case, a token is valid when it consists of both values. Thus, an adversary in possession of a single value cannot replay the token.

Holder-of-Key Web Browser SSO Profile (Klingenstein, 2009) is a forthcoming SSO-profile, which uses the so called "Holder of Key" subject confirmation method according to Cantor, Kemp, Philpott, and Maler (2005b) and hence a cryptographic binding between the user and her assertion.

A main motivation for this profile is the fact that the less secure "Bearer" methods may not be used for the higher security levels according to Radack (2003). The Bearer method in practice means that a client accessing a secured resource at a service provider will be redirected to the inter-site transfer service at the identity provider. After visiting this service, the principal is transferred to the assertion consumer service at the service provider, where the client issues a POST request (with or without user intervention) to set the token. According to the Holder-of-Key profile the client has to authenticate himself using keys supplied through TLS (using client certificates) before issuing the POST request.

ORGANIZATION

The paper is organized as follows: We start with describing SAML assertions and artifacts used in FIM protocols. This is followed by a short introduction to TLS. We then specify a refined SAML Browser Profile, and discuss its integration with the existing SAML specifications. Further, we provide a discussion on its capabilities and restrictions, a security proof, and some implementation issues. Then we present two extensions of our scheme to counter specific attacks in case of a special active adversary, which have different requirements to the IP. Finally, we conclude.

SAML ASSERTIONS AND ARTIFACTS FOR FEDERATED IDENTITY MANAGEMENT

SAML is an XML standard for exchanging authentication and authorization data between an Identity Provider (IP) and a Relying Party (RP). The syntax and semantics for XML-encoded assertions are defined in Cantor, Kemp, Philpott, and Maler (2005a). Several profiles are defined in Cantor, Kemp, Philpott, and Maler (2005b). The most important profile is the Browser SSO profile, which defines how to use SAML to provide the SSO with the client browser. Before describing the operation mode of SAML, we first introduce the two SAML tokens used in this paper: SAML assertion and SAML artifact.

A SAML assertion specifies the claims, and is specified by the saml: Assertion element is defined as follows:

```
<saml:Assertion Version ID IssueInstant>
    <saml:Issuer>
    <ds:Signature>?
    <saml:Subject>?
    <saml:Conditions>?
    <saml:Advice>?
    <saml:Statement>*
    <saml:AuthnStatement>*
    <saml:AuthzDecisionStatement>*
    <saml:AttributeStatement>*
</saml:Assertion>
```

The SAML version used is specified in saml: Version, the assertion's identifier in saml: ID, and the time of issuing in saml: IssueInstant. All these attributes are required. The saml: Issuer element specifies the SAML authority that is making the claim(s) in the assertion (the IP). The assertion's saml: Subject defines the principal that owns all statements within the assertion. For browser-based FIM protocols, this is the browser, or the human user behind the browser, respectively. The identity of the Relying Party (RP) a SAML assertion is issued for is fixed in one or more specific saml: AudienceRestriction elements within the saml: Conditions element. They state that the given SAML assertion is only valid for use with one of the given RP endpoints. The saml:*Statement elements are used to specify user-defined statements relevant for the context of the SAML assertion. In some cases, e.g., if an assertion cannot be sent via the browser due to size constraints, a SAML artifact (Figure 3) is used to indicate where and how to retrieve the assertion. The artifact is specified by a string within a saml: Artifact element and has the format defined in Cantor, Hirsch, Kemp, Philpott, and Maler (2005a).

The MessageHandle identifies the SAML assertion associated with this artifact. It should be a cryptographically strong random or pseudorandom value. After the successful authentication of the user, the IP provides either a SAML assertion or only a SAML artifact (the corresponding assertion is located at the IP's artifact resolution service) to the browser. The received SAML token is then forwarded to the RP. See Figure 2 for an overview. If the received token is a SAML artifact, the RP builds and sends a SAML saml: ArtifactResolve message containing the artifact to the IP's artifact resolution service endpoint (identified by the SourceID and EndpointIndex). The requested assertion is then placed within a saml: ArtifactResponse and sent to the RP.

After receiving the SAML assertion (resolved or not), the RP validates the enveloped XML signature. The assertion with valid signature is then examined by the RP to determine whether the client is allowed to access the specified resource in the RP.

Figure 2. SAML artifact browser profile: protocol overview and generic attacks

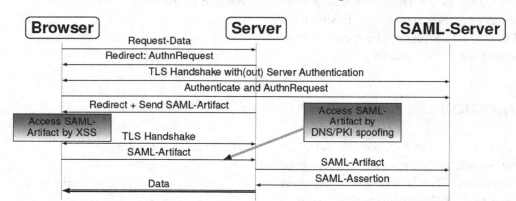

Figure 3. SAML 2.0 artifact format

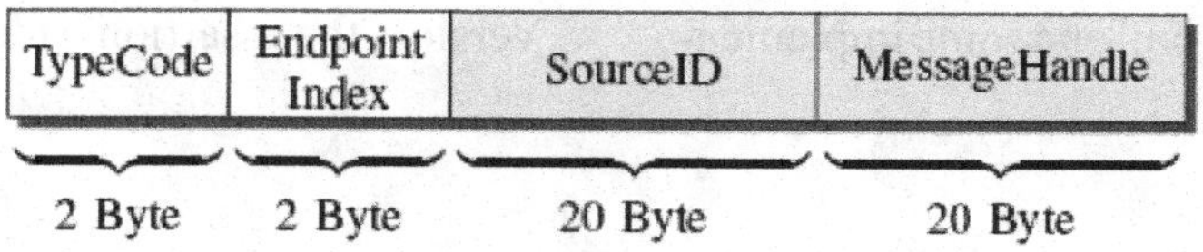

Transport Layer Security

Transport Layer Security (better known as SSL/TLS (Dierks & Allen, 1999; Dierks, & Rescorla, 2006) is the standard method to provide security functionality like privacy and data integrity in the World Wide Web. In a TLS handshake two parties agree upon a cryptographic encryption scheme and (at least partially) authenticate each other. Therefore, they derive a session key out of randomly chosen material that is exchanged between the two parties before. After a TLS handshake has been completed successfully, both client and server know that they can now communicate with each other over a channel guaranteeing confidentiality and integrity of messages. Regarding the identities of their partner, they can rely on the following facts:

1. The client C knows that the server is a machine that knows a private key corresponding to the public key contained in the server certificate. We do not assume that the client is able to verify any other identities of the server such as Fully Qualified Domain Names, thus our protocol is resistant to attacks like Pharming combined with PKI spoofing.
2. If a CertificateVerify message has been sent by the client, the server may deduce that he is talking to a browser that knows the private key corresponding to the public key contained in the client certificate.
3. If the client is not authenticated, the server may nevertheless deduce that any data he sends to the TLS channel will reach exactly the same endpoint that the received data (e.g., a SAML assertion) originates from.
4. If in two consecutive TLS sessions the same master secret is used to derive the keys to protect the TCP byte stream, both communication endpoints (browser and server) may deduce that in the second session they

are talking to the same entity as in the first session.

The first three facts have been used previously to construct secure bindings for SAML to TLS (Gajek, Liao, & Schwenk, 2008): Here we use the last fact to construct a third binding. The idea is the following: If the browser adds a value derived from the master secret of a certain TLS session to his SAML Assertion request, and if this derived value is present in the SAML assertion, the RP may deduce that the other endpoint of the current TLS channel (i.e., the browser) requested this assertion from the IP.

(Modified) SAML Browser Profile

We describe the new binding by highlighting the changes to the Web Browser SSO Profile (Cantor, Kemp, Philpott, & Maler, 2005b). The modifications are marked bold and displayed in Figure 4:

1. **Browser -> RP:** The Browser contacts the Relying Party by sending some HTTP-request over a channel secured by TLS.
2. **RP -> Browser:** The Relying Party answers with an HTTP-response that contains an <AuthnRequest>-element (cf. Cantor, Kemp, Philpott, & Maler, 2005a). The details of the encoding of this element depend on the binding, the options are HTTP Redirect Binding, HTTP POST Binding, and HTTP Artifact Binding (for details see Cantor, Hirsch, Kemp, Philpott, & Maler, 2005a).
3. **Browser -> IP:** The browser sends the <AuthnRequest>-element to the Identity Provider using a simple HTTP GET or POST request. He adds a value dk to this request, derived from the TLS master secret of the current TLS connection with RP (e.g., dk = Hash(mastersecret)).
4. **IP:** In absence of a previously established authenticated session, the Identity

Figure 4. Modified SAML browser profile

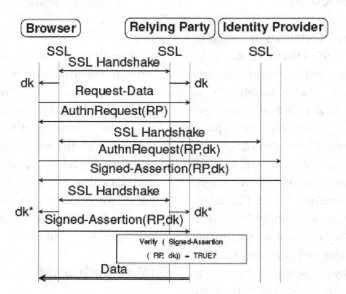

Provider authenticates the user according to the requirements of the Relying Party, which may be specified within the <RequestedAuthentication Context> element inside the <AuthnRequest> element using the authentication classes defined in Kemp, Cantor, Mishra, Philpottl and Maler (2005).

5. **IP -> Browser:** Upon successful authentication, the Identity Provider issues a SAML assertion which contains dk (this value is covered by the XML signature) and returns a credential to the browser, depending on the used binding (see Cantor, Hirsch, Kemp, Philpott, & Maler, 2005a, 2005b, for details).

6. **Browser -> RP:** In case of the HTTP Artifact Binding the browser sends the received SAML artifact to the Relying Party. In case of the HTTP POST Binding, the SAML assertion is directly sent to the Relying Party. In both cases the RP must assure that the same TLS session is used as in the previous communication. This can be achieved by either not releasing the TCP connection, or by ac-

cepting a TLS Session ID from the browser, and performing a fast TLS handshake.

7. **RP:** In this step, the Relying Party needs to verify the signature contained in the <Assertion> which in turn may require the validation of a chain of certificates. If necessary the assertion must first be obtained using the Artifact Resolution Protocol defined in Cantor, Kemp, Philpott, and Maler (2005a). Additionally, the Relying Party must check if the value dk contained in the SAML assertion equals Hash (mastersecret) of the current TLS session.

8. **RP -> Browser:** On success, the Relying Party finally returns an HTTP-response that contains the requested resource.

SAML Assertions

In order to properly implement the proposed SAML protocol, it becomes necessary to slightly extend the syntax of a common SAML assertion (as defined in Cantor, Kemp, Philpott, & Maler, 2005a). Actually, the derived key dk from the

TLS connection between browser and RP must be included both in a SAML assertion request (sent by the browser to the IP) and in the resulting SAML assertion (created by the RP). Both are to be described next.

SAML Assertion Request

The SAML core specification (Assertions and Protocols SAML, 2005) already provides several extension points for specifying arbitrary extensions to SAML assertion requests. For the special purpose intended here, the most appropriate extension to our consideration consists in relying on the usage of the optional saml: Conditions element of the samlp: AuthnRequest element. It is used to provide the IP with conditions restricting the assertion's validity, which are to be included in the resulting SAML assertion. For example, it may be used to specify that the issued SAML assertion is only valid until a certain timestamp has passed (NotOnOrAfter) or that it can be used only once, immediately, and is invalidated on first use (<OneTimeUse>).

Thus, each of these conditions are to be contained in the assertion issued, and thus must be fulfilled on assertion usage, we suggest extending the samlp: AuthnRequest message with a new type of condition that restricts the issued assertion's usage on a certain TLS connection between browser and Relying Party. The TLSRestriction type extends the abstract saml: ConditionAbstract-Type (Cantor, Kemp, Philpott, & Maler, 2005a), and defines a new element nds: TLSDerivedKey, which contains the derived value dk in Base64 encoding. Once a browser has established a valid TLS connection to the Relying Party, it requests a new SAML assertion instant by sending an AuthnRequest message to its IP.

SAML Assertion Syntax

```
<saml:Assertion... ID="theAssertion">
<ds:Signature>
    <ds:SignedInfo>
    <ds:Reference URI="#theAssertion">
    <ds:Transform Algorithm=".../xmldsig
    #enveloped-signature"/>
    </ds:Reference>
    </ds:SignedInfo>
</ds:Signature>
<saml:Issuer>...</saml:Issuer>
<saml:Subject>...</saml:Subject>
<saml:Conditions>
<saml:AudienceRestriction>
<saml:Audience>https://RP.endpoint
</saml:Audience>
</saml:AudienceRestriction>
<saml:Condition
    xsi:type="nds:TLSRestrictionType">
    <nds:TLSDerivedKey>
    AfGuRS3LOiw45dDgV...
    </nds:TLSDerivedKey>
</saml:Condition>
</saml:Conditions>
<saml:AuthnStatement/>
</saml:Assertion>
```

Once the nds: TLSDerivedKey condition is used in the samlp: AuthnRequest, this advises the issuer to include it as-is in the assertion(s) it instantiates for this request. Thus, the dk value derived from the TLS connection between browser and Relying Party will be contained in the resulting SAML assertion token (shown in Figure 5). Furthermore, as the whole assertion is protected by a digital signature, the nds: TLSDerivedKey will be protected against any modification attempt and a cryptographically strong binding between the SAML assertion and the TLS connection between browser and Relying Party is established.

Figure 5. Example assertion containing the dk

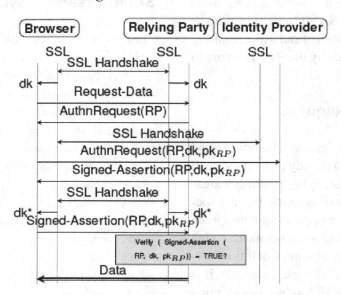

Then, once the browser receives the newly instantiated SAML assertion from the IP, it immediately delivers the assertion via the preexisting TLS connection to the Relying Party. As the Relying Party is capable of both verifying an IP's digital signature and comparing the nds: TLS-DerivedKey value with the dk value derived from the TLS connection to the browser, it can perform the necessary verification tasks by itself and within a reasonable amount of additional workload. As a result, it can make a sound authorization decision based on cryptographically strong credentials.

Merits and Flaws

The proposed scheme provides cryptographically strong guarantees. Further, the protocol does not require any secrets to be stored within the browser. The computational overhead is low as only few altered protocol steps are needed compared to common SSO protocols. The token to identify a client is bound to a temporary TLS session only (instead of a permanent TLS client certificate,

Klingenstein, 2009), and therefore we can preserve anonymity of the browser.

In order to implement the proposed protocol, two additional steps are required. At first, read-access to the TLS master secret (or an appropriate value derived from the master secret) must be given for both client and server, and secondly, both parties also must have access to an identical hash value calculation algorithm.

The modified SAML Browser profile protects the connection between browser and Relying Party against attacks. It does not protect the connection between browser and Identity Provider: By acting as a man-in-the-middle between browser and identity provider, the attacker could exchange the value dk0 sent by the victim in step 3 with the value dk derived from the TLS connection between attacker and Relying Party. He then could intercept the SAML assertion or SAML artifact sent in step 5, and use it to authenticate against the RP. However, the connection between browser and IP can be protected by a variety of means, ranging from using a special browser extension which is capable of automatically verifying the IP server certificate, to the use of TLS client certificates to authenticate against the IP.

It is more difficult to secure the connection between browser and RP, because (a) TLS client certificates would be traceable across several RPs, thus creating privacy problems, and (b) a variety of TLS server certificates could be used by the different RPs.

On the downside of the approach stands that it requires a SAML assertion to be instantiated for about every login request. By setting multiple AudienceRestrictions, a SAML issuer may support SAML assertions that are valid for a set of RPs and can be reused within their timespan of validity. Omitting the AudienceRestriction elements completely may even grant unlimited access to a user, as long as the other conditions given in the assertion hold. However, since the derived key approach binds the use of the SAML assertion to a specific pre-existing TLS connection, that SAML assertion is rendered unusable for all other—legitimate—RPs listed within (unless they are located on the same server). This flaw puts additional load to the IP, since it is forced to issue way more SAML assertions than without the derived key technique. However, this comes to the benefit of improved security guarantees. Besides that, it may be questionable if real-world applications really are frequently required to do simultaneous logins to disjunct systems within the lifetime of a single SAML assertion. Nevertheless, additional investigations regarding SAML assertions containing multiple derived keys instead of a single one are to be performed as part of our ongoing work.

Security Proof

In the following we first define some assumptions for our poposed protocol in Theorem 1. Then we sketch a proof of security for our protocol under this theorem.

Theorem 1: Assume that the connection between browser and IP is secure against attacks, that the received value dk = Hash (mastersecret$_{browser-RP}$), and that all parties follow the protocol. Then this protocol is secure against man-in-the-middle attacks on the connection between browser and RP.

Proof. If the Relying Party receives a SAML assertion that contains a value dk that matches the computed value of Hash (mastersecret$_{browser-RP}$), he may conclude the following:

- Mastersecret$_{browser-RP}$ is only known to RP and one unique, but anonymous browser. Thus dk can only be computed by RP, or by this unique browser.
- Since RP did not send dk to IP, RP may conclude that this unique browser has sent dk to IP.
- RP may additionally conclude that this unique browser successfully authenticated itself (or/and the user behind the browser) to IP (Otherwise the SAML assertion would not have been issued).
- Since dk only matches Hash (mastersecret$_{browser-RP}$) if the two endpoints of the current TLS session are the unique browser and RP, and since a single TLS instance is secure against man-in-themiddle attacks, RP may conclude that the unique, anonymous browser from which he received the SAML assertion indeed successfully authenticated against IP, and may thus grant access to the requested ressource.

Implementation Issues

Since the master secret is the central secret value in each TLS session, it must be protected in the browser from access by scripts or browser plugins. The same holds for TLS implementations in web servers.

Thus in both cases, a minor modification of the TLS implementation itself is required: After successful establishment of a master secret, a derived value that does not compromise the secrecy of the master secret must be made accessible to scripting languages or programming languages like JAVA through a defined interface.

Active Adversary Attacks

The proposed solution heavily depends on XML technology. Hence, we remark that without proper treatment of the particular XML security standards we cannot exclude some additional vulnerabilities existing due to weaknesses in the XML standards and/or their implementation (see e.g., Jensen, Gruschka, & Herkenhöner, 2009). Our approach so far is already fending all cases of eavesdropping adversaries, so in this chapter we will additionally examine a special case, namely active adversary attacks between the browser and RP or IP, respectively, in possession of some valid certificate (e.g., self-signed) for the embodied party. This special case leads to an extension of our proposed scheme.

This attack is not an attack on TLS itself but merely on the fact that one could allow unsecure certificates in certain situations. Under the assumption that an adversary cannot guess or compute the private key according the public key contained in the targeted server's certificate, and that we only trust certificates issued by trusted CAs, we remain secure against active man-in-the-middle attacks.

Active Adversary between Browser and IP

One can easily see that an active adversary between browser and IP does not have any advantage to a passive adversary. We differ between two cases: either the adversary is in possession of the proper private key associated to the certificate of IP, or the adversary is in possession of a self-signed certificate similar to the real certificate of IP (along with the corresponding keys). We estimate the probability of the first case as negligible and require that if a browser encounters a self-signed certificate for an IP it aborts the connection.

We conclude that active adversary attacks in this setting are only possible under very strong assumptions on the adversary's capabilites (i.e., having access to the IP's private key).

Active Adversary between Browser and RP

In this scenario, the assumption is that there exists some RP possessing only self-signed certificates. As a result, the browser cannot abort the connection if such a certificate is encountered. We introduce Lemma 1, which will later be used for construction of the master secret by the adversary.

Lemma 1: Given a pseudorandom function $f(x) = y$ with x being the input parameter and y the output, then

$$f(x) = y = f(x'); \text{ only, if } x = x'$$

A man-in-the-middle (in the following we call this adversary Eve or E) could now perform the following attack:

1. E waits for the browser to establish a connection to RP. Then, E acts as a man-in-the-middle and impersonates RP.
2. E notes the random value sent by the browser along with the session id (client.hello), and establishes herself a secure connection to the real RP, using these received values.
3. Once the RP has sent its random value (server.hello), E passes on the same values to the browser.
4. In the ClientKeyExchange message, the browser sends an encrypted premaster secret to E, which is again passed to the real RP (reencrypted by E for the real RP).

5. According to Lemma 1 (Dierks & Rescorla, 2008), the connection between E and the RP now is secured with the same master secret as the connection between the browser and E, as all inputs to the PRF computing the master secret have been chosen accordingly.

6. After receiving the SAML Assertion bound to dk, E is granted access to RP. This follows from the fact that using the same master secret leads to the computation of the same derived value as well.

To counter this kind of attacks, two options arise. One could enforce the use of CA-signed certificates for all Relying Parties or one could ensure that the SAML Assertion is valid only for the endpoint the client is connected to. We propose an extension of the original approach in the following section, in which we "fix" the client's endpoint, so the Assertion issued by the IP becomes invalid when trying to be used with any endpoint other than the one the client is connected to.

Extended SAML Assertion using Endpoint Fixation

To ensure that a SAML Assertion cannot be used by an adversary as described, we bind the Assertion's validity to the RP to which the browser is connected to. We do so by forwarding the public key extracted from the TLS connection between browser and RP (or, in the adversarial model, E) together with dk to the IP for inclusion in the issued SAML Assertion. Hence, the IP can check the public key against a database including all public keys of all registered RPs, and the original RP can later on verify that the public key contained in the Assertion matches its own (and hence detect such man-in-the-middle attacks). However, we remark that it is an additional effort for the IP to maintain such a public key database in order to be able to match received public keys against expected keys.

We now differ between two cases: a) the adversary is impersonating the RP and behaves as described, or b) the adversary remains passive until the browser has received the Assertion from the IP, and then tries to impersonate the RP.

In the first case, E may succeed in "distributing" the same master secret for the connections browser-to- E and E-to-RP. She could then pass on the Assertion from the browser to RP, but as the Assertion contains the public key used by the adversary, RP will not accept it and abort the connection. As described, the data contained in the Assertion is signed by the IP, and the adversary is not able to alter the public key to validate the Assertion afterwards.

In the second case, E cannot establish herself as man-in-the-middle between browser and RP, as she does not have any information regarding the master secret (and therefore the derived key dk) computed by the browser/RP. However, to be able to authenticate to the RP, E would have to use the same master secret, thus resulting in a failed attack attempt.

Figure 6 shows the extended Browser Profile. Figure 7 shows an example of a SAML assertion containing both the derived key dk and the Relying Party's public key as used in the TLS connection to the Browser. This way, the Relying Party can verify that the Browser is part of the same TLS session, hence it can verify that no man-in-the-middle attack based on other certificates is going on. Optimizing Modifications, in opposition to the model described, requiring a database held by the IP, we also present a "stateless" solution. To achieve this goal, the browser includes the public key of the contacted RP in the derivation function, resulting in the derived key now being dependant on the master secret of the TLS session and the public key of the RP. This solution is easier to achieve, as it does not require the IP to know all recent public keys of all registered RPs, and no additional overhead occurs (compared to sending the public key along with a derived value all the time).

However, this approach implies giving up the ability of the IP to control the browser's connec-

Figure 6. Extended SAML browser profile

```
<saml:Assertion ... ID="theAssertion">
 <ds:Signature>
  <ds:SignedInfo>
   <ds:Reference URI="#theAssertion">
    <ds:Transform
         Algorithm=".../xmldsig
                  #enveloped-signature"/>
   </ds:Reference>
  </ds:SignedInfo>
 </ds:Signature>
 <saml:Issuer>...</saml:Issuer>
 <saml:Subject>...</saml:Subject>
 <saml:Conditions>
  <saml:AudienceRestriction>
   <saml:Audience>https://RP.endpoint
      </saml:Audience>
  </saml:AudienceRestriction>
  <saml:Condition
      xsi:type="nds:TLSRestrictionType">
   <nds:TLSDerivedKey>
     AfGuRS3LOiw45dDqV...
   </nds:TLSDerivedKey>
   <nds:TLSPublicKey>
     Kfgg3SD4Ao8hu91zT...
   </nds:TLSPublicKey>
  </saml:Condition>
 </saml:Conditions>
 <saml:AuthnStatement/>
</saml:Assertion>
```

tions before issuing any token. However, this does not influence the security of the proposed solution, as an adversary using a public key different than the one from the original RP cannot use a token issued for her public key to gain access to the real RP.

Malicious Protocol Participants

In order to give a complete analysis of all adversary scenarios it becomes necessary to also consider the case of a malicious or corrupted protocol participant. If the Relying Party itself is operated by the adversary, or if it got compromised (e.g., via malware; it even suffices for the adversary to gain access to the private key corresponding to certificate of RP (Holz, Engelberth, & Freiling,

2009), the security implications to the overall protocol obviously are tremendous. Since the RP hosts the service that the browser wants to access, it can decide by itself to execute that service, regardless of whether a browser actually triggered its execution or not. In the same line, it can decide on incoming service requests placed by any browser on whether these are to be performed as intended, not performed, or misused to perform any other services. Hence, the given SMLbased SSO protocol is rendered completely useless in such scenarios.

More interesting is the case of a malicious IP. First of all, since it owns the property of being a trusted third party of both browser and RP, its corruption or maliciousness implies a fundamental flaw in the overall system. Being the security token

Figure 7. SAML assertion containing both dk value

```
<saml:Assertion ... ID="theAssertion">
 <ds:Signature>
  <ds:SignedInfo>
   <ds:Reference URI="#theAssertion">
    <ds:Transform
       Algorithm=".../xmldsig
               #enveloped-signature"/>
   </ds:Reference>
  </ds:SignedInfo>
 </ds:Signature>
 <saml:Issuer>...</saml:Issuer>
 <saml:Subject>...</saml:Subject>
 <saml:Conditions>
  <saml:AudienceRestriction>
   <saml:Audience>https://RP.endpoint
      </saml:Audience>
  </saml:AudienceRestriction>
  <saml:Condition
      xsi:type="nds:TLSRestrictionType">
   <nds:TLSDerivedKey>
     AfGuRS3LOiw45dDgV...
   </nds:TLSDerivedKey>
   <nds:TLSPublicKey>
     Kfgg3SD4Ao8hu91zT...
   </nds:TLSPublicKey>
  </saml:Condition>
 </saml:Conditions>
 <saml:AuthnStatement/>
</saml:Assertion>
```

issuer, an IP can obviously also create arbitrary SAML assertions for himself. Since the Relying Party is not able to verify the validity of such tokens—besides verifying its legitimation from the IP—it will accept them. This enables the IP to hijack the identity of every individual to perform every kind of request on every RP that relies on the IP. Then given approach of using derived keys in SAML assertions is not able to mitigate this threat, besides that it requires the IP to stick to the protocol, i.e. instantiate a TLS connection, derive a key, and create a SAML assertion token containing that derived key. However, since the RP is not able to differentiate between the IP and an arbitrary browser, this puts no real restrictions to a malicious or compromised IP.

Last but not least, a malicious or compromised browser induces some level of uncertainty to the proposed derived key approach. There are two different threats here that must be differentiated. The first consists in that the individual using the browser may try to trigger a service execution it is not allowed to perform. However, this threat is fend completely with the usage of SAML assertions, since those explicitly list all actions a user is allowed or prohibited to do at a certain Relying Party. This protection mechanism is not affected by adding a derived key to the SAML assertion token. The second threat consists in an adversary that tries to "steal" the login credential from the browser. Alternatively, the browser's user may try to pass an issued SAML token to another, unauthorized entity, in order to share access rights without RP's permission. An example for such a setting would be a flatrate-style accounting for RP's services, where each user that paid its bill is allowed to access, but is not allowed to pass its login credentials to other users. In the plain SAML scenario, a malicious browser may issue a SAML token, then pass that valid SAML token to its unauthorized peer, who then can use it to perform the particular services on the RP. Using the derived key approach, a SAML token is bound to a specific TLS session, hence it can not be used by other entities than the browser that originally issued it. However, the browser can still act as a proxy, channeling requests from the unauthorized entity to the Relying Party using its own TLS connection. Nevertheless, this requires active involvement of the malicious/compromised browser, hence is way more complicated than simple token forwarding. To conclude, the derived key approach is not preventing attacks in the presence of malicious protocol participants. It may only pose minor restrictions to what a malicious protocol participant must stick to when performing an attack.

CONCLUSION

In this paper we have presented a novel TLS binding for SAML assertions. This binding creates a cryptographically strong dependency between a certain SAML assertion and a TLS channel, thus achieving a binding between a level 5 (application) and a level 4 (transport) protocol according to the ISO/OSI reference model. By embedding a cryptographic value that was derived from a TLS session's master secret into a SAML Assertion token, we enable the Relying Party to determine whether the SAML Assertion was issued for the same Browser that tries to trigger a particular service execution. This way, the approach renders the confidentiality requirement for SAML Assertions to be no longer necessary.

Since the approach is a generic one, it is also applicable to other scenarios where cryptographic protocols are operating in different levels of a protocol stack. Future research hence may cover its adaptation to other application-level security mechanisms like e-mail protection or secure http cookies. Either way, the clear advantage of the presented approach consists in that it effectively counters most kinds of attacks that deal with credential theft, with a minimal footprint in terms of complexity and overhead.

REFERENCES

Backes, M., Cervesato, I., Jaggard, A. D., Scedrov, A., & Tsay, J.-K. (2006). *Cryptographically sound security proofs for basic and public-key kerberos.* Retrieved from http://faculty.nps.edu/gwdinolt/ProtocolExchange/Fall2006/ProtocoleXchange092806_CompProofsKerberos.pdf

Boldyreva, A., & Kumar, V. (2007). *Provable-security analysis of authenticated encryption in kerberos.* Retrieved from http://www.cc.gatech.edu/~virendra/papers/BK07.pdf

Cantor, S., Hirsch, F., Kemp, J., Philpott, R., & Maler, E. (2005). *Bindings for the OASIS security assertion markup language (SAML) v2.0.* Retrieved from http://docs.oasis-open.org/security/saml/v2.0/saml-bindings-2.0-os.pdf

Cantor, S., Kemp, J., Philpott, R., & Maler, E. (2005a). *Assertions and protocol for the OASIS security assertion markup language (SAML) v2.0.* Retrieved from http://docs.oasis-open.org/security/saml/v2.0/saml-core-2.0-os.pdf

Cantor, S., Kemp, J., Philpott, R., & Maler, E. (2005b). *Profiles for the OASIS security assertion markup language (SAML) v2.0.* Retrieved from http://docs.oasis-open.org/security/saml/v2.0/saml-profiles-2.0-os.pdf

Dhamija, R., Tygar, J. D., & Hearst, M. A. (2006). Why phishing works. In *Proceedings of the SIGCHI Conference on Human Factors in Computing Systems* (pp. 581-590).

Dierks, T., & Allen, C. (1999). *RFC 2246: The TLS protocol version, 1.0.* Retrieved from http://www.ietf.org/rfc/rfc2246.txt

Dierks, T., & Rescorla, E. (2006). *RFC 4346: The transport layer security (TLS) protocol, version 1.1.* Retrieved from http://www.ietf.org/mail-archive/web/ietf-announce/current/msg02442.html

Dierks, T., & Rescorla, E. (2008). *RFC 5246: The transport layer security (TLS) protocol, version 1.2.* Retrieved from http://tools.ietf.org/html/rfc5246

Gajek, S. (2008). *Foundations of provable browser-based security protocols.* Bochum, Germany: Ruhr University.

Gajek, S., Jager, T., Manulis, M., & Schwenk, J. (2008). A browser-based kerberos authentication scheme. In *Proceedings of the 13th European Symposium on Research in Computer Security* (pp. 115-129).

Gajek, S., Liao, L., & Schwenk, J. (2008). Stronger tls bindings for SAML assertions and SAML artifacts. In *Proceedings of the ACM Workshop on Secure Web Services* (pp. 11-20).

Gajek, S., Schwenk, J., & Chen, X. (2008). *On the insecurity of Microsoft's identity metasystem cardspace (Tech. Rep. No. HGI TR-2008-004).* Bochum, Germany: Horst Görtz Institute for IT-Security.

Groß, T. (2003). Security analysis of the SAML single sign-on browser/artifact profile. In *Proceedings of the 19th Annual Computer Security Applications Conference* (p. 298).

Grob, T., & Pfitzmann, B. (2006). *SAML artifact information flow revisited.Saml artifact information flow revisited (Research report RZ 3643 99653).* Armonk, NY: IBM Research.

Herzberg, A. (2009). Why Johnny can't surf (safely)? Attacks and defenses for web users. *Computers & Security, 28*(1-2), 63–71. doi:10.1016/j.cose.2008.09.007

Holz, T., Engelberth, M., & Freiling, F. C. (2009). Learning more about the underground economy: A case-study of keyloggers and dropzones. In *Proceedings of the 14th European Symposium on Research in Computer Security* (pp. 1-18).

Jensen, M., Gruschka, N., & Herkenhöner, R. (2009). A survey of attacks on web services. *Computer Science - Research + Development, 24*(4), 185-197.

Kaminski, D. (2008). *Black ops 2008: It's the end of the cache as we know it: DNS server+client cache poisoning, issues with SSL, breaking *forgot my password* systems, attacking autoupdaters and unhardened parsers, rerouting internal traffic.* Retrieved from http://www.blackhat.com/presentations/bh-jp-08/bh-jp-08-Kaminsky/BlackHat-Japan-08-Kaminsky-DNS08-BlackOps.pdf

Kemp, J., Cantor, S., Mishra, P., Philpott, R., & Maler, E. (2005). *Authentication context for the OASIS security assertion markup language (SAML) v2.0.* Retrieved from http://docs.oasis-open.org/security/saml/v2.0/saml-authn-context-2.0-os.pdf

Klingenstein, N. (2009). *SAML v2.0 holder-of-key web browser SSO profile.* Retrieved from http://docs.oasis-open.org/security/saml/Post2.0/sstc-saml-holder-of-key-browser-sso.pdf

Kormann, D., & Rubin, A. (2000). Risks of the passport single signon protocol. *Computer Networks, 33*(1-6), 51-58.

Microsoft. (n. d.). *Passport.* Retrieved from https://accountservices.passport.net/ppnetworkhome.srf?vv=1000&mkt=EN-US&lc=1033

MIT. (2011). *Kerberos: The network authentication protocol.* Retrieved from http://web.mit.edu/Kerberos/

OASIS. (2008). *Security services (SAML) TC.* Retrieved from http://www.oasis-open.org/committees/tc_home.php?wg_abbrev=security

Pfitzmann, B., & Waidner, M. (2003). Analysis of Liberty single-signon with enabled clients. *IEEE Internet Computing, 76,* 38–44. doi:10.1109/MIC.2003.1250582

Radack, S. (2003). *Electronic authentication: Guidance for selecting secure techniques.* Retrieved from http://www.itl.nist.gov/lab/bulletns/bltnaug04.htm

Schechter, S., Dhamija, R., Ozment, A., & Fischer, I. (2007). The emperor's new security indicators. In *Proceedings of the IEEE Symposium on Security and Privacy* (pp. 51-65).

Slemko, M. (2001). *Microsoft passport to trouble.* Retrieved from http://www.znep.com/~marcs/passport/

Soghoian, C., & Jakobsson, M. (2007). *A deceit-augmented man in the middle attack against Bank of America's sitekey service.* Retrieved from http://paranoia.dubfire.net/2007/04/deceit-augmented-man-in-middle-attack.html

Stamm, S., Ramzan, Z., & Jakobsson, M. (2006). *Drive-by pharming* (Tech. Rep. No. 641). Bloomington, IN: Indiana University.

This work was previously published in the International Journal of Mobile Computing and Multimedia Communications, Volume 3, Issue 4, edited by Ismail Khalil and Edgar Weippl, pp. 20-35, copyright 2011 by IGI Publishing (an imprint of IGI Global).

Chapter 7
An Integrated Approach for the Enforcement of Contextual Permissions and Pre-Obligations

Yehia Elrakaiby
TELECOM Bretagne, France

Frédéric Cuppens
TELECOM Bretagne, France

Nora Cuppens-Boulahia
TELECOM Bretagne, France

ABSTRACT

Pre-obligations denote actions that may be required before access is granted. The successful fulfillment of pre-obligations leads to the authorization of the requested access. Pre-obligations enable a more flexible enforcement of authorization policies. This paper formalizes interactions between the obligation and authorization policy states when pre-obligations are supported and investigates their use in a practical scenario. The main advantage of the presented approach is that it gives pre-obligations both declarative semantics using predicate logic and operational semantics using Event-Condition-Action (ECA) rules. Furthermore, the presented framework enables policy designers to easily choose to evaluate any pre-obligation either (1) statically (an access request is denied if the pre-obligation has not been fulfilled); or (2) dynamically (users are given the possibility to fulfill the pre-obligation after the access request and before access is authorized).

DOI: 10.4018/978-1-4666-2163-3.ch007

INTRODUCTION

Traditional security policy systems provided a simple yes/no answer to access requests. However, it was recognized that access often depends on some user-actions being performed before access is granted. For instance, an access rule may specify that users are allowed to download music files provided that they pay 1$ first. In this case, if a user requests to download, for example, the latest single of Muse, s\he is asked to pay 1$. If the payment is made successfully, the user is allowed to download the requested file. Such requirements are called pre-obligations. Neither traditional access control models such as DAC (NCSC, 1987) and RBAC (Ferraiolo & Kuhn, 1992) nor more recent contextual security models such as ASL (Jajodia, Samarati, & Subrahmanian, 1997) and OrBAC (Abou El Kalam et al., 2003) support pre-obligations: In these models, an access request is only allowed if the conditions associated with a permission authorizing the access are true when the access request is made.

There are several advantages of supporting pre-obligations in the policy language. First, this provides additional expressiveness since it enables policy administrators to specify that subjects may fulfill some of the access requirements after the access request. Furthermore, it separates the expression of requirements from the functional specification (the code) of the application. Thus, the analysis of policy requirements is simplified and administrators are able to modify the behavior of the system by updating policy rules without recoding the application.

To support pre-obligations, a number of works (Bettini, Jajodia, Wang, & Wijesekera, 2002, 2003 ; Ni, Bertino, & Lobo, 2008) subordinate obligations to access control rules. This approach has some limitations. For instance, obligations are only activated after access requests and general obligations are not supported. In addition, this approach generally produces intricate access control policies since permissions and obligations are often speci-

fied within the same rule. This is the approach used in (Ni et al., 2008) to specify permissions and their associated pre-obligations. The main limitation of previous works on pre-obligations is however that none formalized the effects of supporting pre-obligations on the evolution of the authorization and obligation policy states. This is essential to provide a deeper understanding of pre-obligations and their enforcement in information systems. In addition, this formal approach allows the study and the analysis of change in the authorization and obligation policy states in the presence of pre-obligations. Therefore, it enables, for instance, to derive plans to reach some particular authorization states (Becker & Nanz, 2008 ; Craven et al., 2009) or to explain the deactivation of pre-obligations after permission activation.

In this paper, we study the specification and the enforcement of pre-obligations. In our approach, we formalize the enforcement of pre-obligations using an extension of the language "Lactive" (Baral & Lobo, 1996). Lactive enables the description of change in state using concepts from action specification languages (Gelfond & Lifschitz, 1993). Thus, it enables reasoning about state evolution and the study of interactions between pre-obligations and the authorization and obligation policy states. Lactive also supports the specification of reactive behavior using active rules. This feature enables us to provide formal operational semantics for the enforcement of pre-obligations.

To simplify the expression of pre-obligations in access control rules, we specify pre-obligations in the form of contexts. A security rule context (Cuppens & Cuppens-Boulahia, 2008) denotes a set of conditions which have to be true for the security rule to be effective. For instance, a context *during_working_hours* may hold (be true) every working day from 8 in the morning until 6 in the afternoon. In our approach, context rules may be used to specify requirements which state that some user-action should be taken. These contexts are called pre-obligation contexts. We support two evaluations of pre-obligation contexts: The static (traditional) evaluation requires that pre-obligation actions be taken before access requests are made. The dynamic evaluation, on the other hand, enables the fulfillment of pre-obligation requirements after access requests.

This is an extended version of the paper (El-rakaiby, Cuppens, & Cuppens-Boulahia, 2010) which appeared in ARES 2010. In particular, we extend our pre-obligation selection algorithm to clarify the formal model and we detail the different aspects of our approach. Furthermore, we consider *state* contexts in the policy language to simplify policy specification. The remainder of the paper is organized as follows. Section two presents some motivating examples. In Section three, we present our formalization language and introduce the basic entities used to describe the application domain. In Section four, we introduce our policy language. Section five formalizes policy management and enforcement using active rules. In Section six, we present the derivation of pre-obligations from the domain description and then present the enforcement of the policy. In Section seven, we present an application example. Finally, Section eight discusses related works and Section nine concludes the paper.

Motivating Example

We consider the following access control requirement:

r1: Mobile users may use the Video on Demand (VoD) service provided that they have paid 2$. In a traditional access control system, this requirement is enforced as follows: when a user requests to use the VoD service, the request is authorized only if the subject has paid 2$. Otherwise, the request is denied. This means that the verification of the fulfillment of pre-obligations consists of checking a history of previous action occurrences. This approach is inflexible for the enforcement

of *r1* since it would be more convenient to allow the subject to pay for the service after s\he requests to use it. Then, when the subject successfully makes the payment, s/he is allowed access.

Thus, when pre-obligations are evaluated dynamically, the system would appear more flexible to the user. To provide such flexibility in the enforcement of access control requirements, we consider that requirements denoting user-actions may be defined as pre-obligations. In this case, when an access request is made, the subject is requested to satisfy the missing pre-obligation requirements (pay 2$). When these pre-obligations are fulfilled, the requested access is granted. Figure 1 compares the traditional enforcement of access control policies with their enforcement when pre-obligations are supported.

r2: Mobile users having WiFi coverage may use the VoD service provided that they have paid 1$.

Assume that the policy includes both the rules r1 and r2 and that it is possible to ask users to move to an area where there is WiFi coverage. In this case, when a user who has not paid for the VoD Service and has not WiFi coverage requests to use the VoD service, two alternative sets of pre-obligations are possible: (1) pay 2$ as specified in *r1*, (2) or pay 1$ and move to a WiFi covered area as specified in *r2*. One possible way to deal with this situation is to randomly select one of these two pre-obligation sets and ask the user to fulfill it. This however clearly represents an unacceptable behavior. Therefore, we choose to allow the association of pre-obligations with weights. For instance, if the pre-obligation to pay 2$ is given a lower weight than the sum of the weights of the two preobligations to pay 1$ and to move to a WiFi covered area, the pre-obligation set with the lowest weight (pay 2$) is selected.

Figure 1. Enforcement of access control policies

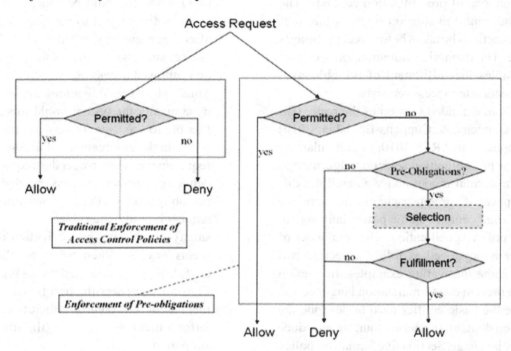

On the other hand, if the user is located in an area which has WiFi, s/he is asked to pay 1$ since the pre-obligation to pay 1$ would have lower weight than the one associated with the pre-obligation to pay 2$. This situation illustrates the importance of the dynamic selection of pre-obligations which takes into account which pre-obligations are and which are not fulfilled at the moment of the access request.

The Formalization Language

To formalize the effects of the support of pre-obligations on the authorization and policy states and to enable the study of their properties, we consider the language Lactive (Baral & Lobo, 1996). Lactive enables the description of change in state using concepts from action languages. It also supports the specification of reactive behavior in the form of Event Condition Action (ECA) rules. This gives operational semantics for the enforce-

ment of pre-obligations. Sorts and propositions of Lactive are given in Tables 1 and 2.

In the language, a state is a set of fluents. A fluent literal is either a fluent symbol or a fluent symbol preceded by $\neg$ ($\neg\neg$f is equivalent to f). The semantics of Lactive defines a transition function which given a state and a (possibly empty) sequence of actions produces a new state as follows. Actions in the input sequence are processed successively. For every action, effect laws are evaluated and the fluent state is updated. If after the execution of the action, conditions in some event definition are true, the event is generated. The newly generated events trigger active rules. Identifiers of these triggered rules are added to the triggered rules set. When the last action in the input sequence is evaluated, if the triggered rules set is not empty, an action selection function selects the sequence of actions appearing in one of the rules in the triggered rules set to process. Active rules are assigned priorities.

Table 1. Sorts of Lactive

Type	Description
Fluents	Facts describing the system state.
Actions	Possible actions in the system. Action occurrences update the fluent state by adding or removing fluents to or from the state.
Events	Define moments at which the policy needs to be updated.
Rule Names	ECA rule identifiers. An ECA rule states that when some *event* occurs and if some *conditions* are true, then some *actions* are executed. ECA rules (also called active rules) update the applied policy when particular events are detected.

Table 2. Propositions of Lactive

Type	Syntax	Description
Effect Law	*a* **causes** *f* **if** $p_p ..., p_n$	An effect law proposition states that the execution of *a* in a state where the fluents $p_p ..., p_n$ are true causes *f* to be true in the next state.
Event Definition	*e* **after** *a* **if** $p_p ..., p_n$	An event definition proposition states that if the conditions $p_p ..., p_n$ are true in the state following the execution of the action *a*, then event *e* is produced.
Active Rule	*R: e* **initiates** α **if** $p_p ..., p_n$	An active rule proposition states that every new detection of the event *e* triggers the execution of the sequence of actions α if the rule conditions are true.

Therefore, the action selection function returns the sequence of actions appearing in one of the rules which have the highest priority in the triggered rule set. The state stops evolving after the processing of all the actions in an input sequence if the triggered rule set is empty.

Basic Entities of the Application Domain

We consider that the application domain includes finite sorts of the entities: subjects *S*, objects *O*, actions *A* and contexts *C*. Entities may have attributes. For instance, the application dependent *Name(s,n)* means that the name of *s* is *n*. We also consider three relations to enable the specification of security rules for groups of subjects, actions and objects respectively: Subjects are empowered into roles using the relation *Empower(Subject;Role)*, actions, *i.e.* programs, are considered implementation of some activity using the relation *Consider(Action; Activity)* and objects are used

in views using the relation *Use(Object; View)*. Security rules may be specified using the abstract entities of roles, activities and views or using the concrete entities of subjects, actions and objects.

Description of Change in the Application Domain

To study the evolution of the policy state when change in state occurs, we assume that the system state is dynamic. More precisely, the system state may change after the execution of actions. We consider that actions of the form *Do(S,A,O)* indicate that subject *S* has taken the action *A* on the object *O*. The effects of the execution of actions on the state are described using effect law propositions.

For instance, we may specify the effect of the action *pay_2$* on the state as follows.

```
Do(S,pay_2$,payment server)
causes Paid_2$(S)
```

This effect law specifies that the fluent *Paid_2$(S)* starts to hold (be true) in the state after the action *pay_2$* is executed by *S* on a payment server. In our example, we will assume that a payment of 2$ is consumed when users use the VoD service. Therefore, we specify that the fluent *Paid_2$(S)* ceases to hold when *S* uses the VoD service as follows.

```
Do(S,use,video_on_demand)
causes ¬Paid_2$(S)
```

A set of effect laws is consistent if it does not contain two effect laws for the same action which have contradictory effects and whose conditions are not disjoint. These conditions are verified by considering the ground instances of effect laws in the application domain: If there is two effect laws "*a* **causes** *f* if $p_1, ... p_i ...,p_n$" and "*a* **causes** *g* if $q_1, ..., q_j ...,q_m$", then they should have either non-contradictory effects (f ≠ ¬g) or disjoint conditions ($\exists i; j: p_i = \neg q_j$).

The Policy Language

In this section, we first introduce our context language and show how we manage context activation and deactivation. We then present our security rules and show how they are used to specify system requirements.

CONTEXT LANGUAGE AND CONTEXT MANAGEMENT

We separate the definition of security rule conditions from the definition of security rules using contexts (Cuppens & Cuppens-Boulahia, 2008). A context defines a set of security rule conditions. The association of security rules with contexts allows the abstraction of complex conditions in security rules and thus, simplifies the interpretation of the policy. Contexts also allow context reuse in different security rules.

Context Rules

Security rule conditions define when some subject S is allowed, prohibited or obliged to take some action A on some object O. Therefore, contexts enable the definition of constraints on the security rule triple (S,A,O). Our context rules are expressions of the following form:

```
Hold_e(S,A,O, start/end(Ctx))
after Do(S,A,O)
if p_1,...,p_n
```

Context rules define the moments at which the conditions identified by the context *Ctx* start and seize to be true for the subject *S*, action *A* and object *O*. More precisely, the context rules for *start(Ctx)* define the conditions at which *Ctx* begins to hold. On the other hand, context rules for *end(Ctx)* specify when *Ctx* ceases to hold.

For instance, consider the following context rules.

```
Hold_e(S,A,O, start(in_WiFi_Area))
after Do(S,enter,L)
if WiFi_Area(L)
Hold_e(S,A,O, end(in_WiFi_Area))
after Do(S,exit,L)
if WiFi_Area(L)
```

These two rules specify that the context *in_WiFi_Area* remains true for some subject *S* from the moment this subject enters a location which is covered by WiFi until the moment the subject exists such location. These two moments are defined in terms of the event contexts *start(in_WiFi_Area)* and *end(in_WiFi_Area)*.

We also consider a second type of context rules which we call state context rules. State context rules define conditions on the system state and are particularly suitable for the specification of conditions of permission and prohibition rules. State contexts are specified using expressions of the following form.

```
Hold(S,A,O,Ctx) ← L₁,...,Lₙ
```

where $L_1,...,L_n$ are conditions on the state. To support this form of context rules called state context rules, we transform state context rules into event context rules (given a domain description) (Elrakaiby, Cuppens, & Cuppens-Boulahia, 2009b). In other words, we transform every state context rule into event context rules of the form *start(Ctx)* and *end(Ctx)*. For instance, consider the following rule.

```
Hold(S,A,O,paid_2$) ← Paid_2$(S)
```

The rule above specifies that the context paid 2$ holds for the subject *S* and any action/object while the fluent *Paid_2$(S)* is true. Given this state context rule and the effect laws presented in the previous section, we use an algorithm (Elrakaiby et al., 2009b) which transforms this state context into two event contexts *start(Ctx)* and *end(Ctx)*. For instance, the following event context rules are derived for the context *paid_2$*.

```
Holdₑ(S,A,O,start(paid_2$))
after Do(S,pay_2$,payment_server)
Holdₑ(S,A,O,end(paid_2$))
after Do(S,use,video_on_demand)
```

Our context language allows the expression of other important context types. For example, our context language supports the specification of temporal contexts. Temporal contexts are specified using the action *Clock*. This action updates fluents which represent calendars available in the system, such as Minutes, Hours, Day, etc. Temporal contexts enable the specification of absolute and periodic temporal conditions.

For instance, we may specify a temporal context working hours which holds everyday from 8 until 18 as follows.

```
Holdₑ(S,A,O, start(working_hours))
after Clock
```

```
if Hours(08)
Holdₑ(S,A,O,end(working_hours))
after Clock
if Hours(18)
```

We also consider the specification of relative temporal deadlines for obligations using the state context *delay(Nb.TimeUnit)*. This special context holds for some security rule after the elapse of Nb time units after its activation. We also allow context composition (Cuppens & Cuppens-Boulahia, 2008) using the logic operators of conjunction (&), disjunction (⊕) and negation (−). The semantics of these operators is defined by the following rules.

```
Hold(S,A,O, C1&C2) ←
Hold(S,A,O,C1)∧ Hold(S,A,O,C2)
Hold(S,A,O, C1⊕C2) ←
Hold(S,A,O,C1)∨ Hold(S,A,O,C2)
Hold(S,A,O, -C1) ← ¬Hold(S,A,O,C)
```

Context Management

In this paper, we consider persistent contexts. A persistent context *Ctx* holds from the moment the event *start(Ctx)* until the occurrence of *end(Ctx)*. To enable the reasoning about which contexts hold in every state, we associate every persistent context *Ctx* with a fluent *Hold(S,A,O,Ctx)*. This fluent holds from the detection of the event context *start(Ctx)* until the occurrence of the event context *end(Ctx)*. This is enforced using the following two active rules.

```
activate_Context:
Holdₑ(S,A,O,start(Ctx))
initiates Insert(Hold(S,A,O,Ctx))
deactivate_Context:
Holdₑ(S,A,O,end(Ctx))
initiates Remove(Hold(S,A,O,Ctx))
```

The rules above specify that the fluent *Hold(S,A,O,Ctx)* should be inserted into (removed from) the state when *start(Ctx)* (*end(Ctx)*) is detected. We consider the context state to be the subset of fluents which are of the form *Hold(S,A,O,Ctx)*. In our framework, the context state is always updated before the evaluation of the policy. Therefore, the previous active rules are given higher priority than the rules which enforce the security policy. We present policy enforcement in the following section.

Security Policy Language

We consider security rules which are close ground facts of the following form.

```
Permission(N, SR, AA, OV, Ctx)
Obligation(N, SR, AA, OV, Ctx, Ctxv)
```

where *N* is a rule identifier, *SR* is a subject or a role, *AA* is an action or an activity and *OV* is an object or a view. These expressions are called abstract security rules. A permission rule has one state context *Ctx*. This context is called the permission context. A permission is effective only while this context is true, *i.e.* after the event context *start(Ctx)* occurs and before the event context *end(Ctx)* occurs.

For example, consider the permission "mobile users may use the VoD service if they have paid 2$". This permission is specified as follows:

```
Permission(p, mobile_users, use,
video_on_demand,
paid_2$)
```

This permission specifies that subjects assigned to the role of mobile users may use the VoD service when the context *paid_2$* is true.

On the other hand, obligations are associated with two contexts: an obligation context (*Ctx*) and a violation context (*Ctxv*). The obligation is effective while the context *Ctx* holds. It is violated if the context *Ctxv* is detected while the obligation is effective. An obligation ceases to be effective

when it is fulfilled, *i.e.* when the subject executes the obliged action on the corresponding object.

For instance, consider the obligation "When users are in a WiFi covered area, they should turn on their WiFi connectivity within 3 minutes". This rule may be specified as follows:

```
Obligation(o1,mobile_users,turn_
on,wifi_connectivity,
in_WiFi_ area,delay(3.minutes))
```

Specification of Pre-Obligations

A permission rule is contextual. For instance, permission *p* specifies that users are allowed to use the VoD service if they have paid 2$. This contextual permission is enforced as follows in traditional systems: When a request to use the VoD service is made, if a payment of 2$ had been made, access is authorized. Otherwise, the request is denied. This enforcement model may be sometimes too inflexible since it may be required to ask users to pay after the access request (if the payment is not already made). To simplify the specification that some requirements should be evaluated dynamically, we associate every user defined context in the policy *Ctx* with another context denoted *d_Ctx*, called the dynamic version of *Ctx*. When some context *d_Ctx* is used in some security rule, this means that this requirement may be fulfilled dynamically after the access request.

For instance, consider our example. To specify that users may be allowed to pay 2$ for the VoD service after they request to use it, we specify a permission rule using the context *d_paid_2$* as follows.

```
Permission(p1, mobile_users, use,
video_on_demand,
d_paid_2$)
```

In this case, when a user requests to use the VoD service and s\he has not paid for the service, the user is asked to pay 2$. This requirement is enforced using an obligation to pay 2$ for using the service. When this obligation is fulfilled, access is allowed.

It is necessary to associate every obligation with a deadline condition. For instance, it may be required to specify that the mobile user should pay within 5 minutes. For this reason, we allow the association of every dynamic context with a deadline in the form of an attribute *Violation*. For instance, we specify that the obligation associated with the context *d_paid_2$* has a deadline of 5 minutes by updating the value of its attribute *Violation* to *Violation(d_paid_2$,delay(5.minutes))*. For every dynamic context, a default deadline defined by the policy administrator is used unless this attribute is updated. We also give pre-obligations weights to enable the selection of the simplest set of pre-obligations for a given access request. Therefore, we consider a second attribute *Weight* for dynamic contexts. The default value of this attribute is 1. For instance, consider the following permission.

```
Permission(p2, mobile_users, use,
video_on_demand,
d_paid_1$ & d_in_WiFi_area)
```

Where the context *paid_1$* is defined similarly to the context *paid_2$*. To specify that a 1$ payment is simpler to a 2$ payment, we assign the contexts *d_paid_1$* and *d_paid_2$* the weights of 2 and 3 respectively. Now, assume that the context *d_in _WiFi_area* is given a weight of 4. In this setting, when a user requests to use the VoD service, there are several possibilities. For instance, if s\he has not paid and is in a WiFi covered area, s\he is asked to pay 1$. If s\he has not paid and is not in a WiFi covered area, s\he is asked to pay 2$.

Policy Management and Enforcement

We distinguish between abstract and concrete security rules as follows: Abstract policy rules describe the global system policy and is specified by policy administrators. Concrete rules, on the other hand, are the security rules which are derived from the abstract policy as follows.

```
Permission(N,S,A,O,Ctx) ←
Permission(N,SR,AA,OV,Ctx) Empower'
(S,SR),Consider'(A,AA),Use'(O,OV)
```

The predicate *Empower'(S,SR)* specifies that *S* should be either *SR* if *SR* is a subject or a subject empowered into the role of *SR* if *SR* is a role. It is specified as follows.

```
Empower'(S,SR) ← Subject(SR)
Empower'(S,SR) ← Role(SR,
Empower(S,SR)
```

Similarly, the predicate *Consider'(A,AA)* states that *A* should be either the action *AA* if *AA* is an action or an action considered in *AA* if *AA* is an activity. The predicate *Use'(O,OV)* dictates that *O* should be either the object *OV* or an object used in *OV* if *OV* is a view. Concrete obligation rules are also derived for individual subjects, actions and objects from abstract obligation rules. In the following, we give formal operational semantics for policies which consist of concrete security rules using active rules.

Permission Activation and Deactivation

Every concrete permission rule is associated with a context which defines when it is effective. We therefore associate every permission in the state with a fluent *Permitted(N,S,A,O,Ctx)*. This fluent starts to hold when the permission's context begins to hold. It ceases to hold when the permission's context is ended. This is specified using the following active rules:

```
activate_Permission:
Hold_e(S,A,O,start(Ctx))
initiates
Insert(Permitted(N,S,A,O,Ctx))
if Permission(N,S,A,O,Ctx)
deactivate_Permission:
Hold_e(S,A,O,end(Ctx))
initiates
Remove(Permitted(N,S,A,O,Ctx))
if Permitted(N,S,A,O,Ctx)
```

The rules above specify that the action *Insert(Permitted(N,S,A,O,Ctx))* should be taken when the context of some permission's is activated. This action makes the fluent *Permitted* hold as specified in the following effect law.

```
Insert(Permitted(N,S,A,O,Ctx))
causes Permitted(N,S,A,O,Ctx)
```

Reciprocally, we specify that *Permitted* ceases to hold after the execution of the action *Remove* on the fluent *Permitted*. In the policy, an access may be authorized by more than one permission. Therefore, we consider an additional fluent *Permitted(S,A,O)* which holds for some access (S,A,O) while this access is allowed. This fluent begins to hold for some access (S,A,O) whenever some permission for (S,A,O) is activated. It ceases to hold after the deactivation of a permission for (S,A,O) only if there is no other permission for (S,A,O) in the state.

Obligation Activation and Deactivation

To manage obligations, we associate every concrete obligation with a fluent *Obliged(N,S,A,O,Ctx,Ctxv)*. This fluent represents that there is an effective obligation for *S* to take *A* on *O* before *Ctxv* is detected. An obligation is deactivated when its context *Ctx* is ended while it is effective. When an obligation is deactivated, the fluent *Obliged* ceases to hold. This is formalized using the following two active rules.

```
activate_Obligation:
Hold_e(S,A,O,start(Ctx))
initiates Insert(Obliged(N,S,A,O,
Ctx,Ctxv))
if Obligation(N,S,A,O,Ctx,Ctxv)
deactivate_Obligation:
Hold_e(S,A,O,end(Ctx))
initiates Remove(Obliged(N,S,A,O,
Ctx,Ctxv))
if Obliged(N,S,A,O,Ctx,Ctxv)
```

Obligation Fulfillment and Violation

As opposed to permissions, obligations may additionally be violated and fulfilled. An effective obligation is fulfilled when its required action is taken. Actions required by obligations are monitored using the following context.

```
Hold_e(S,A,O,start(ctx_fulfillment))
after Do(S,A,O)
if Obliged(N,S,A,O,Ctx,Ctxv)
```

The context *ctx_fulfillment* holds for some (S,A,O) when the action *Do(S,A,O)* is taken and there is an effective obligation requiring (S,A,O). When *start(S,A,O,start(ctx_fulfillment))* is detected, effective obligations for (S,A,O) are fulfilled using the following active rule.

```
fulfill_Obligation:
Hold_e(S,A,O,start(ctx_fulfillment))
initiates Fulfill(N,S,A,O)
if Obliged(N,S,A,O,Ctx,Ctxv)
```

Reciprocally, the detection of the deadline context of an effective obligation violates this obligation. This is specified as follows.

```
violate_Obligation:
Hold_e(S,A,O,start(Ctxv))
initiates Violate(N,S,A,O)
if Obliged(N,S,A,O,Ctx,Ctxv)
```

The actions *Fulfill* and *Violate* indicate the fulfillment and violation of obligations respectively. In this paper, we assume for simplicity that obligations are deactivated whenever they are violated/fulfilled. Therefore, the fluent *Obliged* ceases to hold when the actions *Fulfill* and *Violate* are taken.

Derivation of Dynamic Contexts and Enforcement of Pre-Obligations

To simplify the specification of pre-obligations, we consider that every user-specified context *Ctx* has a corresponding dynamic context *d_Ctx*. This simplifies the specification of the policy by enabling policy administrators to easily choose whether a context should be statically or dynamically evaluated.

Dynamic contexts and their associated pre-obligations are automatically derived from the definition of user-specified contexts using the algorithm in Figure 2. This algorithm takes the set of user-defined event context definitions *E* as input, and produces the definition of dynamic contexts. It also derives for every dynamic context *d_C* an obligation rule *O(d_C)*. This obligation *O(d_C)* defines the action which should be taken for the context *d_C* to be activated. The fulfillment of this obligation activates the context *d_C* (as well as the context *C*) for the access requester.

The algorithm verifies every user-defined event context rule as follows. First, if the context is of the form *start(C)* and is started by some action *A* (line 5), then a dynamic context *d_C* is defined similarly to *C*, *i.e. d_C* is associated with the same

actions which start and end *C* (lines 7-10). An obligation is then constructed. The obligation's identifier is *O(d_C)* (line 12). Its role and view are initialized using the role *any_subject* and the view *any_object* (line 13). These entities represent all subjects and all objects in the system respectively.

Constraints over the parameters of the action which starts *C* in the *after* part (lines 13-14) and in the *if* part (lines 15-19) of the context definition of *start(C)* are then checked. If some constraint over the action's subject or object (S,A,O) is specified, it is used as the subject/role and object/view of the obligation respectively.

An event context identifier of the form *start(O(d_C))* is then used to denote the activation conditions of the obligation (line 20). The context *start(O(d_C))* is then defined (lines 21-23). Its definition states that it should be detected after the execution of the action *Find_Obligations(S',A',O')* if the fluent *Obl_For_Access(O(dC),S,A,O,S',A',O')* holds. The action *Find_Obligations* checks the policy for possible pre-obligations when the access (S',A',O') is not authorized. The fluent *Obl_For_Access*, on the other hand, denotes that the obligation associated with *d_C* for the subject *S* to take the action *A* on the object *O* has been selected for the authorization of (S',A',O').

Finally, if a user-specified Violation Context attribute for *d_C* exists, it is used as the obligation violation context. Otherwise, the default context is used (lines(24-27)). The algorithm returns the constructed event definitions, obligation rules and context attributes. These elements are added to the policy.

For instance, the application of the algorithm to the context *start(paid_2$)* produces: (1) the dynamic context definition for *d_paid_2$*. This context is defined similarly to the user-defined context *paid_2$*, (2) The context attribute *Type(d_paid_2$,dynamic)*, and (3) The obligation and the event context rule specified below.

Figure 2. Derivation of dynamic contexts

```
Input  : (1) Event Definitions ℰ
Output: (1) A Set of Event Context Definitions (ED)
        (2) A Set of Obligation Rules (Obl)
        (3) A set of context attributes (CA)
1  begin
2     ED = Obl = CA = ∅;
3     foreach User-defined Event Context Definition of the form
4        "Hold_e(S',A',O',Ctx) after Do(S,A,O) if P_1, ..., P_n" in ℰ do
5        if Ctx = start(C) and A is an action then
6           CA = CA ∪ {Type(d_C,dynamic)};
7           ED = ED ∪ { Hold_e(S',A',O',start(d_C)) after Do(S,A,O) if
                        P_1,..., P_n }
8           foreach User-defined Context in ℰ of the form
9              "Hold_e(S',A',O',end(C)) after Do(S_1,A_1,O_1) if Q_1, ...,Q_m"
              do
10                ED = ED ∪ { Hold_e(S',A',O',end(d_C)) after
                             Do(S_1,A_1,O_1) if Q_1,...,Q_m }
11           N' = 𝒪(d_C);
12           SR' = any_subject; OV' = any_object;
13           if S is a subject then SR' = S;
14           if O is an object then OV' = O;
15           foreach Condition P_i in P_1, ..., P_n do
16              if P_i == (S = SR) or P_i == Empower(S,SR) then
17                 SR' = SR
18              else if P_i == (O = OV) or P_i == Use(O,OV) then
19                 OV' = OV
20           Ctx' = start(𝒪(d_C));
21           ED = ED ∪ { Hold_e(S,A,O,start(𝒪(d_C)))
22                       After Find_Obligations(S',A,O')
23                       If Obl_For_Access(𝒪(d_C),S,A,O,S',A',O')}
24           if Violation_Context(d_C,Ctx_v) then
25              Ctx'_v = Ctx_v
26           else
27              Ctx'_v = Default_Violation_Context
28           Obl = Obl ∪ { Obligation(N',SR',A,OV',Ctx',Ctx'_v) }
29     return (CA,ED,obl)
30 end
```

```
Obligation(O(d_paid_2$),any_
subject,pay_2$,any_object,
start(O(d_paid_2$))), delay(3.Minutes))
Hold_e(S, pay_2$, O, start(O(d_paid_2$)))
after Find Obligations(S',A',O')
if Obl_For_Access(O(d_paid_2$),S,
pay_2$,O, S',A',O')
```

This obligation rule defines an obligation *O(d_paid_2$)* which states that the action *pay_2$* should be taken by any subject on any object when the context *start(d_paid_2$)* is detected. This context is detected for the subject S and object O if S and O were selected to fulfill the obligation after the execution of the action *Find_Obligations* for the access request (S',A,O'). The selected S and O for the obligation are the ones specified using the fluent *Obl_For_Access(O(d_paid_2$),S, pay_2$,O,S',A',O')*.

Authorization Policy Enforcement

When pre-obligations are supported, the authorization policy is enforced as follows: When an access request is made, access is granted if it is authorized by an effective permission. Otherwise, the authorization policy is checked for pre-obligations which would allow the access. If none is found, access is denied. If pre-obligations are activated, they are enforced as follows. Whenever an effective permission for the requested access is activated or if one of the pre-obligations is violated/deactivated, pre-obligations are deactivated. When all pre-obligations are successfully fulfilled, access is granted.

To enforce the authorization policy, we consider the context *access_req_ctx*. This context is specified as follows.

```
Hold_e(S,A,O,start(access_req_ctx))
after Request(S,A,O)
```

The context *access_req_ctx* holds for an access (S,A,O) after the occurrence of the special action *Request(S,A,O)*. This action indicates that *S* has requested to take *A* on *O*. This context holds until this access request is honored, *i.e.* when the access is either allowed or denied. The end of *access_req_ctx* is therefore specified as follows.

```
Hold_e(S,A,O,end(access_req_ctx))
after Allow(S,A,O)
Hold_e(S,A,O,end(access_req_ctx))
after Deny(S,A,O)
```

When an access request is made, it is directly granted if it is authorized by an effective permission. This is specified using the following rule.

```
allow_Access:
Hold_e(S,A,O,start(access_req_ctx))
initiates Allow(S,A,O)
if Permitted(N,S,A,O,Ctx,Ctxv)
```

If there is no effective permission for the requested access, we check the authorization policy for pre-obligations.

```
find_Obligations:
Hold_e(S,A,O,start(access_req_ctx))
initiates Find_Obligations(S,A,O)
if ¬Permitted(N,S,A,O,Ctx,Ctxv)
```

The action *Find_Obligations* selects (if possible) the simplest set of pre-obligations required to allow (S,A,O) by executing the algorithm in Figure 3. This algorithm works as follows: it checks every permission which permits (S,A,O). First, the permission context *Ctx* into the disjunctive normal form (DNF) to identify the sets of basic contexts which have to hold simultaneously to allow the requested access. A set of basic contexts (*CN*) is considered valid if: (1) all its non-dynamic contexts are true, (2) each of its dynamic contexts which does not hold can be activated. A dynamic context *C* can be activated if there exists (S′,A′,O′) and a dynamic event definition *Hold_e(S,A,O,start(C))* such that the conditions of this event definition are true. This ensures that when *Do(S′,A′,O′)* is preformed, *C* is activated. For every inactive dynamic context which can be activated, a fluent of the form *Obl_For_Access(O(C),S′,A′,O′,S,A,O)* is added to the set *Obligations*. This fluent specifies that *Do(S′,A′,O′)* should be taken to activate the dynamic context *O(C)* and, subsequently allow the requested access (S,A,O). Then, the weight assigned with *O(C)* is added to the *CN_Weight*. After the evaluation of every CN_i, if the sum of the weights of its pre-obligations *CN_Weight* is less than the minimum weight *Min_Weight*, the pre-obligations of this CN_i are selected. After the evaluation of the authorization policy, the algorithm returns *No_Obl_For_Access(S,A,O)* if no preobligations are possible for the access. Otherwise, the set of pre-obligations selected for the access is returned.

If no pre-obligations are returned after the execution of *Find_Obligations*, the context *no_pre_obligations* holds and access is denied. We specify access denial as follows.

Figure 3. Selection of pre-obligations

```
Input  : (1) access_Request(S,A,O)
         (2) The Authorization Policy 𝒫
         (3) Event Definitions ℰ
Output: Selected Pre-obligations
1  begin
2  │   Selected = ∅, Min_Weight = ∞;
3  │   foreach Permission(N,S,A,O,Ctx)∈ 𝒫 do
4  │   │   Ctx = DNF(Ctx);
5  │   │   foreach conjunction CN of the form ⋀ⁿⱼ₌₁ Cⱼ in Ctx do
6  │   │   │   CN_Weight = 0;
7  │   │   │   Obligations = ∅;
8  │   │   │   Valid = true;
9  │   │   │   foreach Basic Context Cⱼ in CN do
10 │   │   │   │   if ¬Type(Cⱼ,dynamic) & ¬Hold(S,A,O,Cⱼ) then
11 │   │   │   │   │   Valid = false;
12 │   │   │   │   if Type(Cⱼ,dynamic) & ¬Hold(S,A,O,Cⱼ) then
13 │   │   │   │   │   if (∃S′∃A′∃O′ :"Holdₑ(S,A,O,start(Cⱼ)) after
   │   │   │   │   │      Do(S′,A′,O′)  if p₁,...,pₙ" in ℰ & p₁,...,pₙ hold)
   │   │   │   │   │   then
14 │   │   │   │   │   │   Obligations =
   │   │   │   │   │   │   Obligations ∪ Obl_For_Access(𝒪(Cⱼ),S′,
   │   │   │   │   │   │   A′,O′,S,A,O);
15 │   │   │   │   │   │   if Weight(Cⱼ,X) then
16 │   │   │   │   │   │   │   CN_Weight = CN_Weight + X;
17 │   │   │   │   │   else
18 │   │   │   │   │   │   Valide = false;
19 │   │   │   if Valid == true & Min_Weight > CN_Weight then
20 │   │   │   │   Selected = Obligations;
21 │   │   │   │   Min_Weight = CN_Weight;
22 │   if Selected == ∅ then
23 │   │   return No_Pre_Obligations_For(S,A,O)
24 │   else
25 │   │   return Selected;
26 end
```

```
Holdₑ(S,A,O,start(no_pre_obliga-
tions))
after Find_Obligations(S,A,O)
if No_Obl_For_Access(S,A,O)
deny_Access: Holdₑ(S,A,O,start(no_
pre_obligations))
initiates Deny(S,A,O)
```

The fluent *No_Obl_For_Access(S,A,O)* as well as the context *no_pre_obligations* seize to hold when the access request is honored to allow the reevaluation of the authorization policy at subsequent access requests.

Enforcement of Pre-Obligation Sets

After the activation of a set of pre-obligations for an access (S,A,O), pre-obligations are enforced as follows.

Permission Activation

Whenever a permission is activated for (S,A,O) and there is a request to take (S,A,O), pre-obligations for (S,A,O) are deactivated and access is allowed. The following context *authorized_request* starts to hold when some requested access (S,A,O) become authorized.

```
Hold_e(S,A,O,start(authorized_request))
after Insert(Permitted(N,S,A,O,Ctx))
if Hold(S,A,O,access_req_ctx)
```

When an access request for (S,A,O) is authorized, the following rule deactivates pending pre-obligations for (S,A,O) (if any exists).

```
deactivate_Pre:
Hold_e(S,A,O,start(authorized_request))
initiates Remove(Obl_For_
Access(N,S',A',O',S,A,O))
if Obl_For_Access(N,S',A',O',S,A,O)
```

We also accept the requested access by initiating the action *Allow* using the following active rule.

```
Allow_access*:
Hold_e(S,A,O,start(authorized_request))
initiates Allow(S,A,O)
```

Violation of Pre-Obligations

When a pre-obligation is violated, the fulfillment of other pre-obligations becomes unnecessary since the access will not be allowed. Therefore, we deactivate in this case other related pre-obligations (*i.e.* pre-obligations for the same access request) and deny access. We define the context *pre_obl_violated* which holds when pre-obligations are violated as follows.

```
Hold_e(S,A,O,start(pre_obl_violated))
after Violate(N,S',A',O')
if Obl_For_Access (N,S',A',O',S,A,O)
```

When *pre_obl_violated* starts to hold, we deactivate pre-obligations and deny the access requested.

```
violate_Pre: Hold_e(S,A,O,start(pre_
obl_violated))
initiates Remove(Obl_For_
Access(N,S',A',O',S,A,O)
```

```
if Obl_For_Access(N,S',A',O',S,A,O)
deny_access*: Hold_e(S,A,O,start(pre_
obl_violated))
initiates Denys(S,A,O)
```

Pre-Obligation Fulfillment

When pre-obligations are fulfilled, they are removed from the state using the following active rule:

```
violate_Pre: Hold_e(S,A,O,start(ctx_
fulfillment))
initiates Remove(Obl_For_
Access(N,S,A,O,S',A',O'))
if Obl_For_Access(N,S,A,O,S',A',O')
```

Application Example

To illustrate the concepts presented in this paper and discuss the evolution of the authorization and obligation policy states when pre-obligations are supported, we consider an example policy that includes the following permission rules.

```
Permission(p1,mobile_users,use,video_
on_demand, d_paid_2$)
Permission(p2,mobile_users,use,video_
on_demand,
d_in_WiFi_area & d_paid_1$)
```

Table 3 shows the values given to the attributes *Weight* and *Violation* of each context. We first discuss the selection of pre-obligations after a user requests to use the VoD service in the following situations:

Table 3. Context attributes

Context	Weight	Violation
d_paid_1$	2	delay(3.minutes)
d_paid_2$	3	delay(4.minutes)
d_in_WiFi_area	4	delay(5.minutes)

- (S1): The user has paid 2$. Access is directly granted since permission p1 is effective.
- (S2): The user has paid 1$ and is not in a WiFi covered area: the user is asked to pay 2$ since this pre-obligation is assigned lower weight than the weight given to the obligation to move to a WiFi covered area.
- (S3): The user has not paid and is in an area having WiFi: the user is asked to pay 1$. Assume we replace the permission *p1* in the policy above with the following permission:

```
Permission(p'1,mobile_
users,use,video_on_demand,
working_hours & d_paid_2$)
```

The permission *p'1* specifies that users may use the VoD service during working hours provided that they have paid 2$. In this case, pre-obligations are selected as follows:

- (S4): During working hours, the user has not paid nor is in a WiFi covered area and is requesting to use the VoD service. The user is asked to pay 2$.
- (S5): Outside of working hours, the user has not paid nor is in a WiFi area and is

requesting to use the VoD service. The user is asked to pay 1$ and to move to an area with WiFi since only *p2* can be activated.

Table 4 and Figure 4 show the selection of pre-obligations and discusses the evolution of the state of authorizations and obligations in the different situations just described. Each table row represents the state obtained by the execution of the action appearing in the rightmost column of the row above. The obligations to pay 2$, to pay 1$ and to move to a WiFi covered area are denoted o_{2s}, o_{1s} and o_{wf} respectively. We only give identifiers for situations when it is necessary. We will now consider the evolution of the authorization and obligation policy states for the situation (S3) where a user is asked to pay 1$ (within 3 minutes). In this scenario, the following may occur:

- The user pays 1$ successfully and access is granted.
- The user pays 2$. In this case, the permission *p1* is activated and the obligation to pay 1$ is deactivated.
- The user fails to pay within 3 minutes and access is denied.

Table 4. Policy state evolution

	Ctx_State			A_State		O_State			
	Paid_2$	Paid_1$	Wifi_area	p_1	p_2	o_{2s}	o_{1s}	o_{wf}	Action
s_1	X	.	.	X	.	.	.	.	Req(use_vod)
	X	.	.	X	.	.	.	.	Allow(use_vod)
s_2	.	X	.	.	.	.	.	.	Req(use_vod)
	.	X	.	.	.	.	.	.	Do(pay_2$)
	X	X	.	X	.	.	.	.	Allow(use_vod)
s_3	.	.	X	.	.			.	Req(use_vod)
s'_3	.	.	X	.	.	X	X	.	Do(pay_1$)
s''_3	.	X	X	.	X	,	.	.	Allow(use_vod)
s'_3	.	.	X	.	.	X	X	.	Do(pay_2$)
	.	X	X	.	X	.	.	.	Allow(use_vod)
s'_3	.	.	X	.	.	X	X	.	Delay(3.minutes)
	.	.	X	.	.	.	.	.	Deny(use_vod)

Figure 4. Policy state evolution

	Ctx_State				A_State		O_State			Action
	paid_2$	paid_1$	wifi_area	work_hours	p'_1	$p2$	$o_{2\$}$	$o_{1\$}$	o_{wf}	
s_4	.	.	.	X	.	.	.	.	.	req(use_vod)
	.	.	.	X	.	.	X	.	.	Do(pay_2$)
	X	.	.	X	X	.	.	.	.	Allow(use_vod)
s_5	.	.	.	.	.	.	.	.	.	req(use_vod)
s'_5	.	.	.	.	.	.	.	X	X	Do(pay_1$)
s''_5	.	X	.	.	.	.	.	.	X	Do(enter_wifi_area)
	.	X	X	.	.	X	.	.	.	Allow(use_vod)
s'_5	.	.	.	.	.	.	.	X	X	Delay(3.minutes)
	.	.	.	.	.	.	.	.	.	Deny(use_vod)
s''_5	.	X	.	.	.	.	.	.	X	Delay(5.minutes)
	.	X	.	.	.	.	.	.	.	Deny(use_vod)

We now consider the situation (S5) where a user is asked to pay 1$ (within 3 minutes) and to move to a WiFi covered area within (5 minutes). The following may happen.

- The user successfully fulfills the two pre-obligations. In this case, the permission *p2* will be activated and access is granted.
- The user fails to pay within 3 minutes. In this case, the second pre-obligation to move to a WiFi covered area is deactivated and access is denied.
- The user pays within 3 minutes but fails to move to a WiFi covered area within 5 minutes. In this case, access is denied.

Related Work

Other models have been proposed to support preobligations in access control policies. To our knowledge, the notion of provisional actions was first introduced by Kudo and Hada (2000) to enable the association of access control security rules for XML documents with actions that should be triggered by access requests. In Kudo (2002), multiple hierarchies and property propagation are studied. In contrast, we study provisional actions in the form of user actions which are monitored for fulfillment/violation and formalize policy enforcement and evolution.

In (Jajodia, Kudo, & Subrahmanian, 2001), the ASL access control language (Jajodia et al., 1997) is extended to allow the association of security rules with provisional actions. An architecture for the enforcement of these provisional actions is proposed. Bettini et al. (2002, 2003) study the association of access control rules with provisions and obligations and propose algorithms for the computation a minimal provisions and obligations set. Obligation definition and monitoring in the framework is discussed in (Bettini, Wang, Jajodia, & Wijesekera, 2002). In comparison, the main advantage of our work is that we consider a formal description of change in state using the concepts of action specification languages. This enables us to formalize the activation, deactivation, violation and fulfillment of pre-obligations and the effects of these operations on the authorization and obligation states. Consequently, we clarify the semantics of pre-obligations by giving their enforcement declarative semantics. In addition, our formal model for pre-obligations is given operational semantics using ECA rules.

In Ni et al. (2008), an obligation model supporting the specification of pre- and post-obligations is presented. The paper studies two interactions between permissions and obligations namely invalid permission due to obligation cascading and the dominance of obligations. With respect to our work, the model subordinates obligations to permissions, only considers temporal obligation deadlines and does not consider the selection of pre-obligations after access requests. Furthermore, in our policy language, obligations are specified separately from access control rules and provisions are specified in the form of contexts in permission rules (as opposed to the specification of obligations embedded in access control rules). This simplifies the representation of the access control policy and, additionally, enables us to support general obligations which do not depend of access requests. Moreover, we provide formal declarative semantics for the enforcement of pre-obligations.

The UCON model (Park & Sandhu, 2004) introduces obligations to deal with usage control requirements and introduces the notion of attribute mutability. The model is formalized in Zhang, Parisi-Presicce, Sandhu, and Park (2005). Pre-obligations in UCON are evaluated using the functional predicate "preB" which checks, when an access request is made, whether pre-obligations required for this access have been fulfilled. Formally, checking pre-obligation fulfillment in UCON is similar to checking regular permission conditions. By contrast, in our framework, pre-obligations are activated just after an access request if their fulfillment is required to enable the access. This is an important advantage since, whenever necessary, subjects may be assisted by the system in accessing resources. Additionally, the UCON model does not support the specification of general or global obligations since obligations are always associated with resource usage.

Other works on trust management (Becker & Nanz, 2008 ; Bonatti, Olmedilla, & Peer, 2006 ; Koshutanski & Massacci, 2004) studied the use of abduction in explaining access denials to users by searching for missing facts or credentials which would allow the requested access. The work that is most relevant to ours is Becker and Nanz (2007) where a logic and an inference system for reasoning about sequences of user-actions and

their effects on the authorization policy state are presented. This work is complementary to ours since we essentially study the enforcement and management of pre-obligations as opposed to how to derive the actions that should be taken to obtain particular permissions.

CONCLUSION

In this paper, we studied the specification, selection and enforcement of pre-obligations. First, we have proposed to specify pre-obligations in access control rules in the form of permission contexts to simplify both the specification and interpretation of the access control policy. We have also considered the notion of dynamic context attributes to allow the association of dynamic contexts (denoting preobligations) with different weights and deadlines. We have then studied the selection of pre-obligations after access requests and formalized the enforcement of pre obligations and its effects on the policy state.

Future work consists of modeling consent requirements in the form of special pre-obligations and the integration of group pre-obligations (El-rakaiby, Cuppens, & Cuppens-Boulahia, 2009a) to enable the specification of pre-obligations which may be fulfilled in different ways.

REFERENCES

Abou El Kalam, A., Benferhat, S., Balbiani, P., Miège, A., El Baida, R., Cuppens, F., et al. (2003). Organization based access control. In *Proceedings of the 4th IEEE International Workshop on Policies for Distributed Systems and Networks* (pp. 120-131). Washington, DC: IEEE Computer Society.

Baral, C., & Lobo, J. (1996). Formal characterization of active databases. In *Proceedings of the International Workshop on Logic in Databases* (pp. 175-195).

Becker, M. Y., & Nanz, S. (2007). A logic for state modifying authorization policies. *ACM Transactions on Information and System Security*, *13*(3), 20.

Becker, M. Y., & Nanz, S. (2008). The role of abduction in declarative authorization policies. In *Proceedings of the 10th International Conference on Practical Aspects of Declarative Language* (pp. 84-99).

Bettini, C., Jajodia, S., Wang, X. S., & Wijesekera, D. (2002). Provisions and obligations in policy management and security applications. In *Proceeding of the 28th International Conference on Very Large Data Bases* (pp. 502-513). Washington, DC: IEEE Computer Society.

Bettini, C., Jajodia, S., Wang, X. S., & Wijesekera, D. (2003). Provisions and obligations in policy rule management. *Journal of Network and Systems Management*, *11*(3). doi:10.1023/A:1025711105609

Bettini, C., Wang, X., Jajodia, S., & Wijesekera, D. (2002). Obligation monitoring in policy management. In *Proceedings of the IEEE International Workshop on Policies for Distributed Systems and Networks* (pp. 2-12). Washington, DC: IEEE Computer Society.

Bonatti, P. A., Olmedilla, D., & Peer, J. (2006). Advanced policy explanations on the web. In *Proceeding of the 17th European Conference on Artificial Intelligence* (pp. 200-204). Amsterdam, The Netherlands: IOS Press.

Craven, R., Lobo, J., Ma, J., Russo, A., Lupu, E., & Bandara, A. (2009). Expressive policy analysis with enhanced system dynamicity. In *Proceedings of the 4th International Symposium on Information, Computer, and Communications Security* (pp. 239-250). New York, NY: ACM Press.

Cuppens, F., & Cuppens-Boulahia, N. (2008). Modeling contextual security policies. *International Journal of Information Security*, *7*(4), 285–305. doi:10.1007/s10207-007-0051-9

Cuppens, F., Cuppens-Boulahia, N., & Sans, T. (2005). Nomad: A security model with non atomic actions and deadlines. In *Proceedings of the 18th IEEE Workshop on Computer Security Foundations* (pp. 186-196). Washington, DC: IEEE Computer Society.

Elrakaiby, Y., Cuppens, F., & Cuppens-Boulahia, N. (2009a). Formalization and management of group obligations. In *Proceedings of the 10th IEEE International Conference on Policies for Distributed Systems and Networks* (pp. 158-165). Los Alamitos, CA: IEEE Press.

Elrakaiby, Y., Cuppens, F., & Cuppens-Boulahia, N. (2009b). From state-based to event-based contextual security policies. In *Proceedings of the Fourth International Conference on Digital Information Management*, Ann Arbor, MI (pp. 1-7). Washington, DC: IEEE Computer Society.

Elrakaiby, Y., Cuppens, F., & Cuppens-Boulahia, N. (2010). From contextual permission to dynamic preobligation: An integrated approach. In *Proceedings of the International Conference on Availability, Reliability, and Security* (p. 70). Washington, DC: IEEE Computer Society.

Ferraiolo, D. F., & Kuhn, D. R. (1992). Role-based access control. In *Proceedings of the 15th National Computer Security Conference* (pp. 554-563).

Gelfond, M., & Lifschitz, V. (1993). Representing action and change by logic programs. *The Journal of Logic Programming*, *17*, 301–322. doi:10.1016/0743-1066(93)90035-F

Jajodia, S., Kudo, M., & Subrahmanian, V. (2001). Provisional authorizations. In *E-commerce security and privacy* (pp. 133–159). Amsterdam, The Netherlands: Kluwer Academic.

Jajodia, S., Samarati, P., & Subrahmanian, V. S. (1997). A logical language for expressing authorizations. In *Proceedings of the IEEE Symposium on Security and Privacy* (p. 0031). Washington, DC: IEEE Computer Society.

Jordan, C. (1987). *A guide to understanding discretionary access control in trusted systems.* Retrieved from http://oai.dtic.mil/oai/oai?verb=getRecord&metadataPrefix=html&identifier=ADA392813

Koshutanski, H., & Massacci, F. (2004). Interactive access control for web services. In *Proceedings of the 19th International Conference on Information Security* (pp. 151-166).

Kudo, M. (2002). PBAC: Provision-based access control model. *International Journal of Information Security, 1*(2), 116–130. doi:10.1007/s102070100010

Kudo, M., & Hada, S. (2000). Xml document security based on provisional authorization. In *Proceedings of the 7th ACM Conference on Computer and Communications Security* (pp. 87-96). New York, NY: ACM Press.

Ni, Q., Bertino, E., & Lobo, J. (2008). An obligation model bridging access control policies and privacy policies. In *Proceedings of the 13th ACM Symposium on Access Control Models and Technologies* (pp. 133-142). New York, NY: ACM Press.

Park, J., & Sandhu, R. (2004, February). The UCONABC usage control model. *ACM Transactions on Information and System Security, 7*(1), 128–174. doi:10.1145/984334.984339

Zhang, X., Parisi-Presicce, F., Sandhu, R., & Park, J. (2005). Formal model and policy specification of usage control. *ACM Transactions on Information and System Security, 8*(4), 351–387. doi:10.1145/1108906.1108908

This work was previously published in the International Journal of Mobile Computing and Multimedia Communications, Volume 3, Issue 2, edited by Ismail Khalil and Edgar Weippl, pp. 35-51, copyright 2011 by IGI Publishing (an imprint of IGI Global).

Chapter 8
Online Authentication Using Smart Card Technology in Mobile Phone Infrastructure

Teddy Mantoro
International Islamic University Malaysia, Malaysia

Admir Milišić
International Islamic University Malaysia, Malaysia

Media A. Ayu
International Islamic University Malaysia, Malaysia

ABSTRACT

The widespread of Internet usage has resulted in a greater number and variety of applications involving different types of private information. In order to diminish privacy concerns and strengthen user trust, security improvements in terms of authentication are necessary. The solutions need to be convenient, entailing ease of use and higher mobility. The suggested approach is to make use of the already popular mobile phone and to involve the mobile network, benefiting from Subscriber Identity Module (SIM) card's tamper resistance to become trusted entities guarding personal information and identifying users. Mobile phone's SIM card is convenient for safely storing security parameters essential for secured communication. It becomes secure entity compulsory for getting access to privacy sensitive Internet applications, like those involving money transfers. Utilizing the NFC interface passes the personal user keys only when needed, giving additional strength to the traditional public key cryptography approach in terms of security and portability.

DOI: 10.4018/978-1-4666-2163-3.ch008

INTRODUCTION

Perhaps due to the lack of experience and knowledge among most of the Internet users, combined with unsatisfying security level regarding online software and websites, Internet user privacy becomes more of an issue each year. As numbers are constantly increasing in terms of services available, connected users and networked devices, Internet community is faced with inherited, new risks that need to be dealt with. Firstly, due to the rise of social networking sites, most notably Facebook, typical user names are becoming less common and real data is used instead. Now ramifications of compromised accounts are more serious and could possibly lead to identity theft. Recent case of personal data leakage involving Facebook, when private details of 100 million users were exposed, illustrates the gravity of situation (Hough, 2010). Secondly, the proliferation of the Internet has given rise to electronic commerce or e-commerce, based on buying and selling online. Because the trust is essential for successful business transactions, the difficulties in protecting information confidentiality and integrity have the greatest impact on e-commerce development. The problem is significant decrease of confidence in online payment system when there is even the slightest possibility or mere rumor of potential flaws in terms of security or convenience. Most of the users still have concerns about the privacy when dealing with "faceless" e-commerce web sites. Similarly, some users are more cautious and more reluctant to adopt new trends, like social networking web sites, due to the fears of their personal information being unrightfully exposed. Even though most of the people are reckless unless material well being (i.e., the money) is involved, in time, as the dangers of stolen private information become apparent, service providers in general will definitely be compelled to do more in order to reassure customers and keep their trust.

Computers could be compared to buildings, due to the fact that both keep some objects and, more or less, guard them against intruders and limit the access to those who are authorized. Considering the buildings, most of them have doors and locks, which is the basic security measure. However, throughout history, with new technologies and ideas, new mechanisms were invented and then used in combination with common locks. These new, different mechanisms are normally not considered as a replacement to one another, but rather an additional security layer to be used together with what was already there. So today, breaking into a museum and retrieving a valuable artifact is not an easy task and requires highly skilled team of diverse expertise and skills. In addition to locked doors there are guards, security cameras, lasers and bulletproof glass boxes that need to be faced.

The reason some buildings have more security layers than others, is because they host objects which are of greater value. In the same way, as the Internet applications become more diverse and more complex, the value of user account relevant information becomes higher and of greater importance. Therefore, with increasing number of applications handling private information, the time has come to consider another layer for user authentication, in addition to common method of user name and password combination. The chances of assuming other person's identity or tampering with their account information would be smaller that way, since more resources would be required on attacker's side in terms of money, skill and work force. Furthermore, the users of various Internet services would be reassured and thus feel more confident to entrust their private information to the providers. However, there is additional factor that needs to be kept in mind while devising a solution. No matter how effective authentication method may be, the success of it also depends on user convenience which entails ease of use and mobility.

There are three general methods to validate user's identity: something they know (username and password), something they have (smart card) and something about them (biometrics) (Stamp,

2006). In addition to common username and password login, the proposed solution is the involvement of mobile phone hosting SIM (Subscriber Identity Module) card with additional functionality of securely storing critical information related to the client side computer application. Among things that smart card (i.e., SIM) stores could be keywords that acknowledge user's identity or cryptography keys that can be employed to secure the communication channels. These parameters can be combined as well or supplemented with additional ones if developers find them necessary and see it as an improvement. The key point and foundational idea is the combination of smart card's security-wise robustness (it cannot be accessed without appropriate driver and authorized reader) and convenience of using familiar and common mobile phone in the secured Internet authentication and communication. This provides more efficient protection against Trojans and malicious individuals that seek to deceive and exploit. Computer application, or certain parts of it (those dealing with money transfer, for example), can work only in conjunction with mobile phone equipped with such card, which passes required data such as encryption keys or credit card number trough the proximity access technology.

Consequently, sensitive information (such as encryption keys) is more secured, being stored within the SIM card and transferred/updated through more private mobile phone network instead of the Internet. In other words, specific money transaction related information still travels through the internet, but the data required for public key encryption (or any other algorithm for information protection purposes) is separated, traveling through the different channel, namely mobile phone network. Upon online payment or access to some other privacy sensitive feature, consumers are required to merely present their mobile phone, which they are familiar and comfortable with. The knowledge of technical details is unnecessary.

Although the involvement of mobile phone and mobile phone network are assumed, due to the resource and hardware availability limitations, actual mobile phone was not used during the prototype development and testing. At the current stage, contactless smart card was utilized working on the similar principle in order to make a proof of concept. The difference is that mobile phones bring convenience in terms of usage and SIM card parameters are easier to update (using mobile phone network), without user being required to be aware of the procedure.

1. LITERATURE REVIEW

The literature review initiated the research and partially served as an inspiration for the ideas developed. There were two different periods of focused reading activity. The first part focuses more on opinions related to the successful e-commerce planning and discussions dealing with user preference, rather than technical details and specifications. E-commerce is explored as currently most discussed area when it comes to user trust and acceptance, because loss of money seems to be greater issue at the time compared to personal data theft. After that, technical foundations are established and reviewed through the research of related technologies. It includes introduction to smart cards as well as explanation of some more specific card types and technologies that are useful for expressing imagined solution.

Online Payment/Banking Issues

There are three social aspects regarding electronic payment systems that provide users' trust and acceptance:

- **Anonymity:** Protecting consumers' privacy by establishing security measures as well as preventing financial institutions and companies from tracking users by storing their relevant data, such as product preferences.

- **User Friendliness:** Important factor for users when choosing the payment method entails convenience and ease of usage.
- **Mobility:** Users do not want to be tied to the PC when making an online purchase. Since many PCs have multiple users, preferred feature is payment system independence on computer hardware, i.e. system can be used anywhere (Lee, Yu, & Ku, 2001).

Many other researchers in the field confirm these three requirements based on their observations, experiments or discussions. They are sometimes partially mentioned (one or two of the three being omitted), or one aspect is given more importance over the other. Still, unless the literature review is very narrow, none of the three characteristics can be overlooked.

Issues of anonymity and privacy are related to proper authentication, data integrity and non-repudiation (whereby participants are prevented from denying commitments made in a transaction). When talking about the convenience, questions of user friendliness and mobility come into the picture.

In order to improve user experience, online payment or banking systems should guarantee security while money transaction activities remain simple and easy. Systems should be stable, update relevant information on time and record it accurately for proper account management (Sheng & Lu, 2009). Customers realize greater risk they are exposed to while conducting payments over the internet and that is one of the main obstacles for faster acceptance of e-commerce trend. A survey presented in one of the reviewed papers shows that, among consumers that do not use online payments, 43.44% are not confident because of "the security risk," 19.67% are not paying online because "they do not like online banking," 22.13%

feel the payment procedure lacks convenience and the remaining 14.75% are not making online payments for "other reasons". The 63.76% of the participants believe that their personal financial information might go to a third party while using online payment systems. The survey also shows that a great number of participants lack awareness related to the security issues. So, for instance, 66.41% are not familiar with the concept of phishing (Karim, Rezaul, & Hossain, 2009).

The different privacy or security risks are related to different payment methods. While purchasing online, people generally prefer to use credit cards because under the Fair Credit Billing Act, buyers have the right to withhold payment on poor-quality or damaged merchandise purchased with a credit card. Even though this is the most popular method in e-commerce, there is a great number of potential online buyers that are afraid to put their trust in it. The main concerns are possibility of card information being intercepted by malicious third party during the transaction over the Internet and misusage of the information by the sellers (Li & Zhang, 2004).

Most of the banks are not ready to face the challenge of a steady number of increases concerning various cyber threats that constantly change and evolve. Single-factor authentication system is still predominant, whereby customers are only required to provide user name and single password for accessing their account (Karim, Rezaul, & Hossain, 2009). Even though, to some extent, protection can be offered to customers through comprehensive international legislation and surveillance (Araujo, 2005), establishing trust requires innovation and continuous service improvement (Sheng & Lu, 2009). Involving another security layer is one of the recommendations for security enhancement (Forman, 2008), yet since the convenience plays important role in making shopping and online money transactions acceptable online (Li & Zhang, 2004), this angle cannot be neglected either.

Since one of the three general methods to validate users' identity is to provide something that they have, there have been some proposals mentioning involvement of external secure element, like smart card or hardware device (Puente, Sandoval, Hernandez, & Molina, 2005).

User identity and information filtering are important in validating user and delivering process/service. Riordan and Sorensen provided an overview of the developments that have occurred in the field of information filtering (Riordan & Sorensen). In 1993, a system used Bayesian interface network for representing documents and user profile is also has been proposed (Callan, Groft, & Harding, 1993). Buckley suggested a smart model for retrieval information (Buckley, 1985). Yan and Garcia-Molina are proposed a retrieval system allows users to submitting their profiles via WWW browser (Buckley, Salton, Allan, &Singhal, 1994).

The secure element holds information (for instance, a key or digital signature) that is required for successful login or communication. In this context, there are several examples involving the mobile phone. Some of those are the online banking authentication protocol that involves the use of mobile phones to securely store clients' digital certificates (Fang & Zhan, 2010) and the use of a mobile phone that acts as a security device to protect the privacy of a buyer's private payments details (credit card number) in an online payment transaction (Al-Dala'in, Summons, & Luo, 2009). In the latter case, the study examined the influence of using mobile devices to enhance an online shopper's trust in the use of e-payment systems. The results demonstrate that the adoption of mobile devices have significant and direct effects on shoppers' trust. However, the ways of storing, securing or managing the critical information was not addressed in depth.

Related Technologies

Smart card or integrated circuit card (ICC) is self-programmable one chip microcomputer (SPOM) that has its own microprocessor, memory,

and communication port. Smart card operating system with own applications can be embedded in these devices and files can be managed and stored (Urien, 2000, 2008). The most importantly, smart cards are tamper resistant devices that can be accessed only with respective driver, so they can be used to preserve integrity of the data. The Smart Card Simulator, which is freely available, was used for initial tests, that were more focused on understanding of smart card inner design and ways it communicates with the reader. In context of our work, the role of the smart card is to ensure that user related information, unique for each person, is secured so that it is not illegally accessed or tampered with.

Although use of typical plastic cards is well established today, next generation smart card applications should adopt different approach for the following reasons:

- Card application is often subject to fraud.
- Number of physical cards per user is ever increasing.
- Card provision takes time and money.
- Card typically needs to be manually inserted into service client user interface (Steffens, Nennker, Ren, Yin, & Schneider, 2009).

Based on the above mentioned points, the popular trend is migration of multiple cards functionality to a single mobile device. While adopting the common principle whereby, sensitive data used for configuration (Lahlou & Urien, 2003; Badra & Urien, 2004; Segura, Sanchez, Madrid, & Seepold, 2005; Urien, 2008) and authentication (Loutrel, Urien, & Pujolle, 2003) is secured within the smartcard, we want to eliminate aforementioned problems related to the smart card when in plastic card form. Mobile phone is the best alternative, since everyone is familiar with the device, meaning that there is no need to introduce new kinds of hardware that user would have to adapt to. Instead, the mobile phone functionality is merely being extended. Secure element that keeps all sensitive data safe is Universal Integrated Circuit Card (UICC), which is next generation of SIM cards. Used primarily in GSM and UTMS networks to keep account information, it can hold number of other applications. In other words, SIM is just one of the applications running on the smart card (Park, Kim, & Kim, 2008; Alimi & Pasquet, 2009). Theoretically, a single UICC could contain multiple SIMs (meaning additional accounts or phone numbers), or any other kind of applications given by card issuer or other authorized parties. Memory is the only limit for number of services that can be provided through UICC, so conceptually, a mobile phone equipped with it becomes universal personal token represent each individual. It can be used as ID, bank card, bus ticket, or as this paper proposes - a security element that confirms person's identity on the Internet and protects personal privacy when needed.

In addition to remote service access (GSM or UTMS), a mobile phone needs proximity access as well, so that previously mentioned new functions can be implemented successfully. The Near Field Communication (NFC) provides the feature, turning a mobile device into payment, ticketing, or access rights entity. One of the motivations for the designers was secured transfer of information. Therefore, NFC is a short-range wireless technology (10 cm maximum distance), operating at 13.56 MHz and exchanging data between two devices at up to 424 Kbits per second. There is a wide range of electronic devices that can utilize this technology, like cameras, game consoles, SD cards etc. However, NFC applications are mostly related to the mobile phone usage. Nokia launched first NFC-enabled phone in November 2004. Perhaps due to the lack of convincing business plans or market demands, NFC is not widely spread at the moment. But in spite of challenges faced, Nokia has recently announced that from 2011 every Nokia smart phone will have NFC. A study from year 2008 predicted over 700 million NFC-enabled mobile phones in usage by the 2013 (Reveilhac & Pasquet, 2009).

The NFC forum, founded in June 2006, outlines three operating modes for NFC:

- **Peer-To-Peer Mode:** Communication needs to be established between two NFC-enabled devices before data can be exchanged,
- **Reader/Writer Mode:** NFC-enabled device is able to read/write information from smart cards or tags (embedded on posters, for example),
- **Card Emulation Mode:** NFC-enabled device emulates contactless smart card. Secure element, such as UICC for mobile phone, ensures data safety, meaning that high security dependent services are acceptable (Reveilhac & Pasquet, 2009).

2. OUR APPROACH

A SIM card, a type of smart card, is installed in the mobile phone, so a typical user does not have to be aware of its presence while benefiting from its security characteristics. By securely storing the critical information, the SIM card causes the mobile phone to inherit its security capabilities and thus become the secure entity. For this purpose typical SIM card functionality would have to be extended, so it would also hold the information which is relevant for the internet authentication.

Moreover, it is thought of authentication in general terms, relating to the all Internet applications, in an attempt to make this approach universal making the mobile phone standard secure element that everyone will use.

To initiate application functionality that involves private data, besides requirement to log in using their user name and password, a customer needs to present the mobile phone, a security token, which should establish the communication with personal computer in use and pass the information that user/client application expects. With this kind of arrangement, SIM card hosted information is protected from unauthorized access and malware threats while being at application's disposal when needed. At the same time, convenience component is taken into consideration, since everyone is familiar with the mobile phone, meaning that there is no need to introduce new kinds of hardware that user would have to adapt to. Instead, the mobile phone functionality is merely being extended.

In our proposed solution, mobile phone goes into card emulation mode to communicate with a computer trough contactless NFC interface, so that the information relevant for the authentication process can be exchanged. Figure 1 shows an NFC-enabled phone.

That information can be anything that developers find appropriate, but in the following discus-

sions and prototypes, public key pair was used. Storing keys in the smart card serves to the purpose of strengthening the public key cryptography approach, by making illegal access to the keys harder. Sometimes also called Diffie-Hellman encryption after its inventors Whitfield Diffie and Martin Hellman in 1976, public key cryptography is fundamental technology, well known and widely used, serving as a foundation for several Internet standards such as Transport Layer Security (TLS), Pretty Good Privacy (PGP) and GNU Privacy Guard (GPG). Asymmetric key algorithm is employed to create mathematically related key pair for each user: public key and private key. Whatever is encrypted with the public key can only be decrypted with corresponding private key. Public key is known to everyone and freely distributed by the user, so that others can encrypt a message for them, whereas the private key that

Figure 1. Smart card authentication architecture for internet applications using NFC enabled phone

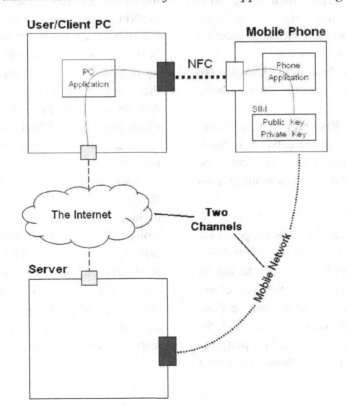

decrypts the data is kept locally, known only to the recipient. No private key is ever transmitted or shared, so there is no need for secured channel or other kind of pre-existing arrangement.

Proposed approach is the placement of user keys in the SIM card, thus enabling the mobile phone to become trusted, secured authentication entity for Internet applications. The keys are passed and kept within computer memory only when they need to be used or to get transferred via the Internet. Once the job is done, sensitive data is discarded. This approach has several advantages:

- **Improved Robustness:** Securing sensitive data, private key primarily, in tamper-resistant smart card memory and accessing/updating it trough trusted gateway (PC application) or mobile network when requested.
- **Multiple Access Technologies (GSM/ UTMS and NFC):** Objects to the SIM card can be passed directly through the mobile network (rather than using NFC interface and the Internet), thus splitting delivery of the content, making connection tracking much more difficult.
- **Portability and Seamless Usage:** No need to manually configure or memorize anything.
- **Mobile Network Provider as Certificate Authority (CA):** Mobile network is trusted third party in user communication, verifying identities of each participant and assigning the keys.

It is important to note that this proposal introduces only a new security layer. When doing authentication, user would still have to log in using their user name and password. Therefore, merely possessing someone else's phone does not mean immediate access to their account. So in case of theft or loss, privacy and property remains protected. When mobile phone is reported

missing, local mobile service provider should block the SIM making it useless and preventing potential dangers.

Four usage scenarios are presented as example for better understanding of the architecture, i.e. signing in, e-mail encryption and ensuring record integrity and non-repudiation and online payment procedure. In all cases, the mobile phone interacts with the user computers connected to the Internet. The mobile phone is equipped with SIM card that holds data required for public key cryptography. Depending on the memory available, encryption/decryption can be performed by the card itself or the user computer hosted gateway application that communicates with it.

Signing In

In this case user utilizes his mobile phone to get access rights for certain Internet application. Rather than providing any information through the keyboard, they present the mobile phone to the NFC interface installed on the PC. Then public key should be transferred to the application server in one of the two possible ways. First possibility is that public key is passed directly through the gateway application and on the Internet. Alternatively, the SIM card could only give the phone number. With that information, application server could request for user's public key from the telecommunication company using mobile phone network. This approach is more secure as it splits the information distribution in two channels. Once in the possession of user's public key, the server would use it to encrypt random word or phrase and then send the result back. Now the data can be decrypted only with the recipient's private key, so if user can give expected response they are allowed to go through. To add more security, user could use server's public key to encrypt the response, or their own private key to provide signature that could be verified with appropriate public key on the server side.

E-Mail Encryption

E-mail encryption aims to establish confidential communication and preserve message integrity. Similar to previous case, the sender would require recipient's public key to encrypt the e-mail. Only the addressee will be able to decrypt it using their private key. One of the two aforementioned channels is used to deliver public key if the system is meant for the Internet users in general. The drawback is that the phone number needs to be known, in addition to e-mail, when number of possible recipients is unlimited. On other hand, depending on preferences and needs, the solution could be applied only for a specific group. If there are 20 users that would be involved, then each of the SIM cards that are distributed among them would hold a personal private key and 19 public keys mapped to the 19 email addresses. Therefore, no data exchange between the cards is needed. The security level is higher, however, at the expense of encrypted communication being available only to these selected individuals.

Ensuring Record Integrity and Non-Repudiation

In the last scenario, the web browser monitoring system is revisited as an example for non-repudiation and integrity. Non-repudiation means the ability to prove that a transaction, communication or access originated from a particular party. Therefore, that party cannot deny that they performed a certain action. A receiver cannot deny that he received a certain message from a sender, and a sender cannot deny that he sent a message to the receiver.

Browsing record file is the output, signed by user's private key to guarantee integrity and provide non-repudiation. The person in charge of the records would browse through them on regular basis and take action when necessary. The public key is used to verify the integrity of the record by the administrator. If the record is not clear when public key is applied to it, the administrator will know that something is amiss.

Online Payment Procedure

In this particular case, where secure element is used for online payment purposes, encryption/decryption keys are placed in the SIM card. They are transferred to the PC only when needed and discarded afterwards. Besides interacting with the PC with mobile phone as an intermediary, the SIM card can be accessed by the telecommunication company. The telecommunication company becomes certification authority in this case, being able to regularly update the keys without need for customers' participation. Data transfer can be performed on two channels with mobile network being used for key transportation. Like this, possibility of key theft is brought to a minimum because they would not be passed over the Internet. In addition to the keys, SIM card may be used to hold other information, if it is deemed more convenient and more secured (e.g., credit card number).

3. PROTOTYPES

Classroom Booking and Management System

The Classroom Booking and Management System is an application used to demonstrate security enhancements that smart card driven authentication provides. The application uses Mifare 1k card and ACR122U NFC reader.

Booking a venue is usually a tedious process which requires office visits and a lot of paperwork. This sometimes causes confusion and mistakes which later cause trouble for everyone. The system intends to eliminate paper driven procedures and make things simple and easy. Booking works on point and click basis. The application screen is dominated by classroom timetable which is the main part of the program. In order to log in and use the application, each user is required to provide name and password. Users are lecturers who intend to book the venue and administrators with the role of overlooking the whole process making sure that everything goes smoothly.

The difference between administrator and lecturer is in terms of privileges and functions. Both of them can change password, or switch classroom timetable. But on the other hand, an administrator has an ability to book more slots and can cancel the booking for anyone. On top of that, administrator is also allowed to add or remove new users (Figure 2).

However, in order to access "Administrator's Control Panel," which enables the addition of new users and removal of existing ones, every administrator has to provide appropriate smart card. This way, when performing action that can cause more damage, additional security measures are imposed. Administrators are still able to login using their user name and password, but they would be allowed only to manage the timetables

if smart card is not presented. So even if administrator's password was stolen and unauthorized access occurred, possible corrupted time tables are not as serious problem as tempering with user list and user personal details would be.

For this implementation ACR122U NFC Reader from Advanced Card Systems was used together with Mifare 1k contactless cards. Instead of public key cryptography, simpler approach was used in this application. A certain word is stored in both smart card and program. The comparison between program's string variable value and string retrieved from the smart card determines the validity of authentication attempt. If words are equal, "Administrator's Control Panel" gets enabled. Figure 3 shows a few different outcomes depending on smart card validity or presence.

To get key word from the smart card, there are four compulsory steps. Functions for each one of them are part of the sample program provided by the ACR122U manufacturer. The first step is the initialization of smart card/NFC reader. Then using the second function reader gets connected to the smart card. In our case the reader is ACS ACR122 as shown in Figure 4(a). After that, coming to the third part, reader needs to get authenticated in relation to the specific block within smart card that it wants to read from or

Figure 2. The classroom booking and management system generally has standard user name and password login for the users

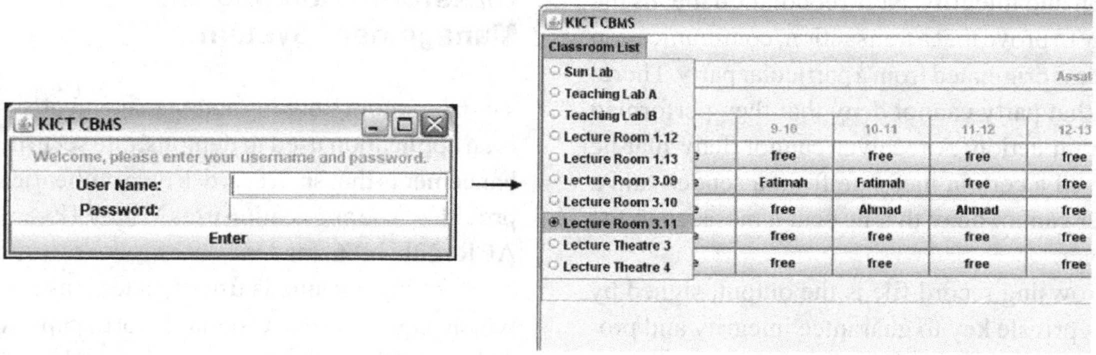

Figure 3. For the classroom booking and management system administrator privileges, smart card holding certain keyword is required

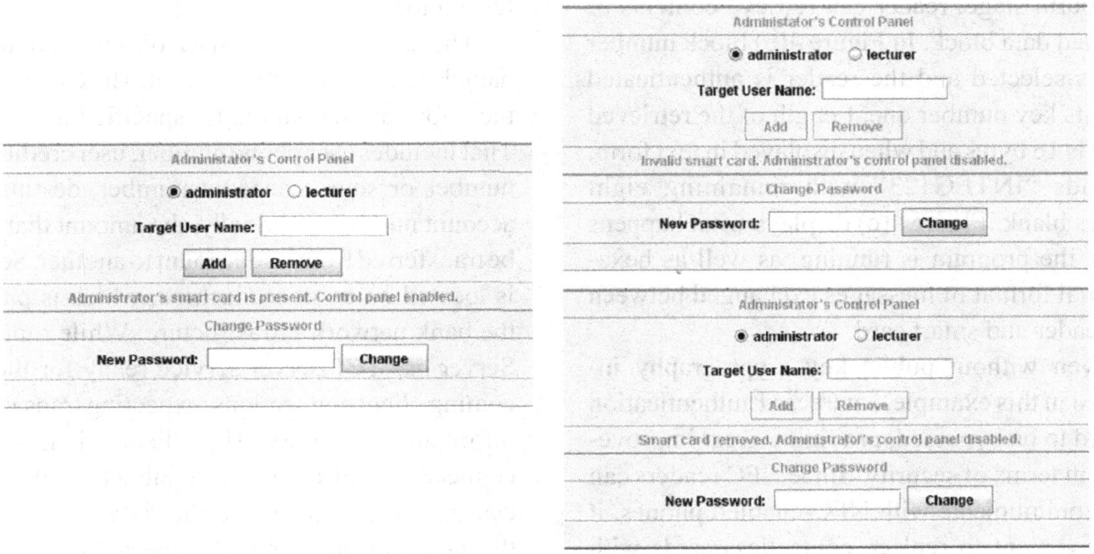

Figure 4. Mifare card programming compiled from ACR122U reader

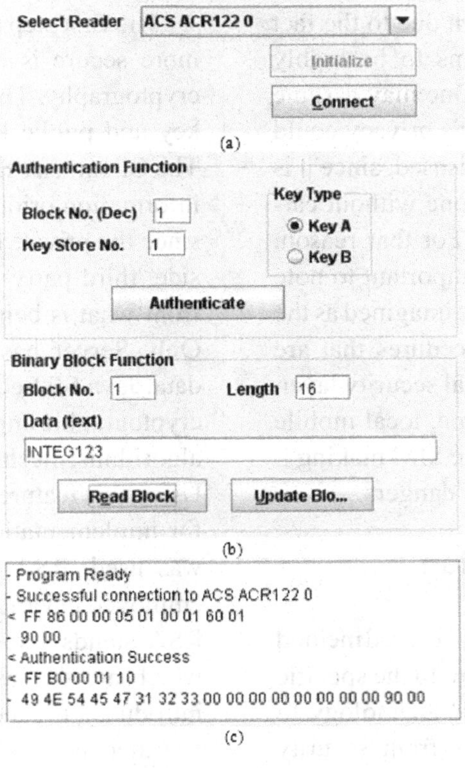

```
- Program Ready
- Successful connection to ACS ACR122 0
< FF 86 00 00 05 01 00 01 60 01
- 90 00
< Authentication Success
< FF B0 00 01 10
- 49 4E 54 45 47 31 32 33 00 00 00 00 00 00 00 00 90 00
```

(c)

write to. In this case it is data block that is known for storing the application key word. Finally, in the fourth stage, reader can retrieve contents of targeted data block. In Figure 4(b) block number one is selected and the reader is authenticated with its key number one. Length of the retrieved word is 16 bytes and when displayed in text form, it reads "INTEG123" with remaining eight spaces blank. Figure 4(c) displays what happens while the program is running, as well as hexadecimal format of messages exchanged between the reader and smart card.

Even without public key cryptography involved in this example, smart card authentication is hard to be bypassed, providing great improvement in terms of security. Since NFC readers can also communicate with NFC-enabled phones, it is convenient to replace contactless cards with them in the future. In the later mentioned money transfer prototype application that was developed later, the public key cryptography was used for further improvement in security-wise robustness.

There might be some concern due to the fact that proposed architecture seems to be highly dependable on mobile device. One may assume that in case of theft or loss, user's privacy could be jeopardized and privileges misused, since it is only required to display the phone without carrier's confirmation of identity. For that reason, as it is mentioned earlier, it is important to note that this authentication method is imagined as the supplement to the existing procedures that are used, having the role of additional security layer. In cases of missing mobile phone, local mobile service provider should block the SIM making it useless and preventing potential dangers.

Money Transfer Application

This prototype is given to illustrate secured method of money transfer from credit card to the specific bank account by using the NFC technology to pass encryption/decryption keys from security element to the computer application. As in the previous case, Java Standard Edition 6 Development Kit (JDK) was utilized as development and testing tool.

The application consists of two programs, namely the Client and the Server. The Client takes the information required for specific transaction. That includes user phone number, user credit card number or source account number, destination account number and finally, the amount that is to be transferred from one account to another. Server is located on another machine, which is part of the bank network infrastructure. While running, Server has TCP server service ready for the incoming client connections, expecting transaction information to come. The Client initiates TCP connection and after it is established, the data can be transferred. Once the data is available, the bank can carry on with expected protocol by executing appropriate transaction. However, the focus, in relation to this prototype, is security and protection of privacy during the process of data being sent from Client to the Server.

The first step towards making the application more secure is involvement of the public key cryptography. The Server side keeps the private key and public key is available for the Client. The Client uses the public key to encrypt critical information prior to sending it to the Server and since the private key is safely kept on the Server side, third party is unable to gain any meaning from what is being passed through the Internet. Only Server has the means of decrypting the data. Java SE Security API contains a number of cryptographic implementations as well as security algorithms, mechanisms and protocols in general. Using this feature as part of JDK, RSA algorithm for implementation of public key cryptography was used. RSA is widespread and commonly employed in variety of e-commerce applications. RSA stands for Rivest, Shamir and Adleman, which are the last names of the scientists that introduced the method in 1978 (Rivest, Shamir, & Adleman, 1978). After key pair is generated, the private key is kept within the Server and corresponding public key is given to the Client, so that the private and secured communication can be established.

However, this application is different from other similar solutions in terms of key storage. In order to additionally enhance security, public key that Client uses, is stored in the smart card that needs to be presented before any transaction details can be transmitted. In case that user logs in with his user name and password without the smart card (Figure 5) being available, his information and transactions details are available, but payment cannot be made.

The ACR122U NFC Reader from Advanced Card Systems (ACR), a PC-linked contactless smart card reader/writer, is used, as in previous

case, to satisfy the hardware requirement. Being compliant with PC/SC (short for "Personal Computer/Smart Card") specification for smart-card integration into computing environments, it is compatible and interoperable across different applications and platforms. Via the USB interface, the reader is the intermediary device between the contactless communication device (smart card, tag, or NFC enabled device) and the personal computer. With this prototype Mifare 1K contactless card is utilized, but in addition to Mifare 1K and 4K cards, the ACR122U supports other types of cards, NFC tags and devices, as stated in accompanying user manual. That means that with additional programming, it is possible to replace current contactless card component with some-

Figure 5. Money transfer application: information available without the smart card

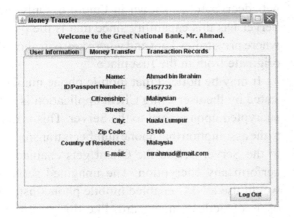

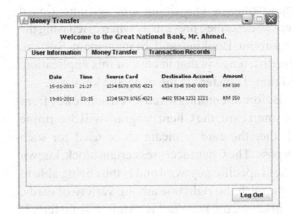

thing else viewed as more suitable and convenient for the application (i.e., NFC enabled phone, Figure 1). Mifare 1K has around 1Kbyte of user accessible memory, organized in 16 sectors with 4 blocks. Each block consists of 16 bytes.

In money transferring application, public key cryptography key pair that belongs to the Server is used, i.e. it is assumed that they are generated at the Server side. Private key is kept with the server and corresponding public keys are distributed to the Clients when need for money transfer arises. However, for security and practical benefits, the public key is not kept at the same machine with the money transferring application. Instead, public key is maintained within security token, Mifare 1K contactless card in this particular case, which needs to be presented upon attempt to use the application. With RSA, both public encryption and private decryption keys are pairs of positive integers. The public key is partitioned in words of 16 bytes and stored in some of the Mifare 1K data blocks. The number of blocks occupied, depends on the size of integer pair that represents the public key.

The Client application reads data from specific blocks of contactless card known to hold the information it needs. To get a word from the card data block, four steps are required. Software development kit, which the ACR122U NFC Reader is part of, also provides sample applications, codes, tools and utilities demonstrating reader's features and capabilities. Among them, there is a sample program explicitly examining four aforementioned steps as described previously when discussing the Classroom Booking and Management System. The difference is that in case of this application, "Money Transfer" is the expected keyword.

Before attempting to retrieve a public key from the smart card, the Client program will determine whether the card is meant to be used for such purpose. The Client accesses certain block, known to hold specific keyword and is thus being able to distinguish the right one among variety of cards. In this case, the keyword is "Money Transfer". If

the Client detects expected keyword, the "Send" button is available which enables the user to initiate connection with the Server and transfer the data which is previously typed into the text boxes. The message under "Money Transfer" tab reads: "Please provide the information required for the transfer." However, if the retrieved keyword is different than "Money Transfer," the "Send" button is unavailable and message displayed is: "Invalid smart card." There are other types of problem related to the process of getting the keyword that may occur, in which case transfer of data is not allowed as well. Depending on the situation, diagnostic message might appear as one of the following: "No PC/SC reader detected," "No Smart Card detected," or "Reader access authentication failed."

If the card is proved to be valid, then the public key is fetched from it. The public key is provided from number of card's data blocks. Words from each one of these blocks are collected one by one and concatenated together to form the integer pair that represents the public key. Once the Client is in possession of public key, the "Send" button will also be active and required data from text boxes can be sent to the Server. After user clicks on "Send" button, TCP connection to the Server will be initiated. Assuming that Server is online, the connection is established and the critical information from text boxes, such as account and credit card numbers, is encrypted. The information, including cipher text, arrives to the Server and gets decrypted, as shown in Figure 6. Only the Server has this capability since that is the place where private key kept and where key pair should originate from in the first place.

It may be noticed that mobile phone number stated by the user using Client application is not encrypted upon arrival to the Server. This is due to the assumption that phone number is transferred to the Server before the Client gets enabled to perform any encryption. The imagined service would use a NFC enabled mobile phone instead of a contactless smart card, like this prototype

Figure 6. Money transfer application: smart card information needs to be accessed in order to send money transfer particulars to the server

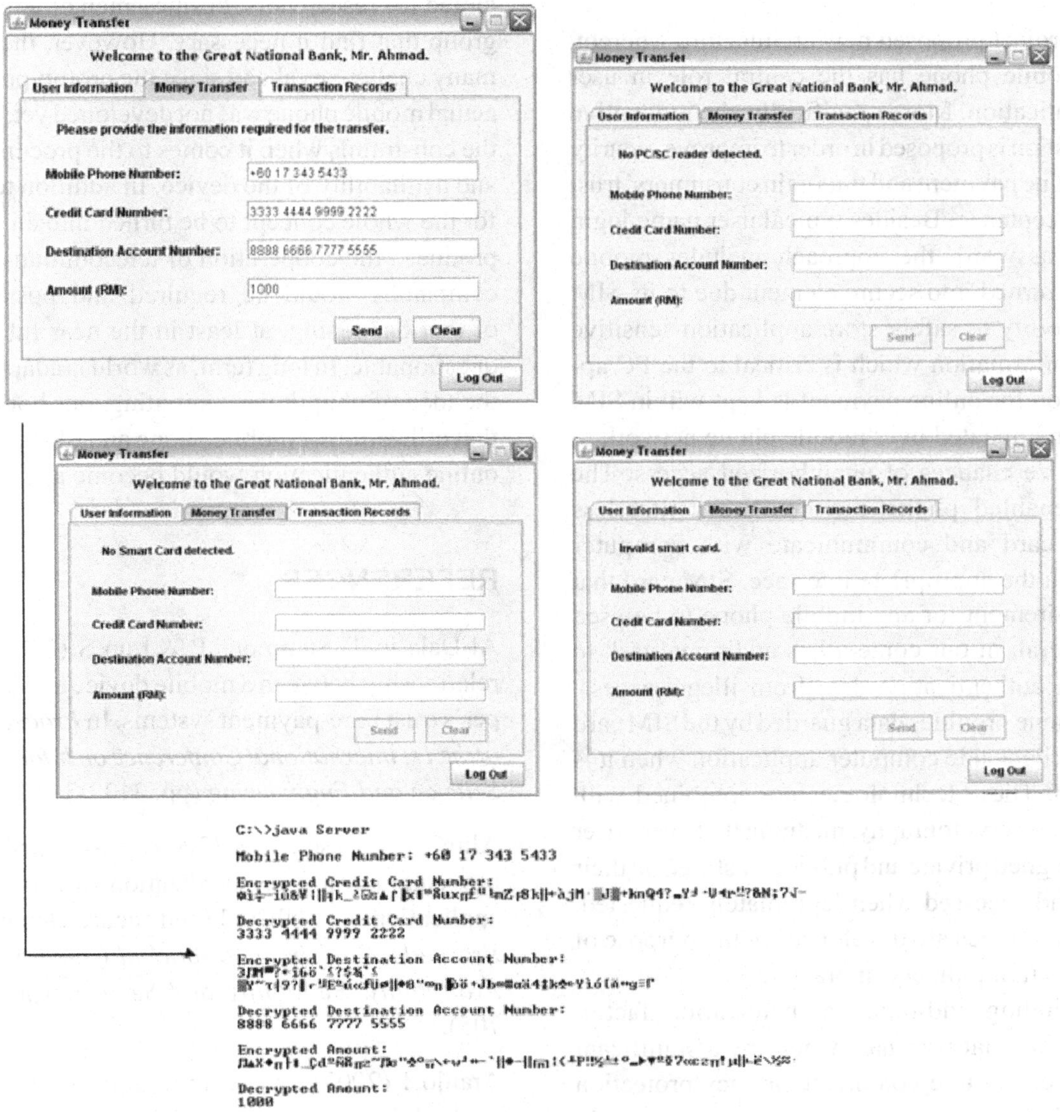

does. And since the information holder will be a SIM card within the phone, it means that both, mobile service provider and the user machine, will interact with it, while NFC enabled mobile phone is being just intermediary. So, the Client can encrypt data only after it receives the public key from the Server trough the mobile service network. Phone number needs to be given, in order for Server to know where to send the key. Therefore, the Client provides the phone number through the Internet, utilizing TCP connection.

4. CONCLUSION AND FUTURE WORKS

This project proposed new architecture whereby the mobile phone has the central role in user authentication. More specifically, the innovative suggestion is proposed in order to improve security for online payment and thus gain consumers' trust and acceptance. Besides typical user name login with password, the approach includes mobile phone turned into secure element due to its SIM card ability to safely store application sensitive data. Information which is critical to the PC application for online payment is kept within SIM card and updated over mobile phone network to minimize chances of unauthorized access. The NFC-enabled phone can emulate contactless smart card and communicate with computer through the appropriate interface. SIM card that is requirement for any mobile phone to be used in general, in our context has additional task to protect authentication data from illegal access. The phone provides data guarded by the SIM card to the client side computer application when it is needed. These technologies are combined with public key cryptography, meaning that every user has assigned private and public key stored on their card and accessed when legitimately requested. Two prototypes are developed for the purpose of demonstrating theory in practice.

Including additional authentication factor, something that user has, would be a significant improvement to e-commerce privacy protection and cyber security in general. However, to gain user acceptance, convenience and familiarity are almost as important as privacy. Because of that, omnipresent and universally known mobile phone seems to be a perfect candidate for general authentication device.

The primary aim was to devise and ponder upon ideas that would improve security, ease of access and promote development and employment of new technologies in practice, such as NFC. Plan for the future work is a development of complete applications working on this principle aimed for researchers, businessmen or any other group that find it necessary. However, there are many challenges ahead since the prototype using actual mobile phone was not developed yet, due to the constraints when it comes to the procurement and availability of the device. In addition to that, for the whole concept to be turned into an actual product - the cooperation of telecommunication companies would be required and possibility of that happening, at least in the near future, is questionable. In long term, as world is adapting to the idea of ubiquitous computing, our hopes are that utilization of mobile phone and SIM card for online authentication would become a standard.

REFERENCES

Al-Dala'in, T., Summons, P., & Luo, S. (2009). The relationship between a mobile device and a shopper's trust for e-payment systems. In *Proceedings of the 1st International Conference on Information Science and Engineering* (pp. 3132-3135).

Alimi, V., & Pasquet, M. (2009). Post-distribution provisioning and personalization of a payment application on a UICC-based secure element. In *Proceedings of the International Conference on Availability, Reliability and Security* (pp. 701-705).

Araujo, I. (2005). Privacy mechanisms supporting the building of trust in e-commerce. In *Proceedings of the 21st International Conference on Data Engineering Workshops* (pp. 1193-1193).

Badra, M., & Urien, P. (2004). Toward SSL integration in SIM SmartCards. In *Proceedings of the Wireless Communications and Networking Conference* (pp. 889- 893)

Buckley, C. (1985). *Implementation of the smart information retrieval system* (Tech. Rep. No. TR85-686). Ithaca, NY: Cornell University.

Buckley, C., Salton, G., Allan, J., & Singhal, A. (1994). *Automatic query expansion using smart: Trec 3*. Ithaca, NY: Cornell University.

Callan, J. P., Groft, W. B., & Harding, S. M. (1993). *The inquiry retrieval system*. Amherst, MA: University of Massachusetts.

Fang, X., & Zhan, J. (2010). Online banking authentication using mobile phones. In *Proceedings of the 5th International Conference on Future Information Technology* (pp. 1-5).

Forman, A. E. (2008). E-commerce privacy and trust: Overview and foundation. In *Proceedings of the First International Conference on the Applications of Digital Information and Web Technologies* (pp. 50-53).

Hough, A. (2010). *Facebook security fears after private details of 100m users leaked to web*. Retrieved from http://www.telegraph.co.uk/technology/facebook/7915572/Facebook-security-fears-after-private-details-of-100m-users-leaked-to-web.html

Karim, Z., Rezaul, K. M., & Hossain, A. (2009). Towards secure information systems in online banking. In *Proceedings of the International Conference on Internet Technology and Secured Transactions* (pp. 1-6).

Lahlou, A., & Urien, P. (2003). SIM-filter: User profile based smart information filtering and personalization in smartcard. In *Proceedings of the 15th Conference on Advanced Information Systems Engineering*.

Lee, Z.-Y., Yu, H.-C., & Ku, P.-J. (2001). An analysis and comparison of different types of electronic payment systems. In *Proceedings of the Portland International Conference on Management of Engineering and Technology* (pp. 38-45).

Li, H., & Zhang, H. (2004). How people select their payment methods in online auctions? An exploration of eBay transactions. In *Proceedings of the 37th Annual Hawaii International Conference on System Sciences* (p. 10).

Loutrel, M., Urien, P., & Pujolle, G. (2003). A smartcard for authentication in WLANs. In *Proceedings of the IFIP/ACM Latin America Conference on Towards a Latin American Agenda for Network Research*.

Park, J., Kim, K., & Kim, M. (2008). The Aegis: UICC based security framework. In *Proceedings of the Second International Conference on: Future Generation Communication and Networking* (pp. 264-269).

Puente, F., Sandoval, J. D., Hernandez, P., & Molina, C. (2005). Improving online banking security with hardware devices. In *Proceedings of the 39th Annual International Carnahan Conference on Security Technology* (pp. 174-177).

Reveilhac, M., & Pasquet, M. (2009). Promising secure element alternatives for NFC technology. In *Proceedings of the First International Workshop on Near Field Communication* (pp. 75-80).

Riordan, C., & Sorensen, H. (1994). Information filtering and retrieval: An overview. In *Proceedings of the IEEE 16th Annual International Conference on Engineering in Medicine and Biology Society*, Baltimore. *MD Medical Newsmagazine, 1*, 42–49.

Rivest, R., Shamir, A., & Adleman, L. (1978). A method for obtaining digital signatures and public-key cryptosystems. *Communications of the ACM, 21*(2), 120–126. doi:10.1145/359340.359342

Segura, J. A. V., Sanchez, J. J. S., Madrid, N. M., & Seepold, R. (2005). Integration of smart cards into automation networks. In *Proceedings of the Third International Workshop on Intelligent Solutions in Embedded Systems* (pp. 185-193).

Sheng, M., & Lu, X.-X. (2009). An empirical study on influencing factors of customer satisfaction to individual internet banking. In *Proceedings of the International Symposium on Computer Network and Multimedia Technology* (pp. 1-4).

Stamp, M. (2006). *Information security principles and practice*. Hoboken, NJ: John Wiley & Sons.

Steffens, E., Nennker, A., Ren, Z., Yin, M., & Schneider, L. (2009). The SIM-based mobile wallet. In *Proceedings of the 13th International Conference on Intelligence in Next Generation Networks* (pp. 1-6).

Urien, P. (2000). Internet Card, a smart card as a true Internet node. *Computer Communications*, *23*(17). doi:10.1016/S0140-3664(00)00252-8

Urien, P. (2008). TLS-tandem: A collaborative technology for trusted WEB applications. In *Proceedings of the International Symposium on Collaborative Technologies and Systems* (pp. 540-546).

This work was previously published in the International Journal of Mobile Computing and Multimedia Communications, Volume 3, Issue 4, edited by Ismail Khalil and Edgar Weippl, pp. 67-83, copyright 2011 by IGI Publishing (an imprint of IGI Global).

Section 2
Commerce

Chapter 9
Systems Development Methodology for Mobile Commerce Applications

Muazzan Binsaleh
Prince of Songkla University, Thailand

Shahizan Hassan
Universiti Utara Malaysia, Malaysia

ABSTRACT

There are several methodologies, including traditional and agile methodologies, being utilized in current systems development. However, it could be argued that existing development methodologies may not be suitable for mobile commerce applications, as these applications are utilized in different contexts from fixed e-commerce applications. This study proposes a system development methodology for mobile commerce applications. In order to achieve this aim, four objectives are proposed: investigating existing systems development methodologies used to develop mobile commence applications, identifying strengths and weaknesses of existing development methodologies, construction of a suitable methodology for mobile commerce applications, and testing for its applicability and practicality. The research methodology used in the study is the design research, which includes the steps of awareness of problems, suggestion, development, evaluation and conclusion. However, this paper only focuses on the first two phases of the whole study, which are awareness of the problem and making suggestions, while the evaluation and conclusion will be conducted as future works.

INTRODUCTION

Mobile commerce, commonly known as m-commerce, typically designates the use of wireless devices (particularly mobile phones) to conduct electronic business transactions, such as product ordering, fund transfer, and stock trading, (Kalakota & Robinson, 2002). According to Liang, Huang, Yeh, and Lin (2007), mobile commerce refers to any transactions, either direct or indirect, via mobile devices, such as phones or Personal Digital Assistants (PDAs). While many different

DOI: 10.4018/978-1-4666-2163-3.ch009

definitions of mobile commerce exist in the literature (Truel & Yuan, 2006), these usually refer to e-commerce activities conducted through mobile devices such as mobile phones and Personal Digital Assistants (PDAs).

Mobile commerce is viewed as the next generation e-commerce (Liang et al., 2007). With the rapid proliferation of mobile devices, including mobile phones, PDAs, and handheld computers, mobile commerce is widely considered to be a driving force for next generation e-commerce (Liang & Wei, 2004). It is therefore necessary to investigate how to design and develop mobile commerce applications to ensure the successfulness of their deployment. The power of m-commerce is primarily due to the anytime-anywhere connectivity of wireless devices, which provide enormous opportunities for business process innovation and location-sensitive services (Zwass, 2003). And with the increasing popularity of mobile appliances, the most effective means of providing these services in a wireless mobile environment should be found (Zhou, Islam, & Ismael, 2004). However, careful consideration should be taken when developing mobile commerce applications since they are utilized in different contexts from those typical e-commerce, they are mobility and portability.

There are several systems development methodologies including traditional and agile methodologies which are being utilized in current systems development (Blum, 1996; Highsmith, 1999; Krutchen, 2001; Cao & Ramesh, 2007). However, based on the analysis of the related literature, it could be argued that existing development methodologies may not be suitable for mobile commerce applications as these applications are utilized in different contexts from typical ecommerce applications such as they are displayed on a small screen device, they are utilized in an unstable or movable environment and they need to be used in a secured environment to deliver financial transactions over mobile network (Varshney &

Vetter, 2002; Tarasewich, 2003; Lee & Benbasat, 2004; Khalifa & Shen, 2008).

There are many research problems which are related to m-commerce applications and services that are raised by researchers. One of them is proposed by Varshney and Vetter (2002) who argue that there is a need for a research to identify strategies and methodology that carriers, vendors, providers, and managers can use in the development of m-commerce applications and services. Henceforth, this study attempts to partly tackle this issue by examining and investigating the suitable system development methodology for mobile commerce applications which carriers, vendors, providers, and managers can utilize. The system development methodology to be proposed should conform to the most significant features of mobile technology, which are mobility and portability (Liang et al., 2007).

Ngai and Gunasekaran (2007), on the other hand, found that if considering the research published in the field of mobile commerce theory and research, it was revealed that the research in the field of development of m-commerce applications and guidelines is only 7.7% comparing to 30.7% in m-commerce behavioral issues (consumer behavior, acceptance of technology, and diffusion of technology), 29.2% in m-commerce economics, strategy and business models, 10.7% in m-commerce legal and ethical issues, and 21.77% in m-commerce overview, context, and usage. Thus this number illustrated that there is a research gap in the field of the development of m-commerce applications and guidelines and henceforth this research area should be examined to fill the knowledge gap.

In order to construct the suitable development methodology for mobile commerce applications, there are several areas to be focused including existing systems development methodologies, mobile commerce, mobile commerce applications, mobile devices and mobile networking. With these related subject areas, there are several issues that should be addressed. In particular, as these applications hold e-commerce activities conducted through mobile devices such as mobile phones and Personal Digital Assistants (PDAs), it therefore poses several development issues (Turel & Yuan, 2006) that will be addressed in this study which include:

- The context awareness issue in the analysis phase of development process.
- Integration of the principles of user interface design for small screen mobile device hardware in the design phase of development process.
- Tackling the issues of transaction security over mobile network in the early phases of development process.
- The integration of all the issues above into the systems development life cycle of mobile commerce applications in order to formulate a suitable system development methodology for mobile commerce applications.

The main research objective is to identify a suitable methodology for developing mobile commerce applications. In order to achieve this objective, four sub-objectives are proposed as follows:

- To identify current methodologies used for mobile commerce application development.
- To identify strengths and weaknesses of current methodologies used for mobile commerce application development.
- To propose a suitable methodology used for mobile commerce applications.
- To test the applicability and practicality of the methodology proposed. However, this objective is not shown in this paper but will be presented as the future work.

The system development methodology that was proposed is specific to mobile commerce applications including mobile financial services, mobile shopping and mobile information. The research methodology used in the study is the design research, which include the steps of awareness of problems, suggestion, development, evaluation and conclusion. The research methods used to assist the mentioned research methodology include literature analysis, industry visits, semi-structured interview, survey, formulative research and proof by demonstration. It is to be noted that in this paper we only focus on the first two phases of the whole study including awareness of problems and suggestion while the development and evaluation will be presented as future works.

PREVIOUS WORKS

Relevant previous works and their implications on the study are summarized in Table 1.

RESEARCH THEORETICAL FRAMEWORK

Traditional and Agile Development Methodologies

The classification of development methodologies in this study is based on the classification by Blum (1996), Highsmith (1999), Krutchen (2001), and Cao and Ramesh (2007), which classifies the development methodology into heavyweight (traditional) and lightweight (agile). Heavyweight methodology commonly refers to traditional plan based methodology while lightweight or agile is an emerging methodology. Table 2 illustrates the differences between the two methodologies suggested by Cao and Ramesh (2007).

Table 1. Previous works relevant to the study and their implications

Previous Work	Contributions	Implications on the Study
'The e-commerce value matrix and use case model: A goal-driven methodology for eliciting B2C application requirements' by Hsia, Wu, and Li (2008)	Developed a goal-driven methodology for eliciting and modeling the requirements of a business-to-consumer application.	Their methodology provides a systemic approach that makes the eliciting and modeling of EC system requirements easier. However when eliciting and modeling of mobile commerce system requirements, additional attentions should be paid to the main characteristics of mobile commerce which are mobility and portable and therefore this methodology needs to be adapted.
'Integrating Human-Computer Interaction Development into the Systems Development Life Cycle: A Methodology' by Zhang et al. (2005)	Examined the roles of HCI in systems development, justifies the importance of considering HCI throughout the entire systems development life cycle, presents a methodology for human-centered IS development, and demonstrates how to apply this methodology to develop human-centered information systems.	The proposed human-centered SDLC model is an integrated methodology that emphasizes human-centeredness and considers HCI issues together with systems analysis and design issues throughout the entire systems development life cycle.\nThis methodology is applicable to general applications, so an arising question is 'how to integrate this methodology into the systems development life cycle of mobile commerce applications effectively'.
'Agile Development of Secure Web Applications' by Ge, Paige, Polack, Chivers, and Brooke (2006)	Presented an agile process to deliver secure web applications.	Many developments omit security consideration from the development process, attempting to add on security mechanisms in an ad hoc way after implementation which is sometimes too late to prevent or correct the security problem. Therefore security mechanisms and new attack paths that might have been opened should be noted in the early phase of systems development life cycle. An agile process addresses a security issue in the early iteration of the development process and it should be integrated into the development process of mobile commerce applications appropriately.
'Agile Software Development: Adaptive Systems Principles and best Practices' by Meso and Jain (2006)	Examined how complex adaptive systems (CAS) theory can be used to increase our understanding of how agile software development practices can be used to develop this capability.	Agile software development practices including frequent releases and continuous integration, need for frequent feedback, proactive handling of changes to the project requirements and etc. should be further investigated to identify: what agile development practices are suitable for the process development of mobile commerce applications?, and the mapping of agile practices along with mobile commerce applications characteristics should also be examined.
'Mobile Commerce: Framework, Applications and Networking Support' by Varshney and Vetter (2002)	Discussed how to successfully define, architect, and implement the necessary hardware/software infrastructure in support of mobile commerce.\nOne of several interesting research problems raised by Varshney and Vetter is 'what strategies carriers, vendors, providers, and managers in the development of m-commerce applications and services should use?'	The research problem raised will be examined by further investigating: 'what systems development methodology carriers, vendors, providers, and managers in the development of mobile commerce applications and services should use?'
'Introduction to the Special Issue: Mobile Commerce Applications' by Liang and Wei (2004)	Proposed a two dimensional matrix that uses fit and viability to evaluate Internet investment portfolios and suggested that the investment focus on the high fit and high viability category.	The Fit-Viability framework will be integrated into the planning phase of systems development life cycle for mobile commerce applications in this study.

continued on following page

Table 1. Continued

Previous Work	Contributions	Implications on the Study
'Designing mobile commerce applications' by Tarasewich (2003)	Proposed the challenges of designing context aware mobile commerce applications.	As mobile commerce applications are utilized in different context with counterpart fixed e-commerce. Therefore context awareness should be addressed in the design phase of mobile commerce application development.
'A framework for the Study of Customer Interface Design for Mobile Commerce' by Lee and Benbasat (2004)	Suggested an extended framework for user interface design based on elements of the 7C framework proposed by Rayport and Jaworski (2001).	An extended framework for user interface design based on elements of the 7C framework can be further analyzed by emphasizing on how to integrate this framework into the systems development life cycle of mobile commerce applications during the design phase.

Table 2. Differences between traditional and agile methodologies

Factors for Comparison	Traditional Methodologies (Heavyweight)	Agile Methodologies (Lightweight)
Environment	More appropriate in a relatively stable environment in which quality is the major concern.	Focus on system development in a dynamic environment with volatile requirements, changing technology, and critical time to market.
Values	Value planning, predictability, high assurance, and control.	As specified in the "Manifesto for Agile Software Development" (see http://www.agilealliance.com), agile methodologies value interaction, collaboration, and adaptability.
Beliefs	Demand complete and accurate requirement specification, preferably before development.	Stress that requirements emerge throughout the product development cycle. Also, agile methodologies presume that change is unavoidable and should be embraced (Beck, 2000) while traditional methods strive to control change.
Implementation of practices	Long process of development life cycle, complicated design with complete requirements, formal team review, customer participation in early phases.	Short iterations, frequent releases, simple and emerging design, peer review, and on-site customer participation.

Dynamic Capabilities Theory

Dynamic capabilities theory is proposed by Teece, Pisano, and Shuen (1997), they are "the firm's ability to integrate, build, and reconfigure internal and external competences to address rapidly changing environments". This theory draws upon research in multiple areas including management of R&D, product and process development, technology transfer, intellectual property, manufacturing, human resources, and organizational learning (Cao & Ramesh, 2007).

The nature of dynamic capabilities varies with market dynamism. In moderately dynamic markets, these capabilities resemble organizational routines that rely on existing knowledge and linear execution to produce predictable outcomes. In high-velocity markets, they resemble simple, experiential, and unstable processes that produce adaptive, but unpredictable outcomes (Cao & Ramesh, 2007).

Software applications of most business organizations are being developed in a changing environment to gain advantages in a competitive business. Thus, dynamic capabilities perspective should be investigated to explain the dynamic capabilities of software development methodologies. The integration of dynamic capabilities in software development process could contribute to effective application development.

Single and Double Loop Learning Theory

The concepts of single and double-loop learning emerged from Agyris and Schon's theory of action (Argyris & Schon, 1974). Single and double-loop theory has three important elements which are:

- Governing variables which are dimensions that people try to keep within acceptable limits.
- Action strategies which are the moves and plans used by people to keep their governing variables within the acceptable range.
- Consequences which are the results of an action.

In single-loop learning, when something goes wrong, people often look for another strategy that will work with the current governing variables. Alternately, in double-loop learning, people question the governing variables themselves and subject them to critical inspection. Such learning might then lead to an alteration of the governing variables and, thus, a shift in the way people frame strategies and consequences (Cao & Ramesh, 2007).

Single-loop learning is common in many organizations and it's "highly unlikely to alter its governing variables, norms, and assumptions" (Argyris & Schön, 1996). Double-loop learning, which is rarely observed, is more important for organizations operating in dynamic environments (Cao & Ramesh, 2007). Figure 1 illustrates the cycle of single- and double-loop learning theory proposed by Argyris and Schön.

In software development projects, learning or project revision is an essential activity conducted to rectify problems and accommodate changes effectively in the early stages of software development. Single- and double-loop learning mode should thus be investigated to define the appropriate one for each software development project.

Research Methodology

The research paradigm used in this study is more toward the 'Design Science' paradigm, which focuses on man-made objects and phenomena that are purposely designed to meet certain goals (Shiratuddin & Hassan, 2010). By referring to the General Methodology for Design Research (GMDR) as suggested by Vaishnavi and Krechler (2004) as presented in Figure 2, it can be explained next.

Step 1: Awareness of Problem

In this study, the problem was formulated by conducting the literature reviews and investigation of relevant works. The outcome of this step is the research proposal.

Step 2: Suggestion

After the problem was presented in the proposal, the tentative design was constructed. The outcome of this step in this case is the suitable development methodology used to develop mobile commerce applications.. In this step, by linking to the research sub-objectives, there are several activities conducted to satisfy the first three research sub-objectives which are:

Sub-Objective 1: To identify current methodologies used for mobile commerce application development.

Figure 1. Single- and double-loop learning (source: Agyris & Schon, 1974)

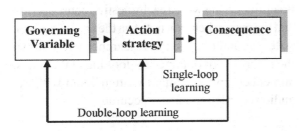

Figure 2. General methodology for design research (GMDR) (source: Vaishnavi & Kuechler, 2004)

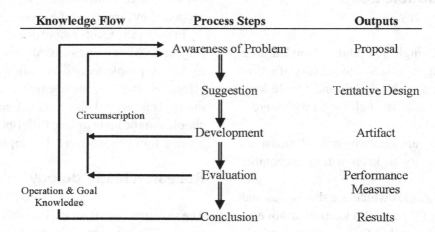

Sub-Objective 2: To identify strengths and weaknesses of current methodologies used for mobile commerce application development.

Sub-Objective 3: To propose a suitable methodology used for mobile commerce applications.

The research methods used to satisfy the first two sub-objectives are the combination of semi-structured interviews and surveys. These methods/ techniques are used to obtain information focusing on practitioner's perspective on their development methodology used when developing mobile commerce applications.

The practitioners from seven organizations were asked to provide information about their development methodologies by answering the questions regarding mobile commerce application development. The questions are opened and aimed to explore practitioner's perspectives on the development methodologies, these questions are included in the interviews:

- Identify a system development methodology being used for mobile commerce application development in your organization.
- Explain guidelines to follow for completing activities in the application development, including specific models, tools, and techniques.

- Does this methodology address essential factors (for examples, HCI, mobile setting, security issue and etc.) in each phase of systems development life cycle of mobile commerce applications? If yes, how?
- Identify strengths and weaknesses of your development methodology.

To obtain this information, the researcher visited the first two organizations and conducted the semi-structured interviews to acquire the information regarding their development methodologies by using the questions structure stated earlier. The benefit of visiting these first two organizations is to ensure that the questions raised are valid, and in that the practitioners could understand and answer the questions clearly. The interviews took place in a small meeting room; the practitioners were given the questions several days before the interview date so that they can prepare for the answers. During the interview session, an electronics audio recorder was used to record the conversation, the practitioners answered each question consequently and the researcher took notes on the answers given. After the interviews, the researcher wrote down the information obtained by looking at the notes, and check up the content written again with the audio recorded to ensure accuracy.

With the last five organizations, after the questions structure were approved and confirmed as they have been tested with the first two organizations, those practitioners were invited to join the open-ended survey via electronics e-mail, they were required to write down the answers for each question in the form provided. The advantage of this survey technique is that it can be conducted in the same period of times with various organizations and practitioners, thus it saved cost and times. However as this survey technique requires a fair amount of times for the practitioners to write down the answers for each question, additional follow up communication thus needed to ensure that the information needed can be obtained in appropriate time.

To satisfy the third sub-objective, all information obtained from the interviews, surveys and analysis were analyzed to formulate the suitable methodology used for mobile commerce applications. The systems development methodology contains the integration of essential factors in each phase of systems development life cycle of mobile commerce applications as well as guidelines to follow for conducting activities in the systems development life cycle, including specific models, tools, and techniques.

Step 3: Development

The system development in this study is there to test the development methodology that was proposed. The reason for having the system development in this study is to test for the applicability and practicality of the proposed development methodology. The method used in this phase is 'proof by demonstration' which is the way 'to build something and then let that artifact stand as an example for a more general class of solutions' (Johnson, 2008). In this study a mobile commerce application prototype was implemented by two teams of developers, the first team uses existing methodology while another team uses the new proposed methodology.

Step 4: Evaluation

The evaluation step in this study is directly connected to the previous development step. In this evaluation, the researcher closely observed and analyzed both the development process and the products made by the development teams using the measurements identified. The main purpose of this evaluation step is to investigate the last research sub-objective which is to test the applicability and the practically of the proposed methodology. At the end of the evaluation step, two experts from the system development field were invited to validate the testing approach, development results and findings.

Step 5: Conclusion

The main activity of this conclusion step is to present the results and findings from the previous evaluation step; future research direction was also suggested here.

However, as stated earlier, this paper only focuses on the first two steps which are awareness of problems and suggestion while the development and evaluation will presented as future works.

SUITABLE DEVELOPMENT METHODOLOGY FOR MOBILE COMMERCE APPLICATIONS

From the practitioner's perspectives, it was found that there are several development methodologies being used in mobile commerce application development and these can be classified into two different development frameworks which are heavyweight (traditional) and lightweight (agile) methodologies. The suitable methodology framework for mobile commerce application development thus was identified.

In order to identify suitable methodology framework for mobile commerce application development, the alignment between mobile commerce application characteristics and the two development methodologies was made. This alignment suggested that mobile commerce applications are more aligned with agile methodologies as they share the same environment, values, beliefs and implications of practices. This suggestion illustrates that agile software development framework is appropriate for mobile commerce application development. In order to support appropriate selection of development methodology framework for mobile commerce applications, two organizational theories stated in the section "Research Theoretical framework" which are dynamic capabilities and double loop learning theories were used.

As it was found from the analysis that agile development methodology framework is appropriate for mobile commerce application development, the suitable development methodology that was proposed thus initially constructed under the agile umbrella by investigating of best practices of each leading agile development methodologies

focusing on the ones mentioned in the practitioner's perspectives and these include Extreme Programming (XP), Feature-Driven Development (FDD), and Scrum. Once the best practices of each leading development methodology were identified, the practices which are suitable with the characteristics of mobile commerce application development were then be chosen and adapted in the proposed methodology.

Apart from investigation of best practices of each leading development methodology, the information and findings obtained from the practitioner's perspectives were also taken into considerations and these include guidelines to follow for conducting activities in the development, essential factors in each phase of systems development life cycle as well as strengths and weaknesses of each development methodology. Figure 3 illustrates how to propose the adapted methodology.

In order to propose this methodology, leading agile development methodologies found in the

Figure 3. How to propose an adapted methodology for mobile commerce application development

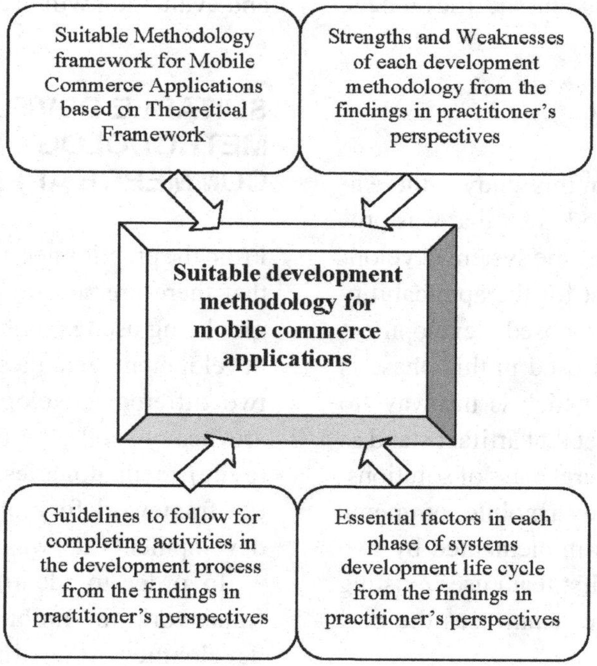

practitioner's perspectives were firstly investigated, and these include Extreme Programming (XP), Scrum, and Feature-Driven Development (FDD). The investigation and analysis then revealed that Extreme Programming practices wrapped with Scrum management structure is suitable for mobile commerce applications development with certain advantages including coverage of certain aspects of software development focusing on management activities and engineering practices, adjustment for each situation and empirical evidence. Once the development methodology structure (XP and Scrum) were identified, an appropriate development methodology for mobile commerce applications is then constructed. The suitable development methodology for mobile commerce applications proposed is derived from suitable methodology structure found from the analysis (XP and Scrum in this case), strengths and weaknesses of each development methodology framework (traditional and agile methodologies), and essential issues for mobile commerce applications to be integrated in the systems development life cycle.

To make the methodology be able to followed, the systems development life cycle (SDLC) for mobile commerce applications were suggested, this SDLC is based on the development lifecycle and practices of Extreme Programming wrapped by Scrum management structure. With the combination of XP and Scrum practices and rules, they provide a structure within which a customer can evolve a software product that best meets his or her needs, and can implement quality functionality incrementally to take advantages of business opportunities, several shared practices between Extreme Programming and Scrum that facilitate this functionality (Mar & Schwaber, 2002) include iterations, increments, emergence, self-organization, and collaboration.

Phases to be included in the development process of mobile commerce applications include Exploration, Release Planning, Iterations to Release, Productionizing and Maintenance. Table

3 illustrates Essential Phases and Steps for the proposed m-commerce application development in the study.

The significant aspect of the development methodology proposed is the integration of essential issues for mobile commerce application development including the user interface design for small screen devices, transaction security over mobile networks, mobile settings, cost of connection, variety of mobile devices and power consumption. These issues are integrated into the development process (focusing on exploration, iterations to release and productionizing phases) to fulfill the requirements of the unique characteristics of mobile commerce applications. Table 4, on the other hand, illustrates when to address these issues in the development process. Essential issues to be addressed in the exploration phase of mobile commerce application development should be initially addressed in this phase by identifying of the requirements for each issue. Table 5 illustrates the requirements found from this study.

When it comes to the design phase in which the solutions for those issues should be designed. The following design guidelines for those issues are presented as follows.

1. User Interface Design for Small Screen Devices

One of the main characteristics of mobile devices is 'portability,' and this implies that the devices should be small enough to be portable. Thus in most mobile device models, the screen size is relatively small and therefore the design principles applied to fixed personal computer cannot be directly used in this case. Therefore the user interface design guidelines for small screen devices should be used.

Standard methods for application design often fail when they are directly applied with small screen mobile device interface (Schmidt et al., 2000). Therefore the appropriate guidelines for designing the interface of small screen mobile devices should be used. The next sub-sections

Table 3. Essential phases and steps for the proposed m-commerce application development

Phase	Step		Technique	Deliverable
Exploration Phase	Determine Business Requirements		User Stories	Requirements Test Scenarios
	Identify a system metaphor		Architectural Spike	System Metaphor
Release Planning Phase	Identify tasks for a given user story		A model in figure format Task cards	Release Plan
	Specify which user stories are going to be implemented for each system release and dates for those releases			
Iterations to Release Phase	Iteration Planning		Revisions of Tasks to Complete	Iteration Plan
	Development	Stand Up Meeting	Sketch on whiteboard	Advice on a specific issue
		Quick Design Session with these practices: -Pair Design & Develop -Model to understand -Apply The Right Artifact(s) -Create Several Models in Parallel -Iterate to Another Artifact when stuck -Consideration of Non-functional requirements for m-commerce	Design Architecture: Architecture Design Hardware & Software Selection	Architecture Report Hardware & Software Specification
			Design Interface: User story Interface Structure Interface Standards Interface Template Design Design Prototype Interface Evaluation	Interface Design
			Design Program: Dataflow Diagramming Program Structure Chart	Physical Process Model Program Design
			Design Database and Files: Database Format Selection Entity Relationship Modeling	Database & File Specification Physical Data Model
		Prove the Design With Code	Programming	Programs
		Refactor	Remove Redundancy, eliminate unused functionality, and refresh obsolete designs	Clean and Concise Program
Productionizing Phase		Certify that the application is ready to go into production	Acceptance Test	Small Release
			Documentation	Documents
Maintenance Phase		Start to produce the new release system when the project are evolved and grown over time.	Conduct Release Planning, Iterations to release and Productionizing phases again for the next releases.	New Small Release

provide guidelines suggested by Schmidt et al. (2000) which can be used to design the small screen mobile devices of mobile commerce applications. These guidelines include general issues for designing mobile commerce applications, input design, and output design.

General Issues for Designing Mobile Commerce Applications3

Several technologies can be utilized to implement mobile commerce applications such as Java (J2ME) and Wireless Markup Language (WML). J2ME applications are installed and run on client

Table 4. Identification of essential issues in the development process of mobile commerce application

Essential Issues / Development Phases			User Interface Design for Small Screen Devices	Mobile Settings	Transaction Security over Mobile Networks	Cost of Connection	Variety of Mobile Devices	Power Consumption
Exploration			✓	✓	✓	✓	✓	✓
Release Planning								
Iterations to Release	Iteration Planning							
	Development	Stand Up Meeting						
		Quick Design Session	✓	✓	✓	✓	✓	✓
		Prove the Design With Code	✓	✓	✓	✓	✓	✓
		Refactor						
Productionizing			✓	✓	✓	✓	✓	✓
Maintenance								

Table 5. Requirements for each essential issue of mobile commerce application development

Essential Issues	Requirements
User Interface Design for Small Screen Devices	As mobile commerce applications have to run on mobile devices containing unique characteristics including 'mobility' and 'portability'. For portability issue, it implies that the devices should be small enough to be portable. Thus in most mobile device models, the screen size is relatively small and therefore the design principles applied to fixed personal computer cannot be directly used in this case. Therefore the user interface design guidelines for small screen devices should be used.
Mobile Settings	With the mobility characteristic of mobile commerce, the applications may be used in some mobility context. The system should thus require less attention from the users.
Transaction Security over Mobile Networks	As mobile commerce applications encompass the transmission of privacy and commercial data over mobile networks, the security issue should thus be addressed in the development process.
Cost of Connection	According to various price plans for connection charge of mobile network, the connection time required should be kept to minimum.
Variety of Mobile Devices	According to various mobile devices used, the system should be able to run and displayed properly on the target mobile devices.
Power Consumption	According to the limitation of power supply of mobile devices, the system should provide mechanism for recovering the data when the power is run out.

devices, while WML applications are installed and run on the servers. If developers decide to use WML pages for the system, Schmidt et al. (2000) suggests the general issues for the designing of small screen mobile devices as follows.

The navigation space and implied interaction with the application should be reflected in the structure of decks and cards in the implementation. According to Giorgis and Agurto (2004), WML pages are called decks; they are constructed as a set of cards, related to each other with links. Even one deck could contain a set of cards, but the WAP browsers normally display only one card at a time. When the mobile system receives the deck, it will display the first card of the deck and then users can navigate from one card to different cards, this navigation among the cards can be operated until a new deck is requested and loaded. The deck is the minimum transmission unit between the server and the mobile system.

Wherever possible (if cards do not rely on user input) provide a maximal navigation space within one deck to avoid reloading during navigation.

Schmidt et al. (2000) also suggested that if information is already provided on a Web site and should also be available on WAP the following approach can be used for porting:

- Define a typical path or more general a graph and build a navigational structure for this path, which is then represented by a deck consisting of multiple cards.
- Use the titles and headlines of Web pages along the path to have the content framework. Reduce text to a minimum and design information chunks that fit *on the* smallest devices you are designing for.

2. Input Design

As most current phones are designed and optimized for inputting numbers rather than text. Based on this the following recommendations for input design suggested by Schmidt et al. (2000) should be considered, these recommendations are also based on one basic principle which is to reduce user attention for user input as much as possible:

- Use numbers for input whenever possible.
- Use common abbreviations like country codes.
- If letters are used keep the input mechanisms in mind, e.g. prefer first letter on key.
- Offer choices (e.g., numbers, listboxes, radio-buttons, link-lists) or default values when applicable; even longer link list prove usable because of scrolling.

- Provide labels to hardware buttons where possible.
- Use standard conventions on buttons (e.g., back).

3. Output Design

Displays on mobile devices contain several limitations including small screen size with low resolution and color depth. With these limitations in mind, Schmidt et al. (2000) suggests the following practices in output design:

- Assess the screen size and quality of the target devices with text and graphics.
- Reduce the output by customizing to the users need such as to have the feature of one click ordering by using customer data storage technique (Sae-Tankg & Esichaikul, 2001).
- Design information chunks that are seen at once on the screen, larger text blocks (more than 20 words!) should be structured.
- Considering the range of devices and their capabilities, it is advisable to design input and output for certain devices classes individually. However if there is any technology that can accommodate several device classes then it should be considered.

Mobile Settings

Mobility is one of the unique characteristics of mobile commerce applications. In some contexts, mobile commerce applications are used in mobility, the system should thus require less attention from the users.

According to Kristoffersen and Ljungberg (1999), Direct manipulation, which is the dominating "interaction style" for mobile computers, fails to meet the conditions of many mobile use situations and in particular, it demands too much visual attention of the user. They introduce a new, complementing interaction style (and system) for mobile computers which addresses three main requirements of interaction with mobile computers:

1. No visual attention needed.
2. Structured, tactile input such as only use four buttons for user input.
3. The use of audio feedback or output.

In the case of mobile commerce applications these requirements should be adapted such as visual attention may still be needed but keep it to minimal.

Transaction Security over Mobile Networks

As addressed in the exploration phase that mobile commerce applications require secured transmission of privacy and commercial data over mobile networks, the security issue should thus be addressed throughout the development process especially in this design phase.

It was mentioned in the previous works that Ge et al. (2006) has presented an agile process to deliver secure web applications. The process suggested encompass an iterative approach to risk analysis that integrates security design throughout the development process. The mentioned process also suggested that security consideration should be embedded throughout the development life cycle to avoid adding on security mechanisms in an ad hoc way after implementation which is occasionally too late to prevent or correct the security problem. In this case, mobile commerce application development, the security considerations will be integrated into the development life cycle in 2 steps:

1. The security policy decision should be made during the Exploration Phase of mobile commerce application development. According to Ge et al. (2006), a security policy is the

set of rules, principles, and practices that determine how security is implemented. They addressed that the development team should create and update a document describing the system security policy integral with the rest of the development process. The security policy settled could assist developers to plan and implement the application with security in mind. With the nature of agile development conducting under a fast changing environment like mobile commerce applications, when the requirements are changed in any iterations, the security policy should thus be revised and changed as necessary. The changes made to the security policy should also be rewritten in the document to make it easier to make changes in coding if required.

2. Security risk analysis should be conducted in the Design Phase of mobile commerce application development. From the view of a project manager, security risk analysis is an iterative, incremental, ongoing process (Ge et al., 2006). In this agile methodology, the activities of designing and implementation focus on one feature for each iteration, when adding another feature in any particular iteration, risk analysis should again be performed as new vulnerabilities may be opened when the new feature is built and added existing features, this is particularly essential for mobile commerce applications. After risk analysis is conducted, the content design may have to be adapted and then a feature including security controls is implemented afterward.

There is a model to be based for risk analysis. Ge et al. (2006) advised that the underlying risk model is that attackers seek to harm assets by obtaining access via system vulnerabilities and the only harms that matter are specific unwanted outcomes or concerns, with associated impacts. They also define that the set of potential attack paths between attackers and the assets of concern are threats that are considered during risk analysis. When treats are found, the responses can be vary from simply deciding that the risk can be accepted but if not, then the modification of content design should be made or additional security controls will have to be implemented.

Cost of Connection

According to various charges and price plans when connecting to a mobile network, connection time required should be kept to minimum to save cost for users. The system implemented should be connected to mobile network only when needed to decrease the connection charge. Thus, in some cases some data should be stored in the phone memory first to avoid all time connection.

Variety and Power Consumption

There are various mobile devices used for mobile commerce applications, the system implemented should be able to run properly on the target mobile devices. And therefore the system should be tested with various mobile device models in each iteration to ensure that the system will run properly on target mobile devices. Any technology platforms that support variety of mobile devices should be utilized.

According to the limitation of power supply of mobile devices, the system must be able to roll back when the power is run out.

CONCLUSION AND FUTURE WORK

This study has suggested the suitable systems development methodology for mobile commerce applications. The major outcome is the systems development methodology for mobile commerce applications which is based on agile development framework. The proposed methodology contains:

- Integration of essential factors in each phase of systems development life cycle of mobile commerce applications.
- Guidelines to follow for conducting activities in the application development, including specific models, tools, and techniques.

The essential aspect of the proposed development methodology is the integration of essential issues for mobile commerce application development including the user interface design for small screen devices, transaction security over mobile networks, mobile settings, cost of connection, variety of mobile devices and power consumption. These issues are integrated into the development process to fulfill the requirements of the unique characteristics of mobile commerce applications.

In future work, after a suitable development methodology for mobile commerce applications was proposed, the testing should then be conducted to assess the applicability and practicality of the proposed methodology. The method used in this testing phase could be 'proof by demonstration' which is the way 'to build something and then let that artifact stands as an example for a more general class of solutions' (Johnson, 2008). In this study a mobile commerce application prototype should be developed by two teams of developers, who have the same experiences in application development, the first team use existing methodology while another team uses the new proposed methodology. In order to control the development environments, developers with the same skills and background are dedicated to each team and they have to come for development work during office hours, so that the evaluator is able to observe their development activities, progress and other issues. In order to evaluate the systems development methodologies, the measurements framework should also be developed.

REFERENCES

Argyris, C., & Schön, D. (1974). *Theory in practice: Increasing professional effectiveness*. San Francisco, CA: Jossey-Bass.

Argyris, C., & Schön, D. (1996). *Organizational learning II: Theory, method and practice*. Reading, MA: Addison-Wesley.

Beck, K. (2000). *Extreme programming explained: Embrace change*. Reading, MA: Addison-Wesley.

Blum, B. (1996). *Beyond programming: To a new era of design*. New York, NY: Oxford University Press.

Cao, L., & Ramesh, B. (2007). Agile software development: Ad hoc practices or sound principles? *IT Professional, 9*(2), 41–47. doi:10.1109/MITP.2007.27

Ge, X., Paige, R. F., Polack, F. A. C., Chivers, H., & Brooke, P. J. (2006). Agile development of secure web applications. In *Proceedings of the 6th ACM International Conference on Web Engineering* (pp. 305-312).

Giorgis, R. S. D., & Agurto, N. R. (2004). *New UML 2.0 based models to design WAP applications*. Paper presented at the 5th Aspect-Oriented Modeling Workshop, Lisbon, Portugal.

Hsia, T. L., Wu, J. H., & Li, E. Y. (2008). The e-commerce value matrix and use case model: A goal-driven methodology for eliciting B2C application requirements. *Information & Management, 45*, 321–330. doi:10.1016/j.im.2008.04.001

Kalakota, R., & Robinson, M. (2002). *M-business: The race to mobility*. New York, NY: McGraw-Hill.

Khalifa, M., & Shen, K. N. (2008). Explaining the adoption of transactional B2C mobile commerce. *Journal of Enterprise Information Management, 21*(2), 110–124. doi:10.1108/17410390810851372

Kristoffersen, S., & Ljungberg, F. (1999). Designing interaction styles for a mobile use context. In *Proceedings of the 1st International Symposium on Handheld and Ubiquitous Computing* (pp. 281-288).

Krutchen, P. (2001). Agility with the RUP. *Cutter IT Journal, 14*(12), 27–33.

Lee, Y. E., & Benbasat, I. (2004). A framework for the study of customer interface design for mobile commerce. *International Journal of Electronic Commerce, 8*(3), 79–102.

Liang, T., Huang, C., Yeh, Y., & Lin, B. (2007). Adoption of mobile technology in business: A fit-viability model. *Industrial Management & Data Systems, 107*(8), 1154–1169. doi:10.1108/02635570710822796

Liang, T., & Wei, C. (2004). Introduction to the special issue: Mobile commerce applications. *International Journal of Electronic Commerce, 8*(3), 7–17.

Mar, K., & Schwaber, K. (2002). *Scrum with XP*. Retrieved from http://www.informit.com/articles/article.aspx?p=26057&seqNum=3

Meso, P., & Jain, R. (2006). Agile software development: Adaptive systems principles and best practices. *Information Systems Management, 23*(3), 19–30. doi:10.1201/1078.10580530/46108.23.3.20060601/93704.3

Ngai, E. W. T., & Gunasekaran, A. (2007). A review of mobile commerce research and applications. *Decision Support Systems, 43*(1), 3–15. doi:10.1016/j.dss.2005.05.003

Sae-Tankg, S., & Esichaikul, V. (2001). Web personalization techniques for e-commerce. In *Proceedings of the 6th International Computer Science Conference on Active Media Technology* (pp. 36-44).

Schmidt, A., Schröder, H., & Frick, O. (2000). WAP – Designing for small user interfaces. In *Proceedings of the CHI Extended Abstracts on Human Factors in Computing Systems*, The Hague, The Netherlands.

Shiratuddin, N., & Hassan, S. (2010). *Design research in software development*. Sintok, Malaysia: Universiti Utara Malaysia Press.

Tarasewich, P. (2003). Designing mobile commerce applications. *Communications of the ACM*, *46*(12), 57–60. doi:10.1145/953460.953489

Teece, D. J., Pisano, G., & Shuen, A. (1997). Dynamic capabilities and strategic management. *Strategic Management Journal, 18*(7), 509–533. doi:10.1002/(SICI)1097-0266(199708)18:7<509::AID-SMJ882>3.0.CO;2-Z

Turel, O., & Yuan, Y. (2006). Investigating the dynamics of the m-commerce value system: A comparative viewpoint. *International Journal of Mobile Communications*, *4*(5), 532–557.

Vaishnavi, V., & Kuechler, W. (2004). *Design research in information systems*. Retrieved from http://desrist.org/design-research-in-information-systems

Varshney, U., & Vetter, R. (2002). Mobile commerce: Framework, applications and networking support. *Mobile Networks and Applications*, *7*, 185–198. doi:10.1023/A:1014570512129

Zhang, P., Carey, J., Te'eni, D., & Tremaine, M. (2005). Integrating human-computer interaction development into the systems development life cycle: A methodology. *Communications of the Association for Information Systems, 15*, 512–543.

Zhou, D., Islam, N., & Ismael, A. (2004). Adaptive replication for mobile services. In *Proceeding of the 13th World Wide Web Conference* (pp. 131-142).

Zwass, V. (2003). Electronic commerce and organizational innovation: Aspects and opportunities. *International Journal of Electronic Commerce*, *7*(3), 7–37.

This work was previously published in the International Journal of Mobile Computing and Multimedia Communications, Volume 3, Issue 4, edited by Ismail Khalil and Edgar Weippl, pp. 36-52, copyright 2011 by IGI Publishing (an imprint of IGI Global).

Chapter 10
FlexRFID Middleware in the Supply Chain:
Strategic Values and Challenges

Mehdia Ajana El Khaddar
ENSIAS Rabat, Morocco

Hamid Harroud
Alakhawayn University in Ifrane, Morocco

Mohammed Boulmalf
Alakhawayn University in Ifrane, Morocco

Mohammed El Koutbi
ENSIAS Rabat, Morocco

ABSTRACT

Radio Frequency Identification (RFID) has been used since the Second World War to identify "friend or foe" aircrafts. It has become an enabling wireless technology that is widely used in a number of application areas, such as product tracking through manufacturing and assembly, inventory control, and supply chain management (SCM). By 2006, Wal-Mart used RFID for all of its suppliers. The use of RFID in supply chain networks has allowed Wal-Mart to create value through greater visibility in its networks, higher product velocity, reduce human error and labor cost, and more efficient inventory management, which led to the achievement of Quick Response (QR) and improved Customer Relationship Management (CRM) in the supply chain. However, RFID system challenges and uncertain Return-On-Investment (ROI) must be overcome to fully achieve these objectives. This paper introduces RFID technology and its key components and concepts, and presents an RFID middleware solution called FlexRFID that achieves the maximum benefits of RFID technology independently of the interested backend applications. This paper illustrates how RFID technology is used to solve the main problems in SCM, the advantages and key issues when implementing RFID in SCM networks, and the relationship between RFID and the main SCM processes.

DOI: 10.4018/978-1-4666-2163-3.ch010

INTRODUCTION

Radio Frequency Identification (RFID) is one of the Automatic Identification and Data Capture (AIDC) techniques (Ishikawa et al., 2003). RFID uses low-power, and radio waves to automatically identify people or objects, and to provide radically enhanced data handling capabilities (Tektronix, 2004). It is convenient, easy to use, and well suited for automatic operations (ADC Technologies Group, 2002). RFID technology can be used to track objects in a manner similar to using barcode based systems (Ishikawa et al., 2003) and Optical Character Recognition (OCR) systems (Phoenix Software International, 2006), but RFID also combines additional advantages not available in these technologies. RFID does not require line of sight readings, can function under a variety of environmental conditions, can read multiple tags simultaneously, store large amounts of data in addition to the ID of the object tracked, and provide a high level of data integrity (ADC Technologies Group, 2002; Ajana et al., 2009).

While existing for decades as an enabling technology, RFID does not provide much value on its own, however the creation of RFID based applications is the key that creates value for the companies. Although RFID can be a complicated and costly business technology, it appears that RFID will overcome the implementation obstacles and become a breakthrough technology throughout the supply chain for manufacturing, packaging, logistics, distributions, and retailing (Chuang & Shaw, 2007).

A supply chain is "a network of facilities and distribution options that performs the functions of procurement of materials, transformation of these materials into intermediate and finished products, and the distribution of these finished products to customers". The complexity of supply chain varies greatly from industry to industry (Ganeshan & Harrison, 1995). The supply chain starts and ends with the customer, and is made up of several elements that are linked by the movement of products along it. The supply chain consists of the following elements: customer, planning, purchasing, inventory, production, and transportation (Murray, 2010).

Supply Chain Management is the "management and control of all materials and information in the logistics process from acquisition of raw materials to delivery to the end user" (Michael & McCathie, 2005). Companies have adopted SCM processes and associated technology in order to ensure that the supply chain is operating as efficient as possible and generating the highest level of customer satisfaction at the lowest possible price (Murray, 2010).

RFID technology has the potential of helping retailers provide the right product at the right place at the right time, thus maximizing sales and profits. The integration of RFID technology in the SCM systems has helped in optimizing inventory management, reducing losses, increasing ROI and information accuracy, and improving visibility in various stages of SCM (Sheng et al., 2008). RFID offers item-level data visibility; a revolutionary advance that can improve product availability and reduce losses associated with shrinkage and product obsolescence (IBM Global Business Services, 2005).

Mandating RFID, Wal-Mart and other companies believe that it benefits their own supply chains as well as their suppliers. However, not all these possible benefits are fully achieved. Uncertainty exists about how RFID will affect supply chains and what benefits and risks it will bring, and evidence suggests that companies will not be able to see RFID ROI for the first two or three years (Chuang & Shaw, 2007). RFID integration in the SCM happens in stages; therefore its benefits accrue in phases throughout the supply chaining activities.

The paper is organized as follows. We talk briefly about RFID system components, and then we present FlexRFID middleware architecture. We show how RFID technology is used for supply chain management networks, its benefits and risks, and its integration stages in SCM. Then we showcase the relationship between RFID and SCM processes. Finally we describe how an SCM application for inventory control can be developed based on the FlexRFID middleware architecture, followed by conclusions and future work in the last section.

RFID SYSTEM COMPONENTS

RFID systems consist basically of three main components: a tag/transponder, a reader, and a middleware running at a host computer. RFID tags are the data carrier part of the RFID system; they store information about the object being tracked. Specific object data is stored in the memory of the tag and is accessed via the radio signal of the reader (Knowledgeleader, 2006). Data stored in RFID tags can consist of serial numbers, security codes, product codes and other object specific data. Various types of tags exist and are classified with respect to different parameters. For example with respect to powering, tags may be passive, semi-passive, and active (Sheng et al., 2008; United States Government Accountability Office, 2005). Passive tags present the simplest version of RFID tags which do not contain a battery as their own power source, and cannot initiate communication with the reader. The passive tag derives its power from the energy waves transmitted by the reader and responds to the reader's radio frequency emissions. Semi-passive tags, called also semi-active tags, also do not initiate communication with the reader but contain batteries that allow the tag to perform other functions, such as monitoring environmental conditions and powering the tag's internal electronics. Active tags, unlike passive tags, they contain a power source and a transmitter in addition to the antenna and chip, and send a continuous signal. These tags typically have read/write capabilities (United States Government Accountability Office, 2005). In terms of access to memory, the tags may be read-only, read-write,

Electrically Erasable Programmable Read-Only Memory, Static Random Access Memory, and Write-once Read-many (Al-Mousawi, 2004; United States Government Accountability Office, 2005). Tags may also be classified with respect to geometrical parameters such as size and shape, or serve different environmental conditions e.g. tags suited to cardboard cases containing plastic items may not be ideal for wooden pallets, metal containers or glass (Intermec, 2007).

The RFID reader is a device that transmits and receives data through radio waves using the connected antennas. RFID reader can read multiple tags simultaneously without line-of-sight requirement. The reading happens even when tagged objects are embedded inside packaging, or even when the tag is embedded inside an object itself (e.g. RFID implants). There exist different types of RFID readers; fixed and handheld/portable, and they can be equipped with tag collision and reader collision prevention techniques, and also tag-reader authentication algorithms (Glasser et al., 2007). RFID deployment is becoming more attractive due to the decreasing prices of RFID tags and readers over the years. The first operation to happen is that the reader sends energy through its antennas and forms an interrogation zone. When a tag enters this zone, it gets activated to exchange data with the reader. The reader then decodes this data and sends it to a software system known as RFID middleware for processing (Al-Mousawi, 2004).

The RFID middleware refers to the software layer which resides between the physical layer components (RFID tags, and RFID readers), and the upper layer standalone or distributed enterprise applications. Hence it is a key component for managing the flow of information between tag readers and enterprise applications (Burnell, 2008). In the traditional applications of RFID such as access control, there was a little need for RFID middleware because networking among RFID readers was not a concern. In contrast to the novel application areas such as SCM, a number of RFID readers are networked to capture data which is disseminated to a variety of backend applications. There is no longer a one-to-one relationship between RFID reader and application, and therefore there is a strong need for RFID middleware to give better device control, and enable users to infer intelligent decisions from the raw RFID data coming from the readers. A successful middleware design solution depends on how well the different components of the middleware in different layers fit together and work to provide valuable processed data to the enterprise applications (Ajana et al., 2009).

FLEXRFID MIDDLEWARE

We developed FlexRFID, which is a multi-layered middleware that has a simple and robust design, satisfies applications' needs, and allows for an easy management of devices as described in (Ajana et al., 2009). Herewith we provide a summary of the FlexRFID middleware architecture focusing on each of its layers separately.

As shown in Figure 1, FlexRFID is part of a three-tier architecture consisting of: the backend applications layer, FlexRFID middleware layer, and hardware layer. We will proceed below through a bottom-up description of these layers.

Figure 1. FlexRFID middleware architecture (©2009, Ajana, M. E., used with permission)

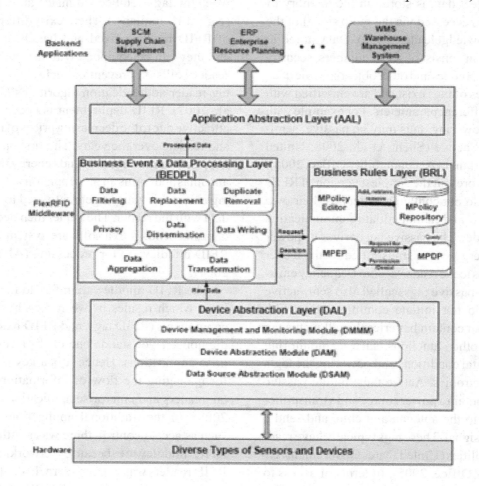

The hardware layer contains diverse types of sensors and devices such as RFID readers, barcode scanners, sensors, and other industrial automation devices. This approach allows creating an intelligent sensor network by offering incredible flexibility in the selection of devices, and enables companies to build their enterprise solutions without handling low-level programming. This diversity in makes and models of sensing devices requires a middleware layer for device management, monitoring and coordination. Our approach consists of using a Device Abstraction Layer (DAL) that abstracts the interaction with the physical network of devices. The FlexRFID middleware incorporates three other layers which are: Business Event and Data Processing Layer (BEDPL), Business Rules Layer (BRL), and Application Abstraction Layer (AAL).

The Device Abstraction Layer (DAL) uses the Data Source Abstraction Module (DSAM) and the Device Abstraction Module (DAM) to handle various data sources and devices independently of their characteristics. The Device Management and Monitoring Module (DMMM) of the DAL is responsible for dynamic loading and unloading of the driver libraries and device adaptors, as well as configuration, monitoring and status reporting of the devices.

The Business Event and Data Processing Layer (BEDPL) acts as a mediator between the DAL and the AAL, and provides the following services: data dissemination, data aggregation, data transformation, data filtering, duplicate removal, data replacement, data writing and privacy management. The BEDPL acts in parallel with the Business Rules Layer (BRL) when performing the services cited above. When an application requests a service from the FlexRFID middleware, its specific rules loaded in the BRL are given as input to the service, which then applies these rules to issue commands to the DAL to access raw data and process it accordingly. Similarly raw data is carried from the DAL, processed by the BEDPL, and passed on to the AAL.

The BRL is a policy-based management engine that hosts the rules applied to the services of the FlexRFID middleware. This is achieved by determining the policies to apply when an application requests access to a service in the BEDPL. Policies are operating rules used to maintain order, security, consistency, or other ways of successfully achieving a service.

As shown in Figure 1 the BRL has four main components. The Middleware Policy Editor (MPE) allows storing, retrieving, and removing policies from the middleware policy repository database. If an application needs to access a service that is protected by the Business Rules Layer, the request goes through the Middleware Policy Enforcement Point (MPEP) which asks the Middleware Policy Decision Point (MPDP) whether to permit or deny access to the service. The MPEP gives the MPDP the authority of decision making whether or not to grant the application access to the service based on the description of the application attributes. The MPDP makes its decision based on the applicable policies stored in the system. The returned decision is Permit, Deny, Indeterminate or Not Applicable. Indeterminate is returned if there is an error in processing the request and Not Applicable if no policy that applies to the request could be found.

Examples of policies included in the BRL are: data filtering policy, location transformation policy, and data aggregation policy. The data filtering policy filters data according to predefined policies by the applications. For example to filter the duplicate reading reported by different readers in the network, the filtering policy will scan data within a sliding window to find if there are duplicate RFID tag readings, and delete the duplicate if it exists. An example of duplicate removal policy could state that if readings from readers R_x and R_y have the same tag ID value within time T, then one of them is dropped according to the application's needs. The location transformation policy transforms RFID readers' observations into location changes. For example, Reader R is mounted at a warehouse departure zone and will scan objects before their departure. A policy for this transformation could specify that any observation generated from reader R will change the object's location to a value different from its current location. The data aggregation policy is used to detect a sequence of ordered events and generate an aggregation relationship from them. For instance when pallets are loaded into a truck to depart, a sequence of readings on the pallets is done, followed by a separate reading of the truck's tag. This sequence of events will aggregate as a containment relationship between the pallets and the truck.

The Application Abstraction Layer (AAL) provides various applications with an interface to the hardware devices, through which the applications request the set of services provided by the FlexRFID middleware with hidden complexity. This layer provides a high level of software abstraction that allows for communication among the enterprise applications and the FlexRFID middleware.

To sum up FlexRFID middleware provides the following distinguishing aspects: a device and data source neutral interface for the applications to communicate simultaneously with different hardware creating an intelligent RFID network, a hardware management and monitoring interface, and data processing capabilities enforced by a policy based management layer. The modular and layered design of FlexRFID allows integrating new services and policies with little effort, and enables seamless integration of many enterprise applications.

RFID TECHNOLOGY FOR SUPPLY CHAIN NETWORKS

RFID technology has gained greater prominence and a higher level of adoption due to its recent advancements and decreasing costs across the years. The applications of RFID in the SCM have

vast potential in improving effectiveness and efficiencies in solving supply chain problems. In the very near future, by adding RFID to every product, tool, resource, and item, manufacturers will be able to get better demand signals from customers (AME Info, 2005). All products in motion are traced throughout the supply chain from manufacturer's shop floor, to warehouses, to retail stores. Such a visibility of accurate data brings opportunities for improvement and transformation in various processes of the supply chain, and allows a wide range of organizations to realize significant productivity gains and efficiencies (Sabbaghi & Vaidyanathan, 2008).

In the next sections we try to answer the following questions: (1) what would be the benefits of RFID integration in supply chain? (2) What are the risks, challenges, and recommendations in adopting and implementing RFID in supply chain? (3) What processes in supply chain will be affected by RFID, and where this technology has the potential of creating the most business value?

The Benefits of RFID

RFID promises to revolutionize supply chains and usher in a new era of cost savings, efficiency and business intelligence. As follows is a description of the main benefits of integrating RFID in SCM.

Automatic non-line-of-sight scanning means that items do not require particular orientation for scanning, unlike barcodes. Also RFID readers can communicate to tags in milliseconds and have the ability to scan multiple items simultaneously. This attractive offering significantly aids the automation of many SCM tasks that have been labor intensive, gives an accurate data about stock levels for organizations which in turn leads to lower inventory costs and less out-of-stock occurrences (Michael & McCathie, 2005).

RFID leads to labor reduction throughout the supply chain process. RFID could yield labor savings of up to 36% in order picking and 90% reduction in verification costs for shipping processes. Labor is the major cost component of typical distribution centers accounting for around 50-80% of total distribution costs. Therefore, these reductions in labor by using RFID can deliver considerable financial savings (Michael & McCathie, 2005).

RFID technology offers greater visibility to all stakeholders in the supply chain. This offered visibility could provide real-time and accurate information about products, allowing organizations to use this information to increase efficiency. Inventory visibility can also be used to make faster response to customer demands and market trends. Smart shelves including inbuilt RFID tag readers are used for real-time reporting of information, and help retailers track the exact number of products they hold (Michael & McCathie, 2005; RFID4U, 2006).

RFID is ideal for asset tracking and returnable items, improving asset utilization by tracking asset's movement, use, and placement. RFID can also log an asset history and ensure that government requirements and regulations are adhered to. RFID tags enable greater visibility of the asset pool which impacts six main areas: operating costs, shrinkage, lead times, inventory visibility and accuracy, customer service and integration among parents (Michael & McCathie, 2005; RFID4U, 2006).

Item level tracking using RFID opens the door to a whole range of potential benefits, for example theft detection or customized manufacturing. It is a necessity for smart shelves to achieve their maximum potential, and will allow identifying and storing individual product properties such as expiry date. This level of tracking will be fully introduced for around 10 years. Currently, most organizations have decided to focus on pallet and case level tracking (Michael & McCathie, 2005).

Faulty instances of a product often lead to the destruction of a perfectly good brand. Using RFID to track affected products will allow manufacturers to issue targeted recalls of these products only. Plus, tagged items that require repair and are covered by a warranty can be authenticated, ensuring that the warranty period of the product has not expired. The item can also be monitored as the product moves back up the supply chain to the manufacturer or authorized repairer, allowing customers to receive detailed information on where their item is in the process (Michael & McCathie, 2005).

RFID permits to monitor the quality of products not only internally in an organization, but also when products move along the supply chain. This allows lowering the chance of customers receiving poor quality products as well as reducing the time spent monitoring and reworking orders. Some RFID tags can monitor things like temperature, and bacteria levels, which is an important capability where many products are shipped around the world, and exposed to countless environmental forces which could affect the quality of the finished good (Michael & McCathie, 2005).

RFID can continue to work perfectly in harsh conditions, such as high or low temperature degrees, and in acids, dirty, oily, or wet industrial and commercial environments (Michael & McCathie, 2005).

The Risks of RFID

Despite the enticing benefits of RFID, some thoughts about its implementation issues in the global supply chain must be taken, including sizes of the chips because they cannot be placed on all products, environment limitations, and personal privacy (Lin et al., 2006). These issues are well known to the industry, and solutions are under development. Here we examine a list of the most prominent problems facing RFID implementation today that are important strategy considerations.

One of the major issues that inhibited RFID growth has been the cost of RFID and uncertain Return on Investment. The costs of a fully functional RFID system include tags, readers, printers, middleware, infrastructure, consulting, and a changed system. Today, tag prices have dropped and are projected to drop much further. A cost driver that should be considered in supply chain is whether the tags will be reused or disposed of. This driver is influenced by the level of partnering achieved by downstream partners who would return, reuse or discard the tags. In addition to tag cost, there are other significant RFID system incurring costs such as software including middleware, integration, and process redesign (Chuang & Shaw, 2005; United Parcel Service of America, 2005).

Whether tag readability is an issue depends on many factors such as tag range and frequencies, reader capabilities and locations, interference from other devices, operating environment variations (temperature, humidity, vibration, and shock), and the type of assets being tagged; for e.g. metal objects and liquid containers tend to create reading problems for some types of tags. Readability issues will become manageable for most applications, given the incremental improvement of RFID technology (United Parcel Service of America, 2005).

Due to RFID data volume and its unique characteristics, new structures for RFID data management should be considered, because most ERP and WMS systems are not designed for RFID capture (United Parcel Service of America, 2005).

The implementation of RFID in SCM may suffer from the issue of data ownership and sharing. The benefits of sharing item specific data as it progresses throughout the supply chain between multiple trading partners can be significant; however the willingness of the partners to do so has historically been a challenge (United Parcel Service of America, 2005).

There are significant efforts undertaken by standard bodies to converge on common requirements for RFID data, but there will be differences based upon applications and other factors. The standardization issue concerning how RFID data is structured, communicated and managed among trading partners should not be a major stumbling block to determine the business value of RFID (United Parcel Service of America, 2005).

RFID implementation involves significant business process changes. Therefore the design of any RFID strategy should consider organizational changes as new processes for automating tasks and decision making will be made (United Parcel Service of America, 2005).

Individual privacy concern is an issue in RFID. Consumers do not want themselves or the products they take to be tracked once they own them. In order to counter the privacy concerns, the industry has developed a "kill tag" feature that will disable the RFID tags in the checkout point at retail. Also some fears of compromised privacy can be alleviated by the fact that RFID tags could not be read from long distances (United Parcel Service of America, 2005).

Competing standards have been one of the most difficult issues for RFID. The problem is that there exists no universally accepted standard, and therefore most RFID applications have been closed systems. Standards can include an agreement about the format and content of the codes placed on the tags, the protocols and frequencies used by the tags and readers to exchange data, the security issues involved on placing tags on packaging and freight containers, and applications use (Modrak et al., 2010).

RFID Integration Stages in SCM

A key success factor when implementing RFID is to start from a pilot RFID infrastructure and make it scalable while taking time to analyze and plan. Chuang & Shaw (2007) suggested a model for RFID integration in SCM that contains three different RFID implementation stages:

Stage 1: Functional RFID Integration
Stage 2: Business Unit RFID Integration
Stage 3: Inter-Company RFID Integration

This model takes into consideration the involvement of business partners and addresses the benefits and risks as more supply chain partners are part of the integration.

Functional RFID Integration addresses companies that apply RFID to a single process or internal activity, such as distribution center processes, Just-In-Time manufacturing processes, and asset tracking activity. By starting a RFID project in this category, the organization addresses several key questions. What process does the company want to change? What results does the company want to see by implementing RFID in this process? What are the expectations from this implementation? The benefits at this stage are improved functional process efficiency and effectiveness, and reduction of labor cost and human errors. The risks and complexity are relatively low at this level since this stage specializes on a single process or activity (Chuang & Shaw, 2007).

Business Unit RFID Integration is extended to different business units within an organization such as distribution centers, warehouses, or headquarters. This integration requires a scalable RFID architecture designed to meet a number of intra-organization expectations. The benefits of Business Unit RFID implementation include reduced labor costs and human errors in logistics operations, and better inventory management between the manufacturing and distribution centers. The involvement of several entities at the same time in the integration process makes the risk level relatively high (Chuang & Shaw, 2007).

Inter-Company RFID Integration means that a company implements RFID in its supply chain networks in collaboration with its business partners. Examples of companies that fall into this category are Wal-Mart, Metro Group, and Target. This integration type consists of having a collaboration relationship between upstream suppliers and downstream customers. Downstream customers communicate their needs from RFID implementation with their supply chain partners. Suppliers in turn would implement RFID with downstream

users in mind to ensure that their expectations are met. Since the majority of organizations are both suppliers and consumers of goods and services, this stage becomes complex and with great technical and business risks (Chuang & Shaw, 2007).

Organizations can experience the overlap between each stage of integration; they can therefore carry the implementation experience and benefits to the next level of integration. Upstream suppliers tend to consider that RFID requires a big investment and uncertain ROI because typically they do not have RFID infrastructure in their current business processes and external supply chains. As a start, upstream suppliers can integrate RFID into their production and distribution systems first and then gradually integrate with their downstream customers (Chuang & Shaw, 2007).

RELATIONSHIP BETWEEN RFID AND SCM PROCESSES

There are eight key processes that make up the SCM, and provide a framework for various aspects of strategic and tactical issues present in the management of the supply chain. As follows is a description of these processes and their functions (Sabbaghi & Vaidyanathan, 2008):

1. **Customer Relationship Management (CRM):** A business philosophy which provides a vision for how a company wants to deal with its customers. A CRM strategy is needed to deliver that vision, and helps giving shape to many activities such as sales, marketing, customer service, and data analysis. Therefore the aim of CRM strategy is to maximize profitable relationships between the company and its customers (Atos Origin, 2002). CRM provides processes that help identifying and targeting the best customers, generating quality sales leads, and implementing marketing campaigns with clear goals and objectives.

2. **Customer Service Management (CSM):** Offers benefits to both providers and customers by allowing the monitoring of service level agreement negotiated between the two parties. CSM offers a competitive advantage to providers, and enables customers to control up-to-date and adequate information about service specific QoS parameters (Langer, 1998). It can also provide real-time information to customers such as shipping dates, and product availability.

3. **Demand Management:** A highly iterative process that uses prioritization of customers, channels, products, and the demand stimulation programs in order to achieve revenue. Demand Management relies on highly sophisticated quantitative analytics and advanced modeling techniques to pre-set tolerance levels, predict problem areas, adjust strategies dynamically, and achieve real-time visibility and synergy across all channels (IBM Business Consulting Services, 2005). This process helps to forecast demand and manage the demand in production, distribution and in all other outputs of the company. Therefore, it helps balancing the customers' requirements with the company's supply capabilities.

4. **Order Fulfillment Management:** Concerns the management of the company's partnerships to meet the customer requirements. This would include the integration of the company's manufacturing, logistics and marketing plans.

5. **Manufacturing Flow Management:** Helps to manage product flow and establish the manufacturing flexibility required to service target markets. This process includes all activities necessary to obtain, implement, and manage manufacturing flexibility in the supply chain and to move products through it.

6. **Supplier Relationship Management:** Defines how companies interact and manage partnership with their core suppliers providing a competitive advantage. This process helps improving the selection and management of global suppliers, and therefore streamlining the other processes by making sure that the company is working with the most capable and economical suppliers.

7. **Product Development and Commercialization:** Provides structure for developing new products and reducing time to market by jointly integrating customers and suppliers. This process enables management to coordinate the efficient flow of new products across the supply chain, and also assists supply chain members with the logistics, marketing and other related activities to support the commercialization of the product. It is one of the most important keys to firm's success.

8. **Returns Management:** Concerns the management of all logistic operations related to returns of products from their original user to their supplier. When the product is returned, it incurs inventory carrying costs, and takes up warehouse space. Returns management allows encountering these problems by allowing a company to monitor productivity improvements and identify valuable ideas related to its products and services.

Out of these eight processes, RFID may be used in demand management, order fulfillment, manufacturing flow management, and returns management. The relationship between RFID and these four supply chain management processes is described in detail as following (Sabbaghi & Vaidyanathan, 2008).

Demand Management and RFID

The lack of reliable data has been one of the major difficulties in Demand Management. Adopting RFID would enhance data accuracy related to inventory of finished goods, work in-progress, and reliable due dates. RFID can eliminate inaccuracies in data due to human error or absence of data, and provide timely data both at the item-level and in aggregate about the market demand of a particular product. Therefore, the integration of RFID would help to develop more successful strategies in production, marketing, and distribution.

Order Fulfillment and RFID

Order fulfillment is a key process in meeting customer requirements and improving the effectiveness of the supply chain. RFID can reduce the cost of operations in order fulfillment. RFID enables suppliers to automatically and accurately determine the location of an item, to track its movement through the supply chain, and to make instantaneous business decisions. This will free up labor-intensive work involved in the quantity check-in and receiving operations.

Manufacturing Flow Management and RFID

The use of RFID in manufacturing helps streamlining the assembly line operations, and therefore reducing cycle time, increasing production throughput, and improving the velocity and visibility of products in the supply chain. This will help manufacturers with their Just-in-Time (JIT) assembly lines by tracking where every item is in the manufacturing process and supply chain.

Returns Management and RFID

RFID can facilitate returns management by helping retailers track the history of the item being returned. Through the Electronic Security Marker (ESM) (Pearson, 2006), RFID can tie the relationship of a particular product to a given sale and then to the return. The tagging of products with electronic security markers enables them to have automated track-and-trace capabilities, and provides real-time visibility of the products through the supply chain.

FLEXRFID-BASED SCM APPLICATION

Among the most important aspects that SCM applications target is inventory control. Inventory control aims at minimizing the total cost of inventory, and has three main factors in its decision making process: the cost of holding the stock, the cost of placing an order, and the cost of shortage; what is lost if the stock is insufficient to meet all demand.

We will focus herewith on the use of FlexRFID middleware to provide input to existing tools and applications for inventory control. FlexRFID middleware deals with RFID data streaming, reactivity, integration, and heterogeneity that represent a challenge for e-logistics and SCM systems.

Data Streaming

RFID devices are becoming cheaper and widely deployed and it is now increasingly important to perform continual intelligence analysis of data captured. To relieve the SCM applications from dealing with the streaming nature of data and the fact that the data might be redundant, even unreliable in certain cases, the FlexRFID middleware is able to process such unreliable real time sensing data before delivering it to the backend system.

Data Reactivity

RFID and other sensing technologies have promised real time global information visibility for SCM participants. To benefit from such visibility, the

SCM participants have to be able to identify the interested situations and react to such situations when they happen. The events associated with the triggers have to be reported in a timely manner and notification has to be sent to interested SCM participants. The FlexRFID middleware handles this through its Business Event and Data Processing Layer, and policy based Business Rules Layer.

Data Integration

The design of FlexRFID middleware allows it to scale and support different devices and data sources that may be used at numerous points of inventory control such as Point of Sale (PoS), and smart shelves.

The advantages of using FlexRFID for inventory control can therefore be summarized as follows:

- Report RFID data about location and inventory level in real time so that the inventory control application could place an automatic order whenever the total inventory at a warehouse or distribution center drops below a certain level.
- Report and aggregate accurate data at the PoS that will be used by the SCM application to monitor demand trends or to build a probabilistic pattern of demand that could be useful for products exhibiting high levels of dynamism in trends.
- Reduction of the Bullwhip effect, which means an exaggeration of demand in upward direction in a supply chain network. FlexRFID will provide accurate and real time information on actual sales of items that can be used for decision making and that will diminish the magnitude of the bullwhip effect. Reducing the bullwhip effect would benefit industries where instances of supply-demand imbalances have high costs attached to them.

- Capturing data that gives total visibility of product movement in the supply chain. This will help to make early decisions about inventory control in case there is any interruption in the supply. This results into reduction of total lead-time for arrival of an order. Pharmaceutical and perishable product industries could benefit from this to increase total useful shelf life of items.
- Reduced inventory shrinkage: FlexRFID can transform the capture of RFID data into inventory shrinkages events including thefts and misplacement of items.
- FlexRFID allows issuing policies by the inventory control applications for items as per the requirements, e.g., first-in-first-out (FIFO) policy for items such as, vegetables, and bread.

CONCLUSION AND FUTURE WORK

Radio Frequency Identification is expected to become a critical and ubiquitous infrastructure technology for SCM related processes and services. It promises automatic data capturing and entering and makes it possible for real time information visibility for supply chain. In this paper we presented the benefits of using RFID in the supply chain networks, and its integration stages within the SCM processes. We developed the FlexRFID middleware and presented how it can be integrated with an SCM application especially for inventory control. Among the tasks that could be achieved while using FlexRFID with an inventory control application are: allowing inventory status to be determined in real time, shipping and receiving documents to be generated automatically, and triggering automatic orders for products that are low in inventory.

With respect to the future works, we intend to integrate the FlexRFID middleware with an open source system for inventory control (e.g.

TechLogic Inventory Control System, Opentaps, etc.), define the different scenarios and events that could be triggered by this system, and show how the different layers of FlexRFID middleware will work to deliver enhanced visibility of inventory in various stages of supply chaining.

ACKNOWLEDGMENT

We would like to express our sincere appreciation to the Wireless and Mobile Computing Lab (WML) at Al Akhawayn University in Ifrane, Morocco, and Systèmes d'Information Multimédia et Mobile Lab (SI2M) at Ecole Nationale Supérieure de l'Informatique et d'Analyse des Systèmes (ENSIAS), Morocco, for the support of this research work.

REFERENCES

ADC Technologies Group. (2002). *RFID overview*. Retrieved from http://www.adctech.com/Documents%5CWhite%20Paper,%20RFID%20Overview.pdf

Ajana, M. E., Boulmalf, M., Harroud, H., & Hamam, H. (2009). A policy based event management middleware for implementing RFID applications. In *Proceedings of the International Conference on Wireless and Mobile Computing, Networking and Communications*, Marrakesh, Morocco (pp. 406-410).

Al-Mousawi, H. (2004). *Performance and reliability of radio frequency identification (RFID)*. Unpublished master's thesis, Agder University College, Kristiansand, Norway.

Atos Origin. (2002). *Customer relationship management*. Retrieved from http://www.es.atosorigin.com/NR/rdonlyres/9C826F13-D59C-456B-AC57-416E686A4C30/0/crm_wp.pdf

Burnell, J. (2008). *What is RFID middleware and where is it needed?* Retrieved from http://www.rfidsolutionsonline.com/article.mvc/RFID-Middleware-What-Is-RFID-Middleware-And-W-0001

Chuang, M. L., & Shaw, W. H. (2005). How RFID will impact supply chain networks. In *Proceedings of the IEEE Engineering Management Conference*, Newfoundland, Canada (pp. 231-235).

Chuang, M. L., & Shaw, W. H. (2007). RFID: Integration stages in supply chain management. *IEEE Engineering Management Review*, *35*(2), 80–87. doi:10.1109/EMR.2007.899757

Ganeshan, R., & Harrison, T. P. (1995). *An introduction to supply chain management*. Retrieved from http://lcm.csa.iisc.ernet.in/scm/supply_chain_intro.html

Glasser, D. J., Goodman, K. W., & Einspruch, N. G. (2007). Chips, tags and scanners: Ethical challenges for radio frequency identification. *Ethics and Information Technology*, *9*(2), 101–109. doi:10.1007/s10676-006-9124-0

IBM Business Consulting Services. (2005). *Demand management: The next generation of forecasting*. Retrieved from http://www-935.ibm.com/services/us/imc/pdf/g510-6014-demand-management.pdf

IBM Global Business Services. (2005). *Supply chain management—logistics services: Cost-effective logistics capabilities to meet today's supply chain challenges.* Retrieved from http://www-935.ibm.com/services/us/gbs/bus/pdf/g510-3793-supply-chain-management-logistics-services-cost-effective-logistics-capabilities.pdf

Info, A. M. E. (2005). *How RFID can help optimize supply chain management.* Retrieved from http://www.ameinfo.com/66090.html

Intermec. (2007). *Supply chain RFID: How it works and why it pays.* Retrieved from http://epsfiles.intermec.com/eps_files/eps_wp/SupplyChainRFID_wp_web.pdf

Ishikawa, T., Yumoto, Y., Kurata, M., Endo, M., Kinoshita, S., Hoshino, F., et al. (2003). *Applying Auto-ID to the Japanese publication business to deliver advanced supply chain management, innovative retail applications, and convenient and safe reader services.* Retrieved from http://www.autoidlabs.org/uploads/media/KEI-AUTOID-WH004.pdf

Knowledgeleader. (2006). *Overview of RFID components.* Retrieved from http://www.theiia.org/download.cfm?file=93793

Langer, M., Loidl, S., & Nerb, M. (1998). Customer service management: A more transparent view to your subscribed services. In *Proceedings of the IEEE International Workshop on Distributed Systems: Operations & Management.*

Lin, H. T., Lo, W. S., & Chiang, C. L. (2006). Using RFID in supply chain management for customer service. In *Proceedings of the IEEE International Conference on Systems, Man, and Cybernetics,* Taipei, Taiwan (pp. 1377-1381).

Michael, K., & McCathie, L. (2005). The pros and cons of RFID in supply chain management. In *Proceedings of the International Conference on Mobile Business,* Sydney, Australia (pp. 623-629).

Modrak, V., Knuth, P., & Novak-Marcinein, J. (2010). Advantages and risks of RFID in business applications. *International Business Management, 4*(1), 28–34. doi:10.3923/ibm.2010.28.34

Murray, M. (2010). *Introduction to supply chain management.* Retrieved from http://logistics.about.com/od/supplychainintroduction/a/into_scm.htm

Pearson, J. (2006). *Increasing security in the supply chain with electronic security markers.* Retrieved from http://www.ti.com/rfid/docs/manuals/whtPapers/wp_eSecurity_Markers.pdf

Phoenix Software International. (2006). *Optical character recognition (OCR): What you need to know.* Retrieved from http://www.phoenixsoftware.com/pdf/ocrdataentry.pdf

RFID4U. (2006). *Benefits of RFID-enabled supply chain.* Retrieved from http://www.rfid4u.com/downloads/Benefits%20of%20RFID-Enabled%20Supply%20Chain.pdf

Sabbaghi, A., & Vaidyanathan, G. (2008). Effectiveness and efficiency of RFID technology in supply chain management: Strategic values and challenges. *Journal of Theoretical and Applied Electronic Commerce Research, 3*(2), 71–81. doi:10.4067/S0718-18762008000100007

Sheng, Q. Z., Li, X., & Zeadally, S. (2008). Enabling next-generation RFID applications: Solutions and challenges. *IEEE Computer, 41*(9), 21–28.

Tektronix. (2004). *Radio frequency identification (RFID) overview.* Retrieved from http://www.isotest.es/web/Soporte/Formacion/Notas%20de%20aplicacion/TEKTRONIX/TEKTRONIX%20RSA/RFID.pdf

United Parcel Service of America, Inc. (2005). *Demystifying RFID in the supply chain: An overview of the promise and pitfalls.* Retrieved from http://www.ups-scs.com/solutions/white_papers/wp_RFID.pdf

United States Government Accountability Office. (2005). *Information security radio frequency identification technology in the federal government.* Retrieved from http://epic.org/privacy/surveillance/spotlight/0806/gao05551.pdf

United States Government Accountability Office. (2005). *Radio frequency identification technology in the federal government.* Retrieved from http://epic.org/privacy/surveillance/spotlight/0806/gao05551.pdf

Section 3
Networks

Chapter 11
Prioritization Schemes in Queuing Handoff and New Calls to Reduce Call Drops in Cellular Systems

Allam Mousa
An-Najah National University, Palestine

ABSTRACT

This paper proposes different queuing scenarios to avoid dropping of handoff and new calls in a cellular phone network, which is essential when the network has certain restrictions on the available frequencies. This limitation degrades the performance of the system and more sites are required to achieve the desired capacity and coverage. However, this leads to a higher percentage of call drops during handoff. This paper presents a queuing technique for both new and handoff calls to reduce the probability of call drop in such a system, leading to improvement in QoS. The proposed scenarios show better system performance. The blocking probability is reduced from 2% down to 0.04% for queuing handoff calls and from 2% to 1.14% when queuing new calls using the same technique. The four different presented approaches are: 1) only new calls are queued; 2) only handoff calls are queued; 3) by using all available channels; 4) by using only half. The queuing size also plays an important role for both new and handoff calls.

DOI: 10.4018/978-1-4666-2163-3.ch011

1. INTRODUCTION

Over the last few years, one of the major successes in the telecommunications world has been the widespread diffusion of cellular mobile telephone which provides full mobility of users (Stallings, 2005). This implies that it is possible for a mobile set (MS) to roam from one cell to another, while information transfer over the network is in progress. In order for the communication to continue, it is necessary that the network be capable of transferring the connection from the old cell (the source BS) to the new one (the destination BS). This operation is normally referred to as call-handover or handoff (Ekiz, Salih, Kucukoner, & Fidanboylu, 2005). Hence, handovers are considered a key element for providing this mobility (Ahmed, Ibrahim, & El-Tamally, 2010). Network operators give emphasis to optimize the handover issue, since it is strongly related to drop calls rate (Markopoulos, Pissaris, Kyriazakos, & Sykas, 2004).

The transfer of a current communication channel could be in terms of a time slot, frequency band, or a code word to a new base station (BS). If a new BS has some unoccupied channels then it assigns one of them to the handed off call. However, if all of the channels are in use at the handoff time there are two possibilities: to drop the call or to delay it for a while (Stallings, 2005).

Call blocking is the phenomenon of dropping new or handoff calls, or it can be defined as suddenly dropping already established calls (for special reasons). In cellular networks, blocking occurs when a base station has no free channel to allocate to a mobile user (Raskutti, Zalesky, Wong, & Zuckerman, 2007). The two kinds of blocking are the new call blocking and handoff blocking (refers to blocking of ongoing calls) due to the mobility of the users. The phenomenon of drop calls has been analyzed to allow the network operator to optimize system performance (Boggia, Camarda, D'Alconzo, De Biasi, & Siviero 2005;

Vassilakis, Kallos, Moscholios, & Logothetis, 2008).

The Quality of Service (QoS) or the Grade of Service (GoS) in cellular networks is mainly determined by the two quantities; the first determines the fraction of new calls that are blocked, while the second is closely related to the fraction of admitted calls that terminate prematurely due to dropout. Hence, the main aim of this work is to achieve a good QoS in cellular network by putting handoff and new calls in a queue until it can be processed, the Queuing theory allows the design of communication links that can provision the quality of service in time-varying channels (Negi & Goel, 2005). This will reduce the percentage of lost calls (Falowo & Chan, 2010).

This paper is organized such that section two describes the handoff initialization decision based on the received signal strength with four techniques; relative signal strength, with threshold, with hysteresis and with hysteresis and threshold. Section three explains the point at which handoff must be initiated and the action protocols MCHO, NCHO, and NCHO/MAHO. The prioritization schemes are illustrated in section four. Section five discusses the queuing schemes used with handoff or new calls. Simulation environments are illustrated in section six which talks about queuing new and handoff calls. The obtained results are analyzed in section seven.

2. HANDOFF INITIATION

The principle parameter used to make the handoff initiation decision is the received signal strength (RSS); four techniques are available to decide the necessity to initiate a handoff request, which are: Relative signal strength, Relative signal strength with threshold, Relative signal strength with hysteresis, Relative signal strength with hysteresis and threshold (Tranter, Shanmugan, Rappaport, & Kosbar, 2004; Lee, 2006; Mullett,

2006). Handoff algorithms for WLAN have also been investigated (Kwon & Lee, 2004).

Relative Signal Strength

While the mobile station is moving from point A to point B, then the mobile unit is handed off from BS A to BS B when the signal strength of BS B exceeds that of BS A. The received power from two adjacent base stations is shown in Figure 1. This handoff occurs at the points L1, L2, L3 and L4 depending on the threshold value Th1, Th2, Th3 and Th4 and based on the selection criteria.

Relative Signal Strength with Threshold

The hand off occurs when two conditions are satisfied; the signal at the current BS should be sufficiently weak (i.e. less than a predefined threshold) and the signal from the new BS should be higher than both threshold and old BS signal strength. Three suggested levels of threshold can be seen in Figure 1, namely; Th1, Th2 and Th3. When Th1 is chosen, then it will operate the same as relative signal strength, if Th2 is chosen then the handoff will take place at point L2 and if the lowest threshold, Th3, is chosen, then the handoff will take place late at point L4, this may cause a bad communication link due to the weak signal.

Relative Signal Strength with Hysteresis

The handoff occurs only when the new BS is sufficiently stronger than the current one by a margin H as displayed in Figure 1, this margin prevents the ping pong effect (Stallings, 2005), because when the handoff occurs the effect of the margin H is reversed; this Hysteresis mechanism is shown in Figure 2.

Figure 1. Received power from two adjacent BSs

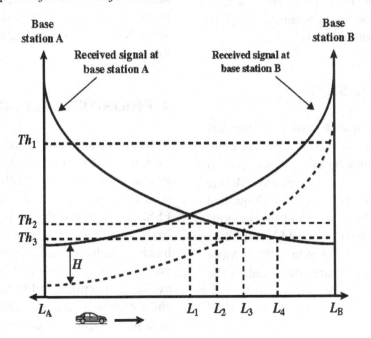

Figure 2. Hysteresis mechanism

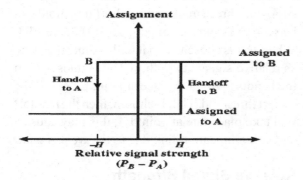

Relative Signal Strength with Hysteresis and Threshold

This method ensures that the handoff will not happen unless the current signal level drops under a threshold and the target base station is stronger than the old one by a hysteresis margin as shown in Figure 1 where the handoff occurs at L3 if the threshold is chosen to be either Th1 or Th2 and occurs at L4 if the threshold is set to Th3.

In all these techniques, the handover initiation must take place before the point where weakness of the RSS may cause link disconnection (Dahmouni, Morine, & Vaton, 2005).

3. HANDOFF DECISION

The measuring techniques to assign the handoff initiation point are used to determine the point at which a handoff must be initiated, to perform an action three protocols exist, namely, Mobile Controlled Handoff (MCHO), Network Controlled Handoff (NCHO), Network Control Handoff/ Mobile Assisted Handoff (NCHO/MAHO) (Ekiz, Salih, Kucukoner, & Fidanboylu, 2005). More details of these protocols are illustrated in the following subsections;

MCHO

MS and BS make the necessary measurements, and the BS sends them to the MS, then, the MS decides when to handoff based on the information gained from the BS and itself. Digital European Cordless Telephone (DECT) is a sample cellular system using MCHO.

NCHO

It is used in first generation cellular systems such as Advanced Mobile Phone System (AMPS); where the mobile telephone switching office (MTSO) is responsible for the overall handoff decision in NCHO; the network handles the necessary RSS measurements and handoff decision and the handoff execution time is in the order of many seconds because of the high network load.

NCHO/MAHO

The MS makes the necessary measurements and sends them into the BS which forwards them into the base station controller (BSC), in the BSC the handoff decision is taken, this technique is used in GSM.

4. PRIORITIZATION SCHEMES

Typical GSM systems usually use Fully Shared Scheme (FSS), in which all free channels are available for both new calls and handoff calls which are treated the same way, when a BS has FSS, it is assigned due to first-come first-serve basis regardless of whether the call is new or handoff, such a scheme is preferred by the service providers since it insures best utilization of the available spectrum, and its less desired by users since dropping an active call is much annoying than blocking a new call (Candan & Salamah, 2007; Salamah & Lababidi, 2006).

For better performance handling handoff calls (ongoing calls), Guard Channel Scheme (GCS) exists. GCS reserves some fixed or adaptively changing number of channels for handoff calls only, the rest of the channels are used by new and handoff calls, so the handoff calls are better served and the blocking probability is decreased. The costs of such a scheme are an increase new call blocking probability and a decrease in total carried traffic. Other techniques are used to combine the benefits of FSS and GCS.

Queuing handoff calls prioritization scheme queues the handoff calls when all of the channels are occupied in a BS; when a channel is released, it is assigned to one of the handoff calls in the queue. Also, some systems queue new calls to decrease call blocking probability, the time interval between handoff initiation and receiver threshold makes it possible to use queuing handoff calls.

5. QUEUING SCHEME

Queuing means to put a call (handoff or new) in a queue if no channels are available instead of dropping or blocking them off, queuing calls may not use GCS thus the available spectrum cam be fully utilized expecting better performance handling handoff calls (Candan & Salamah, 2007).

In order to compare two systems, one uses queuing scheme and the other does not, common parameters should exist, including the number of available channels and maxim traffic taking into account the accepted value of blocking

To determine the maximum traffic a single site can handle according to an accepted value of blocking, Erlang-B formula was used as given in Equation 1. This formula provides the blocking probability versus the total number of channels, where the blocking probability in typical cellular systems that do not use queuing scheme are equal in the case of new and handoff calls (Tranter, Shanmugan, Rappaport, & Kosbar, 2004; Lee, 2006).

$$\mathrm{BP} = A^N / N! * \sum_{n=0}^{N} A^N / n! \qquad (1)$$

where:

- N: number of channels at the site
- A: traffic, which may be seen as call requests times holding time (Erlang)

The maximum traffic at certain blocking probability and for various blocking capacity can be obtained using the Erlang-B formula, from which is shown in Figure 3. The available channels in a TDMA system (i.e. GSM) will be 8 channels per frequency, one channel is used for signaling, the remaining seven channels are used for traffic, and thus a single frequency can serve seven users at a time (Dahmouni, Morin, & Vaton, 2005). At an acceptable blocking probability the maximum traffic can be obtained (to be shown in the simulation section).

6. SIMULATION

The system performance will be investigated in case of queuing new calls and in case of queuing handoff calls. The system to be investigated has 12 available frequencies for call traffic. Thus the total number of channels available for users will be 84, in the case of using all the frequencies at each cell site. The detailed environments of the simulation are discussed below; using all available frequencies, queuing new calls and queuing handoff calls and using half the available frequencies in each cell.

Using All the Available Frequencies in Each Cell Site

In order to do the simulation, the maximum traffic the cell can handle must be found at an accepted level of blocking probability. As shown in Figure

Figure 3. Erlang-B formula simulation

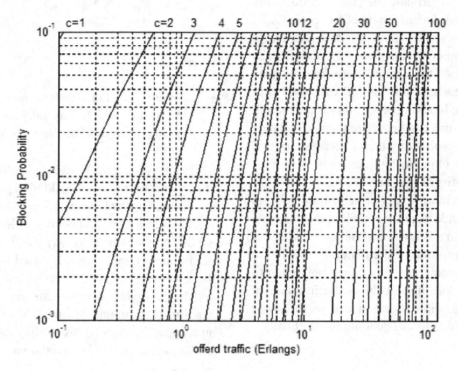

3 (Erlang-B formula), at blocking probability of 2% and 84 channels available the maximum traffic is 69.7 Erlangs, the traffic caused by a single user equals requests for new calls times holding time, assuming each user makes 5 requests and each ones holding time is about 1 minute then the traffic generated by a single user will 0.083 Erlang, the total number of users that can be handled at a single cell site in this case will be 69.7/0.083=840 user.

Queuing New Calls

In this case, if all the channels are busy at the cell site, new calls are put in a queue until a channel is available, handoff calls which don't find available channels will not be handed off or even queued, channels will remain on the old link until dropped off or terminated successfully. A representation of this blocking probability case is given in Equation 2.

$$BP = \left(\frac{b1}{N}\right)^{M1} \bigg/ \left[N! * \frac{\sum_{n=0}^{N-1} A^{n-N}}{n!} + \frac{1 - \left(\frac{b1}{N}\right)^{M1}}{1 - \left(\frac{b1}{N}\right)} \right]$$

(2)

where:

- N: number of channels at the site
- A: traffic, call requests*holding time (Erlang)
- b1: traffic of new calls only
- M1: size of queue for new calls

Assuming handoff percentage to all calls is 5%, then b1=(840*95%)*0.083=66.234 Erlangs. The relation between blocking probability of new calls and queue size used as shown in Figure 4 where queuing new calls fails to improve the blocking probability of handed off calls it even makes it

Figure 4. Blocking probability of handoff calls vs. queue size, new calls are queued

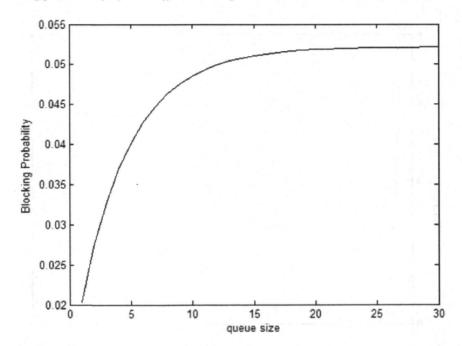

much worse than using no queuing scheme, at queue size of 1 the blocking probability is a little bit over the desired system performance of 2%.

Queuing Handoff Calls

If all channels are busy the handed off call is put in a queue until a channel is available, the period between initiating the handoff request and dropping the call due to signal weakness makes it possible to delay and queue the requests, new calls are assigned a channel if there is no handoff request queue and available free channels, otherwise the call is blocked as illustrated by Equation 3 and simulated as shown in Figure 5 where the values of M1 and M2 are set to have the desired queuing criteria.

$$ BP = \frac{1 - \left(\frac{b2}{N}\right)^{M2}}{1 - \left(\frac{b2}{N}\right)} \bigg/ \left[N! * \sum_{n=0}^{N-1} \frac{A^{n-N}}{n!} + \frac{1 - \left(\frac{b1}{N}\right)^{M1}}{1 - \left(\frac{b1}{N}\right)} \right] \qquad (3) $$

where:

- N: number of channels at the site
- A: traffic, call requests*holding time (Erlang)
- b1: traffic of new calls only
- b2: traffic of handoff calls only
- M1: size of queue for new calls
- M2: size of queue for handoff calls

A large drop in blocking probability of handoff calls can be seen, the performance of the system improved in a noticeable way when dealing with handoff calls. On the other hand, the system's performance when dealing with new calls must be investigated. This may be given in Equation 3 where the values of M1 and M2 are set to have the desired queuing criteria. The simulated results are shown in Figure 6 where new calls blocking probability drops as the queue size increases leading to improvement of the system's performance.

Figure 5. Blocking probability of handoff calls vs. queue size, handoff calls are queued

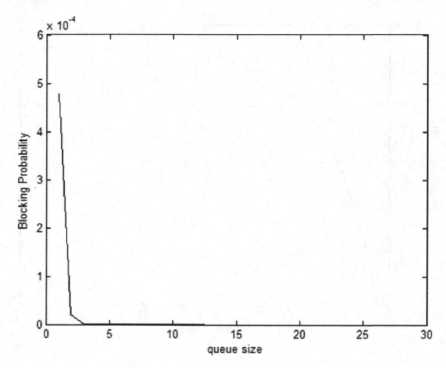

Figure 6. Blocking probability of new calls vs. queue size, handoff calls are queued

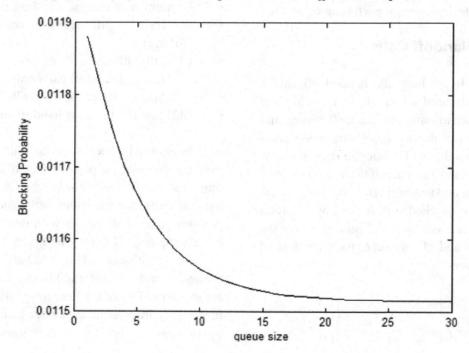

Using Half the Available Frequencies in Each Cell Site

In this case the maximum traffic the cell can handle at blocking probability of 2% and 42 channels available is 31 Erlangs, the traffic caused by a single user is 0.083 Erlang (as calculated previously), the total number of users that can be handled at a single cell site in this case will be 31/0.083=374 users.

The blocking probability of various cases given in Equations 2 and 3 were utilized using the following parameters, and the results are shown in Table 1:

- N: number of channels at the site: (42)
- A: traffic, call requests -times- holding time: (31Erlang)
- b1: traffic of new calls only: (29.5 Erlang)
- b2: traffic of handoff calls only: (1.55 Erlang)

The system has shown a similar performance as in the case of using all the available frequencies, it is noticed for queuing handoff calls with

Table 1. Simulation results for queue size of 1

Queue Size=1	New Calls Queued	Handoff Calls Queued
BP new calls	0.7%	1.14%
BP HO calls	1.8%	0.04%

a queue size of one, that is the system has shown better performance when dealing with both new and handoff requests.

7. SIMULATION ANALYSIS

For the cases where half and full available frequencies are used, queuing handoff calls has shown a noticeable performance increase for both new and handoff calls. For the case where full frequency is used then the blocking probability of handoff calls at a queue size of one is 0.04%, and that due to new calls is 1%. Hence, using queuing handoff calls technique with a queue size of only one will increase the overall system performance. The blocking probability of new and handoff calls, in terms of queue size, is shown in Figure 7.

Figure 7. New and handoff calls blocking probability vs. queue size

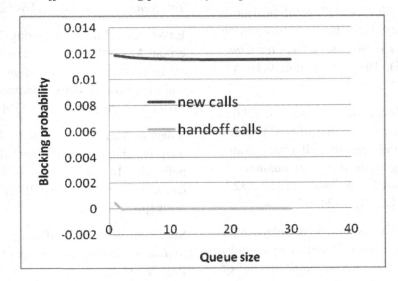

8. CONCLUSION

Queuing both handoff and new calls in GSM communication system has been introduced to reduce the blocking probability of such calls whenever it is needed. A blocking probability reduction factor of 50 was achieved for the handoff calls and a factor of less than 2 was achieved for new calls. A queue size of one was suffecient to improve the performance. However, increasing the queue size for values more than 5 is useless since the blocking probability of both new and handoff calls will stabilize despite the increase in queue size.

REFERENCES

Ahmed, M. A., Ibrahim, N. M., & El-Tamally, H. H. (2010, March). Performance evaluation of handoff queuing schemes. In *Proceedings of the Second International Conference on Communication Software and Networks* (pp. 83-87).

Boggia, G., Camarda, P., D'Alconzo, A., De Biasi, A., & Siviero, M. (2005). Drop call probability in established cellular networks: From data analysis to modeling. In. *Proceedings of the Vehicular Technology Conference, 5*, 2775–2779.

Candan, I., & Salamah, M. (2007). Analytical modeling of time-threshold based bandwidth allocation scheme for cellular networks. *Computer Communications, 30*(5), 1036–1043. doi:10.1016/j.comcom.2006.10.015

Dahmouni, H., Morin, B., & Vaton, S. (2005, March). Performance modeling of GSM/GPRS cells with different radio resource allocation strategies. In. *Proceedings of the Wireless Communications and Networking Conference, 3*, 1317–1322. doi:10.1109/WCNC.2005.1424707

Ekiz, N., Salih, T., Kucukoner, S., & Fidanboylu, K. (2005). An overview of handoff techniques in cellular networks. *International Journal of Information Technology, 2*(2).

Falowo, O. E., & Chan, H. A. (2010). Heuristic RAT selection policy to minimize call blocking probability in next generation wireless networks. *Wireless Communications and Mobile Computing, 10*(2), 214–229.

Kwon, K., & Lee, C. (2004). A fast handoff algorithm using intelligent channel scan for IEEE 802.11 WLANs. In *Proceedings of the 6th International Conference on Advanced Communication Technology* (Vo. 1, pp. 46-50).

Lee, W. (2006). *Wireless and cellular telecommunications* (3rd ed.). New York, NY: McGraw-Hill.

Markopoulos, A. E., Pissaris, P., Kyriazakos, S., & Sykas, E. D. (2004). Cellular network performance analysis: Handoff algorithms based on mobile location and area information. *Wireless Personal Communications, 30*(2-4), 97–117. doi:10.1023/B:WIRE.0000049393.01548.30

Mullett, G. J. (2006). *Wireless telecommunications systems and networks*. Florence, KY: Delmar Cengage Learning.

Negi, R., & Goel, S. (2004, December). An information-theoretic approach to queuing in wireless channels with large delay bounds. In. *Proceedings of the IEEE Conference on Global Telecommunications, 1*, 116–122.

Raskutti, G., Zalesky, A., Wong, E. W. M., & Zuckerman, M. (2007). Enhanced blocking probability evaluation method for circuit-switched trunk reservation networks. *IEEE Communications Letters, 11*(6), 543. doi:10.1109/LCOMM.2007.062119

Salamah, M., & Lababidi, K. (2006). Dynamically adaptive channel reservation scheme for cellular networks. In *Proceedings of the International Conference on Personal Wireless Communications* (pp. 269-272).

Stallings, W. (2005). *Wireless communications and networks* (2nd ed.). Upper Saddle River, NJ: Prentice-Hall.

Tranter, W. H., Shanmugan, K. S., Rappaport, T. S., & Kosbar, K. L. (2004). *Principles of communication systems simulation with wireless applications*. Upper Saddle River, NJ: Prentice-Hall.

Vassilakis, V. G., Kallos, G. A., Moscholios, I. D., & Logothetis, M. D. (2008, June). On the handoff-call blocking probability calculation in W-CDMA cellular networks. In *Proceedings of the Fourth Advanced International Conference on Telecommunications* (pp. 173-179).

Chapter 12
A Proposal for Enhancing the Mobility Management in the Future 3GPP Architectures

Joel Penhoat
Orange Labs, France

Karine Guillouard
Orange Labs, France

Servane Bonjour
Orange Labs, France

Pierrick Seïté
Orange Labs, France

ABSTRACT

The management of the mobility between radio networks composed of heterogeneous radio technologies, called inter-access mobility management, provides the capability to tie together heterogeneous radio networks into an integrated network. The 3GPP architectures with well-designed inter-access mobility management capabilities are a part of the solution to cope with the growth of the mobile data traffic. This paper reviews the 3GPP architectures to highlight those with these capabilities. In order to evaluate if the mobility management is well-designed into these architectures, the authors describe the phases making up the management of the mobility and design an evaluation grid to assess the integration of these phases into the highlighted architectures. Since the assessment shows the existence of loopholes in the design of the inter-access mobility management, this paper proposes to enhance the 3GPP architectures by implementing a method called Hierarchical and Distributed Handover.

DOI: 10.4018/978-1-4666-2163-3.ch012

INTRODUCTION

Seamless mobility, i.e., a set of solutions that provide uninterrupted session continuity, has been performed thanks to the development of cellular technologies and was dedicated to voice services. Once addicted to this seamless mobility, mobile users ask for mobility for their data services also. In Europe, 3rd Generation Partnership Project (3GPP) mobile networks are used to transmit voice and data over long distances. The arrival of new radio technologies, such as Wi-Fi or WiMAX, enhances the radio coverage, thus should potentially satisfy the increasing demand of mobility for data services. But in order to offer a seamless mobility for data services across heterogeneous radio technologies, for example between Universal Mobile Telecommunications System (UMTS) and Wireless Local Area Network (WLAN), a network operator has to deploy an architecture that ties together heterogeneous radio networks into an integrated network. This architecture should allow network operators to cope with the exponential growth of the mobile data traffic by offloading data traffic from their overburdened 3GPP mobile networks to unloaded radio networks without noticeable impact on the Quality of Service (QoS).

Because we consider that 3GPP architectures with well-designed inter-access mobility management capabilities are a part of the solution to cope with the growth of the mobile data traffic mainly fuelled by flat rate subscriptions, smartphones and new uses such as social communities, we want to identify these architectures and evaluate if the management of the mobility is well-designed within these ones.

Our paper is organized as follows. In the first section we describe the phases making up the management of the mobility. This description will help us to assess the accuracy of the design of the mobility management within the 3GPP architectures. In the second section we survey the related works in the inter-access mobility management domain. In the third section, we identify the 3GPP architectures implementing inter-access mobility management functions. In the fourth section, we examine if the mobility management is well-designed within the identified architectures. Since our assessment shows the existence of loopholes in the design of the inter-access mobility management, in the fifth section, we propose to introduce a new method, called Hierarchical and Distributed Handover, into the future 3GPP architectures for enhancing their mobility management. Finally, the conclusion offers insights into our future work.

DESCRIPTION OF PHASES OF THE MOBILITY MANAGEMENT

By carefully analysing the management of mobility, we can split the mobility management into three phases, namely handover information gathering, handover decision and handover execution. The handover information gathering phase gathers information (link monitoring, new incoming call...) and triggers the handover decision phase based on criteria. The handover decision phase selects one or more target network(s) taking into account user's preferences, operator's policies, and so on, and then triggers the handover execution phase. The handover execution phase asks the User Equipment (UE) to connect to the selected network(s). This phase encompasses a preparation phase (context transfer, QoS renegotiation, authentication...) before the execution phase itself consisting of a UE network interface attachment to the new network, a terminal location update, a data forwarding and a resource release on the previous network. Together, the three phases define a handover management chain as shown in Figure 1. These phases may be carried out separately by various entities comprising User Equipments and network nodes.

A question arises: which entity should manage the mobility of a user? His user equipment? One

Figure 1. The handover management chain

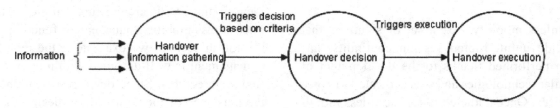

or several network nodes? Zdarsky and Schmitt (2004) proposed to shift the mobility management to the users. But if the viewpoint of the operator managing the networks differs from the viewpoint of a user, a conflict might appear between a user and the operator because the operator might want to choose a different target network from that chosen by a user. The debate whether the user-centric approach, i.e. the approach in which the users manage their mobility, or the network-centric approach, i.e. the approach in which the network operators manage the mobility of the users, is far from being over.

RELATED WORKS IN THE INTER-ACCESS MOBILITY MANAGEMENT DOMAIN

The inter-access mobility management is studied since the early 2000s. Akyildiz, Xie, and Mohanty (2004) reviewed the protocols and architectures managing the mobility. They classified the mobility management solutions according to the layers of the TCP/IP stack in which they are implemented. Then they analysed solutions implemented within the link-layer, within the network-layer, and solutions called cross-layer solutions in which the link-layer assists the network-layer during a handover. Their study is interesting because it shows that cross-layer solutions enhance the mobility management. However, it has two loopholes. Firstly, the definition of the mobility management phases, which dates from 1999, is incomplete because it does not take into account

the information gathering phase and the decision phase. Secondly, the examined solutions do not take into account the 3GPP architectures.

Atiquzzaman and Reaz (2005) reviewed the protocols managing the mobility within the transport-layer. Their study is interesting for three reasons. Firstly, the mobility management implemented within the transport-layer has no impact on the network equipment because only the terminals are concerned. Secondly, the study presents criteria to classify the protocols according to the way they implement the mobility management requirements. Thirdly, within each class, an assessment of the efficiency of each protocol is done against criteria. However, their study has two loopholes. Firstly, the definition of the mobility management phases does not take into account the information gathering phase and the decision phase. Secondly, the study describes no architecture.

Le, Fu, and Hogrefe (2006) reviewed the solutions implemented within the TCP/IP stack. This study is interesting for four reasons. Firstly, it defines the requirements that these solutions have to take into account. Secondly, it defines metrics measuring the performances of the solutions. Thirdly, it presents and evaluates the performances of the solutions implemented within the network-layer, within the transport-layer, within the session-layer, and within a layer between the transport-layer and the network-layer. Fourthly, it shows that all the solutions have shortcomings. Only a solution based on the cooperation of all the layers of the TCP/IP stack will be able to satisfy all the requirements of the mobility management. However, their study has two loopholes. Firstly, it does not define the mobility management phases. Secondly, it does not describe the 3GPP architectures.

Lataste and Tossou (2008) reviewed the solutions implemented within the session-layer. This study is interesting because it lists the 3GPP architectures with inter-access mobility management capabilities. However, it has two loopholes. Firstly, the mobility management phases are not defined. Secondly, the study only focuses on the session-layer. Our work completes their study by identifying the 3GPP architectures with inter-access mobility management capabilities implemented within the link-layer and within the network-layer.

OVERVIEW OF 3GPP ARCHITECTURES WITH INTER-ACCESS MOBILITY MANAGEMENT CAPABILITIES

We reviewed the 3GPP architectures to highlight the architectures with inter-access mobility management capabilities. We found five architectures implementing these capabilities: two architectures implement the mobility management within the session-layer, two architectures implement it within the network-layer, and one within the link-layer. The overview of the mobility management implemented within the session-layer is based on Lataste and Tossou's (2008) work.

3GPP ARCHITECTURES IMPLEMENTING MOBILITY MANAGEMENT WITHIN THE SESSION LAYER

At the session-level, Voice Call Continuity (VCC) and IP Multimedia Subsystem Service Continuity (IMS Service Continuity) implement inter-access mobility management functions. They provide session continuity for IMS based services. IMS based services (Camarillo & Garcia-Martin, 2008), which are based on Session Initiation Protocol (SIP) defined in (Camarillo, Johnston, Peterson, Sparks, Handley, & Schooler, 2002), can be provided with the use of Circuit-Switched (CS) networks or Packet-Switched (PS) networks. VCC provides session continuity for voice services during handovers between CS networks and PS networks; IMS Service Continuity extends session continuity beyond voice services (video, data, etc.) and beyond handovers between CS and PS networks.

Voice Call Continuity

The 3GPP specifies VCC in (3rd Generation Partnership Project, 2007) to offer session continuity for voice services between CS and PS networks. Session continuity is based on a dedicated Application Server (AS) called VCC AS which anchors voice calls. In other words, the VCC AS, which is located in the user's home IMS, is a Mobility Anchor Point. The VCC AS splits into two parts the signaling path between a UE and a Remote Equipment: the signaling path between a UE and its VCC AS is called access leg, and the signaling path between the VCC AS and the Remote Equipment is called remote leg. When a UE performs a handover between an IMS domain and a CS domain (Figure 2), it requests its VCC AS to transfer the access leg. The new access leg is established, then the remote leg is updated and the old access leg is removed. The update of the signaling path between the access leg and the remote leg results in the switch of the media path from the old access network to the new access network and the release of resources in the old access network.

A VCC AS implements four functionalities:

- **Domain Selection Function:** Chooses the appropriate domain to be used for delivering incoming calls to a User Equipment. For choosing the appropriate domain, it

Figure 2. Transfer of an access leg during a handover between IMS and CS domains

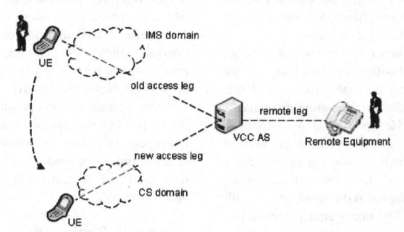

checks the UE registration in the IMS domain and the UE attachment in the CS domain.

- **Domain Transfer Function:** Performs the transfer of voice calls between the CS domain and the IMS domain. All the sessions of the terminal are transferred during a handover, i.e. the transfer is not per session, and only the voice components of a session can be transferred, i.e. the other session components are released.
- **Customised Applications for Mobile network Enhanced Logic (CAMEL) Service:** CAMEL (3rd Generation Partnership Project, 2009a) is a means of adding supplementary services to 3GPP networks, such as prepaid roaming services, fraud control, special numbers... The CAMEL Service enforces the CS domain policy, reroutes CS calls to the IMS domain when CS to IMS handover is requested, and resolves the VCC Domain Transfer Number (3rd Generation Partnership Project, 2007) when IMS to CS handover is requested.
- **CS Adaptation Function:** Responsible for the adaptation of the voice services between CS domain and IMS domain. It acts

as a SIP User Agent on behalf of the User Equipment to establish the call with the remote party and may collaborate with the CAMEL Service for interworking with the CS domain.

The VCC architecture is shown in Figure 3.

IMS Service Continuity

IMS Service Continuity (ISC), defined in (3rd Generation Partnership Project, 2009b), enhances VCC by defining the transfer of multimedia flows (audio, video ...) in four session continuity scenarios. The first one is CS-PS session continuity. The second one is PS-PS session continuity. The third one is PS-PS session continuity in conjunction with CS-PS session continuity. The fourth one is session continuity when transferring part or all media of a session from one terminal to another terminal. In the first scenario, IMS Centralized Services (ICS) as specified in (3rd Generation Partnership Project, 2009c) are used to treat IMS sessions using CS networks as standard IMS sessions. In the second scenario, a user moves from an IP radio network, such as Wi-Fi, to another IP radio network, such as WiMAX. In the third scenario, a session, initially transmitted on a

Figure 3. VCC architecture providing session continuity between CS and PS networks

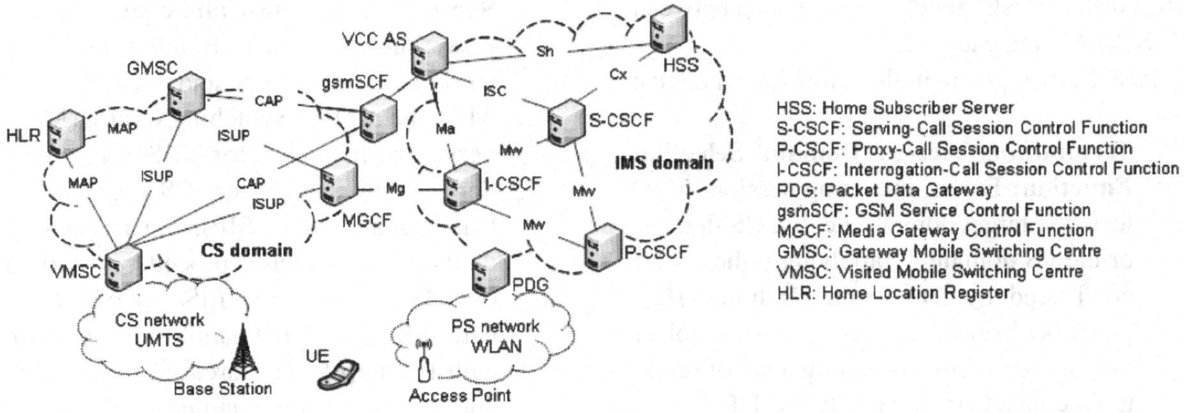

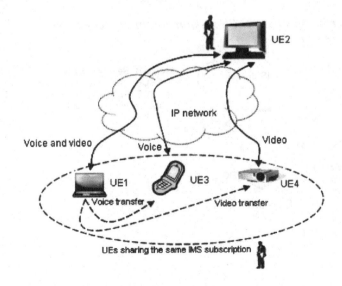

HSS: Home Subscriber Server
S-CSCF: Serving-Call Session Control Function
P-CSCF: Proxy-Call Session Control Function
I-CSCF: Interrogation-Call Session Control Function
PDG: Packet Data Gateway
gsmSCF: GSM Service Control Function
MGCF: Media Gateway Control Function
GMSC: Gateway Mobile Switching Centre
VMSC: Visited Mobile Switching Centre
HLR: Home Location Register

network supporting CS and PS communications, like Universal Terrestrial Radio Access Network (UTRAN), is transferred to a network supporting only PS communications, like Evolved UTRAN (Lescuyer & Lucidarme, 2008), or vice versa. In the fourth scenario, one or more media flows of a session are transferred among a set of User Equipments belonging to a user, i.e. sharing the same IMS subscription, connected via the same or different access networks. Figure 4 illustrates an example where UE1, UE3, and UE4 share the

same IMS subscription. Initially, the UE1 communicates with the UE2; then it requests the transfer of the voice flow from the UE1 to the UE3, and the video flow from the UE1 to the UE4.

The architecture designed to support the four scenarios relies on a dedicated AS, located in the user's home IMS network, called Service Centralization and Continuity Application Server (SCC AS), acting as a Mobility Anchor Point with regard to IMS sessions. The case where both User Equipments are mobile nodes is supported, be-

Figure 4. Transfer of multimedia flows between equipments sharing the same IMS subscription

cause, when the sessions are anchored in the SCC AS, a different SIP dialog is established between the SCC AS and each UE.

A SCC AS implements the following functions:

- **Terminating Access Domain Selection Function:** For an incoming session, it selects the target domain, i.e. the CS domain or the PS domain by applying policy rules configured by the operator's home IMS network. In the PS domain, it may select one or more contacts among a set of registered contacts for each selected UE.
- **CS Access Adaptation Function:** Provides adaptation of signaling messages exchanged between a UE and IMS Application Servers, when the UE is engaged in a session via the CS domain.
- **ICS User Agent Function:** Provides SIP User Agent behaviour on behalf of a UE engaged in a session via the CS domain.

In the CS-PS session continuity scenario, two interfaces have been added in the IMS (Figure 5):

- **I1 Interface Between User Equipment and SCC AS:** Used to control a service over the CS domain.

- **I2 Interface Between Enhanced MSC Server and Serving-Call Session Control Function (S-CSCF):** Handles the interworking between CS and IMS domains when the Mobile Switching Centre (MSC) Server is enhanced for IMS Centralized Services by converting CS signaling to IMS signaling (i.e. SIP); otherwise standard Circuit-Switched procedures apply at the MSC Server. The MSC Server is the part of the MSC that handles the signaling path (Camarillo & Garcia-Martin, 2008), the data path being handled by the Media Gateway.

The SCC AS is always triggered by the S-CSCF via the ISC interface (Figure 5). Like in VCC, when a UE performs a handover, it requests its SCC AS to transfer the access leg. The SCC AS establishes the new access leg and updates the remote leg. Then it removes the old access leg. The update of the signaling path between the access leg and the remote leg results in the switch of the media path from the old access network to the new access network and the release of resources in the old access network.

Figure 5. I1 and I2 interfaces in the CS-PS session continuity scenario

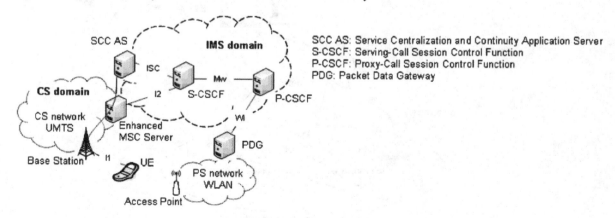

3GPP ARCHITECTURES IMPLEMENTING MOBILITY MANAGEMENT WITHIN THE NETWORK LAYER

At the network-level, WLAN Interworking (I-WLAN) and Evolved Packet Core (EPC) implement inter-access mobility management functions. I-WLAN and EPC provide access to Packet-Switched services located in a Packet Data Network (PDN), i.e. an IP network. I-WLAN aims at extending the radio coverage for PS services by complementing GSM EDGE Radio Access Network (GERAN)/UTRAN with WLAN, while EPC complements GERAN/UTRAN with E-UTRAN and with non-3GPP radio access technologies, such as WLAN, WiMAX. I-WLAN and EPC envisage roaming and non-roaming scenarios. In this paper we focus on the non-roaming scenario.

Interworking-WLAN

In (3rd Generation Partnership Project, 2009d) the 3GPP builds inter-access mobility management functions on top of I-WLAN (3rd Generation Partnership Project, 2008). In this architecture, the mobility management relies on a user-centric approach. To access a PS service through a WLAN, the UE uses a manual or an automatic

WLAN selection mechanism. It can be simultaneously connected to both a WLAN and a GERAN/UTRAN, i.e. it supports multi-homing. During the handovers, the preservation of the IP address of the UE is based on Dual Stack Mobile IPv6 (DSMIPv6) defined in (Soliman, 2009). The architecture requires deploying a Home Agent (HA) in the core network, as shown in Figure 6. The HA, which acts as a Mobility Anchor Point, communicates with the UE and exchanges DSMIPv6 signaling messages to keep track of the network the UE is recently camping on. The UE contains a DSMIPv6 client to enable the DSMIPv6 based signaling and user's data transfer towards the Home Agent. Three new interfaces have been added to the I-WLAN architecture:

- **H1 Interface:** This interface between the UE and the HA is used for DSMIPv6 signaling and data transfer between the UE and the HA. It may be transported over a WLAN or a GERAN/UTRAN. When transported over the WLAN, the Internet Key Exchange protocol (Kaufman, 2005) secures the communications between the UE and the HA.

- **H2 Interface:** This interface between the Authentication Authorization Accounting (AAA) server and the HA is used to trans-

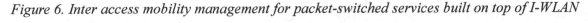

Figure 6. Inter access mobility management for packet-switched services built on top of I-WLAN

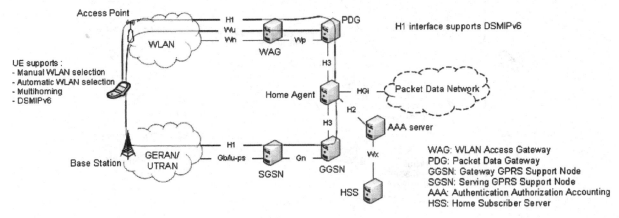

port authentication, authorization and charging information in a secure manner.

- **H3 Interface:** This interface between the Gateway General Packet Radio Service (GPRS) Support Node (GGSN) and the HA, and between the Packet Data Gateway (PDG) and the HA, is used to carry DSMIPv6 messages towards the HA.

Evolved Packet Core

EPC, defined in (3rd Generation Partnership Project, 2009e, 2009f), is the all-IP core network architecture that supports IPv4 only, IPv6 only, and dual stack IPv4/IPv6. It enables operators to deploy one IP packet core network that supports Packet-Switched services over Evolved UTRAN (E-UTRAN), GERAN, UTRAN, and Non-3GPP IP networks. Non-3GPP IP networks are classified in trusted and untrusted networks as shown in Figure 7. An untrusted network requires the deployment of an evolved Packet Data Gateway

(ePDG) that secures the access of the UE to the EPC between itself and the UE. For trusted networks, an ePDG is not required. In Figure 7, the Serving Gateway (S-GW) acts as a link-layer Mobility Anchor Point as the UE moves within E-UTRAN, GERAN and UTRAN; the Access Gateway (A-GW) acts as a link-layer Mobility Anchor Point as the UE moves within trusted non-3GPP IP networks; the PDN Gateway (P-GW) provides access to the Packet Data Network and assigns an IP address to the UE. The 3GPP also introduces an Access Network Discovery and Selection Function (3rd Generation Partnership Project, 2009f) that is used to help the UE to perform the discovery and the selection of non-3GPP IP networks. It provides to a UE a policy that identifies which radio access technologies are allowed for the handovers. For example, the policy may indicate that handovers from WLAN to E-UTRAN/UTRAN/GERAN are allowed, and that E-UTRAN is more preferable than GERAN; it may also provide criteria that must be met to perform a handover and indicates

Figure 7. High level view of the EPC architecture for packet-switched services

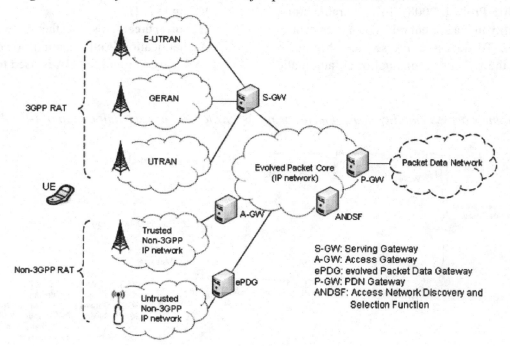

conditions when the policy is valid, for example a location or a time duration.

A requirement of the EPC is to provide seamless mobility for PS services at the IP-level. To achieve this goal, the 3GPP relies on the network-centric and user-centric approaches. The network-centric approach relies on Proxy Mobile IPv6 (PMIPv6) defined in (Gundavelli, Leung, Devarapalli, Chowdhury, & Patil, 2008) and on Mobile IPv4 (MIPv4) in Foreign Agent mode defined in (Perkins, 2002). Recently, PMIPv6 has integrated the support of IPv4 (Wakikawa & Gundavelli, 2010). The P-GW, which acts as a Mobility Anchor Point, includes the PMIPv6 Local Mobility Anchor (LMA) functionality; the A-GW and the S-GW include the PMIPv6 Mobile Access Gateway (MAG) functionality. The user-centric approach relies on DSMIPv6 and on MIPv4. To support the two approaches, the 3GPP defines four interfaces, called S2a, S2b, S2c, and S5. Figure 8 shows the S2a, S2b and S5 interfaces. The S2a interface is defined between the P-GW and the A-GW; it supports PMIPv6 and MIPv4 in Foreign Agent mode. The S2b interface is defined between the P-GW and the ePDG; it supports PMIPv6. The S5 interface is defined between the P-GW and the S-GW; it supports PMIPv6 and GPRS Tunnelling Protocol (GTP).

Figure 9 shows the S2c interface. It is defined between the P-GW and the UE; it supports DSMIPv6.

Because the EPC is able to support four different mobility management protocols, the 3GPP specifies in (3rd Generation Partnership Project, 2009f) an IP Mobility Management Selection (IPMS) function. Upon an initial attachment to a non-3GPP network (trusted or untrusted), and during a handover from 3GPP to a non-3GPP network, IPMS is performed based on the UE and the network capability to support a specific IP mobility management protocol. The decision is made by the AAA Server upon the UE authentication in the trusted non-3GPP network or in the ePDG. The decision is based on the information the AAA server has regarding the UE, the local/home network capabilities and the local/home network policies.

3GPP ARCHITECTURES IMPLEMENTING MOBILITY MANAGEMENT WITHIN THE LINK LAYER

At the link-level, Generic Access Network (3rd Generation Partnership Project, 2009g) implements inter-access mobility management func-

Figure 8. S2a, S2b, S5 interfaces

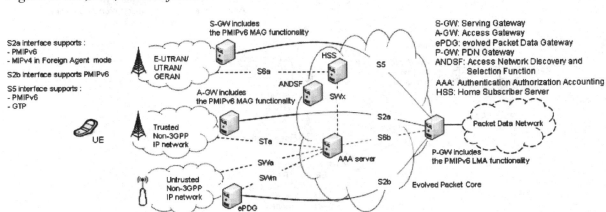

Figure 9. S2c interface

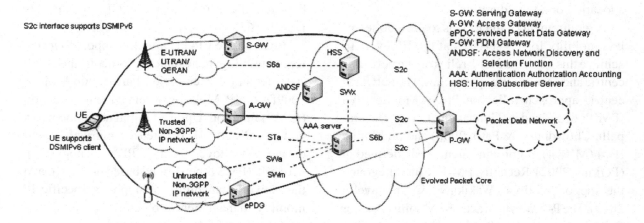

tions. Generic Access Network (GAN) aims at extending the radio coverage for Circuit-Switched and Packet-Switched services by complementing GERAN/UTRAN with WLAN. To provide seamless mobility for CS and PS services, GAN defines an entity, the Generic Access Node Controller (GANC) that appears as a GERAN Base Station Controller (BSC) or an UTRAN Radio Node Controller (RNC) from the point of view of the 3GPP cellular core network (Figure 10). In other words, the MSC and the Serving GPRS Support Node (SGSN) interact with the GANC as though it was a GERAN BSC or a UTRAN RNC.

A UE can be configured by the user or by the network operator to operate in one of the four possible modes: GERAN/UTRAN only mode,

Figure 10. Generic access network architecture for CS and PS services

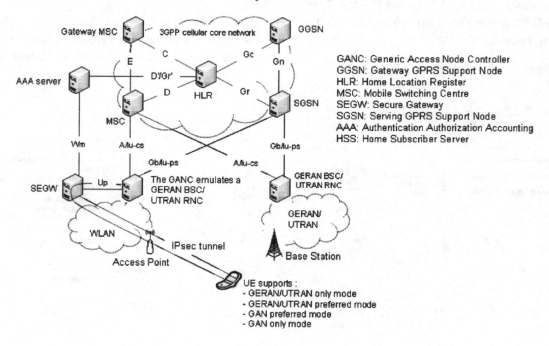

GERAN/UTRAN preferred mode, GAN preferred mode, GAN only mode. Multihoming is not possible, i.e. a UE can't be simultaneously in GAN mode and in GERAN/UTRAN mode. GAN provides two modes of operation: GAN A/Gb mode and GAN Iu mode. The GAN A/Gb mode is an extension of GERAN services that is achieved by tunnelling Non Access Stratum (NAS) protocols (i.e. the protocols used for mobility management and session management) between the UE and the MSC over the A interface of the GANC for CS services and between the UE and the SGSN over the Gb interface of the GANC for PS services. The GAN Iu mode is an extension of UTRAN services that is achieved by tunnelling NAS protocols between the UE and the MSC over the Iu-cs interface of the GANC for CS services and between the UE and the SGSN over the Iu-ps interface of the GANC for PS services.

GAN envisages roaming and non-roaming scenarios. For sake of clarity we focus on the non-roaming scenario. The architecture (Figure 10) relies on the following entities:

- The UE that integrates GERAN/UTRAN mode, GAN A/Gb mode, and GAN Iu mode.
- The Up interface between the UE and the GANC.
- The Security Gateway (SEGW) that secures the access between the UE and itself through an IPsec tunnel. It interacts with the AAA server to set up the required security association. For that purpose the SEGW relays the Subscriber Identity Module (SIM) authentication to the Home Location Register (HLR).
- The GANC that emulates a GERAN BSC or a UTRAN RNC. It is connected to the MSC and the SGSN and enables access to CS and PS services via a WLAN.

ANALYSIS OF DESIGN OF INTER-ACCESS MOBILITY MANAGEMENT IN 3GPP ARCHITECTURES

Having highlighted the 3GPP architectures with inter-access mobility management capabilities, we examine if the mobility management is well-designed within them. For that purpose, we assessed the integration of the three phases making up the mobility management within these architectures by means of an evaluation grid composed of twelve criteria. The criteria number 1 through 6 evaluate the integration of the handover information gathering phase, the criteria number 7 through 9 are related to the handover decision phase, and the criteria number 10 through 12 are related to the handover execution phase:

- **Criterion 1:** Is there an information gathering?
- **Criterion 2:** Is the gathered information described?
- **Criterion 3:** Which entity collects the information?
- **Criterion 4:** Are there criteria to start the handover procedure?
- **Criterion 5:** Are these criteria described?
- **Criterion 6:** Which entity starts the handover procedure?
- **Criterion 7:** Are there methods of decision?
- **Criterion 8:** Are these methods described?
- **Criterion 9:** Which entity makes the decision?
- **Criterion 10:** Are there methods to execute the decision?
- **Criterion 11:** Are these methods described?
- **Criterion 12:** Which entity executes the decision?

For sake of clarity, we provide the assessment for only two architectures: I-WLAN (Table 1) that implements the mobility management within the network-layer, and GAN (Table 2) that implements it within the link-layer.

The analysis of the tables shows that the criteria 2, 5, 8 are not met. In other words, the information collected is not described, the criteria for starting a handover are not described, and the methods for selecting a target network are not described. In addition, the criterion 9 shows that in the I-WLAN architecture, the selection process of the target network is only performed by the User Equipment without taking into account the viewpoint of the operator managing the networks. But if a User Equipment has no information about the load of the target networks, for example because the operator managing the networks considers this information as confidential, the user's QoS could be degraded during a handover when the selected network is overloaded.

Table 1. PS handover between 3GPP networks and I-WLAN

Criterion	PS Handover from I-WLAN to 3GPP Networks	PS Handover from 3GPP Networks to I-WLAN
1	Yes	Yes
2	No	No
3	UE	UE
4	Yes	Yes
5	No	No
6	UE	UE
7	Yes	Yes
8	No	No
9	UE	UE
10	Yes	Yes
11	Not entirely described	Not entirely described
12	UE, PDG, SGSN, GGSN, HA	UE, PDG, GGSN, HA

PROPOSAL FOR ENHANCING 3GPP ARCHITECTURES WITH INTER-ACCESS MOBILITY MANAGEMENT CAPABILITIES

Since our assessment showed the existence of loopholes in the design of the inter-access mobility management, we propose to enhance the 3GPP architectures with inter-access mobility management capabilities by implementing a method that takes into account the viewpoint of all the entities involved in the selection process of a target network. This method is called Hierarchical and Distributed Handover (Suciu, Benzaid, Bonjour, & Louin, 2009).

The Hierarchical and Distributed Handover (HDHO) method distributes the three mobility management phases between logical entities called Mobility Management Entities (MME) and dynamically builds a handover management chain. Since HDHO manages the mobility of each flow of a multimedia session, it defines a chain for each couple (UE, session flow). A chain is composed of several MME that interact with each other in a peer-to-peer way and in a hierarchical way. The addition of hierarchical decision levels in the distributed mobility management is necessary to come to a decision when entities involved in the decision process have contradictory objectives. Entities located in higher hierarchical decision levels enforce partial decisions that must be followed by entities located in lower hierarchical decision levels. For each couple (UE, session flow) the network selection process is as follows. In the first step, each MME calculates a score, noted S, to each possible target network by means of a utility function. In decision theory, when an individual can choose between several commodities, a utility function allows him to indicate his preference for a particular commodity. This concept is implemented in each MME (in this case a commodity is a network) to choose a possible target network

Table 2. CS and PS handover between GERAN/UTRAN and GAN A/Gb mode, GERAN/UTRAN and GAN A/Gb mode, GERAN/UTRAN and GAN Iu mode, GERAN/UTRAN and GAN Iu mode

Criterion	CS and PS Handover			
	CS from GERAN to GAN A/Gb mode	**CS from UTRAN to GAN A/Gb mode**	**CS from GAN A/Gb mode to GERAN**	**CS from GAN A/Gb mode to UTRAN**
1	Yes	Yes	Yes	Yes
2	Not entirely described	Not entirely described	Not entirely described	Not entirely described
3	BSC, UE	RNC, UE	GANC, UE	GANC, UE
4	Yes	Yes	Yes	Yes
5	No	No	No	No
6	BSC	RNC	UE	UE
7	Yes	Yes	Yes	Yes
8	No	No	No	No
9	BSC, UE	RNC, UE	GANC, UE, MSC	GANC, UE
10	Yes	Yes	Yes	Yes
11	Yes	Yes	Yes	Yes
12	UE, GANC, BSC, MSC	UE, GANC, RNC, MSC	UE, GANC, BSC, MSC	UE, GANC, RNC, MSC
	PS from GERAN to GAN A/Gb mode	**PS from UTRAN to GAN A/Gb mode**	**PS from GAN A/Gb mode to GERAN**	**PS from GAN A/Gb mode to UTRAN**
1	Yes	Yes	Yes	Yes
2	Not entirely described	Not entirely described	Not entirely described	Not entirely described
3	BSC, UE	RNC, UE	GANC, UE	GANC, UE
4	Yes	Yes	Yes	Yes
5	No	No	No	No
6	BSC	RNC	UE	UE
7	Yes	Yes	Yes	Yes
8	No	No	No	No
9	BSC, UE	RNC, UE	GANC, UE	GANC, UE
10	Yes	Yes	Yes	Yes
11	Yes	Yes	Yes	Yes
12	UE, GANC, BSC, SGSN	UE, GANC, RNC, SGSN	UE, GANC, BSC, SGSN	UE, GANC, RNC, SGSN
	CS from GERAN to GAN Iu mode	**CS from UTRAN to GAN Iu mode**	**CS from GAN Iu mode to GERAN**	**CS from GAN Iu mode to UTRAN**
1	Yes	Yes	Yes	Yes
2	Not entirely described	Not entirely described	Not entirely described	Not entirely described
3	BSC, UE	RNC, UE	GANC, UE	GANC, UE
4	Yes	Yes	Yes	Yes
5	No	No	No	No
6	BSC	RNC	UE	UE
7	Yes	Yes	Yes	Yes

continued on following page

Table 2. Continued

Criterion	CS and PS Handover			
8	No	No	No	No
9	BSC, UE	RNC, UE	GANC, UE	GANC, UE
10	Yes	Yes	Yes	Yes
11	Yes	Yes	Yes	Yes
12	UE, GANC, BSC, MSC	UE, GANC, RNC, MSC	UE, GANC, BSC, MSC	UE, GANC, RNC, MSC
	PS from GERAN to GAN Iu mode	**PS from UTRAN to GAN Iu mode**	**PS from GAN Iu mode to GERAN**	**PS from GAN Iu mode to UTRAN**
1	Yes	Yes	Yes	Yes
2	Not entirely described	Not entirely described	Not entirely described	Not entirely described
3	BSC	RNC	GANC, UE	GANC, UE
4	Yes	Yes	Yes	Yes
5	No	No	No	No
6	BSC	RNC	UE	UE
7	Yes	Yes	Yes	Yes
8	No	No	No	No
9	BSC	RNC	GANC, UE	GANC, UE
10	Yes	Yes	Yes	Yes
11	Yes	Yes	Yes	Yes
12	UE, GANC, BSC, SGSN, GGSN	UE, GANC, RNC, SGSN	UE, GANC, BSC, SGSN, GGSN	UE, GANC, RNC, SGSN

according to several criteria. In the second step, each MME score is weighted and a final score for each possible target network is calculated by adding the weighted scores. The weighting coefficient of a MME, noted W, allows assigning a greater or smaller weight to the score of this MME in the final score. In the third step, the final MME of the HDHO chain selects for a flow the target network with the highest final score. Figure 11 shows an example of four entities interacting with each other to come to a decision. MME1 takes a local decision and enforces a partial decision that must be followed by MME2 and MME3. MME2 and MME3 come to a partial decision by interacting among them in a peer-to-peer way, and MME2 enforces a partial decision that must be followed by MME4.

For the flow number i and the target network number j, the final score, noted SC_{ij}, is computed as follows:

$$SC_{ij} = \sum_{n=1}^{n=4} W_n * S_n(i, j)$$

To come to a decision, each MME implements three functions (Figure 12):

- **HDHO Initiation (HDHOI) Function:** A handover information gathering function. It collects and stores the information used in the decision process.

Figure 11. Four MME interacting among them to come to a decision

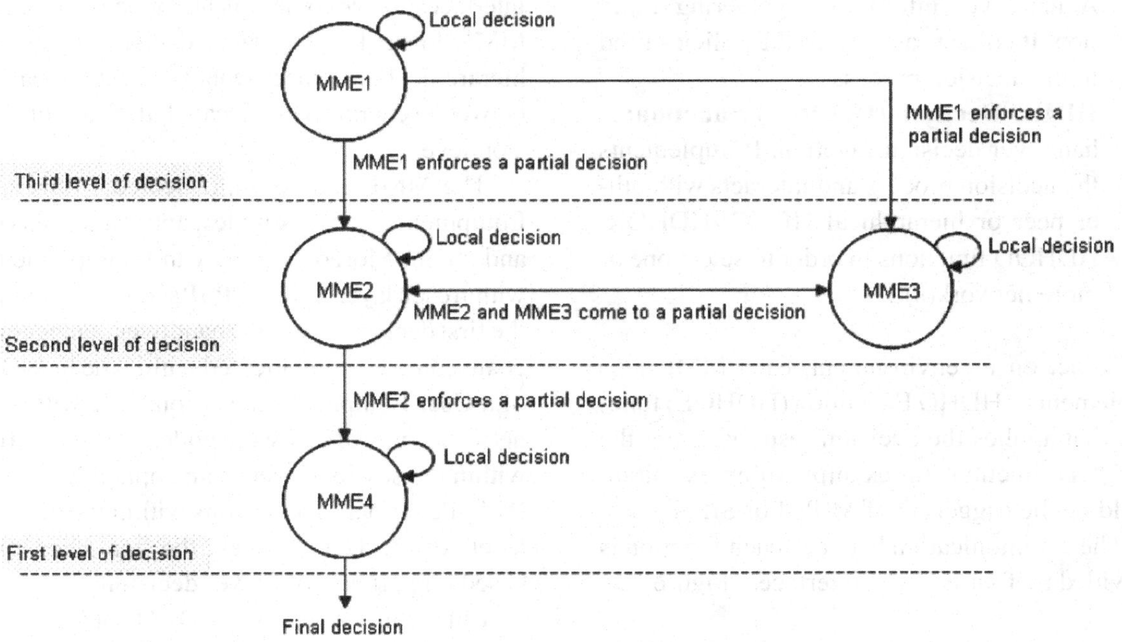

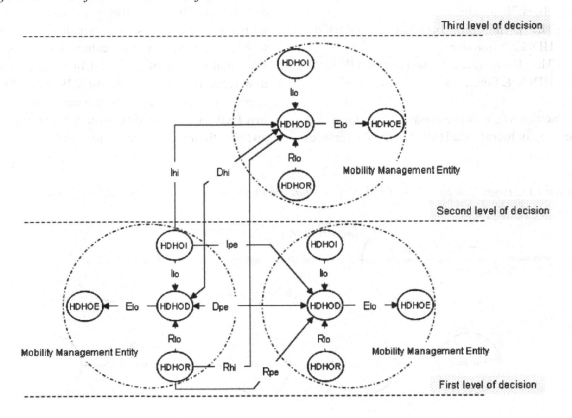

Figure 12. MME functions and interfaces

- **HDHO Repository (HDHOR) Function:** A handover information gathering function. It collects and stores the policies used in the decision process.
- **HDHO Decision (HDHOD) Function:** A handover decision function. It implements the decision process and interacts with other peer or hierarchical HDHOI/HDHOR/HDHOD functions in order to select one or more network(s).

To act on its environment, each MME also implements a HDHO Execution (HDHOE) function that applies the decision resulting from the HDHOD function. An example of an execution could be the triggering of MIPv4 or SIP.

The communication between each function is provided by four types of interfaces (Figure 12):

- The I interface between the HDHOD/HDHOI functions
- The R interface between the HDHOD/HDHOR functions
- The D interface between the HDHOD/HDHOD functions
- The E interface between the HDHOD/HDHOE functions

Each interface can be classified into local (lo), peer (pe), or hierarchical (hi). The local interfaces

enable communications within a MME. The peer interfaces enable communications between several MME located at the same decision level. The hierarchical interfaces enable communications between several MME located at different decision levels.

The MME can be implemented within User Equipments, network nodes, application servers, and so on. Moreover, they can be implemented within each layer of the TCP/IP stack. For example, the first decision level of a handover management chain could be implemented within the link-layer of a User Equipment, the second one within the network-layer of a network node, and the third one within the session-layer of an application server. By building partial decisions within the different layers of the TCP/IP stack, the final decision is based on partial cross-layer decisions.

But the introduction of HDHO could increase the complexity of the mobility management because it manages the mobility for each session flow. The works on autonomous mobility (Radier & Salaun, 2010), that aim to create self-managing mobility architectures, is a part of the solution to overcome this growing complexity. We consider that the use of Artificial Intelligence (AI) in wireless networks (Rondeau & Bostian, 2009) is another part of the solution because the actors involved in the mobility management become aware of their radio environment. In Figure 13 we

Figure 13. Integration of the OOPDA cycle within the three mobility management functions

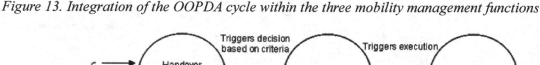
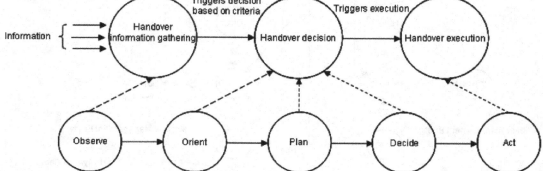

propose a way to integrate AI methods within the three mobility management functions: based on the Observe-Orient-Plan-Decide-Act (OOPDA) cycle (Fette, 2009), we propose to integrate one or more steps of the cycle within each function. For example the Observe step is integrated within the handover information gathering function.

CONCLUSION

Because we consider that 3GPP architectures with well-designed inter-access mobility management capabilities are a part of the solution to cope with the growth of the mobile data traffic, we reviewed the 3GPP architectures and identified five architectures with these capabilities. In order to evaluate if the mobility management is well-designed within the identified architectures, we split the mobility management into three phases and we designed an evaluation grid to assess the integration of these phases into the five 3GPP architectures. Since our assessment showed the existence of loopholes in the design of the inter-access mobility management, we proposed to enhance the 3GPP architectures with inter-access mobility management capabilities by implementing a method, called HDHO, that takes into account the viewpoint of all the entities involved in the selection process of a target network. A lot of work must be done to successfully integrate HDHO because each terminal, each network node, and each server, are potentially impacted. Currently we are implementing HDHO within the Access Network Discovery and Selection Function of the EPC architecture. Moreover, we are studying the HDHO integration within enhanced multicast architectures, like those described in the C-Cast project (Antoniou et al., 2009), because by using networks with multicast capabilities, network operators will be able to deliver their services to a greater number of users and will optimize their network resources.

ACKNOWLEDGMENT

This research was supported by grants from Orange Labs. It includes contributions from the following people: P. Bertin, K. Daoud Triki, S. El Moumouhi, O. Le Grand, A. Mouquet, B. Radier, L. Suciu and B. Tossou. The authors would like to thank T. Lemlouma for his relevant comments.

REFERENCES

Akyildiz, I. F., Xie, J., & Mohanty, S. (2004). A survey of mobility management in next-generation all-IP-based wireless systems. *IEEE Wireless Communications, 11*(4), 16–28. doi:10.1109/MWC.2004.1325888

Antoniou, J., Christophorou, C., Janneteau, C., Kellil, M., Sargento, S., Neto, A., et al. (2009). Architecture for context-aware multiparty delivery in mobile heterogeneous networks. In *Proceedings of the International Conference on Ultra Modern Telecommunications & Workshops* (pp. 1-6).

Atiquzzaman, M., & Reaz, A. (2005). Survey and classification of transport layer mobility management schemes. In *Proceedings of the 16th Annual IEEE International Symposium on Personal, Indoor and Mobile Radio Communications* (Vol. 4).

Camarillo, G., & Garcia-Martin, M. A. (2008). *The 3G IP multimedia subsystem (IMS): Merging the Internet and the cellular worlds* (3rd ed.). Chichester, UK: John Wiley & Sons. doi:10.1002/9780470695135

Camarillo, G., Johnston, A., Peterson, J., Sparks, R., Handley, M., & Schooler, E. (2002). *RFC 3261: Session initiation protocol.* Retrieved from http://www.ietf.org/rfc/rfc3261.txt

Fette, B. A. (2009). *Cognitive radio technology* (2nd ed.). Burlington, MA: Academic Press.

Gundavelli, S., Leung, K., Devarapalli, V., Chowdhury, K., & Patil, B. (2008). *RFC 5213: Proxy mobile IPv6.* Retrieved from http://tools.ietf.org/html/rfc5213

Kaufman, C. (2005). *RFC 4306: Internet key exchange (IKEv2) protocol.* Retrieved from http://www.ietf.org/rfc/rfc4306.txt

Lataste, S., & Tossou, B. (2008). From network layer mobility to IMS service continuity. In *Proceedings of the 12th International Conference on Intelligence in Service Delivery Networks.*

Le, D., Fu, X., & Hogrefe, D. (2006). A review of mobility support paradigms for the internet. *IEEE Communications Surveys and Tutorials, 8*(1), 38–51. doi:10.1109/COMST.2006.323441

Lescuyer, P., & Lucidarme, T. (2008). *Evolved packet system (EPS) the LTE and SAE evolution of 3G UMTS.* Chichester, UK: John Wiley & Sons. doi:10.1002/9780470723678

Perkins, C. (2002). *RFC 334: IP mobility support for IPv4.* Retrieved from http://www.ietf.org/rfc/rfc3344.txt

Radier, B., & Salaun, M. (2010). A vehicle gateway to manage IP multimedia subsystem autonomous mobility. *International Journal of Autonomous and Adaptive Communications Systems, 3*(2), 159–177. doi:10.1504/IJAACS.2010.031089

3rd Generation Partnership Project. (2007). *3GPP TS 23.206 V7.5.0: 3rd generation partnership project: Technical specification group services and system aspects: Voice call continuity (VCC) between circuit switched (CS) and IP multimedia subsystem (IMS): Stage 2 (Release 7).* Retrieved from http://www.arib.or.jp/IMT-2000/V810Jul10/2_T63/ARIB-STD-T63/Rel7/23/A23206-750.pdf

3rd Generation Partnership Project. (2008). *3GPP TS 23.234 V8.0.0: 3rd Generation Partnership Project; Technical Specification Group Services and System Aspects; 3GPP system to Wireless Local Area Network (WLAN) interworking; System description (Release 8).* Retrieved from http://www.quintillion.co.jp/3GPP/Specs/23234-800.pdf

3rd Generation Partnership Project. (2009a). *3GPP TS 22.078 V9.0.0: 3rd generation partnership project: Technical specification group services and system aspects: Customised applications for mobile network enhanced logic (CAMEL): Service description: Stage 1(Release 9).* Retrieved from http://ofdm.jp/3GPP/Specs/23078-900.pdf

3rd Generation Partnership Project. (2009b). *3GPP TS 23.237 V8.6.0: 3rd Generation Partnership Project Technical Specification Group Services and Architecture IP Multimedia Subsystem (IMS) Service Continuity Stage 2 (Release 8).* Retrieved from http://www.quintillion.co.jp/3GPP/Specs/23237-860.pdf

3rd Generation Partnership Project. (2009c). *3GPP TS 23.292 V9.5.0: 3rd Generation Partnership Project; Technical Specification Group Services and System Aspects; IP Multimedia Subsystem (IMS) centralized services; Stage 2 (Release 9).* Retrieved from http://www.quintillion.co.jp/3GPP/Specs/23292-950.pdf

3rd Generation Partnership Project. (2009d). *3GPP TS 23.327 V8.4.0: 3rd Generation Partnership Project; Technical Specification Group Services and System Aspects; Mobility between 3GPP-Wireless Local Area Network (WLAN) interworking and 3GPP systems (Release 8).* Retrieved from http://www.quintillion.co.jp/3GPP/Specs/24327-860.pdf

3rd Generation Partnership Project. (2009e). *3GPP TS 23.401 V8.8.0: 3rd Generation Partnership Project; Technical Specification Group Services and System Aspects; General Packet Radio Service (GPRS) enhancements for Evolved Universal Terrestrial Radio Access Network (E-UTRAN) access (Release 8)*. Retrieved from http://www.quintillion.co.jp/3GPP/Specs/23401-880.pdf

3rd Generation Partnership Project. (2009f). *3GPP TS 23.402 V8.8.0: 3rd Generation Partnership Project; Technical Specification Group Services and System Aspects; Architecture enhancements for non-3GPP accesses (Release 8)*. Retrieved from http://www.quintillion.co.jp/3GPP/Specs/23402-870.pdf

3rd Generation Partnership Project. (2009g). *3GPP TS 43.318 V9.0.0: 3rd Generation Partnership Project Technical Specification Group GSM/EDGE Radio Access Network Generic Access Network (GAN): Stage 2 (Release 9)*. Retrieved from http://www.quintillion.co.jp/3GPP/Specs/23003-900.pdf

Rondeau, T. W., & Bostian, C. W. (2009). *Artificial intelligence in wireless communications*. Norwood, MA: Artech House.

Schneeweiss, C. (2003). *Distributed decision making* (2nd ed.). Berlin, Germany: Springer-Verlag.

Soliman, H. (2009). *RFC 5555: Mobile IPv6 support for dual stack hosts and routers*. Retrieved from http://tools.ietf.org/search/rfc5555

Suciu, L., Benzaid, M., Bonjour, S., & Louin, P. (2009). Assessing the handover approaches for heterogeneous wireless networks. In *Proceedings of the 18th International Conference on Computer Communications and Networks* (pp. 1-6).

Wakikawa, R., & Gundavelli, S. (2010). *IPv4 support for proxy mobile IPv6*. Retrieved from http://tools.ietf.org/html/draft-ietf-netlmm-pmip6-ipv4-support-18

Zdarsky, F. A., & Schmitt, J. B. (2004). Handover in mobile communication networks: Who is in control anyway? In *Proceedings of the 30th EUROMICRO Conference* (pp. 205-212).

This work was previously published in the International Journal of Mobile Computing and Multimedia Communications, Volume 3, Issue 2, edited by Ismail Khalil and Edgar Weippl, pp. 62-81, copyright 2011 by IGI Publishing (an imprint of IGI Global).

Chapter 13
Reducing Network Overhead with Common Junction Methodology

Shashi Bhushan
Haryana Engineering College Jagadhri, India

Mayank Dave
National Institute of Technology Kurukshetra, India

R.B. Patel
DCRUST Murthal, India

ABSTRACT

In structured and unstructured Peer-to-Peer (P2P) systems, frequent joining and leaving of peer nodes causes topology mismatch between the P2P logical overlay network and the physical underlay network. This topology mismatch problem generates high volumes of redundant traffic in the network. This paper presents Common Junction Methodology (CJM) to reduce network overhead by optimize the overlay traffic at underlay level. CJM finds common junction between available paths, and traffic is only routed through the common junction and not through the conventional identified paths. CJM does not alter overlay topology and performs without affecting the search scope of the network. Simulation results show that CJM resolves the mismatch problem and significantly reduces redundant P2P traffic up to 87% in the best case for the simulated network. CJM can be implemented over structured or unstructured P2P networks, and also reduces the response time by 53% approximately for the network.

1. INTRODUCTION

A peer-to-peer (P2P) network is an abstract, logical network called an overlay network, deployed on the peers already connected with the internet. Instead of strictly decomposing the system into

clients (which consume services) and servers (which provides them), peers in the system can elect to provide services as well as consume them. All participating peers form a P2P network over a physical network. The network overlay abstraction provides flexible and extensible application-

DOI: 10.4018/978-1-4666-2163-3.ch013

level management techniques that can be easily and incrementally deployed despite the underlay network. When a new peer wants to join a P2P network, a bootstrapping node provides the IP address list of existing peers in the P2P network. The new peer then tries to connect with these peers. If some attempts succeed then the connected peers will be the new peer's neighbors. Once this peer connects into a P2P network, the new peer will periodically ping the network connections and obtain the IP addresses of some other peers in the network. These IP addresses are cached by this new peer. When a peer leaves the P2P network and later wants to join the P2P network again, the peer will try to connect to those peers whose IP addresses are present in the cache.

In unstructured P2P systems, the mechanism of a peer randomly joining and leaving a P2P network causes topology mismatch between the P2P logical overlay network and the physical underlay network, causing a large volume of redundant traffic in the Internet (Sen et al., 2002; Saroiu et al., 2002). Studies by Ritter (2001) and Ripeanu et al. (2002) have shown that the flooding-based routing algorithm generates 330 TB/month in a Gnutella network with only 50,000 nodes considering the fact that Internet consists of nodes much more in number. A large portion of the heavy P2P traffic is due to topology mismatch problem between overlay topology and underlay topology, which makes the unstructured P2P systems being far from scalable (Ritter, 2001).

In P2P networks peer nodes rely on one another for service rather than solely relying on dedicated and often centralized infrastructure. Decentralized data-sharing and discovery algorithms/mechanisms will be the boosting option for the deployment of P2P networks (Andersen et al., 2001; Huebsch et al., 2003 & Rowstron et al., 2001). The challenges for the researchers are to chase the topology mismatch problem for avoiding unnecessary redundant traffic from the network.

In this paper we have proposed a Common Junction Methodology (CJM) that resolves the topology mismatch problem and also reduce the large amount of redundant traffic over the network. CJM finds the optimal physical links for routing the messages/queries. It works for both the structured and unstructured P2P networks. For implementing our methodology an overlay network model is also identified. The identified model makes information placement and dissemination easy on the P2P networks. It supports the scalability and optimizes the communication cost of the system. CJM also minimizes redundant network traffic in the P2P networks.

The rest of the paper is organized as follows. Section 2 gives the related work. Section 3 presents a case of topology mismatch problem and Section 4 explores System Model. Section 5 introduces CJM, System. Analysis is given in Section 6. Section 7 explores on implementation and performance study of CJM and the paper is concluded in Section 8

2. RELATED WORKS

There are several traditional topology optimization approaches. The end system multicast is used in NARADA (Chu et al., 2000). NARADA first constructs a rich connected graph on which it further constructs shortest path spanning trees. Each tree rooted at the corresponding source uses well-known routing algorithms (Chu et al., 2000). This approach introduces large overhead of forming the graph and trees in a large scope, and does not consider the dynamic joining and leaving characteristics of peers. The overhead of NARADA is proportional to the multicast group size. Further this approach is impractical in large-scale P2P systems.

Researchers have also considered clustering of closely located peers based on their IP addresses

(Krishnamurthy et al., 2001; Padmanabhan et al., 2001). In this approach there are two limitations- (a) mapping accuracy is not guaranteed and (b) searching scope is affected with increase in volume of traffic in P2P networks.

In Xu et al. (2003) authors measure the latency between peers using multiple stable Internet servers called "landmarks". The measured latency is used to determine the distance between peers. This measurement is conducted in a global P2P domain and needs the support of additional landmarks. Similarly, this approach also affects the search scope in P2P systems.

In GIA, Chawathe et al. (2003) introduces a topology adaptation algorithm to ensure that high capacity nodes are the ones with high degree and low capacity nodes are within short reach of high capacity nodes. It addresses a different matching problem in overlay networks. To chase topology mismatch problem Minimum Spanning Tree (MST) based approaches are used by Liu et al. (2007) and Xiao et al. (2005). In these, peers build an overlay MST, among the source node and certain hop neighbors, and then optimize connections that are not on the tree. An early attempt at alleviating topology mismatch is called LTM (Liu et al., 2007), in which each peer issues a detector message in a small region so that the peers receiving the detector can record relative delay information. Based on the delay information, a receiver can detect and cut most of the inefficient and redundant logical links as well as add closer nodes as direct neighbors. The major drawback of LTM is that it needs to synchronize all peer nodes and thus requires the support of NTP (NTP, 2007), which is critical. In Liu et al. (2008) authors presented the relationship between message duplication in overlay connections and the number of overlay links. Authors proposed Two Hop Neighbor Comparison and Selection (THANCS) to optimize the overlay network, which may change the overlay topology. This change in overlay topology may not be accept-

able in many cases. In most of the above said approaches, overlay network is considered for optimization. These approaches are not considering the physical path at underlay network.

We have considered all above challenges lying in both overlay and underlay networks for both structured and unstructured P2P networks without modifying network topology. We have also designed the architecture for overlay network to reduce the network traffic. The response time and traffic cost is measured and compared as performance measure for the network. This architecture is suitable for dissemination of dynamic information in the P2P network. This model implements CJM for minimizing the message transfer between the peers at physical level. It also chases the topology mismatch problem. Simulation results show that CJM saves redundant traffic caused by the topology mismatch problem, while retaining the search scope and minimizing the response time of the network.

3. TOPOLOGY MISMATCH PROBLEM

As shown in Figure 1, the eight peers, numbered 1 to 8 are participating in underlay network, out of which only four peers are in overlay network. Any P2P systems logically deals in overlay networks, i.e., the queries/messages are sent from one overlay peer to another overlay peer. There are two types of query/message communication in overlay networks: direct and indirect link. Direct link, i.e., message is sent logically from peer 1 to peer 6 itself. The actual path in underlay network traversed by the messages is

$$[1 \rightarrow 2 \rightarrow 3 \rightarrow 5 \rightarrow 6]$$

This path is described as:

$$Path_{(1,2,3,5,6)}^{(1)}$$

where superscripts represent the path number assigned to the path and subscripts represents intermediate ordered set of peers in underlay network. Other paths in present example are described as follows:

$$Path_{(1,2,3,5,6)}^{(1)} = \{1,2,3,5,6\}$$
$$Path_{(6,5,3,4)}^{(2)} = \{6,5,3,4\}$$
$$Path_{(4,3,7,8)}^{(3)} = \{4,3,7,8\}$$

Secondly, an indirect link i.e., message sent logically from peer 1 to peer 4 through peer 6, $[1 \rightarrow 6 \rightarrow 4]$ in overlay network (two hop count path). The physical path traversed by the messages is

$$[1 \rightarrow 2 \rightarrow 3 \rightarrow 5 \rightarrow 6 \rightarrow 5 \rightarrow 3 \rightarrow 4]$$

Figure 1. Example of underlay networks of 8 peers, out of which 4 are participating in overlay network. Each connection between two peers represents the traffic cost to send the unit data from one peer to another

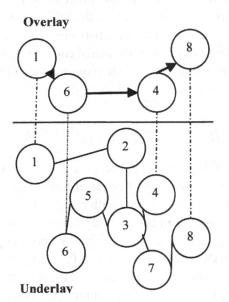

The path is described as:

$$Path_{(1,2,3,5,6,5,3,4)}^{(1,2)}$$

This path is combination of two paths, i.e., path 1 and path 2. Two paths can be merged only if when the destination of first path and the source of second path are same peer. In present case this peer is peer 6. In both cases the physical messages have to travel through multiple peers in underlay network corresponding to single transfer of message from one peer to another in overlay network. Hence, both the direct and indirect links causes a heavy redundant traffic on the physical network due to topology mismatch problem. This is one of the major reasons for unwanted heavy traffic in any of the peer-to-peer network that takes P2P network less scalable. However, we can optimize the traffic at physical level or at underlay level.

4. SYSTEM MODEL

Figure 2 presents a New System Architecture (NSA) for Overlay Networks. NSA is divided into three layers. First layer is under the control of overlay topology, i.e., it provides the interface to the P2P system and receives query or sub queries from the network. This layer is implemented over the application layer of the network. All the data transfer policies are implemented over this layer, e.g., peer selection criteria. All logical connections are implemented over this layer. The second layer comprises of four components. The Query Analyzer accepts the queries, resolve and forwards same to Query Optimizer. The Query Analyzer is also responsible for breaking query into subqueries. The Query Optimizer decides whether a peer is suitable for a particular subquery or not. The Query Execution Engine is responsible for executing the subquery and produces partial results corresponding to the subquery. This partial

Figure 2. New system architecture (NSA) for overlay networks

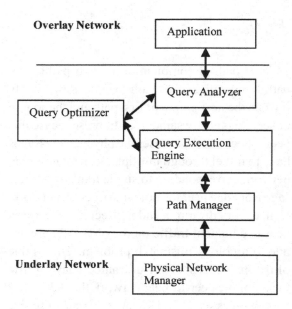

result is further sent to the requesting peer or to the peer responsible for the refinement of partial result. The Path Manager is responsible for optimizing the path and for implementing the CJM. CJM is responsible for optimizing the logical path between the peers in overlay network. All paths are checked and optimized using the database of the underlay peers. Third layer is the Physical Network Manager which is responsible for managing the underlay. This layer works as usual in the directions received from the path manager.

5. COMMON JUNCTION METHODOLOGY (CJM)

To reduce the unnecessary traffic from the network, the query should be routed through optimized/shortest path. Let us again consider the example (Figure 1), if a query is sent logically from peer 1 to peer 4 through peer 6, in overlay network, a two hop count path. The physical path traversed by the messages is

$$[1 \rightarrow 2 \rightarrow 3 \rightarrow 5 \rightarrow 6 \rightarrow 5 \rightarrow 3 \rightarrow 4]$$

The path is described as:

$$Path^{(1,2)}_{(1,2,3,5,6,5,3,4)}$$

This path is combination of two paths, i.e., path 1 and path 2. Two paths can be merged only if when the destination of first path and the source of second path are same peer using conventional methodology. At this point we can save the traffic cost of the path by sending the query through path

$$[1 \rightarrow 2 \rightarrow 3 \rightarrow 4]$$

instead of

$$[1 \rightarrow 2 \rightarrow 3 \rightarrow 5 \rightarrow 6 \rightarrow 5 \rightarrow 3 \rightarrow 4]$$

In this path the traffic cost to send the query through path

$$[3 \rightarrow 5 \rightarrow 6 \rightarrow 5 \rightarrow 3]$$

is saved. As it is redundant traffic in the network, we can save this portion of the traffic cost. Here peer 3 is common junction between the two paths. CJM is based on the key idea of common junction between the two paths. This common junction can be identified as

$$Path^{(1)}_{(1,2,3,5,6)} \cap Path^{(2)}_{(6,5,3,4)} = CJ\{3,6\}$$

where CJ{} is ordered set of peers common in both the paths. Here peer 3 and peer 6 is the common junction of two paths, path1 and path 2, from where query can be diverted. If query is diverted through peer 6, it becomes a conventional path. But in case of choosing peer 3 for query routing, we can save a lot of traffic cost (as described in example). Similarly this common junction can be identified between any two paths available. These paths may or may not be continuous. CJM is based upon the above said technique. CJM saves traffic cost without modifying the network topology, and search space. Other advantages of CJM are that it saves the traffic cost of the P2P network. Secondly it finds the path in underlay network for the two paths in overlay network (may be discontinuous paths in overlay network). Thirdly CJM find the shortest path of any hop count path i.e., CJM is also suitable for any length paths. The saved traffic cost is increase by increase in hop count of the path.

Every path in the overlay network is assigned a number. Let m be the number of such paths. Let path $P_{(a,b)}^{(i)}$ from peer a to peer b in logical topology, be the ordered set of peers in the underlay topology. Let n is the hope count of the path for which we want to find the shortest path. The problem is to find the optimum path of length n. This path and total traffic cost is identified using the algorithm described as follows:

Step 1. Intialize variables:

Let n be the hop count of the path.

$S_1..S_n$ be the source peer of respective individual paths.

$D_1..D_n$ be the destination peer of respective individual paths.

$r_1..r_n$ be the common peer find in respective individual paths.

$Start\ Peer = S_1$;

$TTC = 0$; // TTC is Total Traffic Cost;

Step 2. for all values of i from $[1..n-1]$;

j varies from $[n..i+1]$;

Step 3. While $(j > i)$ go to step 4;

Else go to step 8;

Step 4. Find Common Junction using

$$Path_{(S_i,D_i)}^{(i)} \cap Path_{(S_j,D_j)}^{(j)} = CJ\{\};$$

Step 5. If $CJ\{\} = \phi$ Then $j = j - 1$, and go to step 3;

Else: let r_i is the common junction

$$Path_{(S_i,D_j)}^{(i,j)}CJM = Path_{(S_i,r_i)}^{(i)}.Path_{(r_i,D_j)}^{(j)};$$

where $Path_{(S_i,D_j)}^{(i,j)}CJM$ the shortest path identified through CJM;

Step 6. $TTC = TTC + TC[Start\ Peer, r_i]$;

// TC is traffic Cost between two peers;

Step 7. $i = j$;

$Start\ Peer = r_i$;

goto step 3;

Step 8. End;

$//Path_{(S_i,D_j)}^{(i,j)}CJM$ holds shortest path;

//TTC holds total traffic cost of the shortest path;

6. SYSTEM ANALYSIS

Let $P_{(l,k)}^{(i)}$ and $P_{(m,n)}^{(j)}$ be i^{th} and j^{th} paths, an ordered set of peers come across the path from source peer l to destination peer k and source peer m to destination peer n. These ordered set of peers are the peers in underlay networks. Conventionally, to find the two hop path from $l(n)$, query has to travel first from l to k then m to n for $k=m$. This path is described as $P_{(l,n)}^{(i,j)}$ such that $P_{(l,k)}^{(i)}.P_{(m,n)}^{(j)}$. In case of CJM, this path is also described by $P_{(l,n)}^{(i,j)}$ but the query may traverse through optimized path calculated using CJM. $C_{(l,k)}^{(i)}Normal$ is the cost to transfer the unit data from peer l to peer k using conventional methodology. $C^{(i,j)}_{(l,n)}Normal$ is the total cost to transfer the unit data from peer l to peer n, of two hop count distance. This cost is calculated using the Equation 1.

$$C^{(i,j)}_{(l,n)}Normal = \begin{cases} C^{(i)}_{(l,k)} + C^{(j)}_{(m,n)} & iff & k = m \\ \infty & & otherwise \end{cases} \tag{1}$$

$C^{(i,j)}_{(l,n)}CJM$ is the cost to transfer the unit data from peer l to peer n using CJM. The cost of two hop path $P^{(i,j)}_{(l,n)}$ is calculated using Equation 2.

$$C^{(i,j)}_{(l,n)}CJM = C^{(i)}_{(l,r)} + (C^{(j)}_{(m,n)} - C^{(j)}_{(m,r)}) \tag{2}$$

where $r \in CJ\{\}$ is the Common Junction between $P^i_{(l,k)}$ & $P^j_{(m,n)}$ paths, calculated by the Equation 3:

$$P^i_{(l,k)} \cap P^j_{(m,n)} = CJ\{\} \tag{3}$$

CJM finds the minimum possible underlay path between two paths, using common junction in two paths.

In case of CJM, if $CJ\{\} = \varphi$ then there is no Common Junction. If $CJ\{\} \neq \varphi$ there exist a Common Junction and CJM finds the cost according to the Equation 2. To prove the correctness of the above said methodology, CJM should provide the traffic cost less than or equal to the cost calculated by conventional methodology. The correctness of CJM is as follows:

Case 1: $CJ\{\} = \varphi$. In (1), there is no common junction between two paths, i.e., no continuous path and no common junction peer are present in the two paths. From Equation 1:

$$C^{(i,j)}_{(l,n)}Normal = C^{(i)}_{(l,k)} + C^{(j)}_{(m,n)} = \infty \tag{4}$$

as there is no r hence the cost is infinity. Then from Equation 2:

$$C^{(i,j)}_{(l,n)}CJM = C^{(i)}_{(l,r)} + (C^{(j)}_{(m,n)} - C^{(j)}_{(m,r)}) = \infty \tag{5}$$

From (4) and (5), both the cases have total traffic cost infinity, i.e., no continuous path is available from source to destination.

- **Case 2:** $CJ\{\} \neq \varphi$. Further, there exist two cases, Case (a) and Case (b).
  - **Case (a):** When $k=m$, this is the case when the paths are continuous, i.e., the destination of path 1st is equal to the source of 2nd path. In this case the common junction between two paths is the destination of 1st path and source of the 2nd path. Here r is the destination peer of 1st path and source peer of 2nd path.

$$C^{(i,j)}_{(l,n)}Normal = C^{(i)}_{(l,k)} + C^{(j)}_{(m,n)} \tag{6}$$

Here $r=k=m$, hence from Equation 2.

$$C^{(i,j)}_{(l,n)}CJM = C^{(i)}_{(l,r)} + (C^{(j)}_{(m,n)} - 0) \tag{7}$$

From (6) and (7) the traffic cost in both the cases is same, i.e.:

$$C^{(i,j)}_{(l,n)}CJM = C^{(i,j)}_{(l,n)}Normal \tag{8}$$

  - **Case (b):** When $k \neq m$ we find a Common Junction between the two paths, there exists peer r. The traffic cost of the paths is calculated as follows:

$$C_{(l,n)}^{(i,j)}CJM = C_{(l,r)}^{(i)} + (C_{(m,n)}^{(j)} - C_{(m,r)}^{(j)}) \tag{9}$$

From Equations 6 and 9:

$$(C_{(m,n)}^{(j)} - C_{(m,r)}^{(j)}) \leq C_{(m,n)}^{(j)} \tag{10}$$

Hence, $C_{(l,n)}^{(i,j)}CJM \leq C_{(l,n)}^{(i,j)}Normal.$

From Equations 4, 5, 8 and 10 it is proven that the traffic cost in case of CJM is less than or equal to the traffic cost calculated conventionally. Hence the correctness of Common Junction Methodology is proved. It can be concluded from our simulation study that CJM reduces the response time of the system by large extent.

7. IMPLEMENTATION AND PERFORMANCE STUDY

Assumptions

CJM is based upon the assumption that to send a query/message from one peer to another peer in overlay network, there should be corresponding physical path from source to destination in underlay network. Other assumptions are summarized as follows.

A path is present between source and destination peers participating in overlay networks. It is also assumed that a peer is joined at the same position from where it lefts from. Each edge of the graph represents the total traffic cost, to transfer the unit data from source to destination. If path is broken, a usual strategy is used to find the new path. We have used 2000 peer nodes in the simulation for underlay network out of which 10% of nodes are considered for the overlay network. All the nodes

in underlay are randomly connected, i.e., at most a peer is connected with 7 peers. Uniform random number is used to generate the cardinality of the peer participated in underlay network. Nodes in overlay are selected such that they are connected with the cardinality factor lying in between 1 and 4. Uniform random numbers are used to generate the cardinality of overlay network. All the paths of various hop count are measured and average is taken. The unstructured overlay topology is used in overlay network. The traffic cost is used to measure the cost for transferring the message from source to destination. Traffic cost comprises the bandwidth, latency, processing cost, etc. For computing the average reduction in traffic cost and response time we are using the following relation.

$$\left[\%STC = \frac{(ATTC - ATCJM)}{ATTC} \times 100 \right] \tag{11}$$

where

- STC: Saved Traffic Cost
- ATTC: Average total traffic cost by conventional method
- ATCJM: Average total traffic cost with CJM

$$\left[\%RRT = \frac{(ART - ARTCJM)}{ART} \times 100 \right] \tag{12}$$

where

- RRT: Reduced response time
- ART: Average response time with conventional method
- ARTCJM: Average response time with CJM

The THANCS technique (Liu et al., 2008) is used to optimize the overlay network for the simulation. Two cases- distributed overlay with

CJM and optimized overlay without CJM are considered for the simulation of overlay network.

Result and Discussion

Figure 3 presents CJM based response time for message delivery across the network. From the result it is clear that CJM significantly reduced the response time of the network. This result shows that after optimizing the overlay network, there still exists scope to reduce the traffic at underlay. Approximately 60% of the traffic cost is saved and

53% of response time of the network is reduced on average using CJM. It is also observed from the results that a significant amount of response time is reduced in case of 7 hops. The reduction in response time is minor in case of higher hop count paths.

Figure 4 shows the average saving of traffic cost is increased with the increase in hop count of the path, i.e., the longest is the path in overlay maximum saving will be in traffic cost. The best traffic cost saved is 87% for the hop count 11. After that average saving traffic cost becomes

Figure 3. Graph of reduced response time

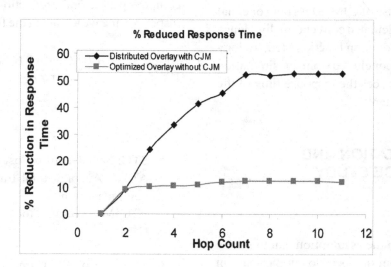

Figure 4. Graph average saved traffic cost

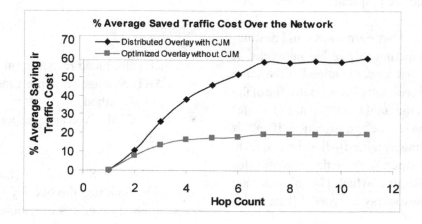

almost constant. It is observed that initially the average saving of traffic cost increases drastically shown by the slope of the graph and after a limit the slope reduced, which indicates the average saving in traffic cost is small. It is also observed that up to 7 hop count the proposed technique CJM gives amazing results. The proposed technique produces good results in both the cases, i.e., for structured and unstructured overlay networks.

8. CONCLUSION AND FUTURE WORKS

In this paper we have presented Common Junction Methodology (CJM) for optimizing the cost of information delivery in the Overlay and Underlay networks. CJM has shown amazing results in saving the traffic cost and reducing the response time of the network. It solved the topology mismatch problem on large extent. CJM works on any of the overlay topology, whether it is centralized or decentralized topology. It produces good results in saving average traffic cost. Maximum of 87% of the traffic cost is saved through the CJM for 11 hop count in overlay topology. 57% of the traffic cost is saved for 7 hop count in overlay network which is the maximum hop length of Gnutella (Ripeanu et al., 2002; Ritter, 2001), a decentralized P2P network. CJM reduces the response time of network by 53% approximately which is an amazing result of the technique. It also works in any of the overlay topology, structured as well as unstructured. CJM can be implemented in any of the overlay topology without changing the topology. Other salient feature of the CJM having fast convergent speed, search scope of the network is also maintained by CJM. In future we will trans-

port the CJM over the global network for testing the feasibility of it.

REFERENCES

Andersen, D. G., Balakrishnan, H., Kaashoek, M. F., & Moms, R. (2001). Resilient overlay networks. *ACM SIGOPS Operating Systems Review*, *35*(5), 131–145. doi:10.1145/502059.502048

Chawathe, Y., Ratnasamy, S., Breslau, L., Lanham, N., & Shenker, S. (2003). Making Gnutella-Like P2P systems scalable. In *Proceedings of the Conference on Applications, Technologies, Architectures, and Protocols for Computer Communications*, Karlsruhe, Germany (pp. 407-418).

Chu, Y., Rao, S. G., & Zhang, H. (2001, June). A case for end system multicast. In *Proceedings of the ACM SIGMETRICS Conference*, Santa Clara, CA (pp. 1-12).

Huebsch, R., Hellerstein, J. M., Lanham, N., Loo, B. T., Shenker, S., & Stoica, I. (2003). Querying the Internet with PIER. In *Proceedings of the 29th Very Large Data Bases Conference*, Berlin, Germany (Vol. 29, pp. 321-332).

Krishnamurthy, B., & Wang, J. (2001, November). Topology modeling via cluster graphs. In *Proceedings of SIGCOMM Internet Measurement Workshop*, San Francisco, CA (pp. 19-23).

Liu, Y. (2008). A two-hop solution to solving topology mismatch. *Transactions on Parallel and Distributed Systems*, *19*(11), 1591–1600. doi:10.1109/TPDS.2008.24

Liu, Y., Xiao, L., & Ni, L. M. (2007). Building a scalable bipartite P2P overlay network. *Transactions on Parallel and Distributed Systems*, *18*(9), 1296–1306. doi:10.1109/TPDS.2007.1059

NTP. (2007). *The network time protocol*. Retrieved from http://www.ntp.org/

Padmanabhan, V. N., & Subramanian, L. (2001). An investigation of geographic mapping techniques for Internet hosts. In *Proceedings of the ACM Conference on Applications, Technologies, Architectures, and Protocols for Computer Communications*, San Diego, CA (pp. 173-185).

Ripeanu, M., & Foster, I. T. (2002). Mapping the Gnutella network: Macroscopic properties of large-scale peer-to-peer systems. In *Proceedings of the 1st International Workshop on Peer-to-Peer Systems*, London, UK (pp. 85-93).

Ritter, J. (2001). *Why Gnutella can't scale. No, really*. Retrieved from http://www.globalspec.com/reference/123320/why-gnutella-can-t-scale-no-really

Rowstron, A., & Druschel, P. (2001). Scalable, distributed object location and routing for large-scale peer-to-peer systems. In *Proceedings of the 18th IFIPIACM International Conference on Distributed Systems Platforms*, Heidelberg, Germany.

Saroiu, S., Gummadi, K. P., Dunn, R. J., Gribble, S. D., & Levy, H. M. (2002, December 9-11). An analysis of Internet content delivery systems. In *Proceedings of the 5th Symposium on Operating Systems Design and Implementation*, Boston, MA (Vol. 36, pp. 315-327).

Sen, S., & Wang, J. (2002). Analyzing peer-to-peer traffic across large networks. *IEEE/ACM Transactions on Networking*, *12*(2), 219–232. doi:10.1109/TNET.2004.826277

Xiao, L., Liu, Y., & Ni, L. M. (2005). Improving unstructured peer-to- peer systems by adaptive connection establishment. *IEEE Transactions on Computers*, *54*(9), 1091–1103. doi:10.1109/TC.2005.146

Xu, Z., Tang, C., & Zhang, Z. (2003). Building topology-aware overlays using global soft-state. In *Proceedings of the 23rd International Conference on Distributed Computing Systems* (pp. 500-508).

This work was previously published in the International Journal of Mobile Computing and Multimedia Communications, Volume 3, Issue 3, edited by Ismail Khalil and Edgar Weippl, pp. 51-61, copyright 2011 by IGI Publishing (an imprint of IGI Global).

Chapter 14
Resource Allocation for Multi Access MIMO Systems

Shailendra Mishra
Kumaon Engineering College, India

Durg Singh Chauhan
Uttrakhand Technical University, India

ABSTRACT

In this paper, the authors discuss the emergence of new technologies related to the topic of the high-speed packet data access in wireless networks. The authors propose an algorithm for MIMO systems that optimizes the number of the transmit antennas according to the user's QoS. Scheduling performance under two types of traffic modes is also discussed: one is voice or web-browsing and the other is for data transfer and streaming data.

INTRODUCTION

During the last few years, MIMO technology has attracted a lot of attention in the area of wireless communications since significant increases in throughput and range are possible at the same bandwidth and at same overall transmit power expenditure. Wireless MIMO communication exploits phenomena such as multipath propagation to increase data throughput and range, or reduce bit error rates rather than attempting to eliminate effects of multipath propagation as traditional SISO (Single-Input Single-Output) communication systems (Yang, 2005; Chuah, Tse, Kahn, & Valenzuelai, 2002).Multi-user multi-antenna transmission architecture with channel estimators cascaded at the receiver side is proposed so that each user can feedback channel state information (CSI) for the further process of antenna resource allocation (Jun Zhang & Letaief, 2005).

In MIMO, "multiple in" means a WLAN device simultaneously sends two or more radio signals into multiple transmitting antennas. "Multiple out" refers to two or more radio signals coming

DOI: 10.4018/978-1-4666-2163-3.ch014

from multiple receiving antennas. These views of "in" and "out" may seem reversed; but MIMO terminology focuses on the system interface with antennas rather than the air interface. Whatever be the terminology, the MIMO's basic advantage seems simple, i.e. multiple antennas receive more signal and transmit more signal (Yang, 2005). Maximal receiver combining takes the signals from multiple antennas/receivers and combines them in a way that significantly boosts signal strength. This technique is fully compatible to 802.11a/b/g (Atheros Communications Inc., 2005). The capacity of the phased array system grows logarithmically with increasing antenna array size, whereas the capacity of the MIMO system grows linearly (Caire & Shamai, 2003).

MIMO TECHNIQUES

There are four unique multi-antenna MIMO techniques available to the system designer namely: spatial multiplexing (SM-MIMO), space-time coding (STC-MIMO), diversity systems (DIV-MIMO), smart antenna (SA-MIMO):

Spatial multiplexing maximizes the link capacity, for spatial multiplexing the number of receive antennas must be greater than or equal to the number of transmit antennas. It makes the receivers very complex, and therefore it is typically combined with orthogonal frequency-division multiplexing (OFDM) (Yang, 2005; Zhang & Letaief, 2004). The IEEE 802.16e standard incorporates MIMO-OFDMA. The IEEE 802.11n standard which is expected to be finalized soon, recommends MIMO-OFDM. Compared to spatial multiplexing systems, space-time code STC-MIMO systems provide robustness of communications without providing significant throughput gains against spatial multiplexing systems (Gesbert, Shafi, Shiu & Naguib, 2003). Moreover, to support fully the cellular environments MIMO research consortiums including IST-MASCOT, proposed to develop advanced MIMO communication

techniques such as cross-layer MIMO, multi-user MIMO and ad-hoc MIMO.

Cross-layer MIMO enhances the performance of MIMO links by solving cross-layer problems occurred when the MIMO configuration is employed in the system (Jiang, Zhuang, & Shen, 2005). A Cross-layer technique has been enhancing the performance of SISO links as well. Examples of cross-layer techniques are Joint source-channel coding, Link adaptation, or adaptive modulation and coding (AMC), Hybrid ARQ (HARQ) and user scheduling. Multi-user MIMO can exploit multiple user interference powers as a spatial resource at the cost of advanced transmit processing while conventional or single-user MIMO uses only the multiple antenna dimension (Zhang & Letaief, 2004). Examples of advanced transmit processing for multi-user MIMO are interference aware precoding and SDMA-based user scheduling.

Ad-hoc MIMO is a useful technique for future cellular networks which considers wireless mesh networking or wireless ad-hoc networking. To optimize the capacity of ad-hoc channels, MIMO concept and techniques can be applied to multiple links between transmit and receive node clusters. Unlike multiple antennas at the single-user MIMO transceiver, multiple nodes are located in a distributed manner. So, to achieve the capacity of this network, techniques to manage distributed radio resources are essential like the node cooperation and dirty paper coding (DPC) (Caire & Shamai, 2003).

CHANNEL MODELS AND DIVERSITY

The capacity of the channel has been calculated with some assumption. The H matrix represents gain of complex channel and will be normalized in a way that makes it possible to compare the capacity for the MIMO system with a SISO system. A communication link with N_T transmitting antennas and N_R receiving antennas are taken into consideration.

During communication the packets is of shorter time span than the coherence time of the channel (Soysal & Ulukus, 2010). With these assumptions we can use this mathematical model:

$$r_t = Hs_t + v_t$$

where

$$r_t = \left[r_t^1 r_t^2 ... r_t^{n_r} \right]^T$$

is the received signal at time instant t,

$$s_t = \left[s_t^1, s_t^2, ..., s_t^{n_T} \right]^T$$

is the sent signal, and v_t is AWGN with unit variance and uncorrelated between the n_r receiver antennas.

The N_R x N_T transition matrix is made up of elements $h_{i,j}$ as follows:

$$H = \begin{pmatrix} h_{1,1} & ... & h_{1,n_T} \\ ... & .... & ... \\ h_{n_R,1} & ... & h_{n_R,n_T} \end{pmatrix}$$

where $h_{i,j}$ denotes the complex channel coefficient between the j:th transmit antenna and the ith receiver antenna.

During comparison of different size systems, we need to normalize the channel matrix as normalization removes variation in frequency and time. The channel matrix is normalized such that

$$\left\| H \right\|_F^2 = n_T \cdot n_R$$

where $\left\| \cdot \cdot \right\|_F^2$ represents the Frobenius norm.

SCHEDULING ALGORITHMS

For the wireline communications, several scheduling techniques such as weighted fair queuing and packetized general processor sharing have been proposed to furnish fair channel access among contending hosts. However, an attempt to apply these wireline scheduling algorithms to wireless systems is inappropriate because wireless communication system presents many new challenges such as radio channel impairments. Therefore, late researches investigate some resources such as code, power, and bandwidth to exploit more efficient transmission under wireless MIMO environment (Telatar, 1999; Fochini, 1996; Tarokh, Jafarkhani, & Calderbank, 1999). We explore an antenna allocation scheme with dynamic allotment of multiple antennas for each real-time user to satisfy their QoS requirements.

ANTENNA SCHEDULING AND SELECTION

Although fairness is an important criterion in judging the design of a scheduling algorithm, overemphasizing it is not good in reality because "fairness" does not equal to user's satisfaction. Hence we propose a different algorithm which targets to satisfy user's QoS by allocating the number of transmit antennas. In this algorithm, we have to calculate how many antennas a user should use in order to satisfy user's time-varying data rate requests. Since we assume that the SNR and spatial correlation are known at the transmitter and the receive antenna amounts are naturally known. So we can compute the channel capacity as the function of the number of transmit antenna. Which antenna should be added or taken off as the next step would be dependent upon how many antennas are to be used.

In this algorithm, we have to calculate how many antennas a user should use in order to satisfy user's time-varying data rate requests. Since we assume that the SNR and spatial correlation are known at the transmitter and the receive antenna amounts are naturally known. So we can compute the channel capacity as the function of the number of transmit antenna. Which antenna should be added or taken off as the next step would be dependent upon how many antennas are to be used. In the algorithm Firstly, the indemnity $R_i(t)$ is included to make up for the scheduling false or incapability in the former time slot with the multiplying of a forgetting factor β, which fades out the compensation when time goes to infinity.

$$R_i(t) = C_i(t) - \left[d_i(t) - \sum_\tau \beta^\tau [C_i(t-\tau) - d_i(t-\tau)] \right]$$

The number of transmit antennas is decided to minimize the gap between requirements and offers with assistance of the channel capacity approximation. In brief, the entire algorithm is to minimize the cost function

$$\left\| f(P) - d_i(t) - R_i(t) \right\|^2$$

SIMULATIONS RESULT

Antenna Scheduling Algorithm

We also discussed the scheduling performance of our algorithm under two different types of traffic mode: one is voice or web-browsing in that bursts of data rate happen in some time intervals, sometimes it occurs silently also. The other one is for data transfer and streaming data. The requirement of data is self-similar and constantly high or low with only few fluctuations. The former is modeled by Pareto distribution while the later one is modeled by Weibull distribution. In the follow-

ing simulations, channel matrix change every 10 time index with a total 12 transmit antennas for 3 users, and the algorithm trigger threshold at 1.5 bits/Hz/sec.

The data streaming traffic mode is modeled by Weibull distribution with given pdf:

$$f(x) = aBx^{B-1} e^{-axB}$$

where a is the scale parameter and B is the shape parameter. The pdf distribution is shown is shown in Figure 1. Data rate request and indemnity curves for Weibull Distribution are shown in Figure 2, Figure 3, and Figure 4, respectively.

PARETO DISTRIBUTION

The former described traffic flow is modeled by Pareto distribution with given pdf as:

$$f(x) = B\, a^B / x^{B+1}$$

where a is the scale parameter and B is the shape parameter. The pdf distribution is shown is shown in Figure 5. Data rate request and indemnity curves for Pareto Distribution are shown in Figure 6, Figure 7, and Figure 8, respectively.

Composite data request rate and indemnity curves for Weibull distribution and Pareto distribution are shown in Figure 9 and Figure 10 respectively.

Weibull distribution traffic mode is for high-data rate transmission (with average throughput request about 20 bits/HZ/sec); so using single receive antenna is not enough for handling the constantly high data rate and in the end it has compensation diverge, i.e. system crashes depicted in Figure 2(a,b). Making forgetting factors smaller could somehow relieve the traffic pressure shown in Figure 8(a,b), but it doesn't solve the problem from the bottom line. Four receive antennas are suggested at least for such high-data rate system requirement.

Figure 1. Weibull distribution

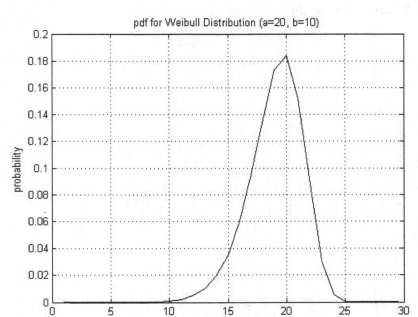

Though applying smaller forgetting factors can alleviate the divergence of compensation, the system turns out to be sensitive to the sudden change of 'data rate request' particularly for the case of Weibull distribution. The indemnity can avoid numbers of antennas being taken off when the data rate request abruptly drops; for the sake of this, the system doesn't have to increase the number of transmit antennas when the data rate request goes back to normal. What's more, excessive small forgetting factor equals to no compensation. So by choosing an appropriate forgetting factor more users can be accommodated by the system.

Either the higher signal-to-noise ratio or the less correlation, offer a better environment for transmission and exploration of more capacities. Therefore, either of them shortens the indemnity delay depicted in Figure 9 and in Figure 10.

In the time domain analysis, we also evaluate how many transmit antennas are needed to reach certain service quality (to guarantee the average indemnity under certain level). Again under the condition $\eta = 25$dB, three users are accommo-

dated in the system. In the case of Pareto distribution not too many transmit antennas are used at a time. Actually using more transmit antennas offer more choices when the allocation scheme seeks the best uncorrelated antenna then the mean values of indemnity are smaller. When all users are with four receive antennas, for example, if 12 transmit antennas are used, it would results in 2.7672 bits/Hz/sec average indemnity which is much smaller than the case of using of eight antennas. Meanwhile, we perceive that in the case of Weibull distribution when there are only 3 receiver antennas and 12 transmit antennas, the allocation scheme is capable of handling the high data rate request.

To wrap up, we do not really use all transmit antennas at a time instant; instead, only a few antennas are taken for transmission. Consequently, a large number of radio frequency power amplifiers, low noise amplifiers, etc are required since numerous transmit antennas can augment for these devices at lower cost and consequent lower power consumption.

Figure 2. (a) Data rate request curves for Weibull distribution (a=20, b=10) with Rx=1 (b). indemnity curves for Weibull distribution (a=20, b=10) with Rx=1

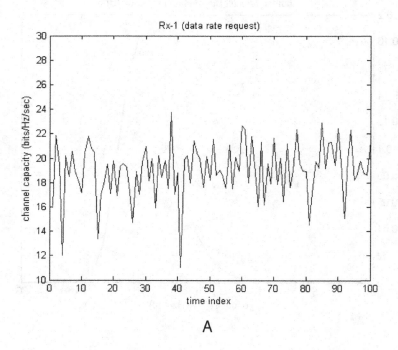

A

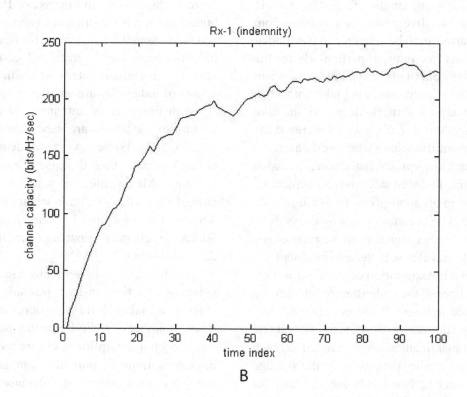

B

Figure 3. (a) Data rate request curves for Weibull distribution (a=20, b=10) with Rx=2 (b). indemnity curves for Weibull distribution (a=20, b=10) with Rx=2

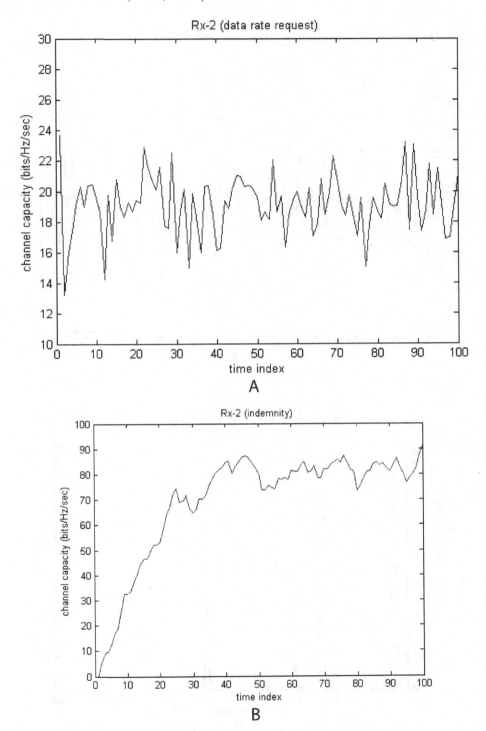

Figure 4. (a) Data rate request curves for Weibull distribution (a=20,b=10) with Rx= 3 (b). indemnity curves for Weibull distribution (a=20,b=10) with Rx= 3

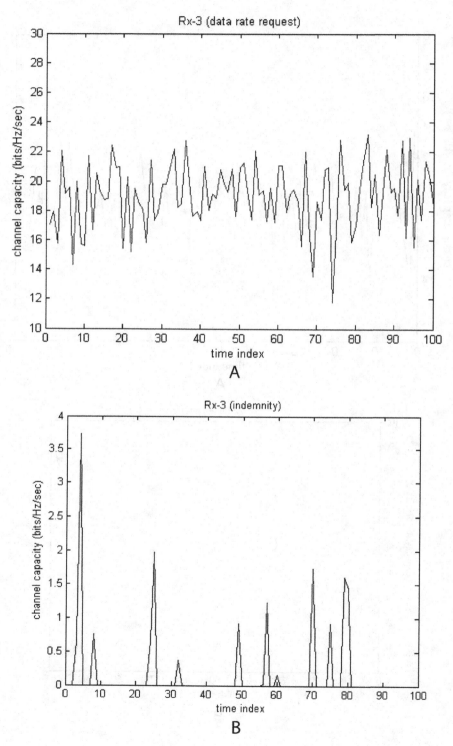

Figure 5. Pareto distribution

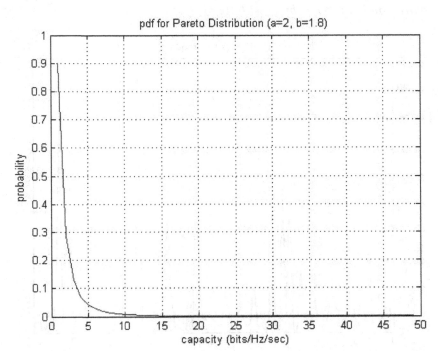

POSSIBLE APPLICATIONS

The current Wireless LAN standard IEEE 802.11a can at most offer 54Mbps via occupying 16.6MHz bandwidth; that is to say, utilized spectral efficiency is about 3.25 bits/Hz/sec for the best transmission case. Our proposed antenna allocation algorithm is decent for average 6.5 bits/Hz/sec under Pareto distribution with two receive antennas and average 20 bits/Hz/sec under Weibull distribution with four receive antennas. Since channel estimator works under block-fading environment, the proposed system is not suggested for high moving-speed application. The present experiments of MIMO system such as IEEE 802.11n which ensures the usage of multiple receive antennas often make use of four transmit antenna. Owing to the advance of RF component manufacture, it is possible that the future high data-rate-demand communication system would require more transmit antennas to overcome the bottleneck of limited capacity. Our algorithm requires as many transmit antennas as that of receive antennas approximately and it would be very helpful to enhance the overall usage of channel resource for high-speed wireless network physical layer design.

FUTURE WORKS

The proposed antenna scheduling could not be perfectly optimum since adding one more transmit antennas might improve the capacity of the system. A potential solution is to assess the possible capacity improvement. If it is much larger than the real needs, then increase the power (to raise the SNR) instead of increasing a transmit antenna. Such a problem involving joint resource allocation is also interesting.

In this work, we make the assumption that the co-relation is known. However, the implementation of system needs to measure the real co-relation by some existent or newer algorithmic implementations.

Figure 6. (a) Data rate request curves for Pareto distribution (a=1.8, b=2) with Rx=1 (b). indemnity curves for Pareto distribution (a=1.8, b=2) with Rx=1

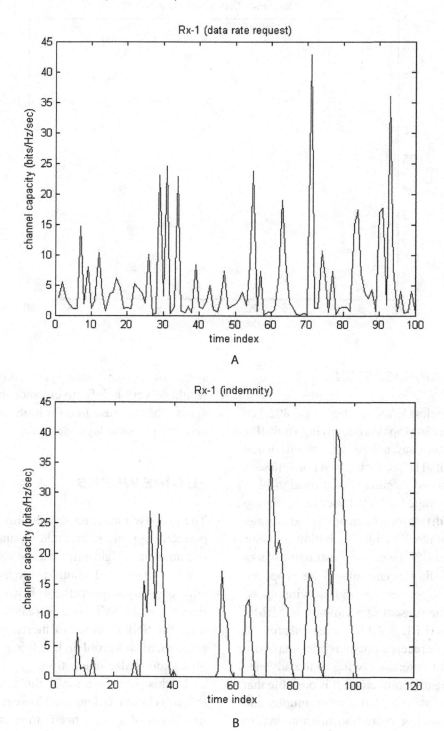

Figure 7. (a) Data rate request curves for Pareto distribution (a=1.8, b=2) with Rx=2 (b). indemnity curves for Pareto distribution (a=1.8, b=2) with Rx=2

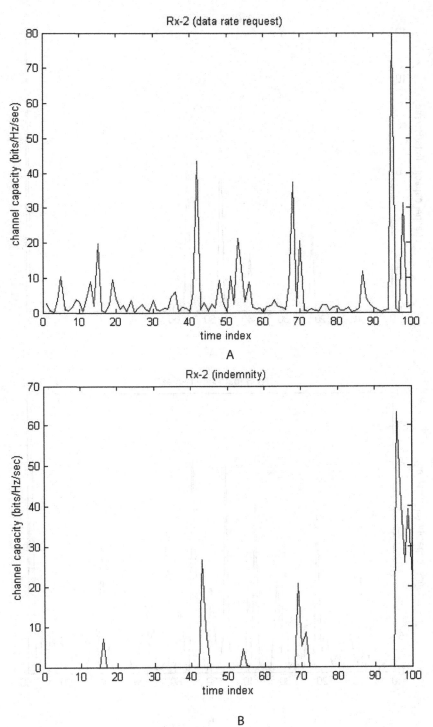

Figure 8. (a) Data rate request curves for Pareto distribution (a=1.8,b=2) with Rx= 3 (b). indemnity curves for Pareto distribution (a=1.8,b=2) with Rx= 3

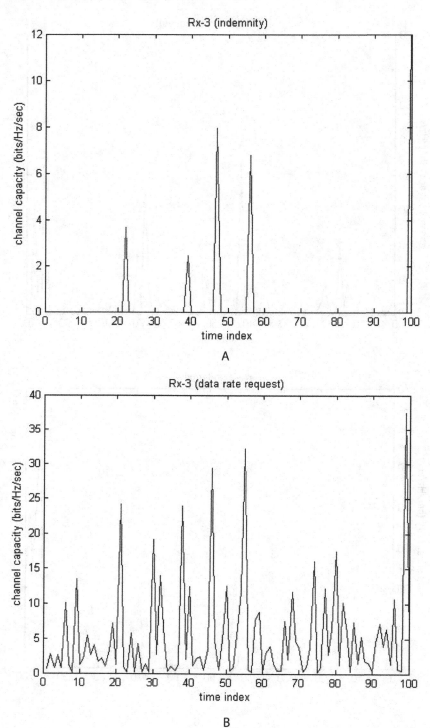

A

B

Figure 9. Composite data request rate and indemnity curves for Weibull distribution

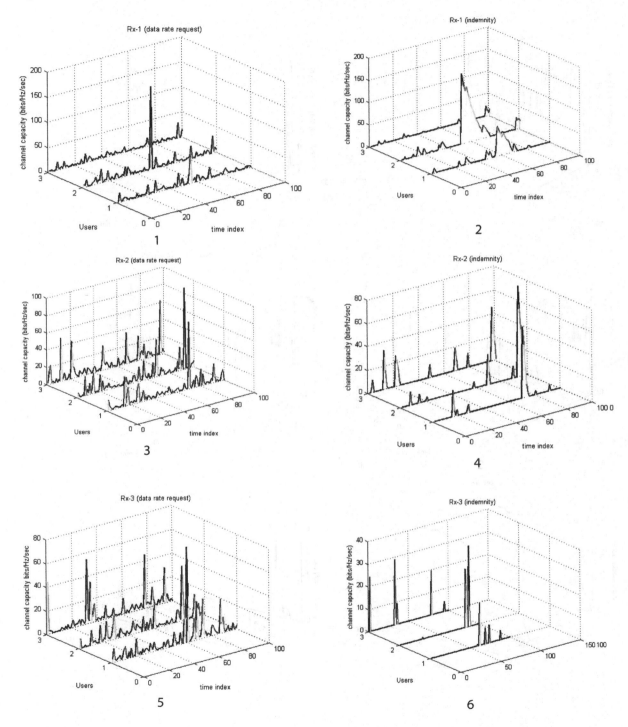

Figure 10. Composite data request rate and indemnity curves for Pareto distribution

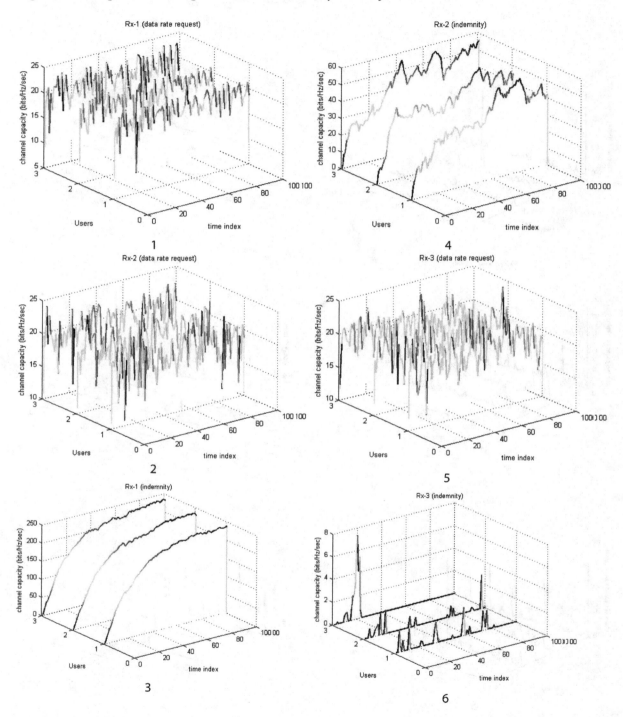

CONCLUSION

In this research, we have proposed scheduling and selection algorithm for MIMO system which targets to satisfy user's QoS by allocating the number of transmit antennas. The basic motive was to consider correlated channel and toward this a thorough discussion was made about applying antenna scheduling and its selection. A broader scope of MIMO channel modeling methods was presented. We briefly went through diverse scheduling policies and proposed a novel, different optimizing target of antenna selection and scheduling. Simultaneously, results of antenna scheduling algorithm under random traffic mode - Weibull and Pareto - are discussed.

REFERENCES

Atheros Communications, Inc. (2005). *Getting the most out of MIMO: Boosting wireless LAN performance with full compatibility.* Retrieved from http://www.opulan.com/pt/whitepapers/MIMO_WLAN_Perf_whitepaper.pdf

Caire, G., & Shamai, S. (2003). On the achievable throughput of a multiantenna gaussian broadcast channel. *IEEE Transactions on Information Theory*, *49*(7), 1691–1706. doi:10.1109/TIT.2003.813523

Chuah, C.-N., Tse, D. N. C., Kahn, J. M., & Valenzuela, R. A. (2002). Capacity scaling in MIMO wireless systems under correlated fading. *IEEE Transactions on Information Theory*, *48*(3).

Fochini, G. J. (1996). Layered space-time architecture for wireless communication in fading environment when using multi-element antennas. *Bell Labs Technical Journal*, *1*, 41–59. doi:10.1002/bltj.2015

Gesbert, D., Shafi, M., Shiu, D., & Naguib, A. (2003). From theory to practice: An overview of MIMO space-time coded wireless systems. *IEEE Journal on Selected Areas in Communications*, *21*(3). doi:10.1109/JSAC.2003.809458

Jiang, H., Zhuang, W., & Shen, X. (2005). Cross-layer design for resource allocation in 3G wireless networks and beyond. *IEEE Communications Magazine*, *43*(12), 120–126. doi:10.1109/MCOM.2005.1561929

Soysal, A., & Ulukus, S. (2010). Joint channel estimation and resource allocation for MIMO systems. *IEEE Transactions on Wireless Communications*, *9*(2), 632–640. doi:10.1109/TWC.2010.02.080100

Tarokh, V., Jafarkhani, H., & Calderbank, A. R. (1999). Space-time block codes from orthogonal designs. *IEEE Transactions on Information Theory*, *45*(5), 1456–1467. doi:10.1109/18.771146

Telatar, E. (1999). Capacity of multi-antenna gaussian channels. *European Transactions on Telecommunication*, *10*(6), 585–596. doi:10.1002/ett.4460100604

Yang, H. (2005). A road to future broadband wireless access: MIMO-OFDM based air interface. *IEEE Communications Magazine*, *43*(1), 53–60. doi:10.1109/MCOM.2005.1381875

Zhang, Y. J., & Letaief, K. B. (2004). Multiuser adaptive subcarrier-and-bit allocation with adaptive cell selection for OFDM systems. *IEEE Transactions on Wireless Communications*, *3*(5), 1566–1575. doi:10.1109/TWC.2004.833501

Zhang, Y. J., & Letaief, K. B. (2005). Adaptive resource allocation for multiaccess mimo/OFDM systems with matched filtering. *IEEE Transactions on Communications*, *53*(11), 1810–1816. doi:10.1109/TCOMM.2005.858665

This work was previously published in the International Journal of Mobile Computing and Multimedia Communications, Volume 3, Issue 3, edited by Ismail Khalil and Edgar Weippl, pp. 36-50, copyright 2011 by IGI Publishing (an imprint of IGI Global).

Chapter 15
An Adaptive Backoff Algorithm for Mobile Ad–Hoc Networks

Yaser Khamayseh
Jordan University of Science and Technology, Jordan

Muneer Bani Yassein
Jordan University of Science and Technology, Jordan

Iman I. Badran
Jordan University of Science and Technology, Jordan

Wail Mardini
Jordan University of Science and Technology, Jordan

ABSTRACT

Collision is a common problem in Mobile Ad Hoc Networks (MANETs). There are several backoff algorithms that have been proposed to avoid this problem. This paper proposes a new backoff algorithm called the Square Root Backoff (SRB). Moreover, it identifies that no algorithm can perform the best in all cases. Therefore, an adaptive strategy is proposed to choose the best backoff mechanism from a set of mechanisms based on network density and mobility parameters. The proposed adaptive algorithm is implemented in two phases: the offline phase and the online phase. Such design aims at reducing the time complexity of the algorithm by performing some of the computations prior to the actual deployment and of the network. Results from simulations demonstrate that the SRB algorithm achieved better performance than BEB and LB. Moreover, the adaptive backoff algorithm obtains the best throughput and end-to-end delay performance over the other backoff algorithms.

DOI: 10.4018/978-1-4666-2163-3.ch015

INTRODUCTION

In the last few decades, studies in networking were concentrated on wireless networks. This is due to the success of wireless networks in many life applications. Wireless networks can be used by devices such as cell phones, laptops, PDAs. Many features discriminate wireless networks over wired networks. A wireless network is less expensive because it eliminates the need to connect nodes by cables which also can help make connecting to the internet much more convenient, and it provides the ability of anytime, anywhere, and unlimited access to the Internet. Two main types of wireless networks have been introduced, infrastructure based and infrastructure-less (ad hoc) wireless networks (Kurose & Ross, 2007). Infrastructure based wireless network has a base station that is connected to a larger wired network such as the Internet. While in infrastructure-less wireless network there is no base station. An example of such infrastructure-less wireless network is Mobile Ad Hoc Network (MANET). MANETs consist of a set of nodes that communicate with each other wirelessly and without the existence of infrastructure, which means that there is not a base station to control the communication between the mobile hosts, so each node will act as both a host and a router (Kurose & Ross, 2007). These networks have many distinguishing features such as self healing, self organizing, multi-hop routing, neighborhood awareness, scarce resources specially bandwidth and batteries, and changing network topology due to the mobility of the nodes in the network (Sun, 2001).

Without the existence of base stations, routers, or any infrastructure, nodes use peer-to-peer communication to interact with each other. Node communication will be direct if the nodes that need to communicate are within the coverage area of each other. But, if they are not within the coverage area of each other then they must communicate via a multi hop route with the cooperation of other nodes in the network (Yi, Gerla, & Kwon, 2002). To find such multi-hop paths between nodes, there must be a method that allows nodes to collect information. This method is known in MANETs as flooding, in which each node receives the message will retransmit it to all its neighbors (Bani Yassein, Ould Khaoua, Mackenzie, & Papanastasiou, 2005, 2006; Bani Yassein & Ould Khaoua, 2007; Sasson, Cavin, & Schiper, 2003). The need to flooding comes from the changing topology of the network in MANETs where the nodes move and may change their location frequently. Many operations in MANETs depend on flooding such as routing protocols, multicast schemes, or service discovery programs. But there is a drawback of using flooding that is redundant transmissions may generate great overhead on the network and cause frequent contentions and collisions which leads to what is called the broadcast storm problem (Tseng, Ni, Chen, & Sheu, 2002).

Wireless links suffer from serious problems such as the shared bandwidth, signal weakening, noise, and interference. With shared medium where we have multiple sending and receiving nodes all connected to the same single shared channel, it is essential to have an efficient and effective Medium Access Control (MAC) mechanism, which is a set of rules or procedures by which a frame is transmitted onto the link, to allow the efficient use of a shared medium, to manage the scarce bandwidth resources among active users, and as a result to avoid collisions (Manaseer, Ould-Khaoua, & Mackenzie, 2006). According to the seven layer Open System Interconnection (OSI) model, IEEE 802.11 MAC represents a sub-layer of the Data Link Control (DLC) layer in that model (Bani Yassein, Manaseer, & Al-Turani, 2009). MAC protocols are essential to control channel access especially multiple-access to the shared medium by multiple nodes at the same time. Another function of MAC protocols is to provide MAC addressing. A mechanism called Carrier Sense Multiple Access with collision Avoidance

(CSMA/CA) is used for controlling the channel access in IEEE 802.11 (Bani Yassein, Manaseer, & Al-Turani, 2009).

The IEEE 802.11 standard can be used in either an ad hoc infrastructure less networks or in base station based networks. In this standard, either a distributed coordination function (DCF) or a point coordination function (PCF) is used for achieving the medium sharing (Pang, Liew, Lee, & Leung, 2004). In Ad Hoc Networks, the MAC protocol includes a backoff algorithm to avoid collisions. Such collisions occur when multiple nodes try to access the shared medium at the same time (Manaseer & Ould-Khaoua, 2006; IEEE, 1999; Song, Kwak, Song, Miller, 2004; Manaseer & Masadeh, 2008). At any time, only one of the nodes can access the channel, while other nodes must wait for some random period of time that is called backoff time which is uniformly selected from the Contention Window (CW).

Many Backoff algorithms have been proposed. But most of the proposed algorithms suffer from increasing the *CW* in case of failure to transmit rapidly to large sizes like the Binary Exponential Backoff (BEB) algorithm (Manaseer, Ould-Khaoua, & Mackenzie, 2006). This leads to long delays and increases the wasted time for which the channel will be idle. On the other hand, other algorithms like the Linear Backoff (LB) don't give the node sufficient time before retrying to transmit which causes more overhead on the node and consumes the battery power because of the very frequent sensing of the channel (Manaseer, Ould-Khaoua, & Mackenzie, 2006). This paper proposes a new backoff algorithm called the Square Root Backoff (SRB) to be implemented in the IEEE 802.11 MAC protocol to reduce collision in MANETs. This new algorithm increases the backoff time by the square root of the current backoff time. When a node tries to start transmission it firstly senses the channel, if it is free the node starts transmission. But when the channel is busy it must wait a backoff time that equals the current backoff time plus the square root of it. We recognize that no

algorithm can perform very well in all environments. Thus, we propose an adaptive mechanism that benefits from the advantages of three backoff algorithms; SRB, LB, and BEB by applying an adaptive strategy that chooses the best backoff algorithm from these three algorithms based on the network density and users' mobility. The metrics used to evaluate the studied backoff algorithms is the network aggregate throughput and end-to-end delay. The proposed Adaptive algorithm is done in two separate phases, the offline phase and the online phase. Such design aims of reducing the time complexity of the algorithm by performing some of the computations and analysis prior to the actual deployment and operation of the network.

The rest of the paper is organized as follows: First we provide a review on some related works. Section 3 presents the proposed backoff algorithms. The parameters used in simulation experiments and the performance results are presented and we conclude the paper.

RELATED WORK

There are many backoff algorithms proposed for the MAC layer within Mobile Ad Hoc Networks. In this section we will present some of these algorithms briefly. A simple backoff algorithm has been proposed by Takahashi and Tsuboi (2003). A dynamic spatial backoff algorithm has been proposed by Yang and Vaidya (2007). This algorithm adapts the space of the transmissions which allows the adjustment of the set of competing nodes and the level of contention in the channel. It used the joint control of carrier sense threshold and transmission rate.

Another backoff algorithm is the Dynamic P-Persistent (DPP) Backoff algorithm (Barcel'o, Bellalta, Cano, & Oliver, 2009). It was based on that under optimal efficiency conditions; number of busy channel slots with collisions is constant.

A Neighborhood Backoff Algorithm (NBA) has been proposed (Taifour, Nat-Abdesselam, &

Simplot-Ryl, 2006) where each node modifies its backoff interval based on the number of its neighbors. Experiments show a better behavior of the NBA scheme in comparison to the BEB scheme. Yeong Han and Abu-Ghazaleh (2008) have proposed three algorithms that aim to distinguish between collisions and transmission errors. When a failure of transmission due to transmission error occurs, it is not necessary to wait for backoff time before retransmission. Another example of the backoff algorithms is the Multiplicative Increase Linear Decrease (MILD) algorithm (Sakakibara et al., 2005). Results shows that this algorithm improves the total throughput of the network, but the cost of this improvement is high because we need to collect a perfect knowledge about collisions happening over the network, which is hard-to-acquire knowledge.

Other works (Anouar & Bonnet, 2007) assume that we can compute the optimal fixed contention window if we know the number of contending stations. Under the assumption that this information about the number of contending stations is directly available at the Access Point or can be calculated using one of the estimation techniques. Performance is increased both in terms of efficiency and fairness by using the fixed optimal contention window. This approach is extended in (Zhao, Zhang, Yang, & Zhang, 2007) to include an estimation technique that helps to estimate the conditional collision probability which is called Virtual-CSMA. Papadimitratos et al. (2005) suggested an algorithm to estimate the BER (Bit Error Rate) of a wireless link to be used in determining the back-off time. The estimated BER was used to perform differentiation for nodes possible, by decreasing fairness for throughput increase. But, finding the BER through link estimation is still a complex process. Yoon et al. (2006) proposed a scheme in IEEE 802.11e networks for service differentiation. Their work is concentrated on modifying the backoff range.

THE PROPOSED BACKOFF ALGORITHMS

This section presents the proposed algorithms in this paper which are temporal algorithms that try to separate nodes transmissions in time to avoid collisions. The first algorithm is a new backoff algorithm called SRB to be implemented in the IEEE 802.11 MAC protocol to reduce collision in MANETs. This new algorithm increases the backoff time by the square root of the current backoff time. We recognize that no algorithm can perform very well in all environments. Thus, we propose the second algorithm in this paper which is an adaptive mechanism that benefits from the advantages of three backoff algorithms; SRB, LB, and BEB by applying an adaptive strategy that chooses the best backoff algorithm from these three algorithms based on the network density and users' mobility.

Square Root Backoff Algorithm

Most of the proposed algorithms suffer from increasing the CW in case of failure to transmit rapidly to large sizes like BEB algorithm (Manaseer, Ould-Khaoua, & Mackenzie, 2006). This leads to long delays and increases the wasted time for which the channel will be idle. On the other hand, other algorithms like LB don't give the node sufficient time before retrying to transmit which causes more overhead on the node and consumes the battery power because of the very frequent sensing of the channel (Manaseer, Ould-Khaoua, & Mackenzie, 2006).

We aim to achieve balanced backoff time increases that are not too long and not too short. To achieve this goal, we have proposed a new backoff algorithm called SRB algorithm. Also, we will apply an adaptive strategy that takes into consideration the network density and users' mobility. The proposed algorithm – the SRB algorithm - uses the square root of the current backoff time as the increment factor to calculate the next backoff. The following formula is used to estimate the new backoff interval where *BO* represents the backoff interval:

$$(BO)_{new} = (BO)_{old} + (sqrt\ (BO)_{old} * Random(1:N)) \tag{1}$$

When a node senses the channel before starting transmission for the first time and finds the channel busy it waits a random time then senses the channel again. If it is free, the node can start its transmission. Otherwise the node waits additional time increased by the square root of the old waiting time multiplied by a random number between 1 and *N*. This random number is used to decrease the opportunity of contention. So there will not be two nodes starting the backoff time together and finish waiting and resense the channel for retransmission at the same time.

Figure 1 shows that the successive values of backoff interval in the BEB algorithm are short intervals increases exponentially as the number

of increments increases. In the LB algorithm, the backoff interval increases in very low ranges. On the other hand, the backoff interval in the SRB algorithm has a smooth increment curve as the number of increments increases.

The Adaptive Backoff Algorithm

From literature and experiments, we recognize that no algorithm can perform very well in all environments. Thus, we propose an adaptive mechanism that combines the advantages of three backoff algorithms (SRB, LB, and BEB) by applying an adaptive strategy that chooses the best backoff algorithm from these three algorithms based on network status. The proposed Adaptive algorithm is done in two separate phases, the offline phase and the online phase. Such design aims of reducing the time complexity of the algorithm by performing some of the computations and analysis prior to the actual deployment and operation of the network. Figure 2 depicts the relationship between the major components of the proposed algorithm.

Figure 1. BO increase behavior is several backoff algorithm

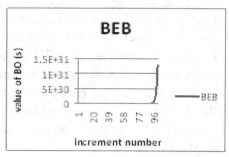
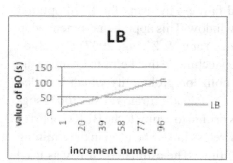

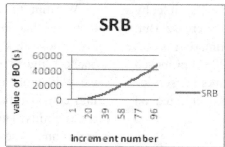

Figure 2. The adaptive backoff algorithm phases

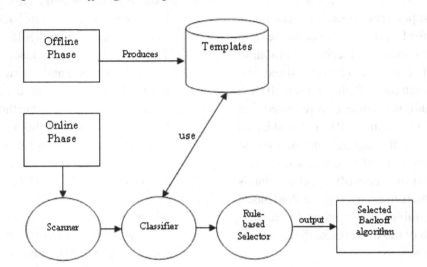

The Offline Phase of the Adaptive Backoff Algorithm

To capture the different possible network states, we define the concept of network template, where each template represents a unique network status expressed by different factors such as mobility and density. The total number of possible templates is $m \times n$, where n and m is the number of characterizing factors for mobility and density of the network respectively. We have classified the mobility of the network into low, medium, high, and highest mobile network. Also, we have classified the network density into low, medium, and high density network. For example, a possible network template is: high mobile and high density network.

In the offline phase, the algorithm scans the network environment and uses a set of factors to generate all possible network templates. In this paper, we use two main factors to build the templates: user mobility, and network density. User mobility is a crucial factor to be considered in designing any wireless network. It is very hard to capture users' mobility with one factor. Thus, we propose to use both nodes speed and pause time to describe this factor but the classification

of the mobility factor is done based on speed only for simplicity. Thus, when we say for example low mobile network it means that it is low speed network but it could have low, medium, or high pause time.

Moreover, ad hoc network operator rely on the concept of multi-hoping to deliver users traffic all over the network. The network area and the number of users in the network are the main limiting factors for multi-hoping. These two parameters can be expressed together by the network density factor. Such combination reduces the number of network templates to be generated and examined.

The algorithm generates and considers all possible Templates according to previously mentioned factors. There are 12 general templates, and each template may have several sub templates. An example of a template is:

Template 1: Low mobility and low density
Template 1.1: Low speed with low pause time and low density
Template 1.2: Low speed with medium pause time and low density
Template 1.3: Low speed with high pause time and low density

241

Each template is then assigned a backoff algorithm that best performs under such template. To better assign the backoff algorithm to the right template we have conducted a series of simulation studies as described in section 3 to investigate the performance of each backoff algorithm with each template. Although the simulation revealed that the three studied algorithms (SRB, LB, and BEB) achieved very close throughput and end-to-end delay performance in most of the cases, we still can say that there is one backoff algorithm that is better than the others in each template. And based on these results, Table 1 summarizes the matching between each of the three backoff algorithms with the templates.

The Online Phase of the Adaptive Backoff Algorithm

The Adaptive algorithm in this phase runs on all nodes independently and estimates the backoff interval according to the procedure to be explained next.

The Online phase consists of three main components as follows:

1. **Scanner:** This component is responsible for gathering information about the network. Network scan is performed on demand.
2. **Classifier:** This component uses the information gathered in the scanning step to estimate the appropriate network template that matches the current network state.

Table 1. Matching backoff algorithms with templates

Backoff Algorithm	Templates
SRB	5, 9, 10.1, 2.3, 6.3, 10.3, 7.2, 11.1, 3.3, 4.1, 8.1, 4.2, 8.3
BEB	2.1, 2.2, 6.2, 10.2, 7.1, 11.2, 11.3, 12.1
LB	1, 6.1, 3.1, 3.2, 7.3, 8.2, 12.2, 4.3, 12.3

3. **Rule-Based Selector:** This component selects the most appropriate backoff algorithm from a set of algorithms (SRB, LB, and BEB). The selection is done based on the current network template and the rules that associate each template with a certain backoff algorithm as determined in the offline phase. We have constructed the Adaptive backoff selector function (F) as follows:

$$F = \alpha1\ F1 + \alpha2\ F2 + \alpha3\ F3 \qquad (2)$$

where:

- *F1*: The formula of computing the backoff value using the SRB algorithm which was shown in Section 2 in (1).
- *F2*: The formula of computing the backoff value using the BEB algorithm:

$$(BO)_{new} = (BO)_{old} * 2 \qquad (3)$$

- *F3*: The formula of computing the backoff value using the LB algorithm:

$$(BO)_{new} = (BO)_{old} + Constant \qquad (4)$$

where the constant used in this thesis equals 1.

$\alpha1$, $\alpha2$, $\alpha3$: represents factors of the three functions *F1, F2, F3* respectively, where $0 \leq (\alpha1, \alpha2, \alpha3) \leq 1$.

The values of the functions factors ($\alpha1$, $\alpha2$, and $\alpha3$) are decided in this thesis to be one or zero for simplification and this value depends on the network status. In other words, if the network environment is in a case where the SRB is the best to use for achieving the highest throughput and end-to-end delay, then $\alpha1$ must equal one while $\alpha2$ and $\alpha3$ will be assigned a zero. The same strategy is used when BEB is preferred: $\alpha2$ is set to one while $\alpha1$ and $\alpha3$ assigned a zero. Also, when the LB is the best choice for the current network status then $\alpha3$ must set to one while $\alpha2$ and $\alpha1$ will be reset to zero.

SIMULATION AND RESULTS

Simulation in this paper was conducted in two steps: In the first step, a preliminary simulation was performed to compare the performance of the three previously mentioned backoff algorithms. Based on the results of this simulation we have decided which algorithm is more suitable for each case of the different density and mobility parameters combinations. Then, the second step starts once the adaptive algorithm is fully constructed and organized to be ready for the next simulation that evaluates its performance in comparison to each of the individual algorithms (SRB, LB, and BEB).

Simulation Environment

We have used the Glomosim 2.03 simulator to conduct intensive experiments to evaluate the performance of the backoff algorithms. The metrics used for comparison is network aggregate throughput and end-to-end delay. The aggregate throughput is the sum of all bits that are delivered per second to all nodes in a network without error (Orenstein, Goodman, Marantz, & Rodriguez, 2004) and can be expressed by the following formula:

$$\text{Aggregate throughput} = \frac{\text{Sum of all correctly delivered bits}}{\text{Time Needed for Delivery}}$$

(5)

The end-to-end delay is the time taken for a packet to be transmitted across a network from source to destination (Kurose & Ross, 2007) and can be expressed by the following formula:

End-to-end delay =
number of routers between source and destination *
(processing delay + queuing delay
+ transmission delay + propagation delay)

(6)

Two key characteristics of the network were taken into consideration in our study: the first characteristic is the mobility of nodes within the network which can be measured by monitoring the changes in neighborhood; this characteristic provides useful information concerning the efficiency of the backoff algorithms for static and highly mobile MANETs as well. The second characteristic is network density which is the number of nodes in area unit. We have used changing density as a method of evaluating the performance of the backoff algorithms for different sizes of networks. We have used the number of nodes as an indicator of the density, and the speed and pause time as indicators of the users' mobility. For each of these three parameters (density, speed, and pause time) we used low, medium, and high values and for speed we added (highest) value. We have considered the network to be low, medium, or high density when the number of nodes in the network is 25, 50, or 100 nodes respectively. Also, we have considered the network to be low, medium, high, or highest mobile network when the speed of the nodes is 1, 10, 20, or 50 m/s respectively.

Also, the values of the functions factors ($\alpha1$, $\alpha2$, and $\alpha3$) that are used in the Rule-based Selector of the online phase are decided in this paper to be one or zero for simplification and this value depends on the network status. In other words, if the network environment is in a case where the SRB is the best to use for achieving the highest throughput and end-to-end delay, then $\alpha1$ must equal one while $\alpha2$ and $\alpha3$ will be assigned a zero. The same strategy is used when BEB is preferred: $\alpha2$ is set to one while $\alpha1$ and $\alpha3$ assigned a zero. Also, when the LB is the best choice for the current network status then $\alpha3$ must set to one while $\alpha2$ and $\alpha1$ will be reset to zero.

Several topologies and mobility scenarios have been created to test the algorithms (LB, BEB, SRB, and the Adaptive) as intensively as possible. The network considered for the performance analysis varies from 25 to 100 nodes placed uniformly on 1000x1000m² area. Other simulation parameters are the speed which ranges between 1 and 50 m/s, pause time that varies between 0 and 40 seconds, simulation time that is 30 minutes, and the random number (N) of the SRB algorithm that is chosen to be 10. The routing protocol used in this simulation is AODV. The simulation parameters are summarized in Table 2.

SRB Algorithm Results

An important parameter that we should consider carefully in SRB algorithm is the random number (N). As mentioned before, this random number is used to decrease the opportunity of contention. So there will not be two nodes starting the backoff time together and finish waiting and resense the channel for retransmission at the same time. We have done several experiments to choose the value of this random number.

In a network with speed of 10m/s and pause time of 0s, when $N = 25$ it achieves slightly better throughput than when $N = 10$ and $N = 50$ in both medium and high density networks. However, in low density networks, it is slightly better to use $N = 50$. In general, the gap in performance of the

Table 2. Simulation parameters

Value	Parameter
30 minutes	simulation time
25,50,100 nodes	density
1,10,20,50 m/s	speed
0,20,40 s	pause time
1000X1000 m²	area
AODV	routing protocol
250 kbps	traffic rate
10	N (random number for SRB)

three tested cases is nominal. The throughput performance of SRB with $N = 10$ is 21181, 22377, and 22397 bit/s. For $N = 25$ it is 21159, 22416, and 22459 bit/s. And for $N = 50$ it is 21183, 22373, and 22374 bit/s in a network with density of 25, 50, and 100 nodes respectively.

For the same setup, the end-to-end delay performance is estimated. For $N = 50$ case, it achieves slightly better end-to-end delay performance than if $N = 10$ and $N = 25$ in both low and medium density networks. However, in high density networks, the $N = 10$ case achieved a slight improvement over the other 2 cases. Again, the achiever improvement is nominal. The end-to-end delay performance of SRB with $N = 10$ is 0.04423816, 0.064961305, and 0.05845339 seconds. For $N = 25$ is 0.042921911, 0.063643303, and 0.062198682 seconds. And for $N = 50$ is 0.042586565, 0.06264321, and 0.06087702 seconds in a network with density of 25, 50, and 100 nodes respectively.

More experiments were conducted, in this set of experiments; we increased the nodes speed to 20m/s and set the pause time to 0s. Again the case in which $N = 25$ achieved slightly better throughput than the other two cases when $N = 10$ and $N = 50$ in both low and medium density networks. However, in high density networks, the case of $N = 10$ achieved slightly better throughput. The performance of the case of $N = 10$ is 19955, 22146, and 22232 bit/s, for $N = 25$ is 20895, 22232, and 22162 bit/s, and for $N = 50$ is 20793, 20817, and 22232 bit/s in a network with density of 25, 50, and 100 nodes respectively.

For the same setup, the end-to-end delay performance is estimated. The case of $N = 10$ achieves slightly better performance than $N = 50$ and $N = 25$ in both medium and high density networks. But in low density networks, the case of $N = 25$ is slightly better. The end-to-end delay of SRB with $N = 10$ is 0.074908742, 0.082938232, and 0.088596009 seconds, with $N = 25$ is 0.065952863, 0.087080885, and 0.09401987 seconds, and with $N = 50$ it was 0.066954144, 0.084585188, and

0.090058981 seconds in a network with density of 25, 50, and 100 nodes respectively.

Increasing the nodes' speed to 50m/s and pause time is set to 0s, the case for $N =$ achieves slightly better throughput in both low and medium density networks. However, in high density networks, the case of $N = 25$ achieved the best performance. The throughput performance of SRB with $N = 10$ is 19744, 20336, and 16848 bit/s, for $N=25$ is 16893, 17412, and 20845 bit/s, and for $N=50$ it was 19841, 20165, and 19536 bit/s in a network with density of 25, 50, and 100 nodes respectively.

The end-to-end delay performance for this setup was the best when $N =10$ in both low and medium density networks. And the best when $N = 25$ in high density networks. The end-to-end delay performance of SRB with $N=10$ is 0.084630507, 0.142586592, and 0.147553824 seconds, with $N=25$ is 0.14851813, 0.145680608, and 0.141664173 seconds, and for $N = 50$ is 0.148660681, 0.146858941, and 0.144047739 seconds in a network with density of 25, 50, and 100 nodes respectively.

The obtained results from the previous set of experiments suggest that no case for N outperforms the other cases in terms of both throughput and end to end delay. However, in general, we may say that when $N = 10$, it achieves more satisfactory performance than $N = 25$ and $N = 50$.

Adaptive Algorithm Results

This section presents the results of our simulation where the network performance is measured in terms of the total network throughput and the end-to-end delay. We have compared the performance of the LB, BEB, SRB, and adaptive algorithms.

In the following figures, each column represents the aggregate throughput or the end-to-end delay of each of the four backoff algorithms (LB, BEB, SRB, and the Adaptive backoff) with different speed and pause time values, and different number of nodes in the network. In most cases we can see that all of the four backoff algorithms

achieve close throughput and end-to-end delay performance. But in each case we still can say there is one that is better than the others by 0.01% up to 76%. The remaining figures show that in most of the cases over different densities and with different mobility states, the four backoff algorithms achieved better throughput and end-to-end delay performance in high density networks than it in low density networks. This is because as the number of nodes in the network increases, the number of routes for transmission will be higher; because MANETs depends on multi-hoping to transmit data. And as a result the network throughput will increase because more bits will be delivered in time unit and the end-to-end delay will decrease because data will be delivered within shorter time. Figure 3 show that the pause time has no effect when the speed is very low. This is clear because when we used low, medium, or high pause time with low speed the results were the same for each of the four algorithms. Also, we can see that all of them achieved relatively close throughput values. But, the SRB gives slightly better throughput performance over all the different density values used by about 0.1% to 0.4% although the BEB algorithm was in the same level of SRB when density is low or high, but when density is medium, BEB achieved lower throughput value. On the other hand, the LB algorithm obtained lower throughput performance than the other algorithms in that case by about 0.1% to 0.4%.

Figure 4 shows that the SRB gives slightly better end-to-end delay performance than the other algorithms when network density is medium or high by about 0.5% to 4%. On the other hand, the LB algorithm obtained better end-to-end delay than BEB and SRB in low density network by about 1% and 9% respectively. From Figures 3 and 4 which represent a network with low speed (and low mobility as mentioned before) and with different pause times, we have decided the adaptive algorithm to be the SRB in medium and high density network because SRB achieved slightly better throughput and end-to-end delay perfor-

Figure 3. Throughput when speed=1 m/s and various pause times

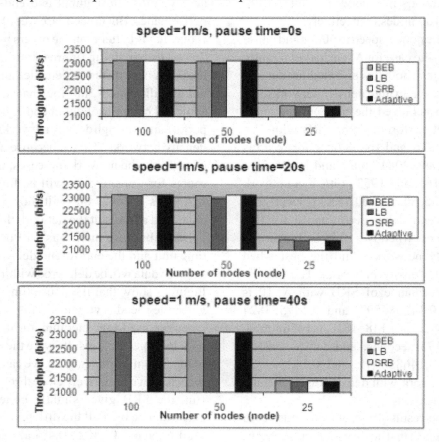

mance than the other algorithms in these cases. But in low density network we have two choices: either SRB because it has the higher throughput value in that case or LB because it has the lower end-to-end delay value. The difference in throughput and end-to-end delay performance between LB and SRB was 0.1% and 9%. We have chosen LB for the adaptive algorithm in that case because it outperforms SRB. In the next Figures, we can notice that the pause time begins to affect the results when the speed is medium or high. Contrary to what was noticed before.

Figure 5 shows that the BEB algorithm has slightly better throughput performance than the other algorithms that is between 0.01% and 18% when density is low or medium, but when density is high, BEB achieved lower throughput

value. On the other hand, the LB Backoff algorithm was the worst in low density networks and with a clear difference that reaches 18% compared to the other backoff algorithms although LB achieved slightly better throughput in high density network than the other algorithms by about 0.2% to 0.3%. While the SRB algorithm obtained the lower throughput performance in both medium and high density networks by about 0.2% and 0.3% respectively.

Moreover, Figure 5 shows that the SRB gives slightly better end-to-end delay performance than BEB and LB when network density is high by about 2% and 20% respectively. On the other hand, the LB and BEB algorithms obtained better end-to-end delay than the other algorithms in medium and low density network by about 6%

Figure 4. End-to-end delay with speed=1 m/s and various pause times

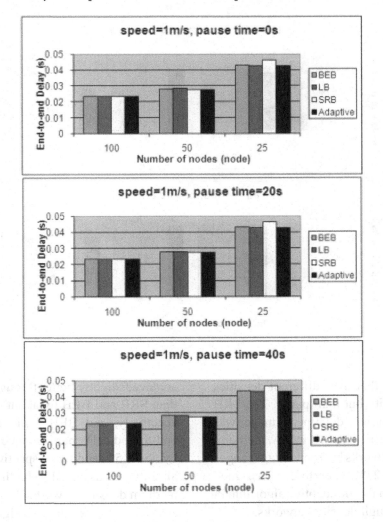

and 7% respectively. From Figure 5, which represent a network with medium speed (and medium mobility as mentioned before) and with low pause time value, we assigned the adaptive algorithm to be the BEB in low density network because BEB achieved slightly better throughput and end-to-end delay performance than the other algorithms in this case. But in medium and high density network we have two choices. In medium density network we have to choose either BEB because it has the higher throughput value in that case or LB because it has the lower end-to-end delay value. The difference in throughput and end-to-

end delay performance between LB and BEB was 0.2% and 4% respectively. We have chosen LB for the adaptive algorithm in that case because it outperforms BEB in higher percentage. While In high density network, we have to choose either LB because it has the higher throughput value in that case or SRB because it has the lower end-to-end delay value. The difference in throughput and end-to-end delay performance between LB and SRB was 0.3% and 20% respectively. We have chosen SRB for the adaptive algorithm in that case because it outperforms LB in higher percentage.

Figure 5. Algorithm performance with speed =10 m/s and pause time = 0 s

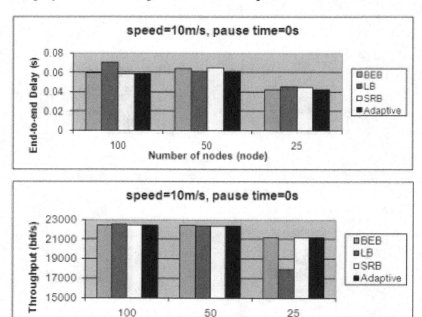

Figure 6 shows that over different densities and medium mobility but high pause. The SRB throughput and end-to-end delay performance was slightly better than BEB and LB in low, medium, and high density networks by a percentage ranges between 0.01% and 24%. Therefore, we assigned the SRB mechanism for the adaptive algorithm in low, medium, and high density networks.

Figure 7 shows the results of using very high speed with low pause time which is the case of highly mobile network and also over different densities. SRB algorithm gained better throughput and end-to-end delay performance than LB and BEB when density is low or medium. In terms of percentages: for throughput SRB outperforms LB and BEB by about 76% and 73% respectively in low density network and by 55% and 4% in medium density network. And for end-to-end delay SRB outperforms LB and BEB by about 0.4% and 18% respectively in low density network and by 0.7% and 6% in medium density network. While when the network density is high, LB

achieved slightly better throughput performance than SRB and BEB by about 25% and 0.6% respectively, and BEB achieved slightly better end-to-end delay performance than SRB and LB by about 5% and 6% respectively. The adaptive algorithm is assigned to be the SRB in low and medium density network. However, in high density networks the adaptive algorithm is assigned the BEB mechanism. The difference in throughput and end-to-end delay performance between BEB and LB was 6% and 0.6% respectively.

Figure 3 also shows the impact of different densities of the network when highest mobility is used but this time we used highest speed value with medium pause time. The LB achieved better throughput performance than BEB and SRB in high density topologies by about 27% and 58% respectively. BEB achieved slightly better throughput performance than LB and SRB in low density networks by about 3% and 0.8% respectively. On the other hand, the SRB Backoff algorithm gained slightly better throughput perfor-

Figure 6. Algorithm performance with speed =10 m/s and pause time = 40 s

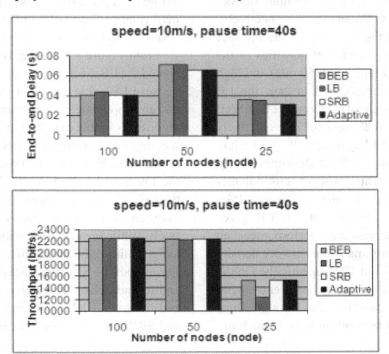

Figure 7. Algorithm performance with speed =50 m/s and pause time = 0 s

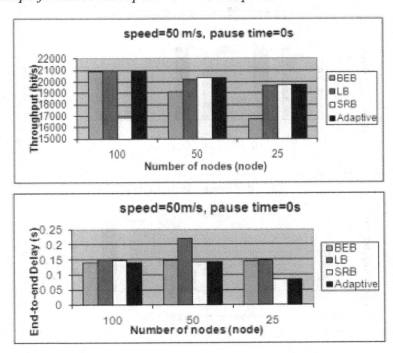

mance than LB and BEB in medium density networks by about 0.2% and 0.4% respectively.

Figure 8 shows the impact of using the four backoff algorithms in different densities of the network with very high speed (50 m/s) and high pause time (40 seconds). In this case the LB achieved better throughput performance than SRB and BEB by about 0.8% and 0.2% respectively in sparse networks and by about 24% for both in dense networks. But, the BEB algorithm gained slightly higher throughput when it is used in medium density networks by about 0.2% to 0.3%.

Also, Figure 8 shows that the LB gives slightly better end-to-end delay performance than SRB and BEB algorithms when network density is low by about 3% and 1% respectively. On the other hand, SRB gives slightly better end-to-end delay performance than BEB and LB algorithms by about 8% when network density is medium.

While BEB gives slightly better end-to-end delay performance than SRB and LB algorithms by about 1% and 5% respectively in dense networks.

From Figure 8, the adaptive algorithm is assigned the LB mechanism in low density network because LB achieved slightly better throughput and end-to-end delay performance than the other algorithms in this case. In high density network, we may either assign LB mechanism (as it has higher throughput) or BEB mechanism (as it has the lower end-to-end delay). The difference in throughput and end-to-end delay performance between LB and BEB was 24% and 5% respectively. While In medium density network, we may assign either BEB mechanism (as it has higher throughput) or SRB mechanism (as it has lower end-to-end delay). The difference in throughput and end-to-end delay performance between BEB and SRB was 0.2% and 8% respectively.

Figure 8. Algorithm performance with speed =50 m/s and pause time = 40 s

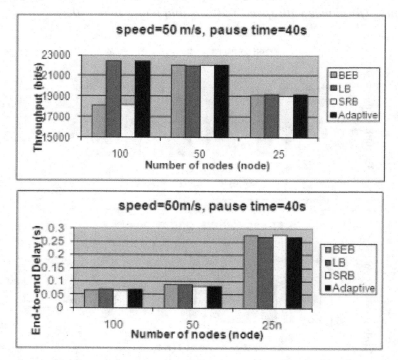

Adaptive Algorithm Results Under Different Scenarios

The algorithm performance were also investigated under different other scenarios as shown next. In the first scenario, the findings of these results are presented in Table 3.

Now, we present the reasoning for such selection.

The results obtained when nodes speed is 10 m/s and pause time is set to 20 seconds, which represent a network with medium mobility and medium pause time, shows that the SRB algorithm achieved slightly better throughput performance than other algorithms when density is low by about 0.2% to 0.3%, but when density is medium it was the worst with percentage that reaches 6%. On the other hand, the LB and BEB Backoff algorithms achieve higher throughput than others in medium and high density networks by percentage that reaches 6% and 0.8% respectively. The results, also shows that the BEB gives slightly better end-to-end delay performance than LB and SRB algorithms by a percentage that reaches 46% and 6% respectively when network density is low, medium, and high.

In this scenario, we assigned the BEB mechanism for the adaptive algorithm in high density network because BEB achieved slightly better

Table 3. Results of Investigated Scenarios

Node Speed	Pause Time	Selected Algorithm		
		Low	Medium	High
10	0	BEB	LB	SRB
10	20	SRB	LB	BEB
10	40	SRB	SRB	SRB
20	0	LB	BEB	SRB
20	20	LB	SRB	BEB
20	40	SRB	LB	BEB
50	0	SRB	SRB	BEB
50	20	SRB	LB	LB
50	40	LB	BEB	SRB

throughput and end-to-end delay performance than the other algorithms in this case. In medium density network we have we assigned the LB mechanism because it has higher throughput value in that case or BEB because it has the lower end-to-end delay value. The difference in throughput and end-to-end delay performance between LB and BEB was 0.3% and 5% respectively. On the other hand, in low density networks, we assigned either SRB because it has higher throughput value or BEB because it has lower end-to-end delay value. The difference in throughput and end-to-end delay performance between BEB and SRB was 0.2% and 0.6% respectively.

The results obtained when nodes speed is 20 m/s and pause time is set to 0 seconds, which represent a network with medium mobility and low pause time. The LB throughput performance was slightly better in both low and high density topologies by about 0.1% to 5%. BEB was slightly better in medium density networks by about 1%. However, the results, shows that the SRB gives slightly better end-to-end delay performance than LB and BEB algorithms when network density is medium, and high by about 1% to 6%. On the other hand, LB gives better end-to-end delay performance than SRB and BEB algorithms when network density is low by about 15% and 0.4% respectively.

For this scenario, the adaptive algorithm is assigned the LB mechanism in low density network. However, in medium density network we have to choose either the BEB mechanism (as it has higher throughput) or SRB mechanism (as it has lower end-to-end delay). The difference in throughput and end-to-end delay performance between SRB and BEB was 1% for both throughput and delay. For high density networks, the LB mechanism achieved higher throughput, while SRB achieved lower end-to-end delay value. The difference in throughput and end-to-end delay performance between LB and SRB was 0.1% and 2% respectively.

The results obtained when nodes speed is 20 m/s and pause time is set to 20 seconds, which represent a network with medium mobility and medium pause time. The SRB algorithm throughput and end-to-end delay performance was slightly better than the other algorithms in medium density topology by about 3% and 16% respectively. While the LB algorithm gained slightly higher throughput and end-to-end delay in low density networks by 0.6% and 1% respectively. On the other hand, BEB was slightly better in both throughput and end-to-end delay in high density networks by 1% and 10% respectively.

The results obtained when nodes speed is 20 m/s and pause time is set to 40 seconds, which represent a network with medium mobility and high pause time shows that the SRB algorithm was slightly better than the other algorithms in both sparse and dense topologies by about 0.4%. While in medium density network, LB gained higher throughput performance than SRB and BEB by about 1% and 0.5% respectively.

Moreover, the results show that the LB gives slightly better end-to-end delay performance than SRB and BEB algorithms when network density is low or medium by about 8% and 2% respectively. On the other hand, BEB gives slightly better end-to-end delay performance than SRB and LB algorithms when network density is high by about 6% and 23% respectively.

In this scenario, the adaptive algorithm is assigned the LB mechanism in medium density network. However, in low density network, the SRB achieved higher throughput while LB achieved lower end-to-end delay. The difference in throughput and end-to-end delay performance between SRB and LB was 0.07% and 0.02% respectively. While In high density network, SRB achieved higher throughput and BEB achieved lower end-to-end delay value. The difference in throughput and end-to-end delay performance between BEB and SRB was 0.2% and 6% respectively.

The results obtained when nodes speed is 50 m/s and pause time is set to 20 seconds, which represent a network with very high mobility and medium pause time shows that the LB gives

slightly better end-to-end delay performance than SRB and BEB algorithms when network density is medium or high by about 1% to 4%. On the other hand, SRB gives slightly better end-to-end delay performance than BEB and LB algorithms when network density is low by about 40% and 25% respectively.

In this scenario, the adaptive algorithm is assigned the LB mechanism in high density network. In low density network, the BEB achieved higher throughput and SRB achieved lower end-to-end delay. The difference in throughput and end-to-end delay performance between SRB and BEB is 0.8% and 40% respectively. While In medium density network, SRB achieved higher throughput and LB achieved lower end-to-end delay. The difference in throughput and end-to-end delay performance between LB and SRB was 0.2% and 4% respectively.

CONCLUSION

In this paper, we have proposed a new backoff algorithm to increase CW reasonably which called SRB algorithm. Then, we have compared the performance of our backoff algorithm (SRB) with standard LB and BEB backoff algorithms based on the network throughput and end-to-end delay metrics and in different density and mobility circumstances. And because we know that there is not one algorithm that is the best in all cases, we decided to develop an adaptive backoff algorithm that combines the three previously mentioned algorithms (LB, BEB, and SRB) in one algorithm in a manner that allows us to benefit from each backoff algorithm in the cases in which it is the best.

The proposed Adaptive algorithm is done in two separate phases, the offline phase and the online phase. Such design aims of reducing the time complexity of the algorithm by performing some of the computations and analysis prior to the actual deployment and operation of the network. In the offline phase, the algorithm scans the network environment and uses a set of factors to generate all possible network templates. Each template is then assigned a backoff algorithm that best performs under such template. The Adaptive algorithm in the online phase runs on all nodes independently and estimates the backoff interval according to a specified procedure. The Online phase consists of three main components: scanner, classifier, and rule-based selector.

Results from simulations demonstrates that SRB algorithm achieved better performance than BEB and LB by a percentage that ranges between 0.01% up to 76% in 47% and 53% of the studied cases of different network density and mobility states for end-to-end delay and throughput respectively. Also, the adaptive backoff algorithm obtains the best throughput and end-to-end delay performance over the other three backoff algorithms (SRB, LB, and BEB) used in the study in 64% and 91% of the studied cases respectively and also by a percentage that ranges between 0.01% up to 76%. And even in the rest of the cases in which the Adaptive backoff algorithm was not the optimal, we can say that it was consistent which means that in any of the cases it was not the worst and also its performance does not degrade to very low levels as it happens to LB, SRB, and BEB.

REFERENCES

Anouar, H., & Bonnet, C. (2007). Optimal constant-window backoff scheme for IEEE 802.11 DCF in single-hop wireless networks under finite load conditions. *Wireless Personal Communications*, 43.

Bani Yassein, M., Manaseer, S., & Al-Turani, A. (2009, July). *A performance comparison of different backoff algorithms under different rebroadcast probabilities for MANET's*. Paper presented at the 25th UK Performance Engineering Workshop.

Bani Yassein, M., & Ould Khaoua, M. (2007). Applications of probabilistic flooding in MANETs. *UBICC Journal, 2*(1).

Bani Yassein, M., Ould Khaoua, M., Mackenzie, L. M., & Papanastasiou, S. (2005, May 23-26). Improving the performance of probabilistic flooding in MANETs. In *Proceedings of the International Workshop on Wireless Ad-hoc Networks*, London, UK.

Bani Yassein, M., Ould Khaoua, M., Mackenzie, L. M., & Papanastasiou, S. (2006). Performance analysis of adjusted probabilistic broadcasting in mobile ad hoc networks. *International Journal of Wireless Information Networks, 13*(2). doi:10.1007/s10776-006-0027-0

Barcel'o, J., Bellalta, B., Cano, C., & Oliver, M. (2009). Dynamic p-persistent backoff for higher efficiency and implicit prioritization. *IEEE Transactions on Wireless Communications*.

Han, S. Y., & Abu-Ghazaleh, N. B. (2008). On backoff in fading wireless channels. In D. Coudert, D. Simplot-Ryl, & I. Stojmenovic (Eds.), *Proceedings of the 7ᵗʰ International Conference on Ad-hoc, Mobile and Wireless Networks* (LNCS 5198, pp. 251-264).

IEEE. (1999). *ANSI/IEEE standard 802.11: Wireless LAN medium access control (MAC) and physical layer (PHY) specifications*. Washington, DC: IEEE Computer Society.

Kurose, J. F., & Ross, K. W. (2007). *Computer networking: A top-down approach* (4th ed.). Reading, MA: Addison-Wesley.

Manaseer, S., & Ould-Khaoua, M. (2006). *Logarithmic based backoff algorithm for MAC protocol in MANETs*. Glasgow, Scotland: University of Glasgow.

Manaseer, S., Ould-Khaoua, M., & Mackenzie, L. M. (2006). *Fibonacci backoff algorithm for mobile ad hoc networks*. Glasgow, Scotland: University of Glasgow.

Manaseer, S. S., & Masadeh, M. (2008). *Pessimistic backoff for mobile ad hoc networks*. Glasgow, Scotland: University of Glasgow.

Orenstein, P., Goodman, D., Marantz, Z., & Rodriguez, V. (2004). Effects of additive noise on the throughput of CDMA data communications. In *Proceedings of the International Conference on Communications* (pp. 3046-3050).

Pang, Q., Liew, S. C., Lee, J., & Leung, V. (2004). Performance evaluation of an adaptive backoff scheme for WLAN. *Wireless Communications & Mobile Computing, 4*(8), 867–879. doi:10.1002/wcm.260

Papadimitratos, P., Mishra, A., & Rosenburgh, D. (2005). A cross-layer design approach to enhance 802.15.4. In *Proceedings of the Conference on Military Communications* (pp. 1719-1726).

Sakakibara, K., Sasaki, M., & Yamakita, J. (2005). Backoff algorithm with release stages for slotted ALOHA systems. *ECTI Transactions on Electrical Engineering, Electronics, and Communications, 3*.

Sasson, Y., Cavin, D., & Schiper, A. (2003). Probabilistic broadcast for flooding in wireless mobile ad hoc networks. *Wireless Communications and Networking, 2*, 1124–1130.

Song, N.-O., Kwak, B.-J., Song, J., & Miller, L. E. (2004). *Enhancement of IEEE 802.11 distributed coordination function with exponential increase exponential decrease backoff algorithm*. Gaithersburg, MD: National Institute of Standards and Technology.

Sun, J. (2001). Mobile ad hoc networking: An essential technology for pervasive computing. In *Proceedings of the International Conferences on Info-tech & Info-net*, Beijing, China.

Taifour, M., Nat-Abdesselam, F., & Simplot-Ryl, D. (2006). *Neighbourhood backoff algorithm for optimizing bandwidth in single hop wireless ad-hoc networks*. Retrieved from citeseerx.ist.psu.edu/viewdoc/summary?doi=10.1.1.76.3509

Takahashi, K., & Tsuboi, T. (2003). *A backoff algorithm for improving saturation throughput in IEEE 802.11 DCF. Tokyo*. Japan: Tokyo University of Technology.

Tseng, Y., Ni, S., Chen, Y., & Sheu, J. (2002). The broadcast storm problem in a mobile ad hoc network. *Journal of Wireless Networks, 8*(2-3).

Yang, X., & Vaidya, N. (2007). A spatial backoff algorithm using the joint control of carrier sense threshold and transmission rate. In *Proceedings of the 4th Annual IEEE Conference on Sensor, Mesh, and Ad Hoc Communications and Networks* (pp. 501-511).

Yi, Y., Gerla, M., & Kwon, T. (2002). *Efficient flooding in ad hoc networks using on-demand (passive) cluster formation*. Paper presented at the Second Annual Workshop on Ad Hoc Networking.

Yoon, J., Yun, S., & Kim, H. (2006). Maximizing differentiated throughput in IEEE 802.11e wireless LANs. In *Proceedings of the IEEE Conference on Local Computer Networks* (pp. 411-417).

Zhao, L., Zhang, J., Yang, K., & Zhang, H. (2007, June 24-27). Using incompletely cooperative game theory in mobile ad hoc networks. In *Proceedings of the International Conference on Communications*, Glasgow, Scotland (pp. 3401-3406).

This work was previously published in the International Journal of Mobile Computing and Multimedia Communications, Volume 3, Issue 3, edited by Ismail Khalil and Edgar Weippl, pp. 1-19, copyright 2011 by IGI Publishing (an imprint of IGI Global).

Chapter 16
Cooperative Caching in Mobile Ad Hoc Networks

Naveen Chauhan
National Institute of Technology Hamirpur, India

Lalit K. Awasthi
National Institute of Technology Hamirpur, India

Narottam Chand
National Institute of Technology Hamirpur, India

Ramesh C. Joshi
Indian Institute of Technology Roorkee, India

Manoj Misra
Indian Institute of Technology Roorkee, India

ABSTRACT

Mobile ad hoc network (MANET) presents a constrained communication environment due to fundamental limitations of client's resources, insufficient wireless bandwidth and users' frequent mobility. MANETs have many distinct characteristics which distinguish them from other wireless networks. Due to frequent network disconnection, data availability is lower than traditional wired networks. Cooperative caching helps MANETs in alleviating the situation of non availability of data. In this paper, the authors present a scheme called global cluster cooperation (GCC) for caching in mobile ad hoc networks. In this scheme, network topology is partitioned into non-overlapping clusters based on the physical network proximity. This approach fully exploits the pull mechanism to facilitate cache sharing in a MANET. Simulation experiments show that GCC mechanism achieves significant improvements in cache hit ratio and average query latency in comparison with other caching strategies.

DOI: 10.4018/978-1-4666-2163-3.ch016

1. INTRODUCTION

Due to information overflow, people can no longer be disconnected from their information systems. Caching plays a vital role in providing access of data to the information systems in case of disconnection. This is a well established way of providing faster data in the area of web caching, proxy servers and browsers (Malpani, Lorch, & Berger, 1996). With the advent of mobile ad hoc networks (MANETs), which is demand based infrastructureless network, being resource poor, caching plays a pivotal role in making MANETs a success in many applications like rescue operations, military operation, etc. A mobile node (MN) is envisioned to be equipped with more powerful capabilities, like sufficient storage space, more processing power, etc. Even though there is no dearth of storage space in present scenario, it is always better to utilize the resources optimally. With caching, the data access delay is reduced since data access requests can be served from the local cache, thereby obviating the need for data transmission over the scarce wireless links. However, caching techniques used in one-hop

mobile environment may not be applicable to multihop ad hoc environment since the data or request may need to go through multiple hops. Variable data size, frequent data updates, limited client resources, insufficient wireless bandwidth and clients' mobility make cache management a challenging task in mobile ad hoc networks. As mobile nodes in ad hoc networks may have similar tasks and share common interest, cooperative caching, which allows the sharing and coordination of cached data among multiple nodes, can be used to reduce the bandwidth and power consumption.

To date there are some works in literature on cooperative caching in ad hoc networks, such as consistency (Yin & Cao, 2004; Chiu & Young, 2009), and placement (Tang, Gupta, & Das, 2008). In this paper, we investigate the data retrieval challenge of mobile ad hoc networks and propose a novel scheme, called global cluster cooperation (GCC) for caching. The goal of GCC is to reduce the cache discovery overhead and provide better cooperative caching performance. GCC partitions the whole MANET into equal size clusters based on the geographical network proximity (Figure 1). To enhance the system performance,

Figure 1. Partitioning of MANET into clusters

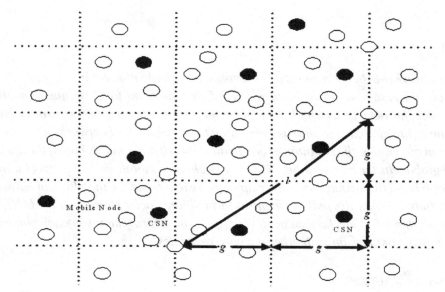

within a cluster, individual caches interact with each other and within a network, the designated CSN of clusters interact with each other such that combined result is a larger cumulative cache. In each cluster, GCC dynamically chooses a "super" node as cache state node (CSN), to maintain the global cache state (GCS) information of different nodes within the network. The GCS for a client is the list of cached items along with their time-to-live (TTL) field. Simulation experiments are performed to evaluate the proposed GCC caching scheme and compare it with existing strategies in the ad hoc networks.

The rest of the paper is organized as follows. Related work is described in Section 2. Section 3 describes the system model. Clustering strategy employed in GCC is presented in Section 4. Section 5 describes the proposed GCC caching scheme for data retrieval. Section 6 is devoted to performance evaluation. Section 7 concludes the paper.

2. RELATED WORK

In context of ad hoc networks, it is beneficial to cache frequently accessed data not only to reduce the average query latency but also to save the wireless bandwidth. Hara (Hara & Madria, 2006) proposed several replica allocation methods to increase the data accessibility and tolerate network partitions in MANETs. In these schemes, the replicated data are relocated periodically based on access frequency and overall network topology. Although replication can improve data accessibility, the overhead for relocating replicas periodically is significantly high. Due to updates at server, the cost of maintaining the consistent copy of replicas is quite high. Lim et al. (2006) suggested a caching algorithm to minimize the delay while acquiring data. To the best of our knowledge, only few of previous works (Chand, Joshi, & Misra, 2006; Chiu & Young, 2009; Chand, Joshi, & Misra, 2007) have exploited clustering as a caching mechanism in MANETs. Cooperative

caching has been studied in web environment (Malpani, Lorch, & Berger, 1996), but efficient cache management is still a hot research area in MANETs. CacheData and Cachepath have been proposed in (Yin & Cao, 2004). Unlike the previous methods, these protocols do not rely on flooding or broadcast for discovering a cached copy of the requested data item. With CacheData, intermediate nodes may cache a data item to serve future requests while forwarding the item for another node. In contrast, CachePath caches the information of a path to the request originator and uses the information to redirect future requests to the nearby caching site. The Hybrid protocol HybridCache combines CacheData and CachePath in an attempt to avoid their weakness. In HybridCache, when a mobile node forwards a data item, it caches the data or the path based on some criteria. These criteria include the data item size and time-to-live (TTL) of the item. One drawback with these methods is that the caching information of a node cannot be shared if the node does not lie on the forwarding path of a request to data center. In a multihop MANET environment, discovering an available copy of a needed data item is the core of a caching scheme. Existing protocols (Chiu & Young, 2009; Lim, Lee, Cao, & Das, 2004) rely on flooding mechanism to locate a data item. Although flooding may potentially reduce the response time for a data request, it leads to excessive communication overhead. The problem could be dealt by imposing a threshold on route existence probability of request packet (Chiu & Young, 2009). A scheme for caching, locating and streaming multimedia objects in mobile networks was proposed in (Lau, Kumar, & Venkatesh, 2002). In this proposal, application manager (APGR) is put between multimedia application and the network layer at each node. AGPR determines the suitable node to cache the multimedia object. Using the definition of route stability, the route existence probability of a request become smaller as it is forwarded hop by hop. By loading a threshold of route existence probability into the header of a request packet beforehand, the range of cache querying can be limited. However, choosing an appropriate threshold for route existence probability is a challenge in itself. CoCa, a cooperative caching protocol (Chow, Leong, & Chan, 2004) have been proposed, which reduces the number of server requests as well as number of cache miss by sharing the cache contents. Further built on the CoCa framework a group based cooperative caching scheme called GroCoCa has been proposed in (Chow, Leong, & Chan, 2004) in which a centralized incremental clustering algorithm is adopted by taking into consideration node mobility and data access pattern. GroCoCa improves system performance at the cost of extra power consumption. Chiu and Young (2009) proposed two protocols IXP and DPIP. In IXP each node shares its cache contents with the nodes in its zone. The disadvantage of the IXP protocol is that when a node enters into a new zone, the nodes of the new zone are not aware about the cache contents of the new entrant.

3. SYSTEM MODEL

This section outlines some of the properties and assumptions of GCC. In this paper, we consider a MANET environment where mobile hosts access the data items stored by other nodes. A mobile host that holds the original copy of a data item is called data center. A data request initiated by a host is forwarded hop-by-hop along the routing path until it reaches the data center and then it sends back the requested data. Mobile hosts frequently access the data, and cache some data locally to reduce network traffic and data access delay. We assume that weak cache consistency is required and time to live (TTL) based consistency model is used (Chow, Leong, & Chan, 2004). As mobile hosts may not have sufficient cache storage e.g.

for multimedia data, hence a caching strategy is to be devised efficiently. We make the following assumptions and introduce some common definitions

Assumptions

- The network is divided into several non-overlapping clusters where in each cluster; a node could be in one of two roles: cache state node (CSN) or ordinary node. CSN is a node that maintains global cache state (GCS) information of different clusters, whereas ordinary node maintains cluster cache state (CCS) information corresponding to all the nodes in its cluster. The ordinary node also maintains local cache as per its requirement.

- Unique host identifier is assigned to each mobile host in the system. The system has total of M hosts and MH_i ($1 \leq i \leq M$) is a host identifier. The set of one hop neighbors of a host MH_i is denoted by MH_i^1.

- Clients can physically move, so there is no guarantee that a neighbor at time t will remain in the cluster at time $t+\tau$. The devices might be turned off or on at any time, so the set of active clients varies with time and has no fixed size.

- The set of data items is denoted by D = {d_1, d_2, ... d_n}, where N is the total number of data items and d_j ($1 \leq j \leq N$) is a data identifier. D_i denotes the actual data for id di. Size of data item di is si. The original of each data item is the data source/center.

- Each mobile host has a cache space of C bytes.

- Each data item is periodically updated at source. After a data item is updated, its cached copy (maintained on one or more hosts) may become invalid.

Definitions

- **Grids:** The ad hoc network topology is divided into equal size parts called grids. Grids are formed to cluster the ad hoc network. Grid size is such that two nodes located in adjacent grids (horizontally, vertically & diagonally) are at a distance of one hop. A grid consists of a cache state node (CSN) and a number of ordinary nodes, and each node belongs to only one grid.

- **Cache State Node (CSN):** In each cluster area, a super node is selected to act as the cache state node (CSN), which is responsible for recording the global cache state (GCS) of all clusters in the network area. When a node in any cluster stores/deletes some data item into/from its cache, it sends the information to its CSN so that the corresponding GCS can be updated. Since a CSN handles additional load of GCS maintenance, it must be relatively stable and capable to support this responsibility. In order to ascertain such qualification of a node, we assign to each node a candidacy factor to qualify as CSN, which is a function of node staying period in the cluster, available battery power and memory space. A node with the highest candidacy factor is elected as CSN.

- **Cluster Cache State (CCS):** Cluster cache state (CCS) for a node is the list of cached items along with Time to Live (TTL) field. When cache content at a node changes, it broadcast the information to all the nodes of its cluster. CCS is maintained at each node of the cluster.

- **Global Cache State (GCS):** Global cache state (GCS) for a network is the list of cached items maintained at different clusters along with their Time To Live (TTL) field. When cache content changes, it

sends the information to the CSN and the CSN updates the corresponding GCS of the cluster. The information at other CSN is updated periodically after certain time period.

4. CLUSTER HANDLING

Our clustering algorithm divides the network topology into predefined equal sized geographical grids called clusters. The problem of finding an optimal clustering is out of the scope of this paper. For the sake of simplicity, we assume that clustering phase gives a partition of the network into grids. However, any clustering algorithm can be used as our GCC caching scheme is compatible with any non-overlapping clustering strategy. Grid size captures the maximum distance between two nodes in adjacent clusters (horizontally, vertically and diagonally). It is ensured that the coordinators in adjacent grids are within the transmission range of each other. Network area is assumed to be virtually extended such that boundary clusters also have same size as other clusters. Beginning with the left lower cluster, the clusters are named as 1, 2,..., in a column-wise fashion. In each cluster area a "super" node is selected to act as CSN, which is responsible for maintaining the global cache state (GCS) information of different clusters within its network domain. GCS for a network is the list of data items along with their TTL stored in its cache. When a node caches/replaces a data item, its GCS is updated at the CSN.

It may be noted that CSN is quite different from conventional "clusterhead" that is used to forward requests for a group of nodes. In each cluster of such a clusterhead networked system, all the requests from/to a client are forwarded by the clusterhead, which tends to make it a bottleneck and/or a point of failure when the system has high network density. Unlike this, CSN works only as GCS holder to save the information about the cached items by different clients belonging to the entire network partitioned into clusters, and provides additional service during cache discovery, admission control and replacement. Compared to clusterhead, CSN deals with much less workload and does not have to as powerful as a clusterhead. In the proposed clustering method, grid side g is a key factor to the clustering. A node in one cluster can communicate with a node in adjacent cluster (horizontally, vertically and diagonally), the required side g is derived as follows. The maximum distance l between two hosts MH_i and MH_j is given as:

$$\sqrt{2g^2 + (2g)^2} = \sqrt{8}g$$

To ensure one hop communication among the hosts within a cluster, l should be less than or equal to transmission range (r), i.e.:

$$\sqrt{8}g \leq r$$

Hence,

$$g = r \big/ \sqrt{8}$$

and all MHs in a cluster can connect to one another in one hop communication.

In GCC, a typical cluster consists of a CSN and a number of clients and a client only belong to one cluster. Since a CSN is expected to handle additional load in the system, it must be relatively stable and capable to support this responsibility. In order to ascertain such qualification of a node, we assign to each node a candidacy factor to be CSN, which is function of node staying period in the cluster and available battery power. A node with the highest candidacy factor is elected as CSN.

5. GLOBAL CLUSTER COOPERATIVE (GCC) CACHING

The design rationale of GCC is that, there is no dearth of storage space in present scenario, so the information regarding the cached contents of various clients in a cluster would be kept with each node in the cluster. In GCC, when a client suffers from a cache miss (called local cache miss), the client will look up the required data item from the cluster members. Only when the client cannot find the data item in the cluster members' caches (called cluster cache miss), it will request the CSN which keeps the global cache state (GCS) and maintains the information about the node in the network which has copy of desired data item. If a cluster other than requesting nodes' cluster has the requested data (called remote cache hit), then it can serve the request without forwarding it further towards the server. Otherwise, the request will be satisfied by the server. For each request, one of the following four cases holds:

1. **Local Hit:** When a node requires a data and found it in the local cache.
2. **Cluster Hit:** When a node requires the data, it checks its local cache, in case of local miss, node consults its CCS which is maintained by this node only, to check whether data is available in one of the neighboring nodes within the cluster.
3. **Remote Hit:** When the requested data item is not stored by a client within the cluster of the requester. The requester checks with CSN which is maintaining GCS and then returns the address of the client that has cached the data item.
4. **Global Hit:** When the data is not found even remotely data is retrieved from data center.

Based on the above idea, we propose a cache discovery algorithm to determine the data access path to a node having the requested cached data or to the data source. Assume that MH_i denotes mobile node/client i. In Figure 2, let us assume MH_i sends a request for a data item d_x and MH_k is located along the path through which the request travels to the data source MH_s, where $k \in \{a, c, d\}$. The discovery algorithm is described as follows:

When MH_i needs d_x, it first checks its own cache. If the data item is not available in its local cache, it checks with CCS which is maintained by MH_i to see whether any of neighboring node in the cluster has a copy of desired data. If it is not available at cluster level, it sends a lookup packet to the CSN MH_j in its cluster. Upon receiving the lookup message, the CSN searches in the GCS for the requested data item. If the item is found, the CSN replies with an ack packet con-

Figure 2. Request packet from client MH_i to data source

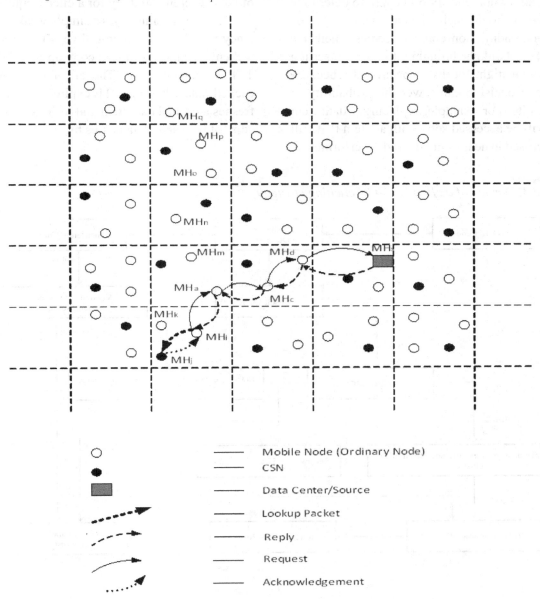

○	———	Mobile Node (Ordinary Node)
●	———	CSN
�	———	Data Center/Source
	———	Lookup Packet
	———	Reply
	———	Request
	———	Acknowledgement

taining id of the client who has cached the item. MH_i sends a request packet to the client whose id is returned by MH_j and the client responds with reply packet that contains the requested data item. When a node/MH_s receives a request packet, it sends the reply packet to the requester. The reply packet containing item id d_x, actual data D_x and TTL_x, is forwarded hop-by-hop along the routing path until it reaches the original requester. Once a node receives the requested data, it triggers the cache admission control procedure to determine whether it should cache the data item.

Cache admission control decides whether a data item should be brought into cache. Inserting a data item might not always be favorable because incorrect decision can lower the probability of cache hits. For example, replacing a data item that will be accessed soon with an item that will be accessed in near future degrades performance.

In GCC, the cache admission control allows a client to cache a data item based on the location of data source or other client that has the requested data. If the origin of the data resides in the same cluster of the requesting client, then the item is not cached, because it is unnecessary to replicate data item in the same cluster since cached data can be used by closely located hosts. In general, same data items are cached in different clusters without replication. Figure 3 shows the behavior of GCC caching strategy for a client request.

The GCC caching uses a simple weak consistency model based on time-to-live (TTL), in which a client considers a cached copy up-to-date if its TTL has not expired. The client removes the cached data when the TTL expires. A client refreshes a cached data item and its TTL if a fresh copy of the same data passes by.

Figure 3. Service of a client by GCC caching strategy

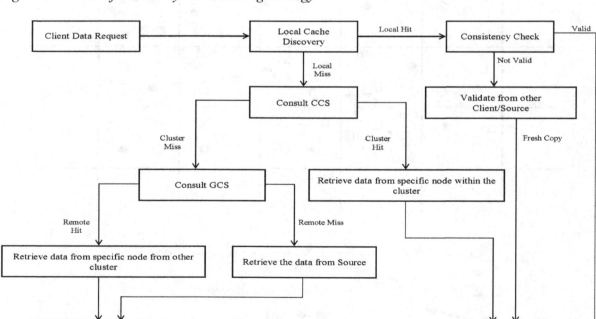

Table 1. Simulation parameters

Parameter	Default Value	Range
Database Size (N)	1000 items	
s_{min}	10 KB	
s_{max}	100 KB	
Number of clients (M)	70	50~100
Client cache size (C)	800 KB	200~1400 KB
Client speed (v_{min}~v_{max})	2 m/s	2~20 m/s
Bandwidth (b)	2 Mbps	
TTL	5000 sec	200~10000 sec
Pause time	300 sec	
Mean query generate time (T_q)	5 sec	2~100 sec
Transmission range (r)	25 m	25~250 m
Skewness parameter (θ)	0.8	0~1

6. PERFORMANCE EVALUATION

In this section, we evaluate the performance of GCC through simulation. The simulation area is assumed of size 1500 m x 1500 m. The clients move according to the random waypoint model (Bettstetter, Resta, & Santi, 2003). The time interval between two consecutive queries generated from each client follows an exponential distribution with mean Tq. Each client generates accesses to the data items following Zipf distribution with a skewness parameter θ. There are N data items at the server. Data item sizes vary from smin to smax such that size si of item di is

$$s_i = s_{min} + \left\lfloor random().(s_{max} - s_{min} + 1)\right\rfloor$$

i = 1, 2,...,N

where random() is a random function uniformly distributed between 0 and 1. The simulation parameters are listed in Table 1. For performance comparison with GCC, two other schemes non-cooperative (NC) caching and CacheData [1, 3] are also implemented. In NC received data are cached only at query node and locally missed data items are always fetched from the origin server. In our experiments, the same data access pattern and mobility model are applied to all the three schemes. All the schemes use LRU algorithm for cache replacement. We evaluate three performance metrics.

1. **Average Query Latency (Tavg):** The query latency is the time elapsed between the query is sent and the data is transmitted back to the requester, and average query latency (Tavg) is the query latency averaged over all the queries.

2. **Byte Hit Ratio (B):** Byte hit ratio is defined as the ratio of the number of data bytes retrieved from the cache to the total number of requested data bytes. Here byte hit ratio (B) includes local byte hit (Blocal), cluster byte hit (Bcluster) and remote byte hit (Bremote). If nlocal, ncluster and nremote denote the number of local byte hits, cluster byte hits and remote byte hits respectively out of total ntotal requested bytes, then

$$B_{local} = n_{local}/n_{total} \times 100\%, \quad B_{clutser} = n_{cluster}/n_{total} \times 100\%$$

$$B_{remote} = n_{remote}/n_{total} \times 100\%$$

3. **Message Overhead:** A commonly used message overhead metric is the total number of messages injected into the network by the query process. Since each broadcast message is processed (received and then rebroadcasted or dropped) by every node that receives it, "number of messages processed per query" is used as the message overhead metric to reflect the efforts (battery power, CPU time, etc.) of the mobile node to deal

with the messages. The message overhead includes all the query and response messages of locating and retrieving data. Because the number of messages due to routing is the same for both the caching schemes under study therefore the overhead for routing messages is ignored.

Effects of Cache Size

Figure 4 shows the effects of cache size on byte hit ratio, average query latency and message overhead by varying the cache size from 200 KB to 1400 KB. Figure 4(a) and 4(b) show that all schemes exhibit better byte hit and average query latency with increasing cache size. This is because more required data items can be found in local cache as the cache gets larger. From Figure 4(b), we can see that the GCC scheme performs much better than NC scheme. Because of the high byte hit ratio due to cluster cooperation, the proposed scheme also performs much better than CacheData. When the cache size is small, more required data could be found in local+cluster+global cache for GCC as compared to CacheData which utilizes only the local cache. Because the hop count of cluster data hit is one and is less than the average hop count of remote data hit, GCC scheme achieves lower average query latency. As the cache size is large enough, the nodes can access most of the required data items from local and cluster cache, so reducing the query latency. It is worth noting that GCC reaches its best performance when the cache size is 800 KB. This demonstrates its low cache space requirement.

Figure 4(c) shows that GCC performs much better than NC and CacheData in terms of message overhead. The reason is that due to cache cooperation among clusters GCC gets data from nearby clusters instead of far away data source. Therefore, the data requests and replies need to travel smaller number of hops and mobile nodes

need to process lower number of messages. As the cache size grows, the byte hit ratio of GCC increases and its message overhead decreases.

Effects of Mean Query Generate Time

The byte hit ratio improves with an increase in Tq. At very large value of Tq, the byte hit ratio is low because query generate rate is so low that the number of cached data is small and many cached data items are not usable because their TTL has already expired before queries are generated for them. Figure 5a verifies this trend. Figure 5(b) shows the average query latency as a function of the mean generate time Tq. The GCC scheme performs better than NC and CacheData schemes at all values of Tq. At small value of Tq, the query generate rate is high and system workload is more. This results in high value of average query latency. When Tq increases, fewer queries are generated and average query latency drops. If Tq keeps increasing, the average query latency drops slowly or even increases slightly due to decrease in cache byte hit ratio. Under extreme high Tq, most of the queries are served by the remote data server and the difference between different schemes is not very large. Figure 5(c) shows that NC has worst message overhead among all the schemes.

Effects of Mobility

Figure 6 shows the comparison of caching strategies, where each node is moving with a speed uniformly distributed between 0 and a given value along x-axis. We vary the maximum speed of nodes from 2, 4, 8, 12, 16, to 20 m/sec. From Figure 6(a), we can see that local byte hit ratio in NC is not affected due to client mobility. The local byte hit ratio of CacheData and GCC decreases slightly as the mobility speed increases because some of the invalid data items may

Figure 4. Effects of cache size on (a) byte hit ratio, (b) average query latency, and (c) message overhead

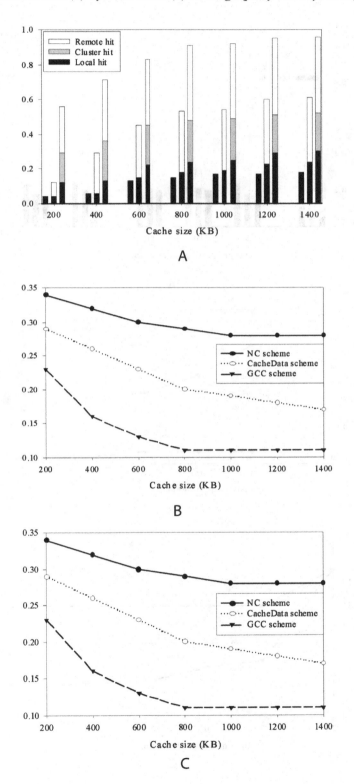

Figure 5. Effects of mean query generate time on (a) byte hit ratio, (b) average query latency, and (c) message overhead

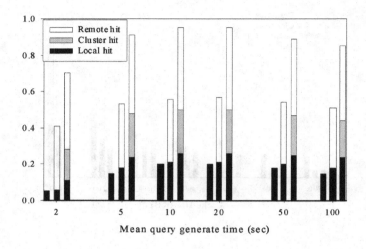

A

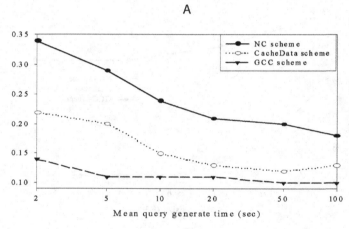

B

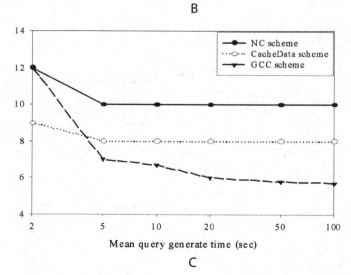

C

Figure 6. Effects of mobility on (a) byte hit ratio, (b) average query latency, and (c) message overhead

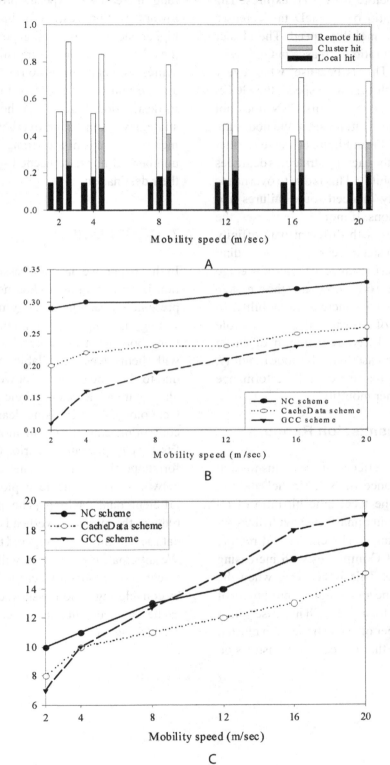

not be refreshed before their TTL expires. The remote byte hit ratio of CacheData decreases with an increase in mobility speed. The cluster and remote byte hit ratio decreases in GCC with increasing speed. This is because, when every node is moving with very high speed, the GCCS recorded for each node with its CSN does not help much in the near future, since the nodes are moving arbitrarily. From Figure 6(b), we see that performance of all the caching strategies degrades with increasing mobility. This is due to overheads caused by mobility induced route failures and route re-computations. If mobility increases, the frequency of nodes with different data affinity leaving/joining a cluster increases, thus, degrading the GCC caching performance in terms of average query latency. Figure 6(c) shows that the message overhead increases with increasing mobility. In GCC, the number of messages due to CSN role change/election and new registration of cache states with CSN increases with the node mobility. Experiments show that the overall performance degrades with higher mobility.

Effects of Transmission Range

Figure 7(a) shows effects of the transmission range on performance of NC, CacheData and GCC strategies. The local byte hit ratio of all the strategies remains unaffected with increasing transmission range. The cluster and remote byte hit ratio of GCC improves with increasing transmission range. This is because, when the transmission range becomes higher, the number of one-hop neighbors for a node will increase which increases the number of cache nodes in a cluster. Figure 7(b) shows that increase in transmission

range increases the expected progress of the packet towards its final destination but at the expense of higher energy consumption per transmission. On the other hand, a shorter transmission range consumes less per transmission energy, but it requires a large number of hops for the packet to reach its destination. Figure 7(c) shows that for all the strategies the message overhead decreases with increasing transmission range because smaller numbers of hops are needed for packet to reach their destination.

7. CONCLUSION

In this paper, we have addressed cache cooperation issue in mobile ad hoc networks. We have presented a caching strategy named GCC. This strategy is unique that in a cluster, the information about what all other clusters are retaining with themselves is available. All this is possible due to the emergence of powerful mobile node along with advances in wireless communication technology. As there is no dearth of storage and computing capabilities in mobile nodes, GCC fits best in present scenario. GCC is proposed for supporting efficient data retrieval in ad hoc networks. This scheme exploits clustering for efficient data caching. The proposed scheme reduces the message overheads and enhances the data accessibility as compared to other strategies. We anticipate that our work will stimulate further research on cooperative cache based data access by considering various issues such as cooperative cache replacement, strong cache consistency, prefetching, etc.

Figure 7. Effects of transmission range on (a) byte hit ratio, (b) average query latency, and (c) message overhead

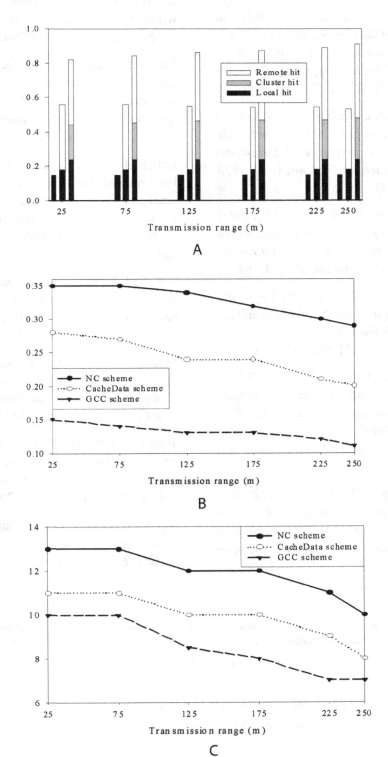

REFERENCES

Bettstetter, C., Resta, G., & Santi, P. (2003). The node distribution of the random waypoint mobility model for wireless ad hoc networks. *IEEE Transactions on Mobile Computing*, 257–269. doi:10.1109/TMC.2003.1233531

Chand, N., Joshi, R. C., & Misra, M. (2006). A zone co-operation approach for efficient caching in mobile ad hoc networks. *International Journal of Communication Systems*, 1009–1028. doi:10.1002/dac.795

Chand, N., Joshi, R. C., & Misra, M. (2007). Cooperative caching strategy in mobile ad hoc networks based on clusters. *International Journal of wireless Personal Communication*, 41-63.

Chiu, G. M., & Young, C. R. (2009). Exploiting in-zone broadcast for cache sharing in mobile ad hoc networks. *IEEE Transactions on Mobile Computing*, 384–396. doi:10.1109/TMC.2008.127

Chow, C. Y., Leong, H. V., & Chan, A. (2004a). Cache signature for peer-to-peer cooperative caching in mobile environments. In *Proceedings of the 18th International Conference on Advanced Information Networking and Applications* (pp. 96-101).

Chow, C. Y., Leong, H. V., & Chan, A. (2004b). Peer-to-peer cooperative caching in mobile environments. In *Proceedings of the 24th International Conference on Distributed Computing Systems Workshop* (pp. 528-533).

Hara, T., & Madria, S. K. (2006). Data replication for improving data accessibility in ad hoc networks. *IEEE Transactions on Mobile Computing*, 1515–1532. doi:10.1109/TMC.2006.165

Lau, W., Kumar, M., & Venkatesh, S. (2002). A cooperative cache architecture in supporting caching multimedia objects in MANETs. In *Proceedings of 5th International Workshop on Wireless Mobile Multimedia* (pp. 56-63).

Lim, S., Lee, W. C., Cao, G., & Das, C. R. (2004). Performance comparison of cache invalidation strategies for Internet based mobile ad hoc networks. In *Proceedings of the IEEE International Conference on Mobile Ad Hoc and Sensor Systems* (pp. 104-113).

Lim, S., Lee, W. C., Cao, G., & Das, C. R. (2006). A novel caching scheme for improving Internet based mobile ad hoc networks performance. *Journal of Ad Hoc Networks*, 225-239.

Malpani, R., Lorch, J., & Berger, D. (1995). Making World Wide Web cache servers cooperate. In *Proceedings of the 4th International World Wide Web Conference* (pp. 107-117).

Tang, B., Gupta, H., & Das, S. R. (2008). Benefit based data caching in ad hoc networks. *IEEE Transactions on Mobile Computing*, 289–303. doi:10.1109/TMC.2007.70770

Yin, L., & Cao, G. (2004). Supporting cooperative caching in ad hoc networks. In *Proceedings of the IEEE Conference INFOCOM* (pp. 77-89).

This work was previously published in the International Journal of Mobile Computing and Multimedia Communications, Volume 3, Issue 3, edited by Ismail Khalil and Edgar Weippl, pp. 20-35, copyright 2011 by IGI Publishing (an imprint of IGI Global).

Chapter 17
Enhancing Data Availability in MANETs with Cooperative Caching

Prashant Kumar
National Institute of Technology Hamirpur, India

Naveen Chauhan
National Institute of Technology Hamirpur, India

Lalit K. Awasthi
National Institute of Technology Hamirpur, India

Narottam Chand
National Institute of Technology Hamirpur, India

ABSTRACT

Mobile Adhoc Networks (MANETs) are very popular solutions where network infrastructure installation is not possible. In MANETs, nodes are mobile, and due to this mobility, topology of the network changes rapidly. This dynamic topology reduces the data availability in MANETs. Cooperative caching provides an attractive solution for this problem. In this paper, a new cooperative caching algorithm, ProCoCa, is proposed. This algorithm is based on a proactive approach. Each node will be associated with a zone and the data of leaving node will be cached. The authors simulate the algorithm on OMNET++ simulator, and simulation results show that ProCoCa improves the data availability as well as overall performance of the network.

DOI: 10.4018/978-1-4666-2163-3.ch017

INTRODUCTION

In recent years there has been a rapid growth in mobile communication. Mobile Adhoc Networks (MANETs) are very popular solution in the situation where network infrastructure is not available. MANETs can be extended by connecting with some other wired or wireless networks like Internet (Sun et al., 2002). In adhoc networks, mobile nodes communicate with each other using multihop wireless links. As there is no infrastructure support, mobile nodes cooperate with each other to forward data. Each node acts as a router, forwarding data packets for other nodes and mobile nodes have peer to peer connection among themselves. Most previous research in ad hoc networks focused on the development of dynamic routing protocols that can efficiently find routes between two communicating nodes. Although routing is an important issue, but the ultimate goal of adhoc networks is to provide mobile nodes with access to information. However, MANETs are limited by intermittent network connections, restricted power supplies, and limited computing resources. These restrictions raise several new challenges for data access applications with the respects of data availability and access efficiency. In adhoc networks, due to frequent network partition, data availability is lower than that in traditional wired networks. Cooperative caching provides an attractive solution for this problem. Cooperative caching is a technique that allows the sharing and coordination among the mobile nodes.

However, the movement of nodes, limited storage space and frequent disconnections limit the availability. By the caching of frequently accessed data in adhoc networks we can improve the data access, performance and availability. Due to mobility and resource constraints of adhoc networks, caching techniques designed for wired network may not be applicable to ad hoc networks.

In many applications, mobile nodes in a MANET share common interests. In this scenario, sharing cache contents between mobile nodes offers significant benefits. Typically, nodes cache data items for serving their own needs. Cache sharing, however, allows geographically neighboring mobile nodes to access each other's cache contents. By doing so, the number of long-distance data accesses to the data center can be reduced. The key to this technique is that a node has to know if there is some node in its vicinity that has cached the data it requires and where it is, if any. One approach to deal with this requirement is to let a mobile node record the caching information about a nearby node while forwarding the data requested by the node. Since MANETs are mobile and constrained by limited energy, bandwidth, and computation power, which is a big concern when designing protocols for such networks.

Consider a scenario in which mobile devices always retrieve data from the data center. This may result in a large amount of traffic in the network. This, apparently, is undesirable as traffic directed to the data center consumes wireless bandwidth as well as power of mobile devices. In addition, a mobile host suffers from high access latency if it is distant from the data center, and packet loss probability for long-distance data access is high. Furthermore, traffic near the data center will be heavy, and this leads to a potential performance bottleneck. These problems are more pronounced when the network size is large, which results in poor scalability of the system. The above observations motivate us to investigate a new data caching technique for MANETs. With data cached in mobile nodes, a data request may be satisfied by a nearby mobile node, instead of being serviced by the data center. By cooperative caching the data we can:

1. Improve the data availability.
2. Improve the data access time.
3. Reduce the traffic near the data center.
4. Reduce the consumption of bandwidth.

In general, a good cooperative cache management technique for MANETs should address these issues:

1.   A cache discovery algorithm that is efficient to discover and deliver requested data items from the neighbors node and able to decide which data items can be cached for future use. In cooperative caching this decision is taken not only on the behalf of the caching node but also based on the other nodes need.
2.   There should be a cache replacement algorithm to replace the cached data items when the caching space is not enough to cache the new ones.
3.   A cache consistency algorithm to ensure that the cached data items are updated.

In this paper we considered all these issues and proposed a new cooperative cache algorithm, ProCoCa. The ultimate goal of ProCoCa is to improve the data availability that means data is available in minimum time and by utilizing fewer resources. The idea of ProCoCa is based upon the fact that each node in the network is willing to share its cache contents with its neighbors. In this algorithm we consider that each node is associated with a zone. Each node in the zone will maintain a Caching Information Table (CIT). When a node caches a new data item or updates its CIT it will broadcasts these updates to all its neighbors. Further when a node wants to move out from its zone then it will broadcast a "LEAVE" message to its neighbors. Now these neighbors will decide whether the data of leaving node can be cached for future use. These decisions will be taken based upon their local cache and the CIT. For cache replacement we will use an access count policy with the TTL (Time-to-Live) value. The cache consistency algorithm will be based upon the TTL value. When a node updates its local cache it broadcasts these updates to all neighbors node in the zone.

RELATED WORK

Caching In Wired Network

Caching is an important technique to enhance the performance of both wired and wireless network. Cooperative caching has been applied to different contexts, such as Web caches/proxies and file systems. These schemes can be categorized as hierarchical, directory-based, and hash table-based approaches. Harvest (Chankhunthod et al., 1996) organizes Web caches hierarchically. A user's request is forwarded up the cache hierarchy until cache hits at some level. As a directory-based approach, Summary (Fan et al., 2000) keeps directory information of which caches has what content. When cache miss happens, the request is forwarded to the cache which contains the requested data potentially. For hash table- based approach, in Squirrel (Iyer et al., 2002), data items or their location information are cached on the correspondent home nodes, and the home nodes are assigned and located using distributed hash tables. These schemes have been evaluated and designed performance improvement for web accessing. However, these schemes are designed for Internet caching, which generally considers the cooperation between dedicated cache servers with high speed network connections. They impose some kind of structure on the network of cooperative nodes, such as hierarchical, hash-table based, a directory-based etc., to facilitate the search of desired data. But for generic MANETs, its dynamic topology and inefficient multi-hop communications make it extremely difficult to maintain information for traditional structures. Comparison of various cooperative caching schemes is given in Table 1.

Table 1. Comparison of cooperative caching schemes

Schemes	Cache Resolution	Cache Management
Harvest (1996)	Hierarchical	No specification
Summary (2000)	Directory-based	LRU
Squirrel (2002)	Hash-based	LRU
Yin(2004, 2006)	CacheData, CachePath,	
HybridCache	LRU	
Yu (2005, 2009)	COOP	Inter-category, intra-category rules
N. Chand (2007)		
	Zone Cooperative	LUV (Least Utility Value)
Chiu (2009)	IXP, DPIP	Count Vector

Caching In Wireless Networks

A lot of researches have been done to improve the caching performance in mobile adhoc network environment. The two basic types of cache sharing techniques are push based and pull based. With push-based caching technique, when a node acquires and caches a new data item, it actively advertises the caching event to the nodes in its neighborhood. Mobile nodes in the vicinity will record the caching information upon receiving such an advertisement and use it to direct subsequent requests for the same item. This scheme enhances the usefulness of the cached contents but this introduce communication overhead for the advertisement and further an advertisement may become useless if no demands for the cached item arise in the neighborhood.

In the push-based scheme, the caching information known to a node may become obsolete due to node mobility or cache replacement. This problem is resolved in pull-based approach. With pull-based caching technique, when a mobile node wants to access a data item that is not cached locally it will broadcast a request to the nodes in its vicinity. A nearby node that has cached the data will send a copy of the data to the request originator. Thus pull-based caching technique allows the node to utilize the latest cache contents. However, as compare to the pushing technique, the pulling scheme has two disadvantages:

1. In case the requested data item is not cached by any node in the neighborhood, the requester node will wait for the time-out interval to expire before it proceeds to send another request to the data center. This will cause extra access latency, and the pulling effort is in vain.

2. Pulling technique uses broadcast to locate a cached copy of an item so it may happens that more than one copy will be returned to the requester node if multiple nodes in the neighborhood cache the requested data. This introduces extra communication overhead (Chiu et al., 2009).

Moriya et al. (2003) proposed a "self-resolver" paradigm, in which a client itself queries and measures which node it should access. In this method if a node *M* requests the data *D* then it forwards a query packet to its neighbor nodes. If some node has the data *D* then it returns a *REPLY* packet to *S*. Otherwise it recursively sends *QUERY* packets to its neighboring nodes. The disadvantage of this approach is that it uses flooding which introduce high discovery overhead. Furthermore in this paper this issue is not discussed that how the request of

M is fulfilled if the requested data is not cached any neighboring node. Chow et al. (2004) have proposed a cooperative caching protocol, called *CoCa*, for mobile computing environments. In this protocol, mobile nodes share their cache contents with each other to reduce both the number of server requests and the number of access misses. Further, built upon the *CoCa* framework, a group-based cooperative caching scheme, called *GroCoCa*, has been proposed in 2004, in which a centralized incremental clustering algorithm is adopted by taking into consideration node mobility and data access pattern. *GroCoCa* improves system performance at the cost of extra power consumption.

Chand et al. (2007) investigate the data retrieval challenge of mobile adhoc networks and proposed a scheme, called Zone Cooperative (ZC) for caching that exploits data utility value for cache replacement. In ZC when a client requested a data item then the node first will check its local cache, if the data item is not found then node broadcast the request to its home zone. If the data is found in the home zone it called zone cache hit. If the data is not found in the home zone then the request is forward to the data source along the routing path. Before forwarding the request each node along the path will check their local cache or zone is the data is found then it returned to the requester otherwise finally the request is complete by the data source. A caching algorithm is suggested by Lim et al. (2006), to minimize the delay when acquiring data. In order to retrieve the data as quickly as possible, the query is issued and broadcast to the entire network. All nodes that have this data are supposed to send an acknowledgment back to the source of the broadcast. The requesting node will then issue a request for the data (unicast) to the first acknowledging node it hears from. The main advantage of this algorithm is its simplicity and the fact that it does achieve a low response delay. However, the scheme is inefficient in terms of bandwidth usage because of the broadcasts, which,

if frequent, will largely decrease the throughput of the system due to flooding the network with request packets (Moriya et al., 2003). Additionally, large amounts of bandwidth will also be consumed when data items happen to be cached in many different nodes because the system does not account for controlling redundancy.

Yin and Cao (2004, 2006) presented three cache resolution schemes: *CacheData*, *CachePath*, and *HybridCache*. In *CacheData*, forwarding nodes check the passing-by data requests. If a data item is found to be frequently requested, forwarding nodes cache the data, so that the next request for the same data can be answered by forwarding nodes instead of travelling further to the data server. A problem for this approach is that the data could take a lot of caching space in forwarding nodes. To overcome this problem the authors present another cache resolution scheme *CachePath*. In *CachePath* forwarding nodes cache the path to the closest caching node instead of the data and redirect future requests along the cached path. This scheme saves caching spaces compared to *CacheData*, but since the caching node is dynamic, the recorded path could become obsolete and this scheme could introduce extra processing overhead. Trying to avoid the weak points of those two schemes the authors proposed *HybridCache*. In *HybridCache*, when a mobile node forwards a data item, it caches the data or the path based on some criteria. These criteria include the data item size and the time-to-live (TTL) of the item. Due to the mobility of nodes the collected statistics about the popular data may become useless. One another drawback of these schemes is that if the node does not lie on the forwarding path of a request to the data center the caching information of a node cannot be shared.

Du et al. (2005, 2009) proposed a cooperative caching scheme called *COOP* for MANETs. To improve data availability and access performance, *COOP* addresses two basic problems of cooperative caching. For cache resolution, *COOP* uses the cocktail approach which consists of two basic schemes: hop-by-hop resolution and zone-based resolution. By using this approach, *COOP* discovers data sources which have less communication cost. For cache management, *COOP* uses the inter- and intra-category rules to minimize caching duplications between the nodes within a same cooperation zone and this improves the overall capacity of cooperated caches. Disadvantage of the scheme is flooding that introduce extra discovery overhead.

Chiu et al. (2009) proposed to protocol *IXP* and *DPIP*. The idea of *IXP* is based on having each node share its cache contents with the nodes in its zone. To facilitate exposition, authors call the nodes in the zone of a node *M* the buddies of *M*. A node should make its cache contents known to its buddies, and likewise, its buddies should reveal their contents to the node. *IXP* requires that, whenever a node caches a data item, it broadcasts an index packet to its buddies to advertise the caching event. Index Push (*IXP*) is push based in the sense that a mobile node broadcasts an index packet in its zone to advertise a caching event. The Data Pull/Index Push (*DPIP*) is a pull based one. *DPIP* is offers an implicit index push property by exploiting in-zone request broadcasts. The disadvantage of the *IXP* protocol is that when a node *M* enters in a new zone, the nodes of the new zone are not aware about *M*'s update. Further in their approaches the authors use a cache replacement policy that based on the Count Vector. According to the policy the data item with higher Count Vector is replaced. A data item with a Count Vector 0 will never be replaced. This may cause the waste of cache memory space.

SYSTEM MODEL

Let us consider a mobile adhoc network shown in Figure 1. This network has no fixed infrastructure and node are free to move anywhere in the net-

Figure 1. System model

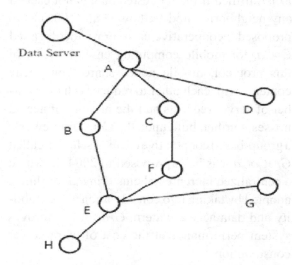

work. Since nodes are mobile so the topology is dynamic and temporary. There exists a data server that contains the database of n items D1, D2,..., Dn. This data server may be connected to some external wired or wireless network like Internet. When a node requires some data item it sends request to data server. When a node receives a data item it caches the data item locally for future use. Each mobile node is associated with a zone and refers to the set of nodes that can be reached by the node within the given number of hops, called the radius of the zone (Chiu et al., 2009). When a node wants to moves out from the zone it will broadcast a "LEAVE" message before leaving the zone.

Each node in the zone will maintain a Caching Information Table denoted as CIT. This CIT will contain n elements where n is the number of the data items. There will be four entries related to each element. Let us consider the entries related of node A for the data item *d*. The first entry is *d.available* that shows whether d is locally cached at node A. This is binary value and is TRUE if data is locally available. The second entry is d.nnode and shows which neighbor node has cached *d*. The third entry maintained to access

Table 2. Entries of cit

S No.	Entry Name	Meaning	Initial Value
1	d.available	shows whether *d* is locally cached at node	FALSE
2	d.nnode	shows which neighbor node has cached *d*	Null
3	d.accesscount	shows how many times *d* is cached by neighbors node of node *A* after *d* is cached by node *A*	Zero
4	d.TTL	shows after how much time *d* is expired.	assigned by the data server

count that show how many times d is cached by neighbors node of node A after *d* is cached by node A. This entry is denoted by *d.accesscount*. The final entry is d.TTL shows the TTL (time-to-live) value that after how much time d has expired. This value is assigned by the data server. Initially *d.available* is set to FALSE, *d.nnode* is set to NULL and *d.accesscount* is set to zero. For example node A will contain some data (in its local cache) maintained a CIT that contains the details about the data which is maintained by its neighbors. The entries of CIT are summarized in Table 2.

Here we will assume that each mobile node has limited cache space and only some data items can be cached. When the cache space of a node is full then the node will select some data items to remove from the cache, when it has to cache the new one. Before forwarding the request of a data item from a node, each forwarding node will check it local cache if it has the data then it will send directly and stop the forwarding otherwise it redirect the to some neighbor that it knows has cached the data item.

PROPOSED ALGORITHM

Cache Discovery

Cache discovery addresses the two issues. Firstly it ensure how fulfill a data request with minimum cost of time, energy, and bandwidth. Secondly how to improve request success ratio, because in MANETs a data request/reply can get dropped easily due to interference, network congestion, or more commonly a forwarding node moving out of range and the path breaks. The traditional way of resolving a user's data request is first to check the local cache. If an up-to-date copy of the requested data found in local cache, then cached copy is returned to user. However, if cache miss occurs, then the request is forwarded to the data server to retrieve the up-to-date copy of data. This approach is known as SimpleCache (Yin et al., 2006). This is not an issue when the user is connected to the server through reliable high-speed connections. But for MANETs, every node is a risk because of signal intervention and link breaks due to nodes movement.

In ProCoCa, when a data item *d* is requested by a node (Figure 2), first the node will check its local cache to see whether the data is locally available or not. For this the entry *d.available* is checked. If this is *TRUE* then the data is locally available and returned to the requester. If this entry is *FALSE* then the node will check entry *d.nnode*

Figure 2. Request failure ratio versus cache size

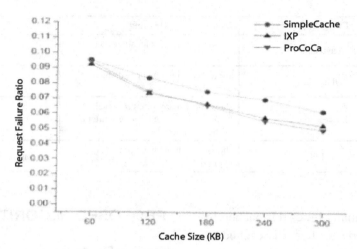

in their CIT to see whether the data item is cached by a node in its neighbor. If the matching entry found then the request is redirect to the node, but in case the matching entries are not found then the request is forwarded towards the data server. However the nodes that are lying on the way to the data server check their own local cache as well as the *d.nnode* entry in their CIT. If any node has data in its local cache then the data is send to requester node and request forwarding is stop and if the data entry is matched in the CIT then the node redirect the request to that node. Here we checks which is close: data center or the node and closer one is selected. Every node is free to move anywhere in the network as the network is mobile. So it is necessary to consider the movement of the nodes. There are two situations one is that a node enters in a new zone and second is a node leaves its zone. We discuss both the cases separately.

1. When a node will enter in a new zone, the nodes in the new zone will not aware with the caching content of this node. To shares its information with other node in that zone, this node will proactively broadcast its up-dates to all its neighbors of the new zone. In other words it will send the information of its local cache. With the help of these broadcasts the neighbor nodes will update their CIT. This will improve the data availability in the zone.

2. When a node wants to leave its zone then the data cached by this node will not be available for future use. So before leaving its zone it will broadcast a *"LEAVE"* message to its neighbors. With this *"LEAVE"* message the node will send the information of its local cache as well. Now when the neighbors receive this information then these neighbors will decide whether the data held by the leaving node can be cached by them. These decisions will be based on following criteria:-

    a. First the nodes will check their local cache if the same data items are found then these data items will not cached by these nodes.

    b. After the local cache the nodes will check their CIT to see whether the same data is cached by some node in their vicinity. If the entries matched then also this data will not be cached by these nodes because this data is already available in the zone.

c. Now if the data is not present in the local cache or in the vicinity then this data will be cached by the node. If the free space is not available in the node then by using cache replacement algorithm some data is removed from the cache to save the new one.

Let us consider that node *B* wants to leave its zone then before leaving it will broadcasts a "*LEAVE*" message to its neighbors i.e. to node *A* and node *E*. Now these neighbor nodes will decide whether the data held by node *B* can be cached by them for future use. Then first these nodes will check their local cache and if the same data is found then they will not cache the data. If the data is not in their local cache then they will check *d.nnode* entry in their CIT to see whether the data is present or not in their vicinity. If the entry matched then neither of these nodes will cache the data as the data is available in the zone. Now if the data is not found in their local cache or in the vicinity then either of the nodes will cache the data items. This will be depending on the fact which node has enough space to cache the data. If either node has not enough space to cache the data then we will choose a node which has to remove less content from its cache in order to make the space free. Both nodes will cache the different data.

Data Caching and Consistency

Data caching management implies how to manage the cached data items and how to create enough free space for the new data items when these items are to be cached by executing the cache replacement. The goal of data caching management is to improve cache hit ratio, which mainly depends on the size of the cache. To accomplish this task in cooperative caching, the focus of data caching management is not only on the local cache of the individual node but also on the whole cooperative caching system. That means we have to try maximizing the effective cache size of the complete cooperative caching system by taking every node into the consideration. To achieve this goal we tries to minimize duplicated caching within the cooperation zone, such that the cache space can be used to acquire more discrete data items.

When a node *A* receives the data item *d*, it caches it. During this process it may happen that the node needs to remove another data item from its cache. Let us assume that the victim item is *c*. How to select this victim data item for to remove, it will be described in the next section. After caching *d* node *A* will set *d.available* is TRUE and *c.available* is FALSE. Now A will reset the *d.accesscount* to 0. Now node will broadcast its updates to its neighbors. These updates will include information about both (cached item *d* and removed item *c*) data items. By doing so the neighbors will make changes in their CIT, this will improve the information accuracy.

Now when *A*'s neighbors receives the update from *A*, they will set their *d.available* to *A*. Further if these nodes have already cached these data items (*d* and *c*) then they will increase *d.accesscount* by 1 and decrease the *c.accesscount* by 1. And also if a node has set *c.nnode* to *A* then they will set it to NULL because the data item *c* is no longer with *A*.

Cache consistency algorithm ensures that the cached data items are updated and clients get fresh copy of data items. There are two widely used cache consistency models one is the weak consistency and the second is strong consistency model. In the weak consistency model, a stale data might be returned to the client. In the strong consistency model, after an update completes, no stale copy of the modified data will be returned to the client (Chand et al., 2007). In MANETs due to bandwidth and power constraints it is too expensive to maintain strong consistency, while the weak consistency model is done well. In Pro-CoCa we use a simple weak consistency model based on the time-to live (*TTL*) value. For this we maintain an entry (*d.TTL*) in the CIT. The data is considered as a fresh copy until its *TTL* value is not expired. When *TTL* value is expired the node removes the cached data and broadcast updates to its neighbors so that they can update their CIT.

Cache Replacements

As in cooperative caching in MANETs the data is not stored only on behalf of caching node but interest of the neighbor's node is also considered. For this reason LRU, LFU (Silberschatz et al., 2004) and SXO (Yin et al., 2006) are not suitable for the MANETs. Here our emphasis to remove such data items whose removals introduce the least effect on the requirement of the neighbor's node and also on the data availability in the zone. Here we use a cache replacement policy based on the access count. As we have maintains an entry *(x).accesscount* in the CIT. in our cache replacement policy we replace a data item which has maximum *(x).accesscount* among all the caching items. We use this replacement policy because by removing a data item with highest access count has least effect on the data availability as other neighbors node has cached the same data item. Because as many times a data item will access by a neighbor's node its *(x).accesscount* will be increased by one. By removing such an item we have the least cache duplicacy in the zone. This is the reason that's why we initially set the *(x).accesscount* to zero. This policy is better than the LRU, LFU and SXO because this is based upon the recent behavior of the nodes.

Now what happens if some data item is not accessed by any of the neighbor node in the zone. Then that item will not be replaced. To overcome this problem we will check the *TTL* values of the

data items. When the *TTL* value is expired then the data item will be removed from the cache.

SIMULATION AND RESULTS

Simulation Environment

The simulation model is constructed on the basis of the OMNeT++ simulator (OMNeT++, 2009). The simulation model is similar to the one used in (Chiu et al., 2009). In our simulation setting, a group of mobile nodes spread randomly in an area of 1,000× m 500 m. The number of mobile nodes varies from 50 to 100 with the default number of nodes being 60. In our simulations, the radius of a zone is set to one hop. One node is considered as the data server, and it is located at the upper left-hand corner of the area throughout the simulation. It is assumed that the wireless transmission range of the nodes is 250 m and the channel capacity is 2 Mbps. A node moves according to the random waypoint model (Broch et al., 1998), in which each node selects a random destination in the specified area and moves toward the destination with a speed selected randomly from the range (Vmin; Vmax). Vmin is fixed at 1 m/s and Vmax varies from 2 to 20 m/s with the default Vmax being 10 m/s. The pause time is set to 300 seconds.

The data server contains 2,000 data items. The default TTL value for the data items is set 4000 sec., but it can vary in the range of 500-5000 sec. Data requests are served on an FCFS basis at each node. The size of each data item is 1,000 bytes; other packets, such as request packets and update packets, are assumed to be 20 bytes long. Each node generates data requests according to a Poisson distribution such that the inter-arrival times of the data requests follow an exponential distribution with a mean of 20 seconds. The default data access pattern is uniformly distributed. We assume that a data request failed if the requested data item is not returned within a specified amount of time.

This is employed to account for packet loss in the unreliable wireless network. In the simulations, this parameter is set to 500 ms. The simulation parameters are listed in Table 3.

The performance metrics used in the simulations are:

1. **Request Failure Ratio:** Request failure ratio is defined as the ratio of data requests that fail to receive the requested data items. Request failures may lead to additional request attempts, which cause even heavier traffic for the bandwidth-constrained wireless network.

2. **Network Traffic:** Another performance metric is the average network traffic, in terms of bytes, introduced by a data request. It is calculated by summing the products of packet sizes and numbers of hops traversed by all packets (data packets and control packets, such as request packets and index packets) involved in a round of data access.

3. **Average Data Access:** The average data access time for a successful data request is also adopted as a performance metric in the simulation.

4. **Data Requests Served by Data Server:** We have measured the ratio of data requests that are served by the data center. Reducing such ratio reduces the workload of the data server.

Results and Discussion

Figure 2 shows the plot of request failure ratio with the cache size. Here we are varying the cache from 60 to 300 Kbytes. This can be seen from the figure that ProCoCa performs better than SimpleCache and IXP. This is due to fact that we maintain CIT at each node, and all the node broadcast update to their neighborhood, so most of the requests are fulfilled from the local cache and the neighborhood. A data request has high probability of failure when the request path is long. It is obvious when the cache size increase the request failure ratio is decreases in all protocols because cache hit ratio at the requester node grows when the cache size is increased.

In Figure 3, we illustrate the average access time of a successful data request. Here we exclude the failed data requests. From Figure 3 we see that ProCoCa performs better when compared to

Table 3. Simulation parameter

Parameter	Default Value	Range
Number of Data Items	2000	
Area(m×m)	1000×500	
Size of data items(bytes)	1000	
Size of update packets(bytes)	20	
Size of request packets(bytes)	20	
Radius of zone(hop)	1	
Bandwidth(Mb/s)	2	
Transmission Range(m)	250	
Number of nodes	50-100	60
Vmin(m/s)	1	
Vmax(m/s)	10	2-20
TTL(secs)	4000	400-5000
Pause Time(secs)	300	

Figure 3. Average data access time vs. cache size

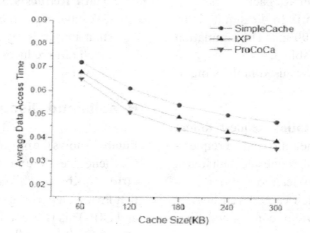

SimpleCache and IXP. As described previously this is due to the fact that each node keep up-to-date with each other in their zone, that increase data availability and more and more requests are fulfilled in the zone itself. Further SimpleCache takes a longer path for a data request to reach a caching site of the needed item.

The average network traffic per data request is plotted in Figure 4. When cache size increases we see that network traffic decreases. As compare to IXP, ProCoCa require more broadcast due to proactively updates. But we argue that these broadcasts are necessary and worthwhile because the probability of locating a copy a requested data item in the zone of requester is increased.

In Figure 5 we plot the ratio of data requests that are fulfilled from the data server. It is essential to reduce the number of data request fulfilled by the data server. This reduces the traffic near the data server and helps to achieve a better load balancing. ProCoCa is out performed when compare to the SimpleCache and IXP.

In Figure 6 analyze the effect the node mobility. We plot request failure ratio versus the maximum speed of the mobile nodes. As obvious, for all three protocols when the nodes move at higher speeds the request failure ratio increase. From the figure, we see that ProCoCa offers the best performance and is least sensitive to node mobility due to proactive updates.

CONCLUSION

In this paper we proposed the cooperative cache algorithm ProCoCa based on proactive approach. This algorithm is unique because this caches the data of leaving node. In order to cache discovery ProCoCa first the node will check its local cache if cache miss occurs then it will check its CIT to see whether the data is available in the neighborhood. If the matching entries are found then the data is returned to the requester otherwise the request is forward to data server. However nodes those are lying on the way to the data server check their own local cache and there CIT. If any node has data in its local cache then the data is send to requester node and request forwarding is stop and if the data entry is matched in the CIT then the node redirect the request to the node. For the cache replacement we use a policy based on the access count in such a way that removing data leave least impact on data availability in the zone. In ProCoCa cache consistency is maintained by using the approach based upon the *TTL* value. The simulation results show that ProCoCa performs better than the previous algorithms.

Figure 4. Average network traffic vs. cache size

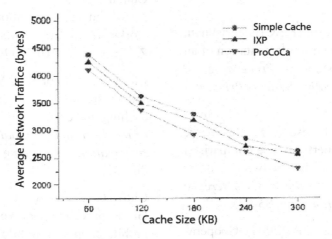

Figure 5. Ratio of access to data server vs. cache size

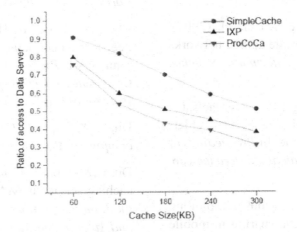

Figure 6. Request failure ratio vs. node mobility

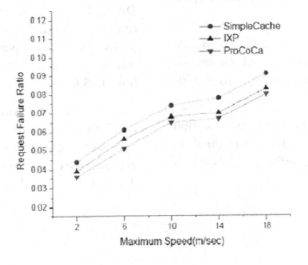

REFERENCES

Adjie-Winoto, W., Schwartz, E., & Balakrishnan, H. (1999). The design and implementation of an intentional naming system. In *Proceedings of the Symposium on Operating Systems Principles* (pp. 186-201).

Broch, J., Maltz, D., Johnson, D., Hu, Y., & Jetcheva, J. (1998). A performance comparison of multi-hop wireless ad hoc network routing protocols. In *Proceedings of the ACM Conference on Mobile Communications* (pp. 85-97).

Cao, G., Yin, L., & Das, C. R. (2004). Cooperative cache-based data access in ad hoc networks. *IEEE Computer*, *37*(2), 32–39.

Chand, N., Joshi, R. C., & Misra, M. (2007). Cooperative caching in mobile ad hoc networks based on data utility. *Mobile Information Systems*, *3*(1), 19–37.

Chankhunthod, A., Danzig, P. B., Neerdaels, C., Schwartz, M. F., & Worrell, K. J. (1996). A hierarchical Internet object cache. In *Proceedings of the USENIX Annual Technical Conference* (pp. 153-163).

Chiu, G. M., & Young, C. R. (2009). Exploiting in-zone broadcasts for cache sharing in mobile ad hoc networks. *IEEE Transactions on Mobile Computing*, *8*(3), 384–397. doi:10.1109/TMC.2008.127

Chlamtac, I., Conti, M., & Liu, J. N. (2003). Mobile ad hoc networking: Imperatives and challenges. *Ad Hoc Networks*, *1*, 13–64. doi:10.1016/S1570-8705(03)00013-1

Chlamtac, I., & Lerner, A. (1986). Link allocation in mobile radio networks with noisy channel. In *Proceedings of the IEEE Conference INFOCOM* (pp. 203-212).

Chlamtac, I., & Lerner, A. (1987). Fair algorithms for maximal link activation in multi-hop radio networks. *IEEE Transactions on Communications*, *7*, 739–746. doi:10.1109/TCOM.1987.1096847

Chow, C. Y., Leong, H. V., & Chan, A. (2004a). Cache signatures for peer-to-peer cooperative caching in mobile environments. In *Proceedings of the 18th International Conference Advanced Information Networking and Applications* (pp. 96-101).

Chow, C. Y., Leong, H. V., & Chan, A. (2004b). Group-based cooperative cache management for mobile clients in mobile environments. In *Proceedings of the 33rd International Conference on Parallel Processing* (pp. 83-90).

Chow, C. Y., Leong, H. V., & Chan, A. (2004c). Peer-to-peer cooperative caching in mobile environments. In *Proceedings of the 24th International Conference on Distributed Computing Systems Workshops* (pp. 528-533).

Du, Y., & Gupta, S. (2004). *Handbook of mobile computing*. Boca Raton, FL: CRC Press.

Du, Y., & Gupta, S. (2005). COOP–A cooperative caching service in MANETs. In *Proceedings of the Joint International Conference on Autonomic and Autonomous Systems and International Conference on Networking and Services* (pp. 58-63).

Du, Y., Gupta, S., & Varsamopoulos, V. (2009). Improving on-demand data access efficiency in MANETs with cooperative caching. *Ad Hoc Networks*, *7*(3), 579–598. doi:10.1016/j.adhoc.2008.07.007

Fan, L., Cao, P., Almeida, J., & Broder, A. Z. (2000). Summary cache: A scalable wide-area web cache sharing protocol. *IEEE/ACM Transactions on Networking*, *8*(3), 281–293. doi:10.1109/90.851975

Gupta, P., & Kumar, P. (2000). The capacity of wireless networks. *IEEE Transactions on Information Theory*, *46*(2), 388–404. doi:10.1109/18.825799

Iyer, S., Rowstron, A., & Druschel, P. (2002). Squirrel: A decentralized peer-to-peer web cache. In *Proceedings of the ACM Symposium on Principles of Distributed Computing* (pp. 156-165).

Lim, L., Lee, W., Cao, G., & Das, C. (2006). A novel caching scheme for Internet based mobile ad hoc networks performance. *Ad Hoc Networks*, *4*(2), 225–239. doi:10.1016/j.adhoc.2004.04.013

Moriya, T., & Aida, H. (2003). Cache data access system in ad hoc networks. In *Proceedings of the Vehicular Technology Conference* (pp. 1228-1232).

OMNeT++ (2009). *Documentation*. Retrieved from http://www.omnetpp.org/

Silberschatz, A., Galvin, P. B., & Gagne, G. (2004). *Operating system concepts*. New York, NY: John Wiley & Sons.

Sun, Y., Belding-Royer, E. M., & Perkins, C. E. (2002). Internet connectivity for ad hoc mobile networks. *International Journal of Wireless Information Networks*, *9*(2), 75–88. doi:10.1023/A:1015399632291

Yin, L., & Cao, G. (2004). Supporting cooperative caching in ad hoc networks. In *Proceedings of the IEEE Conference INFOCOM* (pp. 2537-2547).

Yin, L., & Cao, G. (2006). Supporting cooperative caching in ad hoc networks. *IEEE Transactions on Mobile Computing*, *5*(1), 77–89. doi:10.1109/TMC.2006.15

This work was previously published in the International Journal of Mobile Computing and Multimedia Communications, Volume 3, Issue 4, edited by Ismail Khalil and Edgar Weippl, pp. 53-66, copyright 2011 by IGI Publishing (an imprint of IGI Global).

Chapter 18
An Energy–Efficient Multilevel Clustering Algorithm for Heterogeneous Wireless Sensor Networks

Surender Soni
National Institute of Technology Hamirpur, India

Vivek Katiyar
National Institute of Technology Hamirpur, India

Narottam Chand
National Institute of Technology Hamirpur, India

ABSTRACT

Wireless Sensor Networks (WSNs) are generally believed to be homogeneous, but some sensor nodes of higher energy can be used to prolong the lifetime and reliability of WSNs. This gives birth to the concept of Heterogeneous Wireless Sensor Networks (HWSNs). Clustering is an important technique to prolong the lifetime of WSNs and to reduce energy consumption as well, by topology management and routing. HWSNs are popular in real deployments (Corchado et al., 2010), and have a large area of coverage. In such scenarios, for better connectivity, the need for multilevel clustering protocols arises. In this paper, the authors propose an energy-efficient protocol called heterogeneous multilevel clustering and aggregation (HMCA) for HWSNs. HMCA is simulated and compared with existing multilevel clustering protocol EEMC (Jin et al., 2008) for homogeneous WSN. Simulation results demonstrate that the proposed protocol performs better.

DOI: 10.4018/978-1-4666-2163-3.ch018

INTRODUCTION

In recent years, with the advances in the technology of micro-electromechanical system (MEMS) and developments in wireless communications, wireless sensor networks (WSNs) have gained worldwide attention. WSNs consist of small nodes (sensors) having capabilities like sensing, computation, and communications. These sensors gather data by sensing the surroundings, aggregate this data to form useful information and transmit it to the base station or the neighboring node. WSNs have great potential for many application scenarios such as military sensing (Shen et al., 2010), industrial process monitoring and control (Kay et al., 2004), machine health monitoring (Hadim et al., 2006), environment and habitat monitoring (Hart et al., 2006), healthcare applications (Yan et al., 2009), home automation and traffic control (Chinrungrueng et al., 2006).

With the advances in MEMS, VLSI technology and wireless communication technology, it has become possible to form a large scale WSN with small sensor nodes scattered across some environment. These sensor nodes need to be in touch with far-away base stations. Clustering is an important technique to prolong the lifetime of WSNs and to reduce energy consumption as well, by topology management and routing. Many energy-efficient routing protocols are designed based on the clustering structure (Krishna et al., 1997; McDonald et al., 2001). The clustering technique can also be used to perform data aggregation (Mhatre et al., 2004; Heinzelman et al., 2000). Data aggregation combines the data from source nodes into a small set of meaningful information hence the fewer messages are transmitted thus securing communication energy. Within the clusters, localized algorithms can also efficiently operate. Clustering technique can be extremely effective in broadcast and data query (Ni et al., 1999; Estrin et al., 1999). Cluster-heads help to broadcast messages and collect interested data within their own clusters.

Sensor nodes in WSNs are limited in power, memory and computational capacity. So they may be short lived. A smart way to prolong the lifetime of sensor nodes and WSN is to make efficient use of energy. Many energy efficient algorithms have been proposed in the literature (Abbasi et al., 2007). LEACH (Heinzelman et al., 2000) is one of such algorithms that balances the energy consumption by rotating the clusterhead (CH) role to every node in the cluster. Another way to prolong the lifetime of WSN is to insert a percentage of sensor nodes equipped with additional energy resources i.e. making the WSN heterogeneous in terms of energy. Even though the nodes may have same initial energy in starting, energy of each node will not be same later on due to radio communication characteristics. Therefore, WSNs are more possibly heterogeneous networks rather than homogeneous ones. Many existing schemes for heterogeneous wireless sensor networks (HWSNs) like SEP (Smaragdakis et al., 2004), EEHC (Kumar et al., 2009), DEEC (Qing et al., 2006), etc., demonstrate that HWSNs survive for a longer time as compared to homogeneous WSNs.

Sometimes, direct communication may not be possible with the base station due to certain limitations. This leads to the need of multilevel clustering algorithms for large WSNs. In such algorithms, clusters are formed in hierarchical manner. Sensor nodes sense the events and forward the data to the immediate CH. This CH aggregates and forwards data to the next level CH and so on to the sink node. So the advantage of multilevel clustering algorithms is that the nodes have to transmit data comparatively to short distances so they can conserve their energy. Many energy efficient multilevel clustering algorithms have been proposed till date like (Jin et al., 2008; Rasid et al., 2007; Xinfang et al., 2008). An Energy Efficient Multilevel Clustering Algorithm (EEMC) to minimize the energy consumption in WSNs is proposed in (Jin et al., 2008). EEMC also covers the CH election scheme. The scheme assumes that the sensor network is homogeneous and does not perform well in heterogeneous environment. The low energy nodes will die more quickly than the high energy nodes because the algorithm does not discriminate each node in terms of energy.

In this paper, we apply the concept of multilevel clustering to HWSNs. We propose and evaluate an energy efficient multilevel clustering algorithm for HWSN which is called heterogeneous multilevel clustering and aggregation (HMCA). Similar to EEMC, HMCA forms multilevel clustering hierarchy in each round by rotating the CH role among all nodes. In HMCA, CHs are elected depending upon the probability based on the remaining energy of the nodes. Simulation results show that HMCA can prolong the network life time and stability period. Results are also compared with multilevel clustering scheme EEMC.

Rest of the paper is organized as follows. Related work is described in next section. The assumptions, energy model and heterogeneous model for WSN are presented next. Our proposed algorithm, HMCA, is described and we present the simulation environment and results. We conclude the paper in last section.

RELATED WORK

One of the main goals of clustering algorithms for WSNs is to reduce the energy consumption. In a typically large WSN, it is very difficult for a sensor node to communicate with far away base station and minimize the energy consumption at the same time. Multilevel clustering schemes can provide better connectivity and reduce the energy consumption as well. The impact of heterogeneity of nodes (in terms of energy) on the performance of networks (energy-efficiency and stability) of various sizes and designs is evaluated in (Yarvis et al., 2005). It is also known that if in a network, heterogeneity is used properly, then the response of the network is tripled and the network's lifetime can be increased by 5-fold (Yarvis et al., 2005).

Kumar et al. (2009) proposed an energy efficient clustered scheme for HWSNs based on weighted election probabilities of each node to become CH. It elects the CH in distributed fashion in hierarchal WSN. This algorithm is based on LEACH (Low Energy Adaptive Clustering Hierarchy) (Heinzelman et al., 2000). This algorithm works on the election processes of the CH in presence of heterogeneity of nodes.

Qing et al. (2006) proposed DEEC; a distributed multilevel clustering algorithm for heterogeneous wireless sensor networks. DEEC selects the clusterheads with the help of probability based on the ratio between residual energy of each node and the average energy of the network. How long different nodes would be clusterheads, is decided according to the initial and residual energy. DEEC is also based on LEACH; it rotates the clusterhead role among all nodes to expend energy uniformity. Two levels of heterogeneous nodes are considered in this algorithm and after that a general solution for multilevel heterogeneity is obtained.

In DEEC, all the nodes need to know the total energy and lifetime of the network. When a new epoch begins, each node s_i computes the average probability p_i by the total energy $E_{total,}$ while estimated value R of lifetime is broadcasted by the base station. Now p_i is used to get the election threshold $T(s_i)$. This threshold decides node s_i to be a cluster-head in the current round.

In Rasid et al. (2007), authors propose a multilevel clustering algorithm to reduce the network energy consumption by determining the optimal number of CH nodes in multilevel network. The proposed algorithm chooses a set of nodes to become *level-1* CHs from all the nodes. *Level-2* CHs are selected from the set of *level-1* CHs. This process is repeated until highest level of CHs is reached.

Another multilevel clustering algorithm proposed (Xinfang et al., 2008), is based on mathematical model of clustering virtual back-bone. This algorithm rotates the CH role to all nodes to evenly distribute the energy consumption. It reduces the number of relays for data transmission by reducing the number of nodes in the root tree.

Energy Efficient Multilevel Clustering (EEMC) (Jin et al., 2008) is one of the most recent clustering algorithms for WSN. EEMC works in two phases in each round: cluster set-up phase and network operation phase. The cluster set-up phase works in top-down fashion. Initially, for each round, all nodes are set to regular (non-CH). Each active node u initiates the cluster set-up phase by sending its location information and its current residual energy $E_u(t)$ to the sink. This indicates that algorithm will select *level-1* CH. After receiving these values, the sink node broadcasts a "command" message containing the value of the total remaining energy $E_v(t)$ of the network and the total reciprocal of distance $\sum 1 / dis(n_v, n_{\text{sink}})$ from all active nodes. When an active node u receives this "command" message, it sets its probability of becoming a *level-1* CH, denoted as $p_1(u)$, by using the following relation:

$$p_1(u) = N_{CH1}^{opt} \left[\varphi \frac{E_u(t)}{\sum_{v \in S(t)} E_v(t)} + (1 - \varphi) \left(\frac{1/dis(n_u, n_{\text{sink}})}{\sum_{v \in S(t)} 1/dis(n_v, n_{\text{sink}})} \right) \right]$$

where φ is a parameter and N_{CH}^{opt} is the optimal number of CHs for *level-1*. This means that the nodes with higher energy or a lesser distance will have a greater probability of becoming the CHs. In order to reduce energy consumption, all *level-1* CH send out a *level-1* CHs message with the radio range

$$\frac{R}{\sqrt{N_{CH1}^{opt}}}$$

Selection of *level-2* CH will be done according to the following relation"

$$p_2(u) = \sqrt{N_1} \left[\varphi \frac{E_u(t)}{\sum_{v \in S_1(t)} E_v(t)} + (1 - \varphi) \left(\frac{1/dis(n_u, n_{CH1})}{\sum_{v \in S_1(t)} 1/dis(n_v, n_{CH1})} \right) \right]$$

In general, the probability of each node to become a *level-j* CH can also be calculated.

In network operation phase, when *level-T* clustering topology is formed, the regular nodes start transmitting the sensed data to lower CHs. *Level-T* CHs aggregate the sensed data and send it to *level-(T-1)* CHs and so forth. Finally, all *level-1* CHs transmit the aggregated data to sink node.

One of the drawbacks of EEMC is that all nodes should be equipped with GPS. In Soni et al. (2010), PAMC algorithm is proposed, which uses the concept of Minimum Reachability Power (MRP) to overcome this shortcoming. MRP can be considered as transmission range. Distance parameter $\sum 1 / dis(n_v, n_{\text{sink}})$ of EEMC, is replaced by $\sum 1/P_v$, the Total Reciprocal of Minimum Reachability Power (TRMRP) for all active nodes. PAMC also proceeds in same manner as EEMC: first a cluster set-up phase and then network operation phase.

HETEROGENEOUS MODEL OF WSNS

Here, we present a paradigm of HWSN and discuss the impact of heterogeneous resources described in Yarvis et al. (2005). There are three common types of resource heterogeneity in sensor nodes: computational heterogeneity, link heterogeneity, and energy heterogeneity.

Computational heterogeneity means that the heterogeneous node has a more powerful microprocessor, and more memory, than the normal node. Link heterogeneity means that the heterogeneous node has more bandwidth and a longer distance network transceiver than the normal node. Energy heterogeneity means that the heterogeneous node is line powered, or its battery is replaceable. Among above three types of resource heterogeneity, the most important heterogeneity is the energy heterogeneity because both computational heterogeneity and link heterogeneity will consume more energy resources.

If some heterogeneous nodes are placed in the sensor network, average energy of the network will be higher and hence the network lifetime will increase. Reliability of data transmission is also improved with the help of heterogeneous nodes. Computational and link heterogeneity can decrease the processing latency and waiting time in transmitting queue respectively.

The model proposed here for heterogeneous WSN is same as Qing et al. (2006) that considers two types of nodes: normal nodes and advance nodes. As shown in Figure 1, normal nodes and advance nodes are represented by circle and star respectively. It is assumed that out of total N nodes in the network, there are $(1 - \theta) * N$ normal nodes and $\theta * N$ advance nodes. Advance nodes have γ times more energy than the normal nodes. The initial energies of normal nodes and advance nodes are E_{ini} and $\gamma * E_{ini}$ respectively. Hence total energy of the network:

Figure 1. A typical heterogeneous wireless sensor network with normal nodes and advanced nodes

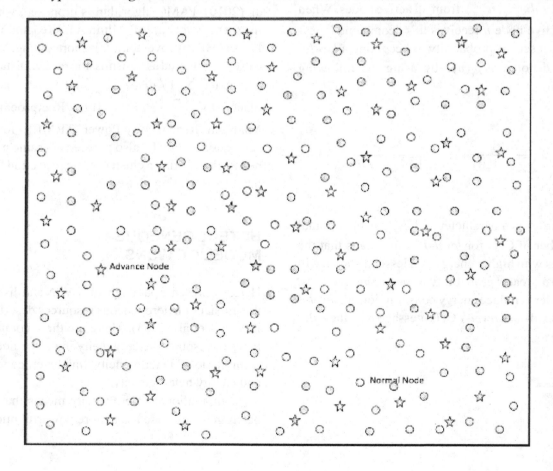

$$E_{total} = (1 - \theta) * N * E_{ini} + \theta * N * \gamma * E_{ini}$$
$$= N * E_{ini}(1 - \theta + \theta * \gamma)$$
$$= N * E_{ini} + N * E_{ini} * \theta * (\gamma - 1)$$

$$(1)$$

This shows that heterogeneous network energy has $\theta * (\gamma - 1)$ more virtual nodes than homogeneous networks with the energy $N * E_{ini}$.

ENERGY MODEL AND ANALYSIS

The same energy dissipation model as in Chinrungrueng et al. (2006) is used here. To achieve an acceptable signal-to-noise ratio (SNR) in transmitting k bit message over a distance d, the energy cost of transmission (E_{Tx}) and reception (E_{Rx}) are given by:

$$E_{Tx}(k, d) =$$
$$\begin{cases} k * E_{elect} + k * \varepsilon_{fs} * d^2 & if \ d \ \leq \ d_0 \\ k * E_{elect} + k * \varepsilon_{mp} * d^4 & if \ d \ \geq \ d_0 \end{cases}$$

where $E_{elect} = 50nJ$ is the energy being used to run the transmitter and receiver circuit.

$$\varepsilon_{fs} = 10pJ \ / \ bit \ / \ m^2$$

and

$$\varepsilon_{mp} = 0.0013pJ \ / \ bit \ / \ m^4$$

are the energies used by transmission amplifiers for short distance and long distance respectively. For $d = d_0$ we can calculate the distance threshold

$$d_0 = \sqrt{\varepsilon_{fs} / \varepsilon_{mp}}$$

To receive a k bit message, the radio expends $E_{Rx} = k * E_{elect}$. The energy to fuse l bits of data is E_F.

First we compute the energy consumption in single level or flat clustering. We assume that sensor nodes are uniformly distributed in a square area of $M * M$. We also assume that base station is located within the square area. So the communication from any node to base station will not be subjected to the multipath fading $(\leq d_0)$. If there are k clusterhead nodes out of N total nodes, energy dissipated by the clusterhead nodes during a round will be

$$E_{CH} =$$
$$l * \left[\left(\frac{N}{k} - 1 \right) * E_{elect} + \frac{N}{k} * E_F + E_{elect} + \varepsilon_{fs} * d_{BS}^2 \right]$$

$$(2)$$

Energy consumed by non-clusterhead nodes is

$$E_{nonCH} = l * \left[E_{elect} + \varepsilon_{fs} * d_{CH}^2 \right] \quad (3)$$

The total energy required for network to sense the environment and send l bits to BS will be summation of energy consumed by k clusterhead nodes and $(N - k)$ non-clusterhead nodes.

$$E_{total} = k * E_{CH} + (N - k) * E_{nonCH}$$

$$E_{total} =$$
$$l * \left[\begin{matrix} 2N * E_{elect} + \frac{\varepsilon_{fs}M^2}{\pi} \left(\frac{N}{k} - 1 \right) \\ + E_F * N + k * \left(\varepsilon_{fs} * d_{BS}^2 - E_{elect} \right) \end{matrix} \right]$$

$$(4)$$

In the following sub-section we present energy consumption model similar to Comeau et al. (2006), for a typical wireless sensor network.

Now we compute the energy consumption in multilevel clustering hierarchy. We assume a two-level hierarchical sensor network with sensor nodes as shown in Figure 2. Here we are following top-down approach. k_1 is the number of the top-level (*level-1*) CHs and k_2 is the number of last-level (*level-2*) CHs.

Sensor nodes send sense data to k_2 (*level-2*) CHs. They collect data, aggregate it and transmit to the k_1 (*level-1*) CHs. Energy consumption at each level can be calculated as follows. Energy expended in transmitting to k_2 clusterheads by non-clusterheads nodes will be

$$E_{nonCH,2} = l * \left[E_{elect} + \frac{\varepsilon_{fs} M^2}{\pi k_2} \right] \quad (5)$$

At *level-2*, clusterhead nodes receive the data and fuse it. The energy expended is

$$E_{CH,2} = l * \left[\left(\frac{N}{k_2} - 1 \right) * E_{elect} + \frac{N}{k_2} E_F \right] \quad (6)$$

Since there are (N-k_2) non-clusterhead nodes and k_2 clusterhead nodes. Expected energy expended to process *l*-bits of data at *level-2* includes the energy of sensing data by nodes and receiving data by k_2 CHs.

$$E_2 = l * [(N - k_2) * E_{nonCH,2} + k_2 * E_{CH,2}]$$

$$E_2 = l * \left[2 * (N - k_2) * E_{elect} + \frac{\varepsilon_{fs} M^2}{\pi} \left(\frac{N}{k_2} - 1 \right) + N * E_F \right] \quad (7)$$

k_1 CHs will not participate in selection of lower level CHs like k_2. So, we consider only remaining $(k_2 - k_1)$ CHs for *level-1* energy consumption. In the similar manner, expected energy expended at *level-1*, includes the energy of receiving data from k_2 CHs, energy expended in aggregation and transmission to k_1 CHs.

Figure 2. Two-level wireless sensor network

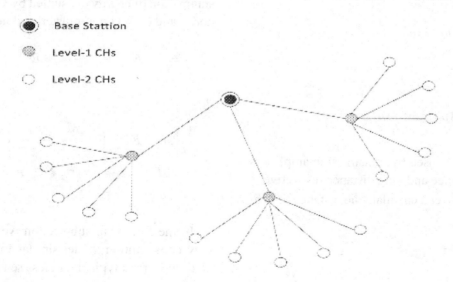

$$E_1 =$$

$$l * \left[2 * (k_2 - k_1) * E_{elect} + \frac{\varepsilon_{fs} M^2}{\pi} \left(\frac{k_2}{k_1} - 1 \right) + k_2 * E_F \right]$$

$$(8)$$

Finally *level-1* CHs transmits to the BS. The energy consumed is

$$E_0 = l * k_1 * \left[E_{elect} + \varepsilon_{fs} * d_{BS}^2 \right] \qquad (9)$$

The total energy expended in each round to transmit *l*-bits for two-level hierarchical network is sum of E_0, E_1 and E_2. We can find out $E_{total,2}$ from Equations 7, 8, and 9.

$$E_{total,2} = E_2 + E_1 + E_0$$

$$E_{total,2} =$$

$$l * \begin{bmatrix} 2NE_{elect} + \frac{\varepsilon_{fs} M^2}{\pi} \left(\frac{N}{k_2} + \frac{k_2}{k_1} - 2 \right) \\ + E_F \left(N + k_2 \right) + k_1 \left(\varepsilon_{fs} d_{BS}^2 - E_{elect} \right) \end{bmatrix}$$

$$(10)$$

Generalizing above equation for *n* levels gives

$$E_{total,n}$$

$$= l * \begin{bmatrix} 2NE_{elect} + \frac{\varepsilon_{fs} M^2}{\pi} \left(\frac{N}{k_n} + \sum_{i=2}^{n} \frac{k_i}{k_{i-1}} - n \right) \\ + E_F \left(N + k_n \right) + k_n \left(\varepsilon_{fs} d_{BS}^2 - E_{elect} \right) \end{bmatrix}$$

$$(11)$$

Lifetime of the network in terms of number of rounds can be calculated for homogeneous as well as heterogeneous wireless sensor network. Number of rounds can be calculated by dividing total network energy by energy expended in one round. For least energy consumption we have to select the optimal value of CHs at each level.

Theorem 1. Number of CHs at various levels $(k_1, k_2, ... k_n)$ will be optimal if and only if they satisfy following equations:

$$\frac{N}{k_2^2} - \frac{1}{k_1} = \frac{\pi E_F}{\varepsilon_{fs} M^2} \quad for \ two \ level \qquad (12)$$

$$\frac{k_{i+1}}{k_i^2} - \frac{1}{k_{i-1}} = \frac{\pi E_F}{\varepsilon_{fs} M^2} \qquad (13)$$
$$for \ n > 2, \ the \ next \ n \text{ - } 2$$

$$\frac{k_n}{k_{n-1}^2} = \frac{\pi d_{BS}^2}{M^2} - \frac{\pi E_{elect}}{\varepsilon_{fs} M^2} \quad for \ last \ level \qquad (14)$$

Proof. We can find the above equations by taking the derivative of $E_{total,2}$ and $E_{total,n}$ with respect to k_2 and k_n respectively and equating to zero. It can also be shown that second derivative of $E_{total,2}$ and $E_{total,n}$ is always positive. This indicates that Equations 12, 13, and 14 are optimal solutions.

Numerical Example 1. For N=200 and M=100, (and given radio parameters $E_{elect} = 50nJ \ / \ bit$, $\varepsilon_{fs} = 10pJ \ / \ bit \ / \ m^2$) if we consider it as two-level sensor network, number of *level-1* CHs (k_1) and number of *level-2* CHs (k_2) can be found from Theorem 1. If $E_F = 5nJ \ / \ bit$, k_1 and k_2 will be 3.7 and 22 respectively. Energy expended in a round, computed by Equation 10 will be $21.5\mu J$. Obviously, we can get energy consumed in transmission of one data packet of size 500 bits as $10.75 \times 10^{-3} J$.

Total energy of homogeneous WSN having 200 node of $1J$ of initial enegy will be $200J$. Hence total number of rounds (i.e. lifetime) of homogeneous network will be 18600. But for same heterogeneous WSN with $\theta = 0.2$ and $\gamma = 3$ the total energy can be found from Equation 1, hence the number of rounds will be 26000.

The above results show the significant increase in the lifetime.

PROPOSED ALGORITHM

Most of the multilevel clustering schemes consider WSN to be homogeneous. One of such algorithms, EEMC does not consider the heterogeneity of nodes in terms of their initial energy. HMCA deals with the adaptation of the CH election process considering heterogeneous nodes in a multilevel clustering scheme.

This paper considers a HWSN deployed for real life applications. The following assumptions are made about the sensor nodes and the network model:

1. The base station (i.e. sink node) is located inside the sensing field.
2. Nodes are deployed randomly in a square area.
3. Communication within the square area is not subjected to multipath fading.
4. Nodes in the sensor field are heterogeneous in terms of energy.
5. Two type of nodes: normal nodes and advance nodes.
6. The communication channel is symmetric.
7. Data gathered can be aggregated into single packet by CH.

HMCA algorithm is based on EEMC (Jin et al., 2008). It also uses the idea of TRMRP of PAMC, described in Soni et al. (2010). PAMC uses the concept of Minimum Reachability Power (MRP). MRP can be considered as transmission range. Distance parameter $\sum 1/dis(n_v, n_{sink})$ of EEMC, is replaced by $\sum 1/P_v$, the Total Reciprocal of Minimum Reachability Power (TRMRP) for all active nodes.

$$TRMRP = \sum 1/MinPow_i$$

where $MinPow_i$ is minimum power level required by the node i to reach its CH. PAMC protocol also assumes that for any power level L_i, there is corresponding transmission range R_i such that

$$R_i < R_j \forall L_i < L_j$$

The operation of the algorithm can be divided into following two phases.

Cluster Set-Up Phase2

Initially, for each round, all nodes are set to regular (non-CH). Cluster set-up phase is initiated by base station by sending a *Start* beacon. All nodes select its minimum power level needed to reach the base station. The process of MRP discovery to base station is done only once during network life time and cached for subsequent usage. As active nodes receive the *Start* message, they reply by sending their residual energy $E_u(t)$ and the MRP P_u to the sink node to indicate that *level-1* CH will now be selected. On receipt of these values, sink broadcasts a "command" message with values like total remaining energy of the network $\sum E_v(t)$ and TRMRP $\sum 1/P_v$. With help of these values each active node u sets its probability of becoming CH. Since network is heterogeneous, nodes having more energy have greater chances to become CH. The probabilities of becoming CH for normal nodes $p_1^n(u)$ and advance nodes $p_1^a(u)$ can be given by following equations:

$$p_1^n(u) =$$
$$k_1 \left[\varphi \frac{E_u(t)}{\sum_{v \in S(t)} E_v(t)} + (1-\varphi) \left(\frac{1/P_u}{\sum_{v \in S(t)} 1/P_v} \right) \right]$$

$$p_1^a(u)$$

$$= k_1 \left[\varphi \frac{E_u(t) * \gamma}{\sum_{v \in S(t)} E_v(t)} + (1 - \varphi) \left(\frac{1/P_u}{\sum_{v \in S(t)} 1/P_v} \right) \right]$$

Here, φ is a parameter deciding the weightage of the energy factor and distance factor, and k_1 is the optimal number of *level-1* CHs that can be found out from Theorem 1. Here

$$\sum_{v \in S(t)} E_v(t) = N * E_u(t) * (1 - \theta + \theta * \gamma)$$

and $S(t)$ is assumed to be the active node set of the network at time t.

All *level-1* CHs send out a *level-1* CH message associated with MRP. Any node that receives this message replies with a "join" message sending out its residual energy and MRP to the CH.

When *level-1* CHs receive this message, they can construct their active node-set, denoted as $S_i(t)$, and then broadcast a "command" message with following three values: total residual energy of the cluster, the TRMRP within the cluster of each node and the cardinality of its active set N_1. After receiving this message each active node u will then set its probability $p_2^n(u)$ and $p_2^a(u)$ (for normal and advance node respectively) to become a *level-2* cluster-head according to the following equation

$$p_2^n(u) =$$

$$k_2 \left[\varphi \frac{E_u(t)}{\sum_{v \in S_1(t)} E_v(t)} + (1 - \varphi) \left(\frac{1/P_u}{\sum_{v \in S_1(t)} 1/P_v} \right) \right]$$

Here we make an additional assumption that after each round, the percentage of normal nodes and super nodes selected for CH role remains constant i.e. value of θ remains unchanged.

$$p_2^a(u) =$$

$$k_2 \left[\varphi \frac{E_u(t) * \gamma}{\sum_{v \in S_1(t)} E_v(t)} + (1 - \varphi) \left(\frac{1/P_u}{\sum_{v \in S_1(t)} 1/P_v} \right) \right]$$

In general, process of clustering may extend up to *level-j*. For any *level-(j-1)*, the elected CH will broadcast a *level-(j-1)* CH message. Any node that receives this message replies with a "join" message sending out its residual energy and MRP to the CH.

When *level-(j-1)* CHs (denoted as k_j) receive this message, they can construct their active node-set, denoted as $S_{j-1}(t)$, and then will broadcast a "command" message with following three values: total residual energy of the cluster, the TRMRP within the cluster of each node and the cardinality of $S_{j-1}(t)$ active set i.e., N_{j-1}. After receiving this message each active node u will then set its probability $p_j^n(u)$ and $p_j^a(u)$ (for normal and advance node respectively) to become a *level-j* clusterhead according to the following formula:

$$p_j^n(u) =$$

$$k_n \left[\varphi \frac{E_u(t)}{\sum_{v \in S_{j-1}(t)} E_v(t)} + (1 - \varphi) \left(\frac{1/P_u}{\sum_{v \in S_{j-1}(t)} 1/P_v} \right) \right]$$

$$p_j^a(u) =$$

$$k_n \left[\varphi \frac{E_u(t) * \gamma}{\sum_{v \in S_{j-1}(t)} E_v(t)} + (1 - \varphi) \left(\frac{1/P_u}{\sum_{v \in S_{j-1}(t)} 1/P_v} \right) \right]$$

The process of clustering will stop if a node has two or less number of nodes in its regular set.

Network Operation Phase2

As shown in Figure 3, when *level-T* clustering topology is formed, the regular nodes start transmitting the sensed data to their CHs. *Level-T* CHs aggregate the sensed data and send it to *level-(T-1)* CHs and so forth. Finally, all *level-1* CH transmit the aggregated data to sink node. Figure 4 shows the final cluster formation after the first round in HMCA.

The cost of delivering data to the sink is sum of energy spent by nodes to send the data to their respective CH. It may be noted that the process of storing some of the last known MRPs can greatly reduce the communication cost of the network.

SIMULATION RESULTS

In this section we evaluate the performance of HMCA protocol. To validate the performance of HMCA, we have done simulation using ns-2 (Fall et al., 2010), a discrete event network simulator. Advance and normal nodes are randomly distributed over the field. We have compared the performance of HMCA with EEMC. The basic parameters used are listed in Table 1.

We simulate proposed HMCA algorithm and multilevel clustering algorithm EEMC. Results from many runs of each algorithm are recorded for random distribution of nodes. Algorithm having less communication overhead, lower delay and greater network lifetime is considered as efficient one. To evaluate and compare the performance of different clustering algorithms, we use parameters described below as performance metrics.

Performance Measures

We define here the measures we use in this paper to evaluate the performance of clustering protocols.

1. **Network Lifetime:** This is the time interval from start of the operation (of sensor network) until death of nodes start. We use first node dead (FND) and half node dead (HND) to evaluate the network lifetime.

2. **Number of CHs Per Round:** This shows the total number of clusters formed in each rounds and the nodes participating in aggregation and data forwarding to the base station.

3. **Cluster Setup Interval:** This can be thought as the complexity of clustering algorithms in a round. It is obvious that cluster setup interval of single level clustering algorithm would be shorter than multilevel.

4. **Delay:** It is the time between a data packet is generated and reached at the base station. We use here maximum and minimum delay to evaluate the algorithms.

5. **Efficiency:** We evaluate and compare the efficiency of HMCA algorithm in terms of average energy utilization ratio. It is calculated as the ratio of the total current consumed energy of all nodes to the total energy of all nodes at start of the simulation.

6. **Data Delivery Ratio:** It represents the ratio between the number of data packets that are sent by the source and the number of data packets that are received by base station.

Network Lifetime

We used the idea of first node dead (FND) and half node dead (HND) to evaluate the network lifetime. FND and HND are number of rounds that elapse before first node and half of the nodes, respectively, run out of energy. For heterogeneous

Figure 3. Multilevel cluster formation in HMCA. Advance and normal nodes are denoted by star and circle respectively.

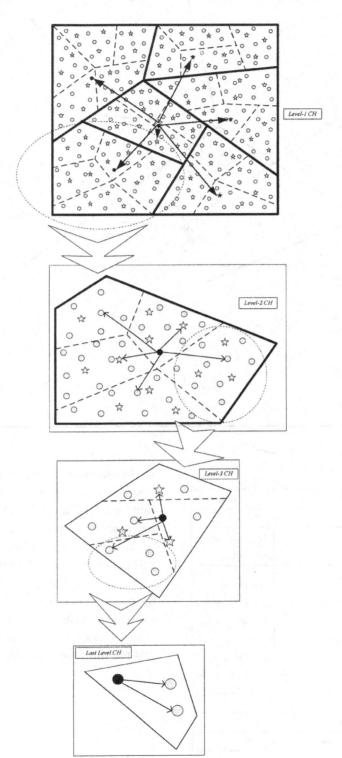

Figure 4. Clusterhead formation after first round

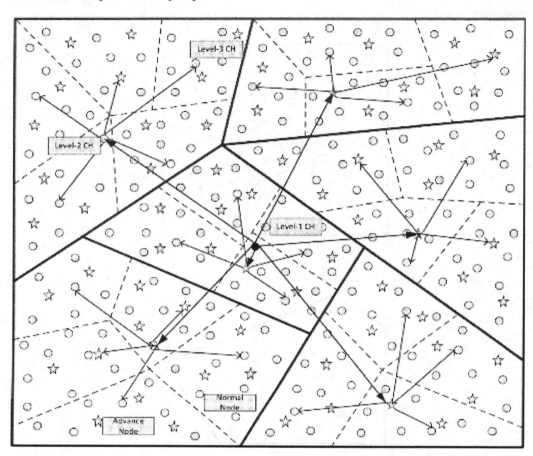

Table 1. Simulation parameters

Parameter	Value
Number of nodes	200-500
Network grid	100 X 100 m²
Base station position	50 X 50 m
ε_{fs}	10 pJ/bit/m²
E_F	5 nJ/bit
E_{elect}	50 nJ/bit
Size of data packet	500 bits
Size of control packet	10 bits
Initial energy of normal nodes	1 J
Transmission range of sensor node	10 m

environment we have two types of nodes: advance nodes and super nodes. We carried out the simulation for EEMC and HMCA for θ=0.2 and γ=3. We increase the number of nodes from 200 to 500.

It is clear from Figure 5 and Figure 6 that HMCA outperforms EEMC in terms of network lifetime. This shows that death of first node and last node occurs earlier in EEMC. In presence of heterogeneity there are more chances for an advance node to become CH. So it is obvious that the time for first node to die will increase.

Figure 5. FND analysis

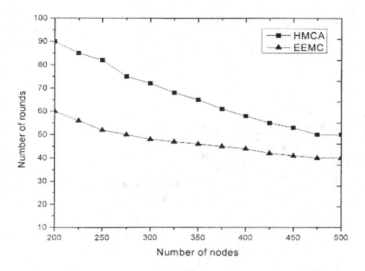

Figure 6. HND analysis

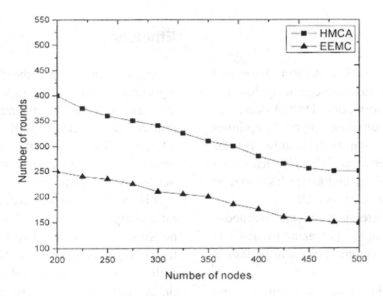

Number of Clusters per Round

We perform the simulation for 200 nodes. If we look at Figure 7, number of clusters per round increase in HMCA. HMCA takes the full advantage of heterogeneity (extra energy of advance nodes), the stable region is increased in comparison to EEMC. Initially both algorithms perform well but after some rounds HMCA outperforms. This is because under HMCA, advance nodes follow the death process of normal nodes, as the probability of electing CHs causes the energy of each node to be consumed in proportion to the nodes residual energy.

Figure 7. Number of clusters per round

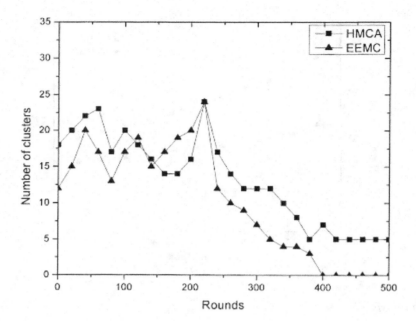

Delay

We simulate EEMC and HMCA for minimum and maximum delay because average delay does not provide so much information. HMCA decreases the delay of data packet in the network by optimizing the cluster formation. HMCA allows regular nodes to join higher level CHs. This leads to a more compact topology and hence less average number of hops and delay as well.

Since HMCA is heterogeneous, advance nodes can transmit with higher power and reach CH in single hop so maximum delay will be less in HMCA.

HMCA uses MRP as closeness criteria. Due to heterogeneity, nodes close to the CHs will not die shortly because of transmission load. So the minimum delay will also be less in HMCA.

We simulated HMCA and EEMC for 200 nodes. The comparison between maximum and minimum delays can be seen in Figure 8 and Figure 9 respectively.

Efficiency

We evaluate and compare the efficiency of HMCA algorithm in terms of average energy utilization ratio. It is calculated as the ratio of the total current consumed energy of all nodes to the total energy of all nodes at start of the simulation. The smaller the average energy utilization ratio, the better the algorithm.

Figure 10 shows the average energy utilization ratio comparison of EEMC and HMCA. Due to heterogeneous nodes, network has comparatively high energy. As described in Numerical example 1, the heterogeneous networks survive for longer times. HMCA dissipate network energy in a slow rate because of heterogeneous nodes, hence performs better in comparison to EEMC in presence of heterogeneity.

We performed simulation for 100 nodes. Energy utilization ratio equal to zero means that no energy is expended till now and energy utilization ratio equal to one means no energy remaining i.e. sensor network is dead.

Figure 8. Maximum delay comparison between HMCA and EEMC

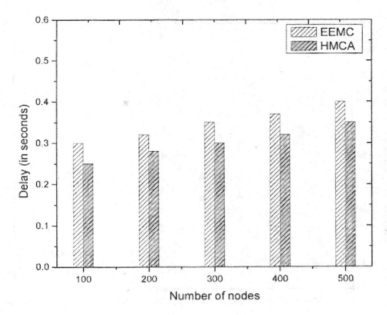

Figure 9. Minimum delay comparison between HMCA and EEMC

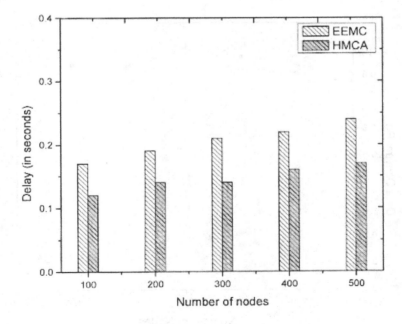

Figure 10. Average energy utilization ratio per round

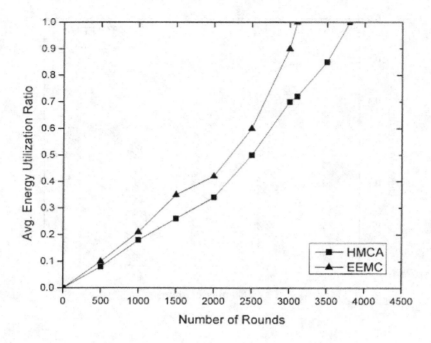

Figure 11. Data delivery ratio under different network size

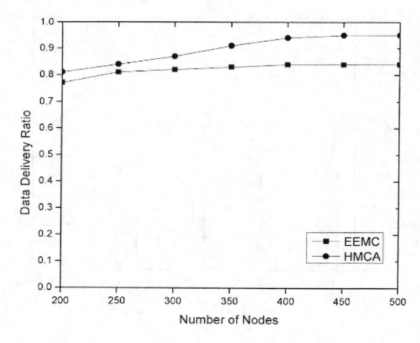

Figure 12. Impact of parameter φ on network lifetime

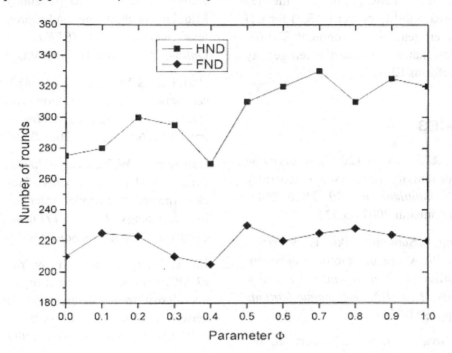

Data Delivery Ratio

Another parameter that we take to compare the performance of the EEMC and HMCA is reliable delivery of packets in terms of data delivery ratio. It is the ratio between the number of packets that are sent by the source and the number of data packets that are received by base station. When we increase the number of nodes in the network the data delivery ratio for HMCA is better than EEMC because new node in EEMC always joins at last level. This means the number of hops that any data packet has to travel will be higher in EEMC. So, there are more chances of data loss in comparison to HMCA.

Another reason for low data delivery ratio in EEMC is that it is a pure homogeneous network, so death of sensor nodes makes the sensor network denser with the time passes. This leads to the drop in data packets reaching at base station. As shown in Figure 11, HMCA outperforms EEMC for reliable data delivery.

Impact of Parameter φ

To study the impact of parameter φ, we simulate the HMCA algorithm for 200 nodes. Value of φ affects the number of nodes eligible for CH role. We have simulated for FND and HND values for HMCA for different values of φ. This shows that FND value is at peak when $\varphi = 0.7$ and least at $\varphi = 0.4$. Figure 12 shows that heterogeneity increases the network lifetime. In general, network lifetime increases with the value of parameter φ.

CONCLUSION

The wireless sensor networks have been designed to help in various monitoring applications. For real life deployments of large scale WSNs, multilevel clustering is needed for better connectivity. In this paper, we have proposed HMCA, a multilevel clustering scheme for HWSNs. Our proposed protocol is based on EEMC [2] and uses the idea of minimum reachability power (MRP) for CH selection in heterogeneous environment. Simulation results show that, in presence of heterogeneity HMCA outperforms EEMC.

REFERENCES

Abbasi, A. A., & Younis, M. (2007). A survey on clustering algorithms for wireless sensor networks. *Computer Communications*, *30*, 2826–2841. doi:10.1016/j.comcom.2007.05.024

Chinrungrueng, J., Sununtachaikul, U., & Triamlumlerd, S. (2006). A vehicular monitoring system with power-efficient wireless sensor networks. In *Proceedings of the ITS Telecommunications Conference* (pp. 951-954).

Comeau, F., Sivakumar, S. C., Robertson, W., & Phillips, W. J. (2006). Energy conserving architectures and algorithms for wireless sensor networks. In *Proceedings of the 39th Annual Hawaii International Conference on System Sciences* (pp. 236-246).

Corchado, J. M., Bajo, J., Tapia, D. I., & Abraham, A. (2010). Using heterogeneous wireless sensor networks in a telemonitoring system for healthcare. *IEEE Transactions on Information Technology in Biomedicine*, *14*(2), 234–240. doi:10.1109/TITB.2009.2034369

Estrin, D., Govindan, R., Heidemann, J., & Kumar, S. (1999). Next century challenges: Scalable coordination in sensor networks. In *Proceedings of the 5th Annual ACM/IEEE International Conference on Mobile Computing and Networking* (pp. 263-270).

Fall, K., & Varadhan, K. (2010). *VINT Project. The ucb/lbnl/vint network simulator-ns*. Retrieved from http://www.isi.edu/nsnam/ns

Hadim, S., & Mohamed, N. (2006). Middleware: Middleware challenges and approaches for wireless sensor networks. *IEEE Distributed Systems Online*, *7*(3), 1. doi:10.1109/MDSO.2006.19

Hart, J. K., & Martinez, K. (2006). Environmental sensor networks: A revolution in the earth system science. *Earth-Science Reviews*, *78*, 177–191. doi:10.1016/j.earscirev.2006.05.001

Heinzelman, W. R., Chandrakasan, A. P., & Balakrishnan, H. (2000). Energy efficient communication protocol for wireless microsensor networks. In *Proceedings of the 33rd Hawaii International Conference on System Sciences* (pp. 3005-3014).

Jin, Y., Wang, L., Kim, Y., & Yang, X. (2008). EEMC: An energy-efficient multi-level clustering algorithm for large-scale wireless sensor networks. *Computer Networks*, *52*(3), 542–562. doi:10.1016/j.comnet.2007.10.005

Kay, R., & Mattern, F. (2004). The design space of wireless sensor networks. *IEEE Wireless Communications*, *11*(6), 54–61. doi:10.1109/MWC.2004.1368897

Krishna, P., Vaidya, N. H., Chatterjee, M., & Pradhan, D. (1997). A cluster-based approach for routing in dynamic networks. *ACM SIGCOMM Computer Communication Review*, *27*(2), 49–65. doi:10.1145/263876.263885

Kumar, D., Aseri, T. C., & Patel, R. B. (2009). EEHC: Energy efficient heterogeneous clustered scheme for wireless sensor networks. *Computer Communications*, *32*(4), 662–667. doi:10.1016/j.comcom.2008.11.025

McDonald, B., & Znati, T. (2001). Design and performance of a distributed dynamic clustering algorithm for ad-hoc networks. In *Proceedings of the Annual Simulation Symposium* (pp. 27-35).

Mhatre, V., Rosenberg, C., Kofman, D., Mazumdar, R., & Shroff, N. (2004). Design of surveillance sensor grids with a lifetime constraint. In *Proceedings of the 1ˢᵗ European Workshop on Wireless Sensor Networks*, Berlin, Germany (LNCS 2920, pp. 263-275).

Ni, S., Tseng, Y., Chen, Y., & Sheu, P. (1999). The broadcast storm problem in a mobile ad hoc network. In *Proceedings of the Annual ACM/IEEE International Conference on Mobile Computing and Networking* (pp. 151-162).

Qing, L., Zhu, Q., & Wang, M. (2006). Design of a distributed energy-efficient clustering algorithm for heterogeneous wireless sensor networks. *Computer Communications, 29*(12), 2230–2237. doi:10.1016/j.comcom.2006.02.017

Rasid, M. F. A., Abdullah, R. S. A. R., Ghazvini, M. H. F., & Vahabi, M. (2007). Energy optimization with multi-level clustering algorithm for wireless sensor networks. In *Proceedings of the International Conference on Wireless and Optical Communications Networks* (pp. 1-5).

Shen, C. C., Srisathapornphat, C., & Jaikaeo, C. (2010). Sensor information networking architecture and applications. *IEEE Personal Communications*, 52-59.

Smaragdakis, G., Matta, I., & Bestavros, A. (2004). SEP: A stable election protocol for clustered heterogeneous wireless sensor networks. In *Proceeding of the International Workshop on SANPA* (pp. 251-261).

Soni, S., & Chand, N. (2010). Energy efficient multilevel clustering to prolong the lifetime of wireless sensor networks. *Journal of Computing, 2*(5), 158–165.

Xinfang, Y., Jiangtao, X., Chicharo, J. F., & Yanguang, Y. (2008). An energy-aware multilevel clustering algorithm for wireless sensor networks. In *Proceedings of the International Conference on Intelligent Sensors, Sensor Networks and Information Processing* (pp. 387-392).

Yan, H., Xu, Y., & Gidlund, M. (2009). Experimental e-health applications in wireless sensor networks. In *Proceedings of the International Conference on Communications and Mobile Computing* (pp. 563-567).

Yarvis, M., Kushalnagar, N., & Singh, H. (2005). Exploiting heterogeneity in sensor networks. In *Proceedings of the 24ᵗʰ Annual Joint IEEE INFOCOM Conference* (pp. 878-890).

This work was previously published in the International Journal of Mobile Computing and Multimedia Communications, Volume 3, Issue 3, edited by Ismail Khalil and Edgar Weippl, pp. 62-79, copyright 2011 by IGI Publishing (an imprint of IGI Global).

Chapter 19
Analysis of Sensors' Coverage through Application–Specific WSN Provisioning Tool

Sami J. Habib
Kuwait University, Kuwait

ABSTRACT

This paper presents an automated provisioning tool for the deployment of sensors within wireless sensor networks (WSN) where we have employed evolutionary approach as a search technique to find the maximal coverage under minimal deployment cost. The coverage area is partitioned into M by N cells to reduce the search space from continuous to discrete by considering the placement of sensors at the centroid of each cell. The author has explored the relationship between various cell's sizes versus the total number of deployed sensors. The experimental results show that when the number of cells to cover the service area from X by X cells to 2X by 2X cells is increased, on average this increases the cost by 3 folds. In this regard, it is due to the increase of the number of required sensors by an average of six folds, while improving the coverage ratio by only 9%. A custom-made graphical user interface (GUI) has been developed and embedded within the proposed automated provisioning tool to illustrate the deployment area with the placed sensors at step of the deployment process.

INTRODUCTION

Wireless sensor network (WSN) offers a platform for many civilian and military applications for monitoring hazard areas with minimal human interventions. The sensors are scattered over the monitoring area with the expectation to adequately cover the target region (Crossbow). This is very

challenging problem to ensure that the area to be monitored is covered adequately; therefore, we have developed and utilized a custom-made provisioning tool to find feasible deployment of minimal sensors to cover the given area. The initial deployment of WSN involves a fundamental problem, which is known as the coverage. The coverage problem has a number of interpretations

DOI: 10.4018/978-1-4666-2163-3.ch019

depending on the characteristics and applications of sensors. However, many researchers have considered the coverage as the measure of quality of service of a sensor network (Dasgupta, Kukreja, & Kalpakis, 2003). For example, in the battle field monitoring, one may ask how well WSN can observe the activity of a tank's movements in the battle field (area to be monitored), and what is the likelihood that a tank's movements in a specific location will be detected in a given time frame.

We used the analogous of placing and integrating modules of integrated circuit (IC) into a circuit board as placing sensor devices in a monitoring area. Since both problems are known to be NP-complete; there is no known polynomial time algorithm to solve either problem. To simplify the placement and integration modules of integrated circuit (IC) into a circuit board, researchers have divided the problem into two sub-problems: floorplan and placement. The floorplan problem is to divide the area into well-defined cells, and then it determines the best cells to place the sensors with maximal coverage, minimal number of deployed sensors. In this paper, we are extending further our previous work (Habib, 2007; Habib & Safar, 2007) by analyzing sensor's coverage with respect to various cell's sizes.

We have employed an evolutionary approach to search the design space for the best coverage, and we have explored the relationship between various cell's sizes versus the total number of deployed sensors. Our experimental results show when we increase the number of cells to cover the service area from X by X cells to 2X by 2X cells, on average this increases the cost by 3 folds. Thus, it is due to the increase of the number of required sensors by an average of six folds, while improving the coverage ratio by only 9%. A custom-made graphical user interface (GUI) has been developed and embedded within the proposed automated provisioning tool to illustrate the service area with the deployed sensors at step of the deployment process.

The rest of the paper is organized into sections. Next, the literature survey of the provisioning tools employed to analyze the coverage problem within WSN is described, followed by the description of typical coverage problem in WSN. Next, the internal view of the provision tool to solve the floorplan and placement sub-problems in an optimal way is presented, followed by the illustration of experimental results generated by the proposed evolutionary methodology. Finally, the conclusion and future developments are presented.

RELATED WORK

Many researchers (Bhardwaj & Chandrakasan, 2002; Haenggi, 2003; Kalpakis, Dasgupta, & Namjoshi, 2002; Krishnamachari & Ordonez, 2003; Pan, Hou, Cai, Shi, & Shen, 2003; Sadagopan & Krishnamachari, 2004) focused their efforts on increasing the lifespan of sensor devices by reducing the coverage. Researchers (Shih, Cho, Ickes, Min, Sinha, Wang, & Chandrakasan, 2001; Woo & Cullar, 2001; Ye, Heidemann, & Estrin, 2002) focused on the physical and media access layers within WSN, where others focused their research on routing and transport protocols (Braginsky & Estrin, 2002; Ganesan, Govidan, Shenkar, & Estrin, 2001; Heinzelman, Chandrakasan, & Balarishnan, 2000). Also, researchers (Bahl & Padmanabhan, 2000; Nicules & Nath, 2003; Savvide, Han, & Strivastava, 2001) focused on localization and position applications of WSN. However, all the above research activities have assumed that the coverage problem is predetermined.

The sensor devices can be deployed in the service area either in arbitrary or random fashion. When we employ either arbitrary or random sensors placement, the service area should be well-covered or monitored by the sensors devices. Thus, the coverage has been formulated in various ways. The coverage problem has been formulated as a decision problem by Huang and Tseng (2005), with an objective to determine whether every point in the service area is covered by at least k sensors, where k is a predefined value. Li, Wan, and Frieder (2003) formulated the coverage problem as a problem of finding the best-coverage path between a source and a destination, where all the nodes in the path represent sensor devices of WSN. Here a path designates the coverage area from source and destination. They developed a distributed algorithm to search for the best-coverage path.

The intrinsic properties of coverage/lifetime were identified in terms of Gaussian distribution parameters of WSN during the design stage by Wang, Bin, and Agrawal (2008). They further determined the sensor deployment strategies for a WSN that could satisfy a predefined coverage and lifetime. They developed two deployment algorithms based on analytical models and their algorithms were shown to effectively increase the WSN lifetime. Few researchers focused on solving coverage problems using homogeneous sensors, having same sensing radii (Meguerdichian, Koushanfar, Potkonjak, & Srivastava, 2001; Quintao, Nakamura, & Mateus, 2004). Kar and Banerjee (2003) proposed an algorithm to solve the coverage problem of a planar region using fewer numbers of homogeneous sensors. They assumed that the sensing radius and communication radius were equal.

Quintao, Nakamura, and Mateus (2004) employed Genetic Algorithm to solve an on-demand coverage problem. Zheng, Pu, Zeng, Liu, and Xiong (2005) discussed the issues and solutions on the coverage problem. A mathematical model was discussed to compute minimum number of nodes under required coverage quality and they employed genetic algorithm to maximize the coverage quality. In this work, we consider a similar formulation of the coverage problem as discussed in (Quintao, Nakamura, & Mateus, 2004; Quintao, Nakamura, & Mateus, 2005; Kar & Banerjee, 2003). However, we have assumed that the cell size is not fixed, and the service area can be floor planned in arbitrary ways. Also, we

used object-oriented classes to represent chromosomes and their genes. Our provision tool coded within Genetic Algorithm is attached with a sensor device library with heterogeneous sensor features, such as the variable radius of coverage (maximum up to 1000 meters) and cost (ranging from $50 to $10,000).

DESCRIPTION OF TYPICAL COVERAGE PROBLEM IN WSN

We are given a rectangular sensor deployment area (A) with two dimensions: width (W) and height (H) as shown in Figure 1. The deployment area is obstacle-free and it can be floorplanned into M x N cells, where all cells can have either the same dimensions or different dimensions, as shown in Figure 2.

The variable $\beta_{m,n}$ represents a center of mass of cell that is located at m^{th} row and n^{th} column as illustrated in Figure 2. We have classified the set of center-of-mass points as the set of demand points, which represent all possible locations to place a sensor device.

Therefore, we have reduced the continuous design space with infinite demand points into discrete design space with finite demand points. Thus, the coverage problem becomes a matching

Figure 1. Deployment area to be monitored by WSN

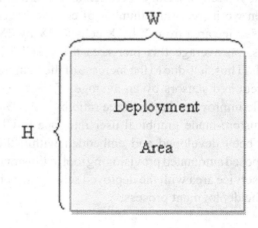

Figure 2. A floorplanned deployment area divided into M x N cells

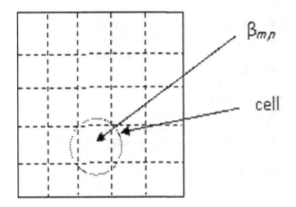

$$\sum_{\forall i} \sum_{\forall j} \alpha_{k,i,j} = 1, \text{ for a given k} \tag{2}$$

$$\sum_{\forall k} \sum_{i \in M, j \in N} \left(\left(\text{COST} \left(\Omega_k \right) \right) \times \alpha_{k,i,j} \right) \leq C \tag{3}$$

$$L \leq \sum_{i \in M} \sum_{j \in N} \beta_{i,j} \leq U \tag{4}$$

$$1 \leq \sum_{\forall k} \Omega_k \leq \left(M \times N \right) \tag{5}$$

$$\Omega \in \left\{ 0, 1 \right\}, \quad \alpha \in \left\{ 0, 1 \right\}, \text{ and } C \in R \tag{6}$$

problem between two sets. The first set represents the demand point $\beta_{m,n}$, and the second set is the sensor device library in Table 1.

In a previous work (Habib, 2007); we formulated the optimization problem for finding the maximum coverage, subject to a set of constraints. The objective function is to achieve a maximum coverage of cells as stated in Equation 1.

$$\max \sum_{k \in S} \sum_{i \in M, j \in N} \left(\Omega_k \times \alpha_{k,i,j} \times RC_k \right) \tag{1}$$

Ω_k represents an allocation variable of a sensor device; $\Omega_k = 1$ indicates that a sensor device k has been allocated to be placed within WSN. Otherwise, it is not allocated. $\alpha_{k,i,j}$ represents a binding variable; $\alpha_{k,i,j} = 1$ indicates that an allocated sensor device k has been placed/assigned at a cell within i row and j column location. RC_k represents the radius of coverage for the sensor device k, which is listed in the sensor device library. Since we assume that the radius of the inscribed circle of the cells in figure 2 have variable radius of coverage, the maximum of coverage is attained, when RC_k equals radius of the cell in which it is allotted. This objective function is subject to a set of Equations 2, 3, 4, 5, and 6.

Equation 2 ensures that an allocated sensor device k is placed at most in one demand point. Equation 3 ensures that the total cost of any solution should satisfy the budget threshold C. Equation 4

Table 1. A library of sensor devices used by our evolutionary methodology

Sensor Device Identification	Sensor Type	Radius of Coverage (meters)	Sensor Device Cost ($)
1	Temperature	3	50
2	Temperature	5	150
3	Temperature	8	160
4	Temperature	10	250
5	Temperature	15	300
6	Temperature	20	600
7	Temperature	25	700
8	Temperature	30	800
9	Temperature	35	825
10	Temperature	40	850
11	Temperature	45	900
12	Temperature	50	1000
13	Temperature	100	2500
14	Temperature	500	6000
15	Temperature	1000	10000

*The library is expected to be updated periodically to cope with the changes in technologies and costs.

ensures that the number of cells generated from the floor-planning is bound between upper and lower values. Equation 5 ensures that the number of allocated sensor devices should not exceed the total number of cells in the service area. Equation 6 defines the allocation and binding variables as a Boolean, and the budget threshold as a real number.

INTERNAL VIEW OF EVOLUTIONARY BASED PROVISIONING TOOL

The computations of floorplan and placement sub-problems require an enormous computational effort to achieve optimal solutions. Therefore, we have selected the Genetic Algorithm (GA), which is a member of the evolutionary algorithm family, to search the discrete design space for good solutions. GA uses a population of chromosomes, which represent the candidate solutions, to evolve toward better solutions. Through some genetic operators such as a mutation and crossover, these chromosomes will reach the optimum or near-optimum solutions. The evolution process starts from a feasible population of completely random chromosomes, and occurs over a number of generations. In each generation, multiple chromosomes are stochastically selected from the current population, modified using different operators to form a new offspring, which becomes the new chromosomes in the next iteration of the algorithm. The basic structure of GA, as shown in Figure 3, is a powerful search technique that is used to solve many combinatorial problems (Michalewicz, 1994).

Genetic Algorithm

The genetic algorithm starts with an initial population $P(t=0)$ of solutions encoded as chromosomes. An initial population is most often generated randomly but a heuristic algorithm can be used.

Figure 3. Basic structure of genetic algorithm

```
1  begin
2    t = 0;
3    initialize_chromosomes_P(t);
4    evaluate_chromosomes_P(t);
5    while (number_of_generations<=Max_Gen)
6    begin
7      t = t + 1;
8      select P(t) from P(t - 1);
9      mutate_subset_of_P(t);
10     crossover_subset_of_P(t);
11     evaluate_chromosomes_P(t);
12   end
13 end
```

Each chromosome is made of a sequence of genes and every gene controls the inheritance of specific attributes of the solution's characteristics. A fitness function measures the quality of the chromosome (total coverage area). A fit chromosome suggests a better solution. In the evolution process relatively fit chromosomes reproduce new chromosomes and inferior chromosomes die. This process continues until a chromosome with desirable fitness is found. These selected chromosomes, known as parents, are used to reproduce the next generation of chromosomes, known as the offspring. The evolution process involves two genetic operations namely, mutation and crossover. A mutation operator arbitrarily alters one or more genes of a randomly selected chromosome. The intuition behind the mutation operator is to introduce a missing feature in the population. Our mutation has two options; either it replaces an existed sensor device with a new one or it selects an empty cell and assigns a new sensor device to it. A crossover operator combines features of two selected chromosomes (parents) to form two similar chromosomes (offspring) by swapping genes of the parent chromosomes. The intuition behind the crossover operator is to exchange information between different potential solutions.

Chromosome Representation

We represent a solution of the coverage problem as two object-oriented link lists, as shown in Figure 4. We combined all chromosomes in the population of size P into one data structure, which comprises of one link list representing all chromosomes and each chromosome has one link list representing all its genes, where each gene symbolizes a sensor device that is allocated to a demand point.

Two types of nodes are declared as two different classes, where the first class represents a chromosome's attributes and the second class represents a gene's features. Also, we maintain a dynamic matrix to illustrate all the cells and demand points.

EXPERIMENTAL RESULTS

We have coded the coverage optimization problem in the evolutionary domain using JAVA as a programming language. For all our experiments, we assigned the population size, the number of generation, the crossover rate and mutation rate to be 100, 1000, 0.5, and 0.2 respectively. The budget threshold C is set to $150,000. In our experiments, we presented our service area by 4 different sizes of cells: 5 cells by 5 cells, 10 cells by 10 cells, 15 cells by 15 cells, and 20 cells by 20 cells. Hence, we varied the cells' sizes from 160 meters by 160 meters to 640 meters by 640 meters. All the experiments are executed on a PC platform and each experimental run took under five minutes. Moreover, in all of our experiments, as the number of generations increased, the behavior of our algorithm changed and then it reached a plateau after 200 generations.

In each of the Figure 5, Figure 6, and Figure 7, we illustrate four curves that tracked the average behavior of the whole population with respect to the increase in the number of cells, used to represent the service area as the number of generation increases. Figure 5 illustrates the average coverage ratio behavior of our solutions. The curves show that as the number of generations increased, the average coverage ratio of our solutions was between 86% and 96% for all different cell sizes.

Figure 4. A population of chromosomes

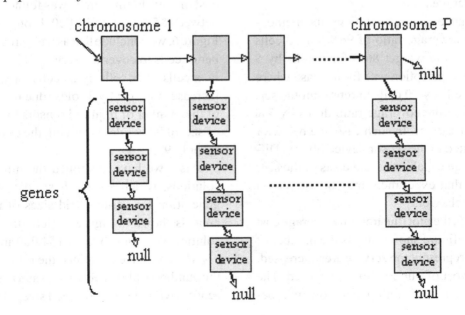

Figure 5. Relation between the average coverage ratio and the number of generations for different numbers of cells used to represent the service area

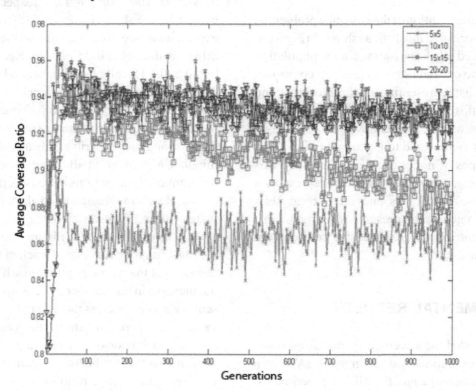

However, as the number of cells used to represent the service area increases, the methodology gets a higher coverage ratio.

On average, over all generations, the methodology gets a coverage ratio of 96% for 20 cells by 20 cells, while we get 86% for 5 cells by 5 cells. The only exception was for the case where we used 10 cells by 10 cells to represent the service area. Here the coverage ratio drops by 7% after 600 generations. In such case, the behavior could be related to the sensor device library. Different coverage capabilities and costs of the sensors used in that experiment may be the reason behind that behavior.

In Figure 6, the plot illustrates the average cost solution. The figure shows that as the number of cells used to represent the service area increased, the average cost of our solutions increased. The average solution cost of all generations was be-

tween $10,000 for 5 cells by 5 cells and $120,000 for 20 cells by 20 cells. In addition, the average cost of 100 chromosomes was found to be bound between $5,600 and $13,000. From Figure 5 and Figure 6, we conclude that as we increase the number of cells to cover the service area from x cells by x cells to 2x cells by 2x cells, on average this increases the cost by 3 folds (due to the increase of the number of required sensors by an average of six folds), while improving the coverage ratio by only 9%.

Also, we have examined the minimum cost solutions, which are the best cost during each generation for various grid sizes of the service area, as shown in Figure 7. Here, the cost of the solution was bound between $4,000 and $90,000.

Also, we have examined the relation between the number of allocated sensors and the cost of the sensors with the grid size (cell size) of the service

Figure 6. Relation between the average solution cost and the number of generations for various cell size representing the service area

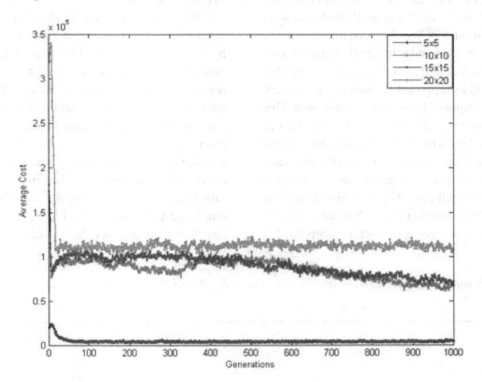

Figure 7. Relation between the minimum cost and the number of generations for various cell size representing the service area

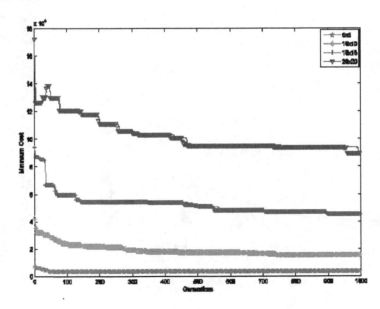

area, as shown in Figure 8. As illustrated, when the number of cells increases, the number of allocated sensors also increases (line graph) thereby showing a linear relationship. We observed the same in the graph between cost and grid size (bar graph). This is due to the fact that as we increase the number of cells used to represent the service area; more sensors are required to cover the whole area. This in turn increases the cost. Here the selection of the sensors should be optimized with the cost and coverage, so that sensors with a smaller coverage range can used to cover smaller service areas to reduce the overall cost. Figure 5 also illustrates that the average number of neighbored cells covered by a sensor's coverage radius is around 2-4

neighbors regardless of the number of cells used to cover the service.

Hence, our optimization algorithm strives to reduce the cost by trying to cover smaller areas by each sensor. This would be cost effective if the cost of a sensor increases more than linearly with respect to its coverage radius. We concluded from these early experiments that the number of cells used to cover a service area affects the coverage ratio and design cost. This is due to the fact that one sensor with its radius of coverage is able to cover an entire cell and some of its neighbors rather than allocating multiple sensors to cover one large cell. Finally, in Figure 9 we show a snapshot of our Sensor CAD Visualizer. It provides

Figure 8. Relationship between the average coverage level and the grid size

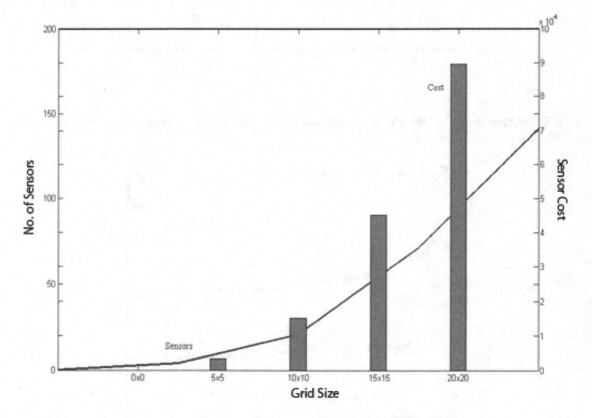

Figure 9. Sensor CAD visualizer snapshot shows 88 sensors used as coverage sensors in the 90 generation of the run costing $57,855 with a coverage ratio of 98.6%

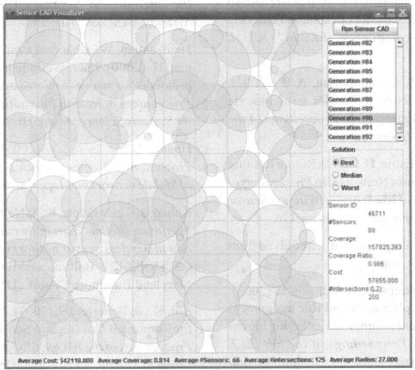

a graphical user interface that lets the user control the genetic algorithm, visualizes the solutions graphically, shows how it would look like in real life, and lets you go through different generations that were produced by the GA.

CONCLUSION AND FUTURE WORK

We have modeled the coverage problem in the wireless sensor networks as two sub-problems: floorplan and placement. Such modeling has reduced the design space into a discrete one by assigning sensors into the cells. We combined the two sub-problems into one optimization problem so that it can achieve the maximum coverage possible. An evolutionary approach was used to search the design space for optimal placement of sensors with an objective to maximize the coverage area, and our early experiments demonstrate very promising results, especially when we vary the number of cells used to cover the service area. We will continue to improve our methodology to consider the transmission power during the coverage problem while reducing the energy utilization. In addition, we will experiment on increasing the number of neighbors that could be covered by a sensor to more than its direct four neighbors.

ACKNOWLEDGMENT

The author would like to knowledge the support of Research Administration, Kuwait University under Research Grant no. EO05/06.

REFERENCES

Bahl, P., & Padmanabhan, V. (2000). RADAR: An In-Building RF-Based User Location and Tracking System. In *Proceedings of the IEEE INFOCOM*, Tel-Aviv, Israel.

Bhardwaj, M., & Chandrakasan, A. P. (2002). Bounding the lifetime of sensor networks via optimal role assignments. In *Proceedings of the IEEE INFOCOM*, New York.

Braginsky, D., & Estrin, D. (2002). Rumor Routing Algorithm for Sensor Networks. In *Proceedings of ACM International Workshop on Wireless Sensor Networks and Applications*, Atlanta, GA.

Crossbow Technology Inc. (n.d.). Retreived from http://www.xbow.com

Dasgupta, K., Kukreja, M., & Kalpakis, K. (2003). Topology-aware placement and role assignment for energy-efficient information gathering in sensor networks. In *Procesedings of the 8th IEEE International Symposium on Computers and Communication*, Turkey.

Ganesan, D., Govindan, R., Shenker, A., & Estrin, D. (2001). Highly Resilient Energy Efficient Multipath Routing in Wireless Sensor Networks. In *Proceedings of ACM Mobile Computations and Communications Review* (Vol. 5, No. 4, pp. 11-25).

Habib, S. (2007). Modeling and simulating coverage in sensor networks. *Computer Communications*, *30*, 1029–1035. doi:10.1016/j.comcom.2006.08.026

Habib, S. J., & Safar, M. (2007). Sensitivity Study of Sensor's Coverage within Wireless Sensor Networks. In *Proceedings of the 16th International Conference on Computer Communications and Networks* (pp. 876-881).

Haenggi, M. (2003). Energy-balancing strategies for wireless sensor networks. In *Proceedings of the International Symposium on Circuits and Systems*, Bangkok, Thailand.

Heinzelman, W., Chandrakasan, A., & Balarishnan, H. (2000). Energy-efficient communication protocols for wireless microsensor networks. In *Proceedings of Hawaii International Conference on Systems Science*, Maui, HI.

Huang, C., & Tseng, Y. (2005). The coverage Problem in a Wireless Sensor Network. *Journal of Mobile networks and applications, 10*, 519-528.

Kalpakis, K., Dasgupta, K., & Namjoshi, P. (2002). *Maximum lifetime data gathering and aggregation in wireless sensor networks* (Tech. Rep. No. CS TR-02-12). Baltimore, MD: University of Maryland Baltimore County (UMBC).

Kar, K., & Banerjee, S. (2003). Node Placement for Connected Coverage in Sensor Networks. In *Proceedings of the WiOpt, Modeling and Optimization in Mobile, Ad Hoc and Wireless Networks*.

Krishnamachari, B., & Ordonez, F. (2003). Analysis of energy-efficient, fair routing in wireless sensor networks through non-linear optimization. In *Proceedings of Workshop on Wireless Ad hoc, Sensor, and Wearable Networks, IEEE Vehicular Technology Conference*, Orlando, FL.

Li, X., Wan, P., & Frieder, O. (2003). Coverage in wireless ad hoc sensor networks. *IEEE Transactions on Computers, 52*(6), 753–763. doi:10.1109/TC.2003.1204831

Meguerdichian, S., Koushanfar, F., Potkonjak, M., & Srivastava, M. (2001). Coverage Problems in Wireless Ad-Hoc Sensor Networks. In *Proceedings of the IEEE INFOCOM*, AK.

Michalewicz, Z. (1994). *Genetic Algorithms + Data Structure = Evolution Programs*. Berlin: Springer Verlag.

Nicules, D., & Nath, B. (2003). Ad-Hoc Positioning System (APS) Using AoA. In *Proceedings of IEEE INFOCOM*, San Francisco.

Pan, J., Hou, Y. T., Cai, L., Shi, Y., & Shen, S. X. (2003). Topology Control for Wireless Sensor Networks. In *Proceedings of the International Conference on Mobile Computing and Networking*, San Diego.

Quintao, F., Nakamura, F., & Mateus, G. (2004). An Evolutive Approach for the Coverage Problem in Wireless Sensor Networks. In *Proceedings of the 24th Brazilian Computer Society*.

Quintao, F., Nakamura, F., & Mateus, G. (2005). Evolutionary Algorithm for the Dynamic Coverage Problem Applied to Wireless Sensor Networks Design. In *Proceedings of IEEE Congress on Evolutionary Computations*, Edinburgh, UK.

Sadagopan, N., & Krishnamachari, B. (2004). Maximizing Data Extraction in Energy-Limited Sensor Networks. In *Proceedings of the IEEE INFOCOM*, Hong Kong, China.

Savvide, A., Han, C., & Strivastava, M. (2001). Dynamic Fine-Grained Localization in Ad-Hoc Networks of Sensors. In *Proceedings of the ACM International Conference on Mobile Computing and Networking*, Rome, Italy.

Shih, E., Cho, S., Ickes, N., Min, R., Sinha, A., Wang, A., & Chandrakasan, A. (2001). Physical Layer Driven Protocol and Algorithm Design for Energy-Efficient Wireless Sensor Networks. In *Proceedings of the ACM International Conference on Mobile Computing and Networking*, Rome, Italy.

Wang, D., Bin, X., & Agrawal, D. P. (2008). Coverage and life time optimization of wireless sensor networks with Gaussian distribution. *IEEE Transactions on Mobile Computing*, 7(12), 1444–1458. doi:10.1109/TMC.2008.60

Woo, A., & Culler, D. (2001). A Transmission Control Scheme for Media Access in Sensor Networks. In *Proceedings of the ACM International Conference on Mobile Computing and Networking*, Rome, Italy.

Ye, W., Heidemann, J., & Estrin, D. (2002). An Energy-Efficient MAC Protocol for Wireless Sensor Networks. In *Proceedings of the IEEE INFOCOM*, New York.

Zhang, S., Pu, J., Zeng, X., Liu, Y., & Xiong, Z. (2008). Issue and Solution on coverage and performance for wireless sensor networks. In *Proceedings of the AINTEC'08*, Bangkok, Thailand (pp. 131-137).

This work was previously published in the International Journal of Mobile Computing and Multimedia Communications, Volume 3, Issue 1, edited by Ismail Khalil and Edgar Weippl, pp. 50-61, copyright 2011 by IGI Publishing (an imprint of IGI Global).

Section 4
Audiovisual Recognition

Chapter 20
Primary Research on Arabic Visemes, Analysis in Space, and Frequency Domain

Fatma Zohra Chelali
Houari Boumedienne University of Sciences and Technologies, Algeria

Amar Djeradi
Houari Boumedienne University of Sciences and Technologies, Algeria

ABSTRACT

Visemes are the unique facial positions required to produce phonemes, which are the smallest phonetic unit distinguished by the speakers of a particular language. Each language has multiple phonemes and visemes, and each viseme can have multiple phonemes. However, current literature on viseme research indicates that the mapping between phonemes and visemes is many-to-one: there are many phonemes which look alike visually, and hence they fall into the same visemic category. To evaluate the performance of the proposed method, the authors collected a large number of speech visual signal of five Algerian speakers male and female at different moments pronouncing 28 Arabic phonemes. For each frame the lip area is manually located with a rectangle of size proportional to 120*160 and centred on the mouth, and converted to gray scale. Finally, the mean and the standard deviation of the values of the pixels of the lip area are computed by using 20 images for each phoneme sequence to classify the visemes. The pitch analysis is investigated to show its variation for each viseme.

INTRODUCTION

Speech comprises of a mixture of audio frequencies, and every speech sound belongs to one of the two main classes known as vowels and consonants. Vowels and consonants belong to the basic linguistic units known as phonemes, which can be mapped to visible mouth shapes called visemes. Visemes and phonemes can be used as the basic units of visible articulatory mouth shapes (Waters et al., 1993). A phoneme is an abstract representation of a sound, and the set of phonemes in a

DOI: 10.4018/978-1-4666-2163-3.ch020

language is defined as the minimum number of symbols required to represent every word in that language (Breen et al., 1996).

The set of visemes in a language is often defined as the number of visibly different phonemes in that language. A simple definition of viseme would be that a viseme could be generated from a set of archetypal sounds in a language based on the phonemes of that language (Breen et al., 1996). Möttönen et al. (2000) define a viseme set as phoneme realizations that are visually inextricable from each other. In lip reading studies viseme categories can be defined as clustering response distributions to observed phoneme articulations. These clusters are then used to find those phoneme articulations, which are perceived to be similar. Typically a cluster is considered as a viseme category if the proportion of within cluster responses is at least 70% of the total amount of responses to the phoneme articulations that are included in the cluster (Möttönen et al., 2000).

To date, there has been no precise definition for the term, but in general it has come to refer to a speech segment that is visually contrastive from another (Möttönen et al., 2000; Ezzat et al., 1999). In their work, they define a viseme to be a static lip shape image that is visually contrastive from another.

It is also important to point out that that the map from phonemes to visemes is also one-to-many: the same phoneme can have many different visual forms. This phenomenon is termed coarticulation, and it occurs because the neighboring phonemic context in which a sound is uttered influences the lip shape for that sound (Ezzat et al., 2000).

However, current literature on viseme research indicates that the mapping between phonemes and visemes is many-to-one: there are many phonemes which look alike visually, and hence they fall into the same visemic category. This is particularly true, for example, in cases where two sounds are identical in manner and place of articulation, but differ only in voicing characteristics (Ezzat et al., 2000).

Several standards for visemes (Tiddeman et al., 2002) exist but they were developed for English language. Since each language comprises of a different phonetic set (sounds) therefore, visemes have to be identified separately for each language. Möttönen et al. (2000) developed a Finnish talking head, which had to identify Finnish visemes for each Finnish phoneme (Rafay et al., 2003; Ezzat et al., 1999).

Bastanfard et al. (2009) proposed a novel method adopting an image-based approach for grouping visemes in the Persian language considering coarticulation effect. In their work, visemes can be recognized in two ways: Model-based, and image-based. In model based approach, lip is identified by its parameters, in that various geometrical factors are specified to lip shape. Model-based approach has low accuracy and high execution time while the iteration of this algorithm may cause local minimum. In image-based approach, lip images are considered, where all work is done on lip pixels (Bastanfard et al., 2009).

In addition, Bastanfard et al. (2009) investigate the coarticulation effect and phoneme position in syllable and a new image-based approach is used for Persian viseme extraction and classification. The focus is on cv and cvc combinations in Persian (Bastanfard et al., 2009).

Abou Zliekha et al. (2006) present an emotional audio-visual Text to speech system for the Arabic language. The system described is based on two entities: an emotional audio text to speech system which generates speech depending on the input text and the desired emotion type, and an emotional Visual model which generates the talking heads, by forming the corresponding visemes. For their Arabic audio-visual speech synthesis system, they've built an inventory of Arabic visemes classes and developed a phoneme-viseme mapping. Thirteen (13) Arabic visemes were investigated for Arabic language (Abou Zliekha et al., 2006).

Foo et al. (2004) develop the performance of automatic speech recognition (ASR) system that can be significantly enhanced with additional information from visual speech elements such as the movement of lips, tongue, and teeth, especially under noisy environment. The approach makes use of adaptive boosting (AdaBoost) and hidden Markov models (HMMs) to build an AdaBoost-HMM classifier. Their study on lip dynamics shows that the motion of the lips can be partitioned into three phases during viseme production. The first is the initial phase, starting from a closed mouth or the end of the last viseme production to the beginning of sound production of the viseme investigated. During this interval, the sound of the target viseme is not fully articulated and the lips are characterized with sharp changes. The next phase is the articulation phase, which is the time when the sound is produced. The third phase is the end phase when the mouth restores to the relaxed state or transits to the production of the next viseme (Foo et al., 2004).

APPLICATIONS OF VISEME IDENTIFICATION

In lip-reading, audiovisual recognition, speech/ speaker recognition, visemes are used as basic speech units. A viseme is a group of phonemes, whose visual expression is the same. For example phonemes p, b, and m create one viseme. A big problem in lip-reading is the influence of subsequently pronounced visemes in one word (co-articulation effect). Visemes can be classified as influencing and influenced. The shape of viseme can be altered by impact of surrounding visemes. This phenomenon complicates the lip-reading.

Identifying the viseme or viseme categories is the basic problem faced while designing realistic computer facial animations. In order to lip-synch the mouth shape to different sounds in a language, the mouth shapes i.e., visemes corresponding to each phoneme have to be calculated. Computer facial animation has found wide applications in the fields of visual speech synthesis, deaf children

education and other kinds of language training techniques.

One of the earliest applications of visual speech synthesis was to use it to understand the mechanism of speech perception. It was discovered that there are three mechanisms involved in speech perception: auditory, visual and audio-visual. So perception of speech could only be well studied with the help of visual speech (visual auditory) experiments (Rafay et al., 2003). Moreover, improvement in visual speech synthesis can only be brought by studying in detail, how real humans produce speech (Rafay et al., 2003; Cohen et al., 1993).

By using both auditory and visual modalities scientists were able to better understand the speech than by relying only on audition, especially if the speech was exposed to noise, bandwidth limitations, hearing limitations or other disturbances (Rafay et al., 2003).

In one of the recent applications, visual speech synthesis is being used to explore new ways of presenting information and enhancing computer user interfaces. Facial animations combined with speech synthesizers to provide a unique form of computer user interaction, which will make computers accessible to a much wider range of people. This application will help realize the dream of a true personable computer (Rafay et al., 2003; Möttönen et al., 2000).

Another application of this technology is in Deaf Children Education. Deaf and hearing-impaired children use auditory visual speech (visual auditory) perception in order to lip-read the words. Children with hearing impairment require guided instruction in speech perception and production. Some of the distinctions in spoken language cannot be heard with degraded hearing, even when the hearing loss has been compensated by hearing aids or cochlear implants. To overcome this limitation, visual speech can be used as speech targets for the child with hearing loss. It was observed by Möttönen et al. (2000) that visual information improves the intelligibility of both synthetic and natural acoustic speech by approximately 15% to 50%. Lip reading research has shown that deaf children can receive 70% of the information in speech if the combined approach of sight with sound (visual auditory) is used (Rafay et al., 2003; Cohen et al., 1993; Möttönen et al., 2000).

Moreover, human teachers have proved insufficient for teaching deaf children. Due to specific articulatory and phonetic features associated with a human teacher many deaf children complain that they can only understand their teacher. This provides motivation to develop an automated facial animation whose parameters can be changed at runtime to model the viseme shapes of persons of different ages and sex. This technology can also be used in general language training, as in the learning of non-native languages and in remedial instruction with language disabled children. Speech therapy during the recovery from brain trauma could also benefit from this. Children with reading disabilities could profit from interactions with animation of talking head (Rafay et al., 2003; Cohen et al., 1993).

The purpose of our work is to introduce an Arabic viseme system based on visual speech database through statistics analysis. We haven't taken co-articulation of visemes in context. Experiments were carried in the "laboratoire de communication parlée et traitement du signal (LCPTS)" of the Electronics and computer Sciences Faculty, Algiers, ALGERIA

The corpus was recorded with a Canon camera acquiring audio and video signals in a synchronized and unsynchronized manner in order to analyze an audiovisual sequence for speakers saying a monosyllabic sequence, and to analyze separately the unsynchronized signals: the still images and the speech signals for speakers pronouncing the Arabic phonemes.

The paper is organised as follows. A brief description of the Arabic language is presented. We detail the Arabic phoneme database acquisition used in the experiments, we focus in our article on the visual data, this section presents the theory of visemes developed in our work, and the investigation of Pitch was developed for two visemes as illustration. Finally, results obtained are discussed and we close with discussions and conclusion and also suggest future work in this area of research.

ARABIC LANGUAGE

Arabic is a Semitic language, and it is one of the oldest languages in the world. It is the 5th most widely used language nowadays. Standard Arabic has 35 basic Pharyngealized (L) which is rarely used); six are vowels, three long and three short (Satori et al., 2005).

Vowels can be arranged depending on the degree of constriction at the articulation point and on the tongue hump position as presented in Satori et al. (2005). They are relatively easy to identify because of their high energy resulting in instance formant patterns. The vowels are voiced sounds.

Arabic phonemes contain two distinctive classes, which are named pharyngeal and emphatic phonemes. These two classes can be found only in Semitic languages like. The allowed syllables in Arabic language are: CV, CVV, CVC, CVVC, CVCC and CVVCC where V indicates a (long or short) vowel while C indicates a consonant. Arabic utterances can only start with a consonant (Satori et al., 2005).

All Arabic syllables must contain at least one vowel. Also Arabic vowels cannot be initials and can occur either between two consonants or final in a word. Arabic syllables can be classified as short or long. The CV type is a short one while all others are long.

DESCRIPTION OF THE SYSTEM

A Phoneme Database

The corpus is a repetition of the 28 Arabic phonemes spoken by ten (10) native Algerian speaking male and female subjects. A database of facial and speaker features is assigned for one of each known individuals. The recordings were made on camera canon video with 25 frames of size 576*720pixels per second at the speech communication and signal processing Laboratory in Algiers. Then, the data were transferred into computer through IEEE1394 card. The corpus consists of 20 repetitions of every syllabus (phoneme with short vowel) produced by each speaker, 20 still images in format bmp and 20 repetitions for audio file in format wav. We haven't taken co-articulation of visemes in context. For every phoneme, 20 different samples were recorded by ten subjects (Algerian university students: Fazia, Naima, Zohir, Amine, Halim, Nabil, khadidja, Dalila, Mohamed and Hanane). This gives 200 versions of each of 28 Arabic phonemes in our database. The database includes 5600 face images from ten (10) different subjects. The speech signals are acquired during different sessions with a sampling frequency of 22 KHz. Table 1 presents the API representation of the Arabic phonemes.

THE CONSONANT VISEMES

In lip-reading, audiovisual recognition, speech/speaker recognition, visemes are used as basic speech units. A viseme is a group of phonemes, whose visual expression is the same. For example phonemes p, b, and m create one viseme.

To date, there has been no precise definition for the term, but in general it has come to refer to a speech segment that is visually contrastive from another. In this work, we define a viseme to be a static lip shape image that is visually contrastive from another.

Table 1. The phonetic transcription and symbol used for phoneme

Arabic Alphabet	Phonetic Transcription (A P I)	Symbol
ء	[?]	A
ب	[b]	ba
ت	[t]	Ta
ث	[θ]	Tha
ج	[z]	Dja
ح	[h]	H
خ	[x]	Kha
د	[d]	Da
ذ	[ð]	Dha
ر	[r]	Ra
ز	[Z]	Za
س	[s]	Saa
ش	[š]	Cha
ص	[ś]	Ssa
ض	[ð]	Daa
ط	[tˤ]	Taa
ظ	[ð]	Dhaa
ع	[ʕ]	Aa
غ	[ɣ]	Gha
ف	[F]	Fa
ق	[q]	Qua
ك	[k]	Ka
ل	[l]	La
م	[m]	Ma
ن	[n]	Na
ه	[h]	Ha
و	[w]	Wa
ي	[j]	ya

For example, aba /? b?/ and ama /?m?/ are two bilabial signals which differ only in the fact that the former is voiced while the latter is voiceless. This difference, however, does not manifest itself visually, and hence the two phonemes should be placed in the same visemic category (Ezzat et al., 2000).

Visemes are used as basic speech units in lip-reading, audiovisual recognition and speech/speaker recognition. A viseme is a group of phonemes, whose visual expression is the same. Phonemes p, b, and m create one viseme for French/English language.

In our work, we investigate visemes representing the 28 consonantal Arabic phonemes using two techniques, the statistical parameters (mean and standard deviation) for lip, the geometrical parameters for the internal and the external lip contour. Hierarchical Clustering is used to show the intrapersonal and extrapersonnal variation for the same viseme (Figure 1).

STATISTICAL PARAMETERS

For each frame the lip area is manually located with a rectangle of size proportional to 120*160 and centred on the mouth, and converted to gray scale (Figure 2). Finally, the standard deviation of the values of the pixels of the lip area (of size n*m) is computed by using 20 images for each phoneme sequence to classify our visemes. The standard deviation of the values of the pixels of the lip area is computed (Equations 1 and 2): we have 20 images for each monosyllabic sequence. We note that we have used still images for this purpose.

Figure 1. Overview of system acquisition

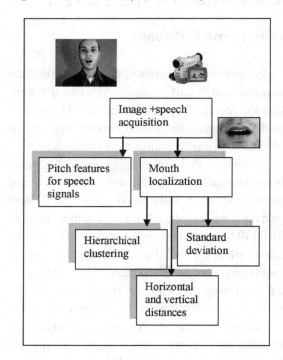

$$\sigma_I = \sqrt{\frac{1}{n*m}\sum_{i,j}(I(i,j)-\bar{I})^2} \qquad (1)$$

where the mean is described as:

$$\bar{I} = \frac{1}{n*m}\sum_{i,j}I(i,j) \qquad (2)$$

Figure 2. Manual mouth extraction

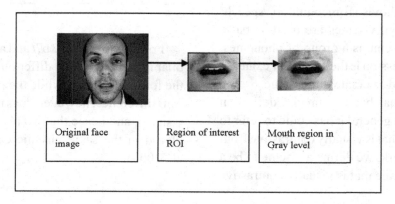

GEOMETRICAL PARAMETERS FOR VISEMES

We use a set of geometrical parameters (Figure 3) based on the internal and external lip shape of the speaker. Several studies have underlined a certain correlation between these geometrical parameters, which allows us to reduce their number to only two corresponding to the height and the width of the internal lip contour (Benoit et al., 1992; Revéret, 1999; Magno et al., 1997). We have chosen to add the parameters of the external contour as mentioned in the work of Wang et al. (2000).

Wang et al. (2000) show the importance to choose appropriate features to represent visual speech. Traditional phonetics research indicates that lip and jaw are the most important among articulators that can be seen from the outside. The shape of other parts of the vocal tract might also be estimated from measurements of the facial movements. Consequently, authors demonstrate that the visual features to be measured all correlate to the lip area. And they are: the height of inner lip, the width of inner lip, the height of outer lip, the width of outer lip, the visible upper teeth, the visible lower teeth, the position of upper lip, the position of jaw, the degree of upper lip protrusion, the degree of lip corner protrusion, the degree of lower lip protrusion, and so on (Wang et al., 2000).

In our work, the region of interest (ROI) containing the speaker's mouth of the different syllabus is considered as the most relevant information used for lip reading. The corresponding region was extracted; the result images of 120*160 pixels of the Region of Interest (ROI) are stored in a BMP format.

EXPERIMENTAL RESULTS

We present in this section results obtained first for Arabic visemes using statistical and geometrical parameters, and then we investigate the hierarchical clustering on one visemic class. A viseme could include several phonemes, since we cannot for example visually differentiate between pronouncing a /b/ or a /m/. Thus, both sounds have the same lip-based realisation. Figure 4 shows the different lip shape for each Arabic phoneme pronounced by a female speaker.

Figure 3. Geometrical parameters (A, A', B, B')

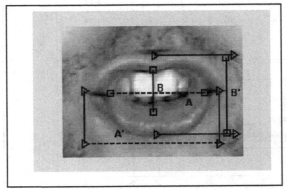

A: the width of the internal lip contour (the first horizontal distance).
A': the width of the external lip contour (the second horizontal distance).
B: the height of the internal lip contour (the first vertical distance).
B': the height of the external lip contour (the second vertical distance).

ARABIC VISEMES

Visemes are used as basic speech units in lip-reading, audiovisual recognition and speech/speaker recognition. A viseme is a group of phonemes, whose visual expression is the same. Phonemes p, b, and m create one viseme for French/English language.

In our work, we investigate visemes representing the 28 consonantal Arabic phonemes using the two methods described earlier. For each frame, the lip area is manually located with a rectangle of size proportional to 120*160, centered on the mouth, and converted to gray scale. Finally, the standard deviation of the values of the pixels of the lip area is computed: we have 20 images for each monosyllabic sequence. We note that we've used still images for this purpose.

Figure 5 and Figure 6 show the standard deviation variation for the ten speakers when pronouncing the syllabic (/ba, ma/ {ب, م }) and (/dja, cha/ {ج, ش}).

Figure 4. Mouth extraction for the 28 Arabic phonemes pronouncing by a female speaker

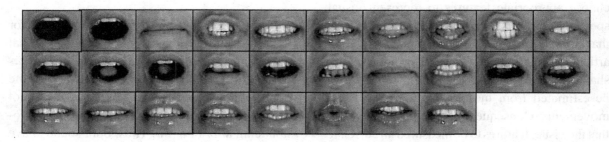

Figure 5. The standard deviation for viseme /ba/ and /ma/

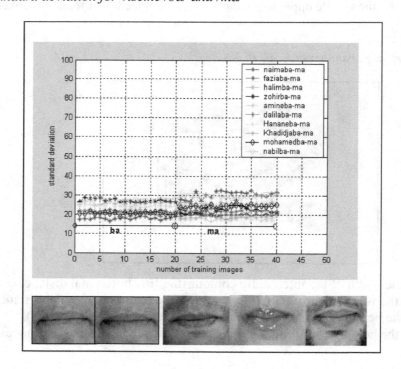

Figure 6. The standard deviation for viseme /dja/ and /cha/

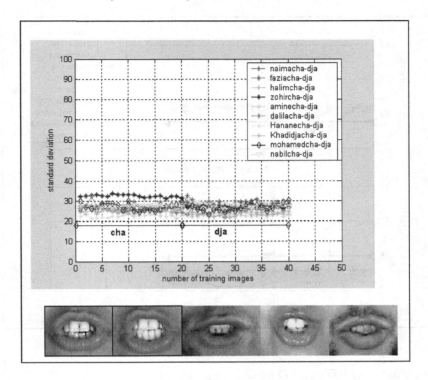

We notice that the standard deviation is quasi stationary for the first visemic category and for the ten speakers. This study is insufficient since the existing significant variation for each class.

The second method for classifying visemes uses the geometric parameters described (The two horizontal variation (HD: A and A'), the two vertical opening distances (VD: B and B')). Each image is presented as a matrix containing the four (4) values of the horizontal (HD) and vertical (VD) distances stored in a file (.mat). These parameters are used to classify our visemes.

Figure 7 shows the two parameters calculated for ten (10 images) for each phoneme (ba and ma), we are interested only on the two distances A' and B' for the first viseme, the distance B for the internal contour is not significant.

Figure 7 demonstrates the variation for the horizontal distance HD and the vertical distance VD for the ten speakers, it's clear that the range of variation is between (100 and 125) for the HD

and from 30 to 50 for VD. This variation deals with a lot of parameters like: intrapersonal variation, extrapersonal variation, acquisition conditions, and light variations....etc.

We investigate some observations on the intraclass and interclass confusions that were found from this study (Figure 8).

The following figure shows the four geometric parameters calculated for ten (10 images) for each phoneme (dja and cha) that describes the second viseme (Figure 9).

We noticed that there is a great correlation between each parameter for all speakers, the two opening vertical distance B and B' varied for 50 to ~100 for all speakers. The mouth openness area is bigger than the first viseme where it was not insignificant.

In Arabic language, approximately 11 visemes are distinguished. Table 2 shows the visual representation of Arabic visemes obtained from the statistics analysis and the geometric parameters

Figure 7. Variation of the horizontal and vertical distance for the first viseme ba&ma

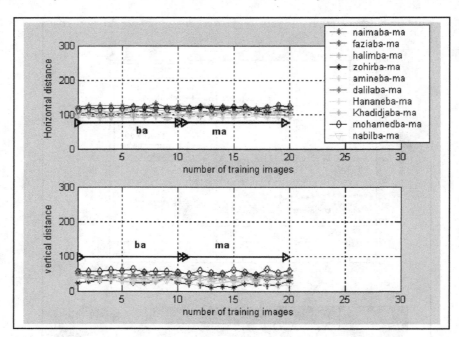

Figure 8. The distribution of HD and VD for the ten speakers

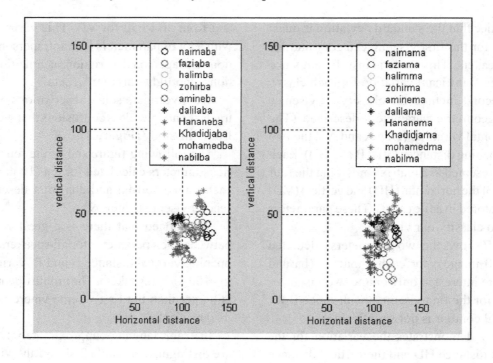

Figure 9. Variation of the horizontal and vertical distance for the second viseme dja&cha

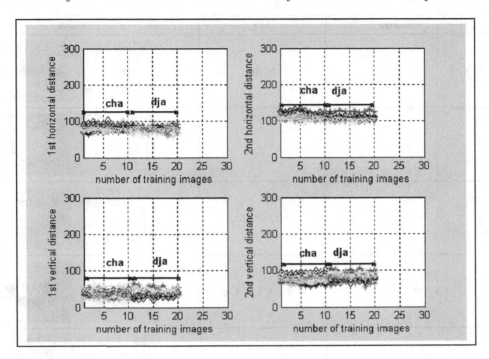

calculated for each frame representing phonemes and for the ten speakers.

Therefore, we developed a phoneme-viseme mapping for Arabic. There were 11 final visemes representing the 28 consonantal Arabic phonemes.

The visual characteristics of these classes are: Lip closed (1st viseme /b/, /m/), friction between lips and teeth(6th viseme/F/), friction between tongue and teeth(3rd viseme / θ/,/ δ/,/ δ/), lips protrusion(2nd viseme/ š /, / z/), lips neutral and mouth open(4th viseme Ha), lips partially rounded (9th viseme / w/, neutral lip and jaw position.

We describe in the following paragraph the use of the Hierarchical clustering applied to our viseme results to demonstrate the intrapersonnel and extrapersonnel variation.

CLASSIFY VISEMES USING HIERARCHICAL CLUSTERING

The definition of clustering leads directly to the definition of a single "cluster." Many definitions have been proposed over the years. Most of them are based on loosely defined terms, such as "similar," "alike," etc. (Theodoridis et al., 2003).

The vectors are viewed as points in the l-dimensional space and the clusters are described as "continuous regions of this space containing a relatively high density of points, separated from other high density regions by regions of relatively low density of points. We try to give some definitions for clustering (Theodoridis et al., 2003).

Let X be our data set, that is:

$$X = \left\{ x_1, x_2, ..., x_N \right\} \tag{3}$$

Table 2. The 11 Arabic visemes

Viseme	Phoneme	API	Mouth
1. Ba	{ب, م}	/b/, /m/	
2. Cha	{ش, ج}	/ š /, / z/	
3. dha	{ ث, ذ, ظ}	/ θ/,/ ð/, / ð/	
4. Ha	{ أ, ع, غ, ح, هـ, ك, خ, ق }	/ʔ, ç, γ, ħ, h, k, x, q/	
5. Ta	{د, ن, ت, س, ز, ط, ص, ي, ض }	/d,n,t,s,Z, t', ś,j, d'/	
6. Fa	{ف}	/F/	
7. La	{ل}	/l/	
8. Ra	{ر}	/r/	
9. wa	{و}	/ w/	
10	ظمه ممالة	/u/	
11	ممالة كسرة	/i/	

We define as an m-clustering of X, R, the partition of X into m sets (clusters), $c_1,...,c_m$, so that the three following conditions are met:

$$c_i \neq \varphi, \ j = 1,...,m \tag{4}$$

$$\cup_{i=1}^{m} c_i = X$$
$$c_i \cap c_j = \varphi \tag{5}$$
$$i \neq j, i, j = 1,...,m$$

In addition, the vectors contained in a cluster ci are "more similar" to each other and "less similar" to the features vectors of the other clusters (Theodoridis et al., 2003).

However, not all clustering algorithms are based on proximity measures between vectors. For example, in the hierarchical clustering algorithms one has to compute distances between pairs of sets of vectors of X. In the sequel, we extend the preceding definitions in order to measure "proximity" between subsets of X. That is:

$$D_i \subset X, i = 1,...,k$$
$$U = \left\{ D_1,...,D_k \right\}$$

A proximity measure $\wp \ on \ U$ is a function

$$\wp : U * U \rightarrow R$$

Usually, the proximity measures between two sets D_i and D_j are defined in terms of proximity measures between elements of D_i and D_j (Theodoridis et al., 2003).

In order to better understand the structure of visual speech data and hence to determine the visemes for further automatic lip-reading, we use hierarchical classification using the k nearest neighbour. We've used the Euclidean distance to construct the Hierarchical clustering based on the pairwise distance between observations. The pairwise distance between observations defined

by: Y=pdist. (X) returns a vector Y containing the Euclidean distances between each pair of observations in the M-by-N data matrix X Rows of X correspond to observations (pixels), columns correspond to variables (different images).

$$L = \left\| X_i - X_j \right\| = \sqrt{\sum_{k=1}^{N} X_{ik} - X_{jk})^2} \tag{6}$$

The defined function dendrogram (Z) generates a dendrogram plot of the hierarchical binary cluster tree Z. Z is an (M-1)-by-3 matrix, generated by the LINKAGE function, where M is the number of objects in the original dataset.

We analyse the dendrogram generated for the hierarchical binary cluster tree (Figure 10) using 3 images for each phoneme (ba & ma) and for each speaker, the training images is about 30 images on greyscale of size 120*160 pixels.

L1: 03 images for sequence ba and 03 images for sequence ma for the first speaker.

We conclude some observations on the intraclass (s1) and interclass (s2) confusions that were found from this study for the first class of viseme (ba-ma).the minimum distances using hierarchical clustering demonstrate that for the same viseme varied from 8 to 10. This difference makes the study more difficult. The dynamic features must be investigated to take co-articulation into account.

This variation can be discussed in frequency domain by exploiting the pitch analysis. The following paragraph demonstrates the pitch variation for each viseme.

ANALYSIS IN FREQUENCY DOMAIN: PITCH ANALYSIS

The pitch determination is very important for many speech processing algorithms, a commonly used method to estimate pitch (fundamental frequency)

Figure 10. The dendrogram of hierarchical clustering

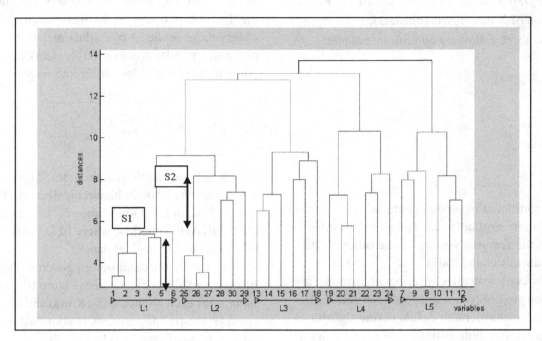

is based on detecting the highest value of the autocorrelation function in the region of interest. Our perception of pitch is strongly related to periodicity in the waveform in the time domain.

In practice, we need to obtain an estimate the autocorrelation $\hat{R}[m]$ from knowledge of only N samples. The empirical autocorrelation function is given by (Naotoshi, 2008):

$$\hat{R}[m] = \frac{1}{N} \sum_{n=0}^{N-1-|m|} (w[n] x[n] w[n + |m|] x[n + |m|])$$

(7)

where $w[n]$ is a window function of length N so that we can find the pitch period by computing the highest value of the autocorrelation which has a maxima for m=lT$_0$.

Since pitch periods can be as low as 40Hz (for a very low-pitched male voice) or as high as 600 Hz (for a very high-pitched female or child's voice), the search for the maximum is conducted within a region (Naotoshi, 2008).

For the same visemic category, (ba and ma) and also (dja and cha), we investigate the variability of the pitch parameter for the ten speakers, ten repetitions of each phoneme were used, and the simulation results are shown in Figure 11 and Figure 12.

We noticed that pitch varies from 180Hz to 240Hz for the same visemic class ba&ma for the first speaker. This variation explains correctly the difference for audio features for the same viseme.

The subplot of the pitch variation demonstrates the intrapersonel and the extrapersonel variation for the same viseme, this study permits us to show the importance of the speech analysis in order to improve the audiovisual speech recognition or the lip reading system for future work.

This study demonstrates also the parallel and interactive processing: speech perception is based on multiple sources of information, e.g. Lip move-

Figure 11. Pitch variation for viseme ba and ma

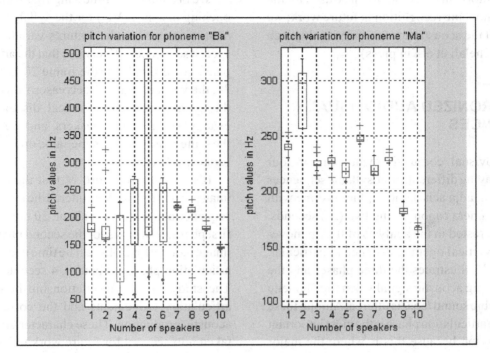

Figure 12. Pitch variation for viseme dja and cha

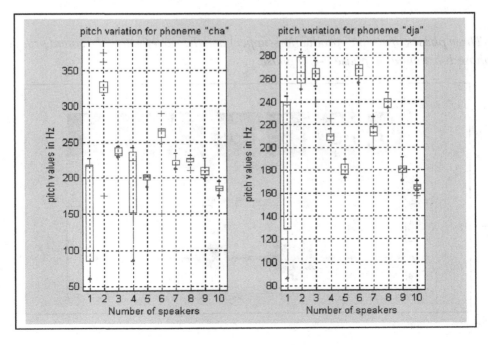

ments, auditory information. It can be used for the bimodal phoneme recognition in future work; we can exploit the acoustic speech and visual speech analysis (Chelali et al., in press).

SYNCHRONIZED AUDIOVISUAL SEQUENCES

The audiovisual corpus is evaluated for four speakers saying different monosyllabic sequences as (aba ama, adja acha); the capture is done with the same camera canon during two (2s) seconds. We are interested in the analysis of the lip movement, the vertical opening distance in particular.

Figure 13 illustrates the three phases and the corresponding acoustic signal when the phonetic monosyllabic sound /aba/ is uttered. Among these phases, the articulation phase is the most important for recognition because this is where the major difference among visemes lies and it is relatively independent to the context. The initial phase and end phase are transitional phases.

We present in the following figure the vertical opening distance (VD) for the syllable /aba/ and /ama/, it describes the features variation for the speech sequences. We can see that the articulation phase corresponds for the frame 20 to the frame 30, the vertical distance decreases from 60 to 20, the syllable sequence vertical distance is not exactly equal for all speakers, and we have not the same mouth size and the same opening mouth for al speakers.

It's clear from Figure 14 that the number of images when the speakers uttered the monosyllabic sequence aba and ama is about: 20 images for the first phase, 10 images for the second phase and 20 images for the final phase. The time needed for the articulation phase is about 0, 4 second (400ms). The study shows the relationship between the articulatory movements and the corresponding acoustic production. These characteristics can be taken into account for future work to investigate the audiovisual synchrony.

Figure 13. Three phases of visemes production (upper) and the waveform of the sound produced (lower) a- initial phase b-articulation phase c-end phase

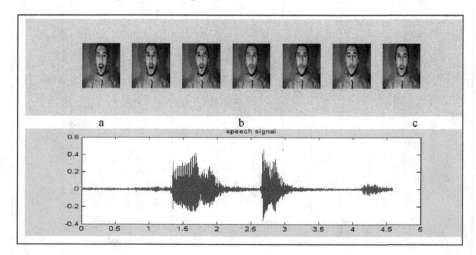

Figure 14. Variation of the vertical opening distance (aba&ama sequence)

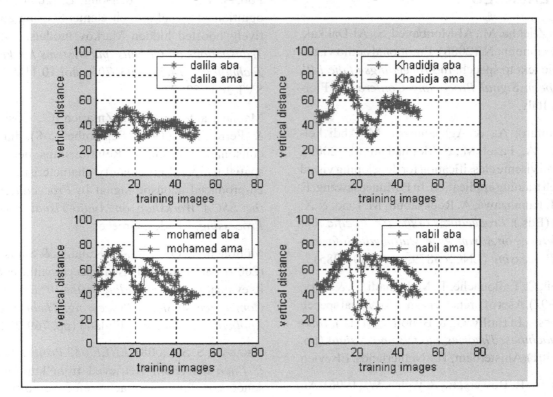

CONCLUSION

In this paper we introduced an Arabic viseme system based on visual speech database through statistics analysis. This study demonstrates that the use of statistical parameters like the standard deviation and the geometrical parameters like height and weight of lip permits to distinguish visual speech in Standard Arabic.

We have recorded a small visual speech database, all the 28 Arabic consonants were pronounced as monosyllabic sequences, and these 11 groups of consonants should probably correspond to the 11 visemes of Arabic.

This primary work in viseme classification for Arabic language needs to be improved. The spatio-temporal characteristics of articulatory movements and their relationships with the co-produced acoustic signal should be taken into consideration for future work.

This work demonstrates the efficiency of the visual speech-recognition systems, particularly in noisy audio conditions. The fusion of audio and lip texture modalities can be investigated in future work to study a speaker/ speech recognition system.

REFERENCES

Abou Zliekha, M., Al-Moubayed, S., Al-Dakkak, O., & Ghneim, N. (2006). Emotional audio visual Arabic text to speech. In *Proceedings of the 14th European Signal Processing Conference*, Florence, Italy.

Bastanfard, A., & Aghaahmadi, M. Abdi kelishami, A., Fazel, M., & Moghadam, M. (2009). Persian viseme classification for developing visual speech training application. In P. Muneesawang, F. Wu, I. Kumazawa, A. Roeksabutr, M. Liao, & X. Tang (Eds.), *Proceedings of the 10th Pacific Rim Conference on Advances in Multimedia Information Processing* (LNCS 5879, pp. 1080-1085).

Benoît, C., Lallouache, T., Mohamadi, T., & Abry, C. (1992). A set of French visemes for visual speech synthesis. In Bailly, G., & Benoît, C. (Eds.), *Talking machines: Theories, models and designs* (pp. 485–501). Amsterdam, The Netherlands: Elsevier.

Breen, A. P., Bowers, E., & Welsh, W. (1996). An investigation into the generation of mouth shapes for a talking head. In *Proceedings of the Fourth International Conference on Spoken Language Processing* (pp. 2159-2162).

Chelali, F. Z., & Djeradi, A. (in press). Audiovisual speech/speaker recognition, application to Arabic language. In *Proceedings of the IEEE-ICMCS International Conference on Multimedia and Computing Systems*, Ouarzazate, Morroco.

Cohen, M. M., & Massaro, D. W. (1993). Modeling coarticulation in synthetic visual speech. In Thalmann, N. M., & Thalmann, D. (Eds.), *Models and techniques in computer animation* (pp. 139–156). Berlin, Germany: Springer-Verlag.

Ezzat, T., & Poggio, T. (2000). Visual speech synthesis by morphing visemes. *International Journal of Computer Vision*, *38*(1), 45–57. doi:10.1023/A:1008166717597

Foo, S. W., Lian, Y., & Dong, L. (2004). Recognition of visual speech elements using adaptively boosted hidden Markov models. *IEEE Transactions on Circuits and Systems for Video Technology*, *14*(5), 693–705. doi:10.1109/TC-SVT.2004.826773

Magno-Caldognetto, E., Zmarich, C., Cosi, P., & Ferrero, F. (1997, September 5-8). Italian consonantal visemes: Relationships between spatial/temporal articulatory characteristics and co-produced acoustic signal In *Proceedings of the ESCA Workshop on Audio-Visual Speech Processing*, Rhodes, Greece.

Möttönen, R., Olivés, J.-L., Kulja, J., & Sams, M. (2000). Parameterized visual speech synthesis and its evaluation. In *Proceedings of the 10th European Conference on Signal Processing: Theories and Applications*, Tampere, Finland (pp. 769-772).

Naotoshi, S. S. (2008). *ENEE 632 Project 4 Part I: Pitch detection*. Retrieved from http://note.sonots.com/?plugin=attach&refer=SciSoftware%2FPitch&openfile=pitch.pdf

Rafay, A. A., & Ahmad, N. (2003). *CRULP annual student report* (pp. 68-71). Retrieved from http://www.crulp.org/research/reports/streport03.htm

Revéret, L. (1999). *Conception et évaluation d'un système de suivi automatique des gestes labiaux en parole*. Thèse de doctorat préparée au sein de l'Institut de la Communication Parlée, Grenoble, France.

Satori, H., Hiyassat, H., Harti, M., & Chenfour, N. (2005). Investigation Arabic speech recognition using CMU Sphinx system. *International Arab Journal of Information Technology*, *6*(2).

Theodoridis, S., & Koutroumbas, K. (2003). *Pattern recognition* (2nd ed.). San Diego, CA: Academic Press.

Tiddeman, B., & Perret, D. (2002). Prototyping and transforming visemes for animated speech. In *Proceedings of the Conference on Computer Animation* (pp. 248-251).

Wang, A., Bao, H., & Chen, J. *(2000). Primary research on the viseme system in standard Chinese. In* Proceedings of the International Symposium on Chinese Spoken Language Processing, *Beijing, China.*

Waters, K., & Levergood, T. M. (1993). *DEC-face: An automatic lip-synchronization algorithm for synthetic faces* (Tech. Rep. No. CRL93/4). Cambridge, MA: Digital Equipment Corporation, Cambridge Research Lab.

Werda, S., Mahdi, W., & Hamadou, A. B. (2007). Lip localization and viseme classification for visual speech recognition. *International Journal of Computing & Information Sciences*, 5(1).

This work was previously published in the International Journal of Mobile Computing and Multimedia Communications, Volume 3, Issue 4, edited by Ismail Khalil and Edgar Weippl, pp. 1-19, copyright 2011 by IGI Publishing (an imprint of IGI Global).

Compilation of References

3rd Generation Partnership Project. (2007). *3GPP TS 23.206 V7.5.0: 3rd generation partnership project: Technical specification group services and system aspects: Voice call continuity (VCC) between circuit switched (CS) and IP multimedia subsystem (IMS): Stage 2 (Release 7).* Retrieved from http://www.arib.or.jp/IMT-2000/V810Jul10/2_T63/ARIB-STD-T63/Rel7/23/A23206-750.pdf

3rd Generation Partnership Project. (2008). *3GPP TS 23.234 V8.0.0: 3rd Generation Partnership Project; Technical Specification Group Services and System Aspects; 3GPP system to Wireless Local Area Network (WLAN) interworking; System description (Release 8).* Retrieved from http://www.quintillion.co.jp/3GPP/Specs/23234-800.pdf

3rd Generation Partnership Project. (2009). *3GPP TS 22.078 V9.0.0: 3rd generation partnership project: Technical specification group services and system aspects: Customised applications for mobile network enhanced logic (CAMEL): Service description: Stage 1 (Release 9).* Retrieved from http://ofdm.jp/3GPP/Specs/23078-900.pdf

3rd Generation Partnership Project. (2009). *3GPP TS 23.237 V8.6.0: 3rd Generation Partnership Project Technical Specification Group Services and Architecture IP Multimedia Subsystem (IMS) Service Continuity Stage 2 (Release 8).* Retrieved from http://www.quintillion.co.jp/3GPP/Specs/23237-860.pdf

3rd Generation Partnership Project. (2009). *3GPP TS 23.292 V9.5.0: 3rd Generation Partnership Project; Technical Specification Group Services and System Aspects; IP Multimedia Subsystem (IMS) centralized services; Stage 2 (Release 9).* Retrieved from http://www.quintillion.co.jp/3GPP/Specs/23292-950.pdf

3rd Generation Partnership Project. (2009). *3GPP TS 23.327 V8.4.0: 3rd Generation Partnership Project; Technical Specification Group Services and System Aspects; Mobility between 3GPP-Wireless Local Area Network (WLAN) interworking and 3GPP systems (Release 8).* Retrieved from http://www.quintillion.co.jp/3GPP/Specs/24327-860.pdf

3rd Generation Partnership Project. (2009). *3GPP TS 23.401 V8.8.0: 3rd Generation Partnership Project; Technical Specification Group Services and System Aspects; General Packet Radio Service (GPRS) enhancements for Evolved Universal Terrestrial Radio Access Network (E-UTRAN) access (Release 8).* Retrieved from http://www.quintillion.co.jp/3GPP/Specs/23401-880.pdf

3rd Generation Partnership Project. (2009). *3GPP TS 23.402 V8.8.0: 3rd Generation Partnership Project; Technical Specification Group Services and System Aspects; Architecture enhancements for non-3GPP accesses (Release 8).* Retrieved from http://www.quintillion.co.jp/3GPP/Specs/23402-870.pdf

3rd Generation Partnership Project. (2009). *3GPP TS 43.318 V9.0.0: 3rd Generation Partnership Project Technical Specification Group GSM/EDGE Radio Access Network Generic Access Network (GAN): Stage 2 (Release 9).* Retrieved from http://www.quintillion.co.jp/3GPP/Specs/23003-900.pdf

Abbasi, A. A., & Younis, M. (2007). A survey on clustering algorithms for wireless sensor networks. *Computer Communications, 30,* 2826–2841. doi:10.1016/j.comcom.2007.05.024

Abou El Kalam, A., Benferhat, S., Balbiani, P., Miège, A., El Baida, R., Cuppens, F., et al. (2003). Organization based access control. In *Proceedings of the 4th IEEE International Workshop on Policies for Distributed Systems and Networks* (pp. 120-131). Washington, DC: IEEE Computer Society.

Abou Zliekha, M., Al-Moubayed, S., Al-Dakkak, O., & Ghneim, N. (2006). Emotional audio visual Arabic text to speech. In *Proceedings of the 14th European Signal Processing Conference*, Florence, Italy.

ADC Technologies Group. (2002). *RFID overview*. Retrieved from http://www.adctech.com/Documents%5CWhite%20Paper,%20RFID%20Overview.pdf

Adjie-Winoto, W., Schwartz, E., & Balakrishnan, H. (1999). The design and implementation of an intentional naming system. In *Proceedings of the Symposium on Operating Systems Principles* (pp. 186-201).

Adlam, D. (2009). *Social networking identity fraud*. Retrieved September 2, 2009, from http://ezinearticles.com/?Social-Networking-Identity-Fraud&id=2730177

Ahmed, M. A., Ibrahim, N. M., & El-Tamally, H. H. (2010, March). Performance evaluation of handoff queuing schemes. In *Proceedings of the Second International Conference on Communication Software and Networks* (pp. 83-87).

Ajana, M. E., Boulmalf, M., Harroud, H., & Hamam, H. (2009). A policy based event management middleware for implementing RFID applications. In *Proceedings of the International Conference on Wireless and Mobile Computing, Networking and Communications*, Marrakesh, Morocco (pp. 406-410).

Akyildiz, I. F., Xie, J., & Mohanty, S. (2004). A survey of mobility management in next-generation all-IP-based wireless systems. *IEEE Wireless Communications, 11*(4), 16–28. doi:10.1109/MWC.2004.1325888

Albrechtsen, E. (2007). A qualitative study of users' view on information security. *Computers & Security, 26*(4), 276–289. doi:10.1016/j.cose.2006.11.004

Al-Dala'in, T., Summons, P., & Luo, S. (2009). The relationship between a mobile device and a shopper's trust for e-payment systems. In *Proceedings of the 1st International Conference on Information Science and Engineering* (pp. 3132-3135).

Alimi, V., & Pasquet, M. (2009). Post-distribution provisioning and personalization of a payment application on a UICC-based secure element. In *Proceedings of the International Conference on Availability, Reliability and Security* (pp. 701-705).

Al-Mousawi, H. (2004). *Performance and reliability of radio frequency identification (RFID)*. Unpublished master's thesis, Agder University College, Kristiansand, Norway.

Aloul, F., Zahidi, S., & El-Hajj, W. (2009). Two factor authentication using mobile phones. In *Proceedings of the IEEE/ACS International Conference on Computer Systems and Applications*, Rabat, Morocco (pp. 641-644).

Andersen, D. G., Balakrishnan, H., Kaashoek, M. F., & Moms, R. (2001). Resilient overlay networks. *ACM SIGOPS Operating Systems Review, 35*(5), 131–145. doi:10.1145/502059.502048

Anouar, H., & Bonnet, C. (2007). Optimal constant-window backoff scheme for IEEE 802.11 DCF in single-hop wireless networks under finite load conditions. *Wireless Personal Communications, 43*.

Antoniou, J., Christophorou, C., Janneteau, C., Kellil, M., Sargento, S., Neto, A., et al. (2009). Architecture for context-aware multiparty delivery in mobile heterogeneous networks. In *Proceedings of the International Conference on Ultra Modern Telecommunications & Workshops* (pp. 1-6).

Araujo, I. (2005). Privacy mechanisms supporting the building of trust in e-commerce. In *Proceedings of the 21st International Conference on Data Engineering Workshops* (pp. 1193-1193).

Argyris, C., & Schön, D. (1974). *Theory in practice: Increasing professional effectiveness*. San Francisco, CA: Jossey-Bass.

Argyris, C., & Schön, D. (1996). *Organizational learning II: Theory, method and practice*. Reading, MA: Addison-Wesley.

Asnar, Y., Giorgini, P., & Mylopoulos, J. (2006). *Risk modelling and reasoning in goal models* (Tech. Rep. No. DIT-06-008). University of Trento, Trento, Italy.

Asnar, Y., Giorgini, P., Massacci, F., & Zannone, N. (2007). From trust to dependability through risk analysis. In *Proceedings of the international conference on availability, reliability and security (AReS)* (pp. 19-26). Washington, DC: IEEE Computer Society.

Atheros Communications, Inc. (2005). *Getting the most out of MIMO: Boosting wireless LAN performance with full compatibility*. Retrieved from http://www.opulan.com/pt/whitepapers/MIMO_WLAN_Perf_whitepaper.pdf

Atiquzzaman, M., & Reaz, A. (2005). Survey and classification of transport layer mobility management schemes. In *Proceedings of the 16th Annual IEEE International Symposium on Personal, Indoor and Mobile Radio Communications* (Vol. 4).

Atos Origin. (2002). *Customer relationship management*. Retrieved from http://www.es.atosorigin.com/NR/rdonlyres/9C826F13-D59C-456B-AC57-416E686A4C30/0/crm_wp.pdf

Backes, M., Cervesato, I., Jaggard, A. D., Scedrov, A., & Tsay, J.-K. (2006). *Cryptographically sound security proofs for basic and public-key kerberos*. Retrieved from http://faculty.nps.edu/gwdinolt/ProtocolExchange/Fall2006/ProtocoleXchange092806_CompProofsKerberos.pdf

Badra, M., & Urien, P. (2004). Toward SSL integration in SIM SmartCards. In *Proceedings of the Wireless Communications and Networking Conference* (pp. 889- 893)

Bahl, P., & Padmanabhan, V. (2000). RADAR: An In-Building RF-Based User Location and Tracking System. In *Proceedings of the IEEE INFOCOM*, Tel-Aviv, Israel.

Bani Yassein, M., & Ould Khaoua, M. (2007). Applications of probabilistic flooding in MANETs. *UBICC Journal, 2*(1).

Bani Yassein, M., Manaseer, S., & Al-Turani, A. (2009, July). *A performance comparison of different backoff algorithms under different rebroadcast probabilities for MANET's*. Paper presented at the 25th UK Performance Engineering Workshop.

Bani Yassein, M., Ould Khaoua, M., Mackenzie, L. M., & Papanastasiou, S. (2005, May 23-26). Improving the performance of probabilistic flooding in MANETs. In *Proceedings of the International Workshop on Wireless Ad-hoc Networks*, London, UK.

Bani Yassein, M., Ould Khaoua, M., Mackenzie, L. M., & Papanastasiou, S. (2006). Performance analysis of adjusted probabilistic broadcasting in mobile ad hoc networks. *International Journal of Wireless Information Networks, 13*(2). doi:10.1007/s10776-006-0027-0

Baral, C., & Lobo, J. (1996). Formal characterization of active databases. In *Proceedings of the International Workshop on Logic in Databases* (pp. 175-195).

Barcel´o, J., Bellalta, B., Cano, C., & Oliver, M. (2009). Dynamic p-persistent backoff for higher efficiency and implicit prioritization. *IEEE Transactions on Wireless Communications*.

Basseville, M., & Nikiforov, I. V. (1993). *Detection of abrupt changes: theory and application*. Upper Saddle River, NJ: Prentice Hall.

Bastanfard, A., & Aghaahmadi, M. Abdi kelishami, A., Fazel, M., & Moghadam, M. (2009). Persian viseme classification for developing visual speech training application. In P. Muneesawang, F. Wu, I. Kumazawa, A. Roeksabutr, M. Liao, & X. Tang (Eds.), *Proceedings of the 10th Pacific Rim Conference on Advances in Multimedia Information Processing* (LNCS 5879, pp. 1080-1085).

Becker, M. Y., & Nanz, S. (2008). The role of abduction in declarative authorization policies. In *Proceedings of the 10th International Conference on Practical Aspects of Declarative Language* (pp. 84-99).

Becker, M. Y., & Nanz, S. (2007). A logic for state modifying authorization policies. *ACM Transactions on Information and System Security, 13*(3), 20.

Beck, K. (2000). *Extreme programming explained: Embrace change.* Reading, MA: Addison-Wesley.

Bencsath, B., & Vajda, I. (2004). *Protection against DDoS attacks based on traffic level measurements.* Paper presented at the International Symposium on Collaborative Technologies.

Benoît, C., Lallouache, T., Mohamadi, T., & Abry, C. (1992). A set of French visemes for visual speech synthesis. In Bailly, G., & Benoît, C. (Eds.), *Talking machines: Theories, models and designs* (pp. 485–501). Amsterdam, The Netherlands: Elsevier.

Bettini, C., Jajodia, S., Wang, X. S., & Wijesekera, D. (2002). Provisions and obligations in policy management and security applications. In *Proceeding of the 28th International Conference on Very Large Data Bases* (pp. 502-513). Washington, DC: IEEE Computer Society.

Bettini, C., Wang, X., Jajodia, S., & Wijesekera, D. (2002). Obligation monitoring in policy management. In *Proceedings of the IEEE International Workshop on Policies for Distributed Systems and Networks* (pp. 2-12). Washington, DC: IEEE Computer Society.

Bettini, C., Jajodia, S., Wang, X. S., & Wijesekera, D. (2003). Provisions and obligations in policy rule management. *Journal of Network and Systems Management, 11*(3). doi:10.1023/A:1025711105609

Bettstetter, C., Resta, G., & Santi, P. (2003). The node distribution of the random waypoint mobility model for wireless ad hoc networks. *IEEE Transactions on Mobile Computing,* 257–269. doi:10.1109/TMC.2003.1233531

Bhardwaj, M., & Chandrakasan, A. P. (2002). Bounding the lifetime of sensor networks via optimal role assignments. In *Proceedings of the IEEE INFOCOM,* New York.

Blazek, R. B., Kim, H., Rozovskii, B., & Tartakovsky, A. (2001). *A novel approach to detection of denial-of-service attacks via adaptive sequential and batch-sequential change-point detection methods.* Paper presented at the IEEE Workshop Information Assurance and Security.

Bluetooth, S. I. G. Inc. (2010). *Welcome to Bluetooth.org.* Retrieved from https://www.bluetooth.org/apps/content/

Blum, B. (1996). *Beyond programming: To a new era of design.* New York, NY: Oxford University Press.

Boggia, G., Camarda, P., D'Alconzo, A., De Biasi, A., & Siviero, M. (2005). Drop call probability in established cellular networks: From data analysis to modeling. In. *Proceedings of the Vehicular Technology Conference, 5,* 2775–2779.

Boldyreva, A., & Kumar, V. (2007). *Provable-security analysis of authenticated encryption in kerberos.* Retrieved from http://www.cc.gatech.edu/~virendra/papers/BK07.pdf

Bonatti, P. A., Olmedilla, D., & Peer, J. (2006). Advanced policy explanations on the web. In *Proceeding of the 17th European Conference on Artificial Intelligence* (pp. 200-204). Amsterdam, The Netherlands: IOS Press.

Bose, A., & Shin, K. G. (2006). On mobile viruses exploiting messaging and bluetooth services. In *Proceedings of the Securecomm and Workshops,* Baltimore, MD (pp. 1-10).

Braber, F., Hogganvik, I., Lund, M. S., Stølen, K., & Vraalsen, F. (2007). Modelbased security analysis in seven steps – a guided tour to the CORAS method. *BT Technology Journal, 25*(1), 101–117. doi:10.1007/s10550-007-0013-9doi:10.1007/s10550-007-0013-9

Braginsky, D., & Estrin, D. (2002). Rumor Routing Algorithm for Sensor Networks. In *Proceedings of ACM International Workshop on Wireless Sensor Networks and Applications,* Atlanta, GA.

Breen, A. P., Bowers, E., & Welsh, W. (1996). An investigation into the generation of mouth shapes for a talking head. In *Proceedings of the Fourth International Conference on Spoken Language Processing* (pp. 2159-2162).

British Broadcasting Corporation. (2007). *Web networkers 'at risk of fraud'.* Retrieved September 2, 2009, from http://news.bbc.co.uk/1/hi/uk/6910826.stm

Broch, J., Maltz, D., Johnson, D., Hu, Y., & Jetcheva, J. (1998). A performance comparison of multi-hop wireless ad hoc network routing protocols. In *Proceedings of the ACM Conference on Mobile Communications* (pp. 85-97).

Brocke, J. v., & Buddendick, C. (2005). *Security awareness management - Foundations and Implementation of security awareness.* Paper presented at the 2005 International Conference on Security and Management (SAM'05), Las Vegas.

Buckley, C. (1985). *Implementation of the smart information retrieval system* (Tech. Rep. No. TR85-686). Ithaca, NY: Cornell University.

Buckley, C., Salton, G., Allan, J., & Singhal, A. (1994). *Automatic query expansion using smart: Trec 3*. Ithaca, NY: Cornell University.

Burnell, J. (2008). *What is RFID middleware and where is it needed?* Retrieved from http://www.rfidsolutionsonline.com/article.mvc/RFID-Middleware-What-Is-RFID-Middleware-And-W-0001

Burnside, M., Clarke, D., Gassend, B., Kotwal, T., van Dijk, M., Devadas, S., et al. (2002). The untrusted computer problem and camera-based authentication. In *Proceedings of the First International Conference on Pervasive Computing* (pp. 114-124).

Burr, W. E., Dodson, D. F., & Polk, W. T. (2008). *Electronic authentication guideline, recommendations of the National Institute of Standards and Technology*. Retrieved from http://csrc.nist.gov/publications/nistpubs/800-63/SP800-63V1_0_2.pdf

Burton, D. (2007). Psycho-pedagogy and personalised learning. *Journal of Education for Teaching: International research and pedagogy, 33*(1), 5-17.

Business Enterprise Regulatory Reform. (2008). *The 9th information security breaches survey*. London: Department for Business Enterprise and Regulatory Reform & Pricewaterhouse Coopers.

Caire, G., & Shamai, S. (2003). On the achievable throughput of a multiantenna gaussian broadcast channel. *IEEE Transactions on Information Theory, 49*(7), 1691–1706. doi:10.1109/TIT.2003.813523

Callan, J. P., Groft, W. B., & Harding, S. M. (1993). *The inquiry retrieval system*. Amherst, MA: University of Massachusetts.

Calvert, K., & Zegura, E. (1997). *GT internetwork topology models*. GT-ITM.

Camarillo, G., Johnston, A., Peterson, J., Sparks, R., Handley, M., & Schooler, E. (2002). *RFC 3261: Session initiation protocol*. Retrieved from http://www.ietf.org/rfc/rfc3261.txt

Camarillo, G., & Garcia-Martin, M. A. (2008). *The 3G IP multimedia subsystem (IMS): Merging the Internet and the cellular worlds* (3rd ed.). Chichester, UK: John Wiley & Sons. doi:10.1002/9780470695135

Campbell, R. J., Robinson, W., Neelands, J., Hewston, R., & Mazzoli, L. (2007). Personalised learning: Ambiguities in theory and practice. *British Journal of Educational Studies, 55*(2), 135–154. doi:10.1111/j.1467-8527.2007.00370.x

Candan, I., & Salamah, M. (2007). Analytical modeling of time-threshold based bandwidth allocation scheme for cellular networks. *Computer Communications, 30*(5), 1036–1043. doi:10.1016/j.comcom.2006.10.015

Cantor, S., Hirsch, F., Kemp, J., Philpott, R., & Maler, E. (2005). *Bindings for the OASIS security assertion markup language (SAML) v2.0*. Retrieved from http://docs.oasis-open.org/security/saml/v2.0/saml-bindings-2.0-os.pdf

Cantor, S., Kemp, J., Philpott, R., & Maler, E. (2005). *Assertions and protocol for the OASIS security assertion markup language (SAML) v2.0*. Retrieved from http://docs.oasis-open.org/security/saml/v2.0/saml-core-2.0-os.pdf

Cantor, S., Kemp, J., Philpott, R., & Maler, E. (2005). *Profiles for the OASIS security assertion markup language (SAML) v2.0*. Retrieved from http://docs.oasis-open.org/security/saml/v2.0/saml-profiles-2.0-os.pdf

Cao, G., Yin, L., & Das, C. R. (2004). Cooperative cache-based data access in ad hoc networks. *IEEE Computer, 37*(2), 32–39.

Cao, L., & Ramesh, B. (2007). Agile software development: Ad hoc practices or sound principles? *IT Professional, 9*(2), 41–47. doi:10.1109/MITP.2007.27

Carl, G., Kesidis, G., Brooks, R. R., & Rai, S. (2005). *Denial-of-service attack-detection techniques*. Distributed Systems Online.

Chand, N., Joshi, R. C., & Misra, M. (2007). Cooperative caching strategy in mobile ad hoc networks based on clusters. *International Journal of wireless Personal Communication*, 41-63.

Chand, N., Joshi, R. C., & Misra, M. (2006). A zone cooperation approach for efficient caching in mobile ad hoc networks. *International Journal of Communication Systems*, 1009–1028. doi:10.1002/dac.795

Chand, N., Joshi, R. C., & Misra, M. (2007). Cooperative caching in mobile ad hoc networks based on data utility. *Mobile Information Systems*, *3*(1), 19–37.

Chang, C.-T. (2000). An efficient linearization approach for mixed integer problems. *European Journal of Operational Research*, *123*, 652–659. doi:10.1016/S0377-2217(99)00106-X

Chang, C.-T. (2001). On the polynomial mixed 0-1 fractional programming problems. *European Journal of Operational Research*, *131*(1), 224–227. doi:10.1016/S0377-2217(00)00097-7

Chankhunthod, A., Danzig, P. B., Neerdaels, C., Schwartz, M. F., & Worrell, K. J. (1996). A hierarchical Internet object cache. In *Proceedings of the USENIX Annual Technical Conference* (pp. 153-163).

Chawathe, Y., Ratnasamy, S., Breslau, L., Lanham, N., & Shenker, S. (2003). Making Gnutella-Like P2P systems scalable. In *Proceedings of the Conference on Applications, Technologies, Architectures, and Protocols for Computer Communications*, Karlsruhe, Germany (pp. 407-418).

Chelali, F. Z., & Djeradi, A. (in press). Audiovisual speech/speaker recognition, application to Arabic language. In *Proceedings of the IEEE-ICMCS International Conference on Multimedia and Computing Systems*, Ouarzazate, Morroco.

Chen, Y., Li, Y., Cheng, X.-Q., & Guo, L. (2006). Survey and Taxonomy of Feature Selection Algorithms in Intrusion Detection System. In *Proceedings of Inscrypt 2006* (LNCS 4318, pp. 153-167).

Chen, C. C., Medlin, B. D., & Shaw, R. S. (2008). A cross-cultural investigation of situational information security awareness programs. *Information Management & Computer Security*, *16*(4), 360–376. doi:10.1108/09685220810908787

Chia, P. A., Maynard, S. B., & Ruighaver, A. B. (2002). *Understanding organizational security culture*. Paper presented at the Sixth Pacific Asia Conference on Information Systems, Tokyo, Japan.

Chinrungrueng, J., Sununtachaikul, U., & Triamlumlerd, S. (2006). A vehicular monitoring system with power-efficient wireless sensor networks. In *Proceedings of the ITS Telecommunications Conference* (pp. 951-954).

Chiu, G. M., & Young, C. R. (2009). Exploiting in-zone broadcast for cache sharing in mobile ad hoc networks. *IEEE Transactions on Mobile Computing*, 384–396. doi:10.1109/TMC.2008.127

Chiu, G. M., & Young, C. R. (2009). Exploiting in-zone broadcasts for cache sharing in mobile ad hoc networks. *IEEE Transactions on Mobile Computing*, *8*(3), 384–397. doi:10.1109/TMC.2008.127

Chlamtac, I., & Lerner, A. (1986). Link allocation in mobile radio networks with noisy channel. In *Proceedings of the IEEE Conference INFOCOM* (pp. 203-212).

Chlamtac, I., Conti, M., & Liu, J. N. (2003). Mobile ad hoc networking: Imperatives and challenges. *Ad Hoc Networks*, *1*, 13–64. doi:10.1016/S1570-8705(03)00013-1

Chlamtac, I., & Lerner, A. (1987). Fair algorithms for maximal link activation in multi-hop radio networks. *IEEE Transactions on Communications*, *7*, 739–746. doi:10.1109/TCOM.1987.1096847

Chow, C. Y., Leong, H. V., & Chan, A. (2004). Cache signature for peer-to-peer cooperative caching in mobile environments. In *Proceedings of the 18th International Conference on Advanced Information Networking and Applications* (pp. 96-101).

Chow, C. Y., Leong, H. V., & Chan, A. (2004). Group-based cooperative cache management for mobile clients in mobile environments. In *Proceedings of the 33rd International Conference on Parallel Processing* (pp. 83-90).

Chow, C. Y., Leong, H. V., & Chan, A. (2004). Peer-to-peer cooperative caching in mobile environments. In *Proceedings of the 24th International Conference on Distributed Computing Systems Workshop* (pp. 528-533).

Chu, Y., Rao, S. G., & Zhang, H. (2001, June). A case for end system multicast. In *Proceedings of the ACM SIGMETRICS Conference*, Santa Clara, CA (pp. 1-12).

Chuah, C.-N., Tse, D. N. C., Kahn, J. M., & Valenzuela, R. A. (2002). Capacity scaling in MIMO wireless systems under correlated fading. *IEEE Transactions on Information Theory, 48*(3).

Chuang, M. L., & Shaw, W. H. (2005). How RFID will impact supply chain networks. In *Proceedings of the IEEE Engineering Management Conference*, Newfoundland, Canada (pp. 231-235).

Chuang, M. L., & Shaw, W. H. (2007). RFID: Integration stages in supply chain management. *IEEE Engineering Management Review, 35*(2), 80–87. doi:10.1109/EMR.2007.899757

Cohen, M. M., & Massaro, D. W. (1993). Modeling coarticulation in synthetic visual speech. In Thalmann, N. M., & Thalmann, D. (Eds.), *Models and techniques in computer animation* (pp. 139–156). Berlin, Germany: Springer-Verlag.

Comeau, F., Sivakumar, S. C., Robertson, W., & Phillips, W. J. (2006). Energy conserving architectures and algorithms for wireless sensor networks. In *Proceedings of the 39th Annual Hawaii International Conference on System Sciences* (pp. 236-246).

Cone, B. D., Irvine, C. E., Thompson, M. F., & Nguyen, T. D. (2007). A video game for cyber security training and awareness. *Computers & Security, 26*(1), 63–72. doi:10.1016/j.cose.2006.10.005

Confident Technologies Inc. (2010). *Intuitive and secure image-based authentication solutions.* Retrieved from http://www.confidenttechnologies.com/

Cooper, M. H. (2008). *Information security training: lessons learned along the trail.* Paper presented at the 36th annual ACM SIGUCCS conference on User services conference.

Corchado, J. M., Bajo, J., Tapia, D. I., & Abraham, A. (2010). Using heterogeneous wireless sensor networks in a telemonitoring system for healthcare. *IEEE Transactions on Information Technology in Biomedicine, 14*(2), 234–240. doi:10.1109/TITB.2009.2034369

Cormen, T. H., Leiserson, C. E., Rivest, R. L., & Stein, C. (2001). *Introduction to Algorithms* (2nd ed.). Cambridge, MA: MIT Press.

Craven, R., Lobo, J., Ma, J., Russo, A., Lupu, E., & Bandara, A. (2009). Expressive policy analysis with enhanced system dynamicity. In *Proceedings of the 4th International Symposium on Information, Computer, and Communications Security* (pp. 239-250). New York, NY: ACM Press.

Crescenzo, G. D., Ghosh, A., & Talpade, R. (2005). Towards a theory of intrusion detection. In *Proceedings of the 10th European Symposium on Research in Computer Security (ESORICS'05)* (pp. 267-286). New York: Springer.

Crossbow Technology Inc. (n.d.). Retreived from http://www.xbow.com

Cuppens, F., Cuppens-Boulahia, N., & Sans, T. (2005). Nomad: A security model with non atomic actions and deadlines. In *Proceedings of the 18th IEEE Workshop on Computer Security Foundations* (pp. 186-196). Washington, DC: IEEE Computer Society.

Cuppens, F., & Cuppens-Boulahia, N. (2008). Modeling contextual security policies. *International Journal of Information Security, 7*(4), 285–305. doi:10.1007/s10207-007-0051-9

Dahmouni, H., Morin, B., & Vaton, S. (2005, March). Performance modeling of GSM/GPRS cells with different radio resource allocation strategies. In *Proceedings of the Wireless Communications and Networking Conference, 3,* 1317–1322. doi:10.1109/WCNC.2005.1424707

Dainton, S. (2004). Personalised learning. *Symposium Journals, 46*(2), 56-58.

Dasgupta, K., Kukreja, M., & Kalpakis, K. (2003). Topology-aware placement and role assignment for energy-efficient information gathering in sensor networks. In *Procesedings of the 8th IEEE International Symposium on Computers and Communication*, Turkey.

Denso Wave Inc. (2009). *QR Code.com.* Retrieved from http://www.denso-wave.com/qrcode/index-e.html

Department for Children School and Families. (2010). *Personalised learning approaches used by schools.* Retrieved May 6, 2010, from http://www.dcsf.gov.uk/research/programmeofresearch/projectinformation.cfm?projectId=14664&type=5&resultspage

Dhamija, R., Tygar, J. D., & Hearst, M. A. (2006). Why phishing works. In *Proceedings of the SIGCHI Conference on Human Factors in Computing Systems* (pp. 581-590).

Dierks, T., & Allen, C. (1999). *RFC 2246: The TLS protocol version, 1.0.* Retrieved from http://www.ietf.org/rfc/rfc2246.txt

Dierks, T., & Rescorla, E. (2006). *RFC 4346: The transport layer security (TLS) protocol, version 1.1.* Retrieved from http://www.ietf.org/mail-archive/web/ietf-announce/current/msg02442.html

Dierks, T., & Rescorla, E. (2008). *RFC 5246: The transport layer security (TLS) protocol, version 1.2.* Retrieved from http://tools.ietf.org/html/rfc5246

Dlamini, M. T., Eloff, J. H. P., & Eloff, M. M. (2009). Information security: The moving target. *Computers & Security, 28*(3/4), 189–198. doi:10.1016/j.cose.2008.11.007

Du, Y., & Gupta, S. (2005). COOP – A cooperative caching service in MANETs. In *Proceedings of the Joint International Conference on Autonomic and Autonomous Systems and International Conference on Networking and Services* (pp. 58-63).

Duda, R. O., Hart, P. E., & Stork, D. G. (2001). *Pattern Classification.* New York: Wiley-Interscience.

Du, Y., & Gupta, S. (2004). *Handbook of mobile computing.* Boca Raton, FL: CRC Press.

Du, Y., Gupta, S., & Varsamopoulos, V. (2009). Improving on-demand data access efficiency in MANETs with cooperative caching. *Ad Hoc Networks, 7*(3), 579–598. doi:10.1016/j.adhoc.2008.07.007

Eastlake, D. (2006). *HMAC SHA TSIG algorithm identifiers.* Retrieved from http://www.ietf.org/rfc/rfc4635.txt

Ekiz, N., Salih, T., Kucukoner, S., & Fidanboylu, K. (2005). An overview of handoff techniques in cellular networks. *International Journal of Information Technology, 2*(2).

Eliasson, C., Fiedler, M., & Jorstad, I. (2009). A criteria-based evaluation framework for authentication schemes in IMS. In *Proceedings of the 4th International Conference on Availability, Reliability and Security,* Fukuoka, Japan (pp. 865-869).

Elrakaiby, Y., Cuppens, F., & Cuppens-Boulahia, N. (2009). Formalization and management of group obligations. In *Proceedings of the 10th IEEE International Conference on Policies for Distributed Systems and Networks* (pp. 158-165). Los Alamitos, CA: IEEE Press.

Elrakaiby, Y., Cuppens, F., & Cuppens-Boulahia, N. (2009). From state-based to event-based contextual security policies. In *Proceedings of the Fourth International Conference on Digital Information Management,* Ann Arbor, MI (pp. 1-7). Washington, DC: IEEE Computer Society.

Elrakaiby, Y., Cuppens, F., & Cuppens-Boulahia, N. (2010). From contextual permission to dynamic preobligation: An integrated approach. In *Proceedings of the International Conference on Availability, Reliability, and Security* (p. 70). Washington, DC: IEEE Computer Society.

Estrin, D., Govindan, R., Heidemann, J., & Kumar, S. (1999). Next century challenges: Scalable coordination in sensor networks. In *Proceedings of the 5th Annual ACM/IEEE International Conference on Mobile Computing and Networking* (pp. 263-270).

European Network and Information Security Agency. (2008). *The new users' guide: How to raise information security awareness.* European Network and Information Security Agency.

Ezzat, T., & Poggio, T. (2000). Visual speech synthesis by morphing visemes. *International Journal of Computer Vision, 38*(1), 45–57. doi:10.1023/A:1008166717597

Fabian, B., Gürses, S., Heisel, M., Santen, T., & Schmidt, H. (2010). A comparison of security requirements engineering methods. *Requirements Engineering, 15*(1), 7–40. doi:10.1007/s00766-009-0092-xdoi:10.1007/s00766-009-0092-x

Fall, K., & Varadhan, K. (2010). *VINT Project. The ucb/lbnl/vint network simulator-ns.* Retrieved from http://www.isi.edu/nsnam/ns

Falowo, O. E., & Chan, H. A. (2010). Heuristic RAT selection policy to minimize call blocking probability in next generation wireless networks. *Wireless Communications and Mobile Computing, 10*(2), 214–229.

Fang, X., & Zhan, J. (2010). Online banking authentication using mobile phones. In *Proceedings of the 5th International Conference on Future Information Technology* (pp. 1-5).

Fan, L., Cao, P., Almeida, J., & Broder, A. Z. (2000). Summary cache: A scalable wide-area web cache sharing protocol. *IEEE/ACM Transactions on Networking, 8*(3), 281–293. doi:10.1109/90.851975

Feinstein, L., Schnackenberg, D., Balupari, R., & Kindred, D. (2003). *Statistical approaches to DDoS attack detection and response.* Paper presented at the DARPA Information Survivability Conference and Exposition.

Fernandez, E. B., la Red, M. D. L., Forneron, J., Uribe, V. E., & Rodriguez, G. G. (2007). A secure analysis pattern for handling legal cases. In *Proceedings of the Latin America conference on pattern languages of programming (SugarLoafPLoP)*. Retrieved August 9, 2009, from http://sugarloafplop.dsc.upe.br/wwD.zip

Ferraiolo, D. F., & Kuhn, D. R. (1992). Role-based access control. In *Proceedings of the 15th National Computer Security Conference* (pp. 554-563).

Fette, B. A. (2009). *Cognitive radio technology* (2nd ed.). Burlington, MA: Academic Press.

Fochini, G. J. (1996). Layered space-time architecture for wireless communication in fading environment when using multi-element antennas. *Bell Labs Technical Journal, 1*, 41–59. doi:10.1002/bltj.2015

Foo, S. W., Lian, Y., & Dong, L. (2004). Recognition of visual speech elements using adaptively boosted hidden Markov models. *IEEE Transactions on Circuits and Systems for Video Technology, 14*(5), 693–705. doi:10.1109/TCSVT.2004.826773

Forman, A. E. (2008). E-commerce privacy and trust: Overview and foundation. In *Proceedings of the First International Conference on the Applications of Digital Information and Web Technologies* (pp. 50-53).

Forum, N. F. C. (2010). *NFC forum homepage*. Retrieved from http://www.nfc-forum.org

Furnell, S., & Thomson, K.-L. (2009). From culture to disobedience: Recognising the varying user acceptance of IT security. *Computer Fraud & Security*, (2): 5–10. doi:10.1016/S1361-3723(09)70019-3

Gajek, S., Jager, T., Manulis, M., & Schwenk, J. (2008). A browser-based kerberos authentication scheme. In *Proceedings of the 13th European Symposium on Research in Computer Security* (pp. 115-129).

Gajek, S., Liao, L., & Schwenk, J. (2008). Stronger tls bindings for SAML assertions and SAML artifacts. In *Proceedings of the ACM Workshop on Secure Web Services* (pp. 11-20).

Gajek, S. (2008). *Foundations of provable browser-based security protocols*. Bochum, Germany: Ruhr University.

Gajek, S., Schwenk, J., & Chen, X. (2008). *On the insecurity of Microsoft's identity metasystem cardspace (Tech. Rep. No. HGI TR-2008-004)*. Bochum, Germany: Horst Görtz Institute for IT-Security.

Ganesan, D., Govindan, R., Shenker, A., & Estrin, D. (2001). Highly Resilient Energy Efficient Multipath Routing in Wireless Sensor Networks. In *Proceedings of ACM Mobile Computations and Communications Review* (Vol. 5, No. 4, pp. 11-25).

Ganeshan, R., & Harrison, T. P. (1995). *An introduction to supply chain management*. Retrieved from http://lcm.csa.iisc.ernet.in/scm/supply_chain_intro.html

Ge, X., Paige, R. F., Polack, F. A. C., Chivers, H., & Brooke, P. J. (2006). Agile development of secure web applications. In *Proceedings of the 6th ACM International Conference on Web Engineering* (pp. 305-312).

Gelfond, M., & Lifschitz, V. (1993). Representing action and change by logic programs. *The Journal of Logic Programming, 17*, 301–322. doi:10.1016/0743-1066(93)90035-F

Gesbert, D., Shafi, M., Shiu, D., & Naguib, A. (2003). From theory to practice: An overview of MIMO space-time coded wireless systems. *IEEE Journal on Selected Areas in Communications, 21*(3). doi:10.1109/JSAC.2003.809458

GetSafeOnline. (2009). *Get safe online with free, expert advice*. Retrieved July 23, 2009, from http://www.getsafeonline.org/

Ghiselli, E. E. (1964). *Theory of Psychological Measurement*. New York: Mc GrawHill.

Gil, T. M., & Poletto, M. (2001). *MULTOPS: a data-structure for bandwidth attack detection.* Paper presented at the 10th conference on USENIX Security Symposium.

Giorgini, P., & Mouratidis, H. (2006). Secure Tropos: dealing effectively with security requirements in the development of multiagent systems. In M. Barley, F. Masacci, H. Mouratidis, & P. Scerri (Eds.), *Safety and security in multi-agent systems – selected papers.* New York: Springer.

Giorgini, P., & Mouratidis, H. (2007). Secure tropos: A security-oriented extension of the tropos methodology. *International Journal of Software Engineering and Knowledge Engineering, 17*(2), 285–309. doi:10.1142/S0218194007003240doi:10.1142/S0218194007003240

Giorgis, R. S. D., & Agurto, N. R. (2004). *New UML 2.0 based models to design WAP applications.* Paper presented at the 5th Aspect-Oriented Modeling Workshop, Lisbon, Portugal.

Glasser, D. J., Goodman, K. W., & Einspruch, N. G. (2007). Chips, tags and scanners: Ethical challenges for radio frequency identification. *Ethics and Information Technology, 9*(2), 101–109. doi:10.1007/s10676-006-9124-0

Glenn, C., & Madson, R. (1998). *The use of HMAC-SHA-1-96 within ESP and AH.* Retrieved from http://www.ietf.org/rfc/rfc2404.txt

Google. (2009). *Joid.* Retrieved from http://code.google.com/p/joid/

Google. (2010). *ZXing.* Retrieved from http://code.google.com/p/zxing/

Grob, T., & Pfitzmann, B. (2006). *SAML artifact information flow revisited.Saml artifact information flow revisited (Research report RZ 3643 99653).* Armonk, NY: IBM Research.

Groß, T. (2003). Security analysis of the SAML single sign-on browser/artifact profile. In *Proceedings of the 19th Annual Computer Security Applications Conference* (p. 298).

GS1. (2010). *GS1 barcodes.* Retrieved from http://www.gs1.org/barcodes

Gu, G., Fogla, P., Dagon, D., Lee, W., & Skoric, B. (2006). Towards an information-theoretic framework for analyzing intrusion detection systems. In *Proceedings of the 11th European Symposium on Research in Computer Security (ESORICS'06)* (pp. 527-546). New York: Springer.

Gundavelli, S., Leung, K., Devarapalli, V., Chowdhury, K., & Patil, B. (2008). *RFC 5213: Proxy mobile IPv6.* Retrieved from http://tools.ietf.org/html/rfc5213

Gupta, P., & Kumar, P. (2000). The capacity of wireless networks. *IEEE Transactions on Information Theory, 46*(2), 388–404. doi:10.1109/18.825799

Gürses, S., Jahnke, J. H., Obry, C., Onabajo, A., Santen, T., & Price, M. (2005). Eliciting confidentiality requirements in practice. In *Proceedings of the conference of the centre for advanced studies on collaborative research (CASCON)* (pp. 101-116). IBM Press.

Guyon, I., Gunn, S., Nikravesh, M., & Zadeh, L. A. (2006). *Feature Extraction: Foundations and Applications.* New York: Springer. doi:10.1007/978-3-540-35488-8

Habib, S. J., & Safar, M. (2007). Sensitivity Study of Sensor's Coverage within Wireless Sensor Networks. In *Proceedings of the 16th International Conference on Computer Communications and Networks* (pp. 876-881).

Habib, S. (2007). Modeling and simulating coverage in sensor networks. *Computer Communications, 30,* 1029–1035. doi:10.1016/j.comcom.2006.08.026

Hadim, S., & Mohamed, N. (2006). Middleware: Middleware challenges and approaches for wireless sensor networks. *IEEE Distributed Systems Online, 7*(3), 1. doi:10.1109/MDSO.2006.19

Haenggi, M. (2003). Energy-balancing strategies for wireless sensor networks. In *Proceedings of the International Symposium on Circuits and Systems,* Bangkok, Thailand.

Hall, M. (1999). *Correlation Based Feature Selection for Machine Learning.* Unpublished doctoral dissertation, University of Waikato, Department of Computer Science, Hamilton, New Zealand.

Han, S. Y., & Abu-Ghazaleh, N. B. (2008). On backoff in fading wireless channels. In D. Coudert, D. Simplot-Ryl, & I. Stojmenovic (Eds.), *Proceedings of the 7th International Conference on Ad-hoc, Mobile and Wireless Networks* (LNCS 5198, pp. 251-264).

Hara, T., & Madria, S. K. (2006). Data replication for improving data accessibility in ad hoc networks. *IEEE Transactions on Mobile Computing*, 1515–1532. doi:10.1109/TMC.2006.165

Harris Interactive. (2009). *Online security and privacy study*. Retrieved July 23, 2009, from http://staysafeonline. mediaroom.com/index.php?s=67

Hart, J. K., & Martinez, K. (2006). Environmental sensor networks: A revolution in the earth system science. *Earth-Science Reviews*, *78*, 177–191. doi:10.1016/j. earscirev.2006.05.001

Hatebur, D., Heisel, M., & Schmidt, H. (2007). A security engineering process based on patterns. In *Proceedings of the international workshop on secure systems methodologies using patterns (spatterns)* (pp. 734-738). Washington, DC: IEEE Computer Society.

Hatebur, D., Heisel, M., & Schmidt, H. (2008). Analysis and component-based realization of security requirements. In *Proceedings of the international conference on availability, reliability and security (AReS)* (pp. 195-203). Washington, DC: IEEE Computer Society.

Hawkins, S., Yen, D. C., & Chou, D. C. (2000). Awareness and challenges of Internet security. *Information Management & Computer Security*, *8*(3), 131–143. doi:10.1108/09685220010372564

Hazas, M., Scott, J., & Krumm, J. (2004). Location-aware computing comes of age. *Computer*, *37*(2), 95–97. doi:10.1109/MC.2004.1266301

Heckmann, O., Piringer, M., Schmitt, J., & Steinmetz, R. (2003). *On realistic network topologies for simulation*. Paper presented at the ACM SIGCOMM workshop on Models, methods and tools for reproducible network research.

Heinzelman, W. R., Chandrakasan, A. P., & Balakrishnan, H. (2000). Energy efficient communication protocol for wireless microsensor networks. In *Proceedings of the 33rd Hawaii International Conference on System Sciences* (pp. 3005-3014).

Hernan, S., Lambert, S., Ostwald, T., & Shostack, A. (2006, November). *Uncover security design flaws using the STRIDE approach*. Retrieved from http://msdn. microsoft.com/de-de/magazine/cc163519.aspx

Herzberg, A. (2009). Why Johnny can't surf (safely)? Attacks and defenses for web users. *Computers & Security*, *28*(1-2), 63–71. doi:10.1016/j.cose.2008.09.007

Hinde, S. (2004). Hacking gains momentum. *Computer Fraud & Security*, (11): 13–15. doi:10.1016/S1361-3723(04)00136-8

Holz, T., Engelberth, M., & Freiling, F. C. (2009). Learning more about the underground economy: A case-study of keyloggers and dropzones. In *Proceedings of the 14th European Symposium on Research in Computer Security* (pp. 1-18).

Hough, A. (2010). *Facebook security fears after private details of 100m users leaked to web*. Retrieved from http:// www.telegraph.co.uk/technology/facebook/7915572/ Facebook-security-fears-after-private-details-of-100m-users-leaked-to-web.html

Houmb, S. H., Georg, G., France, R., Bieman, J., & Jürjens, J. (2005). Cost-benefit trade-off analysis using BBN for aspect-oriented risk-driven development. In *Proceedings of the IEEE international conference on engineering of complex computer systems (iceccs)*. Washington, DC: IEEE Computer Society.

Howard, M., & Lipner, S. (2006). *The security development lifecycle*. Redmond, WA: Microsoft Press.

Hsia, T. L., Wu, J. H., & Li, E. Y. (2008). The e-commerce value matrix and use case model: A goal-driven methodology for eliciting B2C application requirements. *Information & Management*, *45*, 321–330. doi:10.1016/j. im.2008.04.001

Huang, C., & Tseng, Y. (2005). The coverage Problem in a Wireless Sensor Network. *Journal of Mobile networks and applications*, *10*, 519-528.

Huebsch, R., Hellerstein, J. M., Lanham, N., Loo, B. T., Shenker, S., & Stoica, I. (2003). Querying the Internet with PIER. In *Proceedings of the 29th Very Large Data Bases Conference*, Berlin, Germany (Vol. 29, pp. 321-332).

IBM Business Consulting Services. (2005). *Demand management: The next generation of forecasting*. Retrieved from http://www-935.ibm.com/services/us/imc/ pdf/g510-6014-demand-management.pdf

IBM Global Business Services. (2005). *Supply chain management—logistics services: Cost-effective logistics capabilities to meet today's supply chain challenges.* Retrieved from http://www-935.ibm.com/services/us/gbs/bus/pdf/g510-3793-supply-chain-management-logistics-services-cost-effective-logistics-capabilities.pdf

IEEE. (1999). *ANSI/IEEE standard 802.11: Wireless LAN medium access control (MAC) and physical layer (PHY) specifications.* Washington, DC: IEEE Computer Society.

Info, A. M. E. (2005). *How RFID can help optimize supply chain management.* Retrieved from http://www.ameinfo.com/66090.html

Infrared Data Association. (2009). *IRDA: The secure wireless link.* Retrieved from http://www.irda.org/

Intermec. (2007). *Supply chain RFID: How it works and why it pays.* Retrieved from http://epsfiles.intermec.com/eps_files/eps_wp/SupplyChainRFID_wp_web.pdf

International Organization for Standardization (ISO) and International Electrotechnical Commission. (IEC). (2000). *Functional safety of electrical/electronic/programmable electronic safty-relevant systems* (ISO/IEC 61508). Retrieved August 9, 2009, from http://www.iec.ch/61508/

Ioannidis, J., & Bellovin, S. M. (2002). *Implementing pushback: Router-based defense against DDoS attacks.* Paper presented at the Network and Distributed System Security Symposium.

Ishikawa, T., Yumoto, Y., Kurata, M., Endo, M., Kinoshita, S., Hoshino, F., et al. (2003). *Applying Auto-ID to the Japanese publication business to deliver advanced supply chain management, innovative retail applications, and convenient and safe reader services.* Retrieved from http://www.autoidlabs.org/uploads/media/KEI-AUTOID-WH004.pdf

Iyer, S., Rowstron, A., & Druschel, P. (2002). Squirrel: A decentralized peer-to-peer web cache. In *Proceedings of the ACM Symposium on Principles of Distributed Computing* (pp. 156-165).

Jackson, M. (2001). *Problem frames. Analyzing and structuring software development problems.* Reading, MA: Addison-Wesley.

Jain, A., & Ross, A. (2008). Introduction to biometrics. In Jain, A., Flynn, P., & Ross, A. (Eds.), *Handbook of biometrics* (pp. 1–22). New York, NY: Springer. doi:10.1007/978-0-387-71041-9_1

Jajodia, S., Samarati, P., & Subrahmanian, V. S. (1997). A logical language for expressing authorizations. In *Proceedings of the IEEE Symposium on Security and Privacy* (p. 0031). Washington, DC: IEEE Computer Society.

Jajodia, S., Kudo, M., & Subrahmanian, V. (2001). Provisional authorizations. In *E-commerce security and privacy* (pp. 133–159). Amsterdam, The Netherlands: Kluwer Academic.

JanRain. (2009). *Relying party stats as of Jan 1st, 2009.* Retrieved from http://blog.janrain.com/2009/01/relying-party-stats-as-of-jan-1st-2008.html

Jensen, M., Gruschka, N., & Herkenhöner, R. (2009). A survey of attacks on web services. *Computer Science - Research + Development, 24*(4), 185-197.

Jiang, H., Zhuang, W., & Shen, X. (2005). Cross-layer design for resource allocation in 3G wireless networks and beyond. *IEEE Communications Magazine, 43*(12), 120–126. doi:10.1109/MCOM.2005.1561929

Jin, Y., Wang, L., Kim, Y., & Yang, X. (2008). EEMC: An energy-efficient multi-level clustering algorithm for large-scale wireless sensor networks. *Computer Networks, 52*(3), 542–562. doi:10.1016/j.comnet.2007.10.005

Jordan, C. (1987). *A guide to understanding discretionary access control in trusted systems.* Retrieved from http://oai.dtic.mil/oai/oai?verb=getRecord&metadataPrefix=html&identifier=ADA392813

Kalakota, R., & Robinson, M. (2002). *M-business: The race to mobility.* New York, NY: McGraw-Hill.

Kalpakis, K., Dasgupta, K., & Namjoshi, P. (2002). *Maximum lifetime data gathering and aggregation in wireless sensor networks* (Tech. Rep. No. CS TR-02-12). Baltimore, MD: University of Maryland Baltimore County (UMBC).

Kaminski, D. (2008). *Black ops 2008: It's the end of the cache as we know it: DNS server+client cache poisoning, issues with SSL, breaking *forgot my password* systems, attacking autoupdaters and unhardened parsers, rerouting internal traffic.* Retrieved from http://www.blackhat.com/presentations/bh-jp-08/bh-jp-08-Kaminsky/BlackHat-Japan-08-Kaminsky-DNS08-BlackOps.pdf

Kar, K., & Banerjee, S. (2003). Node Placement for Connected Coverage in Sensor Networks. In *Proceedings of the WiOpt, Modeling and Optimization in Mobile, Ad Hoc and Wireless Networks*.

Karim, Z., Rezaul, K. M., & Hossain, A. (2009). Towards secure information systems in online banking. In *Proceedings of the International Conference on Internet Technology and Secured Transactions* (pp. 1-6).

Kaufman, C. (2005). *RFC 4306: Internet key exchange (IKEv2) protocol.* Retrieved from http://www.ietf.org/rfc/rfc4306.txt

Kay, R., & Mattern, F. (2004). The design space of wireless sensor networks. *IEEE Wireless Communications*, *11*(6), 54–61. doi:10.1109/MWC.2004.1368897

Kemp, J., Cantor, S., Mishra, P., Philpott, R., & Maler, E. (2005). *Authentication context for the OASIS security assertion markup language (SAML) v2.0.* Retrieved from http://docs.oasis-open.org/security/saml/v2.0/saml-authn-context-2.0-os.pdf

Khalifa, M., & Shen, K. N. (2008). Explaining the adoption of transactional B2C mobile commerce. *Journal of Enterprise Information Management*, *21*(2), 110–124. doi:10.1108/17410390810851372

Klingenstein, N. (2009). *SAML v2.0 holder-of-key web browser SSO profile.* Retrieved from http://docs.oasis-open.org/security/saml/Post2.0/sstc-saml-holder-of-key-browser-sso.pdf

Knowledgeleader. (2006). *Overview of RFID components.* Retrieved from http://www.theiia.org/download.cfm?file=93793

Kormann, D., & Rubin, A. (2000). Risks of the passport single signon protocol. *Computer Networks, 33*(1-6), 51-58.

Koshutanski, H., & Massacci, F. (2004). Interactive access control for web services. In *Proceedings of the 19th International Conference on Information Security* (pp. 151-166).

Krawczyk, H., Bellare, M., & Canetti, R. (1997). *HMAC: Keyed-hashing for message authentication.* Retrieved from http://www.ietf.org/rfc/rfc2104.txt

Krishnamachari, B., & Ordonez, F. (2003). Analysis of energy-efficient, fair routing in wireless sensor networks through non-linear optimization. In *Proceedings of Workshop on Wireless Ad hoc, Sensor, and Wearable Networks, IEEE Vehicular Technology Conference*, Orlando, FL.

Krishnamurthy, B., & Wang, J. (2001, November). Topology modeling via cluster graphs. In *Proceedings of SIGCOMM Internet Measurement Workshop*, San Francisco, CA (pp. 19-23).

Krishna, P., Vaidya, N. H., Chatterjee, M., & Pradhan, D. (1997). A cluster-based approach for routing in dynamic networks. *ACM SIGCOMM Computer Communication Review*, *27*(2), 49–65. doi:10.1145/263876.263885

Kristoffersen, S., & Ljungberg, F. (1999). Designing interaction styles for a mobile use context. In *Proceedings of the 1st International Symposium on Handheld and Ubiquitous Computing* (pp. 281-288).

Krutchen, P. (2001). Agility with the RUP. *Cutter IT Journal*, *14*(12), 27–33.

Kudo, M., & Hada, S. (2000). Xml document security based on provisional authorization. In *Proceedings of the 7th ACM Conference on Computer and Communications Security* (pp. 87-96). New York, NY: ACM Press.

Kudo, M. (2002). PBAC: Provision-based access control model. *International Journal of Information Security*, *1*(2), 116–130. doi:10.1007/s102070100010

Kumar, D., Aseri, T. C., & Patel, R. B. (2009). EEHC: Energy efficient heterogeneous clustered scheme for wireless sensor networks. *Computer Communications*, *32*(4), 662–667. doi:10.1016/j.comcom.2008.11.025

Kurose, J. F., & Ross, K. W. (2007). *Computer networking: A top-down approach* (4th ed.). Reading, MA: Addison-Wesley.

Kwon, K., & Lee, C. (2004). A fast handoff algorithm using intelligent channel scan for IEEE 802.11 WLANs. In *Proceedings of the 6th International Conference on Advanced Communication Technology* (Vo. 1, pp. 46-50).

Lahlou, A., & Urien, P. (2003). SIM-filter: User profile based smart information filtering and personalization in smartcard. In *Proceedings of the 15th Conference on Advanced Information Systems Engineering*.

Lakhina, A., Crovella, M., & Diot, C. (2005). *Mining anomalies using traffic feature distributions*. Paper presented at the Conference on Applications, technologies, architectures, and protocols for computer communications.

Langer, M., Loidl, S., & Nerb, M. (1998). Customer service management: A more transparent view to your subscribed services. In *Proceedings of the IEEE International Workshop on Distributed Systems: Operations & Management*.

Lataste, S., & Tossou, B. (2008). From network layer mobility to IMS service continuity. In *Proceedings of the 12th International Conference on Intelligence in Service Delivery Networks*.

Lau, W., Kumar, M., & Venkatesh, S. (2002). A cooperative cache architecture in supporting caching multimedia objects in MANETs. In *Proceedings of 5th International Workshop on Wireless Mobile Multimedia* (pp. 56-63).

Le, D., Fu, X., & Hogrefe, D. (2006). A review of mobility support paradigms for the internet. *IEEE Communications Surveys and Tutorials*, *8*(1), 38–51. doi:10.1109/COMST.2006.323441

Lee, Z.-Y., Yu, H.-C., & Ku, P.-J. (2001). An analysis and comparison of different types of electronic payment systems. In *Proceedings of the Portland International Conference on Management of Engineering and Technology* (pp. 38-45).

Lee, W. (2006). *Wireless and cellular telecommunications* (3rd ed.). New York, NY: McGraw-Hill.

Lee, Y. E., & Benbasat, I. (2004). A framework for the study of customer interface design for mobile commerce. *International Journal of Electronic Commerce*, *8*(3), 79–102.

Lescuyer, P., & Lucidarme, T. (2008). *Evolved packet system (EPS) the LTE and SAE evolution of 3G UMTS*. Chichester, UK: John Wiley & Sons. doi:10.1002/9780470723678

Li, H., & Zhang, H. (2004). How people select their payment methods in online auctions? An exploration of eBay transactions. In *Proceedings of the 37th Annual Hawaii International Conference on System Sciences* (p. 10).

Liang, T., Huang, C., Yeh, Y., & Lin, B. (2007). Adoption of mobile technology in business: A fit-viability model. *Industrial Management & Data Systems*, *107*(8), 1154–1169. doi:10.1108/02635570710822796

Liang, T., & Wei, C. (2004). Introduction to the special issue: Mobile commerce applications. *International Journal of Electronic Commerce*, *8*(3), 7–17.

Lim, S., Lee, W. C., Cao, G., & Das, C. R. (2004). Performance comparison of cache invalidation strategies for Internet based mobile ad hoc networks. In *Proceedings of the IEEE International Conference on Mobile Ad Hoc and Sensor Systems* (pp. 104-113).

Lim, S., Lee, W. C., Cao, G., & Das, C. R. (2006). A novel caching scheme for improving Internet based mobile ad hoc networks performance. *Journal of Ad Hoc Networks*, 225-239.

Lin, H. T., Lo, W. S., & Chiang, C. L. (2006). Using RFID in supply chain management for customer service. In *Proceedings of the IEEE International Conference on Systems, Man, and Cybernetics*, Taipei, Taiwan (pp. 1377-1381).

Lin, L., Nuseibeh, B., Ince, D., & Jackson, M. (2004). Using abuse frames to bound the scope of security problems. In *Proceedings of the IEEE international requirements engineering conference (RE)* (pp. 354-355). Washington, DC: IEEE Computer Society.

Liu, H., & Motoda, H. (2008). *Computational Methods of Feature Selection*. Boca Raton, FL: CRC.

Liu, Y. (2008). A two-hop solution to solving topology mismatch. *Transactions on Parallel and Distributed Systems*, *19*(11), 1591–1600. doi:10.1109/TPDS.2008.24

Liu, Y., Xiao, L., & Ni, L. M. (2007). Building a scalable bipartite P2P overlay network. *Transactions on Parallel and Distributed Systems*, *18*(9), 1296–1306. doi:10.1109/TPDS.2007.1059

Li, X., Wan, P., & Frieder, O. (2003). Coverage in wireless ad hoc sensor networks. *IEEE Transactions on Computers*, *52*(6), 753–763. doi:10.1109/TC.2003.1204831

Loutrel, M., Urien, P., & Pujolle, G. (2003). A smartcard for authentication in WLANs. In *Proceedings of the IFIP/ACM Latin America Conference on Towards a Latin American Agenda for Network Research.*

Magno-Caldognetto, E., Zmarich, C., Cosi, P., & Ferrero, F. (1997, September 5-8). Italian consonantal visemes: Relationships between spatial/temporal articulatory characteristics and co-produced acoustic signal In *Proceedings of the ESCA Workshop on Audio-Visual Speech Processing*, Rhodes, Greece.

Maguire, A. (2008). *Achieving real personalised learning: Considerations on blended learning*. Retrieved March 30, 2010, from http://www.thirdforce.com/resources/whitepaper/WP_AMaguire01.pdf

Mahajan, R., Floyd, S., & Wetherall, D. (2001). *Controlling high-bandwidth flows at the congested router.* Paper presented at the Proc. 9th International Conference on Network Protocols.

Malpani, R., Lorch, J., & Berger, D. (1995). Making World Wide Web cache servers cooperate. In *Proceedings of the 4ᵗʰ International World Wide Web Conference* (pp. 107-117).

Manaseer, S. S., & Masadeh, M. (2008). *Pessimistic backoff for mobile ad hoc networks*. Glasgow, Scotland: University of Glasgow.

Manaseer, S., & Ould-Khaoua, M. (2006). *Logarithmic based backoff algorithm for MAC protocol in MANETs*. Glasgow, Scotland: University of Glasgow.

Manaseer, S., Ould-Khaoua, M., & Mackenzie, L. M. (2006). *Fibonacci backoff algorithm for mobile ad hoc networks*. Glasgow, Scotland: University of Glasgow.

Mannan, M., & van Oorschot, P. C. (2007). Using a personal device to strengthen password authentication from an untrusted computer. In S. Dietrich & R. Dhamija (Eds.), *Proceedings of the 11th International Conference on Financial Cryptography and the 1st International Workshop on Usable Security* (LNCS 4886, pp. 88-103).

Mar, K., & Schwaber, K. (2002). *Scrum with XP*. Retrieved from http://www.informit.com/articles/article.aspx?p=26057&seqNum=3

Markopoulos, A. E., Pissaris, P., Kyriazakos, S., & Sykas, E. D. (2004). Cellular network performance analysis: Handoff algorithms based on mobile location and area information. *Wireless Personal Communications*, *30*(2-4), 97–117. doi:10.1023/B:WIRE.0000049393.01548.30

May, C. (2008). Approaches to user education. *Network Security*, (9): 15–17. doi:10.1016/S1353-4858(08)70109-0

Mayer, N. (2009). *Model-based management of information system security risk*. Unpublished doctoral dissertation, University of Namur. Retrieved August 9, 2009, from http://nmayer.eu/publis/Thesis Mayer 2.0.pdf

McAfee. (2009). *McAfee security tips - 13 ways to protect your system*. Retrieved September 2, 2009, from http://www.mcafee.com/us/threat_center/tips.html

McDonald, B., & Znati, T. (2001). Design and performance of a distributed dynamic clustering algorithm for ad-hoc networks. In *Proceedings of the Annual Simulation Symposium* (pp. 27-35).

Mead, N. R., Hough, E. D., & Stehney, T. R., II. (2005). *Security quality requirements engineering (SQUARE) methodology* (Tech. Rep. No. CMU/SEI-2005-TR-009). Pittsburgh, PA: Carnegie Mellon Software Engineering Institute.

Meguerdichian, S., Koushanfar, F., Potkonjak, M., & Srivastava, M. (2001). Coverage Problems in Wireless Ad-Hoc Sensor Networks. In *Proceedings of the IEEE INFOCOM*, AK.

Meso, P., & Jain, R. (2006). Agile software development: Adaptive systems principles and best practices. *Information Systems Management*, *23*(3), 19–30. doi:10.1201/1078.10580530/46108.23.3.20060601/93704.3

Mhatre, V., Rosenberg, C., Kofman, D., Mazumdar, R., & Shroff, N. (2004). Design of surveillance sensor grids with a lifetime constraint. In *Proceedings of the 1ˢᵗ European Workshop on Wireless Sensor Networks*, Berlin, Germany (LNCS 2920, pp. 263-275).

Michael, K., & McCathie, L. (2005). The pros and cons of RFID in supply chain management. In *Proceedings of the International Conference on Mobile Business*, Sydney, Australia (pp. 623-629).

Michalewicz, Z. (1994). *Genetic Algorithms + Data Structure = Evolution Programs*. Berlin: Springer Verlag.

Microsoft. (2009). *Consumer online safety education*. Retrieved September 2, 2009, from http://www.microsoft.com/protect/default.aspx

Microsoft. (n. d.). *Passport*. Retrieved from https://accountservices.passport.net/ppnetworkhome.srf?-vv=1000&mkt=EN-US&lc=1033

MIT. (2011). *Kerberos: The network authentication protocol*. Retrieved from http://web.mit.edu/Kerberos/

Modrak, V., Knuth, P., & Novak-Marcinein, J. (2010). Advantages and risks of RFID in business applications. *International Business Management*, *4*(1), 28–34. doi:10.3923/ibm.2010.28.34

Moriya, T., & Aida, H. (2003). Cache data access system in ad hoc networks. In *Proceedings of the Vehicular Technology Conference* (pp. 1228-1232).

Möttönen, R., Olivés, J.-L., Kulja, J., & Sams, M. (2000). Parameterized visual speech synthesis and its evaluation. In *Proceedings of the 10ᵗʰ European Conference on Signal Processing: Theories and Applications*, Tampere, Finland (pp. 769-772).

M'Raihi, D., Bellare, M., Hoornaert, F., Naccache, D., & Ranen, O. (2005). *HOTP: An HMAC-based one-time password algorithm*. Retrieved from http://www.ietf.org/rfc/rfc4226.txt

Mullett, G. J. (2006). *Wireless telecommunications systems and networks*. Florence, KY: Delmar Cengage Learning.

Murray, M. (2010). *Introduction to supply chain management*. Retrieved from http://logistics.about.com/od/supplychainintroduction/a/into_scm.htm

Naotoshi, S. S. (2008). *ENEE 632 Project 4 Part I: Pitch detection*. Retrieved from http://note.sonots.com/?plugin=attach&refer=SciSoftware%2FPitch&openfile=pitch.pdf

National Cyber Security Alliance & Symantec. (2008). *NCSA-Symantec national cyber security awareness study newsworthy analysis*.

Negi, R., & Goel, S. (2004, December). An information-theoretic approach to queuing in wireless channels with large delay bounds. In. *Proceedings of the IEEE Conference on Global Telecommunications*, *1*, 116–122.

Ngai, E. W. T., & Gunasekaran, A. (2007). A review of mobile commerce research and applications. *Decision Support Systems*, *43*(1), 3–15. doi:10.1016/j.dss.2005.05.003

Ni, Q., Bertino, E., & Lobo, J. (2008). An obligation model bridging access control policies and privacy policies. In *Proceedings of the 13th ACM Symposium on Access Control Models and Technologies* (pp. 133-142). New York, NY: ACM Press.

Ni, S., Tseng, Y., Chen, Y., & Sheu, P. (1999). The broadcast storm problem in a mobile ad hoc network. In *Proceedings of the Annual ACM/IEEE International Conference on Mobile Computing and Networking* (pp. 151-162).

Nicules, D., & Nath, B. (2003). Ad-Hoc Positioning System (APS) Using AoA. In *Proceedings of IEEE INFOCOM*, San Francisco.

NIST. (2001). *Federal information processing standards publication: Security requirements for cryptographic modules*. Retrieved from http://csrc.nist.gov/publications/fips/fips140-2/fips1402.pdf

NTP. (2007). *The network time protocol*. Retrieved from http://www.ntp.org/

OASIS. (2008). *Security services (SAML) TC*. Retrieved from http://www.oasis-open.org/committees/tc_home.php?wg_abbrev=security

Okenyi, P. O., & Owens, T. J. (2007). On the Anatomy of Human Hacking. *Information Systems Security*, *16*, 302–314. doi:10.1080/10658980701747237

OMNeT++ (2009). *Documentation*. Retrieved from http://www.omnetpp.org/

Open, I. D. Foundation. (2010). *Get an OpenID*. Retrieved from http://openid.net/get-an-openid

Orenstein, P., Goodman, D., Marantz, Z., & Rodriguez, V. (2004). Effects of additive noise on the throughput of CDMA data communications. In *Proceedings of the International Conference on Communications* (pp. 3046-3050).

Padmanabhan, V. N., & Subramanian, L. (2001). An investigation of geographic mapping techniques for Internet hosts. In *Proceedings of the ACM Conference on Applications, Technologies, Architectures, and Protocols for Computer Communications*, San Diego, CA (pp. 173-185).

Pan, J., Hou, Y. T., Cai, L., Shi, Y., & Shen, S. X. (2003). Topology Control for Wireless Sensor Networks. In *Proceedings of the International Conference on Mobile Computing and Networking*, San Diego.

Pang, Q., Liew, S. C., Lee, J., & Leung, V. (2004). Performance evaluation of an adaptive backoff scheme for WLAN. *Wireless Communications & Mobile Computing*, *4*(8), 867–879. doi:10.1002/wcm.260

Papadimitratos, P., Mishra, A., & Rosenburgh, D. (2005). A cross-layer design approach to enhance 802.15.4. In *Proceedings of the Conference on Military Communications* (pp. 1719-1726).

Park, J., Kim, K., & Kim, M. (2008). The Aegis: UICC based security framework. In *Proceedings of the Second International Conference on: Future Generation Communication and Networking* (pp. 264-269).

Park, J., & Sandhu, R. (2004, February). The UCO-NABC usage control model. *ACM Transactions on Information and System Security*, *7*(1), 128–174. doi:10.1145/984334.984339

Pearson, J. (2006). *Increasing security in the supply chain with electronic security markers*. Retrieved from http://www.ti.com/rfid/docs/manuals/whtPapers/wp_eSecurity_Markers.pdf

Peng, T., Leckie, C., & Ramamohanarao, K. (2003). Detecting distributed denial of service attacks by sharing distributed beliefs. In Safavi-Naini, R., & Seberry, J. (Eds.), *Lecture Notes in Computer Science* (*Vol. 2727*, pp. 214–225). New York: Springer.

Peng, T., Leckie, C., & Ramamohanarao, K. (2004). Proactively detecting distributed denial of service attacks using source IP address monitoring. In Mitrou, N. (Ed.), *Lecture Notes in Computer Science* (pp. 771–782). New York: Springer.

Perkins, C. (2002). *RFC 334: IP mobility support for IPv4*. Retrieved from http://www.ietf.org/rfc/rfc3344.txt

Pfitzmann, B., & Waidner, M. (2003). Analysis of Liberty single-signon with enabled clients. *IEEE Internet Computing*, *76*, 38–44. doi:10.1109/MIC.2003.1250582

Phoenix Software International. (2006). *Optical character recognition (OCR): What you need to know*. Retrieved from http://www.phoenixsoftware.com/pdf/ocrdataentry.pdf

Puente, F., Sandoval, J. D., Hernandez, P., & Molina, C. (2005). Improving online banking security with hardware devices. In *Proceedings of the 39th Annual International Carnahan Conference on Security Technology* (pp. 174-177).

Qing, L., Zhu, Q., & Wang, M. (2006). Design of a distributed energy-efficient clustering algorithm for heterogeneous wireless sensor networks. *Computer Communications*, *29*(12), 2230–2237. doi:10.1016/j.comcom.2006.02.017

Quinlan, J. R. (1993). *C4.5: Programs for Machine Learning*. San Francisco: Morgan Kaufmann.

Quintao, F., Nakamura, F., & Mateus, G. (2004). An Evolutive Approach for the Coverage Problem in Wireless Sensor Networks. In *Proceedings of the 24th Brazilian Computer Society*.

Quintao, F., Nakamura, F., & Mateus, G. (2005). Evolutionary Algorithm for the Dynamic Coverage Problem Applied to Wireless Sensor Networks Design. In *Proceedings of IEEE Congress on Evolutionary Computations*, Edinburgh, UK.

Radack, S. (2003). *Electronic authentication: Guidance for selecting secure techniques*. Retrieved from http://www.itl.nist.gov/lab/bulletns/bltnaug04.htm

Radier, B., & Salaun, M. (2010). A vehicle gateway to manage IP multimedia subsystem autonomous mobility. *International Journal of Autonomous and Adaptive Communications Systems*, *3*(2), 159–177. doi:10.1504/IJAACS.2010.031089

Rafay, A. A., & Ahmad, N. (2003). *CRULP annual student report* (pp. 68-71). Retrieved from http://www.crulp.org/research/reports/streport03.htm

Rasid, M. F. A., Abdullah, R. S. A. R., Ghazvini, M. H. F., & Vahabi, M. (2007). Energy optimization with multi-level clustering algorithm for wireless sensor networks. In *Proceedings of the International Conference on Wireless and Optical Communications Networks* (pp. 1-5).

Raskutti, G., Zalesky, A., Wong, E. W. M., & Zuckerman, M. (2007). Enhanced blocking probability evaluation method for circuit-switched trunk reservation networks. *IEEE Communications Letters*, *11*(6), 543. doi:10.1109/LCOMM.2007.062119

Reveilhac, M., & Pasquet, M. (2009). Promising secure element alternatives for NFC technology. In *Proceedings of the First International Workshop on Near Field Communication* (pp. 75-80).

Revéret, L. (1999). *Conception et évaluation d'un système de suivi automatique des gestes labiaux en parole*. Thèse de doctorat préparée au sein de l'Institut de la Communication Parlée, Grenoble, France.

RFID4U. (2006). *Benefits of RFID-enabled supply chain*. Retrieved from http://www.rfid4u.com/downloads/Benefits%20of%20RFID-Enabled%20Supply%20Chain.pdf

Richardson, R. (2007). 2007 CSI computer crime and security survey. In *Proceedings of the 12th annual computer crime and security survey*. Retrieved August 22, 2008, from http://i.cmpnet.com/v2.gocsi.com/pdf/CSISurvey2007.pdf

Richardson, R. (2008). *2008 CSI computer crime & security survey*. Computer Security Institute.

Riordan, C., & Sorensen, H. (1994). Information filtering and retrieval: An overview. In *Proceedings of the IEEE 16th Annual International Conference on Engineering in Medicine and Biology Society*, Baltimore. *MD Medical Newsmagazine*, *1*, 42–49.

Ripeanu, M., & Foster, I. T. (2002). Mapping the Gnutella network: Macroscopic properties of large-scale peer-to-peer systems. In *Proceedings of the 1st International Workshop on Peer-to-Peer Systems*, London, UK (pp. 85-93).

Ritter, J. (2001). *Why Gnutella can't scale. No, really*. Retrieved from http://www.globalspec.com/reference/123320/why-gnutella-can-t-scale-no-really

Rivest, R., Shamir, A., & Adleman, L. (1978). A method for obtaining digital signatures and public-key cryptosystems. *Communications of the ACM*, *21*(2), 120–126. doi:10.1145/359340.359342

Rondeau, T. W., & Bostian, C. W. (2009). *Artificial intelligence in wireless communications*. Norwood, MA: Artech House.

Røstad, L., Tøndel, I. A., Line, M. B., & Nordland, O. (2006). Safety vs. security. In M. G. Stamatelatos & H. S. Blackman (Eds.), *Proceedings of the international conference on probabilistic safety assessment and management (PSAM)*. New York: ASME Press.

Rotvold, G. (2008). How to create a security culture in your organization. *Information Management Journal*, *42*(6), 32–38.

Rowstron, A., & Druschel, P. (2001). Scalable, distributed object location and routing for large-scale peer-to-peer systems. In *Proceedings of the 18th IFIPIACM International Conference on Distributed Systems Platforms*, Heidelberg, Germany.

Sabbaghi, A., & Vaidyanathan, G. (2008). Effectiveness and efficiency of RFID technology in supply chain management: Strategic values and challenges. *Journal of Theoretical and Applied Electronic Commerce Research*, *3*(2), 71–81. doi:10.4067/S0718-18762008000100007

Sadagopan, N., & Krishnamachari, B. (2004). Maximizing Data Extraction in Energy-Limited Sensor Networks. In *Proceedings of the IEEE INFOCOM*, Hong Kong, China.

Sae-Tankg, S., & Esichaikul, V. (2001). Web personalization techniques for e-commerce. In *Proceedings of the 6th International Computer Science Conference on Active Media Technology* (pp. 36-44).

Sakakibara, K., Sasaki, M., & Yamakita, J. (2005). Backoff algorithm with release stages for slotted ALOHA systems. *ECTI Transactions on Electrical Engineering, Electronics, and Communications, 3*.

Salamah, M., & Lababidi, K. (2006). Dynamically adaptive channel reservation scheme for cellular networks. In *Proceedings of the International Conference on Personal Wireless Communications* (pp. 269-272).

Sardana, A., Joshi, R., & Kim, T. (2008). *Deciding Optimal Entropic Thresholds to Calibrate the Detection Mechanism for Variable Rate DDoS Attacks in ISP Domain.* Paper presented at the International Conference on Information Security and Assurance.

Sardana, A., Kumar, K., & Joshi, R. C. (2007). *Detection and Honeypot Based Redirection to Counter DDoS Attacks in ISP Domain.* Paper presented at the 3rd International Symposium on Information Assurance and Security.

Saroiu, S., Gummadi, K. P., Dunn, R. J., Gribble, S. D., & Levy, H. M. (2002, December 9-11). An analysis of Internet content delivery systems. In *Proceedings of the 5th Symposium on Operating Systems Design and Implementation*, Boston, MA (Vol. 36, pp. 315-327).

Sasson, Y., Cavin, D., & Schiper, A. (2003). Probabilistic broadcast for flooding in wireless mobile ad hoc networks. *Wireless Communications and Networking, 2*, 1124–1130.

Satori, H., Hiyassat, H., Harti, M., & Chenfour, N. (2005). Investigation Arabic speech recognition using CMU Sphinx system. *International Arab Journal of Information Technology, 6*(2).

Savvide, A., Han, C., & Strivastava, M. (2001). Dynamic Fine-Grained Localization in Ad-Hoc Networks of Sensors. In *Proceedings of the ACM International Conference on Mobile Computing and Networking*, Rome, Italy.

Shih, E., Cho, S., Ickes, N., Min, R., Sinha, A., Wang, A., & Chandrakasan, A. (2001). Physical Layer Driven Protocol and Algorithm Design for Energy-Efficient Wireless Sensor Networks. In *Proceedings of the ACM International Conference on Mobile Computing and Networking*, Rome, Italy.

Schechter, S., Dhamija, R., Ozment, A., & Fischer, I. (2007). The emperor's new security indicators. In *Proceedings of the IEEE Symposium on Security and Privacy* (pp. 51-65).

Schlienger, T., & Teufel, S. (2003). *Analyzing information security culture: Increased trust and appropriate information security culture.* Paper presented at the 14th International Workshop on Database and Expert Systems Applications (DEXA'03), Prague, Czech Republic.

Schmidt, A., Schröder, H., & Frick, O. (2000). WAP – Designing for small user interfaces. In *Proceedings of the CHI Extended Abstracts on Human Factors in Computing Systems*, The Hague, The Netherlands.

Schmidt, H. (2010). *A pattern-and component-based method to develop secure software.* Berlin: Deutscher Wissenschafts-Verlag (DWV).

Schneeweiss, C. (2003). *Distributed decision making* (2nd ed.). Berlin, Germany: Springer-Verlag.

Schneier, B. (1999). Attack trees. *Dr. Dobb's Journal.* Retrieved August 9, 2009, from http://www.schneier.com/paper-attacktrees-ddj-ft

Schneier, B. (2000). *Secrets and lies.* New York: Wiley Publishing, Inc.

Schultz, E. (2004). Security training and awareness--fitting a square peg in a round hole. *Computers & Security, 23*(1), 1–2. doi:10.1016/j.cose.2004.01.002

Segura, J. A. V., Sanchez, J. J. S., Madrid, N. M., & Seepold, R. (2005). Integration of smart cards into automation networks. In *Proceedings of the Third International Workshop on Intelligent Solutions in Embedded Systems* (pp. 185-193).

Sen, S., & Wang, J. (2002). Analyzing peer-to-peer traffic across large networks. *IEEE/ACM Transactions on Networking, 12*(2), 219–232. doi:10.1109/TNET.2004.826277

Shen, C. C., Srisathapornphat, C., & Jaikaeo, C. (2010). Sensor information networking architecture and applications. *IEEE Personal Communications*, 52-59.

Sheng, M., & Lu, X.-X. (2009). An empirical study on influencing factors of customer satisfaction to individual internet banking. In *Proceedings of the International Symposium on Computer Network and Multimedia Technology* (pp. 1-4).

Sheng, Q. Z., Li, X., & Zeadally, S. (2008). Enabling next-generation RFID applications: Solutions and challenges. *IEEE Computer*, *41*(9), 21–28.

Shim, S. S., Bhalla, G., & Pendyala, V. (2005). Federated identity management. *Computer*, *38*(12), 120–122. doi:10.1109/MC.2005.408

Shiratuddin, N., & Hassan, S. (2010). *Design research in software development*. Sintok, Malaysia: Universiti Utara Malaysia Press.

Silberschatz, A., Galvin, P. B., & Gagne, G. (2004). *Operating system concepts*. New York, NY: John Wiley & Sons.

Simulator, N. (2005). *2 (NS2)*. Retrieved from http://www.isi.edu/nsnam

Sindre, G. (2007). Mal-activity diagrams for capturing attacks on business processes. In P. Sawyer, B. Paech, & P. Heymans (Eds.), *Proceedings of the international working conference on requirements engineering: Foundation for software quality (REFSQ)* (LNCS 4542, pp. 355-366). New York: Springer.

Sindre, G., & Opdahl, A. L. (2001). Capturing security requirements through misuse cases. In *Proceedings of the Norwegian informatics conference (NIK)*.

Slemko, M. (2001). *Microsoft passport to trouble*. Retrieved from http://www.znep.com/~marcs/passport/

Smaragdakis, G., Matta, I., & Bestavros, A. (2004). SEP: A stable election protocol for clustered heterogeneous wireless sensor networks. In *Proceeding of the International Workshop on SANPA* (pp. 251-261).

Soghoian, C., & Jakobsson, M. (2007). *A deceit-augmented man in the middle attack against Bank of America's sitekey service*. Retrieved from http://paranoia.dubfire.net/2007/04/deceit-augmented-man-in-middle-attack.html

Soliman, H. (2009). *RFC 5555: Mobile IPv6 support for dual stack hosts and routers*. Retrieved from http://tools.ietf.org/search/rfc5555

Song, N.-O., Kwak, B.-J., Song, J., & Miller, L. E. (2004). *Enhancement of IEEE 802.11 distributed coordination function with exponential increase exponential decrease backoff algorithm*. Gaithersburg, MD: National Institute of Standards and Technology.

Soni, S., & Chand, N. (2010). Energy efficient multilevel clustering to prolong the lifetime of wireless sensor networks. *Journal of Computing*, *2*(5), 158–165.

Soysal, A., & Ulukus, S. (2010). Joint channel estimation and resource allocation for MIMO systems. *IEEE Transactions on Wireless Communications*, *9*(2), 632–640. doi:10.1109/TWC.2010.02.080100

Spurling, P. (1995). Promoting security awareness and commitment. *Information Management & Computer Security*, *3*(2), 20–26. doi:10.1108/09685229510792988

Stallings, W. (2005). *Wireless communications and networks* (2nd ed.). Upper Saddle River, NJ: Prentice-Hall.

Stamm, S., Ramzan, Z., & Jakobsson, M. (2006). *Drive-by pharming* (Tech. Rep. No. 641). Bloomington, IN: Indiana University.

Stamp, M. (2006). *Information security principles and practice*. Hoboken, NJ: John Wiley & Sons.

Starnberger, G., Froihofer, L., & Goeschka, K. M. (2009). QR-TAN: Secure mobile transaction authentication. In *Proceedings of the 4th International Workshop on Frontiers in Availability, Reliability and Security*, Fukuoka, Japan (pp. 578-583).

StaySafeOnline. (2009). *Are your defenses up and your instincts honed?* Retrieved July 23, 2009, from http://www.staysafeonline.org/

Steffens, E., Nennker, A., Ren, Z., Yin, M., & Schneider, L. (2009). The SIM-based mobile wallet. In *Proceedings of the 13th International Conference on Intelligence in Next Generation Networks* (pp. 1-6).

Sternberg, R. J., Grigorenko, E. L., & Zhang, L.-f. (2008). Styles of learning and thinking matter in instruction and assessment. *Perspectives on Psychological Science*, *3*(6), 486–506. doi:10.1111/j.1745-6924.2008.00095.x

Suciu, L., Benzaid, M., Bonjour, S., & Louin, P. (2009). Assessing the handover approaches for heterogeneous wireless networks. In *Proceedings of the 18th International Conference on Computer Communications and Networks* (pp. 1-6).

Sun, J. (2001). Mobile ad hoc networking: An essential technology for pervasive computing. In *Proceedings of the International Conferences on Info-tech & Info-net*, Beijing, China.

Sun, Y., Belding-Royer, E. M., & Perkins, C. E. (2002). Internet connectivity for ad hoc mobile networks. *International Journal of Wireless Information Networks*, 9(2), 75–88. doi:10.1023/A:1015399632291

Symantec. (2007). *Symantec Internet security threat report - Trends for January - June 2007*. Symantec Corporation.

Taifour, M., Nat-Abdesselam, F., & Simplot-Ryl, D. (2006). *Neighbourhood backoff algorithm for optimizing bandwidth in single hop wireless ad-hoc networks*. Retrieved from citeseerx.ist.psu.edu/viewdoc/summary?doi=10.1.1.76.3509

Takahashi, K., & Tsuboi, T. (2003). *A backoff algorithm for improving saturation throughput in IEEE 802.11 DCF. Tokyo*. Japan: Tokyo University of Technology.

Tang, B., Gupta, H., & Das, S. R. (2008). Benefit based data caching in ad hoc networks. *IEEE Transactions on Mobile Computing*, 289–303. doi:10.1109/TMC.2007.70770

Tarasewich, P. (2003). Designing mobile commerce applications. *Communications of the ACM*, 46(12), 57–60. doi:10.1145/953460.953489

Tarokh, V., Jafarkhani, H., & Calderbank, A. R. (1999). Space-time block codes from orthogonal designs. *IEEE Transactions on Information Theory*, 45(5), 1456–1467. doi:10.1109/18.771146

Teece, D. J., Pisano, G., & Shuen, A. (1997). Dynamic capabilities and strategic management. *Strategic Management Journal*, 18(7), 509–533. doi:10.1002/(SICI)1097-0266(199708)18:7<509::AID-SMJ882>3.0.CO;2-Z

Tektronix. (2004). *Radio frequency identification (RFID) overview*. Retrieved from http://www.isotest.es/web/Soporte/Formacion/Notas%20de%20aplicacion/TEKTRONIX/TEKTRONIX%20RSA/RFID.pdf

Telatar, E. (1999). Capacity of multi-antenna gaussian channels. *European Transactions on Telecommunication*, 10(6), 585–596. doi:10.1002/ett.4460100604

The National Strategies. (2007). *Leading on intervention: Personalisation questions and answers*. Retrieved March 30, 2010, from http://nationalstrategies.standards.dcsf.gov.uk/downloader/9e2a483e7a1c9191f017c6ddfe2dfc30.pdf

Theodoridis, S., & Koutroumbas, K. (2003). *Pattern recognition* (2nd ed.). San Diego, CA: Academic Press.

Thompson, M. E., & Von Solms, R. (1998). Information security awareness: Educating your users effectively. *Information Management & Computer Security*, 6(4), 167–173. doi:10.1108/09685229810227649

Tiddeman, B., & Perret, D. (2002). Prototyping and transforming visemes for animated speech. In *Proceedings of the Conference on Computer Animation* (pp. 248-251).

Tranter, W. H., Shanmugan, K. S., Rappaport, T. S., & Kosbar, K. L. (2004). *Principles of communication systems simulation with wireless applications*. Upper Saddle River, NJ: Prentice-Hall.

Tseng, Y., Ni, S., Chen, Y., & Sheu, J. (2002). The broadcast storm problem in a mobile ad hoc network. *Journal of Wireless Networks*, 8(2-3).

Turel, O., & Yuan, Y. (2006). Investigating the dynamics of the m-commerce value system: A comparative viewpoint. *International Journal of Mobile Communications*, 4(5), 532–557.

UML Revision Task Force. (2009, February). *OMG unified modeling language: Superstructure*. Retrieved August 9, 2009, from http://www.omg.org/spec/UML/2.2/

Underwood, J., & Banyard, P. (2008). Managers', teachers' and learners' perceptions of personalised learning: evidence from Impact 2007. *Technology, Pedagogy and Education*, 17(3), 233–246. doi:10.1080/14759390802383850

United Parcel Service of America, Inc. (2005). *Demystifying RFID in the supply chain: An overview of the promise and pitfalls*. Retrieved from http://www.ups-scs.com/solutions/white_papers/wp_RFID.pdf

United States Government Accountability Office. (2005). *Information security radio frequency identification technology in the federal government*. Retrieved from http://epic.org/privacy/surveillance/spotlight/0806/gao05551.pdf

United States Government Accountability Office. (2005). *Radio frequency identification technology in the federal government.* Retrieved from http://epic.org/privacy/surveillance/spotlight/0806/gao05551.pdf

Urien, P. (2008). TLS-tandem: A collaborative technology for trusted WEB applications. In *Proceedings of the International Symposium on Collaborative Technologies and Systems* (pp. 540-546).

Urien, P. (2000). Internet Card, a smart card as a true Internet node. *Computer Communications, 23*(17). doi:10.1016/S0140-3664(00)00252-8

Vaishnavi, V., & Kuechler, W. (2004). *Design research in information systems.* Retrieved from http://desrist.org/design-research-in-information-systems

van Lamsweerde, A. (2004). *Elaborating security requirements by construction of intentional anti-models* (pp. 148–157).

van Lamsweerde, A. (2007). Engineering requirements for system reliability and security. In J. G. M. Broy & C. Hoare (Eds.), *Software system reliability and security* (*Vol. 9*, pp. 196–238). Geneva, Switzerland: IOS Press.

van Thanh, D., Jorstad, I., Jonvik, T., & van Thuan, D. (2009). Strong authentication with mobile phone as security token. In *Proceedings of the 6th IEEE International Conference on Mobile Adhoc and Sensor Systems*, Macau, China (pp. 777-782).

Vapen, A., & Shahmehri, N. (2009). *Optical challenge-response authentication.* Retrieved from http://www.ida.liu.se/divisions/adit/authentication/

Vapen, A., Byers, D., & Shahmehri, N. (2010). 2-clickAuth - optical challenge-response authentication. In *Proceedings of the 5th International Conference on Availability, Reliability, and Security*, Krakow, Poland (pp. 79-86).

Varshney, U., & Vetter, R. (2002). Mobile commerce: Framework, applications and networking support. *Mobile Networks and Applications, 7*, 185–198. doi:10.1023/A:1014570512129

Vassilakis, V. G., Kallos, G. A., Moscholios, I. D., & Logothetis, M. D. (2008, June). On the handoff-call blocking probability calculation in W-CDMA cellular networks. In *Proceedings of the Fourth Advanced International Conference on Telecommunications* (pp. 173-179).

von Solms, B. (2000). Information Security -- The Third Wave? *Computers & Security, 19*(7), 615–620. doi:10.1016/S0167-4048(00)07021-8

von Solms, R., & von Solms, S. H. (2006). Information security governance: Due care. *Computers & Security, 25*(7), 494–497. doi:10.1016/j.cose.2006.08.013

Wakikawa, R., & Gundavelli, S. (2010). *IPv4 support for proxy mobile IPv6.* Retrieved from http://tools.ietf.org/html/draft-ietf-netlmm-pmip6-ipv4-support-18

Wallop, H. (2007). *Fears over Facebook identity fraud.* Retrieved September 2, 2009, from http://www.telegraph.co.uk/news/uknews/1556322/Fears-over-Facebook-identity-fraud.html

Wang, A., Bao, H., & Chen, J. *(2000). Primary research on the viseme system in standard Chinese. In* Proceedings of the International Symposium on Chinese Spoken Language Processing, *Beijing, China.*

Wang, D., Bin, X., & Agrawal, D. P. (2008). Coverage and life time optimization of wireless sensor networks with Gaussian distribution. *IEEE Transactions on Mobile Computing, 7*(12), 1444–1458. doi:10.1109/TMC.2008.60

Waters, K., & Levergood, T. M. (1993). *DECface: An automatic lip-synchronization algorithm for synthetic faces* (Tech. Rep. No. CRL93/4). Cambridge, MA: Digital Equipment Corporation, Cambridge Research Lab.

WebWise. (2009). *The BBC guide to using the Internet.* Retrieved July 23, 2009, from http://www.webwise.com/

Werda, S., Mahdi, W., & Hamadou, A. B. (2007). Lip localization and viseme classification for visual speech recognition. *International Journal of Computing & Information Sciences, 5*(1).

Woo, A., & Culler, D. (2001). A Transmission Control Scheme for Media Access in Sensor Networks. In *Proceedings of the ACM International Conference on Mobile Computing and Networking*, Rome, Italy.

Wood, C. C. (1995). Information security awareness raising methods. *Computer Fraud & Security Bulletin*, (6): 13–15. doi:10.1016/0142-0496(95)80197-9

Wu, M., Garfinkel, S., & Miller, R. (2004, July). *Secure web authentication with mobile phones.* Paper presented at DIMACS Workshop on Usable Privacy and Security Software, Piscataway, NJ.

Xiao, L., Liu, Y., & Ni, L. M. (2005). Improving unstructured peer-to- peer systems by adaptive connection establishment. *IEEE Transactions on Computers, 54*(9), 1091–1103. doi:10.1109/TC.2005.146

Xinfang, Y., Jiangtao, X., Chicharo, J. F., & Yanguang, Y. (2008). An energy-aware multilevel clustering algorithm for wireless sensor networks. In *Proceedings of the International Conference on Intelligent Sensors, Sensor Networks and Information Processing* (pp. 387-392).

Xu, Z., Tang, C., & Zhang, Z. (2003). Building topology-aware overlays using global soft-state. In *Proceedings of the 23rd International Conference on Distributed Computing Systems* (pp. 500-508).

Yan, H., Xu, Y., & Gidlund, M. (2009). Experimental e-health applications in wireless sensor networks. In *Proceedings of the International Conference on Communications and Mobile Computing* (pp. 563-567).

Yang, X., & Vaidya, N. (2007). A spatial backoff algorithm using the joint control of carrier sense threshold and transmission rate. In *Proceedings of the 4th Annual IEEE Conference on Sensor, Mesh, and Ad Hoc Communications and Networks* (pp. 501-511).

Yang, H. (2005). A road to future broadband wireless access: MIMO-OFDM based air interface. *IEEE Communications Magazine, 43*(1), 53–60. doi:10.1109/MCOM.2005.1381875

Yan, J., Blackwell, A., Anderson, R., & Grant, A. (2004). Password memorability and security: Empirical results. *IEEE Security & Privacy, 2*(5), 25–31. doi:10.1109/MSP.2004.81

Yarvis, M., Kushalnagar, N., & Singh, H. (2005). Exploiting heterogeneity in sensor networks. In *Proceedings of the 24th Annual Joint IEEE INFOCOM Conference* (pp. 878-890).

Ye, W., Heidemann, J., & Estrin, D. (2002). An Energy-Efficient MAC Protocol for Wireless Sensor Networks. In *Proceedings of the IEEE INFOCOM*, New York.

Yi, Y., Gerla, M., & Kwon, T. (2002). *Efficient flooding in ad hoc networks using on-demand (passive) cluster formation.* Paper presented at the Second Annual Workshop on Ad Hoc Networking.

Yin, L., & Cao, G. (2006). Supporting cooperative caching in ad hoc networks. *IEEE Transactions on Mobile Computing, 5*(1), 77–89. doi:10.1109/TMC.2006.15

Yoon, J., Yun, S., & Kim, H. (2006). Maximizing differentiated throughput in IEEE 802.11e wireless LANs. In *Proceedings of the IEEE Conference on Local Computer Networks* (pp. 411-417).

Zave, P., & Jackson, M. (1997). Four dark corners of requirements engineering. *ACM Transactions on Software Engineering and Methodology, 6*(1), 1–30. doi:10.1145/237432.237434doi:10.1145/237432.237434

Zdarsky, F. A., & Schmitt, J. B. (2004). Handover in mobile communication networks: Who is in control anyway? In *Proceedings of the 30th EUROMICRO Conference* (pp. 205-212).

Zegura, E. W., Calvert, K. L., & Bhattacharjee, S. (1996). *How to model an internetwork.* Paper presented at the IEEE INFOCOM.

Zegura, E. W., Calvert, K. L., & Donahoo, M. J. (1997). A quantitative comparison of graph-based models for Internet topology. *IEEE/ACM Transactions on Networking (TON), 5*(6), 770–783. doi:10.1109/90.650138

Zhang, S., Pu, J., Zeng, X., Liu, Y., & Xiong, Z. (2008). Issue and Solution on coverage and performance for wireless sensor networks. In *Proceedings of the AINTEC'08*, Bangkok, Thailand (pp. 131-137).

Zhang, P., Carey, J., Te'eni, D., & Tremaine, M. (2005). Integrating human-computer interaction development into the systems development life cycle: A methodology. *Communications of the Association for Information Systems, 15*, 512–543.

Zhang, X., Parisi-Presicce, F., Sandhu, R., & Park, J. (2005). Formal model and policy specification of usage control. *ACM Transactions on Information and System Security, 8*(4), 351–387. doi:10.1145/1108906.1108908

Zhang, Y. J., & Letaief, K. B. (2004). Multiuser adaptive subcarrier-and-bit allocation with adaptive cell selection for OFDM systems. *IEEE Transactions on Wireless Communications*, *3*(5), 1566–1575. doi:10.1109/TWC.2004.833501

Zhang, Y. J., & Letaief, K. B. (2005). Adaptive resource allocation for multiaccess mimo/OFDM systems with matched filtering. *IEEE Transactions on Communications*, *53*(11), 1810–1816. doi:10.1109/TCOMM.2005.858665

Zhao, L., Zhang, J., Yang, K., & Zhang, H. (2007, June 24-27). Using incompletely cooperative game theory in mobile ad hoc networks. In *Proceedings of the International Conference on Communications*, Glasgow, Scotland (pp. 3401-3406).

Zhou, D., Islam, N., & Ismael, A. (2004). Adaptive replication for mobile services. In *Proceeding of the 13th World Wide Web Conference* (pp. 131-142).

Zwass, V. (2003). Electronic commerce and organizational innovation: Aspects and opportunities. *International Journal of Electronic Commerce*, *7*(3), 7–37.

About the Contributors

Ismail Khalil (http://www.iiwas.org/ismail/) is a senior researcher and lecturer at the institute of telecooperation, Johanes Kepler University Linz, Austria, since October 2002. He is the president of the international organization of Information Integration and Web-based Applications & Services (WAS). He holds a PhD in computer engineering and received his habilitation degree in applied computer science on his work on agents' interaction in ubiquitous environments in May 2008. He currently teaches, consults and conducts research in Mobile Multimedia, Cloud Computing, Agent Technologies and the Semantic Web and is also interested in the broader business, social and policy implications associated with the emerging information technologies. Before joining Johannes Kepler University of Linz, he was a research fellow at the Intelligent Systems Group at Utrecht University, Netherlands from 2001-2002 and the project manager of AgenCom project at the Software Competence Center Hagenberg - Austria from 2000-2001. Dr. Khalil has authored around 100 scientific publications, books and book chapters. He is the editor of the *Handbook of Research on Mobile Multimedia* series, the book *Mobile Multimedia: Communication Engineering Perspective*, the book *Multimedia Transcoding in Mobile and Wireless Networks*, the book *Innovations in Mobile Multimedia Communications and Applications: New Technologies* and the book *Advancing the Next-Generation of Mobile Computing: Emerging Technologies*. He serves as the Editor-in-Chief of the *International Journal on Web Information Systems* (IJWIS), *International Journal on Pervasive Computing and Communication* (IJPCC) both published by Emerald Group publishing, UK, *Journal of Mobile Multimedia* (JMM) published by Rinton Press, USA, *International Journal of Mobile Computing and Multimedia Communication* (IJMCMC) published by IGI Global, USA, *Advances in Next Generation Mobile Multimedia* book series published by IGI Global, USA and *Atlantis Ambient and Pervasive Intelligence* book series published by Atlantis and Springer. He is on the editorial board of several international journals. His work has been published and presented at various conferences and workshops.

Edgar R. Weippl (CISSP, CISA, CISM) is Science Director of Secure Business Austria and an assistant professor at the Vienna University of Technology. His research focuses on applied concepts of IT-security and e-learning. Edgar has taught several tutorials on security issues in e-learning at international conferences, including ED-MEDIA 2003-2007 and E-Learn 2005. In 2005, he published *Security in E-Learning* (Springer). After graduating with a PhD from the Vienna University of Technology, Edgar worked for two years in a research startup. He then spent one year teaching as an assistant professor at Beloit College (WI, USA). From 2002 to 2004, he worked with the software vendor ISIS Papyrus, as well as he worked as a consultant for HMO (Empire BlueCross BlueShield) in New York and Albany (NY, USA) and for Deutsche Bank (PWM) in Frankfurt (Germany).

* * *

Lalit K. Awasthi received his Ph.D degree from IIT Roorkee in Computer Science and Engineering. Previously he received MTech from IIT Delhi. Presently he is working as Dean (Students & Alumani Affairs) and Head Computer Centre, NIT Hamirpur Since 1989 he has been with the Department of Computer Science and Engineering, NIT Hamirpur, where he is currently a Professor. His research interests are distributed fault tolerant computing, mobile computing, wireless sensor networks.

Media A. Ayu is currently a researcher in the Intelligent Environment Research Group (INTEG) and a Senior Lecturer at the Dept of Information Systems, KICT, International Islamic University Malaysia, Kuala Lumpur. He was awarded a PhD from the Department of Engineering, College of Engineering and Computer Science, the Australian National University (ANU), Canberra, Australia. She has authored several research papers, several book chapters and has three patent pending to her credits in the area of pervasive computing.

Iman I. Badran has finished her bachelor degree in computer information systems and master degree in computer science from Jordan University of Science and Technology in 2008 and 2010 respectively. She is currently working as a school teacher in Jordan. Her main research interest is designing efficient algorithms for wireless networks with emphasis on investigating and designing backoff algorithms for mobile ad hoc networks. Iman graduated with high rank in her bachelor and master degrees. She is currently in the process of applying for doctoral program in computer science.

Shashi Bhushan received his B. Tech. (Computer Technology) degree from Nagpur University, Nagpur in the year 1998. He received his M. Tech. (Computer Science and Engineering) degree from JRN Rajasthan Vidyapeeth, Rajasthan in 2005 and now, he is pursuing PhD in the field of Peer-to-Peer Networks from National Institute of Technology, Kurukshetra, INDIA. Presently he is working as Associate Professor in the Department of Computer Science & Engineering at Haryana Engineering College, Jagadhri, Haryana (India). His fields of interest are Networks, Sensor Networks and Mobile Computing.

Muazzan Binsaleh is a lecturer at the Department of Information and Communication Technology for Management, Faculty of Communication Sciences, Prince of Songkla University (PSU), Thailand. He received his BEng in Mining and Metallurgical Engineering from Prince of Songkla University in 1994, his MSc in Computing from University of Central England, United Kingdom in 2001. Currently, he is doing his PhD at University Utara Malaysia (UUM). Muazzan's research focuses on three areas in the field of information systems: mobile commerce applications, systems development methodology and agile methodology. His current research is related to system development methodology in mobile commerce.

Servane Bonjour has been working at Orange Labs / France Telecom R&D since 1993 as research engineer and then as architect in innovative networks. Servane received her engineering diploma from INSA Rennes in 1993. She has contributed in collaborative European projects such as IST-BRAIN, IST-MIND and CELTIC-MEVICO on IP mobility between heterogeneous networks. Now, she is in charge of a research project in Orange Labs, where several studies dealing with seamless mobility (QoS, security and mobility interworking, mobility and service adaptation) and new distributed mobility architecture are carried out. She was also involved in IEEE P1900.4 standardization body where dynamic reconfiguration of cognitive terminals and base stations is considered.

Mohammed Boulmalf received his B.Eng. degree in Communications from National Institute of Telecommunications "INPT" in 1987, Rabat, Morocco. He worked for 5 years as a Network Engineer at ONCF Company in Rabat Morocco. In August 1992, Boulmalf moved to Canada to pursue his graduate studies at the National Institute for Scientific Research, Montreal, Canada. He received the M.Sc. and Ph.D. degrees both in Wireless Communications and Networking in 1994 and 2001, respectively. From September 1994 to December 1998 he was with INRS-Telecom as a Radio Communications Research Engineer. In January 1999, he joined ETS, Quebec University where he worked as a Lecturer. In September for the same year, Boulmalf moved to Microcell Telecommunications, GSM Operator in Canada, where he worked as a Senior Network Engineer. From 2000 to 2002, he worked as a Principal Engineer at the Multi-vendor Integration Department at Ericsson, Montreal, Canada. In February 2002, he joined the College of Information Technology at the United Arab Emirates University, Abu Dhabi - Al-Ain, where he worked as an Assistant Professor till July 2007. In August 2007, he moved to the same position at the School of Science & Engineering at Al Akhawayn University in Morocco where he is currently Associate Professor of Computer Science. He is the author/co-author of about 50 articles in refereed journals and conferences in the areas of wireless networking and communications, mobile computing, and network security.

Narottam Chand received his PhD degree from IIT Roorkee in Computer Science and Engineering. Previously he received MTech and BTech degrees in Computer Science and Engineering from IIT Delhi and NIT Hamirpur respectively. Presently he is working as Head, Department of Computer Science and Engineering, NIT Hamirpur. He also served as Head, Institute Computer Centre, NIT Hamirpur from February 2008 to July 2009. He has coordinated different key assignments at NIT Hamirpur like Campus Wide Networking, Institute Web Site, Institute Office Automation. His current research areas of interest include mobile computing, mobile ad hoc networks and wireless sensor networks. He has published more than 60 research papers in International/National journals & conferences and guiding six PhDs in these areas. He is member of ISTE, CSI, International Association of Engineers and Internet Society.

Durg Singh Chauhan received his B.Sc.Eng. (1972) in Electrical Engineering at I.T. B.H.U., M.E. (1978) at R.E.C. Tiruchirapalli (Madras University), PhD (1986) at IIT, Delhi, and his post-doctoral work at Goddard space Flight Centre, Greenbelt Maryland. USA (1988-91). His brilliant career brought him to teaching profession at Banaras Hindu University where he was Lecturer, Reader and then has been Professor till today. He was founder vice Chancellor of U.P. Tech. University (2000, 2003, 2006). Currently he has been serving as Vice-Chancellor of Uttarakhand Technical University for (2009-12)

Tenure. He supervised 12 Ph.D., one D.Sc and is currently guiding a half dozen research scholars. He had authored two books and published and presented 85 research papers in international journals and international conferences and wrote more than 20 articles on various topics in national magazines. He is Fellow of institution of Engineers and Member IEEE.

Naveen Chauhan received an M.E. degree from Punjab University, Chandigarh, India. He is currently working toward the Ph.D. degree in computer Science and engineering at National Institute of Technology, Hamirpur. His research interest includes wireless networks, distributed systems, and mobile computing, with a focus on mobile ad hoc networks.

Fatma Zohra Chelali received her engineering degree in electronic engineering from University of science and technology of Algiers; ALGERIA (USTHB) in 1994. She works as Assistant teacher in the high school of aeronautical Technicians (ESTA) from 1998 to 2008, she teaches courses on Analog and digital telecommunications systems, digital electronics, principal functions in electronics and Microwave systems. She spends a year of post graduation from 2002 to 2003.She received a "magister" degree in speech communication from electronic engineering and computing faculty (USTHB) in 2006. She is currently pursuing her Doctorate degree in speech communication and signal processing laboratory (LCPTS, USTHB, Algiers).She teaches courses with telecommunications department on Electromagnetic waves, transmission lines and digital electronics since 2007 in Electronic engineering and computer science Faculty, university of science and technology (USTHB). Her research interests include pattern recognition, audiovisual recognition and human-computer interaction.

Nathan L. Clarke is an Associate Professor in Information Security and Digital Forensics within the Centre for Security, Communications and Network Research at the University of Plymouth. Dr Clarke is also an adjunct scholar at Edith Cowan University, Western Australia. His research interests reside in the area of biometrics, digital forensics and security education; having published 50 papers in international journals and conferences. Dr Clarke is a Certified Biometrics Professional (IEEE CBP), a chartered engineer, a fellow of the British Computing Society (BCS), and a UK representative in the International Federation of Information Processing (IFIP) working groups relating to the Human Aspects of Information Security and Assurance (co-vice chair and co-proposer), Identity Management and Information Security Education.

Frédéric Cuppens is a full professor at the TELECOM Bretagne LUSSI department. He holds an engineering degree in computer science, a PhD and an HDR. He has been working for more 20 years on various topics of computer security including definition of formal models of security policies, access control to network and information systems, intrusion detection, reaction and counter-measures, and formal techniques to refine security policies and prove security properties. He has published more than 120 technical papers in refereed journals and conference proceedings. He served on several conference program committees and was the Program Committee Chair of ESORICS 2000, IFIP SEC 2004, of SARSSI 2006 and general chair of ESORICS 2009, DPM 2010 and SETOP 2010.

Nora Cuppens-Boulahia is an associate researcher at the TELECOM Bretagne LUSSI department. She holds an engineering degree in computer science and a PhD from SupAero and an HDR from University Rennes 1. Her research interest includes formalization of security properties and policies, cryptographic protocol analysis, formal validation of security properties and thread and reaction risk assessment. She has published more than 80 technical papers in refereed journals and conference proceedings. She has been member of several international program committees in information security system domain and the PC Chair of Setop 2008, Setop2009, SAR-SSI 2008, CRISIS 2010 and the co-general chair of ES-ORICS 2009 and SETOP 2010. She is the French representative of IFIP TC11 "Information Security" and she is he co-responsible of the information system security axis of SEE.

Teddy Mantoro, PhD, is currently the head of Intelligent Environment Research Group (INTEG) and a Senior Lecturer at the Dept of Computer Science, KICT, International Islamic University Malaysia, Kuala Lumpur. He holds a PhD, an MSc and a BSc, all in Computer Science. He was awarded a PhD from Department of Computer Science, the Australian National University (ANU), Canberra, Australia. He has authored several research papers, a book on Intelligent Environment, several chapters in a couple of books and has three patent pending and in the process of two other patents to his credits in the area of pervasive/ubiquitous computing.

Mayank Dave received PhD degree from IIT Roorkee, INDIA in 2002, M. Tech degree in Computer Engineering from IIT Roorkee, INDIA in 1991. He is presently working as an associate professor and head in Computer Engineering Department at NIT Kurukshetra, INDIA. He has more than 19 years experience in academic and administrative affairs. He had published approximately 60 research papers in various International / National Journals and International / National Conferences and guided several PhDs, M. Tech and B. Tech students. He coordinated several projects and training programmes.. He is a member of IEEE (Computer Society), Life member of IETE, Life member Institutions of Engineers (India) and Life member of ISTE. His research interests include Peer-to-Peer Computing, Pervasive Computing, and Sensor Networks, Database Systems, QoS in Mobile Networks.

Amar Djeradi received his engineering degree in Electronics in 1984, his magister degree in applied electronics, and Doctorate degree in 1992.He teaches since 1985 in different modules for graduation and post graduation such as Electronics, Television, digital electronics, principals functions of electronics, pattern recognition, human-machine communication. His current research interests are in the area of speech communication, human-machine Communication, multimodal interfaces and signal analysis.

Mehdia Ajana El Khaddar is an IT project manager and engineer at Fondation Mohammed VI de Promotion des Oeuvres Sociales de l'Education-Formation in Rabat, Morocco since June 2009. She obtained, in 2007, her Bachelor of Science in Computer Science from Alakhawayn University in Ifrane, Morocco. In 2009, she obtained her Master of Science in Computer Networks from Alakhawayn University in Ifrane, Morocco. She is currently a second year PhD student at ENSIAS (Ecole National Supérieure de l'Informatique et d'Analyse des Systèmes) in Rabat, Morocco. Her research interests are RFID applications and middleware, context and situation awareness, and wireless sensor networks.

Mohammed El Koutbi is presently working as a full professor at the University Mohamed V - Souissi at ENSIAS (an engineering school in computer science). He held a PhD degree in Computer Science from Montreal University, Canada since July 2000. He has been heavily involved in teaching, research, curriculum development, certification activities, lab developments, and faculty/ staff hiring at the department. He has several years of strong industrial and research experience in software engineering and computer networking. His current research is in the area of computer networking (mobile computing and adhoc networks) and software engineering (software development and model engineering).

Yehia Elrakaiby holds a PhD degree from the National School of Telecommunication (TELECOM-Bretagne), France in 2010. He received his Engineering degree, in 2003, from the Department of Electronics and Communications Engineering, Cairo University, Egypt. He pursued his studies at the National School of Telecommunications (TELECOM-Bretagne) where he obtained an Engineering degree, in 2005. His research interests include the formal modeling of security concepts and the specification and application of security policies to network and information systems.

Katrin Franke is professor of information security at NISlab, Department of Computer Science and Media Technology, Gjøvik University College, Gjøvik, Norway. She received a diploma in electrical engineering from the Technical University Dresden, Germany in 1994 and her Ph.D. in artificial intelligence from the Groningen University, The Netherlands in 2005. Her research interests include computational forensics, biometrics, document and handwriting analysis, computer vision and computational intelligence. She has published several scientific journal articles, peer-reviewed conference papers and edited books.

Steven M. Furnell is the head of the Centre for Security, Communications & Network Research at the University of Plymouth in the United Kingdom, and an Adjunct Professor with Edith Cowan University in Western Australia. His interests include security management and culture, computer crime, user authentication, and security usability. Prof. Furnell is active within three working groups of the International Federation for Information Processing (IFIP) – namely Information Security Management, Information Security Education, and Human Aspects of Information Security & Assurance. He is the author of over 190 papers in refereed international journals and conference proceedings, as well as books including Cybercrime: Vandalizing the Information Society (2001) and Computer Insecurity: Risking the System (2005). Further details can be found at www.plymouth.ac.uk/cscan.

Sebastian Gajek is a postdoctoral fellow at the Tel Aviv University, Israel. He received his PhD from the Ruhr University Bochum, Germany. Sebastian's research interests include theory of cryptography, and information security.

Karine Guillouard graduated from INSA (National Applied Science Institute), France, in 1994, as an Electronics and Radiocommunications engineer and received the Radiocommunications PhD degree from INSA, in 1997. She joined France Telecom R&D, where she was involved in techno-economic studies of radio access networks and feasibility studies of wireless home networks until 1999. She contributed to the Eurescom HINE project. From 2000, her focus was mainly on IP based mobility management within wireless broadband IP accesses. She particularly participated to IST BRAIN and

MIND projects; she was also in charge of the RNRT Cyberté project that conceived a multi-access IPv6 terminal architecture. She is currently focusing her studies on long term network architectures supporting heterogeneous accesses in the context of fixed mobile convergence.

Sami J. Habib received a BS in Computer Engineering from Iowa State University, where he spent a year working as a Lab Engineer in the Department of Electrical and Computer Engineering at Kuwait University. Then, he pursued a graduate study at the University of Southern California, where he earned MS and PhD in Computer Engineering. Currently he is a vice-dean for academic affairs at the College of Graduate Studies and an associate professor at the Department of Computer Engineering at Kuwait University. His researches are focused on developing computer-aided design methodologies and performance analysis techniques for designing/redesigning computer networks.

Hamid Harroud is an assistant professor in Computer Science at the School of Science and Engineering (SSE), at Al Akhawayn University in Ifrane (AUI), Morocco. His research interests include context-aware systems, mobile computing and policy-based management. H. Harroud received his MSc degree in Electrical Engineering from the Mohammadia School of Engineering (EMI), Morocco, and has a Ph.D. in computer science from the University of Ottawa, Canada.

Shahizan Hassan, a PhD degree holder from the University of Newcastle upon Tyne, United Kingdom, is an associate professor in information systems at the College of Business, University Utara Malaysia. He is the editor for Malaysian Management Journal (MMJ) and has published three books and thirteen articles in national and international journals. He is very active in research projects in the area of information systems evaluation, Web design and evaluation, knowledge management, electronic government, and wireless applications. To date, he had completed a total of ten research projects funded by various agencies. He has supervised more than 100 undergraduate and post-graduate students' projects in various IT disciplines. He was previously the director of the Centre for University-Industry Collaboration (CUIC), Universiti Utara Malaysia.

Meiko Jensen studied computer science at the Christian Albrechts University of Kiel, Germany, and received his degree in computer science (a German diploma) in 2007. Currently he is a PhD student, researching in the field of Web Service security, and is particularly interested in service composition security, XML security, security modeling, and attacks on Web Services. Meiko is a member of ACM and GI.

Ramesh C. Joshi was born at Pithoragarh (UA, India) on June 1st, 1946. Dr. Joshi received his B.E. degree in electrical engineering from Allahabad University, Allahabad, India in 1967. He then received his M.E. and Ph.D. degrees in electronics and computer engineering from University of Roorkee, India, in 1970 and 1980, respectively. He joined J. K. Institute, Allahabad University as Lecturer in 1967 and in August 1970 he joined E&CE Dept., University of Roorkee as Lecturer. He then became READER in August 1981 and then PROFESSOR in September 1987. Currently he is working as PROFESSOR in Electronics and Computer Engineering Department, Indian Institute of Technology, Roorkee. He has served as Head of the Department twice from Jan. 1991 to Jan. 1994 and from Jan. 1997 to Dec. 1999. He has been Head of Institute Computer Centre, IITR from March 1994- Dec 2005. Presently he is actively involved in research in the areas of Information Security, Bioinformatics, Databases and Reconfigurable Computing. Dr. Joshi is in expert panel of various national committees like AICTE, DRDO and MIT. He is also a member of National Industrial Research and Development Award Committee. Dr. Joshi has guided about 25 Ph.D. theses M.E./M. Tech. Dissertations (150), M.E./B.E. projects (200+). He has been principal investigator for projects from various national agencies like Ministry of Information and Communication, DRDO, DOE and AICTE He has published over 150 research papers in National/International Journal/Conferences. Dr. Joshi has also done 18 months training at ENSER Grenoble, Franc under Indo French Collaboration program. He has received a gold medal by the Institute of Engineers in 1978 for best research paper.

Vivek Katiyar received his B. Tech. degree from FET-RBS College, Agra. He is currently pursuing M. Tech. at the Department of Computer Science & Engineering, NIT Hamirpur. His research interests include energy efficient clustering and data aggregation in heterogeneous wireless sensor networks. He is currently working on Energy Map construction and application in wireless sensor networks. He has published more than 15 research papers in International journals & International/National conferences.

Yaser Khamayseh received B.Sc degree in computer science from Yarmouk University, Jordan in 1998, and M.Sc from University of New Brunswick, Canada in 2001. He received a PhD degree in computer science in 2007 from University of Alberta, Edmonton, Canada. In 2007 he joined the faculty of computer and information technology at Jordan University of Science and Technology, Jordan, as an assistant professor of computer science. He has served as a technical program committee member of various conferences. His research interests include wireless network optimization, resource management in wireless networks, and protocol design and analysis for future generation wireless communication networks and systems.

Florian Kohlar studied IT Security at Ruhr University Bochum (Germany) between 2002 and 2008. His diploma thesis covered the security of XML based files and messages. After receiving his diploma's degree, he started 2009 as a PhD student at the chair for network and data security collocated with the faculty for Electrical Engineering and Information sciences at the Ruhr University Bochum. He is currently doing research in the field of browser-based protocols and especially security of single sign on and identity management protocols.

Wail Mardini is an assistant professor at the Computer Science department at Jordan University of Science and Technology (JUST) since 2006. Dr. Mardini received his PhD degree in Computer Science from University of Ottawa/Canada at 2006 and his Masters degree from University of New Brunswick/Canada at 2001. Dr. Mardini has many publications in network survivability, wireless networks and optical-wireless networks. He is currently working on Wireless Mesh Networks, Wireless Sensor Networks, Wireless Optical Mesh Networks, Optical Network Survivability, WiMax Technology, Scheduling in Parallel Computing and Intrusion Detection in database Techniques. Dr. Mardini is currently the chairman of the Computer Science department at JUST.

Admir Milišić received a bachelor's degree in Computer Science from Kulliyyah (Faculty) of Information and Communication Technology (KICT), International Islamic University Malaysia. He is currently a research assistant of Intelligent Environment Research Group (INTEG), KICT. His interest areas are pervasive computing, computer networking and security.

Shailendra Mishra received his PhD degree in 2007, Master of Engineering Degree (ME) in Computer Science & Engineering (Specialization: Software Engineering) from Motilal Nehru National Institute of Technology (MNNIT), Allahabad India(2000) Presently he is Professor & Head, Department of Computer Science & Engineering Kumaon Govt. Engineering College, Dwarahat, Uttrakhand India. His recent research has been in the field of Mobile Computing & Communication and Advance Network Architecture. He has also been conducting research on Communication System & Computer Networks with Performance evaluation and design of Multiple Access Protocol for Mobile Communication Network. He handled many research projects during the last 5 years; Power control and recourse management for WCDMA System, Code and Time complexity for WCDMA System, OCQPSK spreading techniques for third generation communication system, "IT mediated education and dissemination of health information via Training & e-Learning Platform, etc. and published 40 research papers in International journals and International conference proceedings.

Manoj Misra obtained his PhD degree from Newcastle upon Tyne, UK in Computer Science and Engineering. He is currently a Professor at the Department of Electronics and Computer Engineering, IIT Roorkee. Dr. Misra's current research interests are in mobile computing, performance evaluation and distributed computing. Currently he is working as Principal Investigator for Data Caching on Planet Lab Project from Intel.

Hai Thanh Nguyen is doctoral researcher of information security at NISlab, Department of Computer Science and Media Technology, Gjøvik University College, Gjøvik, Norway. He received his diploma and Master degree in applied mathematics and computer science from Moscow State University named after M. V. Lomonosov in 2007. His research interests include intrusion detection, cryptography and computational intelligence.

R. B. Patel received PhD from IIT Roorkee in Computer Science & Engineering, PDF from Highest Institute of Education, Science & Technology (HIEST), Athens, Greece, MS (Software Systems) from BITS Pilani and B. E. in Computer Engineering from M. M. M. Engineering College, Gorakhpur, UP. Dr. Patel is in teaching and Research & Development since 1991. He has supervised 30 M. Tech, 7 M. Phil and 3 PhD Thesis. He is currently supervising 3 M. Tech, and 10 PhD students. He has published more than 130 research papers in International/National Journals and Refereed International Conferences. System and Method for Reliable and Flexible Mobile Agent Computing and System, Method, & Computer Program for Routing Data in Wireless Sensor Network are two patents in the credit of Dr. Patel. He had been awarded for Best Research paper many times in India and abroad. He has written numbers books for engineering courses (These are "Fundamentals of Computing and Programming in C," "Theory of Automata and Formal Languages," "Expert Data Structures with C," "Expert Data

Structures with C++," "Art and Craft of C" and "Go Through C". His research interests are in Mobile & Distributed Computing, Mobile Agent Security and Fault Tolerance, development infrastructure for mobile & Peer-To-Peer computing, Device and Computation Management, Cluster Computing, Sensor Networks, etc.

Joel Penhoat has been involved in the telecommunication industry for ten years. He joined France Telecom Orange Labs, France, in 2000. His work is centered around security and QoS in radio networks. Since 2006, his current research interests are in the area of Fixed Mobile Convergence, QoS-aware networks, service-aware networks, IP Multimedia Subsystem and the Future Internet. In 1985, he received a Master degree in Electronics from the University of Brest, France. In 2008, he received a Master degree in Information Technology from the Ecole Nationale Supérieure des Télécommunications Paris, France. He is currently contributing to the networking design of the Future Internet to obtain a Ph.D. degree from the University of Rennes, France.

Slobodan Petrović is professor of information security at NISlab, Department of Computer Science and Media Technology, Gjøvik University College, Gjøvik, Norway. He received his Ph.D. degree in 1994 from the University of Belgrade, Serbia. His research interests include cryptology, intrusion detection, and digital forensic. He is the author of more than 40 papers published in renowned international journals and conferences.

Anjali Sardana, born at Bareilly (UP, India) on August 1, 1982, received her B. Tech degree in Information Technology from U.P. Technical University, Lucknow, India, in 2004. She received her M.Tech degree in Information Technology from Indian Institute of Technology Roorkee in 2006 and her Ph.D. degree in 2009 in Electronics and Computer Engineering Department, Indian Institute of Technology Roorkee, India. She has been gold medalist during her undergraduate studies. Her recent significant work on Honeypots and DDoS includes implementation of low interaction honeypots and simulation of high interaction honeypots. Her research interests include Information Security, Network Evaluation and Protocol Engineering. Dr. Anjali has been recipient of 1st prize at National Level R&D contest organized by Govt. of India, "Best Engineer Award" in the year 2003-2004, has been recipient of three Gold Medals during undergraduate studies, has been honored twice by IMA and been a national level participant at ImagineCup'06 by Microsoft, recipient of prestigious Google Women in Engineering Award 2009.

Holger Schmidt has a post-doc position at Technical University of Dortmund. He received his PhD in computer science at University Duisburg-Essen, Germany. He has authored many papers and presented at numerous international conferences on the topics of secure software engineering and security requirements engineering. He holds a Diploma degree in mathematics from University Münster, Germany. Moreover, he works for about three years as a free-lance consultant in the area of security consultancy for software development and evaluation projects.

Jörg Schwenk has the chair for Network and Data Security at the Horst Görtz Institute for IT Security at RUB since 2003. From 1993-2001 he worked in the security department of Deutsche Telekom on different projects. He has written more than 60 patents, and more than 30 scientific publications. His research interests include cryptographic protocols (especially multi-party protocols), XML and Web Service security and internet security (especially protection against real world challenges such as pharming or WWW-based attacks).

Pierrick Seïté received the PhD in electronic and digital communications from the University of Metz (France) in 1995. He joined France Telecom in 2001 being in charge of architecture studies dealing with mobility management over heterogeneous access systems. He is currently focusing on network-controlled mobility management and convergent network architectures. He was involved in European collaborative projects (IST/CISMUNDUS and IST/OVERDRIVE) and is now contributing to CELTIC/MEVICO. He is also involved in some standardization bodies; namely the IETF where he is contributing to mobility or multiple interfaces terminals related working groups (NetExt, MEXT, MultiMob and MIF).

Nahid Shahmehri received her PhD in 1991, in the area of programming environments. Since 1994 her research activities have been concerned with various aspects of engineering advanced information systems, e.g. security. Examples of current projects are processes for software security, software security in vehicular systems, mobile authentication, spam prevention, and vehicular networks. She has been a full professor in Computer Science at Linköping University since 1998. She is Chairperson of the Swedish Section of the IEEE Chapter for Computer/Software.

Surender Soni received his B. Tech Degree from NIT Hamirpur, and M. Tech Degree from Punjab University Chandigarh. He is currently a Research Scholar at the Department of Computer Science & Engineering, NIT Hamirpur. His research interests include resource management in wireless sensor networks.

Shuhaili Talib is currently a PhD candidate from Centre for Security, Communications & Network Research at the University of Plymouth in the United Kingdom, a lecturer at the Department of Information Systems, Kulliyyah of Information and Communication Technology (KICT), International Islamic University Malaysia (IIUM). She received her Bachelor Degree in Management Information Systems from the International Islamic University Malaysia and a Master of Science Degree in Information Security from Royal Holloway, University of London. In research, she is interested to study about Information Security Awareness. Currently, she researches in improving information security awareness to public users. In addition to topics in Information security, Shuhaili also interested to research in human aspects in security and security management. Before pursuing her study, she was the student advisor at the Department of Information Systems and taught several courses such as Information Technology Security, Internet Applications and Information Technology.

Anna Vapen received her master's degree in computer engineering from Linköping University, Sweden in 2008. She is a PhD student in the field of information security under the supervision of Professor Nahid Shahmehri in the Division of Databases and Information Techniques at the Department of Computer and Information Science at Linköping University. Her research interests are in the areas of security, web authentication and mobile computing. Her current research focuses on the use of mobile phones as secure hardware devices in authentication.

Muneer Bani Yassein received his BSc degree in Computing Science and Mathematics from Yarmouk University, Jordan in 1985 and MSc in Computer Science, from Al Al-bayt, University, Jordan in 2001. And PhD degrees in Computer Science from the University of Glasgow, UK, in 2007, He is currently an assistant professor in the Department of Computer science at Jordan University of Science and Technology (JUST), His research include the development/analysis the performance probabilistic flooding behaviours in MANET optimizations and the refinement of routing algorithms for mobile device communications in heterogeneous network environments.

Index